U.S. ARMY COUNTERINSURGENCY AND CONTINGENCY OPERATIONS DOCTRINE 1942-1976

by
Andrew J. Birtle

MILITARY INSTRVCTION

CENTER OF MILITARY HISTORY
UNITED STATES ARMY
WASHINGTON, D.C., 2007

Library of Congress Cataloging-in-Publication Data

Birtle, A. J. (Andrew James)
  U.S. Army counterinsurgency and contingency operations doctrine,
1942–1976 / by Andrew J. Birtle.
      p. cm.
  Includes bibliographical references and index.
  1. Counterinsurgency—United States—History—20th century. 2.
United States. Army. I. Title.

  U241.B52 2006
  355.4'25—dc22   2006020046

CMH Pub 70–98–1

First Printed 2006

ISBN 0-16-072959-9

FOREWORD

In recent years the U.S. Army has been heavily engaged in performing counterinsurgency and nation-building missions in Iraq, Afghanistan, and elsewhere. These undertakings, together with recent operations in Somalia, Haiti, and the Balkans, have kindled a strong interest in the Army's past experiences in combating irregulars and restoring order overseas. In response, the Center has commissioned its historians to take a close look at the evolution of counterinsurgency and related doctrine in the U.S. Army. This volume, covering 1942 to 1976, is the second volume representing that effort.

During the third quarter of the twentieth century, powerful political and socioeconomic forces created instability in many countries. Watching international communism exploiting such situations, the United States mobilized its resources to fight Communist subversion as part of a post–World War II global "Cold War." While recognizing the underlying problems that made societies vulnerable to Communist exploitation, the U.S. Army played a central role in executing all aspects of this policy. It furnished counterguerrilla training, advice, and assistance to foreign armies and police forces. It occupied conquered or unstable countries, organized governments, and supplied men, money, and materiel to help allied nations redress the socioeconomic and political conditions that American policy makers believed fostered unrest. And when necessary, it fought Communist insurgents, guerrillas, and even regular forces employed in irregular roles.

The Cold War is over and the threat posed by communism much diminished. However, the conditions that can fuel civil unrest and insurrection are still with us and will probably always be features of human affairs. Soldiers, diplomats, politicians, and analysts will thus benefit from learning about how the U.S. Army has historically approached such problems and the successes and failures that those ventures have met. Although every historical event is unique, many of the issues and challenges involved in such actions are as relevant today as they were in the past. By examining evolving Army doctrine, training, and field operations, this work provides an in-depth look at how our institution performed its counterinsurgency and nation-building responsibilities during a previous era of global instability, experiences that might well shed some needed light on the work that must be done today and tomorrow.

Washington, D.C.   JEFFREY J. CLARKE
15 September 2006   Chief of Military History

THE AUTHOR

Andrew J. Birtle received a B.A. degree in history from Saint Lawrence University in 1979 and M.A. and Ph.D. degrees in military history from Ohio State University in 1981 and 1985, respectively. He worked for the U.S. Air Force as a historian for approximately three years before joining the U.S. Army Center of Military History in 1987. He has written several articles, pamphlets, and monographs; a book on the rearmament of West Germany; and *U.S. Army Counterinsurgency and Contingency Operations Doctrine, 1860–1941*, the companion volume to this study. He is currently working on a volume concerning U.S. Army activities in Vietnam between 1961 and 1965.

PREFACE

Stability operations, nation building, and *counterinsurgency:* these are all phrases that are very much in the news today as the United States and its allies attempt to bring peace and order to troubled places like Iraq, Afghanistan, and Kosovo. None of these terms are new. They all originated over forty years ago, when the United States wrestled with an earlier era of global instability. Although the causes of foreign unrest, the nature of the threat, and the circumstances under which the United States has attempted to address those challenges are different today than they were several decades ago, many of the fundamental issues associated with such phenomena remain the same. Indeed, readers of this study and its predecessor volume, *U.S. Army Counterinsurgency and Contingency Operations Doctrine, 1860–1941,* will find many points of similarity in how the U.S. Army has dealt with counterinsurgency, constabulary, and limited contingency situations in the past. The reasons for these similarities and the principles that form the core of American doctrine are described in the book. The volume also examines the nature of counterinsurgency and nation-building missions, the institutional obstacles inherent in dealing effectively with such operations, and the strengths and weaknesses of U.S. doctrine, including the problems that can occur when that doctrine morphs into dogma. Readers should remember, however, that while many threads of continuity exist there are also developments that have no parallel. Continuity and change are the twin muses of history. No two situations are identical, and the fact that something happened in one instance does not mean it will occur in another. This is particularly true with regard to the subject matter of this book, as a plethora of political, socioeconomic, cultural, environmental, and military factors give each counterinsurgency, nation-building, and contingency operation a unique hue. The vagaries of these types of operations encumber both the historian and the doctrine writer. Consequently, writers and readers alike should always bear in mind that history, like military doctrine, is not an exact science, nor does it have determinative or predictive powers. It is an interpretive art that explains the past, helps us understand the present, and provides insights that may assist us in wrestling with the inevitable challenges of the future. Hopefully this volume accomplishes all three goals.

Many people, far too many to name, assisted in the production of this volume. I would like to extend a general word of appreciation to the staffs of the National Archives and Records Administration, the Library of Congress, the U.S. Army Center of Military History (CMH), the U.S. Army Military History Institute (MHI), and the Pentagon, Infantry School, and Command and General Staff College libraries. Individuals worthy of special mention are Wilbert Mahoney of the National Archives; Richard J. Sommers, David Keough, and Pamela Cheney at MHI; and at CMH, Graham Cosmas, Mary Gillett, James Knight, and Geraldine Harcarik. I would also like to recognize the members of the Center's Publishing Division who transformed the manuscript into a book: Keith Tidman, Beth MacKenzie, S. L. Dowdy, and Teresa Jameson. Contractor Anne Venzon created the index. I am especially grateful to Diane Sedore Arms, whose expert editing greatly improved the quality of the work. Thanks also go to the scholars who reviewed all or portions of the manuscript and made many helpful suggestions: Stephen Bowman, Jeffrey Clarke, Robert Doughty, Paul Herbert, Joel Meyerson, Allan Millett, Richard Stewart, and Lawrence Yates. Finally, I would like to thank my parents and my wife, without whose support this work would not have been possible.

Though many people contributed to this volume, the author alone is responsible for all interpretations and conclusions, as well as for any errors that may appear.

Washington, D.C.   ANDREW J. BIRTLE
15 September 2006

Contents

Illustrations courtesy of the following sources: cover and pp. 33, 107, 322, 374, Army Art Collection; 9, 10, 14, 16, 62, 90, 95, 96, 99, 104, 106, 110, 112, 113, 115, 154, 156, 186, 187, 189, 201, 202, 204, 207, 208, 210, 258, 270, 271, 273, 274, 276, 277, 295 (*top/bottom*), 297 (*top/bottom*), 301, 303 (*top/bottom*), 308, 318, 320, 326, 332, 333, 338, 340, 343, 377, 379, 388, 391, 393, 396, 397, 398, 457, 459, 460, 463, 464, 466, National Archives; 45, 47, 55, Library of Congress; 69, 71, 226, 228, 363, 373, 394, 395, U.S. Army Military History Institute; 133, *We Remained*, by Russell Volckmann; 191, United Press International; and 421, U.S. Army Center of Military History.

U.S. ARMY
COUNTERINSURGENCY AND CONTINGENCY OPERATIONS DOCTRINE
1942-1976

1

INTRODUCTION

Rarely do armies have the luxury of being able to prepare for only one mission. Although waging conventional war has always lain at the heart of the military profession, it has never been the soldier's only, or even most frequently performed, role. Historically, U.S. soldiers have spent far more time performing a variety of constabulary, administrative, diplomatic, humanitarian, nation-building, and irregular warfare functions than they have fighting on the conventional battlefield. This work describes the evolution of U.S. Army doctrine for two of the many types of operations other than conventional warfare for which the Army had to prepare during the three decades that followed World War II—counterinsurgency and limited peacetime contingency operations.

Terms and Their Relevance

Fighting insurgents and intervening in the internal affairs of foreign countries had long been missions performed by the Army, but after World War II these missions achieved heightened significance. The United States emerged from the war as a world leader with global interests and obligations. The outbreak of the Cold War magnified these burdens, as the threat of Communist subversion and the need for the United States to project military power into the internal affairs of foreign states led the Army to undertake a variety of counterinsurgency and constabulary missions. The extent of these missions, as well as the doctrinal confusion surrounding them, is illustrated by the plethora of terms employed to describe them. According to one student of the period, soldiers, policy makers, and civilian analysts coined more than fifty terms to describe the military's many counterinsurgency functions, an estimate that is probably too low. Among them were such

3

expressions as *situations short of war, low intensity warfare, cold war operations, stability operations, subbelligerency operations, para-war, revolutionary* (and *counterrevolutionary*) *war, guerrilla* (and *counter-guerrilla*) *war, internal defense and development, sublimited war,* and most exotic of all, *subliminal war.*[1]

Because of this extensive but confusing lexicon, a few definitions must be established. For the purposes of this book, the term *counterinsurgency* embraces all of the political, economic, social, and military actions taken by a government for the suppression of insurgent, resistance, and revolutionary movements. The military's role in counterinsurgency embraces two broad categories of activities: combat, frequently counterguerrilla in nature, and pacification. The latter encompasses a broad array of civil, administrative, and constabulary functions designed to establish or maintain governmental authority in an area that is either openly or potentially hostile.

A *contingency operation*, according to the Department of Defense, is any military operation that is likely to result either in confrontations with an opposing force or the call-up of reserves.[2] Rather than attempt to cover all the many and disparate activities that could conceivably fit under the rubric of contingency operations, this work confines its discussion to limited overseas missions undertaken in peacetime to restore order, quell an insurrection, bolster a friendly government, or otherwise serve as an instrument of American diplomacy short of engaging in full-scale hostilities. Limited contingency operations of this type share with counterinsurgency a number of features that allow the student of doctrine to consider them as a whole. First, the military frequently performs these missions in relatively underdeveloped areas, where transportation systems are often rudimentary and topographical and climatic conditions are difficult. Second, combat in such situations usually pits the Army against irregular or semiregular forces. Finally, and most important, political considerations play a crucial role in these activities at both the operational and tactical level. Not only is the close coordination of political, diplomatic, and military measures crucial during both of these types of operations, but also the ultimate success of these missions often depends on the interaction of soldiers with indigenous civilian populations. Consequently, soldiers engaged in these activities must exercise political and diplomatic skills beyond the martial talents normally required on the conventional battlefield.

One last term that must be defined is *doctrine*. For the purpose of this study, doctrine is that body of knowledge disseminated through officially approved publications, school curriculums, and textbooks that represents an army's approach to war and the conduct of military operations. Doctrine offers a distillation of experience, providing a guide to methods that have generally worked in the past and that are thought to be of some enduring utility. By providing a common orientation, language, and conceptual framework, doctrine helps soldiers navigate through the fog of war.[3]

Despite the importance of formal, written doctrine, informal doctrines composed of custom, tradition, and accumulated experience often play just as significant a role in shaping the conduct of military operations as do officially codified precepts. Informal doctrines, concepts, and beliefs may be preserved and transmitted through a variety of mediums, including official and unofficial writings, curricular materials, conversations, and individual memories. This process, while somewhat haphazard and difficult to document, is particularly important given the fact that doctrinal developments generally occur in an evolutionary fashion in which experience is gradually distilled and codified, only to be eventually modified and replaced after new experiences have demonstrated shortcomings in existing precepts. This study, therefore, approaches the development of Army doctrine for counterinsurgency and contingency operations by examining the formal and informal evolution of Army thought and practice, both in the field and in the classroom.

After taking a cursory look at the Army's pre–World War II doctrinal heritage and relevant wartime experiences, this volume describes the state of national and military affairs at the conclusion of World War II that would influence the development of Army doctrine. With the outbreak of the Cold War, the Army assumed the relatively new role of providing advice and assistance to friendly countries threatened by Communist subversive movements. The study goes on to examine how the Army performed this role in five countries—China, Greece, Korea, Indochina, and the Philippines—during the decade and a half that followed World War II. The Korean War, in which the Army moved from an advisory to a combatant role, will also be discussed, as will the doctrinal writings that emerged during this period. The work then examines Army contingency operations in theory and, in the case of Lebanon and the Dominican Republic, in practice. By the early 1960s interest in counterinsurgency had reached a fever pitch. The volume describes how the Army responded to the counterinsurgency challenge in its manuals, its classrooms, and in the field, either directly in Vietnam or through a number of advisory missions around the globe. By the end of the Vietnam War both the nation and the Army had become disenchanted with overseas entanglements, and the study concludes by tracing the declining emphasis on counterinsurgency and limited contingency

MAP 1

operations in the Army's doctrinal and educational systems by the mid-1970s. (*Map 1*)

Counterinsurgency and contingency operations describe broad operational environments that involve many aspects of the military art, from tactics to unconventional warfare, logistics, transportation, military assistance, psychological operations, and civil affairs. Many of these subjects have doctrines and literatures of their own. This monograph covers only those aspects of Army doctrine that might play a role in conducting a counterinsurgency or peacetime contingency

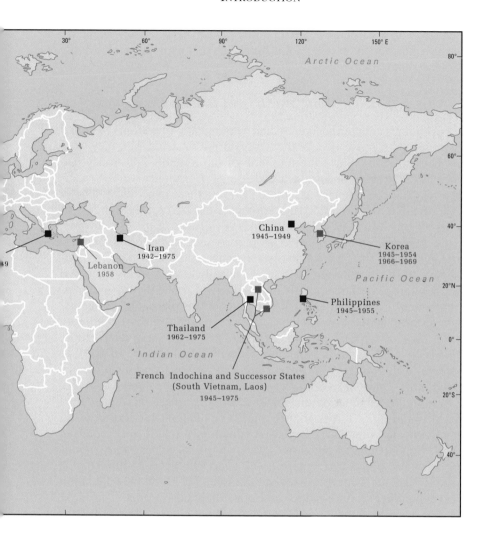

operation. Rather, the study focuses only on those aspects that are uniquely tailored to the counterinsurgency and stability operations environment. Similarly, while the work examines selective episodes of American military advisory and operational activities, it is not meant to be a narrative history of the Army's numerous overseas experiences since World War II. The many activities undertaken by the Army during this period require that the work be selective in its coverage and incorporate only those facts necessary to provide the reader with sufficient background with which to understand the evolution of doctrine.

7

Readers who are interested in obtaining a more detailed understanding of the events touched upon in this book can find many resources in the footnotes and bibliography.

Early Doctrine, World War II, and Postwar Occupations

Although counterinsurgency and contingency operations assumed a heightened significance for the Army during the Cold War, they were not new missions. Since the founding of the Republic, the Army had been called upon to undertake a wide range of irregular warfare, pacification, and constabulary assignments. From these experiences a body of formal and informal doctrine eventually evolved for the conduct of what the pre–World War II Army came to call *small wars*. Small wars, as the Army defined them, were operations undertaken for the purpose of suppressing an insurrection, establishing order, or dispensing punishment in situations where U.S. troops usually faced a poorly equipped or irregular foe. Relatively little of this doctrine found its way into official manuals. However, curricular materials, war plans, and the actual actions taken by the Army in the field reveal a high degree of continuity in the way the service approached irregular warfare and pacification. This body of thought, the evolution of which is discussed in the first volume of this series, *U.S. Army Counterinsurgency and Contingency Operations Doctrine, 1860–1941*, established some broad concepts governing the conduct of small wars. Militarily, these concepts called for the tailoring of forces and techniques to the political, military, and environmental situation. Aggressive small-unit action, incorporating regular and irregular techniques, was emphasized, as were mobility, surprise, population control, and good intelligence. In terms of pacification, the theory recognized the value of courting the population through proper troop conduct and governmental reforms. The latter actions were designed to win favor, redress potential causes of discontent, and in their most acute form, to "uplift" the subject society by introducing "modern" social, political, and economic institutions. This approach to pacification was based on a complex blend of American and Western political and moral thought, international law, and rather paternalistic notions of the "white man's burden."

Army doctrine also followed Western traditions in taking a dim view of guerrillas who violated the laws of war and hid their true identity by shedding their arms and uniforms. When a civilian population spurned the hand of reconciliation and supported illegal combatants, an army was free to employ more severe measures. Among the counterinsurgency methods employed by the United States prior to World War II were the

*U.S. soldiers execute a German guerrilla in the closing days of
World War II.*

taking of hostages; the destruction of food and property; the arrest, trial, and possible execution of guerrillas and their civilian allies; population resettlement; and a host of other restrictive steps. The net result of the Army's thinking about small wars was a loose body of broadly defined concepts that blended aggressive military action, punitive measures, and enlightened administration into a carrot-and-stick approach to the suppression of irregulars and their civilian supporters.[4]

After a century of antiguerrilla operations, the U.S. Army had little occasion for fighting guerrillas during World War II. In the closing months of the war German leader Adolf Hitler launched a "Werewolf" guerrilla movement that harassed the Allies. The movement largely fizzled after Germany surrendered, however, and resistance to the postwar occupation of Germany generally amounted to little more than minor acts of sabotage and hooliganism, often perpetrated by wayward boys.[5]

For the most part, the U.S. Army found itself fighting alongside, rather than against, numerous partisan movements during World War II. U.S. soldiers, either as individuals caught behind enemy lines, as members of special irregular warfare units, as advisers to indigenous resistance forces, or as part of the Office of Strategic Services (OSS), waged guerrilla warfare against Axis forces throughout Asia and Europe. Compared to the millions of men who served in conventional combat assignments, however, the war produced only a small cadre of

Captured "Werewolves" like these posed little danger during the postwar occupation of Germany.

guerrilla warfare practitioners. These men would play an important role in guiding the Army's postwar efforts to establish a guerrilla, and to a lesser extent, counterguerrilla, capability. The fact that the Army did not actually undertake any significant counterguerrilla actions during the war meant that there was no incentive to preserve or expand prewar small wars doctrine. Consequently, counterguerrilla warfare disappeared from the curriculums of wartime service schools. Army doctrine writers similarly ignored the subject, and the meager amount of counterguerrilla information contained in the Army's basic combat manual, Field Manual (FM) 100–5, *Field Service Regulations, Operations,* hardly changed at all between 1939 and 1949.

According to FM 100–5, partisan warfare could result from the defeat and breakup of the main forces of a modern opponent, from civilian resistance to the occupation of enemy territory, or from the rebellions of "semicivilized" peoples. Such campaigns, the manual advised, usually occurred in remote areas under difficult climatic and topographical conditions in which the counterinsurgent would have to employ special weapons, equipment, organizations, and methods to eliminate the resistance. Based in part on a study of French colonial techniques used in fighting Moroccan irregulars during the 1920s and 1930s, the manual called for vigorous and bold action conducted along a broad front. Army doctrine considered encirclement to be the best method for defeating an elusive irregular foe, while air attacks were deemed particularly effective both as an economy of force measure and as a way to weaken the morale of the guerrillas and their civilian supporters. Once the hostile region had been occupied, it was to be prepared for defense, with highly mobile columns organized to operate as reaction and strike forces. The doctrine also recognized the particular utility of enrolling the indigenous population into small, mobile, constabulary-type units. Beyond these limited and largely colonial-oriented prescriptions the manual did not go. And with the disappearance of most of the Army's prewar constabulary veterans due to death and retirement and with its interwar counterguerrilla curricular materials swept aside by the onslaught of global conventional war, the Army emerged from World War II with virtually no written doctrine or corporate expertise on the conduct of counterguerrilla and pacification campaigns.[6]

This did not mean, however, that Army doctrine was devoid of information useful for conducting such campaigns. Wartime texts and manuals covered a wide range of topics that would be of utility in conducting counterguerrilla operations, including small-unit patrol, security, and combat techniques, convoy procedures, Ranger and commando-style operations, mountain and jungle warfare, and logistical and administrative methods required to project military power into the most remote corners of the globe. Moreover, the Army gained significant experience during the war in two doctrinal areas relevant to the conduct of pacification operations: military law and military government.

Traditionally, international law and the U.S. Army's own regulations disapproved of guerrillas and other mufti-clad irregulars for the simple reason that they blurred the line between combatant and noncombatant, a distinction that was essential to ameliorating the harshness of war for civilian populations. FM 27–10, *Rules of Land Warfare*, published in 1940, echoed these long traditions in Western jurisprudence by establishing strict criteria for guerrilla warriors. To be considered legitimate combatants, guerrillas had to be commanded by a person responsible for his subordinates; wear a fixed, distinctive sign recognizable at a distance; carry their arms openly; and conduct themselves in accordance with the laws of war. Irregulars who failed to meet these criteria could be considered criminals, tried by military courts, and sentenced to prison or death. In practice, the Army had often chosen to treat captured guerrillas as legitimate prisoners of war to avoid an escalation of retaliatory violence between the Army and its irregular opponents, although at times it had availed itself of the most extreme sanctions, especially against particularly troublesome guerrilla leaders.[7]

A similar code governed the treatment of civilians in occupied or hostile areas. Since the promulgation in 1863 of General Orders 100, *Instructions for the Government of Armies of the United States in the Field*, the U.S. Army had acted in the belief that it had both a legal and moral obligation to conduct itself in as humane a manner as circumstances permitted in its dealings with civilian populations. Such a policy was not only morally enlightened, but served a practical purpose as well, for as FM 27–5, *Basic Field Manual, Military Government* (1940), noted, "A military occupation marked by harshness, injustice, or oppression leaves lasting resentment against the occupying power in the hearts of the people of the occupied territory and sows the seeds of future war by them against the occupying power when circumstances shall make that possible; whereas just, considerate, and mild treatment of the governed by the occupying army will convert enemies into friends." Since the Army's immediate objective was to minimize any resistance that might hamper the prosecution of the military campaign and since the ultimate object of war was the establishment of a lasting peace, such a creed made sense. Consequently, prewar military government doctrine called for the rapid restoration of normal social and economic life, the protection of personal and property rights, the inculcation among the troops of respect for social and religious customs, the perpetuation of most indigenous law and administrative forms, and the retention, when possible, of indigenous officials in their posts. Military government districts were to conform as closely as possible to preexisting civilian boundaries so as to facilitate the coordination of political and military affairs.[8]

Wartime emotions led some soldiers during the 1940s to react adversely to what they perceived as the overly benevolent tone of this doctrine. When, for example, an Army civil affairs instructor at Yale University told his soldier-students that they should treat Japanese civilians humanely, several officers shouted back, "Let the yellow bastards starve!" Similarly, albeit with less bitterness, Col. Lewis K. Underhill instructed his students at the School for Military Government that the 1940 edition of FM 27–5 was too lenient and

gives us the impression the objective of promoting the welfare of the governed in occupied territory is almost as important as the objective of military necessity. In fact, you get the impression from the text that our principal objective in invading a foreign country is to bring light to the heathen. Now I can assure you that is not realistic. There is only one legitimate objective of military government and that is to win the war. It is a method of fighting behind the lines, and is done by holding the civil population in subjection. . . . Military government is not a missionary enterprise, and while you do pay attention to

12

the welfare of the governed, you do it because you are inherently decent and because paying attention to their welfare where you can will tend to avoid the more violent kinds of outbreaks against you; but it is utterly misleading to put the welfare of the governed on par with military necessity. Everything you do in military government has to be tested in the light of whether it will aid or retard the campaign.[9]

The Army endorsed this view, and the 1943 edition of FM 27–5 dropped "welfare of the governed" and "considerate and mild treatment" as objectives of military government, injunctions that had been a part of U.S. Army doctrine since the Civil War. Nevertheless, while wartime attitudes stiffened some of the language contained in FM 27–5, the revised doctrine still recognized the merits of "just and reasonable" treatment and encouraged moderate policies. Rather than a fundamental alteration in doctrine, the 1943 edition of FM 27–5 merely reflected a modest shift in the pendulum between benevolence and severity, two policies that had always enjoyed a dynamic relationship in Army doctrine. Indeed, Army doctrine continued to view the relationship between soldiers and civilians as a reciprocal one. As long as the population did not resist military authority it was to be treated well; but should the inhabitants take up arms or support guerrilla movements, then they were open to sterner measures. Thus, before, during, and after the war, Army doctrine endeavored to strike a pragmatic, though often uneasy, balance between humanity and severity, the exact proportions of which were left undefined so that commanders could best respond to the particular circumstances of the moment.[10]

Although governing occupied areas was a traditional military function, when the Army established a School for Military Government at Charlottesville, Virginia, in May 1942, the move immediately drew criticism. Many believed that the institution represented a dangerous intrusion of the military into civilian affairs, labeling it a "school for gauleiters." Several civilian departments of government likewise attacked the school because they deemed the training of military specialists in civil administration to be a direct threat to their own bureaucratic interests. For its part, the Army was not at all enthusiastic about undertaking civil administrative burdens, but it maintained that as a practical matter it was the only agency with the training, organization, and personnel to administer foreign populations during wartime. Moreover, military necessity and the principle of unity of command demanded that all civil and military forces be placed at the disposal of a single military commander so as not to impede the successful prosecution of the war. These principles had long been core tenets of U.S. Army doctrine, for as Col. Jesse Miller of the Provost Marshal General's Military Government

The U.S. Army School for Military Government

Division noted in July 1942, "if there is one outstanding lesson to be gained from prior American experiences in military government, it is the unwisdom of permitting any premature interference by civilian agencies with the Army's basic task of civil administration in occupied areas."[11]

Ultimately, experience showed that the Army was right. After civilian agencies proved incapable of meeting their basic obligations during the occupation of North Africa in 1942–1943, the Army assumed nearly complete control of civil affairs and military government functions for the remainder of the war. Despite some failings of concept, policy, and administration, the Army assembled a creditable record under trying circumstances, providing basic governmental services to over 200 million people worldwide.[12]

Much to the Army's chagrin, the end of hostilities did not bring an end to the service's civil affairs and military government responsibilities.[13] When the civilian agencies that ought to have assumed the burdens of administering the occupied territories after the war proved unequal to the task, the Army was forced to take on the mission. These postwar occupations differed in important respects from those conducted during the war. The wartime occupations had endeavored to restore law, order, and basic governmental services for the purpose of facilitating the war effort. The postwar occupations, on the other hand, had as a goal not the restoration of antebellum conditions, but their transformation. In Germany and Japan, the U.S. government endeavored to revolutionize the political, social, and economic foundations of those societies to ensure that they would never again become fertile ground for aggressive militaristic and antidemocratic forces. In Germany, this took the form of the four "Ds": denazification, decartelization, demilitarization, and democratization. A similar program was imposed on Japan.[14]

The job of transforming Germany and Japan was enormous, and it was a task for which most U.S. soldiers had little preparation. The man chosen to bring American-style democracy to Germany, Lt. Gen. Lucius D. Clay, had never cast a ballot in his life. His counterpart in Japan, General of the Army Douglas MacArthur, likewise had no special qualifications as a nation builder. Nor were many of their subordinates much better prepared. Partly because of the Army's traditional disinclination to dabble in politics and partly because civilian criticism had led the School for Military Government to focus on purely administrative matters to the exclusion of policy, the majority of military government personnel were unprepared for the mission of transforming German and Japanese society.[15]

Nevertheless, America's soldier-diplomats did not undertake their assignment in a vacuum. Like U.S. soldiers charged with nation-building duties before them—including MacArthur's own father four decades earlier in the Philippines—they approached their work from a perspective shaped by American political and cultural values. Although their particular views on any given subject might vary, America's overseas governors generally believed in the virtue of the American political, economic, and social system. Like the society from which they were drawn, they believed in liberty, self-reliance, and individualism tempered by civic responsibility; in private property and industry unfettered by overly intrusive government regulation; and in public education's vital role in laying the groundwork for full participation in political and economic affairs. They also brought with them the prides and prejudices of their day, including racist and ethnocentristic attitudes. This complex mosaic of cultural values was what often guided their actions rather than any specific training.

Although charged with the task of transforming German and Japanese society, the Army's social engineers were aware that, in the words of one Army manual, "in general, it is unwise to impose upon occupied territory the laws and customs of another people." Past experience had shown that such endeavors often produced much turmoil and little results, as the indigenous body politic often rejected transplanted institutions. Indeed, Clay believed that "a foreign group cannot establish a successful revolution" in another society, while Army officials in Japan stated that "only insofar as the Japanese leaders and

A U.S. military court tries a German civilian charged with illegally possessing a firearm.

people recognized the goals of the Occupation as desirable could there be hope that the alterations accomplished by the Occupation would endure." Bayonets could impose change, but only a genuine evolution in the values and beliefs of the people could ensure that the subject societies would be transformed—a process that required time and indigenous support. Consequently, U.S. overseas administrators took a conservative and pragmatic approach consistent with that adopted by the Army in its pre-1940 nation-building endeavors. Rather than literally transposing American institutions on foreign societies, America's social engineers in uniform usually worked through existing institutions as much as possible, planting seeds—like reforming educational systems and removing barriers to personal, political, economic, and social expression—in the hope that these ideas would eventually take root and flourish. Generally, they endeavored to build democracy from the ground up, strengthening local institutions and appealing to the will of the people wherever possible. Following military government precedent, the Army rapidly restored most aspects of internal civil and political life to lighten its own administrative burdens, build consensus, and garner legitimacy.[16]

These wise policies were exceedingly difficult to accomplish. Undesirable traits such as racism and wartime hatreds complicated their execution. In fact, the very notion of transforming a foreign society was in itself inherently ethnocentric. No matter how sensitive one tries to be toward another culture—and sensitivity is an absolute prerequisite to any successful aid, advisory, or nation-building mission—not to impose one's own notions is virtually impossible; after all, that is why the mission is usually being undertaken in the first place. Moreover, there are times when reforms are so important, either to the subject society or to the occupier, that they must be imposed whether popular or not.

The postwar occupations illustrated these age-old dilemmas well. When U.S. officials deemed a particular change to be of critical importance, like denazification, they imposed it by fiat regardless of indigenous sentiments. Such impositions sometimes created a backlash from the subject population. On the other hand, the Army's policy of turning over the workings of government as quickly as possible to indigenous officials also undermined reform efforts, as local leaders often had different goals and values than U.S. authorities. For example, once the Army passed the job of denazification over to German authorities in 1946, those officials restored full citizenship rights to most ex-Nazis after imposing only mild admonitions and fines, much to the distress of many Americans. Similar problems occurred in other aspects of the reform effort, with the result that many American-introduced concepts either withered on the vine or were otherwise transformed or subverted. Had America's proconsuls had the luxury of an indefinite tenure and a single agenda, they might have been more successful in transplanting American institutions, but they did not. Neither the Army nor the nation was willing to undertake the costs of indefinite tutelage. Furthermore, military government personnel had to juggle the multiple goals of promoting democracy, reducing the financial burdens of occupation duty, achieving economic health and self-sufficiency, obtaining Allied cooperation, and, with the onset of the Cold War, building bulwarks against the spread of communism. Some of these goals were complementary, but others were not, and in endeavoring to balance them, long-term reforms sometimes gave way to more pragmatic, short-term objectives.[17]

Difficulties notwithstanding, the United States ultimately succeeded in transforming the former Axis powers into stable democratic partners. This achievement encouraged some observers to believe that social engineering was possible in a relatively short time. Such conclusions overlooked both the failure of many American initiatives and the hardiness of indigenous institutions. Moreover, the postwar occupations had enjoyed several significant advantages over the type of nation-building activities that the United States would attempt in many third world countries. The occupations had occurred in peacetime, after conflict had been terminated, law and order restored, and many of the institutions that might have impeded change had been destroyed by the war itself. Having total control over a prostrate society also simplified nation-building programs in Germany and Japan. Conquest facilitated social engineering by discrediting the old ways and by providing a powerful, physical demonstration of the superiority of American methods. Finally, in Germany and Japan, the United States was dealing with modern, industrialized, and ethnically cohesive nations with strong bureaucratic, political, and social institutions. Success in these areas would not necessarily translate into an ability to work similar transformations in less developed and less homogenous societies or in societies whose political and cultural heritages were radically unlike America's own. Future policy makers would not always appreciate these aspects of postwar nation-building endeavors.[18]

The military government experience of the 1940s thus bequeathed America's soldiers, statesmen, and policy makers an ambivalent legacy. Much had been accomplished, yet many problems remained unresolved. One such issue involved the question of government organization for overseas politico-military operations. In theory, the State Department determined policy and the Army executed it. In practice, poor civilian guidance and the press of events often meant that the Army exercised broad powers over the conduct of overseas policy, both during the war and the postwar occupations. Throughout the war the Departments of State, the Treasury, and the Interior had fought fiercely both among themselves and against the War Department over questions of function and jurisdiction, and when President Franklin D. Roosevelt created the Foreign Economic Administration in 1943 to establish some coordination, the civilian agencies had fought against the prospect of unified civilian direction just as vehemently as they had against the prospect of military predominance. The Army's commitment to the principle of unity of command notwithstanding, the philosophical and bureaucratic impediments to achieving centralized direction over overseas politico-military operations had never been fully overcome during the 1940s. The result was an unsettled legacy that did not bode well for future American foreign aid, nation-building, and pacification efforts.[19]

The experience of the 1940s also illustrated the impossibility of separating political from purely military or administrative concerns, no matter how hard soldiers and civilians sought to do so. Political issues and consequences were embedded in even the most technical and seemingly innocuous administrative questions, and by necessity rather than by choice, U.S. soldiers had found that they had to exercise considerable political judgment. The experience demonstrated that the Army needed to be better prepared for politico-military missions.

Yet civilian criticism also reaffirmed for soldiers the old lesson that military government and nation building were arduous and institutionally unrewarding. Thus, while the Army could not ignore the military government function, strong traditions in American political thought—traditions shared by soldiers and civilians alike—continued to retard the development of military capabilities in political affairs. Consequently, the Army's military government training and doctrinal systems emerged from the 1940s much as they had entered it. They focused on the military, technical, and administrative aspects of civil affairs—military government duty while avoiding detailed treatment of political issues—issues that were not only difficult but, since they were often situation specific, were largely irresolvable from a doctrinal standpoint in any case. Nation building, as distinct from occupation duty, was not discussed. Rather, the postwar Army, like its prewar predecessor, confined itself to prescribing some broad principles governing the Army's relationship with foreign populations—principles that stressed pragmatism, flexibility, and "firm-but-fair" policies designed to balance military necessity with the needs and aspirations of the local populace. How such a doctrine would fare under the demands of the postwar world remained to be seen.[20]

Guerrillas, Civilians, and the Geneva Convention of 1949

Although U.S. Army doctrine on the treatment of guerrillas and civilian populations emerged from World War II with its fundamental principles largely intact, one outgrowth of the war that had the potential to alter these principles occurred in 1949, when the victorious powers met at Geneva, Switzerland, to revise international law in light of their wartime experiences. Many of the participating countries had been occupied by the Axis powers during the war, had formed resistance movements to oppose those occupations, and had suffered under exceedingly harsh Axis policies. Consequently, there was a general movement to clarify and expand the protections accorded to civilian populations during wartime. The convention reemphasized the rights of noncombatants and narrowed the definition of military necessity—a clause that armies had often used in the past to justify the harshest of actions.[21]

The conferees also took the extraordinary step of extending international law to internal conflicts. The 1949 agreement required that signatory nations facing an internal war or rebellion treat humanely "persons taking no active part in the hostilities." The convention made illegal the acts of humiliating, mutilating, torturing, or killing such individuals; of taking them hostage; or of denying them due process. These provisions were exceedingly controversial, as many states felt that any rule affecting their internal affairs represented an infringement on their sovereignty. Consequently, the language of the treaty was vague in some respects. Similarly, although the convention attempted to extend the protection of "legitimate belligerents" to members of resistance movements, the treaty still required that individuals meet the same four criteria of the past to qualify for such protection—responsible command, recognizable insignia, exposed weapons, and proper conduct according to the laws of war.[22]

The results of Geneva were thus ambiguous. Champions of human rights could point to significant victories, yet the treaty remained open to conflicting interpretation. To what extent could international law really be applied to the internal affairs of a nation, and at what point did individuals cross the line from being bandits (to which international law did not apply) to "privileged belligerents"? Were civilians who participated in clandestine organizations that fed, clothed, housed, and aided guerrillas "taking no active part in the hostilities," and therefore protected under the convention, or were they acting illegally and therefore outside of its protections? Finally, since most guerrilla organizations were either unable or unwilling to meet the four criteria of legitimacy, the convention had not really improved their status at all. These ambiguities would provide fertile ground for confusion and debate for decades to come.[23]

For the most part the U.S. Army embraced the more humane spirit of the 1949 convention. Collective punishment, reprisals, and hostage taking—three tools the Army had employed in past counterinsurgencies—were banned after the United States ratified the Geneva Convention in 1955, as were all measures of intimidation or terror. The Army also required U.S. soldiers to follow the treaty's internal warfare prescriptions in all advisory and operational missions abroad, including those involving purely indigenous resistance movements. On the other hand, while the Army continued to espouse the same enlightened principles of justice, humanity, and good troop conduct that had long been the foundation of U.S. Army policy, it also continued to apply to irregulars the same strict criteria of legitimacy that had existed prior to World War II. Similarly, the Army continued to maintain that civilians who gave guerrillas supplies, money, or intelligence could be punished. Civilian property could still be destroyed if the destruction served a demonstrable military purpose, and civilian populations could still be relocated as long as such action was performed humanely. The carrot and stick thus remained inextricably linked in the uneasy, yet symbiotic, relationship that had long characterized the conduct of American counterinsurgency operations.[24]

The Army and the Challenges of the Postwar World

The Geneva Convention was just one example of how World War II had altered the political and military landscape in which the postwar Army would have to maneuver. In addition to wrestling with new global responsibilities and Cold War threats, the postwar Army found itself under constant pressure to absorb increasingly sophisticated technologies, from atomic weapons to helicopters, in ever shorter lengths of time. These developments placed enormous strains on the service's doctrinal, materiel, organizational, and training systems, as the Army struggled to prepare for the divergent requirements of nuclear, conventional, and irregular warfare; domestic duties; and overseas constabulary functions. The result of all these pressures and competing needs was a doctrinal treadmill, with the Army's basic statement of fundamental doctrine, FM 100–5, *Operations*, undergoing eight different editions between 1941 and 1976. Force structures underwent similar changes. Over the course of a single ten-year period (1955–1965), the Army twice overhauled its basic divisional structure while dabbling with a number of air cavalry, airmobile, Ranger, Special Forces, and light infantry formations. All of these factors impeded the ability of soldiers to absorb and understand doctrine.[25]

America's superpower status, when coupled with the Cold War and the introduction of weapons of mass destruction, also complicated the Army's world by intertwining political and military affairs to an extent far greater than before. This resulted in an unprecedented degree of military influence on political and diplomatic affairs, and an equally deep penetration of traditionally military spheres by civilian policy makers who believed that war in the nuclear age was too important to be left to generals. The advent of the national security state was accompanied by the development of an entirely new class of civilian strategists, analysts, and scientists who fueled the creation of what one author termed an "era of overthink." Driven by the belief that technology had revolutionized warfare, many national security intellectuals declared history to be irrelevant in establishing future strategies and doctrines. One consequence of this trend was that doctrine, which had traditionally represented a distillation of experience, began to reflect an increasingly theoretical influence in which projections of future technologies and behaviors began to overshadow lessons from the past. Although scholars of strategy initially focused their attention on nuclear affairs, the plethora of civilian think tanks, institutes, and analysts would eventually have a profound influence on how the United States approached counterinsurgency, pacification, and nation-building issues.[26]

The difficulties facing the Army in the realms of organization and doctrine after 1945 were matched by equally daunting foreign policy problems for the nation as a whole. In assessing the challenges of the postwar world, America's attention initially focused on Western Europe, an area with which the United States had strong cultural, economic, and political ties. Six years of warfare had made the region vulnerable to communism, either through internal subversion or by overt aggression from the Soviet Union's new lodgments in Eastern Europe. To counter these threats, the United States during the late 1940s developed a dual strategy of economic development and military assistance that would serve as its fundamental recipe for the containment of communism for the next half-century.

In March 1947 President Harry S. Truman requested that Congress appropriate a mixture of economic and military aid to prevent Greece and Turkey from falling under the shadow of totalitarianism. Three months later Secretary of State George C. Marshall unveiled a massive $13 billion program of economic and technical assistance for the rest of Europe—a sum that, if expressed in 2004 dollars, would exceed $102 billion. The overwhelmingly economic focus of these first Cold War programs reflected the widespread belief that political systems were largely shaped by economic conditions and that communism and other radical ideologies flourished in economically depressed conditions. Eliminate the socioeconomic environment in which communism bred, and the danger of subversion would likewise diminish.[27]

The stunning success of the Marshall Plan in restoring Western Europe encouraged the United States to apply the same formula in various degrees around the world to any nation threatened by communism. U.S. policy makers were aware, however, that economic aid and technical assistance alone could not always keep the Communists at bay, either because the United States lacked the financial resources to uplift every threatened part of the world simultaneously or because the Communists had already established firm footholds before American help could arrive. Moreover, even healthy democratic societies were vulnerable to external aggression. Consequently, in 1949, two years after the announcement of the Marshall Plan, the United States strengthened the military aspects of its effort to contain the spread of communism. The military response to the Cold War took two forms. The first was a system of alliances, begun in Europe with the formation of the North Atlantic Treaty Organization (NATO) but later expanded to other parts of the world with the creation of additional pacts. The second was the establishment of a program of military assistance to flesh out the armed forces of America's new allies with U.S. arms and military expertise.

Two features of the Mutual Defense Assistance Program, as the aid program was initially known, are of interest. First, the legislation authorizing the program stated that the economic recovery of Europe, as well as the other countries that were to receive aid, would receive a higher funding priority than the provision of military assistance. This stipulation reflected the continued belief that internal socioeconomic strength was the ultimate key to both democracy and national security. Second, the military aid program, like America's economic aid programs, was intended to be a short-term, pump-priming measure, rather than a permanent program. Self-help and reciprocity were the program's watchwords—ideals that were not always achieved as promptly and thoroughly as the architects of the program might have hoped.[28]

The advent of the military assistance program represented an immense new undertaking for the U.S. Army, one for which it had relatively little experience. Between 1949 and 1960, the United States provided nearly $24 billion worth of military aid to more than forty nations around the world. By 1956, 20 percent of all Army officers had served as military advisers to foreign forces. Initially, much of this effort focused on creating conventional armed forces to resist Soviet or other external aggression. However, internal subversion, either indigenously generated or assisted by external Communist forces, soon became equally as menacing. This observation was true not so much in Western Europe, but rather in Asia, Africa, and Latin America, where the weakness of the old European colonial powers combined with rising third world nationalism and socioeconomic change to create a world ripe for revolution and civil war. In fact, there were so many internal conflicts during the three decades between 1945 and 1975 that the period has been described as the "era of people's war." Revolution, colonial rebellions, and civil strife were certainly not new phenomena, but their potential exploitation by the forces of communism made them particularly dangerous in the minds of American Cold War strategists. This was especially true after the widespread dissemination of Chinese Communist leader Mao Tse-tung's theories of revolutionary warfare in the 1950s and early 1960s.[29]

Early Communists like Karl Marx, Friedrich Engels, V. I. Lenin, and Leon Trotsky had always considered guerrilla warfare as but one tool in the revolutionary arsenal, and not necessarily the most important one. Rather, they had regarded urban insurrection and conventional warfare as the primary weapons of revolution. Although the world's first Communist state, the Union of Soviet Socialist Republics (USSR), had employed partisan tactics during the revolution and civil war that had given it birth, guerrilla methods never played a central role in Soviet thinking. When the Soviet Union published a manual on insurrectionary warfare in 1928, the book contained only a single chapter on guerrilla warfare—a chapter that was written not by a Soviet, but by an obscure Vietnamese Communist, Ho Chi Minh. Consequently, from the time U.S. soldiers first began to contemplate measures to combat socialist revolutionaries in the 1880s until World War II, they approached the subject largely in terms of urban warfare and domestic disturbances rather than as counterguerrilla warfare.[30]

All this began to change in 1949, when Mao Tse-tung's rural-based insurgency finally toppled Chiang Kai-shek's regime in China after more than two decades of war and revolution. Over those years Mao had been a prolific writer, committing to paper his thoughts on the nature of war, revolution, and the course of the Chinese Civil War. Differing significantly from most Soviet strategists and their disciples among the Chinese Communist Party (CCP), he rejected urban-centered strategies for rural-based guerrilla warfare. Much of what Mao had to say about guerrilla warfare was not new, for the basic tenets of guerrilla combat have been known for centuries. In fact, he shared the traditional view of guerrilla warfare as an inferior tool—one that was unlikely to triumph against a regular army unless the guerrillas eventually created their own conventional forces. But he correctly gauged that rural guerrilla warfare could lay the foundations for a successful revolution, at least under the conditions he found in contemporary China. What made Mao's methods unique were not his military stratagems, but his blending of traditional guerrilla methods with Leninist organizational techniques to create a mass, peasant-based, nationalistic armed movement firmly under the control of the Communist Party.[31]

Although a Marine officer had warned his Army colleagues about the potency of Mao's methods in a 1941 article, the Army would not begin to study Mao until the 1950s, after his final triumph had demonstrated the power of his ideas. Even then, intensive study was slow in coming, partly because of the Army's conventional focus, partly because the import of Mao's methods was not yet fully clear, and partly because the Army's first direct clash with Mao's forces occurred during a largely conventional war on the Korean Peninsula. Moreover, one must remember that Mao's victory had not been certain. China's Communists had come perilously close to being defeated several times during their long struggle, and, had Japan not invaded China and subsequently been defeated by the United States in World War II, the Chinese Communists may well have failed.[32]

But fortune smiled on Mao, and his victory over Chiang Kai-shek in 1949, followed by the triumph of his Vietnamese disciple Ho Chi Minh over French colonialists in neighboring Indochina in 1954, eventually catapulted his methods to the forefront of Cold War strategy. Although most of Mao's writings focused on explaining the nature of China's political and military situation, the leaders of radical movements around the world treated his words as if they were prophecy. In Mao's three stages of revolutionary warfare they thought they had found the ideal formula by which a relatively small, highly disciplined cadre could organize the rural masses of an underdeveloped country to overthrow an unpopular, repressive, or colonial regime. Since, by happy coincidence, World War II had shattered the grip of the old imperial powers and unleashed hitherto suppressed nationalistic sentiments throughout the third world, Mao's revolutionary war philosophy became the very embodiment of the era of people's war.[33]

By the 1960s many Americans had come to share this view, particularly after Soviet Premier Nikita Khrushchev openly embraced "wars of national liberation" as a vehicle with which to further communism's struggle against the West. Taking the challenge to heart, U.S. soldiers, statesmen, and civilian theorists alike rushed to obtain copies of what ultimately became known as Mao's little red book to understand what they believed was the next phase of world communism's master plan. In the process, many theorists—American and foreign, Marxist and non-Marxist—became more doctrinaire than Mao himself, asserting universal applicability to concepts Mao had originally envisioned only for China in the 1930s and 1940s. The Chinese government actively promoted the notion that Mao's precepts were universal, both as a way to make war on the West without risking a nuclear confrontation and as a means of elevating China's standing in its rivalry with the Soviet Union for leadership of the Communist world. Such analysis ignored Mao's own warning that each military and revolutionary situation had its own rules and circumstances that would doom to failure any attempt to apply slavishly a particular doctrine. Nevertheless, many theorists came to believe that Mao had done for guerrilla warfare what the atom bomb had done to conventional warfare—he had revolutionized it. By blending modern techniques of Communist Party organization, propaganda, and population control with the ancient arts of guerrilla warfare, some observers believed Mao had created a whole new form of warfare, unprecedented in scope, for which all previous experience was irrelevant.[34]

One aspect of Communist theory that many Western analysts found appealing was Mao's statement that political, rather than military, considerations were paramount in revolutionary warfare. To many, this idea made Maoist-style warfare qualitatively different from all past guerrilla and revolutionary conflicts. But the assertion by Mao's Western disciples that prior guerrilla conflicts had been apolitical was historically incorrect.[35] Past revolutionary movements may have been less sophisticated in organization and technique, but their leaders certainly had been aware of the political and psychological components of their struggles. Nevertheless, Mao's dictum of political primacy had the effect of further promoting civilian influence in the formulation of military doctrine. Indeed, with the exception of nuclear warfare strategy, no other area of military thought would be so influenced by politicians and civilian theorists during the initial postwar decades than counterinsurgency. There was, of course, nothing wrong with this, as long as the policies and doctrines that emerged from the intellectual tumult of the 1960s were workable and based on reality rather than on theoretical constructs or overly doctrinaire readings of Mao and other Communist theorists. Unfortunately, that was not always the case, and some of the "overthink" that transpired during the era of people's war would prove counterproductive. In fact, fascination with Mao produced a certain rigidity in American counterinsurgency thought during the 1960s and 1970s that earlier doctrine had lacked and that seems particularly dated in the light of the post–Cold War world.

But that is jumping ahead in the story. During the decade that followed World War II the Army grappled with a number of insurgencies that had erupted in areas formerly occupied by the Axis powers, as Communists around the world endeavored to exploit the vacuum created by Axis withdrawal and the frailty of many postwar governments and colonial regimes. For the most part, the Army undertook this job in a doctrinal void, without the benefit of a detailed written doctrine for counterguerrilla warfare or any familiarity with the writings of Mao. How it met the challenges posed by the postwar revolutions is the subject of the next two chapters.

Notes

[1] Edwin Corr and Stephen Sloan, *Low-Intensity Conflict: Old Threats in a New World* (Boulder, Colo.: Westview Press, 1992), p. 6.

[2] Department of Defense, Joint Publication 1–02, *Department of Defense Dictionary of Military and Associated Terms*, 12 Apr 2001, as amended 25 Sep 2002, p. 117.

[3] Robert Doughty, *The Evolution of U.S. Army Tactical Doctrine, 1946–76* (Fort Leavenworth, Kans.: U.S. Army Command and General Staff College, 1979), p. 1; John Mills, "U.S. Army Doctrine—Far Sighted Vision or Transient Fad?" (Master's thesis, U.S. Army Command and General Staff College [CGSC], 1987), pp. 10–12.

[4] Andrew Birtle, *U.S. Army Counterinsurgency and Contingency Operations Doctrine, 1860–1941* (Washington, D.C.: U.S. Army Center of Military History, 1998).

[5] For background on the Werewolf movement, see Perry Biddiscombe, *The Last Nazis: SS Werewolf Guerrilla Resistance in Euorpe, 1944–1947* (Charleston, S.C.: Tempus, 2000), and Charles Whiting, *Werewolf: The Story of the Nazi Resistance Movement, 1944–1945* (Barnsley, England: Pen & Sword Books, 1996).

[6] War Department Field Manual (FM) 100–5, *Field Service Regulations, Operations* (tentative) (Washington, D.C.: Government Printing Office, 1939), pp. 229–31; FM 100–5, *Field Service Regulations, Operations*, 1941, pp. 238–40; FM 100–5, *Field Service Regulations, Operations*, 1944, pp. 284–86; FM 100–5, *Field Service Regulations, Operations*, 1949, pp. 231–33.

[7] For background on the legality of guerrilla warfare, see Lester Nurick and Roger Barrett, "Legality of Guerrilla Forces Under the Laws of War," *American Journal of International Law* 40 (July 1946): 563–83.

[8] FM 27–5, *Basic Field Manual, Military Government*, 1940, p. 4.

[9] First quote from Justin Williams, "From Charlottesville to Tokyo: Military Government Training and Democratic Reforms in Occupied Japan," *Pacific Historical Review* 51 (1982): 417. Second quote from Carl Friedrich et al., *American Experiences in Military Government in World War II* (New York: Rinehart and Co., 1948), p. 27.

[10] William Daugherty and Marshall Andrews, A Review of U.S. Historical Experience with Civil Affairs, 1776–1954, Operations Research Office Technical Paper, ORO–TP–29, Chevy Chase, Md.: Operations Research Office, Johns Hopkins University, 1961, pp. 234–35; FM 27–10, *Rules of Land Warfare*, 1940, pp. 4–5, 7, 85–90; FM 27–5, *United States Army and Navy Manual of Military Government and Civil Affairs*, 1943, pp. 7–8; FM 27–5, *United States Army and Navy Manual of Civil Affairs Military Government*, 1947, pp. 6, 9–10.

[11] First quote from Earl Ziemke, *The U.S. Army in the Occupation of Germany, 1944–1946*, Army Historical Series (Washington, D.C.: U.S. Army Center of Military History, 1975), p. 12. Second quote from Harry Coles and Albert Weinberg, *Civil Affairs: Soldiers Become Governors*, U.S. Army in World War II (Washington, D.C.: U.S. Army Center of Military History, 1964), p. 15, and see also pp. 4–5, 16–17, 22–26. Daugherty and Andrews, Historical Experience with Civil Affairs, pp. 199, 260; Provost Marshal General, History of Military Government Training, 4 vols., 1945, 1:6–10, U.S. Army Center of Military History (CMH), Washington, D.C.

[12] Coles and Weinberg, *Civil Affairs*, pp. 3, 56–66, 92; Ziemke, *Occupation of Germany*, pp. 15–16; Daugherty and Andrews, Historical Experience with Civil Affairs,

pp. 444–50; Martin Kyre and Joan Kyre, *Military Occupation and National Security* (Washington, D.C.: Public Affairs Press, 1968), pp. 19–24; Daniel Fahey, Jr., Findings, Analysis, Conclusions, and Recommendations Concerning U.S. Civil Affairs/Military Government Organization, Department of the Army, 1951, p. 1, CMH (hereafter cited as Fahey Report).

[13] Prior to World War II, the Army had used the terms *civil affairs* and *military government* interchangeably. One of the conceptual changes that emerged during the war was the creation of a distinction between these terms. In the new lexicon, *civil affairs* referred to the exercise of varying degrees of governmental authority short of full control, usually over predominantly friendly areas. The term *military government* was limited to the imposition of absolute military control, usually over hostile areas. During the 1950s the Army broadened the term *civil affairs* to include the entire relationship between the Army and civilian communities. Military government thus became a subset of civil affairs. This change reflected the increasing importance of civil and political matters in the conduct of postwar overseas operations of a constabulary, contingency, and assistance nature, where the Army would not be operating as an occupation power. Kyre and Kyre, *Military Occupation*, pp. 10–16.

[14] Robert Wolfe, ed., *Americans as Proconsuls: United States Military Government in Germany and Japan, 1944–1952* (Carbondale: Southern Illinois University Press, 1984), pp. 59, 93, 96; Fahey Report, p. 2; Ziemke, *Occupation of Germany*, p. 432; John Pappas, "A Review of U.S. Civil Affairs/Military Government, 1778–1955: An Analysis of Concepts" (Student thesis, Army War College, 1955), p. 21; John Mason, "Training American Civilian Personnel for Occupation Duties," *American Journal of International Law* 40 (January 1946): 180–81; Williams, "Charlottesville to Tokyo," pp. 421–22; General Headquarters, Supreme Commander for the Allied Powers (SCAP), History of the Nonmilitary Activities of the Occupation of Japan, 1952, pp. 1–9, CMH.

[15] Wolfe, ed., *Americans as Proconsuls*, p. 105; Pappas, Review of U.S. Civil Affairs/Military Government, p. 20; Eric Bohman, "Rehearsals for Victory: The War Department and the Planning and Direction of Civil Affairs, 1940–43" (Ph.D. diss., Yale University, 1984), pp. 467–68.

[16] First quote from Coles and Weinberg, *Civil Affairs*, p. 146. Second quote from Wolfe, ed., *Americans as Proconsuls*, p. 104, and see also p. 105. Third quote from SCAP, History of Nonmilitary Activities, p. 37. Henry Hille, "Eighth Army's Role in the Military Government of Japan," *Military Review* 27 (February 1948): 9–10.

[17] Wolfe, ed., *Americans as Proconsuls*, p. 66; Koppel Pinson, *Modern Germany* (New York: Macmillan, 1966), pp. 42–45; James Tent, *Mission on the Rhine* (Chicago: University of Chicago Press, 1982), p. 312; SCAP, History of Nonmilitary Activities, pp. 57–58; John Gimbel, *The American Occupation of Germany* (Stanford, Calif.: Stanford University Press, 1968), p. 249.

[18] Tent, *Mission on the Rhine*, p. 318; Conference of Scholars on the Administration of Occupied Areas, 1943–55, 10–11 Apr 70, pp. 71–75, 82, Harry S. Truman Library, Independence, Mo., copy in CMH; Wolfe, ed., *Americans as Proconsuls*, pp. 66, 417–22, 442–43; Michael Latham, *Modernization as Ideology: American Social Science and "Nation Building" in the Kennedy Era* (Chapel Hill: University of North Carolina Press, 2000), pp. 79–80.

[19] Ziemke, *Occupation of Germany*, pp. 21–22.

[20] E. H. Vernon, "Civil Affairs and Military Government," *Military Review* 26 (June 1946): 25–32; FM 27–5, *United States Army and Navy Manual of Military Government*

and Civil Affairs, 1943, pp. 5–10; FM 27–5, *United States Army and Navy Manual of Civil Affairs Military Government*, 1947, pp. 7–15; William Swarm, "Impact of the Proconsular Experience on Civil Affairs Organization and Doctrine," in *Americans as Proconsuls*, ed. Wolfe, pp. 398–415.

[21] FM 27–10, *The Law of Land Warfare*, 1956, pp. 17–23.

[22] Keith Suter, *An International Law of Guerrilla Warfare: The Global Politics of Law Making* (New York: St. Martin's Press, 1984), p. 15.

[23] FM 27–10, *The Law of Land Warfare*, 1956, pp. 107, 152. For comments on the inadequacy of the 1949 convention's treatment of guerrilla and internal conflicts, see Suter, *International Law of Guerrilla Warfare*, pp. 10–17; John Moore, "Low-Intensity Conflict and the International Legal System," in Corr and Sloan, *Low-Intensity Conflict*, pp. 276–87; Robert Powers, "Guerrillas and the Laws of War," *U.S. Naval Institute Proceedings* 89 (March 1963): 82–87; Morris Greenspan, "International Law and Its Protection for Participants in Unconventional Warfare," *Annals* 341 (May 1962): 30–41.

[24] FM 27–10, *The Law of Land Warfare*, 1956, pp. 3, 23–28, 31, 33, 34, 106–07, 144–45, 148–49.

[25] Mills, "U.S. Army Doctrine," pp. 2, 8, 14; Douglas Blaufarb, *The Counterinsurgency Era: U.S. Doctrine and Performance, 1950 to the Present* (New York: Free Press, 1977), p. 71.

[26] Harry Coles, "Strategic Studies Since 1945, the Era of Overthink," *Military Review* 53 (April 1973): 3–16; Dennis Vetock, *Lessons Learned: A History of U.S. Army Lesson Learning* (Carlisle Barracks, Pa.: U.S. Army Military History Institute, 1988), p. 92.

[27] Walter Hermes, Survey of the Development of the Role of the U.S. Army Military Advisor, OCMH Study, Office of the Chief of Military History (OCMH), 1965, p. 61, CMH; "Marshall Plan Changed the Face of Europe," *Washington Post*, 25 May 97, p. 1.

[28] Andrew Birtle, *Rearming the Phoenix: U.S. Military Assistance to the Federal Republic of Germany, 1950–1960* (New York: Garland, 1991), pp. 10–12.

[29] Timothy Lomperis, *From People's War to People's Rule* (Chapel Hill: University of North Carolina Press, 1996), pp. 7–11. For an overview of America's experience in providing military aid, see Hermes, Development of the Role of the U.S. Army Military Advisor; Harold Hovey, *United States Military Assistance* (New York: Frederick A. Praeger, 1965); James Lacy, "Origins of the U.S. Army Advisory System: Its Latin American Experience, 1922–1941" (Ph.D. diss., Auburn University, 1977).

[30] Walter Laqueur, *Guerrilla: A Historical and Critical Study* (Boston: Little, Brown and Co., 1976), pp. 141–46, 151–52, 172–77; Harold Nelson, *Leon Trotsky and the Art of Insurrection, 1905–1917* (London: Frank Cass, 1988), pp. 14–15, 24–25, 31, 126; Conrad Lanza, "Communist Warfare," lecture, General Staff School, 1919–1920; Cassius Dowell, *Confidential Supplement to Military Aid to the Civil Power* (Fort Leavenworth, Kans.: 1925); Bernard Semmel, ed., *Marxism and the Science of War* (New York: Oxford University Press, 1981), pp. 19–24; Franklin Osanka, ed., *Modern Guerrilla Warfare; Fighting Communist Guerrilla Movements, 1941–1961* (Glencoe, Ill.: Free Press, 1962), pp. 58–71.

[31] Robert Asprey, *War in the Shadows: The Guerrilla in History*, 2 vols. (Garden City, N.Y.: Doubleday, 1975), 1:387; John Pustay, *Counterinsurgency Warfare* (New York: Free Press, 1965), p. 35; Laqueur, *Guerrilla*, pp. 245, 376, 385; Frank Trager, "Wars of National Liberation: Implications for U.S. Policy and Planning," *Orbis* 18 (Spring 1974): 61–68; Mao Tse-tung, *Selected Military Writings of Mao Tsetung* (Peking: Foreign Language Press, 1967).

[32] James Griffith, "Guerrilla Warfare in China," *Cavalry Journal* (September–October 1941): 12; Ian Beckett, ed., *The Roots of Counter-Insurgency: Armies and Guerrilla Warfare, 1900–1945* (New York: Blandford Press, 1988), p. 127.

[33] Semmel, *Marxism and the Science of War*, pp. 25–27; Walter Jacobs, "Mao Tse-Tung as a Guerrilla—A Second Look," *Military Review* 38 (February 1958): 26–30.

[34] John Shy and Thomas Collier, "Revolutionary War," in *Makers of Modern Strategy*, ed. Peter Paret (Princeton, N.J.: Princeton University Press, 1986), pp. 840–44; Mao, *Selected Military Writings*, pp. 77–80; J. Bowyer Bell, *The Myth of the Guerrilla: Revolutionary Theory and Malpractice* (New York: Alfred Knopf, 1971), p. 36.

[35] Laqueur, *Guerrilla*, pp. 374, 376, 384–85, 396.

2

THE COUNTERINSURGENCY ADVISORY EXPERIENCE 1945-1955

Revolution was in the air in 1945. The ravages of war and occupation had torn the fabrics of many societies. The end of World War II opened the door for additional strife, as competing social, economic, and political groups sought to reassemble their broken countries in ways that reflected their particular interests. In most cases the antagonists confined their battles to the political arena, but occasionally the struggles turned violent. Although favoring democratization and decolonization, the United States sought to suppress many of these revolutions out of fear that they would lead to the establishment of Communist regimes. Four countries in particular received considerable counterinsurgency support from the United States in the years immediately following World War II: China, Greece, the Philippines, and Indochina.

The Chinese Civil War, 1945–1949

The Chinese Civil War of 1945–1949 continued a struggle that had begun in 1927, when the Chinese government under the leadership of Generalissimo Chiang Kai-shek and his ruling Nationalist Kuomintang (KMT) Party tried to exterminate the Chinese Communist Party. The Japanese invasion of 1937 partially suspended this conflict, as Chiang joined Communist leader Mao Tse-tung in an uneasy alliance against the invader. When Japan surrendered to the Allied powers on

2 September 1945, Chiang and Mao squared off once again to determine China's destiny.

World War II had worked to Mao Tse-tung's advantage. Prior to the Japanese invasion the Chinese Communist Party had been on the run, as the government had forced Mao's army to flee to north China in the famous "Long March." The KMT's conventional forces bore the brunt of the Japanese invasion, enabling Mao not only to regroup, but to expand his guerrilla forces by capitalizing on hostility toward the Japanese invaders. As a result, the Communist movement grew from 40,000 party members and 92,000 guerrillas in 1937 to 1.2 million members and 860,000 soldiers by August 1945, by which point the party controlled nearly 20 percent of China's population. Japan's surrender provided further opportunities for Mao, as the withdrawal of Japanese troops from northern and eastern China created a vacuum that the CCP's northern-based guerrillas were better situated to exploit than Chiang's armies in south-central China. The United States did what it could to help Chiang in the race to reoccupy northeastern China, transporting nearly 500,000 Chinese government soldiers to the north. It also deployed approximately 50,000 U.S. marines to northern China, ostensibly to facilitate the repatriation of Japanese personnel but more pointedly to prevent either the Chinese Communist Party or the Soviets, who had invaded Manchuria in the closing days of the war, from gaining control over key population, transportation, and mining centers.[1] (*Map 2*)

These partisan actions notwithstanding, the United States genuinely hoped for a peaceful resolution to China's internal strife. Although it officially recognized Chiang's government, it realized that his regime was severely flawed. The Nationalist government was oppressive, inefficient, and corrupt, and many U.S. officials sympathized, at least in principle, with the Communists' call for social, political, and economic reform. Moreover, the United States desperately wanted a strong, united China to counterbalance Soviet influence in the Far East. A new civil war, even if it resulted in a Nationalist victory, threatened to invite Soviet encroachment. Consequently, rather than simply backing Chiang, U.S. officials worked toward the peaceful reunification of China. The United States hoped to persuade Mao to lay down his arms while convincing Chiang to create a reformed government in which all political parties could compete through peaceful, democratic processes. Toward this end, President Truman sent retired General George C. Marshall to China in December 1945 to broker a peace between Mao and Chiang. Marshall negotiated a cease-fire in January 1946 that included the provision of nearly 1,000 U.S. soldiers as part of a tripartite truce enforcement mechanism. The effort, which marked one

U.S. soldiers meet with Communist guerrillas in an attempt to negotiate a truce to the Chinese Civil War.

of the U.S. Army's first experiences in international truce enforcement and peacekeeping, failed. Neither Mao nor Chiang was interested in compromise, and by 1947 the civil war was in full swing.[2]

The Nationalist government labored under a number of severe handicaps during the ensuing conflict. Years of war had left the economy in a shambles, and the corrupt and inefficient government had little appeal among the masses, many of whom found Communist promises of agricultural reform and land redistribution attractive. Though he too espoused reform, Chiang proved either incapable or unwilling to make the far-reaching changes needed to strengthen his administration and its appeal to the common man. So frustrated was the United States with Chiang's lackluster leadership that it sought to replace him, but it never found someone equal to the task.

Chiang's political failings were exceeded only, in the words of U.S. Ambassador J. Leighton Stuart, by "the proclivity of the Generalissimo, a man of proved military incompetence, to interfere on a strategic and tactical level with field operations." Foremost among Chiang's strategic errors was his decision—taken against American advice—to rush troops to Manchuria in the wake of the USSR's withdrawal from that

CHINA
1945

0 ——————— 150
Miles

UNION OF SOVIET S

90°   100°

MONGOLIAN

70° 50°   80°

50°

30°

Yangtze R

Lhasa
○

N E P A L

BHUTAN

I   N   D   I   A

20°

B U R M A

80°   90°

MAP 2

region in 1946. This move overcommitted the government's already dispersed military forces. Moreover, Chiang tended to deploy his troops defensively around towns and lines of communications, thereby ceding the initiative to the Communists in the countryside. Chosen for loyalty rather than talent, Chiang's generals were unable to compensate for his misguided policies. The Nationalists' poorly trained, ill-treated, and unmotivated soldiers paid the price for their leaders' inadequacies, exhibiting in turn a callous disregard for the civilian population that further undermined public support for the government.[3]

Mao's methods differed dramatically from Chiang's. He moved fluidly through the countryside, employing the ancient arts of guerrilla warfare, attacking where the Nationalists were weak, retiring to remote sanctuaries when they were strong, and relying on ambush and stratagem to wear down his opponent. Mao's real strength, however, was in his recognition of the political dynamics of warfare. Lacking both the veneer of legitimacy and the coercive tools conferred upon the Nationalists by virtue of their control over the formal machinery of government, he was acutely aware of the necessity of building a firm political and economic base among the people. Beginning at the "rice roots" level, Mao created a tightly organized, hierarchical politico-military structure that mobilized, inspired, and controlled China's rural population. By skillfully blending organizational acumen, propaganda, nationalism, and coercion with an ideological vision, the Communist Party succeeded in harnessing China's resources for its particular ends.[4]

Mao especially stressed the importance of proper troop conduct, impressing upon his soldiers an eight-point creed: speak politely, pay fairly for what you buy, return everything you borrow, pay for anything you damage, do not hit or swear at people, do not damage crops, do not take liberties with women, and do not ill-treat captives. By following this program, Mao hoped to transform China's population into a hospitable ocean through which the guerrillas could move about as easily as fish, taking shelter and sustenance from the human sea that nurtured them.

By the time the civil war renewed in earnest in 1947, the conflict had already reached the last of what Mao had postulated to be the three stages of a protracted, insurrectionary war. The first stage—the development of a mass political movement and an embryonic guerrilla capability controlled by the party—and the second stage—in which that movement blossomed into full-scale guerrilla warfare—had occurred over the past two decades. During the third and final stage, Mao employed both guerrillas and large conventional forces to engage Chiang in open warfare.[5]

As the war escalated, the inner contradictions of U.S. policy became increasingly apparent. Uncomfortable with the Nationalist regime and desirous of a peaceful settlement, President Truman had suspended arms transfers to China in August 1946. He also circumscribed the role of the U.S. Army Advisory Group in China, prohibiting personnel from either visiting combat zones or conducting any training that might improve the operational performance of the KMT army. Moreover, much of the equipment and advice provided by the mission had been based on the premise that China's armed forces would be developed slowly in a peacetime environment with the principal task of defending China from external aggression. The aid program had not been designed for the immediate prosecution of an internal war—a war that U.S. policy was trying to prevent. Thus, when the civil war erupted, the government's military forces were neither trained, organized, nor equipped to meet the circumstances at hand.[6]

Only with the greatest reluctance did Truman gradually loosen the restrictions governing U.S. military aid. This reluctance reflected a belief on the part of senior officials that any increase in military assistance without a concomitant move on Chiang's part to implement political, social, and economic reforms would be futile. Furthermore, U.S. officials feared that an unfettered aid program would lead Chiang to believe that the United States was so desperate to stop communism that it would have no choice but to "sink or swim" with him, thus allowing the Nationalist government to ignore American calls for reform. Still, the United States felt some moral obligation to help the anti-Communists, and in July 1947 it partially lifted the arms embargo. Not until late 1947, however, did Washington permit the Chief, U.S. Army Advisory Group to China, Maj. Gen. David G. Barr, to advise Chiang on military operations. Even then, Washington insisted that Barr confine his advice to informal suggestions, opposing his and Ambassador Stuart's recommendations that the United States assign advisers down to the regimental level and establish a formal operational planning cell lest such moves embroil the United States in what it increasingly regarded as a lost cause.[7]

While Washington continued to limit American involvement in the war, Ambassador Stuart occasionally complained that the advice the U.S. Army was providing was not responsive to Chinese conditions. In fact, most of the guidance proffered by the advisory group was routine in nature, focusing on the establishment of conventional command, staff, and logistical systems. But such advice was usually sound, both because the essentials of military science and administration are broadly applicable to all forms of war and because by 1947 the

Communists were increasingly operating in large division- and corps-size units as Mao implemented the third phase of his revolutionary strategy. Once Washington changed the advisers' mission from building a conventional army to aiding the Nationalists in the internal war, they did indeed adapt to the situation. They advised the government that Chinese troops should be trained for both irregular and conventional operations and that Chinese divisions should be relatively light, mobile formations bereft of the kind of artillery, tanks, and heavy equipment found in American divisions of the day. Strategically, their advice was equally sound, castigating Chiang for overextending his armies and deploying them behind ancient city walls and in innumerable railroad blockhouses where they were unable to implement "the American concept of finding, fixing, and destroying the enemy and are subject to the dry rot of immobility."[8]

Although they were no students of revolutionary warfare, U.S. soldiers also addressed the political aspects of the insurgency. From 1945 on, senior American officers including Marshall (both as Truman's emissary to China in 1946 and as secretary of state thereafter), Lt. Gen. Albert C. Wedemeyer (former commander of Allied forces in China during World War II and another of Truman's special emissaries to China), and advisory chief Barr had recognized that "the military problem in China is inextricably involved in psychological, moral, and economic factors." "The Chinese Communist movement," Wedemeyer told Nationalist leaders in August 1947, "cannot be defeated by the employment of force. Today China is being invaded by an idea instead of strong military forces from the outside. The only way in my opinion to combat this idea successfully is to do so with another idea that will have stronger appeal and win the support of the people. This means that politically and economically the Central Government will have to remove corruption and incompetence from its ranks in order to provide justice and equality and to protect the personal liberties of the Chinese people, particularly the peasants." "It should be accepted," he concluded, "that military force by itself will not eliminate communism." Included in the list of reforms advocated by U.S. soldiers were the introduction of "good government," the end of police terror, and a variety of land and tax reforms.[9]

Reforms of this kind were outside the normal bailiwick of American military advisers. Nevertheless, the advisers spoke out on these matters because they recognized the inextricable link between political and military issues. The areas of political significance to which U.S. military personnel could speak to most directly concerned the indifference with which Chinese officers treated their men and the arrogant way government soldiers treated the population at large. To remedy the situation, U.S. soldiers urged greater troop indoctrination, heightened discipline, and the establishment of a more efficient military justice system. But punishment alone was not enough, and they also advocated the provision of better food, clothing, pay, and medical care for soldiers and their families to raise morale and redress some of the underlying problems that led soldiers to prey on the public.[10]

By late 1947 Ambassador Stuart had come to the conclusion that the U.S. Army could play an even greater role on the civil front than just encouraging better discipline and troop care, and he joined Barr in advocating the creation of a military government section within the Army advisory group. Staffed by soldiers knowledgeable in military government techniques and civilians familiar with Chinese political and economic problems, the proposed section would advise Nationalist forces in civil affairs. Although reflecting certain Maoist influences, at its heart the idea was not revolutionary at all. Rather, it merely sought to apply traditional principles of international law and military government—principles first codified in U.S. Army doctrine by General Orders 100 during the American Civil War—to China's civil war. Stuart and Barr believed that these precepts, which tried to balance humanitarian concerns and enlightened administration with military necessity, would, if properly implemented, greatly increase both the government's popularity and its control over the nation's resources.[11]

Once the Nationalists had been trained in military government techniques, Barr envisioned a multiyear campaign in which the government would slowly and systematically spread its control northward, starting from its bastions south of the Yangtze River. In contrast to the past, Barr recommended that the government not try to increase its territory until it had established firm control over the areas it already possessed. After occupying a region, Nationalist forces, with the aid of U.S. civil and military advisers, would establish "good government" and implement agrarian reforms. Food and other relief measures would alleviate suffering and win popular support, while the army rooted out the remaining guerrillas. To free the army for further offensives, Barr proposed that the government create an extensive system of militias to maintain control over pacified areas, guard lines of communications, and protect the population from any resurgence of Communist intimidation. Only after all of these measures had been undertaken would Nationalist forces move north to repeat the process in another area, until government control gradually spread to the entire country.[12]

Some Nationalist leaders shared Barr's vision of an integrated politico-military campaign. In fact, official government doctrine espoused similar concepts. As early as 1933, Chiang had concluded that anti-Communist warfare was "seventy percent political, thirty percent military," and had supplemented his military operations with efforts to stem corruption, stabilize the economy, and improve local administration. He reiterated this theme after World War II, telling his governors in 1946 that "the government can crush the Communist Army in five months, whereas the political fight will take another five years" and urging them to develop programs that would improve people's lives and win them over from the Communists. The government's "Manual for Bandit Suppression," originally written in 1933 and reissued in 1945, emphasized good troop behavior to gain both popular support and intelligence, noting that "the sure road to the extinction of the Reds must take as its point of departure the abstention from annoying the people. Recruiting soldiers by force is annoying to the people; raping of women is annoying to the people. So is looting; so is squeezing. Anyone committing any of these crimes is certainly to be executed." The manual also espoused vigilance, security, proper march procedures, guerrilla tactics, marksmanship, and night operations. Population-control and counterinfrastructure measures were also a part of Chinese doctrine. As early as 1932 Chiang had imposed a neighborhood watch system—called *pao chia*—based on the principle of collective responsibility.[13]

One person who reportedly took these prescriptions to heart was General Fu Tso-yi, who led the government's counterinsurgency effort in northern China. Considered an outstanding leader by the Americans, Fu believed that an integrated politico-military effort that bound the people to the government's cause through honest administration and social reforms was the only way to defeat the insurgency. He supported the creation of self-defense organizations controlled by local leaders who knew the political and military topography of their areas and who identified with the interests of the local population. Such militias would be the primary vehicles for intensive intelligence, propaganda, and population-control measures designed to mobilize the population and destroy the "bandit cadres" that were the inner fiber of the Communist movement. Like Barr, Fu believed that, "to be effective, this work must be done thoroughly. If it is done only on the surface, it would be useless." He endorsed granting amnesty for rank-and-file Communists, but he also avowed that Communist leaders, agents, and civilians who sheltered guerrillas should be "severely punished and horribly tortured." Areas that strongly sympathized with the Communists or were otherwise under their control were to be cleansed by "scorched earth tactics, hiding grain, carrying away able-bodied men, not leaving a stick of wheat or blade of grass for the enemy."[14]

Neither Barr's nor Fu's prescriptions were fully implemented. Though Chiang often spoke of reform, he made little effort to translate words into deeds. Initiatives to improve troop behavior and governmental administration made little headway. While Washington did not agree to Barr's and Stuart's plan to establish a military government section, Nationalist military leaders proved either unwilling or unable to implement many of the advisory group's military programs. By 1948 most U.S. political and military analysts had concluded that Chiang was doomed. Nearly $2 billion worth of grants and credits (about half of which were military in nature) had failed to stabilize China, and while the Joint Chiefs of Staff advocated additional military aid, even they believed that such assistance would only delay the government's inevitable collapse. Only billions more dollars, and perhaps military intervention on an equally grand scale, could save the government, and no one—politicians, diplomats, or soldiers—wanted that. Rather than become sucked into the Chinese vortex, the Truman administration chose to continue providing limited military aid to the Nationalists while simultaneously keeping them at arm's length. The inevitable result followed. During 1948 Communist offensives gobbled up one isolated and overextended government garrison after another, and the following year Chiang and his supporters fled to Taiwan, leaving Mao free to consolidate his hold over mainland China.

Like Woodrow Wilson during the Russian Civil War, Truman had been confronted with the choice of either supporting an unsavory anti-Communist regime or of acceding to a Communist victory. He had tried to solve the dilemma by walking a policy tightrope, initially assuming the mantle of honest broker and, when that did not work, of providing limited assistance to the anti-Communists, hoping either to coerce them into mending their ways or, should that fail, to minimize U.S. involvement in the ensuing collapse. In the end, Truman succeeded in keeping the United States out of an extremely costly and possibly unwinnable conflict, but, like Wilson before him, he failed to attain his broader policy goals.[15]

For the Army, the Nationalists' defeat was particularly frustrating. Despite the limitations that both the U.S. and Chinese governments had placed on them, the Army's "old China hands" had exhibited a basic appreciation for many counterinsurgency fundamentals. Indeed, many of the principles that Wedemeyer, Barr, and others had recommended in China—including close politico-military coordination; "good government" administration and modest reform; a strategy of progressive area clearance; population security; good troop conduct; and aggressive, mobile, offensive operations—would become the hallmarks of American counterinsurgency doctrine for years to come.

The Greek Insurgency, 1945–1949

While the civil war was raging in China, another insurgency was occurring on the other side of the globe, in Greece. Prior to World War II a multiplicity of factions—republican, monarchist, socialist, and Communist—had struggled to shape the future of that impoverished land. Those divisions continued to simmer during the Axis occupation, as leftists, anti-monarchists, and nationalists banded together under Communist leadership to form a National Popular Liberation Army (ELAS). The liberation army used guerrilla techniques to fight not only the Germans and Italians, but right-wing groups as well, some of which in turn collaborated with the Axis. When British and Greek monarchist troops entered Athens on the heels of withdrawing Axis forces in the fall of 1944, ELAS attacked them in a bid to seize control of the country. The attempt failed, and in February 1945 the warring factions agreed to lay down their arms and to resolve their differences peacefully. The truce was short lived. Elections in 1946 installed a rightist government whose partisans initiated a reign of terror against their political opponents. ELAS, which had secreted many of its weapons rather than surrendering them as called for in the 1945 accord, re-formed as the Democratic People's Army and resumed guerrilla operations.[16] (*Map 3*)

In the ensuing civil war the Communists refined the guerrilla warfare techniques that they had learned during the occupation by studying Russian and Chinese manuals and by attending training camps run by veteran Yugoslav partisans. Operating in small, lightly armed groups, the "bandits," as they were labeled by the government, ambushed patrols, mined roads, and raided villages before fading back to forest and mountain hideaways. Consciously following Mao's ten military principles, the guerrillas avoided unfavorable confrontations, concentrating their forces against weak government detachments and small villages before tackling larger prey. Supporting the people's army was the *yiafka*, a formidable clandestine organization developed during the occupation that provided the guerrillas with labor, supplies, guides, money, and intelligence. Together with Communist Party cells and front organizations, it helped mobilize and control the population in support of the insurgency.[17]

Although the *yiafka* was vital to the insurgents, so too was the external assistance given by Greece's three Communist neighbors—Albania,

MAP 3

Bulgaria, and especially Yugoslavia. These nations provided training, equipment, and cross-border sanctuaries to which the guerrillas could retreat when pressed by government forces. With this outside help, the guerrillas established several base areas along the mountainous northern frontier, where they stockpiled supplies and established "liberated zones" that boosted their claims of political legitimacy.

Thanks in part to resentment over government repression, the insurgency grew to approximately 30,000 guerrillas, 50,000 *yiafka* members, and 750,000 sympathizers by the end of 1947. Still, unsavory conduct on the part of the insurgents—forcibly recruiting soldiers and laborers, extorting supplies, and terrorizing rural communities—also cost the Communists much public support. Caught between two brutal antagonists and demoralized by the prevailing atmosphere of insecurity and economic hardship, many people adopted a passive, apathetic attitude that probably helped the guerrillas, who hoped that prolonged chaos would eventually undermine the government.[18]

Hampered by a collapsed economy and political infighting, the government's response to the insurgency was weak. Advised by the British to treat the insurgency as a problem of law and order rather than a military conflict, the government initially tried to subdue the guerrillas using only the national police, the gendarmerie. Staffed largely by Axis collaborators bent on settling old scores, this force was generally distrusted by the population and incapable of coping with the guerrillas. The government responded by enlarging the gendarmerie to include mobile combat police formations, but this had several disadvantages. Not only did this create a rivalry between the police and the army, but the gendarmes, lacking proper military training and equipment, proved poor soldiers. Conversely, the gendarmerie's preoccupation with counterguerrilla operations only further undermined its ability to perform routine police duties.[19]

In October 1946 the government called in the newly formed Greek National Army (GNA), but it was in no better shape than the police to combat the guerrillas. The officer corps was racked by factional infighting, while the soldiers, many of whom were pre–World War II reservists, were old, tired, poorly trained, and indifferently cared for. Weakened by an inefficient staff system and political interference, the army responded to public pressure for protection from Communist raids by dispersing its soldiers into so many small detachments that it had few men leftover to conduct offensive operations. As in China, such dispersion robbed the government's forces of the initiative, sapped morale, and complicated efforts to improve the organization and training of the army as a whole.[20]

By 1947 the Greeks, with British help, had begun to develop a doctrine for "anti-bandit" warfare that reflected both British colonial experience and German counterguerrilla operations in the Balkans during World War II, some of which the Greeks had experienced firsthand. The emerging doctrine called for aggressive, offensive combat; night movements; and deception, all with the purpose of killing guerrillas rather than taking ground. A well-planned and -executed encirclement with adequate forces was the preferred method of bringing the guerrillas to battle, but such operations went for naught unless accompanied by the systematic destruction of the guerrillas' clandestine politico-military infrastructure. This doctrine was basically sound, but as in China, persuading the Greeks to practice what they taught in their staff schools was not easy.[21]

Greek soldiers engage Communist guerrillas.

The Greek Army launched its first major offensive in 1947. The campaign, which was developed with British advice, set the pattern for the rest of the war. It consisted of a series of sweeps and encirclements, moving progressively from south to north up the Greek peninsula. Once an area was cleared the bulk of the troops moved on to the next area, leaving behind a small garrison for security. The endeavor failed. The insurgents' keen intelligence system usually allowed them to learn of an impending operation and escape, while those guerrillas caught in an encirclement had little difficulty slipping through gaps in government lines. Planning and execution were shoddy, with the army frequently allocating insufficient time and resources to make the operations truly effective. Ultimately, the clearing operations took longer and absorbed more troops than the government had anticipated, so that as the army moved north it had progressively fewer soldiers to conduct new operations. By year's end, over half of the army was tied down performing static guard duties, while the guerrillas emerged largely unscathed.[22]

Meanwhile, in February 1947 Great Britain announced that while it would continue its advisory effort, it could no longer afford the financial costs of rebuilding and rearming Greece. Consequently, President Truman decided to assume much of this burden. In what became known as the Truman Doctrine, the president declared in March that the United States was determined "to support free peoples who are resisting subjugation by armed minorities or outside pressures." As in the case of China and the subsequent Marshall Plan for Europe, the administration

45

believed that the best defense against revolution was "economic stability and orderly political process," and it earmarked less than half of the original $300 million aid package for military assistance.[23]

To oversee the aid program, Truman created an American Mission to Aid Greece (AMAG), headed by Dwight P. Griswold. Griswold shared Truman's priorities, believing that the "defeat of communism [is] not solely a question of military action. . . . Military and economic fronts are of equal importance." He attempted to use his authority to produce a well-integrated effort devoid of the type of bureaucratic infighting that had all too frequently marred past politico-military endeavors. In this he did not succeed. The administration's failure to delineate clearly the relationship between Griswold and the American ambassador to Greece, Lincoln MacVeagh, led to a bitter feud that was not resolved until late 1948, when Truman appointed Henry F. Grady to head both the embassy and the aid mission. Nor did finding the right mix of civil and military programs prove to be an easy task. The military situation in Greece, as in China, proved too precarious to permit any significant civil rehabilitation, while U.S. and British officers alike advocated shifting aid priorities toward military assistance. After some debate, a rough consensus gradually emerged between U.S. diplomatic and military leaders that security concerns had to take precedence over political and economic rehabilitation. Consequently, the United States not only increased the amount of military aid, but devoted an ever larger share of the economic aid package to war-related projects.[24]

Maj. Gen. William G. Livesay headed AMAG's military component, the U.S. Army Group, Greece. As in China, the group's role was entirely logistical, partly because Truman was reluctant to become embroiled in Greek internal affairs and partly because the British already maintained military and police advisory missions in Greece. Consequently, Washington instructed Livesay to limit his advice to "personal" observations. This restriction quickly proved unsatisfactory. Logistical and technical matters had wide-ranging organizational and operational implications that could not be easily segregated. Moreover, as in China, the United States came to the conclusion that indigenous political and military leaders lacked the administrative skill and political will to do what needed to be done to win the war. Whereas China's problems were so massive that they overawed the stoutest of American policy makers, the situation in Greece, a small country the size of North Carolina, seemed much more malleable. Consequently, Truman opted for measures that he had shunned in China. His first move was to insert U.S. experts into Greek ministries where they exercised so much influence that they controlled "almost all segments of the Greek

General Van Fleet (center, in cap) *and Greek officials inspect government troops.*

economy." Then, in December 1947 the Pentagon created the Joint U.S. Military Advisory and Planning Group, Greece (JUSMAPG), through which the United States assumed "operational guidance of the Greek National Army."[25]

Under the command of first General Livesay and then Lt. Gen. James A. Van Fleet, the advisory group provided advice on all aspects of the war. It drew up operational and administrative plans, coordinated these plans with the Greek General Staff, and then helped to implement them. It also stationed advisers at Greek military schools, training centers, and with each corps and division where they introduced American tactical, training, and administrative doctrines. The result, recalled Van Fleet, was that "I really had no orders from Washington that I would command the Greek forces, but in practice I actually did."[26]

The soldiers the Army sent to Greece believed that certain basic principles governed the conduct of all military operations and that a correct application of these principles would eventually bring success. Among these principles were an appreciation for the importance of inspired leadership, professional competence, and high morale; a belief that one must gain the initiative through decisive, aggressive action; and an adherence to the principle of economy of force that led the Americans to shun overly dispersed, passive deployments. With these tenets in mind, the advisory group emphasized small-unit patrol and combat skills, night operations to catch the guerrillas by surprise,

47

winter operations to exploit the government's logistical superiority over the comparatively ill-clad and poorly supplied irregulars, and tactics designed to find, fix, and finish an elusive opponent.

U.S. soldiers were particularly critical of what they regarded as the Greek Army's overreliance on artillery and air support. All too often Greek commanders seemed content to engage the enemy at long distances, cautiously advancing their infantry only after a preliminary bombardment. Such tactics were ineffective, as the insurgents simply withdrew out of harms way, leaving the Greeks to take possession of a meaningless terrain objective without having destroyed the enemy. Instead, the Americans stressed fire and movement in which the infantry advanced to close with and destroy the enemy, either without fire support or under covering fire, rather than sitting back and waiting for the artillery to drive the enemy off.[27]

U.S. Army advisers revamped the Greek Army training system along American lines, introducing unit training and field exercises for the first time and sending demonstration platoons made up of Greek soldiers trained in American tactics to each infantry division. Recognizing that intelligence was critical in bringing the elusive guerrillas and their shadowy support network to heel, the advisory group stressed reconnaissance skills, the use of civilian spies and informants, and improved intelligence staff work. It also supported the British in their contention that the gendarmerie should be relieved of combat duty so that it could focus on the critical tasks of maintaining law and order and ferreting out the *yiafka*. All of these measures eventually paid dividends, although U.S. proposals for creating specially trained long-range reconnaissance companies and establishing a central intelligence agency to coordinate army, police, and paramilitary intelligence efforts were not successfully implemented.[28]

Throughout, American advisers constantly strove to overcome what they regarded as the Greek Army's Achilles heel—its inertia and lack of fighting spirit. They pushed for aggressive, continuous action and relentless pursuit. They pressed the Greek government to remove incompetent officers and to end untoward political interference in operational and personnel decisions. Van Fleet also sought to energize the rank and file, suggesting that the Greek Army replace worn out soldiers with younger draftees, increase its troop propaganda and educational activities, and improve the lot of the common soldier and his family. Ultimately, however, U.S. advisers recognized that military morale reflected national morale and that neither would improve until some measure of economic relief could be brought to the countryside. Consequently, in November 1947 a panel of U.S. Army and British military personnel agreed that "greater attention must be paid to the rapid rehabilitation of liberated areas, so that the people in these areas feel that the Government has their well-being at heart." JUSMAPG therefore suggested that Greek campaign plans include comprehensive civil affairs programs designed to bring economic and social assistance to areas as the Greek Army cleared them of guerrillas.[29] This last proposal was not effectively implemented during 1948, and in November of that year Secretary of the Army Kenneth C. Royall recommended to Secretary of State Robert Lovett and Ambassador Grady that the United States shift its economic aid effort from cities to rural areas where the real battle for the people was taking place. The diplomats agreed, and in 1949 the advisory group and the newly formed Economic Cooperation Administration collaborated on a number of projects. With U.S. aid, the Greek government put men to work on public works projects and provided food, building materials, animals, seed, and farm implements to refugees returning to areas cleared by military operations. These projects were not always sufficiently large or coordinated to ameliorate the harsh conditions in the countryside, but they did good work and helped consolidate military gains.[30]

JUSMAPG also supported the creation of an armed militia, both to free the army from static guard duties and to solidify rural pacification. Many such organizations already existed by 1947, but they were clearly inadequate. Armed with an incredible assortment of weaponry, these groups were unresponsive to military control, poorly trained, indifferently led, and prone to committing excesses that undermined their usefulness in promoting pacification. The British opposed arming civilians, fearing that it would fuel an endless cycle of atrocity and retaliation. Livesay's initial reaction to Greek requests for arms for civilians was similarly cool, partly because he shared British concerns and partly because he felt that the civilian aid program should pay for the weapons, as military aid funds were already overstretched. Still, he considered the idea of arming civilians to be "militarily sound" as it would give the villagers confidence, and "once the confidence of the villagers has been gained they begin to lose their fear of the bandits and give information about the bandits which is so vital to Greek Army success." When in the fall of 1947 the Greek government proposed the creation of a new type of local defense force—the National Defense Corps (NDC)—the United States pledged its support on the condition that the government disband the older, ad hoc militias. Originally conceived of as a type of minuteman formation, the defense corps was to be organized into regionally based battalions, officered by military cadres, and filled out by ex-servicemen and old reservists whose familiarity with the local people and terrain would prove to be a significant asset in combating the guerrillas.[31]

The initiative proved only partially successful, as the Greeks reneged on their promise to disarm the old vigilante organizations and employed the National Defense Corps in mobile roles for which it was not prepared, thereby leaving the villages it was supposed to be guarding vulnerable to guerrilla raids. In 1948 a new bargain was struck, in which some NDC units became static defense troops, while others were infused with younger draftees and transformed into mobile "light infantry" battalions virtually indistinguishable from regular army formations. These units hunted guerrillas on a regional basis and supplemented regular army units during major cordon-and-sweep operations. Meanwhile, the government created a new militia organization, the Home Guard, to replace the paramilitary groups. Outfitted with over 50,000 American-supplied small arms, the Home Guard was led by reservists; received training in guerrilla, patrol, and ambush tactics; and was more tightly controlled by the Army than the older civilian bands. It performed good service in 1949, guarding villages and installations, monitoring subversives, protecting returning refugees, and otherwise freeing the military for more offensive employment.[32]

Closely allied with providing security for the rural population was the need to isolate the people so that they could not provide the insurgents with the information, food, shelter, and recruits that the guerrillas needed to survive. Prior to the time when the United States began giving operational advice, the Greek government had developed three effective, yet harsh, tools to achieve these ends. In addition to employing paramilitaries alternately to protect and terrorize the population, the government arrested tens of thousands of people suspected of supporting the guerrillas. It executed some and exiled others—together with their families and often without trial—to remote island internment camps. Though many innocent people were doubtlessly swept up in the dragnet, the mass arrests effectively weakened the *yiafka*. Finally, the government also removed entire populations from guerrilla-infested areas to drain the "sea" in which the guerrillas "swam." By November 1947 the government had forcibly evacuated 310,000 people, primarily from the insurgents' northern base areas. By 1949 the number of refugees had swollen to 700,000, roughly 10 percent of the Greek population. Some of these refugees had left their homes voluntarily to escape the war. Others had been forced to flee by the guerrillas, who hoped to overburden the government's already strained economic resources. But the majority were the product of government relocation campaigns.[33]

The United States assumed an ambivalent stand on these measures. Officially, it protested the use of terror, mass arrests, and population removal. Certainly these activities made the depiction of the war as a Zoroastrian struggle between democracy and totalitarianism more difficult for the Truman administration. Moreover, U.S. officials were genuinely uncomfortable with such tactics and believed that terror and arrest without due process were ultimately counterproductive. But as the war dragged on, many Americans felt that the goal of destroying communism justified harsh means. "We should realize," Secretary of State Marshall instructed Griswold in 1947, "that stern and determined measures, although of course not excesses, may be necessary to effect the termination of the activities of the guerrillas and their supporters as speedily as possible." Most of the American diplomatic community adhered to this line.[34]

U.S. soldiers were more outspoken. Although eschewing terror, General Van Fleet did not inquire too closely into how the Greeks treated guerrillas, believing that the "only good Communist is a dead one." He approved of the use of mass arrests and population relocations to destroy the *yiafka* and impede guerrilla access to the people. Likewise, Maj. Gen. Stephen J. Chamberlin, detailed by the Pentagon to study the Greek situation, endorsed laying waste to sections of the Greek countryside, noting that the "ruthless removal or destruction of food and shelter in the mountain villages would compel all but insignificant guerrilla forces to either retire to the frontiers or accept combat in the valleys and plains under adverse conditions." Consequently, while the Greek government occasionally curtailed its utilization of terror, mass arrests, and refugee generation in response to outside pressure, American support, at least for the latter two actions, helped ensure their continuation.[35]

Although proffering American methods, Livesay and Van Fleet recognized that to recast the Greek Army into a miniature U.S. Army was inappropriate. When JUSMAPG designed a standard field division for the Greek Army in 1949, it did not try to replicate an American division, but rather created a structure adapted to Greek conditions. Believing that tanks and heavy artillery were useful in only limited situations, the United States provided Greece with weapons suitable for mountain operations, such as mortars, machine guns, and pack artillery. The advisory group reduced the number of motorized vehicles found in infantry battalions and consolidated them into rear echelon formations so that combat units would not be road-bound. Nor did Van Fleet have any tolerance for expensive and complicated "high tech" solutions. He repeatedly rejected proposals by U.S. and British aviators to outfit the

Greek Army with helicopters and specially trained troops capable of operating with aerial resupply, stating that the GNA's problem lay not in moving to a particular location, but rather in motivating it to do something once it arrived. Horses and mules rather than combustion engines were the U.S. Army's prescription for counterguerrilla mobility in Greece. The Army outfitted seven horse cavalry squadrons, improved the efficiency of the Greek Army's pack logistics system, and gave the Greek military more mules than trucks.[36]

Many of the ideas offered by the American advisory group were not new. Rather, they mirrored advice that the British military and police missions had been giving the Greeks since 1946. Though they did not agree on every issue, U.S. and British advisers held similar views about the core problems facing the Greek Army and how to fix them.[37] Consequently, the American-designed campaign plan for 1948 did not differ significantly from the British plan for 1947, consisting of a series of encirclement-and-sweep operations, moving progressively from south to north. After the army cleared each area, the National Defense Corps, police, and paramilitaries were to move in to prevent guerrilla reinfiltration. What made the 1948 plan different from 1947 was thus not its overall conception, but the hope that U.S. advice would make the Greek Army more effective in executing the plan. In this the Americans were destined to be disappointed, for while the Greek Army achieved some success, it continued to suffer from many of the underlying institutional weaknesses that had undermined its efforts in the past. By year's end the guerrillas had made good their losses and counterattacked government forces in the north.[38]

Fortunately for the government, several developments occurred in 1948 and 1949 that drastically altered the strategic equation in the government's favor. In 1948 the Communists began consolidating their forces from bands of 50 to 100 men into "brigades" and "divisions." These larger formations were less mobile, more visible, and more dependent on a regular commissary than the smaller guerrilla bands. Concomitant with this development was a shift to more positional warfare, reflected not only in the creation of fortified base areas along the border, but in assaults aimed at capturing medium-size towns. The change represented a bid on the part of Communist Party chief Nikos Zachariades to transform the guerrilla war into a more conventional conflict akin to Mao's third stage of revolution. Unfortunately for the Greek Communists, they were not blessed by the same constellation of factors that had made this shift possible in China. Rather than increasing the pressure on the government, the change merely rendered the guerrillas vulnerable to the government's superior firepower.[39]

Zachariades' timing was poor, but he was responding to wider developments that he could not entirely control. Growing American aid was one factor. Then, in June 1948 the Cominform, a committee representing the Communist parties of Eastern Europe, expelled Marshal Josip Tito's Yugoslavia over policy differences. This development eventually forced the Greek Communists to choose between staying in the larger Communist camp or siding with Tito, their chief benefactor. Zachariades' shift to larger formations represented a bid to alter the strategic balance inside Greece before that day came. When in early 1949 Zachariades endorsed the Cominform's decision that Greek Macedonia should be granted autonomy—a policy widely regarded as a stepping stone for its eventual acquisition by Tito's arch rival, Bulgaria—he irrevocably alienated Tito, created a split within his own party between nationalists, internationalists, and Macedonian separatists, and gave the Greek government a patriotic platform upon which to rally public opinion against the Communists. In July 1949 Tito retaliated by sealing Yugoslavia's borders, cutting the Greek Communists off from their primary source of sustenance and refuge. Albania eventually followed suit, leaving the guerrillas with nowhere to run during the government's 1949 offensive.[40]

That offensive might still have produced unsatisfactory results had there not been a third major development, the appointment, with strong American support, of Field Marshal Alexander Papagos to the newly created post of supreme commander of the Greek armed forces. An undisputed patriot and man of action, Papagos both rallied the nation and wielded his unprecedented powers to galvanize the military, removing incompetent officers and insisting that his subordinates thoroughly execute Greco-American plans. Working closely with Van Fleet, Papagos built on past U.S. initiatives in a way that ensured that the 1949 offensive would be the most effectively conducted campaign to date. This, when coupled with missteps and divisions within the Communist camp, laid the groundwork for victory.[41]

For 1949, Greco-American planners envisioned a repetition of the familiar north to south "strategy of staggered expansion of control," refined by two years' experience and made more effective by steady improvements in the GNA's command, staff, logistical, and combat systems. Before each operation, Greek security forces conducted mass arrests, depopulating entire areas and taking "the most strong measures against the suspect inhabitants of neighboring villages" who might be aiding the guerrillas. After sealing the targeted area in depth to prevent guerrilla exfiltration, government troops conducted sweeps and small-unit patrols to attack, harass, and pursue the guerrillas, operating at night and in adverse weather more than ever before. The encirclement operations of 1949 also tended to be more systematic than those of earlier years, as the military took the time to comb suspect areas repeatedly rather than simply making a cursory sweep. Special commando units, designed by the British and outfitted by the Americans, often spearheaded these operations, blending elite morale, high firepower, and expertise in small-unit tactics into a potent strike force. Once an area had been cleared of guerrillas, the government resettled the evacuees in selected towns secured by barbed wire, fortifications, and Home Guards, allowing the people to visit their fields during the day before returning to the safety of the protected villages at night. As the situation stabilized, the government opened additional defended villages, gradually resettling the population in a way that extended its control over the countryside. After clearing most of southern and central Greece in this fashion, the government then assaulted the Communists' fortified northern bastions, crushing them in a well-orchestrated drive backed by tanks, artillery, and aircraft that sent the guerrillas reeling across the border into Yugoslav internment camps. The war was over.[42]

Papagos and Van Fleet had not achieved a miracle. Even in this last campaign, many of the GNA's old problems persisted, leading JUSMAPG to conclude that the performance of Greek divisions was still "below the standards expected of infantry troops." Greek soldiers were still too reliant on air and artillery support for American taste, while field advisers complained that Greek commanders still ignored their advice. In evaluating its success, the advisory group freely acknowledged that Yugoslavia's termination of support for the Greek Communists, the guerrillas' tendency to rely on coercion rather than developing stronger ties with the people, and Zachariades' adoption of larger formations and static defenses contributed significantly to the government's victory. Nevertheless, the Greek armed forces still had to win the war. Thanks to American assistance and Papagos' leadership, the Greeks had improved sufficiently to get the job done.[43]

Apart from combat operations, Greek, U.S., and British observers all attributed the government's success to the use of mass arrests, population removal, and village security measures that severed the Communists' hold over the rural population.[44] On the other hand, progressive reforms and benevolent measures designed to win popular favor played only a supporting role. True, American aid resulted in a wide variety of road, harbor, housing, health, agricultural, and industrial improvements, yet these were modest at best. Nine years of war and revolution had left Greece in such a shambles that by 1950 $2 billion worth of American and other foreign aid had barely restored the

Greek soldiers assault a guerrilla bunker.

Greek economy to its pallid 1939 level. Because of the drain caused by the insurgency and the huge refugee problem, few of the economic goals envisioned by U.S. planners in 1947 had been achieved by 1949. American support for civil affairs, refugee relief, and resettlement programs ameliorated much human suffering and possibly won some converts, but such programs were little more than a band-aid for the wounds of a war torn land. Likewise, while the United States was able to impose certain economic and financial programs, the Greek government ignored or subverted many American prescriptions for social, economic, and political reforms. By war's end, the Greek political system had not become significantly more democratic, its economic and tax systems were no less regressive, and its record on human rights was no more exemplary than when the insurgency had started. American wishes notwithstanding, Greece had defeated the insurgency without enacting the full panoply of reforms that the Truman administration had believed necessary to slay the Communist dragon.[45]

The Philippine Insurgency, 1945–1955

China and Greece were not the only countries in the 1940s where war and occupation aggravated prewar conditions to create an environment ripe for internal disorder. A similar case existed in the Philippines, where a prewar peasant movement that sought to redress a variety of oppressive socioeconomic conditions joined forces with a largely urban-based Communist Party and other groups to form a united front against Japanese occupation during World War II. As in Greece, the Communist-led front organized guerrillas—called Huks—and a clandestine, village-based support organization—the Barrio United Defense Corps—that mobilized the rural population and provided the guerrillas with food, shelter, recruits, and intelligence. During the war the Huks fought not only the Japanese and their collaborationist allies, but American-led non-Communist guerrillas as well.[46] (*Map 4*)

The liberation of the Philippines in 1945 brought no relief for the peasants. Economic conditions were abysmal and exploitation by the land-holding class continued unabated. Meanwhile, the new President of the Philippines, Manuel Roxas, not only refused to seat members of the Huk-supported Democratic Alliance who had been elected to congress, but declared war against the Huks. Between 1946 and 1950, President Roxas and his successor, Elpidio Quirino, carried out an ill-conceived and ineffectual campaign that stumbled clumsily between repression and unfulfilled pledges to redress peasant grievances.

Insisting that the suppression of the "bandits" was a police rather than a military problem, Philippine officials turned the campaign over to the Ministry of Interior's security forces—the Military Police Command and its successor, the Philippine Constabulary. Backing the Constabulary were a large number of civilian guards—private armies raised by landowners to protect their property from peasant unrest. These paramilitary forces were undisciplined, poorly paid, and manned largely by Axis collaborators and former pro-American guerrillas who had scores to settle with the Huks. The Constabulary and guards not only acted ruthlessly against the guerrillas and their civilian supporters, but also abused the very people they were supposed to be protecting. The government's forces were also poorly trained and scattered in so many small outposts that they were unable to take effective, coordinated offensive action. Consequently, they confined their activities to conducting road patrols, manning checkpoints, and guarding towns and private estates. Major sweep operations, when they occurred, rarely lasted more than three days and were usually ineffective.[47]

The Constabulary based its counterinsurgency techniques on Japanese methods. This was natural, since many of its members had either employed or experienced Japanese counterguerrilla tactics during the occupation. Government *zona* operations—cordon-and-sweep actions—were modeled after Japanese tactics, as were other elements of the campaign, including the establishment of *pao chia*–style neighborhood watch organizations, which the Japanese had copied from Chinese Nationalists. Government security forces took hostages and

THE PHILIPPINES
1950

▨ Area of Guerrilla Strength

0   150
Miles

SOUTH

CHINA

SEA

LUZON

PHILIPPINE

SEA

Manila

VISAYAN ISLANDS

PALAWAN

SULU SEA

MINDANAO

NORTH
BORNEO

Sulu Archipelago

CELEBES SEA

MAP 4

used Japanese interrogation techniques that included torture, terror, and the "magic eye," in which villagers were brought before a concealed informer who would identify Huk supporters. The government also emulated Japanese destruction operations that denied food to guerrillas and punished barrios suspected of harboring irregulars. During the insurgency the Constabulary reportedly looted and burned more villages than the Japanese, creating a large refugee population in the process. This method stripped Huk-dominated areas of the people whom the guerrillas relied on for support, but it also placed heavy drains on the country's already ravaged economy.[48]

Although the Huks also employed terror and intimidation, their excesses paled in comparison with the behavior of government security forces. The harshness of Constabulary techniques and their similarity to methods so recently employed by the Japanese naturally discredited the government in the eyes of the people and drove many into the Huk camp. The failure of the Roxas and Quirino regimes to follow through on pledges of reform, coupled with the government's blatant manipulation of the 1946 and 1948 elections, merely reinforced in many people's minds the belief that their grievances could only be redressed by force.[49]

Organized in squadrons of 100 men and trained using U.S. Army infantry manuals, the Huks posed as innocent peasants by day only to emerge at night to raid barrios, attack police posts, and ambush security forces before retreating to jungle and mountain base camps to rest and refit. Though poorly armed and equipped, by 1950 the Huks under the inspired leadership of Maj. Gen. Luis M. Taruc had grown to approximately 15,000 guerrillas, 100,000 Barrio United Defense Corps members, and 1 million sympathizers, asserting virtual control over a four-province area in central Luzon. Encouraged by recent events in China, Taruc began to seize larger towns in preparation for what he hoped would be the final phase of the insurgency, issuing to his subordinates the same list of Maoist combat principles used by Greek guerrillas.[50]

By 1950 the Philippine government's position was sufficiently precarious to persuade the United States to play a more active role in suppressing the insurgency. True to its philosophy, the Truman administration considered the Huk situation to be a political problem that could only be resolved by instituting political, social, and economic reforms that eliminated the underlying causes of unrest. Mindful of the reasons for Chiang Kai-shek's recent defeat, U.S. embassy personnel were particularly critical of the Constabulary's poor behavior, believing that it undermined the "political-military campaign for the minds and loyalties of Filipinos." Considering the Filipinos to be "precocious children" who had absorbed only "superficial aspects" of Western culture and American-style democracy, the embassy endeavored through a combination of "continuously applied pressure" and "firm patience and understanding" to alternately entice and cajole the Quirino regime into making the necessary reforms. Chief among these were the need for fair and honest elections to restore confidence in the political process, financial and tax reform, minimum wage legislation, economic growth, and a variety of agrarian reforms designed to ease the crushing burdens born by tenant farmers.[51]

Economic and political reforms, however, were only part of the Truman administration's prescription. Although policy makers differed as to the relative importance of political and military measures, by late 1950 a consensus had emerged within the administration that the military situation had to be stabilized before political and economic measures could take root. Consequently, while the vast majority of the $1.3 billion worth of aid the United States would give to the Philippines between 1946 and 1956 was economic in nature, the U.S. government stepped up its aid program after 1950, providing $117 million in military assistance between 1951–1956, a sum that represented nearly 40 percent of Philippine military expenditures.[52]

The United States had opened a small Joint U.S. Military Advisory Group (JUSMAG) in Manila in 1947, but as elsewhere President Truman initially limited the group to providing logistical assistance and broad organizational advice. American advisers, nearly all of whom were U.S. Army personnel, were prohibited from visiting Philippine military units and bases and had very little firsthand information on the country's deteriorating internal situation. Washington did not grant JUSMAG chief Maj. Gen. Leland S. Hobbs greater latitude in providing advice on the insurgency until 1950.[53]

Hobbs' recommendations were similar to the advice Livesay and Van Fleet had been giving the Greeks, and indeed JUSMAG consciously emulated certain aspects of the recently successful Greek campaign.[54] Like his counterparts in Greece, Hobbs believed that inspirational leadership was needed to shake the Philippine security forces from their lethargy. He urged the government to consolidate its far-flung security detachments into larger units capable of taking offensive action. He also counseled the Philippine government to streamline its security apparatus, realigning the Constabulary under the Department of National Defense to effect better coordination, returning the Constabulary to more traditional police functions, and transferring excess Constabulary men to the army. Once these steps had been taken, the advisory group proposed a combination of cordon-and-sweep operations, active patrolling, night movements, and relentless pursuit to keep the guerrillas off-balance and drive them away from populated areas. It also wanted to wean the Filipinos from their overreliance on indiscriminate firepower, which it believed was not an effective substitute for closing with the enemy.[55]

While aggressive, offensive action represented the American prescription for eliminating the Huks as a military force, Hobbs recognized that the government would have to protect the people if it was going to succeed in obtaining their assistance. He therefore recommended that the Philippine Army reduce military-civilian friction by improving troop discipline. He also proposed that it create fortified villages manned by policemen, both to free the Army from static defense duty and to cut the guerrillas' access to the population. Increased funding and coordination of intelligence programs, an invigorated public information and propaganda campaign, new initiatives to restrict the availability of weapons to the guerrillas, and the establishment of an office specifically charged with the task of destroying the Communist's underground organization were also part of Hobbs' pacification program.[56]

Although JUSMAG strove to improve troop conduct and was leery about relying on paramilitary groups that might become instruments of repression, Hobbs urged the Philippine government to drop certain peacetime restraints that hindered its ability to root out the Huk underground. Specifically, Hobbs recommended that the government outlaw the Communist Party, establish special courts to try dissidents rapidly, and suspend *habeas corpus* for suspected insurgents. The suspension of *habeas corpus* was especially important to Hobbs, not only to strike more effectively at the Communists' covert infrastructure, but to improve troop conduct as well. Philippine law required that all prisoners either be released or charged with a crime within twenty-four hours of being apprehended, with bail being offered to anyone not charged with murder. This created a revolving door through which suspected guerrillas and their civilian supporters quickly regained their freedom and resumed their past behaviors. As had been the case with Union soldiers during the American Civil War, Filipino security forces found such leniency particularly frustrating and, like their American predecessors, soon took matters into their own hands by adopting policies of "no quarter." By suspending *habeas corpus* in cases related to insurgency, the government could improve both its counterinfrastructure capability and the treatment of prisoners, an important step in persuading Huks to surrender. Programs to rehabilitate former Huks, possibly to include the creation of agricultural colonies, were also part of Hobbs' plan to encourage defections and weaken the appeal of Huk propaganda.[57]

Unlike China and Greece, which already had extensive military establishments prior to American involvement, the Philippine Army had only two combat-capable infantry battalions in 1950. This force was clearly inadequate, and JUSMAG pushed for the rapid expansion of the Armed Forces of the Philippines (AFP) into twenty-six battalion combat teams. As designed by the advisory group, each team was a mobile, combined arms force capable of aggressive, independent action in the country's varied and often rugged terrain.[58]

In restructuring the Filipino military, Hobbs and his subordinates were mindful of the special circumstances governing the conflict. Not only was the battalion combat team not a carbon copy of an American formation, but JUSMAG firmly resisted suggestions that the Philippine Army be organized into divisions, noting that it had tailored the armed forces for internal security duties and that the military situation did not warrant a larger, more conventional structure. The advisory group similarly resisted proposals to introduce U.S. combat troops into the Philippines or to assign Americans either to advise or command Filipino units in the field, not only because it felt the military situation did not warrant these measures, but because it believed such actions would Americanize the war, wound Filipino pride, and rob the armed forces of the very sense of initiative and self-responsibility the advisory group was trying to promote.[59]

Although the Philippine government reorganized its armed forces in accordance with JUSMAG proposals, Hobbs was only marginally successful in convincing Quirino to adopt his recommendations. Then, in the fall of 1950, things began to change. The expansion of the Huk insurgency, together with Mao's victory in China and the growth of Communist movements in Korea, Malaya, and Indochina created a sense of urgency. So too did the issuance of a report by a special Economic Survey Mission, which outlined the seriousness of the Philippines' situation and called for major reforms as a prerequisite for additional U.S. aid. Caught between the rising Huk tide and Truman administration threats to withhold further assistance unless America's demands were met, Quirino pledged to enact many elements of the American reform package.

Over the next three years Quirino instituted some significant reforms. He lowered agricultural rents, inaugurated an anti-usury drive, and passed a new minimum wage law. He also acceded to American pressure to hold honest elections, an act that eventually cost him the presidency but which restored public faith in the democratic process, thereby dampening revolutionary sentiments. But perhaps most importantly, in September 1950 President Quirino acquiesced to American

Filipino soldiers of the 7th Battalion Combat Team search for Huk guerrillas.

suggestions that he appoint senator and former World War II guerrilla Ramon Magsaysay as secretary of national defense.

No one played a more central role in defeating the Huks than Ramon Magsaysay. Not only was he a dynamic leader, but, unlike his predecessors, he energetically instituted many of JUSMAG's proposals, thanks in part to his close relationship with the chief of JUSMAG's newly established intelligence and unconventional warfare section, Air Force Lt. Col. Edward G. Lansdale. Magsaysay recognized that the best way to attack the insurgents was through a well-coordinated political and military campaign, what he termed the left hand of friendship and the right hand of force. To strengthen his right hand, Magsaysay realigned the national command and intelligence systems along the lines developed by the advisory group, expanded the army, and created an elite Scout Ranger force patterned on Philippine and American precedents that effectively conducted many long-range reconnaissance, intelligence, and raiding missions, often in the guise of Huks.[60] With Lansdale's help, he developed a significant propaganda apparatus, the two men taking great delight in dreaming up new tricks with which to outmaneuver the Huks. He demanded honest, aggressive leadership, energizing the officer corps through surprise personal inspections, spot promotions, and disciplinary actions in which he sacked over 400 officers. Despite his off-quoted quip to his American-trained officers that they should forget everything they had learned at West Point and Fort

Benning, Georgia, he not only sent hundreds of officers to the United States for training, but made U.S. Army manuals and training materials the basis for the Philippine Army's tactical, intelligence, psychological warfare, and logistics doctrines. American-designed training programs that stressed conventional small-unit patrol and combat tactics, night operations, and offensive action formed the core of military training under Magsaysay. Inspection visits by JUSMAG personnel, as well as the eventual placement of U.S. advisers at AFP regional headquarters, helped ensure that the new programs and doctrines were properly implemented, and although the Philippine advisory group never became involved to the same degree as the Greek advisory group in advising combat units in the field, it drafted tactical guidelines and operational blueprints. In fact, American doctrines required only minor modifications to fit Philippine conditions, and, while the Filipinos demonstrated ingenuity in making such adaptations, they did not develop any new tactics during the course of the war.[61]

Although Magsaysay would have liked to abolish many of the private security forces whose undisciplined conduct undermined pacification, he realized that he could not secure the countryside without them. Consequently, he sought to improve their performance by attaching military personnel to them and giving them radios with which to coordinate their actions with the army. He supplemented the private armies by raising an additional 10,000 civilian commandos, trained and led by AFP regulars, who guarded barrios, gathered intelligence, apprehended members of the Huk underground, and provided guides and auxiliaries to the army. The irregulars freed the Philippine Army for offensive operations, consolidated the army's successes in the field, and kept the population separated from the guerrillas. As such, they played a vital role in the government's pacification campaign, though they continued to commit excesses.[62]

While Magsaysay wielded the stick of "all-out force" in his right hand, he held out with his left the carrot of "all-out friendship." Under the label of "civic action," a term coined by Lansdale, Magsaysay set the armed forces to doing many of the same things the U.S. Army had done fifty years before during the Philippine War of 1899–1902, building over 4,000 schools, repairing roads and bridges, digging wells, distributing food and medical supplies, and performing other public works. Troops carried "candy for kids," military lawyers represented indigent farmers in court, and Filipino and U.S. soldiers observed polling places to ensure fair elections. Magsaysay ameliorated the treatment of prisoners and improved troop discipline by promptly investigating citizen complaints and instituting an American-financed pay raise that helped reduce foraging and corruption. To ensure that these initiatives were being implemented, Magsaysay centralized control over the "attraction program" and propaganda campaigns by creating a civil affairs office within the Department of National Defense, placing what would normally have been civilian programs under military management, and installing about a hundred officers in civil posts to energize the lethargic bureaucracy.[63]

Perhaps the most notable of the AFP's civic actions was the establishment of the Economic Development Corps (EDCOR). The development corps had its genesis in an August 1950 JUSMAG proposal to establish a rehabilitation colony for captured Huks. Magsaysay built on this idea, creating several remote jungle camps where former Huks, leavened by a cadre of reliable veterans, were given land on which to start a new life. The Army assisted by clearing the land, building roads and community facilities, and providing medical care, tools, credit, and advice. The program had tremendous public relations value. It stole the thunder from the Huks' slogan "land for the landless," encouraged Huk defections, and seemed to demonstrate the government's commitment to meaningful land reform. Once Magsaysay became president in 1953, he created a number of other agricultural reform and resettlement initiatives, further cementing the image of progress among foreign and domestic observers alike.[64]

Magsaysay's combined politico-military offensive won praise from U.S. Army observers who noted with some relief that the Filipinos had finally realized "that the key to success in dealing with the Huks is the stopping of their support from the population." By 1952 Filipino-American initiatives had clearly wrested the initiative away from the Huks. Cordon-and-sweep operations broke up guerrilla formations and drove them away from populated areas, while intelligence agents, police, and paramilitary forces controlled the population and attacked the Communist infrastructure. Protected from guerrilla retaliation, encouraged by government successes, and swayed by the government's propaganda and civic action initiatives, an increasing number of people cashed-in on rewards by providing information about the Huks to the government. The year following Magsaysay's election as president, General Taruc surrendered. By 1955 fewer than 1,000 Huks remained under arms, living in remote mountain areas more as fugitives than as guerrillas.[65]

The Philippines succeeded in suppressing the Huks by following America's formula of implementing military measures "hand in hand" with political reforms. Achieving this "judicious combination" had required a significant amount of U.S. intervention—goading the Filipinos into action, designing initiatives, and financing revitalization programs. Thanks in large measure to Magsaysay, the Filipinos rose to the challenge and applied ingenuity and determination to crafting policies along the lines advocated by U.S. representatives.[66]

Yet the government's success should not overshadow significant deficiencies in the counterinsurgency effort. Terror and misconduct had continued, albeit on a lesser scale. Nor had the AFP's professional competence improved overnight. In 1951 JUSMAG bemoaned the fact that the Philippine military was still too widely dispersed in passive deployments, still poorly trained, and still insufficiently attuned to the necessity of unearthing the Huk underground. A year later Filipino performance had improved markedly, yet the advisory group complained that the Philippine armed forces still exhibited a reluctance to come to grips with the enemy. Moreover, after the army had succeeded in breaking up Huk concentrations, both it and JUSMAG had clung to using large encirclement operations once their utility had passed, shifting only belatedly to a strategy of saturation patrolling to meet the changed circumstances of the campaign.[67]

Shortcomings on the military side of the campaign paled, however, in comparison with those on the civil side. Despite making some changes in the nation's fiscal and economic structure in response to American prodding, most of the government's socioeconomic reforms proved cosmetic and superficial. The AFP's civic action program was not fully implemented until after the military had turned the tide against the guerrillas, and it barely began to satisfy the tremendous socioeconomic problems in the countryside. Despite some modest initiatives to help the farmer, meaningful land reform had been "for all practical purposes a dead letter" during the Quirino regime. Under the Quirino administration the plight of many small, independent farmers actually worsened rather than improved. Between 1948 and 1952 the percentage of Filipino farmers who did not own land increased from 37 percent to 46 percent. EDCOR, Magsaysay's much touted resettlement program, proved to be more of a propaganda tool than a meaningful experiment in Huk rehabilitation and land reform. By 1954 the government had resettled only 246 former guerrillas in development corps communities. By September 1959 this number had fallen to 221, a mere 21 percent of 1,046 settlers then living in EDCOR projects. When one considers that the total number of people (both Huk and non-Huk settlers and their families) living in EDCOR settlements in 1959 totaled only 5,709 people in a nation of over 19 million, the propagandistic nature of the development corps becomes clear. Other reform measures initiated by Magsaysay during his presidency (1953–1957), while well intentioned, also failed to make a dent in the nation's rural problems, and by 1963, 70 percent of Filipino farmers were landless tenants.[68]

As in Greece, the United States had lacked the leverage to compel the Filipinos to enact deeper socioeconomic reforms, with the result that the hand of force, rather than the hand of friendship, had played the predominate role in defeating the Huks. Hard measures—including arrest without trial, destruction of food and shelter in guerrilla-controlled areas, hostage taking, reprisals, and the occasional forcible relocation of civilian populations—had all been integral to the government's campaign. Civic and psychological actions, while important, had ultimately played an ancillary role to the military effort. Ironically, many Filipinos and Americans became so caught up in their own propaganda about EDCOR, candy for kids, and other unconventional programs and tricks that they lost sight of the fact that most Huks surrendered because they tired of living on the run from the government's increasingly effective security forces. Unconventional techniques notwithstanding, Philippine and American counterinsurgents had been able to break the back of the Huk rebellion by intelligently adapting the age-old American dictum of "Find 'em, Fight 'em, Finish 'em" to Philippine conditions.[69]

The Indochina War, 1945–1954

In contrast to Greece and the Philippines, where U.S. advisers played a significant part in orchestrating successful counterinsurgency campaigns, the United States assumed a less direct—and ultimately unsuccessful—role in a fourth major conflict of the period, the Indochina War. A French colony, Indochina had been occupied by Japan during World War II. French defeats in Europe and Asia during that war greatly weakened French prestige and fueled proindependence sentiments throughout Indochina. When Allied forces arrived to take control of Indochina from the Japanese in the fall of 1945, they found that much of the region's three political entities—Vietnam, Laos, and Cambodia—were already under the control of nationalist groups. This was particularly true in the northern reaches of Vietnam, where Ho Chi Minh's Communist-dominated Viet Minh organization was quite strong. After a year of political and military sparring, a full-blown war erupted between the Viet Minh and the French in December 1946. (*Map 5*)

In trying to reassert its authority over Indochina, France employed several traditional colonial military techniques, including raids, encirclements, and *tache d'huile* ("oil spot") operations. None of these methods succeeded, as the French attempted to reclaim too quickly far more territory than their meager expeditionary force could effectively control. Moreover, the French seriously underestimated both the depth

CHINA

Lao Cai

CHINA

Red R.

Lang Son

Black R.

BURMA

Dien Bien Phu

HANOI

Haiphong

De Lattre Line

Mekong R.

Luang Prabang

NORTH
VIETNAM

HAINAN

LAOS

GULF
OF
TONKIN

Vinh

VIENTIANE

Udon Thani
(Udorn)

Dong Hoi

DEMARCATION LINE

Savannakhet

Hue

THAILAND

Da Nang

Paksé

Nakhon Ratchasima
(Korat)

BANGKOK

Pleiku

Qui Nhon

CAMBODIA

Tonle Sap

SOUTH
VIETNAM

Kratie

Mekong R.

Loc Ninh

Da Lat

GULF
OF
THAILAND

PHNOM PENH

Sihanoukville

SAIGON

Phu Quoc

Can Tho

SOUTH

CHINA

Con Son

SEA

FRENCH INDOCHINA
1954

0   150

Miles

MAP 5

of nationalist sentiment among the Vietnamese people and the ability of the Viet Minh to harness that sentiment. Using Maoist methods, Ho Chi Minh effectively mobilized large segments of the Vietnamese people in support of a war of national liberation. Under increasing pressure from both the Viet Minh and world opinion, France grudgingly granted a veneer of autonomy to the associated states of Laos, Cambodia, and Vietnam while still preserving its colonial administration—a political half measure that failed to defuse the independence movement.[70]

France's position in Indochina was rather bleak when, in June 1950, the first shipment of American military aid arrived. Despite its general opposition to colonialism, the United States government had decided that it could not permit Indochina to fall under the ever-lengthening shadow of international communism. Growing Cold War tensions and the necessity of winning French help in creating an effective counterweight to the Soviet bloc in Europe heavily influenced the decision, as did the recent Communist takeover of neighboring China.[71]

The aid arrived none too soon. Following his 1949 victory in China, Mao Tse-tung had begun sending truckloads of arms, ammunition, and advisers into Indochina to succor his Vietnamese comrades. With this assistance, Ho and his chief military commander, General Vo Nguyen Giap, had begun to transform the Viet Minh's ragtag guerrilla bands into quasi-conventional 10,000-man divisions. By 1950 Giap had five such divisions at his disposal in northern Vietnam and was ready to launch the third and final phase of Vietnam's Maoist-style revolution.[72]

The 1950 offensive succeeded in limiting French control in the north to the Red River Delta, a region France attempted to secure by constructing a heavily fortified perimeter known as the de Lattre Line after the French commander in Indochina, General Jean de Lattre de Tassigny. Buoyed by his success, Giap tried to take the delta by storm the following year but suffered a bloody repulse. As had happened in Greece just a few years before, the shift to conventional warfare had proved premature, as Giap's divisions were no match for the French in positional combat. Unlike the Greek Communists, however, the Viet Minh enjoyed the benefits of a deep reservoir of popular support, a highly developed and disciplined political infrastructure, and an uninterrupted source of external supply. These factors enabled the Viet Minh to weather the defeats of 1951. Recognizing that they had acted prematurely, Ho and Giap returned to guerrilla warfare, keeping the French off-balance while studiously avoiding set-piece confrontations. Meanwhile, Giap carefully nurtured his regulars back to health in the safety of his northern mountain redoubts. With Chinese help, he

Franco-Vietnamese soldiers search for Viet Minh guerrillas in a village in the Red River Delta.

continuously upgraded their training and armament, so that by 1953 many Viet Minh regular battalions were better armed than their French counterparts.[73]

Thanks in part to American assistance, French military forces in Indochina grew in strength and capability as well, reaching 500,000 men by mid-1953. No less than 350,000 of these men, however, were tied down guarding towns, outposts, and lines of communications, with the de Lattre Line's 1,200 fortifications absorbing some 100,000 soldiers. These static deployments enabled the highly mobile and elusive Viet Minh to gain local superiority at any given point despite France's overall numerical advantage. The result was an enervating stalemate. The Viet Minh dominated virtually all of northern Vietnam and much of the rural south as well, while the French controlled the major cities and the fortified salient in the Red River Delta, although even this supposedly secure area was heavily infiltrated by tens of thousands of Communist guerrillas.[74]

In 1953 a new French commander, Lt. Gen. Henri-Eugene Navarre, pledged to break the stalemate by reorganizing French forces and infusing the army with a more offensive spirit. With the help of some additional troop units from France and materiel from the United States, Navarre planned to consolidate his forces so as to free up a significant strategic reserve capable of taking the war to the enemy. While elite parachute units, Vietnamese light infantry, and tribal irregulars kept the enemy off-balance through raids and guer-rilla-style actions, Navarre proposed to invigorate France's heretofore halfhearted efforts at creating a large Vietnamese National Army whose troops could assume most of the responsibility for pacification and static security missions. This would then allow him to consolidate his veteran French formations—which were not organized into any-thing larger than regiment-size units—into regular divisions capable of conducting sustained, large-scale operations against the enemy's main forces and bases.

The Navarre plan won the approval of both the French and American governments, with the newly installed Eisenhower admin-istration pledging $385 million in additional aid to help implement it. The results, however, were disappointing. The divisions were never formed, the expansion of the Vietnamese National Army proceeded slowly, and the vast majority of French troops remained tied down in static positions. Navarre did initiate greater offensive activity, but his operations were often of questionable military value and had the effect of dispersing his painfully accumulated reserves to little effect. Though he inflicted some damage on his adversaries, all too often the nimble guerrillas managed to elude his nets, fighting when it served their purpose, avoiding the French when it did not. Then, in the winter of 1953–1954, Navarre made the mistake of committing approximately 17,000 of his best troops to a remote outpost called Dien Bien Phu in northwestern Vietnam.[75]

Navarre intended that the deployment to Dien Bien Phu would thwart a possible Viet Minh invasion of Laos. He also thought that the isolated outpost would prove an irresistible lure to the one or two Communist divisions he believed were operating in the area and which he hoped would eviscerate themselves on the garrison's defenses. It proved a serious miscalculation. Rather than facing one or two divisions armed with a few dozen artillery pieces, the defenders of Dien Bien Phu were soon surrounded by five Viet Minh divisions equipped with several hundred artillery pieces and rocket launchers. Outnumbered and outgunned, the French received another shock when a ring of Communist antiaircraft guns made aerial resupply of the besieged outpost problematic. Chinese aid had truly transformed the Viet Minh into a potent, quasi-conventional battle force, and in May 1954 the beleaguered garrison capitulated.[76]

Giap followed up his stunning victory with a ten-division offensive that compelled the French to abandon a large segment of the Red River Delta. Reeling from these defeats, a weary French government has-tened to the peace table. In June an international conference at Geneva

Franco-Vietnamese soldiers parachute into Dien Bien Phu.

granted full independence to Laos, Cambodia, and a divided Vietnam. The Geneva conferees placed all of Vietnam north of the 17th Parallel under Communist control, while everything south of that line was to be administered by an indigenous non-Communist regime backed by the French. Although the convention called for the eventual reunification of Vietnam through general elections, the government of South Vietnam refused to sign the accords. In actuality, both the North and the South were committed to the destruction of the other and the eventual reunification of the entire country under their respective auspices by any means possible, a situation that would ultimately lead to twenty more years of bloody civil war.[77]

The United States Army played virtually no role in shaping the strategies, tactics, and doctrines employed by France in Indochina. A proud people with a rich heritage of colonial warfare, the French neither sought nor accepted U.S. advice on the conduct of the war. Like so many other American aid missions of the period, the military assistance organization in Indochina was devoted entirely to administrative and logistical functions. Its personnel neither advised the French on military operations nor accompanied them in the field. The French tightly restricted the information they gave to the aid mission and rarely revealed their operational plans to their allies. They also barred U.S. military personnel from having any direct contact with the Vietnamese National Army. Thus the French consulted U.S. officers neither about the construction of the de Lattre Line nor the deployment to Dien Bien

Phu, and they did not provide the Army with the operational details of the Navarre plan.[78]

Though U.S. soldiers had virtually no influence over the conduct of the war, they were not without their opinions on the conflict. Throughout the war, senior U.S. officers, including Army Chief of Staff General J. Lawton Collins, had repeatedly warned that American military aid would not be effective in suppressing the insurgency unless that aid was carefully integrated into an overall program of political and economic reforms, including meaningful independence for the people of Indochina. Without such reforms France would not be able to win much support among the Vietnamese people, and without such support the French would never be able to gather the intelligence they needed to successfully root out the shadowy Viet Minh organization. U.S. soldiers also argued, as they had in China, Greece, and the Philippines, that the key to victory lay in continuous, aggressive infantry action. They sharply criticized France for adopting an overly passive, static defensive posture that ceded the moral and military initiative to the Viet Minh. They suggested that the French were too road-bound in their movements and conventional in their thinking and believed that they needed to adjust their organizations and tactics more completely to the realities of Asian guerrilla warfare. U.S. soldiers recommended that France expand its unconventional warfare capabilities and form more effective Vietnamese military institutions, including an army capable of independent operations, light infantry battalions for pacification support, and a village-based militia that could both protect the population from Communist intimidation and free the regular forces for offensive action. Finally, the Americans pressed the French to mimic the Viet Minh by consolidating their disparate, ad hoc formations into regular combat divisions that would have the administrative and logistical wherewithal to undertake sustained offensive operations against enemy main force units and bases. While these formations dislodged the Communists from their redoubts, small units of raiders could harass the Communists using guerrilla tactics while indigenous auxiliaries, backed by intelligence and psychological warfare units, secured and pacified the countryside from the baleful influence of the Viet Minh infrastructure. These concepts mirrored similar sentiments expressed by U.S. military advisers in China, Greece, and the Philippines, and indeed, one American plan for the pacification of Indochina was specifically based on the strategy of progressive area clearance employed by Van Fleet during the recently concluded Greek Civil War.[79]

France did in fact attempt at one time or another to implement many of the suggestions advocated in the American program but never to the satisfaction of U.S. military observers. Civilian analysts were similarly critical of France's performance. Like their uniformed colleagues, U.S. diplomats were forever pressing France to adopt more meaningful political and economic concessions in Indochina. The United States even supplemented its massive military aid program with a modest package of economic and technical assistance designed to improve the lot of the Vietnamese peasant and win his support for the anti-Communist cause. American-funded programs promoted literacy, constructed roads and bridges, dug wells, resettled refugees, inoculated civilians, and regrouped small villages into larger, more defensible settlements. Ultimately, however, the modest size of these efforts, American ignorance about conditions in Indochina, French intransigence, and Vietnamese corruption all conspired to limit the effectiveness of such programs. Unable to influence sufficiently France's conduct of the war and unwilling to intervene directly in what everyone acknowledged was an extremely difficult situation, the United States could do nothing more than watch with despair as northern Vietnam fell into the Communist orbit. As for the newly independent, French-backed government in southern Vietnam, years of colonial maladministration and impolitic policies bequeathed to that unfortunate regime a population that was generally sympathetic to the Viet Minh. Whether the government could overcome this handicap remained to be seen.[80]

Notes

[1] Beckett, *Roots of Counter-Insurgency*, pp. 127–36; Lomperis, *People's War to People's Rule*, p. 138; Laqueur, *Guerrilla*, pp. 241, 247.

[2] For details of the Army's peacekeeping effort in China, see Andrew Birtle, "The Marshall Mission: A Peacekeeping Mission That Failed," *Military Review* 80 (March–April 2000): 99–103; Larry Bland, ed., *George C. Marshall's Mediation Mission to China, December 1945–January 1947* (Lexington, Va.: George C. Marshall Foundation, 1998); *The Complete Records of the Mission of General George C. Marshall to China, December 1945–January 1947* (Wilmington, Del.: Scholarly Resources, 1987); John Beal, *Marshall in China* (Garden City, N.Y.: Doubleday, 1970); Wesley Wilson, "The U.S. Army's Contribution to the Marshall Mission in China, January 1, 1946 to March 1, 1947" (Master's thesis, University of Maryland, 1957); *Marshall's Mission to China, December 1945–January 1947: The Report and Appended Documents*, 2 vols. (Arlington, Va.: University Publishers of America, 1976).

[3] Quote from State Department, *Foreign Relations of the United States [FRUS], 1948*, vol. 8, *The Far East: China* (Washington, D.C.: Government Printing Office, 1973), p. 244, and see also pp. 422–23. State Department, *United States Relations with China* (Washington, D.C.: Government Printing Office, 1949), p. 358; Final Report of the Joint U.S. Military Advisory Group to the Republic of China, pp. 9–10, in 893.20 Mission/4–449, Records of the Department of State, Record Group (RG) 59, National Archives and Records Administration (NARA), Washington, D.C.

[4] Mao, *Selected Military Writings*, pp. 217, 229, 302–03; Blaufarb, *Counterinsurgency Era*, pp. 7–11.

[5] Mao, *Selected Military Writings*, pp. 210–14, 343; Pustay, *Counterinsurgency Warfare*, pp. 32–38; Asprey, *War in the Shadows*, 1:387–91.

[6] *U.S. Relations with China*, pp. xv, 339, 346, 354; *FRUS, 1948*, 8:243–44, 247–48; Final Report of the Joint U.S. Military Advisory Group to the Republic of China, pp. 4–5; Memo, Maj Gen John P. Lucas, Ch, Army Advisory Group, China, 2 Sep 47, in 091 China, 1946–48, Plans and Operations Division (P&O), Records of the Army Staff, RG 319, NARA.

[7] The proposal to create an American planning group was based on the recent establishment of such an entity in Greece. Secretary of the Army Kenneth C. Royall, Army Chief of Staff General Omar N. Bradley, and former Army chief and then Secretary of State George C. Marshall all opposed the idea lest such an action further enmesh the United States in the Chinese imbroglio. *U.S. Relations with China*, p. 324; *FRUS, 1948*, 8:91–96, 244–47; *FRUS, 1947*, vol. 7, *The Far East: China*, pp. 754, 877.

[8] Quote from *FRUS, 1947*, 7:392. *U.S. Relations with China*, pp. 136, 176, 316, 336–37; Msg, Army Advisory Group to War Department (WD), 10 Oct 47, box 3, General files, Entry (E) 90, Joint U.S. Military Advisory Group, Republic of China, RG 334, NARA.

[9] First quote from *U.S. Relations with China*, p. 810, and see also pp. 131, 174, 211–13. Second quote from ibid., pp. 758–59. Third quote from ibid., pp. 257–58. *FRUS, 1947*, 7:389, 754–55, 764–814; Albert Wedemeyer, *Wedemeyer Reports!* (New York: Henry Holt, 1958), pp. 394–95; Edward Cray, *General of the Army: George C. Marshall, Soldier and Statesman* (New York: W. W. Norton, 1990), p. 634; Ltr, Barr

to Stuart, 5 Jun 48, box 4, General files, E 90, Joint U.S. Military Advisory Group, Republic of China, RG 334, NARA.

[10] *U.S. Relations with China*, pp. 759–60.

[11] Ibid., p. 336; *FRUS, 1947*, 7:393, 922; *FRUS, 1948*, 8:248–49, 498.

[12] Ltr, Barr to Stuart, 5 Jun 48; Outline of Two-Year Strategic Plan for the Ministry of National Defense, 21 Jul 48, box 4, General files, E 90, Joint U.S. Military Advisory Group, Republic of China, RG 334, NARA; *FRUS, 1948*, 8:422–23.

[13] First quote from Beckett, *Roots of Counter-Insurgency*, p. 133. Second quote from Wilson, "The U.S. Army's Contribution to the Marshall Mission," p. 83. Third quote from Manual for Bandit Suppression, Sep 45, p. 7, atch to Rpt, Asst Mil Attache, Peiping, China, 23 Jan 47, sub: Handbook for Suppressing Bandits, 339026, Intelligence Document (ID) file, G–2, RG 319, NARA. Mao, *Selected Military Writings*, p. 410.

[14] First and second quotes from Rpt, Asst Naval Attache, Peiping, China, 26 Aug 48, sub: China—Army and Related Organizations, p. 3, 0493142. Fourth quote from ibid., p. 4. Third quote from Rpt, Mil Attache, Nanking, 29 Jun 48, sub: Strategy and Tactics of North China Bandit Suppression HQ, 475708; Rpt, Mil Attache, Nanking, 3 Jun 48, sub: Fu Tso-yi's Principles of Communist Suppression, 471145. All in ID, G–2, RG 319, NARA.

[15] *FRUS, 1947*, 7:659–60; *FRUS, 1948*, 8:132–34; *U.S. Relations with China*, pp. x–xii, 252, 281, 352–53, 380–84, 389–94, 770.

[16] Michael Shafer, *Deadly Paradigms: The Failure of U.S. Counterinsurgency Policy* (Princeton, N.J.: Princeton University Press, 1988), pp. 167–72; Hugh Gardner, Guerrilla and Counterguerrilla Warfare in Greece, 1941–1945, Office of the Chief of Military History, 1962, p. 9, CMH; Thomas Greene, ed., *The Guerrilla, and How To Fight Him* (Washington, D.C.: Frederick A. Praeger, 1967), p. 67.

[17] Greene, *The Guerrilla*, pp. 69–70, 78–79; Edward Wainhouse, "Guerrilla War in Greece," *Military Review* 37 (June 1957): 20–22; Rpt, Mil Attache, Greece, 22 Mar 49, sub: Organization of the Bandit Forces and Tactics Employed, Historians files, CMH. Compare Mao's ten principles as related by Otto Heilbrunn, *Partisan Warfare* (New York: Frederick A. Praeger, 1967), pp. 168–69, with instructions issued by the National Popular Liberation Army during World War II as described by Frank Lillyman, Guerrilla Warfare in Greece (Student paper, Infantry Officer Advanced Course [IOAC], Infantry School, Fort Benning, Ga., 1952–53), pp. 11–12, and by the Democratic People's Army as found in Greek General Staff, Special Intelligence Pamphlet, Bandit Methods, Mar 49, Incl to Rpt, Mil Attache, Greece, 23 May 49, sub: Guerrilla Tactical Methods, Historians files, CMH.

[18] "The Greek Guerrillas—How They Operate," *Intelligence Review* 156 (March 1949): 33.

[19] Edgar O'Ballance, *The Greek Civil War, 1944–1949* (Washington, D.C.: Frederick A. Praeger, 1966), p. 129; Greene, *The Guerrilla*, p. 76; William Needham, Paramilitary Forces in Greece, 1946–1949 (Student paper, Army War College [AWC], 1971), pp. 28–29.

[20] Greene, *The Guerrilla*, pp. 94–95; Rpt, Joint U.S. Military Advisory and Planning Group, Greece (JUSMAPG), 1 Oct 48, sub: Greek Army Operations, 1948, an. A to Rpt, JUSMAPG, 1 Oct 48, sub: Estimate of the Current Military Situation in Greece, 091 Greece, P&O, 1946–48, RG 319, NARA.

[21] Greek General Staff, Suppression of Irregular (Bandit) Operations, n.d., Historians files, CMH; Greek Staff College, curricular material, Precis Internal Security 3, Jan

47, and Anti-Bandit Warfare Supplement to Inf 2, Oct 47, both in NS–16284, CGSC Library archives, Fort Leavenworth, Kans. Compare these materials to British concepts presented to the Greek high command in December 1946, as found in Rpt, Mil Attache, Greece, 2 Jan 47, sub: Anti-Bandit Operations, app. A, British Ideas on Internal Security, 925947, ID, G–2, RG 319, NARA.

[22] Rpt, Maj Gen S. J. Chamberlin to Chief of Staff, Army (CSA), 20 Oct 47, sub: The Greek Situation, pt. 2, p. 3, 868.00/10–2047, RG 59, NARA; Alexander Papagos, "Guerrilla Warfare," *Foreign Affairs* 30 (January 1952): 222–24; Memo, Maj Gen S. B. Rawlins, British Mil Mission, Greece, n.d., sub: Notes on the GNA and Its Problems Prepared in Connection with the Visit of Commander in Chief MELF to Athens, August 1947, 091 Greece, P&O, 1946–48, RG 319, NARA.

[23] Quotes from Robert Packenham, *Liberal America and the Third World* (Princeton, N.J.: Princeton University Press, 1973), p. 26. Shafer, *Deadly Paradigms*, pp. 184–86.

[24] Even with the shift in priorities, economic assistance still accounted for 60 percent of all U.S. aid by war's end. Quote from *FRUS, 1947*, vol. 5, *The Near East and Africa*, p. 361. Walter Hermes, Survey of the Development of the Role of the U.S. Army Military Advisor, OCMH Study, Office of the Chief of Military History, 1965, p. 59, CMH; Ralph Hinrichs, "U.S. Involvement in Low Intensity Conflict Since World War II: Three Case Studies—Greece, Dominican Republic, and Vietnam" (Master's thesis, CGSC, 1984), pp. 3-6 to 3-8; Shafer, *Deadly Paradigms*, pp. 181, 184; Edwin Curtin, "American Advisory Group Aids Greece in War of Guerrillas," *Armored Cavalry Journal* 58 (January–February 1949): 9; Ltr, Livesay to Griswold, 21 Aug 47, sub: Increase in Strength of the Greek Army, in 091 Greece, P&O, 1946–48, RG 319, NARA; Memo, Rawlins, n.d., sub: Notes on the GNA and Its Problems Prepared in Connection with the Visit of Commander in Chief MELF to Athens, August 1947; Msg, Athens 176 to State, 10 Feb 48, sub: Greek Military Situation, in 868.20/2–1048, RG 59, NARA; Ltrs, William Draper, Jr., Actg Secy of Army, to Robert Lovett, Secy of State, 24 Dec 48, and Lovett to Royall, 13 Jan 49, both in 868.20/12–2448, RG 59, NARA; Memos, CSA for Joint Chiefs of Staff (JCS), Situation in Greece, App to Incl B, Report on Greece by Combined Imperial General Staff, JCS 1704/19, 3 May 49, in 091 Greece, P&O, 1949–50, RG 319, NARA, and American Embassy, Greece, for the Secy of State, 20 Dec 48, sub: Visit to Greece of the Secretary of the Army Kenneth C. Royall, 522347, ID, G–2, RG 319, NARA.

[25] First quote from Shafer, *Deadly Paradigms*, pp. 188–92. Second quote from Estimate of the Military Situation, pp. 54–55, atch to Rpt, Chamberlin to CSA, 20 Oct 47, sub: The Greek Situation. Harold Roberts, The Organization and Functions of the Joint U.S. Military Advisory Planning Group for Greece (JUSMAPG) (Student paper, IOAC, Infantry School, 1952–53), pp. 1–7; Monthly Historical Rpt, U.S. Army Group, American Mission to Greece, Sep 47, U.S. Army Section Group, Adjutant General Section History files, 1947–50, Joint U.S. Military Aid Group (JUSMAG), Greece, E 155, RG 334, NARA; William McNeill, *Greece: American Aid in Action, 1947–1956* (New York: Twentieth Century Fund, 1957), p. 67.

[26] Quote from Interv with James A. Van Fleet, U.S. Army Senior Officer Debriefing Program, U.S. Army Military History Institute (MHI), Carlisle Barracks, Pa., p. 26, and see also pp. 14, 16 (hereafter cited as Van Fleet Interv). Lawrence Wittner, *American Intervention in Greece, 1943–1949* (New York: Columbia University Press, 1982), p. 242; Brief History, 1 January 1948 to 31 August 1949, p. 14, U.S. Army Section Group, Adjutant General Section History files, 1947–50, JUSMAG, Greece, E 155, RG 334,

NARA; Robert Selton, "Communist Errors in the Anti-Bandit War," *Military Review* 45 (September 1965): 75.

[27] Van Fleet Interv, pp. 3–4, 15; Estimate of the Military Situation, p. 19, atch to Rpt, Chamberlin to CSA, 20 Oct 47, sub: The Greek Situation.

[28] Robert Siegrist, Victory in the Balkans (Student paper, IOAC, Infantry School, 1952–53), p. 6; O'Ballance, *Greek Civil War*, pp. 173–74; Curtin, "American Advisory Group," p. 13; Memos, Highlight Notes, 30 Jun 49, in 314.7, JUSMAPG, Greece, RG 334, NARA, and JUSMAPG, 18 Dec 47, sub: Minutes of the Seventeenth Meeting of the Committee of the Chiefs of Staff of all Three War Ministries, in 334, JUSMAG, Greece, E 146, RG 334, NARA; Diary, William G. Livesay, 31 Aug 47, William G. Livesay Papers, MHI.

[29] Quote from Rpt, Mil Attache, Greece, 15 Nov 47, sub: Armed Forces of Greece, Expansion Possibilities, 929245, ID, G–2, RG 319, NARA. Van Fleet Interv, pp. 3, 17, 21; Memo, Van Fleet for Grady, 31 Dec 48, sub: General Zervas' Opinions on the Current Military Situation, Incl to Despatch 149, Athens to State, 19 Feb 49, 535816, ID, G–2, RG 319, NARA; Roberts, Organization and Functions, p. 10.

[30] Ltrs, Brig Gen Reuben E. Jenkins, Asst Dir, JUSMAPG, to Lt Gen S. Kitrilakis, Dep Ch, GGS (Greek General Staff), 3 Jun 49, in 322, and Col Temple G. Holland, Comdr, JUSMAPG Det, C Corps, to Commanding General (CG), C Corps, 4 Feb 49, sub: Rifles for Civil Units, in 322; Memos, JUSMAPG, n.d., sub: Minutes of the Meeting of the Executive Committee Held February 25, 1949, in 332, and JUSMAPG Det, C Corps, 16 Jun 49, sub: Addendum to Monthly Report, May 1949, in 319.1. All in JUSMAG, Greece, E 156, RG 334, NARA. McNeill, *Greece*, pp. 49, 132.

[31] Quotes from Rpt, Livesay to Griswold, 24 Jun 47, sub: Requests by the GNA and Gendarmerie for Authorization and Funds To Increase Their Military Strength and Certain Allied Activities, in 868.20/8–147, RG 59, NARA; Livesay Diary, 19 Jun 47; Needham, Paramilitary Forces in Greece, p. 29; Memo, U.S. Army Group Greece (USAGG), 1 Nov 47, sub: Notes of Supreme National Defense Council Meeting, Held at 1800 Hours, 31 Oct 1947, 334, JUSMAG, Greece, E 146, RG 334, NARA; Rpt, Chamberlin to CSA, 20 Oct 47, sub: The Greek Situation, 2:8, 10.

[32] Memo, Highlight Notes, 30 Jun 49; Brief History, 1 January 1948 to 31 August 1949, pp. 12–13. Needham, Paramilitary Forces in Greece, pp. 29–31; Roberts, Organization and Functions, pp. 11–12.

[33] By 1949 refugee relief absorbed 22 percent of the Greek budget and a high percentage of American economic aid as well. O'Ballance, *Greek Civil War*, pp. 15, 136, 150, 163, 167–68; McNeill, *Greece*, pp. 40, 49, 131–32; "The Greek Guerrillas—How They Operate," p. 28; Wittner, *American Intervention*, pp. 137–39.

[34] Quote from Wittner, *American Intervention*, p. 136, and see also pp. 138, 143, 147–49. Shafer, *Deadly Paradigms*, pp. 192–95; *FRUS, 1947*, 5:388n, 402–03.

[35] First quote from Van Fleet Interv, p. 33, and see also pp. 26–27, 32, 34, 49–52. Second quote from Estimate of the Military Situation, p. 3, atch to Rpt, Chamberlin to CSA, 20 Oct 47, sub: The Greek Situation. *FRUS, 1947*, 5:403; O'Ballance, *Greek Civil War*, pp. 150, 167–68, 179, 214; Dimitrios Kousoulas, "The Guerrilla War the Communists Lost," *U.S. Naval Institute Proceedings* 89 (May 1963): 70; Charles Shrader, *The Withered Vine: Logistics and the Communist Insurgency in Greece, 1945–1949* (Westport, Conn.: Frederick A. Praeger, 1999), pp. 124–27.

[36] Memo, Highlight Notes, 30 Jun 49; JUSMAG, Greece, History, 25 March 1949 to 30 June 1950, p. 58; Monthly Historical Rpt, U.S. Army Group American Mission to

Greece, Oct 47, p. 4; Memo, JUSMAPG, n.d., sub: Minutes of Conference Held in the JUSMAPG Conference Room, 3 P.M., 11 Jan 49. All in JUSMAG, Greece, 1947–48, RG 334, NARA. Speech, Livesay to Advisers, 16 Jan 48, pp. 1–4, Livesay Papers, MHI; Memo, Van Fleet for Grady, 31 Dec 48, sub: General Zervas' Opinions, Incl to Des 149, Athens to State, 19 Feb 49; Van Fleet Interv., p. 44; Greene, *The Guerrilla*, pp. 82, 88; Guenther Rothenberg, Guerrilla Warfare and Counterinsurgent Efforts in Greece, 1941–1949, in Historical Evaluation and Research Organization (HERO), Isolating the Guerrilla (Washington, D.C.: HERO, 1966), p. 209.

[37] For British views, see Memo, Rawlins, British Military Mission, Greece, n.d., sub: Notes on the GNA and Its Problems Prepared in Connection with the Visit of Commander in Chief MELF to Athens, August 1947; Rpt, Mil Attache, Greece, 5 Nov 47, sub: Army Commander's Conference, Volos, 17–18 October 1947, 414357, ID, G–2, RG 319, NARA.

[38] Rpt, JUSMAPG, 1 Oct 48, sub: Estimate of the Current Military Situation in Greece, with 2 ans.: A, Rpt, JUSMAPG, 1 Oct 48, sub: Greek Army Operations, 1948, and B, Rpt, British Military Mission, n.d., sub: Estimate of the Bandit War in Greece and of the Steps Required To Bring It to a Successful Conclusion as Quickly as Possible; Rpt, Van Fleet to Dir, P&O, U.S. Army General Staff, 31 Mar 48; Rpt, JUSMAPG, 25 Mar 48, Operations Report 6, 11–19 Mar 48, pp. 9–12. All in 091 Greece, P&O, 1946–48, RG 319, NARA. Roberts, Organization and Functions, pp. 13–14; Rpt, Mil Attache, Greece, 15 Nov 47, sub: Armed Forces of Greece, Expansion Possibilities; Papagos, "Guerrilla Warfare," p. 226; O'Ballance, *Greek Civil War*, pp. 170–73.

[39] Anastase Balcos, "Guerrilla Warfare," *Military Review* 38 (March 1958): 53; Dimitrios Kousoulas, "The Crucial Point of a Counterguerrilla Campaign," *Infantry* 53 (January–February 1963): 18–19. For a partial exposition of Zachariades' philosophy, which had Maoist tones, see Greek General Staff, Special Intelligence Pamphlet, Bandit Methods, Mar 49, Incl to Rpt, Mil Attache, Greece, 23 May 49, sub: Guerrilla Tactical Methods.

[40] O'Ballance, *Greek Civil War*, pp. 179, 200; Selton, "Communist Errors," pp. 72–75.

[41] Greene, *The Guerrilla*, pp. 97–98; Shrader, *Withered Vine*, pp. 253–63.

[42] First quote from Kousoulas, "Guerrilla War the Communists Lost," p. 69. Second quote from Memo, Greek General Staff for A, B Corps, et al., 9 May 49, in 091 Greece, P&O 1949–50, RG 319, NARA. Memo, Brig Gen T. Sfetsios for GGS/A3, 9 May 49, sub: Distribution of 2,000 Rifles, in 322, JUSMAPG, Greece, RG 334, NARA; Papagos, "Guerrilla Warfare," pp. 228–29; Roberts, Organization and Functions, p. 15; O'Ballance, *Greek Civil War*, pp. 156, 161.

[43] Quote from JUSMAG, Greece, History, 25 March 1949 to 30 June 1950, p. 85, and see also pp. 103, 108–09. Memo, Highlight Notes, 30 Jun 49; Monthly Rpts, JUSMAPG B Corps Detachment, 1 Jun, 1 Jul, and 1 Aug 49, in 319.1, JUSMAPG, Greece, E 155, RG 334, NARA; Minutes of Conference Held 9 May 1949 Between JUSMAPG, BMM(G), RAF Delegation, BMM(G), and BPPM, n.d., in 091 Greece, P&O, 1949–50, RG 319, NARA.

[44] For assessments of the war, see O'Ballance, *Greek Civil War*, pp. 175, 192, 210–16; Wainhouse, "Guerrilla War in Greece," p. 25; Kousoulas, "Crucial Point," pp. 19–20; E. Zacharakis, "Lessons Learned in the Anti-Guerrilla War in Greece, 1946–1949," *General Military Review* (July 1960): 186–93.

[45] Balcos, "Guerrilla Warfare," pp. 53–54; Papagos, "Guerrilla Warfare," pp. 229–30; *FRUS, 1949*, 6:273; McNeill, *Greece*, pp. 40, 45, 50–51, 63; Lomperis, *People's War to People's Rule*, p. 167; Packenham, *Liberal America*, pp. 31–32; Shafer, *Deadly Paradigms*, pp. 166, 189–96, 203–04; Wittner, *American Intervention*, pp. 189–91.

[46] "Huk" was shorthand for *Hukbo Ng Bayan Laban Sa Hapon*, which translates as "People's Army to Fight Against Japan." William Moore, "The Hukbalahap Insurgency, 1948–1954: An Analysis of the Roles, Missions, and Doctrine of the Philippine Military Forces" (Student thesis, AWC, 1971), p. 2; Asprey, *War in the Shadows*, 2:818; Benedict Kerkvliet, *The Huk Rebellion: A Study of Peasant Revolt in the Philippines* (Berkeley: University of California Press, 1977), pp. 250–54; Shafer, *Deadly Paradigms*, pp. 206–11; Eduardo Lachica, *The Huks: Philippine Agrarian Society in Revolt* (Washington, D.C.: Frederick A. Praeger, 1971), pp. 41–47.

[47] Blaufarb, *Counterinsurgency Era*, p. 26; Shafer, *Deadly Paradigms*, pp. 211–12; Kerkvliet, *Huk Rebellion*, p. 267; Michael McClintock, *Instruments of Statecraft: U.S. Guerrilla Warfare, Counter-insurgency, and Counter-terrorism, 1940–1990* (New York: Pantheon Books, 1992), pp. 96–98; Dana Dillon, "Comparative Counter-Insurgency Strategies in the Philippines," *Small Wars and Insurgencies* 6 (Winter 1995): 283–84; Richard Leighton et al., The Huk Rebellion: A Case Study in the Social Dynamics of Insurrection (Washington, D.C.: Industrial College of the Armed Forces, 1964), pp. 28–29.

[48] Napoleon Valeriano and Charles Bohannan, *Counter-Guerrilla Operations: The Philippine Experience* (Washington, D.C.: Frederick A. Praeger, 1962), pp. 160–62; Alvin Scaff, *The Philippine Answer to Communism* (Stanford, Calif.: Stanford University Press, 1955), p. 124; McClintock, *Instruments of Statecraft*, pp. 120–22; Charles Bohannan, The Communist Insurgency in the Philippines: The Hukbalahap, 1942–1955, in HERO, Isolating the Guerrilla, pp. 137–38, 142; Mao, *Selected Military Writings*, p. 410; Russell Volckmann, *We Remained* (New York: W. W. Norton, 1954), pp. 108–09; Gene Hanrahan, Japanese Operations Against Guerrilla Forces, ORO–T–268 (Chevy Chase, Md.: Operations Research Office, Johns Hopkins University, 1954); Dillon, "Comparative Strategies," pp. 283–84; Leighton, Huk Rebellion, pp. 28–29, 57–58; Lawrence Greenberg, *The Hukbalahap Insurrection: A Case Study of a Successful Anti-Insurgency Operation in the Philippines, 1944–1946* (Washington, D.C.: U.S. Army Center of Military History, 1987), p. 76; Kerkvliet, *Huk Rebellion*, pp. 160, 189–90, 195; Robert Ross Smith, The Hukbalahap Insurgency: Economic, Political, and Military Factors, Office of the Chief of Military History, 1963, pp. 85–86, CMH.

[49] Uldarico Baclagon, How We Fight the Communist (Student paper, IOAC, Infantry School, 1956–57), p. 10; Greenberg, *The Hukbalahap Insurrection*, p. 129; Bohannan, "Communist Insurgency," p. 134.

[50] Rpts, Mil Attache, Manila, 21 Nov 51, sub: Captured Enemy Document Titled (Military Strategy and Tactics), 858801, and HQ, Philippine Command (PhilCom) (Air Force [AF]), and 13th AF, Ofc of the Dep for Intel, 14 May 51, sub: Hukbong Mapagpalaya Ng Bayan (HMB) Tactics, 811902. Both in ID, G–2, RG 319, NARA. Otto Scharth, The Strategy, Training, and Tactics of the Huks in the Philippine Islands (Student paper, IOAC, Infantry School, 1952–53), pp. 9–12; Fred Barton, Salient Operational Aspects of Paramilitary Warfare in Three Asian Areas, ORO–T–228 (Chevy Chase, Md.: Operations Research Office, Johns Hopkins University, 1953), pp. 204–10, 233–35. Estimates of Huk strength vary. See Charles Bohannan, "Antiguerrilla Operations," *Annals* 341 (May 1962): 21; Tomas Tirona, "The Philippine

Anti-Communist Campaign," *Air University Review* 7 (Summer 1954): 47; Dillon, "Comparative Strategies," p. 285.

[51] First quote from David Greenberg, "The United States Response to Philippine Insurgency" (Ph.D. diss., Fletcher School of Law and Diplomacy, Tufts University, 1994), p. 100. Remaining quotes from *FRUS, 1951*, vol. 6, *Asia and the Pacific*, p. 1561, and see also pp. 1505–12, 1536–39, 1553–54. *FRUS, 1950*, vol. 6, *East Asia and the Pacific*, pp. 1435–37; Shafer, *Deadly Paradigms*, pp. 220–22; Dillon, "Comparative Strategies," p. 287; Richard Kessler, *Rebellion and Repression in the Philippines* (New Haven, Conn.: Yale University Press, 1989), p. 138.

[52] Greenberg, "United States Response to Philippine Insurgency," pp. 123, 174; *FRUS, 1950*, 6:1437, 1483, 1487, 1514–20; *FRUS, 1951*, 6:1495, 1500; Memo, John F. Melby, Chair, Joint State-Defense Mutual Defense Assistance Program (MDAP) Survey Mission to Southeast Asia, for FMACC, 29 Sep 50, pp. 2–3, atch to Rpt, Joint Mutual Defense Assistance (MDA) Survey Mission in Southeast Asia, 27 Sep 50, sub: Report No. 4 of the Joint MDA Survey Mission in Southeast Asia (hereafter cited as Erskine Rpt), in 091 Philippines, 1950–51, G–3, RG 319, NARA.

[53] Hermes, Development of the Role of the U.S. Army Military Advisor, p. 36; Erskine Rpt, p. 10.

[54] For evidence that JUSMAG planners were mindful of the Greek example, see Greenberg, "United States Response to Philippine Insurgency," p. 126; Briefing, JUSMAG to U.S. Ambassador to the Philippines et al., n.d., sub: Ground Forces: Organization, Disposition, Tactics, Logistics, and Recommendations to Philippine Government Made by JUSMAG, p. 14, atch to Rpt, JUSMAG, 29 Sep 50, sub: Weekly Summary of Activities, in 319.1, JUSMAG, Philippines, 1949–53, RG 334, NARA; Memorandum for the Record (MFR), G–3, 26 Oct 51, sub: Request by JUSMAGPHIL on Operational Procedures Utilized in Greece by JAMAG, in 091 Philippines, G–3 1950–51, RG 319, NARA.

[55] John Jameson, "The Philippine Constabulary as a Counterinsurgency Force, 1948–54" (Student thesis, AWC, 1971), pp. 17–18; Greenberg, "United States Response to Philippine Insurgency," p. 117; Erskine Rpt, an. B, pp. 9–10; Rpts, JUSMAG, 18 Jan 51, sub: Semi-Annual Appraisal of the Joint United States Military Advisory Group to the Republic of the Philippines, pp. 29–30, and 25 Mar 50, sub: Semi-Annual Appraisal of the Joint United States Military Advisory Group to the Republic of the Philippines, p. 5. Both in 091 Philippines, G–3 Classified Correspondence, RG 319, NARA.

[56] Rpt, JUSMAG, 25 Mar 50, sub: Semi-Annual Appraisal of the Joint United States Military Advisory Group to the Republic of the Philippines, pp. 5–6; Hermes, Development of the Role of the U.S. Army Military Advisor, pp. 38–38b; Memo, Melby for FMACC, 29 Sep 50, p. 4, atch to Erskine Rpt.

[57] Briefing, JUSMAG to U.S. Ambassador to the Philippines et al., n.d., sub: Ground Forces: Organization, Disposition, Tactics, Logistics, and Recommendations to Philippine Government Made by JUSMAG, pp. 13–15, atch to Rpt, JUSMAG, 29 Sep 50, sub: Weekly Summary of Activities; Jameson, "Philippine Constabulary," pp. 20–21; Bohannan, "Antiguerrilla Operations," p. 21.

[58] A battalion combat team had 1,047 men and consisted of a headquarters and headquarters company, three infantry companies, a heavy weapons company of mortars and machine guns, a reconnaissance company partially outfitted with armored cars, and a service company. Typical attachments included an artillery battery whose crewmen often served as infantry, a scout dog team, an air detachment, a military intelligence team, a

psychological warfare and civil affairs team, a medical detachment, and up to a dozen Scout Ranger teams. Although the formation was not entirely ideal for Philippine conditions, it proved to be an effective adaptation. Luis Villa-Real, "Huk Hunting," *U.S. Army Combat Forces Journal* 5 (November 1954): 32; Donald MacGrain, "Anti-Dissident Operations in the Philippines" (Student thesis, AWC, 1956), pp. 16–18; Rpt, JUSMAG, 25 Mar 50, sub: Semi-Annual Appraisal of the Joint United States Military Advisory Group to the Republic of the Philippines, p. 5.

[59] For State and Defense Department support for greater American involvement and for JUSMAG's opposition, see *FRUS, 1950*, 6:1435–37; *FRUS, 1951*, 6:1534; Erskine Rpt, pp. 12, 16; Rpts, JUSMAG, 18 Jan 51, sub: Semi-Annual Appraisal of the Joint United States Military Advisory Group to the Republic of the Philippines, pp. 45–47, and 14 Feb 52, sub: Semi-Annual Report, 1 July–31 December 1951, p. 3, 091 Philippines, G–3, 1952, RG 319, NARA.

[60] Edward Lansdale, *In the Midst of Wars* (New York: Harper & Row, 1972), pp. 47–49; Boyd Bashore, "Dual Strategy for Limited War," *Military Review* 40 (May 1960): 57. The Scout Rangers were patterned after the U.S. Army's Alamo Scouts, which during World War II had conducted small-scale reconnaissance, observation, and intelligence operations behind Japanese lines, as well as Philippine organizations like Force X and the Nenita unit. Such formations were partly inspired by techniques employed by U.S. Army Brig. Gen. Frederick Funston during the Philippine War of 1899–1902. Christopher Harmon, "Illustrations of 'Learning' in Counterinsurgency," *Comparative Strategy* 11 (January–March 1992): 41; McClintock, *Instruments of Statecraft*, pp. 112, 115, 119–22; Barton, Salient Operational Aspects, pp. 173–77; Rpt, JUSMAG, 18 Jan 51, sub: Semi-Annual Appraisal of the Joint United States Military Advisory Group to the Republic of the Philippines, p. 49.

[61] At its height, JUSMAG numbered but sixty-four individuals and was never allowed to post advisers on a permanent basis with Philippine units. The United States did not allow its personnel to accompany Armed Forces of the Philippines (AFP) units on active operations until 1953. Rpts, JUSMAG, 26 Apr 51, sub: Weekly Summary of Activities, and 1 Dec 51, sub: Weekly Summary of Activities, both in 319.1, JUSMAG, Philippines, RG 334, NARA; Robert Ross Smith, "The Hukbalahap Insurgency," *Military Review* 45 (June 1965): 37–38; Barton, Salient Operational Aspects, pp. 59–60; Jameson, "Philippine Constabulary," p. 64; Uldarico Baclagon, *Lessons from the Huk Campaign in the Philippines* (Manila: M. Colcol, 1960), pp. 66–69, 113, 180, 187; Rpt, Office of the Assistant Chief of Staff (OACS), G–2, 17 Jan 52, sub: Notes on Psychological Warfare, Historians files, CMH; Rpt, Mil Attache, Manila, 9 Jan 52, sub: Tactical Notes for Use by BCT and Company Commanders, 866168, ID, G–2, RG 319, NARA; Clarence Barrens, "I Promise: Magsaysay's Unique Psyop 'Defeats' Huks" (Master's thesis, CGSC, 1965), p. 74; Paul Linebarger, *Psychological Warfare* (Washington, D.C.: Combat Forces Press, 1954), p. 260.

[62] Valeriano and Bohannan, *Counter-Guerrilla Operations*, pp. 117–18, 127–29; MacGrain, "Anti-Dissident Operations," pp. 25–26; McClintock, *Instruments of Statecraft*, pp. 119, 123–25.

[63] First and second quotes from Bohannan, "Antiguerrilla Operations," p. 25. Fourth quote from ibid., p. 26. Third quote from Lansdale, *In the Midst of Wars*, p. 70. Dillon, "Comparative Strategies," p. 288; Greenberg, *The Hukbalahap Insurrection*, pp. 107, 132; Iluminado Mangako, "The Constabulary and Rural Development," *Philippine Armed Forces Journal* (March 1956): 43–45. Both Americans and

Filipinos consciously patterned certain aspects of the counterinsurgency campaign after techniques employed during the Philippine Insurrection. Even the Huks drew inspiration from that conflict, flying the old revolutionary flag. Harmon, "Illustrations of Learning," p. 41; McClintock, *Instruments of Statecraft*, p. 112; Valeriano and Bohannan, *Counter-Guerrilla Operations*, pp. 241–42; CGSC, *Counterinsurgency Case History: The Philippines, 1946–54*, RB 31–3 (Fort Leavenworth, Kans.: U.S. Army Command and General Staff College, 1965), pp. 47–48, 70–71; Kerkvliet, *Huk Rebellion*, pp. 160, 195; Robert Ginsburg, "Damn the Insurrectos!" *Military Review* 44 (January 1964): 59.

⁶⁴ Briefing, JUSMAG to U.S. Ambassador to the Philippines et al., n.d., sub: Ground Forces: Organization, Disposition, Tactics, Logistics, and Recommendations to Philippine Government Made by JUSMAG, pp. 13–15, atch to Rpt, JUSMAG, 29 Sep 50, sub: Weekly Summary of Activities; Rpt, JUSMAG, 18 Jan 51, sub: Semi-Annual Appraisal of the Joint United States Military Advisory Group to the Republic of the Philippines, pp. 28, 43; Blaufarb, *Counterinsurgency Era*, pp. 32–33; Maynard Dow, "Counterinsurgency and Nation-Building: A Comparative Study of Post–World War II Antiguerrilla Resettlement Programs in Malaya, the Philippines, and South Vietnam" (Ph.D. diss., Syracuse University, 1965), p. 139.

⁶⁵ Quote from Rpt, OACS, Intelligence, 24 Jan 52, sub: G–2 Evaluation, atch to Rpt, Army Attache, Manila, 23 Dec 51, sub: Seminar of AFP CAO's, 863148, ID, G–2, RG 319, NARA; Bohannan, "Communist Insurgency," p. 129; Rpt, JUSMAG, 18 Jul 51, sub: Semi-Annual Report, 1 January 1951 to 30 June 1951, pp. 26–27, in 091 Philippines, 1950–51, G–3, RG 319, NARA; Tirona, "Philippine Anti-Communist Campaign," p. 50; Andrew Molnar, *Human Factors Considerations of Undergrounds in Insurgencies*, DA Pam 550–104 (Washington, D.C.: Special Operations Research Office, American University, 1966), p. 213; Rpt, JUSMAG, 14 Feb 52, sub: Semi-Annual Report, 1 July–31 December 1951, p. 3.

⁶⁶ First quote from Erskine Rpt, p. 2. Second quote from Smith, Hukbalahap Insurgency, p. 115. Even the Huks attributed their defeat to American intervention. Lomperis, *People's War to People's Rule*, pp. 190–91; Kerkvliet, *Huk Rebellion*, p. 243; McClintock, *Instruments of Statecraft*, pp. 111–12.

⁶⁷ Rpt, JUSMAG, 18 Jan 51, sub: Semi-Annual Appraisal of the Joint United States Military Advisory Group to the Republic of the Philippines, p. 26; Msg, Manila 1533 to State, 25 Apr 51, sub: MDAP Monthly General Report for the Period Ending March 31, 1951, in 091 Philippines, G–3, 1950–51, RG 319, NARA; Rpt, JUSMAG, 18 Jul 51, sub: Semi-Annual Report, 1 January 1951 to 30 June 1951, pp. 20–21, 27–29; Rpt, JUSMAG, 14 Feb 52, sub: Semi-Annual Report, 1 July–31 December 1951, p. 3; Rpt, OACS, G–2, 28 Mar 52, sub: AFP—1952 Anti-Huk Campaign, 873401, ID, G–2, RG 319, NARA; MacGrain, "Anti-Dissident Operations," pp. 19–20, 29.

⁶⁸ Quote from CGSC, *Counterinsurgency Case History: The Philippines*, p. 140, and see also pp. 132, 145–46. *FRUS, 1952–54*, vol. 12, *East Asia and the Pacific*, pp. 492–94, 497–501; Dillon, "Comparative Strategies," p. 295; Kerkvliet, *Huk Rebellion*, pp. 237–39, 268; Douglas Blaufarb and George Tanham, *Who Will Win?* (New York: Crane Russak, 1989), pp. 115–16; Dow, "Counterinsurgency and Nation-Building," pp. 100, 110–11, 137; Edward Lansdale, "Civic Action in the Military, Southeast Asia," in CGSC, *Internal Defense Operations: A Case History, the Philippines, 1946–54*, RB 31–3 (Fort Leavenworth, Kans.: U.S. Army Command and General Staff College, 1967), p. 22.

[69] Quote from Bohannan, "Antiguerrilla Operations," p. 20, and see also pp. 27–29. In their popular recounting of the insurgency, AFP Col. Napoleon Valeriano and JUSMAG intelligence and guerrilla warfare expert Capt. (later Lt. Col.) Charles T. R. Bohannan admitted that propaganda and modest initiatives, not major reforms, had won the war. They considered most proposals for major socioeconomic reforms to have been misguided and impractical, the product of American civilian officials who were out of touch with Philippine realities. Valeriano and Bohannan, *Counter-Guerrilla Operations*, pp. 75–76, 225; Bohannan, "Communist Insurgency," p. 141; Shafer, *Deadly Paradigms*, pp. 221, 224–25; Smith, Hukbalahap Insurgency, pp. 122–24; Jameson, "Philippine Constabulary," pp. 48, 64; Greenberg, "United States Response to Philippine Insurgency," p. 107; Greenberg, *The Hukbalahap Insurrection*, p. 130; *FRUS, 1951*, 6:1510, 1549; Scaff, *Philippine Answer to Communism*, pp. 123–24, 135; Kerkvliet, *Huk Rebellion*, pp. 236–40.

[70] Asprey, *War in the Shadows*, 2:480–88.

[71] Charles MacDonald, An Outline History of U.S. Policy Toward Vietnam, U.S. Army Center of Military History, 1978, pp. 3–7, CMH; Ronald Spector, *Advice and Support: The Early Years, 1941–1960*, United States Army in Vietnam (Washington, D.C.: U.S. Army Center of Military History, 1983), pp. 97–104.

[72] Edgar O'Ballance, *The Indo-China War, 1945–1954* (London: Faber and Faber, 1964), pp. 104–28; Spector, *Early Years*, p. 124.

[73] O'Ballance, *Indo-China War*, p. 195; Bernard Fall, "Indochina: The Last Year of the War, Communist Organization and Tactics," *Military Review* 36 (October 1956): 1.

[74] O'Ballance, *Indo-China War*, pp. 140–51; Asprey, *War in the Shadows*, 2:502, 513, 576–77.

[75] MacDonald, Outline History, p. 11; Bernard Fall, "Indochina, The Last Year of the War, The Navarre Plan," *Military Review* 36 (December 1956): 48–50; Spector, *Early Years*, p. 181.

[76] Fall, "Navarre Plan," pp. 52–55; Fall, "Communist Organization," pp. 1–2.

[77] MacDonald, Outline History, pp. 13–14.

[78] Disenchantment with the way the French were conducting the war eventually led the United States to insist that it have the opportunity to examine and comment on French plans before approving any additional funding. This demand led to the dispatch of a special military envoy, Lt. Gen. John W. O'Daniel, to Indochina in 1953. O'Daniel consulted closely with Navarre, and his endorsement of the Navarre plan paved the way for the special aid appropriation that followed. However, the Navarre plan was less a detailed blueprint than a short and rather vague list of goals and guiding principles. Efforts in 1953–1954 to post American observers with some French headquarters elements were too limited and came too late in the conflict to affect its outcome. MacDonald, Outline History, pp. 8–10; *United States–Vietnam Relations, 1945–1967: Study Prepared by Department of Defense*, 12 vols. (Washington, D.C.: Government Printing Office, 1971), bk. 1, ch. IV.A.2, pp. 11, 15; Spector, *Early Years*, pp. 127, 185; James Arnold, *The First Domino: Eisenhower, the Military, and America's Intervention in Vietnam* (New York: William Morrow, 1991), pp. 118–22; *FRUS, 1952–54*, vol. 13, *Indochina*, pp. 744–47; Annex D (Navarre Concept), p. 1, atch to Plan, Army G–3, 24 Mar 54, sub: Outline Plan To Achieve a Military Victory in Indochina, Historians files, CMH.

[79] Spector, *Early Years*, pp. 99, 102, 114, 128, 162–65, 195, 221–22; Arnold, *First Domino*, pp. 83, 98; *FRUS, 1952–54*, 13:745, 1017–18, 1110, 1114–15; Chester Cooper,

The American Experience with Pacification in Vietnam, R–185, 3 vols., Institute for Defense Analyses, Mar 72, 3:113, MHI; Lamar Prosser, "The Bloody Lessons of Indochina," *U.S. Army Combat Forces Journal* 5 (June 1955): 30.

[80] O'Ballance, *Indo-China War*, pp. 251–56; "Reasons for the French Failure in Indochina," *U.S. Army Pacific Intelligence Bulletin* (September 1959); Fall, "Navarre Plan," pp. 55–56; Arnold, *First Domino*, p. 386; William Dodds, "Anti-Guerrilla Warfare" (Student thesis, AWC, 1955), pp. 9–10; Ellen Hammer, *The Struggle for Indochina, 1940–1955* (Stanford, Calif.: Stanford University Press, 1966), pp. 315–16.

3

THE KOREAN CIVIL WAR
1945-1954

France's defeat in Indochina left the United States with an even win to loss ratio in its post–World War II counterinsurgency advisory endeavors, as victories in Greece and the Philippines were offset by a partial failure in Indochina and a crushing defeat in China. There was, however, one more conflict to enter into the balance sheet—a bloody conflagration that racked the Korean Peninsula for nearly a decade. The Korean Civil War differed from the other irregular conflicts of the post–World War II decade in that it was the only one in which the United States moved beyond an advisory role to become a full-fledged participant in the hostilities.

Occupation and Advice, 1945–1950

Unlike China, Greece, and the Philippines, Korea had suffered relatively little material damage during World War II, but it did not escape the war's effects. A Japanese colony, Korea bore the weight of the imperial war effort, providing millions of people for overseas service in Japanese military and economic enterprises, while back home the population groaned under the weight of wartime inflation, exploitative landlords, repressive police, and oppressive tax and rice collection systems. Japan's defeat unleashed a torrent of political activity as a host of groups competed to recast the country to their own liking. Communist and leftist organizations were particularly popular in the countryside, where their promises of land reform resonated among poor tenant farmers. Onto this revolutionary situation the Allied powers imposed a temporary military occupation designed to guide Korea through the transition from Japanese colony to an independent nation. Divided geographically between northern (Soviet) and southern (U.S.) zones, each of the occupation regimes cultivated those groups that appealed to their particular ideological interests and repressed those that did not. (*Map 6*)

The commander of U.S. forces in Korea, Lt. Gen. John R. Hodge, followed the same creed of good government, free market economics, and measured reform that characterized the postwar military governments in Germany and Japan. Unfortunately, his attempts at reforming the Korean economic system produced unintended and often disruptive consequences, and in the fall of 1946 serious rioting erupted over Hodge's impolitic decision to continue the hated Japanese rice collection and taxation system. Tensions continued to simmer through 1947 and into 1948, when Cold War pressures led to the final abandonment of the original goal of establishing a single Korean state. In its stead, two rival regimes emerged, Communist North Korea under the leadership of ex-guerrilla chieftain Kim Il Sung, and non-Communist South Korea under Syngman Rhee, a long-time nationalist with close ties to the American Christian missionary community in Korea. Each man was committed to the destruction of the other and the eventual reunification of Korea under his own auspices. Rhee's position, however, was tenuous, as the Republic of Korea (ROK) continued to experience political infighting, peasant unrest, and periodic outbreaks of violence.[1]

The Communist South Korean Labor Party (SKLP) provided the organizational nucleus for the anti-Rhee movement. It infiltrated government organizations, gathered intelligence, spread propaganda, and mobilized the population through a variety of front organizations. Meanwhile, in the countryside SKLP cadres, bolstered by traditional bandits and peasants who had tired of insensitive treatment at the hands of landlords and policemen, took up arms. By the time the U.S. military government officially turned over the reins of power to Rhee in August 1948, Communist guerrillas already controlled several large areas of South Korea, most notably in the southwest, where tenant farmers suffered the greatest exploitation, and in the Chiri, Taebaek, and Odae mountain regions. Acting as "farmers by day and fighters by night," SKLP guerrillas sallied forth from remote mountain bases to attack isolated police detachments and raid villages, alternately propagandizing and terrorizing the population.[2]

By 1949 the SKLP fielded several thousand guerrillas backed by 10,000 party members, 600,000 active sympathizers, and up to 2 million "fellow travelers" in affiliated front organizations. Although indigenous to the South, the movement was increasingly controlled

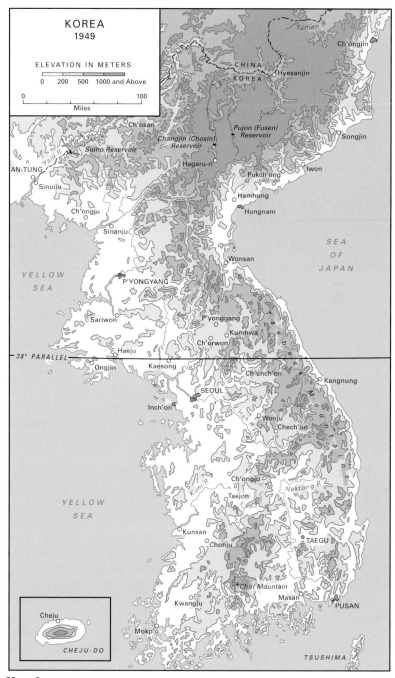

KOREA
1949

ELEVATION IN METERS

0   200   500   1000 and Above

0   100
                    Miles

CHINA
Tumen R.
Ch'ongjin
Hyesanjin
KOREA

Ch'osan
Suiho Reservoir
Changjin (Chosin) Reservoir
Pujon (Fusen) Reservoir
Songjin

Yalu R.
AN-TUNG
Sinuiju
Hagaru-ri
Pukch'ong
Iwon

Ch'ongju
Hamhung
Hungnam

Sinanju
SEA
OF
JAPAN

Wonsan

YELLOW
SEA
P'YONGYANG

Sariwon
P'yonggang
Kumhwa
Ch'orwon
Taebaek Mountains

Haeju
38° PARALLEL
Ongjin
Kaesong
Ch'unch'on
Kangnung

SEOUL
Inch'on
Wonju
Chech'on

Ch'ongju
Kum R.
Taejon
Naktong R.

Han R.

Kunsan
Chonju
TAEGU

Chiri Mountain
Kwangju
Masan
PUSAN

YELLOW
SEA

Cheju
CHEJU-DO

Mokp'o
TSUSHIMA

MAP 6

from the North, as Kim Il Sung sent cadres across the border to act as troop commanders, political leaders, instructors, spies, and eventually as rank-and-file guerrillas as well. In 1949 North Korea formed a Democratic Front for the Liberation of the Fatherland to orchestrate a more concerted campaign of guerrilla warfare and political upheaval, and thereafter northern control predominated, although communications difficulties and lingering regionalism impeded coordination.[3]

The Republic of Korea's counterinsurgency effort suffered from a number of defects. Factionalism, cronyism, and corruption permeated the government, while political and economic instability were exacerbated by the South's failure to redress popular grievances, as Rhee preferred to suppress his political rivals rather than implement reforms that might erode his power base. Suppression, however, was not easy to achieve, as Rhee's security apparatus suffered from serious structural problems. South Korea's first security organization, the National Police, was poorly paid and hated, having inherited from the Japanese colonial police a reputation for brutality and extortion. Scattered across the countryside in small, fortified posts, the police were vulnerable to guerrilla concentrations and had difficulty quelling major uprisings.[4]

In 1946 the United States created the Korean Constabulary as a light infantry reserve to reinforce the police during internal disorders. Unfortunately, a fierce rivalry grew between the police and Constabulary that was never fully overcome and that greatly impeded the execution of the counterinsurgency campaign. The Constabulary had also been infiltrated by leftists during its formation and lacked cohesion until a massive purge in 1948–1949 cleansed it of suspect personnel.[5]

Upon gaining independence in 1948, South Korea redesignated the Constabulary as the ROK Army, but the name change did not result in a more effective force. Organized, trained, and advised by the U.S. Army through the auspices of the Korean Military Assistance Group (KMAG), both the police and army suffered from all the defects one might expect from hastily raised forces immediately thrown into combat. KMAG's job was further complicated by the resistance some Korean officers exhibited toward American advice. U.S. advisers expunged from the South Korean Army with only the greatest difficulty certain outmoded methods, like the *banzai* charge, that its officers had learned while in Japanese service. In fact, the assistance group attributed the ROK Army's heavy losses when fighting guerrillas in 1948–1949 to the refusal of some of its commanders to heed American advice, particularly with regard to march and camp security.[6]

In 1950 South Korea tried to relieve its regular infantry units of counterinsurgency duty so that they could concentrate on fixing their many operational, administrative, and training defects. This was done by creating special counterguerrilla units—National Police combat battalions and Army "antiguerrilla" battalions—as well as units of railroad police. The initiative was only partially successful, as the new forces were also poorly trained and equipped and lacked the numbers necessary to keep the guerrillas in check. Moreover, both the railroad police and antiguerrilla battalions were employed in largely static roles to protect installations and lines of communications, a fact reflected in the government's eventual redesignation of the antiguerrilla battalions as "security" battalions. Consequently, the army was never able to quit the counterinsurgency business, and most major counterguerrilla operations after 1950 continued to require large infusions of regular infantry units.[7]

American advice to Rhee did not differ materially from that given to other nations threatened by internal warfare during the Truman years. Politically, the United States pushed for the establishment of more open, democratic institutions, honest and effective administration, economic development, and social reform, most notably in the areas of land tenancy and labor issues. These had been the goals, imperfectly achieved, of the military government, and KMAG advisers continued such counsel after South Korea achieved its independence. Thus when the first significant wave of sustained guerrilla warfare erupted in South Korea on the island of Cheju-do in 1948, the Army's local representative, Col. Rothwell H. Brown, suggested that economic development, honest and efficient governmental administration, an improved public relations program, and better behavior on the part of the police would go far toward resolving the situation. Three years later, a KMAG document echoed these sentiments, noting that "Communist forces will find it hard to grow or even exist among people who are well fed, well housed, well clothed and gainfully employed. On the other hand, it is useless to believe in the ultimate success of any military operation if conditions continue to foster political or economic discontent."[8]

Since political and economic reforms were outside its purview, the assistance group concentrated its "political" efforts on improving the conduct of ROK security forces. Government forces routinely used torture to extract confessions, executed suspects without trial, appropriated civilian property to supplement their meager wages, and on occasion massacred villagers in retaliation for guerrilla ambushes.[9] Americans attributed Korean brutality to cultural factors and to Japanese precedent. Torture, terror, and abuse had been standard practices throughout

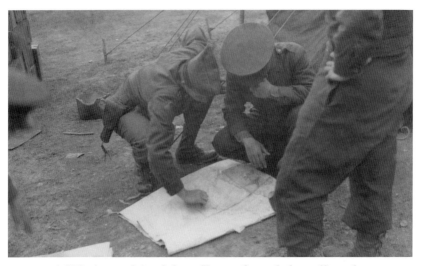

*A U.S. Army adviser helps a Korean Constabulary officer plan
a counterguerrilla operation on Cheju-do.*

the Japanese empire, and a significant proportion of the leadership of
the new Korean security forces had served in Japanese forces during
World War II. KMAG chief Brig. Gen. William L. Roberts considered
the Korean soldier's "desire to kick civilians around like his Jap predecessors used to do, his sadistic tendencies" to be his chief weakness,
and he cautioned new advisers that "one of your greatest problems will
come from Korean Army personnel having the wrong attitude toward
civilians." Roberts directed his subordinates to stress impartial enforcement of the law and humane behavior, instructing them to report all
incidents of abuse and to press for the punishment of offending personnel. The assistance group also drafted regulations for the South Korean
Army that banned foraging and compulsory civilian labor.[10]

By 1949 American pressure for reform had begun to bear fruit. On
Cheju-do the government changed tactics, initiating a new strategy of
"half force, half administration," under which it called "a halt to the
indiscriminate slaying of residents of the hill country villages" while
providing additional relief supplies. Adopting Chiang Kai-shek's formulation of counterinsurgency as seven parts political and three parts
military, Rhee offered amnesty to Communist activists and endeavored
to mobilize public support through propaganda and political action. The
government enacted a land reform program and created the National
Repentance Alliance, an organization of ex-subversives who in return
for their confessions and denunciation of communism were absolved

of their sins and given help finding jobs. The organization, which had 300,000 members, not only rehabilitated former opponents, but served as an effective propaganda, intelligence, and population-control mechanism. In time the government placed some of the penitents into special armed propaganda teams, called Listen to Me units, which proved effective in both propaganda and combat roles.[11]

Local officials supplemented these initiatives with programs of their own. In South Cholla, the provincial government reopened schools and imposed a program of political reeducation in guerrilla-dominated districts. It reinforced this effort by forming a special pacification unit composed of local dignitaries and army musicians that attempted alternately to coax and serenade the guerrillas into surrendering. Meanwhile, in neighboring South Kyongsang the provincial governor established a rural education program in which teams of officials and youths armed with pamphlets, loudspeakers, and films praised the government and vilified the Communists. Such actions received a boost from Rhee's growing concern over allegations of human rights abuses, a concern that led him occasionally to punish individuals for committing or tolerating atrocities. By January 1950 the assistance group was able to report that whereas "the Army and police were once despised just as much as the rebels for their looting by the villagers, this feeling has been corrected for the most part and an encouraging amount of cooperation is being experienced between the villagers and the protective forces. This program of placating the villagers has been successful to the point where villagers are reporting to the Army and police locations of guerrilla food caches and movements."[12] (*Map 7*)

While KMAG supported efforts to integrate political, economic, and psychological initiatives into a combined politico-military campaign, it naturally concentrated most of its efforts on the military aspects of the insurgency. Most of the information imparted to the South Koreans by their American advisers concerned conventional subjects such as organization, administration, logistics, and training. These were subjects essential to the effectiveness of any military organization, and while naturally patterned on U.S. Army concepts, the assistance group was aware that it had to take Korean conditions into account. From the start, KMAG molded the armed forces of South Korea for internal security duties. It outfitted them with light weapons and equipment rather than the heavier ordnance required for conventional operations, while its troop training curriculum focused almost exclusively on marksmanship, patrolling, march and camp security, and small-unit tactics—fundamentals that were equally applicable to both conventional and unconventional situations. The assistance group issued guidelines

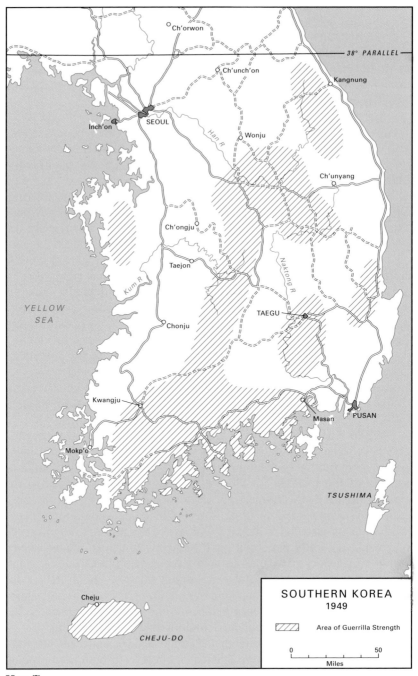

Ch'orwon

38° PARALLEL

Ch'unch'on

Kangnung

Inch'on

SEOUL

Wonju

Ch'unyang

Han R.

YELLOW
SEA

Ch'ongju

Kum R.

Taejon

Naktong R.

Chonju

TAEGU

Kwangju

Masan

PUSAN

Mokp'o

TSUSHIMA

Cheju

CHEJU-DO

SOUTHERN KOREA
1949

////// Area of Guerrilla Strength

0   50

Miles

MAP 7

for antiguerrilla training, wrote campaign plans, and helped execute those plans through advisers posted to infantry regiments and major police and military commands. It thus exercised a great amount of influence over the conduct of the counterguerrilla campaign.[13]

Trial and error played a significant part in KMAG's efforts, as few advisers had any counterguerrilla experience. American advice was neither the only, nor necessarily the most important, influence on the conduct of counterguerrilla warfare in Korea because the Koreans also looked to Asian examples. Several high-ranking South Korean officers had served in either the Chinese Nationalist or the Japanese armed forces during the 1930s and 1940s, where they learned how these two armies conducted counterguerrilla operations. Among the techniques they had observed were active police and counterintelligence measures to unearth the Communist underground, the *pao chia* system, reprisals, the forcible relocation of rural dwellers into fortified villages in order to separate them from the guerrillas, the creation of village self-defense and militia groups, and even the development of political, economic, and propaganda programs to win popular support. Encirclement, sometimes on a massive scale, had been a standard Sino-Japanese technique, while the Japanese had particularly favored winter operations, when leafless trees and harsh weather complicated the guerrillas' ability to move, hide, and survive relative to their more logistically endowed opponents. Finally, in guerrilla base areas that were either too strong or remote to be controlled, the Japanese had employed a strategy of "Three All"—take all, burn all, kill all—in which they laid waste to the countryside, both to deny the guerrillas human and material resources and to break the people's will to resist. Ultimately, the South Koreans would employ all of these Sino-Japanese techniques, blending them with American organizational and tactical methods to create an increasingly effective—if sometimes harsh—counterinsurgency campaign.[14]

The counterguerrilla war in South Korea represented a multilayered effort. At the rice roots level, police detachments housed in medieval-style forts guarded villages and conducted patrols. They were assisted by a variety of paramilitary organizations. These groups had first emerged in 1945 as the private armies of rival political factions and personalities. In time Rhee asserted control over these organizations, occasionally integrating their personnel into police and military units and supplementing their numbers by drafting villagers into militia and "voluntary police" organizations. Undisciplined and prone to committing atrocities, the paramilitaries were invaluable for waging street battles and controlling the behavior of the civilian population. Together with the police, they gave Rhee the means for enforcing a variety of population-control measures, including the *pogap*, South Korea's version of the *pao chia* system. Granted sweeping powers by the legislature to arrest and detain suspected Communists, the police and paramilitaries were Rhee's primary instrument for "ruthlessly stamping out the communist party organization and guerrilla resistance, employing whatever methods were considered necessary." By the end of 1949 the government had arrested approximately 30,000 suspected subversives, adopting in time the Greek custom of conducting mass arrests prior to launching a counterguerrilla offensive to disrupt the enemy's command, intelligence, and supply systems.[15]

U.S. Army advisers and Counter Intelligence Corps personnel took an active part in the counterinfrastructure campaign, both by helping establish indigenous intelligence systems and by participating in the interrogation of Communist suspects. During the Cheju-do rebellion of 1948, Army advisers created a "central intelligence agency" to collect, coordinate, analyze, and disseminate all insurgency-related information from police, military, and civilian sources. This system was so successful that the assistance group directed that similar entities be established in every South Korean division and counterguerrilla command. Meanwhile, U.S. Counter Intelligence Corps agent Lt. Tero Miyagishima formed a network of civilian informers in the Chiri-San guerrilla base area that, while failing to penetrate the guerrilla bands, succeeded in gathering useful information from area villages. Eventually, the South Koreans developed their own spy networks that, together with the police and paramilitaries, helped break the Communists' underground organization.[16]

Despite their value in controlling the population and attacking the Communist infrastructure, the local police and paramilitaries lacked the training, discipline, support structure, and morale needed to take the offensive against the guerrillas. Indeed, their dispersed deployment made them vulnerable to annihilation by superior guerrilla concentrations. Relief for beleaguered garrisons and impetus for offensive sweeps came from the second tier in the government's security apparatus—mobile police combat battalions, Army security battalions, combat youth regiments, and regular infantry formations detailed for that purpose. These forces conducted patrols and sent columns into the hills to hunt the guerrillas. Cordon and sweeps, in which security forces surrounded a village, searched it, and interrogated its inhabitants, were common. Manpower shortages and logistical difficulties, however, often reduced the effectiveness of such operations, most of which lasted no more than three days. Consequently, the government found that it had to resort to a third

A U.S. Army adviser (right) *to the Korean National Police helps display captured guerrilla flags.*

layer of effort—large-scale drives spearheaded by Army regulars—to disperse large guerrilla concentrations.[17]

ROK Army offensives typically lasted up to several months and involved tens of thousands of soldiers, policemen, and paramilitaries. They usually took the form of an initial encirclement followed by either a linear sweep or a concentric advance. Army units conducted what contemporary American documents referred to as "extensive search and destroy" operations to break up major guerrilla units, while police and paramilitary formations lent support and formed cordons to prevent escape. Once the major sweep had been completed, police and army units would break down into smaller units to exert "constant pressure" on the remaining insurgents. The regulars would then depart, leaving the local police and paramilitaries to consolidate the gains and prevent a guerrilla resurgence. Like the Japanese and KMAG's counterparts in Greece, KMAG advisers also recognized the wisdom of undertaking operations at a time when seasonal conditions rendered the irregulars most vulnerable, and consequently the assistance group made winter campaigning a staple of the counterguerrilla war, crafting major offensives for every winter between 1949 and 1955.[18]

Large-scale encirclements were no panacea to the guerrilla problem. They required large numbers of troops and had to be executed with speed and stealth, lest the guerrillas escape before the trap could be sealed. All too often, these criteria were unmet. Coordinating

Korean National Policemen inspect captured guerrilla weapons.

the movements of police, military, and paramilitary formations over considerable distances in mountainous terrain with inaccurate maps, inadequate communications equipment, and meager intelligence was exceedingly difficult. All of these problems were magnified in winter, when cold temperatures inflicted great hardships on the troops. Even under the best conditions, rooting out the guerrillas in their mountain lairs was, recalled one U.S. adviser, "an almost impossible task. The mountains were thickly wooded with trees and underbrush, precipitous and extremely rocky and rough in nature, which not only provided excellent cover for the guerrilla groups, but confined troop movement to single trails and made ambushing a constant threat."[19]

These handicaps notwithstanding, large operations, such as the Winter Punitive Operation of 1949–1950, Operation RATKILLER (December 1951–March 1952), and Operation MONGOOSE (July–August 1952)—all of which employed the equivalent of two or more divisions—could be effective. When carefully conceived and executed, operations like these could inflict serious losses on the enemy, killing and capturing many guerrillas, destroying their food and shelter, and imposing hardships that led some guerrillas and their civilian supporters to defect. Moreover, by compelling the guerrillas to break down into smaller units, the government not only gained the initiative, but created circumstances under which it too could operate in smaller formations. Although the South Koreans and their U.S. advisers tended to adhere to large-scale operations beyond the point of diminishing returns, government forces nevertheless did break down into smaller units to harass the irregulars, furthering their disintegration until the guerrillas, like their Huk contemporaries, were little more than small bands of fugitives.[20]

While encirclement operations and infantry tactics were the mainstays of the shooting war, concentration and devastation were the primary methods by which the government drained the "sea" of the human and material "nutrients" the guerrilla "fish" needed to survive. Beginning in 1948 with the first major counterguerrilla offensive of the insurgency, the South Korean government embraced a strategy of removing civilians from guerrilla-controlled areas. The government placed the evacuees in refugee camps and fortified towns—known variously as "collective villages" and "assembly villages"—where police and militiamen protected them from subversive influences. The security forces then put to the torch everything that could be of use to the guerrillas—buildings, villages, and crops. Anyone remaining in these areas was considered suspect and liable to arrest and detention if not outright death. By 1949 South Korea had relocated approximately 100,000 people from guerrilla-infested Cheju-do, evacuating over half the island's villages and destroying nearly 40,000 houses, though guerrilla raids accounted for some of this destruction. While harsh, this policy succeeded in breaking the back of the rebellion, for it increased the guerrillas' vulnerability to famine and inclement weather, undermined the willingness of both the guerrillas and the civilian population to continue their resistance, and materially weakened the irregulars by cutting them off from the population upon which they depended for intelligence, recruits, and supplies.[21]

Success on Cheju-do led to imitation elsewhere. KMAG plans for the Winter Punitive Operation of 1949–1950, the first major counterguerrilla offensive on the mainland, called for the relocation of over 100,000 civilians, followed by the confiscation of all food and the destruction of all villages in several guerrilla base areas. Such activities were not without cost, however. As in Greece they disrupted agricultural production and created huge numbers of destitute refugees. For some the experience became a catalyst for joining the rebellion, while others sank into a sullen apathy. Caught between callous government officials by day and unforgiving guerrillas at night, many people initially decided that placating the guerrillas was their best chance for survival and refused to cooperate with authorities. The government's occasional use of devastation and other severe measures to retaliate against guerrilla acts further discredited it in the eyes of the people. Yet the detrimental effects of government-imposed hardships and abuse were not always clear-cut. This was partially because guerrilla excesses also alienated people and partly because the increasingly war-weary population tended to support whoever seemed to have the upper hand. By improving the population's security against guerrilla retaliation through increased military activity, strict population- and resources-control measures, and the establishment of defended villages, the government created conditions that enabled the people not only to withhold their support from the irregulars, but to aid the government. Thus, while the government paid a high price for its heavy-handed policies, that price did not prove to be unbearable, and ultimately population relocation, protected villages, and devastation were the primary means by which the government cut the guerrillas off from the population.[22]

South Korean Counterguerrilla Operations in an Expanded War, 1950–1954

By early 1950 the South Korean government had gained the upper hand in its battle against internal dissidents. Through mass arrests, combat operations, and amnesties, Seoul had dealt the labor party a severe blow, and while discontent remained widespread, it was fragmented and disorganized. Yet Rhee's success had come dearly in terms of lives, resources, and military readiness. The counterguerrilla campaign tied down a third of the ROK Army, thereby weakening the government's ability to protect itself against external aggression and exacerbating the military's logistical and organizational weaknesses. The army's administrative systems were overburdened, its officers uneducated, and its troops poorly trained. Indeed, by the end of 1949 less than half of the South Korean Army had completed company-level training, and KMAG advisers openly complained of the army's poor performance. Oriented toward internal warfare, the ROK Army was clearly unprepared for waging a conventional war.[23]

These points were not lost on Kim Il Sung. Having failed to overthrow the southern government through subversive means, in June 1950 he initiated a new chapter in the Korean Civil War by launching a major conventional invasion of the South. Backed by tanks and heavy artillery, the northerners overran most of the country in a matter of weeks. Only the southeastern corner of the Korean Peninsula around Pusan managed to escape submersion in the Communist tide, thanks to the intervention of United Nations (UN) military forces spearheaded by the Eighth U.S. Army in Korea (EUSAK).

The *North Korean People's Army* was a formidable foe. Some of its members had fought with Mao during World War II and the subsequent civil war in China. Others had served in Russian partisan and regular units during the war. All received training in guerrilla-style tactics according to precepts laid down in Russian and Chinese manuals. Like their mentors, the North Koreans employed partisan warfare as an integral adjunct to conventional operations. Armed and equipped as light infantry and often disguised as civilians, North Korean troops infiltrated allied lines to disrupt UN rear areas, laying ambushes, creating roadblocks, destroying lines of communications, and attacking command and support installations. Many of these operations were conducted at night so as to avoid UN air attacks while exploiting allied weaknesses in night fighting. Espionage too was

A Korean soldier checks the identity papers of a refugee in an effort to prevent Communist infiltrators from getting behind allied lines.

a Communist specialty. The Communists routinely employed women and children to gather information. One notable agent was "Poison Mary," whose daily visits to American positions around Pusan begging for food were invariably followed by mortar barrages of uncanny accuracy—until a search of her skirts revealed a hidden radio by which she had relayed target coordinates to North Korean artillerists. So disruptive were these activities that one senior U.S. general declared in August 1950 that "the North Korean guerrillas are . . . at present the single greatest headache to U.S. forces."[24]

Disorganized by the South Korean government's counterinsurgency campaign and caught off guard by the rapidity of the North Korean advance, South Korean Communists did not play a significant role during the first few weeks of the invasion. In time, however, they became more active, encouraged by the apparent inevitability of a northern victory. They disrupted UN rear areas, acted as guides, and gathered intelligence. The southern Communists also helped their northern brethren organize conquered territory, establishing Communist administrations and instituting a wave of reprisals against former officials. These actions proved premature, for in September 1950 the United Nations counterattacked by landing deep behind the front lines at Inch'on. The envelopment, coupled with a frontal attack at Pusan, sent the *North*

Korean People's Army reeling back north. The following month UN forces invaded North Korea, capturing most of that country before the Communist Chinese *People's Liberation Army* intervened and drove UN forces back across the inter-Korean border. The war would see-saw around this boundary for another two years.[25]

North Korea's near conquest of South Korea in the summer of 1950 and the rapidity of the UN's counteroffensive had significant consequences for the southern insurgency. The ebb and flow of the battle lines disrupted the South Korean government and created huge numbers of refugees. Reestablishing the government and caring for the refugees were difficult tasks that created conditions conducive to further internal disorder. The rapidity of the UN counteroffensive had also cut off large numbers of North Koreans from their homeland, swelling the number of enemy troops operating behind UN lines to 40,000. This represented a potential windfall for the insurgency, and by November 1950, 30 percent of UN forces were tied down performing rear area security duty.[26]

Yet on balance, North Korea's near victory proved disastrous for the insurgency. In their belief that the war had been won, many South Korean Communists had abandoned their covert habits in the summer of 1950 and emerged into the light of day. When South Korean authorities returned on the coattails of UN forces later that year, the Communists were caught in the open. Some succeeded in going back underground, but many were apprehended. Still others chose to flee, either to North Korea or, failing that, to the mountains where they joined the ranks of the guerrillas. This had a devastating effect on the party's village-level apparatus, as the southern Communists were never fully able to restore their infrastructure among the people, despite repeated urging from the North that they do so. This in turn compelled the guerrillas to take what they needed by force, a policy that merely exacerbated their standing among the population. Even the prospect of being reinforced by the large number of North Korean soldiers cut off by the UN counteroffensive proved chimerical, for although some of these men continued to act in a partisan capacity, the majority attempted to exfiltrate back to North Korea.[27]

The widening war increased American influence over the conduct of South Korean counterinsurgency operations, as Rhee subordinated the ROK Army to American command and the United States deployed additional advisers. Several of the new U.S. personnel had had significant counterguerrilla experience prior to deploying to Korea. Foremost among these was General Van Fleet, who assumed control over allied ground forces in Korea in the spring of 1951. Fresh from his triumph over Communist guerrillas in Greece, Van Fleet used his experience to shape the counterguerrilla campaign. Other individuals of note were Lt. Col. John Beebe, who applied what he had learned as a military attache in China to his duties as the senior adviser to the Southern Security Command—a major counterguerrilla organization—and Col. William A. Dodds, a veteran of the Greek insurgency whom Van Fleet purposefully appointed as the chief adviser for the largest counterguerrilla action of the war, Operation RATKILLER.[28]

With the additional U.S. personnel came additional equipment, as the United States sought to bolster South Korea's battered armed forces. The infusion of materiel naturally had an effect on the counterguerrilla war, as it allowed the South Koreans to employ more firepower than had been available in the past. Tanks and armored cars escorted convoys, artillery shelled suspect areas cordoned off by police, and American warplanes bombed guerrilla mountaintop strongholds. Still, the counterguerrilla effort remained largely an infantryman's war, partly because the allies needed to concentrate the majority of their heavy weaponry on the conventional battlefront and partly because U.S. officers continued to doubt the utility of heavy equipment, given the nature of the guerrilla war and Korea's rugged terrain. General Van Fleet was particularly skeptical in this regard. Though not eschewing firepower, Van Fleet recognized that fire support was highly addictive, especially to mediocre combat formations that tended to employ it as a substitute for closing with the enemy. An overreliance on artillery sapped military units of aggressiveness, encouraged road-bound movements, and produced indecisive results, as the irregulars often took a preliminary bombardment as a signal to withdraw out of harm's way. These were the lessons Van Fleet had learned in Greece, and when he drafted the plans for Operation RATKILLER he deliberately ordered the South Koreans to leave their artillery behind, promising them a modest amount of tactical air support for those occasions when additional firepower was necessary.[29]

While the infusion of additional American expertise and materiel thus altered the guerrilla war somewhat, it did not fundamentally transform the conflict. Essentially, the South Koreans and their U.S. advisers continued to apply the same concepts and techniques after June 1950 as they had before that date. As had been the case before the North Korean invasion, the National Police continued to bear most of the counterinsurgency burden, as the demands of the conventional war were such that regular troops, other than some fairly static "security battalions," were rarely available for counterguerrilla work for more than a few months at a time. Moreover, when ROK Army units were assigned to counterguerrilla operations, the commitment was usually on a rotating basis during which the units were also expected to rest, refit, and absorb replacements. This policy led to the creation of ad hoc task forces whose commanders and staffs lacked the type of familiarity with local conditions so necessary for effective counterguerrilla work.

The government rectified this situation somewhat in 1951 by creating several headquarters organizations called Combat Police Commands to coordinate regional police activity. The following year, Seoul replaced the police commands with Security Commands that integrated regional police and military efforts. These entities provided important stability with regard to staff and headquarters functions, but they still required augmentation from external sources to conduct major offensives. The assistance group also tried to replace the combat police with regiments of light infantry specifically earmarked for counterguerrilla work. This measure would have created a permanent counterguerrilla force within the ROK Army while allowing the police to concentrate on their civil duties, thereby improving the administration of civil law and reducing unnecessary duplication and friction between the two security services. The initiative, however, did not come to fruition during the war, and consequently the government never fully overcame the inherent weaknesses in relying upon ad hoc troop deployments.[30]

As had been the case prior to 1950, large-scale cordon-and-sweep operations backed by the removal of civilians and the destruction of property remained the centerpiece of government efforts to clear vital rear areas and reduce guerrilla strongholds. During the summer of 1950 U.S. and South Korean authorities evacuated several towns inside the Pusan Perimeter, deporting some 12,000 people from the town of Masan to isolated islands from which they were forbidden to leave. South Korean troops made liberal use of the torch during counterguerrilla operations in the winter of 1950, and by the end of the following year intense guerrilla and counterguerrilla activity had generated over 500,000 refugees in South Cholla Province alone. The winter of 1951–1952 brought more of the same as ROK soldiers destroyed all structures and evacuated all civilians in the areas targeted by Operation RATKILLER, and the South Koreans continued to employ such methods for the duration of the war.[31]

U.S. Army Counterguerrilla Operations, 1950–1953

While the South Koreans and their KMAG advisers continued to bear the brunt of the irregular conflict after June 1950, America's entry into the Korean Civil War meant that U.S. Army combat units would perform counterguerrilla missions for the first time since America's intervention in the Russian Civil War thirty years before. U.S. commanders, however, deliberately minimized their participation in the internal war. This was a sensible policy because it maximized the respective strengths of the two armies—American firepower was best suited for the conventional battlefront, while the lightly armed South Koreans had the linguistic and cultural skills necessary to deal with the population. Respect for Korean sovereignty and the necessity of closely coordinating political and military initiatives further favored this division of responsibility. Consequently, direct American participation in the counterguerrilla war was largely confined to the period between June 1950 and June 1951, when South Korean weaknesses and rapid fluctuations in the battlefront necessitated the commitment of U.S. forces to counterguerrilla operations. Once the front had stabilized, U.S. combat units rarely executed major counterguerrilla actions.

Two other factors influenced the conduct of American antiguerrilla operations during the Korean War. First, the dire situation in which U.S. forces found themselves in 1950–1951 necessitated that U.S. commanders initially focus their efforts on maintaining the security of critical lines of communications rather than pacifying the countryside. Second, as noted earlier, many Korean Communists responded to the UN's 1950 counteroffensive by attempting to flee back into North Korea. Their activities, while conducted in an irregular fashion and disruptive to UN rear areas, were not aimed at establishing a permanent presence in the countryside. This greatly simplified American operations, as did the fact that many Communist units were demoralized in the wake of the Inch'on landings and chose to surrender rather than fight when cornered by UN forces.[32]

To accomplish the largely defensive task of securing rear areas against Communist partisans, U.S. commanders fell back on their World War II experiences for guidance. This was necessary because the 1949 edition of FM 100–5, *Field Service Regulations, Operations*, did not provide a doctrine for rear area security. In time, and with the help of Army Chief of Staff General J. Lawton Collins who gave a copy of the procedures he had implemented to secure rear areas as a corps commander in Europe during World War II, the Eighth Army developed an extensive rear area security system. This system was based on the principle of economy of effort because it called for service troops to bear most of the burden for their own defense. Eighth Army sited and grouped installations for defensibility against partisan attack, protecting them with perimeter defenses, fortifications, and minefields. Mobile reaction units stood ready to reinforce beleaguered posts, while

*An armored railway car used by U.S. Military Police to keep South
Korea's railroad lines free of guerrilla interference*

armed convoys and armored trains manned by U.S. and South Korean
military policemen shuttled back and forth along defoliated routes
where trespassers could be shot on sight. The Korean Communications
Zone supervised the security effort, organizing elaborate communications and intelligence networks that coordinated the actions of installation garrisons, civil and military police, security units, and mobile
reaction forces to keep vital lines of communications and supply free
of partisan interference. Since the Communications Zone also handled
much of the UN Command's civil affairs responsibilities and oversaw
the activities of South Korea's two major territorial counterguerrilla
organizations—the Central and Southern Security Commands—it was
in an excellent position to coordinate the civil and military aspects of
the antipartisan campaign, although in practice things did not always
run smoothly.[33]

While World War II precedent helped Army officers establish
defensive measures against partisans, they had little other than a few
brief paragraphs in FM 100–5 to guide them on the offensive aspects
of antipartisan warfare. Maj. Robert B. Rigg, a veteran observer of
irregular warfare operations in Iraq and China, attempted to fill the
gap in an article that appeared in the September 1950 edition of
the *U.S. Army Combat Forces Journal.* After calling on the Army to
devote more attention to counterguerrilla warfare in its training and
doctrinal systems, Rigg prescribed a number of techniques, including

counterambush drills, raids and encirclements, refugee screening, village searches, and the employment of natives as guards and spies. Finally, Rigg impressed upon his readers that the "guerrillas depend a lot on the local population. And so it is essential to get the local people on your side. . . . It will save you time and effort. You'll never succeed without them."[34]

Rigg's advice was sound, and shortly after the publication of his article the Department of the Army rushed newly developed counter-guerrilla doctrinal materials to Far East Command. Both the article and the new doctrine were undoubtedly helpful, but their appearance in late 1950 meant that they were not fully digested by field commanders until after the Army had begun to exit the counterguerrilla business in early 1951. Consequently, U.S. counterguerrilla operations during the Korean War are best understood by studying the operations themselves rather than the emerging written doctrine, which is considered more fully in the following chapter.

American participation in the counterguerrilla war reached its height between October 1950 and February 1951. Following the Inch'on landings and the breakout from the Pusan Perimeter, Eighth Army ordered IX Corps to clear a large swath of South Korea of Communist troops cut off by the rapid U.S. advance. By the end of October IX Corps estimated that it had killed, wounded, or captured over 35,000 enemy troops behind UN lines. After the ROK III Corps assumed the job of securing South Korea in early November 1950, the U.S. IX Corps moved into North Korea where it was again involved in clearing out guerrillas and bypassed enemy troops between Kaesong and P'yonggang. Meanwhile, along North Korea's eastern coast the 3d Infantry Division struggled to secure the X Corps' rear area from an estimated 25,000 Communist partisans. After the Chinese had pushed the X Corps out of North Korea in December, the corps' 7th Infantry Division joined with South Korean troops to combat Communist partisans in South Korea's Taebaek Mountains. These efforts ultimately culminated in the "Pohang Guerrilla Hunt" of January–February 1951, a major encirclement operation conducted near Andong by the 1st Marine Division, South Korean forces, and some U.S. Army units.[35]

When faced with the task of mopping up Communist irregulars behind UN lines in late 1950 and early 1951, U.S. corps commanders adopted a territorial approach, assigning divisions to specific geographical areas of responsibility. These areas were often quite large. The zone of responsibility in October 1950 of the X Corps' 25th Infantry Division spanned about 16,835 square kilometers, while the 3d Infantry Division in November was responsible for over 8,029 square

Soldiers from the 65th Infantry bring in captured guerrillas.

kilometers. Commanders of these and other divisions assigned to counterguerrilla duty likewise assigned their subordinate units to subsidiary zones in what the X Corps called the "war of areas." Once fortified base camps had been established, the units extensively patrolled their assigned sectors. In the case of the 25th Infantry Division, most patrols were conducted at the platoon level until several reversals at the hands of larger North Korean formations led to the institution of company-size patrols. Once a patrol had located a guerrilla unit, it usually established a base of fire while sending a detachment to outflank and surround the enemy. The most successful operational technique consisted of establishing a battalion-size blocking position while one or more additional units swept in from another direction, driving the enemy onto the blocking force.[36]

The dispersed and irregular nature of counterguerrilla operations in Korea's mountainous terrain led to some modifications in standard procedures. Regimental combat team commanders frequently split their heavy mortar companies to provide each of their battalions with some organic fire support. Likewise, division commanders assigned artillery battalions to the regimental combat teams, occasionally attaching batteries to individual rifle companies. Because of the threat of surprise attacks, commanders established defensive perimeters around all camp, fighting, and battery positions, detailing infantrymen to protect artillery batteries. Artillery firebases in guerrilla regions deployed their guns so that each piece was aimed in a different direction in order to provide immediate 360 degree coverage. Fear of ambush initially led the 25th Infantry Division to prohibit its subordinate units from operating outside the range of supporting artillery. The division also banned unobserved artillery fire to reduce the chance of inflicting civilian casualties.[37]

U.S. ground commanders found that spotter aircraft were invaluable in keeping tabs on the guerrillas, while fighter-bombers provided fire support in areas that were inaccessible to artillery. Korea's rugged terrain, communication difficulties, and inadequate liaison arrangements reduced the effectiveness of air and artillery fire support. So too did the guerrillas' habits of moving at night and hiding in caves and forests. Nevertheless, under the right circumstances fire support from artillery, aircraft, and warships could inflict significant casualties. Most guerrilla casualties were from ground action, however, and at one point during its counterguerrilla operations in the fall of 1950 the 25th Infantry Division transferred most of its artillery and tanks to the conventional battlefront because it concluded that it no longer needed such weapons once the guerrillas in its area had become scattered and dispersed.[38]

An American convoy, supported by aircraft, defends itself against a guerrilla ambush in the Korean mountains.

The extensive employment of infiltrators by the North Koreans and Chinese also led the Army to modify its tactics on the conventional battlefield. Concerned that bypassed enemy units would initiate partisan operations, Eighth Army adopted a policy of conducting offensive operations by broad sweeps in which units advanced line-abreast at a slow pace regulated by phase lines and territorial boundaries. But such tactics also made exploitation of momentary breaches in enemy lines difficult and permitted the Communists to withdraw and regroup. Nevertheless, Eighth Army adhered to the technique in the belief that it was more cost effective than having to hunt down bypassed units.[39]

Modifications such as these improved American military effectiveness, but the real key to enhanced performance was better training. Although the 25th Infantry Division concluded after its counterguerrilla duty in 1950 that "the war in Korea has not, as yet, revealed any necessity for a change in established U.S. training doctrines," significant problems did in fact exist. Most U.S. soldiers were poorly trained during the early phases of the war and neglected to practice proper security procedures, often suffering heavily from Communist ambushes as a result. U.S. soldiers also exhibited deficiencies in patrolling techniques and rarely operated at night, when the guerrillas were most active. These facts reinforce the conclusion that the heavy casualties inflicted on Communist partisans in October 1950 by the IX Corps were due more to the overall military situation than to American tactical expertise.[40]

Eventually the situation improved, as General Collins directed that all troops undergo counterguerrilla training. Collins' order included rear echelon soldiers like bakers, mechanics, and truck drivers who were especially unprepared for the type of combat and security roles that the irregular war imposed on them. Soon stateside training centers were instructing Army service personnel in basic infantry skills, perimeter defense, psychological warfare, night movements, and counterguerrilla operations in order to enable the rear echelon soldier "to withstand successfully the pressures imposed on him by enemy infiltration tactics, guerrilla operations, and unorthodox fighting methods."[41]

Such training programs helped U.S. soldiers adapt to the challenges they faced in Korea. Yet for the most part these adaptations were minor because conventional doctrines for small-unit action, patrolling, march and camp security, and night, mountain, and forest operations proved sufficiently effective. In fact, Army Field Forces concluded that while the Korean experience had demonstrated deficiencies in training and execution, it had essentially ratified prewar doctrine, and, consequently, the Army did not push for an overhaul of U.S. doctrine after the war.

The only truly innovative counterguerrilla tactic to emerge from the war came from the marines, who experimented with using helicopters to transport counterguerrilla patrols.[42]

One area where the Army did experiment was in the use of special units for counterguerrilla action. Stung by Communist infiltration tactics, in August 1950 Eighth Army created a Ranger company for conducting a variety of infiltration, reconnaissance, raiding, and guerrilla warfare missions. The Eighth Army placed the unit under the command of Col. John H. McGee, a former guerrilla leader in the Philippines who based his training program on those of the prewar Philippine Scouts and Merrill's Marauders, a World War II raiding outfit. Meanwhile, in the fall of 1950 General Collins established a Ranger Training Command at Fort Benning, Georgia, that eventually trained and deployed six additional Ranger companies to Korea. Because field commanders often did not have suitable offensive missions for the Rangers to perform, they frequently used them in rear area security and counterguerrilla roles—missions for which the Rangers had not been intended but which put to good use their intense training in small-unit tactics and night operations.[43]

Occasionally, commanders supplemented the Rangers with task forces drawn from conventional infantry formations in corps reserve status. An even more exotic organization was Far East Command's Special Activities Group, a combined force of U.S. Army Rangers, U.S. Marine Raiders, Royal Navy Commandos, Royal Navy volunteers, South Korean police, and a South Korean Special Attack Battalion. Originally intended for coastal raiding, the British and U.S. Marine Corps elements failed to materialize, and the group ended up pulling mostly counterguerrilla duty.

The Special Activities Group conducted intensive saturation patrolling throughout the X Corps area from December 1950 until its disestablishment in April 1951. Seek-and-destroy operations, night movements, and ambushes, including squad-size stay-behind ambushes, were also part of its *modus operandi*. The unit screened refugees, destroyed villages and buildings that could be used by guerrillas, and provided medical treatments to civilians. Its effectiveness was enhanced by the provision of radios down to the squad level and the establishment of an extensive intelligence network in conjunction with local authorities and Korean and American intelligence services.[44]

Although they performed well in counterguerrilla roles, special autonomous units like the Rangers and the Special Activities Group were expensive to maintain and were bedeviled by logistical, manpower, and administrative problems. Many commanders were unenthusiastic about

Special Activities Group soldiers engage guerrillas.

the special units, whom they rarely used in roles for which they had originally been intended. As the South Koreans increasingly assumed responsibility for rear area security, even this mission fell by the wayside. Consequently, the Army disbanded all such units in 1951, choosing to boost combat performance by providing Ranger training to the Army as a whole, rather than by relying on special formations.[45]

Counterguerrilla operations inevitably brought U.S. soldiers into close contact with South Korean civilians. Thrown among people with whom they could neither communicate nor readily tell friend from foe, U.S. soldiers occasionally took out their frustrations on the population. U.S. Army doctrine had long recognized that troop misconduct was counterproductive, and U.S. commanders urged their subordinates to prevent and punish all transgressions. Still, given the uncertainties of the irregular war, soldiers needed "to be suspicious of any civilians in front line areas." U.S. commanders removed civilians from sensitive areas on both humanitarian and security grounds and imposed nighttime curfews that permitted troops to shoot anyone found moving around in civilian dress. U.S. units on counterguerrilla duty routinely took all males whom they encountered as prisoners, sending them to camps where Korean-American interrogation teams determined their fate. Similar procedures were employed to screen refugees and search villages. Typically, U.S. soldiers would surround a village, using artillery fire to block escape avenues that could not be covered by troops, while South Korean police combed the hamlet looking for suspects and contraband. Once a village had been cleared, the Americans helped reestablish local government and police organizations, creating central intelligence agencies to better coordinate military-police intelligence efforts.[46]

The Army also sometimes inflicted reprisals on Korean civilians for guerrilla actions, evacuating towns and destroying villages. Most of these actions occurred during the early stages of the war, when U.S. troops felt particularly vulnerable and had the most opportunity to come into contact with Korean irregulars. Although punitive measures tended to alienate people, their effects were complex, as villagers often allied with one side for reasons of self-preservation rather than ideology. Noting this phenomenon, one American who had been commissioned by the U.S. Army to study the guerrilla war in Korea endorsed the use of collective punishments against communities where guerrillas were active, writing that "it is well recognized that an innocent person punished singly or collectively for crimes he did not commit will tend to take an almost extreme initiative to prove his innocence; suffer the punishment with growing and sincere indignation; and finally turn with acute wrath against the real culprit in his midst because of whom he, the innocent, is suffering. It may be quite desirable to use this method no matter how harsh it be, at least to arouse the sentiments of the bulk of the population against [the guerrilla]." Far East Command, however, rejected this conclusion, stating that "communal punishment in retaliation for the misdeeds of a few is not considered justifiable or wise." Consequently, U.S. officials generally discouraged retaliatory actions in all but extreme cases.[47]

Although many of the Army's dealings with the civilian population were restrictive in nature, Far East Command's comments on retaliation indicate that Americans were mindful of the human aspects of the conflict. Indeed, between 1951 and 1953, the Civil Assistance Command waged a relentless war on poverty and disease. Manned largely by U.S. Army military and civilian personnel, the UN Civil Assistance Command, Korea, fed and clothed 4 million refugees, established health care facilities that treated nearly 3 million civilians, and provided over 60 million inoculations. It helped plan and implement programs that restored water, sanitation, and other public utilities, constructed and repaired transportation and communications systems, and improved agricultural and industrial production. U.S. soldiers chipped in on their own time, building orphanages, clinics, schools, and churches. This charity work eventually gave birth to the Armed Forces Assistance to Korea (AFAK) program in 1953. Conceived by Eighth Army commander Lt. Gen. Maxwell D. Taylor, the assistance

American and Korean soldiers deliver food to indigent civilians.

program combined American financial aid with the voluntary labor of U.S. soldiers to construct over 3,780 facilities by the end of the decade. Few of these efforts were undertaken specifically in response to the guerrilla war. Most were performed either out of humanitarian concerns or to facilitate the prosecution of the war. Yet they reflected an old principle of U.S. military government and civil affairs doctrine, for by ameliorating the hardships of war, the Army was also reducing the risk of civil unrest.[48]

U.S. commanders tried to treat the civilian population humanely, but they sometimes had difficulty exercising similar restraint toward their enemies, especially during the darker moments of 1950 and 1951. Although Far East Command demanded that captured North Korean soldiers be treated as prisoners of war, U.S. commanders were somewhat confused by the status of guerrillas and North Korean regulars disguised as civilians. One senior commander opined that "we cannot execute them but they can be shot before they become prisoners," while another solved the problem by "turning them over to the ROK's and they take care of them."[49] Eventually the UN Command clarified the situation, insisting that all guerrillas be treated as prisoners of war. South Korean treatment of captured guerrillas, on the other hand, continued to be "less sympathetic," and in 1952 the government redefined all "guerrillas" as "bandits" so that it would not have to treat captured irregulars according to the precepts laid down in the 1949 Geneva Convention.[50]

A civil affairs soldier organizes a village election.

While proper treatment of civilians and captured guerrillas remained thorny issues, the most heavy-handed tactic employed by U.S. counterinsurgency forces involved devastation. Like their KMAG and South Korean counterparts, U.S. field commanders recognized that the guerrillas depended on local food and shelter to survive the harsh Korean winters, and they embraced devastation as a means of denying such sustenance to the guerrillas. Although devastation was designed to achieve military as opposed to punitive ends, Eighth Army commander Lt. Gen. Matthew B. Ridgway was disturbed by the political and humanitarian ramifications of such policies, ordering on 2 January 1951 that "destruction for destruction's sake will not be permitted, nor will anything approaching 'scorched earth' tactics be condoned." Pressed by a major Communist Chinese offensive to their front and harried by thousands of Korean irregulars to their rear, U.S. commanders found adhering to the spirit of his instructions difficult.[51]

For example, on 16 January 1951, Maj. Gen. Edward M. Almond, commander of the X Corps, asked Ridgway for additional air liaison teams, noting that "air strikes with napalm against these guerrilla bands wherever found is a most effective way to destroy not only the bands themselves, but the huts and villages in the areas they retire to. . . . As you know, I have instituted a campaign of burning these huts in guerrilla-infested areas, and an increased number of planes, with an effective means for controlling them, will greatly assist in this program." Ridgway did not object, and by the end of the month Almond reported

113

that "by air and artillery fire and by infantry patrols those villages, buildings and shelters which are used, or suspected of being used, by enemy personnel are being eliminated. This program is driving the enemy into the open where he is more readily located and destroyed and also where he suffers from the elements to the full extent." The destruction in some areas was quite intense, as Almond reported conducting 436 incendiary operations in just one nine-day period in what he labeled the "zone of destruction."[52]

Maj. Gen. David G. Barr, commander of the 7th Infantry Division that was charged with conducting the incineration campaign around Tangyang, reported after flying over the area on 18 January that the "smoke from flaming villages and huts has filled valleys [in the] vicinity [of] Tangyang with smoke three thousand feet deep and blinded all my observations and created [a] flying hazard." Having seen the damage that heavy-handed tactics could inflict on a government's popularity from his days in China, Barr openly worried that

methodical burning of dwellings is producing hostile reaction. . . . People cannot understand why US troops burn homes when no enemy present. . . . Methodically burning out poor farmers when no enemy present is against the grain of U.S. soldiers. From house burning we already have estimated 8,000 refugees and expect more. These are mostly the old, crippled, and children. My view is that the meager gain from this program is infinitesimal when compared to the disastrous psychological effect it will produce. I recommend that selective burning be substituted for the methodical burning.[53]

Almond quickly approved Barr's recommendation stating that his intention had never been to authorize indiscriminate destruction. Yet he continued to use fire as a weapon, instructing Barr to "select and burn out those villages in which guerrillas or enemy forces were being harbored, willingly or unwillingly, by the inhabitants, and those habitations . . . from which guerrillas could not otherwise be barred." Almond further cautioned that "it would be most unfortunate if the impression described in your message were allowed to become widespread or publicized," and to help avoid a public outcry, unit commanders were advised to describe their activities as "clearing fields of fire" rather than "scorched earth" tactics.[54]

By March 1951 Ridgway had become so concerned with the amount of destruction being inflicted by both the conventional and unconventional aspects of the war that he reaffirmed his ban on the "wanton destruction of towns and villages, by gun-fire or bomb, unless there is good reason to believe them occupied." American incendiarism subsided somewhat thereafter, if for no other reason than the fact that

*U.S. soldiers depart from a village that they have just set on fire
in order to prevent guerrillas from using it.*

American participation in counterguerrilla operations also declined after the spring of 1951. Nevertheless, destruction remained an integral part of America's counterguerrilla repertoire, and in the fall of 1951 the U.S. Marines added a new dimension when, in Operations HOUSEBURNER I and II, they pioneered the use of helicopters to ferry incendiary patrols to their targets.[55]

By the spring of 1951 exfiltration, surrenders, and combat casualties had cut the number of guerrillas and North Korean partisans in South Korea by nearly 50 percent. A year after the breakout from the Pusan Perimeter, American intelligence estimated that the number of guerrillas operating in South Korea had fallen to about 7,500. Of these, approximately 20 percent were North Koreans and another 20 percent were southerners forcibly recruited into guerrilla ranks. The change in the composition of the guerrillas from a nearly all-southern, all-volunteer force to one that was increasingly composed of northerners and impressed men reflected the heavy toll inflicted by government counterguerrilla operations and the inability of the guerrillas to attract new recruits, both because of their own weaknesses and the success of the government's countermeasures. By 1952 the allies had reduced the guerrilla problem to a nuisance level. The guerrillas struggled on after the July 1953 armistice, more as fugitives than as a viable combat force, and by 1955 they were all but eliminated.[56]

Assessment

South Korea and its UN partners defeated the insurgency through a mixture of political and military means. Of the two, however, force had proved to be the most important ingredient. Harried by increasingly effective police and military operations, cut off from external aid by the establishment of a solidified battlefront, and denied access to local succor by government policies of devastation, population removal, and population and resources control, the guerrilla movement gradually withered and died. As in the Philippines, Korean guerrillas usually surrendered not because of the lure of government aid programs, but because they tired of living on the run, without proper food, clothes, shelter, or security. Military action thus proved to be the key.[57]

This is not to say that political action did not play an important role, but in the end, that role was a complementary one marred by flaws in conception and execution. Of all of the political programs, improvements in troop behavior probably had the most immediate effect on the counterguerrilla war, as many commanders reported positive results when the troops behaved more civilly toward the populace. Nevertheless, this problem was never fully rectified, as misconduct, terror, and reprisal remained features of the war.[58]

The record of the allied propaganda campaign was similarly spotty. Although the assistance group had begun developing counterguerrilla propaganda materials in 1948, by 1950 it was forced to concede that "no concentrated program of anti-guerrilla propaganda of any import has been accomplished to date." As the war progressed, the allies stepped up the propaganda campaign, linking it with troop behavior and civil assistance initiatives. During Operation RATKILLER in the winter of 1951–1952, the U.S. Air Force dropped 12 million propaganda leaflets while teams from the South Korean Ministries of Education, Social Affairs, Justice, and Home Affairs fanned out to assist the population and restore local government services. The Army Staff in Washington welcomed the news, noting that "reports of good treatment of civilians by the ROK forces during the current antiguerrilla campaign reflect an awareness of the importance of popular support in checking the guerrillas."[59] The results of such endeavors, however, were mixed. In the case of RATKILLER, the 12 million leaflets produced only 300 surrenders, while the 100,000 counterguerrilla leaflets dropped per month by the Air Force in the fall of 1952 produced few defectors.[60]

Most of the allies' early propaganda efforts had been directed at the guerrillas themselves, but by the end of the war the allied propaganda machine had redirected its attention from the guerrillas to the wider population upon whom the guerrillas depended for their survival.[61] Even so, much of this effort missed the mark. In contrast to Communist propaganda, allied propaganda failed to touch home, focusing too often on "high-sounding idealistic phrases that have been just empty words to the peasant and worker." The allies also did not sufficiently coordinate their propaganda with meaningful civil relief and reform programs. In either case, the Army's Office of the Chief of Psychological Warfare concluded after the war that the consolidation psychological warfare effort—the branch of psychological warfare aimed at friendly and occupied populations—had been unsatisfactory.[62]

While sporadic misconduct and inadequate propaganda may have weakened the anti-Communist drive, the real limits to its effectiveness came from the civil front. The civil war had created massive social and economic turmoil, so much so that the people of South Korea were significantly worse off by the end of the conflict than they had been before it had begun. By the time of the armistice, 1 million South Koreans were dead and 7.5 million were either refugees or destitute. At least 600,000 homes had been destroyed, while both rice production and per capita income were 30 percent lower than 1949 levels.[63] Foreign aid had barely enabled the country to survive, and by June 1953 the United States believed that restoring South Korea to its preinvasion standard of living would take three years and an additional $1 billion in aid. Nor had the political situation improved. The government had not had a chance to implement the 1949 land reform program before the North Korean invasion threw the country into chaos, while the State Department ruefully noted that the Rhee administration evinced a "tendency toward irresponsible, capricious administration, stultifying mediocrity and widespread corruption," which, when coupled with its willingness to use the police to intimidate voters and members of the political opposition, created an "unfortunate trend toward autocratic, one-man, unrepresentative government." Thus, while U.S. policy makers might have wished that victory had been achieved under different circumstances, in the end the South Koreans had defeated the insurgency without making any significant social, economic, or political improvements.[64]

The Truman-Era Counterinsurgencies in Retrospect

In 1945 the U.S. Army did not have a significant body of doctrine concerning the suppression of insurgencies. A half-decade of global warfare had washed away virtually all of the Army's institutional memory regarding its many prewar experiences in irregular combat and overseas nation building. Nor did Americans find applying the lessons of one postwar insurgency to the next easy, partly because each event was governed by its own set of circumstances and partly because the insurgencies occurred virtually simultaneously. True, the conclusion of the Chinese and Greek Civil Wars in 1949 had permitted the transference of some ideas and personnel to the Philippines and Korea, but for the most part U.S. advisers approached their duties without any detailed knowledge about revolutionary warfare. Although American ignorance was hardly blissful, it had, at least, permitted advisers to adapt to the situation at hand, taking into account the unique political, military, cultural, and topographical circumstances under which each conflict was fought, unencumbered by preconceived notions, pedantic doctrines, or slavish parroting of Mao.

The doctrinal void notwithstanding, U.S. soldiers addressed the postwar insurgencies with surprising consistency. The fact that all of the insurgencies were guided by Communists who shared to one degree or another a common insurrectionary creed contributed to these similarities, as did the very nature of guerrilla warfare itself, whose age-old principles naturally begot similar responses. Yet there were also other elements at work.

On the political front, the consistency with which the U.S. Army approached the postwar conflicts stemmed in part from the foreign policies of the Truman administration. In the administration's opinion, political unrest flourished in situations where governments were unstable and undemocratic, where social problems went unaddressed, and economic hardships abounded. Rectify these problems, and communism would not be able to flourish. Social, political, and economic reform thus became Truman's primary weapon in the war against communism, an approach reflected in each of the postwar insurgencies as well as in the Marshall Plan.

The Truman administration's philosophy set the parameters under which the Army operated in the postwar decade, but it was not unique. In fact, Truman's policy was entirely consistent with the way the United States had traditionally approached nation-building and counterinsurgency tasks. Fueled by a heady blend of American democratic and progressive values, sociological and anthropological theory, missionary zeal, and ethnocentric conceptions of the "white man's burden," American civil and military policy makers had been prescribing the same troika of good government, socioeconomic improvement, and military action for nearly a century.[65]

U.S. soldiers shared the administration's faith in this creed, though they tended to believe that meaningful social and economic progress could not be achieved until after military security had been established. In time many, though not all, American diplomats came to agree with them, citing both the necessities of the situation and the difficulty of transforming indigenous institutions in the midst of a war. Indeed, American policy makers were destined to relearn what previous generations of U.S. soldiers and statesmen had already found to be true—that reshaping foreign societies was exceedingly difficult, especially when the indigenous elites whose cooperation the United States needed had a vested interest in the status quo. All too often American officials found that they lacked the leverage necessary to force America's allies to enact meaningful internal reforms. This proved true not only in Greece and South Korea, where the indigenous governments triumphed without making significant reforms, but in the Philippines as well, where many of the reforms turned out to be rather superficial. Only in China was the United States willing to stick to its principles and allow an inflexible regime to fall. The terrible ramifications of that fall—the loss of 20 percent of the world's population to communism and acrimonious debates at home over "who lost China," further undermined U.S. leverage, as did the growing stakes of the Cold War. Thereafter, when forced to chose between supporting a less than democratic regime or permitting a Communist overthrow, the United States frequently chose to stand by its imperfect allies, still urging them to reform but refusing to abandon them when they did not.[66]

Frustrated by their inability to reshape foreign societies, U.S. officials often sought solace in the idea that a change of leadership in the country in question would provide the necessary impetus for overcoming the many cultural and institutional barriers to reform. Speaking of Chiang Kai-shek, Secretary of State Dean Acheson concluded that "if there is one lesson to be learned from the China debacle it is that if we are confronted with an inadequate vehicle, it should be discarded or immobilized in favor of a more propitious one." There was merit in this idea, and, by helping to elevate Alexander Papagos and Ramon Magsaysay, the United States had indeed succeeded in infusing life into otherwise pallid counterinsurgency efforts. Such an approach was not a panacea, however, as the United States would soon learn.[67]

Although many U.S. soldiers were unfamiliar with the Army's many irregular warfare and nation-building experiences of the previous century, the Army had distilled the lessons of these experiences into a doctrine that reflected the many subtleties and ambiguities of operations of this nature. On the political front, FM 27–5, *United States Army and Navy Manual of Civil Affairs Military Government* (1947), called for unified and coordinated civil-military action, flexible plans, clear and consistent policies, honest and efficient administration, sensitivity to indigenous cultural norms, and humane treatment of civilians and prisoners. For the most part, the Army endeavored to follow this doctrine during the postwar insurgencies, although it often found that personal, political, bureaucratic, and national differences and rivalries impeded the attainment of these goals. Indeed, Army leaders soon discovered that implementing a clear and coordinated civil-military program was no easier in the 1940s and 1950s than it had been during the previous century in places like the American South during Reconstruction, the western frontier, Cuba, the USSR, or the Philippines. Still, enlightened benevolence, no matter how hard to achieve in practice, remained the goal.

Yet while FM 27–5 called for intelligent and humane policies to cultivate public favor, it also recognized that "restrictive or punitive measures," including "the taking of hostages, the imposition of collective fines, or the carrying out of reprisals," were often necessary to suppress a restive population. Humanity and political acumen alike dictated that commanders resort to the severest measures only in extreme circumstances and when conditions were most favorable for their success. But such weapons remained an essential part of the military's arsenal, just as Magsaysay's right hand of force had backed the left hand of friendship, and in every postwar insurgency the twin principles of attraction and chastisement had guided U.S. Army actions and advice.[68]

Militarily, U.S. soldiers adhered to the broad antipartisan principles that had been included in every edition of FM 100–5 since 1939. They consistently pressed for inspired leadership and aggressive action, urging their counterparts to break free from blockhouse mentalities and enervating piecemeal deployments. Killing the enemy and breaking his will to resist, not seizing and holding terrain, were the U.S. Army's counterinsurgency goals. Cutting the guerrilla off from cross-border sanctuaries and external support was also a cardinal American tenet. But U.S. soldiers also realized that victory could not be achieved without isolating the guerrilla from his sources of internal support. Here, once again, attraction and chastisement played their intricate dance. In one hand, the United States and its allies offered civil, medical, and economic palliatives to ease wartime suffering and attract public support, while in the other they wielded a variety of repressive measures designed to attack the insurgents' presence among the population and control antigovernment behavior. Among these were the establishment of effective police and counterintelligence systems; the issuance of identity cards; the imposition of restrictions on travel, on communications, and on the possession of arms, food, and other commodities; the suspension of certain democratic rights, like *habeas corpus*; and, when necessary, devastation and population relocation. Some soldiers fretted that such steps smacked of totalitarianism, yet most came to accept them as unpleasant but necessary weapons in the war against subversion.

Operationally, Americans favored large-scale encirclements and sweeps, coordinated with civil and police measures, to break the hold of large guerrilla units over rural base areas. In China and Greece, U.S. planners recommended a strategy of systematic and progressive area clearance. In the Philippines, where the guerrillas were more localized, and in Korea, where external forces greatly disrupted the prosecution of the internal campaign, less systematic approaches were used, with the Americans usually counseling that the indigenous government attack the largest guerrilla concentrations first before targeting less important areas. In either case, such operations were difficult to execute but could, under favorable conditions, yield impressive results. Once the guerrillas had been dispersed, smaller operations followed to further the disintegration of the insurgents, although both the Americans and their allies often had trouble making this shift in a timely manner.

In every insurgency U.S. advisers followed the guidance contained in FM 100–5 and sought to establish defended villages and local self-defense units to free the regular army for offensive operations, to protect the people from guerrilla harassment, and to prevent those same people from aiding the insurgents. Concern over the reputation of paramilitary groups for lawlessness and brutality, however, led the Army to move cautiously on creating such entities, lest their excesses undermine the goals of pacification. But U.S. advisers had very little control over indigenous governments on this score, especially since many governments organized paramilitary forces without American material aid. Consequently, the best the United States could do was to urge indigenous authorities to impose tighter control and discipline over the paramilitaries, and occasionally, as in Greece, to use the provision of material assistance as leverage to win such improvements.

Tactically, American advisers adhered to the old credo of finding, fixing, and finishing the enemy that had guided U.S. soldiers since the Indian wars.[69] They consistently tried to wean their counterparts from relying too heavily on fire support, believing that close infantry action represented the only way to destroy the enemy effectively. Careful reconnaissance, rapid deployments, vigorous attacks, and relentless pursuits were the principal methods by which the Army hoped to defeat the guerrillas in the field. Consequently, American advisers emphasized the basics of infantry warfare—small-unit tactics, marksmanship, fire discipline, patrolling and reconnaissance, ambush and counterambush drills, night movements, and march and camp security. Although they recognized that mobility was essential, they preferred to inculcate old-fashioned foot mobility rather than to foster a dependency on trucks or expensive, "high tech" fixes like parachutists and helicopters. U.S. soldiers were less united, however, with respect to the advisability of creating specially trained counterguerrilla units, endorsing such initiatives in Greece, the Philippines, and to a lesser extent South Korea, while ultimately deciding against the incorporation of specialist units into their own force structure during the Korean War.

The overall consistency with which the United States Army approached the insurgencies of 1945–1954 indicates the existence within the officer corps, in practice if not on paper, of a set of commonly held assumptions and responses to wars of this type. These responses represented less a fixed doctrine than a conglomeration of tools bound loosely together by a set of concepts and principles taken from a variety of sources—conventional military doctrine, indigenous methods, Axis precedents, American ideology and foreign policy, and more generally from certain broad continuities in Western political, legal, and cultural thought. During the 1950s, the Army began to translate and interpret this loose body of thought and experience into a formal, written doctrine for counterinsurgency.

Notes

[1] Bruce Cumings, *The Origins of the Korean War*, 2 vols. (Princeton, N.J.: Princeton University Press, 1981–1990), 1:66–67, 201–04, 350–67, 375–79, and 2:247; Allan Millett, "Understanding Is Better Than Remembering: The Korean War, 1945–1954," Dwight D. Eisenhower Lectures in War and Peace (Manhattan: Kansas State University, 1997); HQ, Far East Command (FEC), History of the U.S. Army Forces in Korea, vol. 3, pt. 3, pp. 18–24, copy in CMH.

[2] Quote from FEC, History of U.S. Army Forces in Korea, vol. 3, pt. 3, p. 17. Cumings, *Origins of the Korean War*, 2:280; Despatch, Seoul 389 to State, 15 Apr 50, sub: Guerrilla Strength and Activity, 658644, ID, G–2, RG 319, NARA.

[3] John Merrill, "Internal Warfare in Korea, 1948–50: The Local Setting of the Korean War" (Ph.D. diss., University of Delaware, 1982), pp. 321–22, 345–48; Cumings, *Origins of the Korean War*, 2:238–40, 282–83; Msg, Seoul 706 to State, 8 Nov 49, sub: Guerrilla Raid on Chinju, 612081, ID, G–2, RG 319, NARA; Jon Halliday and Bruce Cumings, *Korea, The Unknown War* (New York: Pantheon, 1988), p. 34. For background on the organization of the guerrilla movement, see Fred Barton, Operational Aspects of Paramilitary Warfare in South Korea, ORO–T–25 (FEC) (Chevy Chase, Md.: Operations Research Office, Johns Hopkins University, 1952); W. Phillips Davison and Jean Hungerford, North Korean Guerrilla Units, RM–550 (Santa Monica, Calif.: RAND, 1951); Aerospace Studies Institute, Guerrilla Warfare and Airpower in Korea, 1950–1953 (Maxwell Air Force Base [AFB], Ala.: Air University, 1964).

[4] John Lord et al., A Study of Rear Area Security Measures (Washington, D.C.: Special Operations Research Office, American University, 1965), p. 116; Memo, Lt Gen Hodge for Lt Gen Wedemeyer, c. 1946, sub: Joint Korean-American Conference, box 83, U.S. Army Forces in Korea (USFIK), RG 332, NARA.

[5] Robert Sawyer, *Military Advisors in Korea: KMAG in Peace and War*, Army Historical Series (Washington, D.C.: U.S. Army Center of Military History, 1962), pp. 15, 26; Allan Millett, "Captain James H. Hausman and the Formation of the Korean Army, 1945–1950," *Armed Forces and Society* 23 (Summer 1997): 503–39; Riley Sunderland and Marshall Andrews, Guerrilla Operations in South Korea, 1945–53, in HERO, Isolating the Guerrilla, 2:262; Samuel Sampson, Training Mission of Officers Assigned to the Korean Military Advisory Group (Student paper, IOAC, Infantry School, 1952–53), p. 7.

[6] Ltrs, Maj Gen Orlando Ward, CG, 6th Inf Div, to Col Rothwell H. Brown, Comdr, 20th Inf, 6 Feb 48 and 10 Mar 48, Rothwell H. Brown Papers, MHI; Rpt, U.S. Military Advisory Group Korea (KMAG), Ofc of the Chief, 15 Oct 49, sub: G–3 Summary, sec. I, an. 7, pp. 1–2, 091 Korea, 1949–50, P&O, RG 319, NARA; Ltr, Brig Gen William L. Roberts, Ch, KMAG, to Maj Gerald E. Larson, Senior Adviser, ROK 8th Div, 4 May 50, 333, KMAG, RG 338, NARA.

[7] Rpt, FEC Intel Sum 2704, 3 Feb 50, 633512; Despatch, Seoul 325 to State, 1 Apr 50, sub: Formation of Police Battalions, with atch, 655899. Both in ID, G–2, RG 319, NARA.

[8] Quote from Rpt, KMAG, G–2, n.d., sub: Guerrilla Activity for the Period Ending 19 Dec 51, p. 3, and see also pp. 4–5, 950126, ID, G–2, RG 319, NARA. For an account of

the Cheju-do rebellion, see John Merrill, "The Cheju-do Rebellion," *Journal of Korean Studies* 2 (1980): 139–98.

[9] For examples of government terror, see Briefing Paper, National Police Force, atch to Provisional Military Advisory Group (PMAG), Extension of Notes, Data on Korean Security Forces for Mr. Kenneth C. Royall, Secretary of the Army, 1949, 091 Korea, 1949–50, P&O, RG 319, NARA; Merrill, "Internal Warfare in Korea," pp. 236–38, 255, 265, 357–59; Despatch, Seoul 788 to State, 10 Dec 49, sub: Summary of Political Affairs of the Republic of Korea, November 1949, p. 5, 620368, ID, G–2, RG 319, NARA; MFR, U.S. Adviser to the Director, Uniform Bureau, Korean National Police, 3 Aug 48, sub: Beating and Torture Cases, box 83, USAFIK, RG 332, NARA.

[10] First quote from Ltr, Brig Gen William L. Roberts to Maj Gen Charles L. Bolte, 19 Aug 49, 091 Korea, P&O 1949–50, RG 319, NARA. Second quote from KMAG, Advisers' Handbook, 1949, p. 4, KMAG, RG 338, NARA. Memos, Roberts for All Advisers with Regiments and Divisions, 21 Mar 50, sub: Reporting Violations of Standing Orders, and Tubb for American Advisers, 3 May 50, sub: Special Subject for Korean Army. Both in 353, KMAG, RG 338, NARA.

[11] Quotes from Merrill, "Internal Warfare in Korea," pp. 300–301, and see also pp. 331, 358–61. Cumings, *Origins of the Korean War*, 2:403, 472; Despatches, Pusan 27 to State, 23 Jul 52, sub: Guerrilla Movement in South Korea (hereafter cited as Pusan 27), Incl 1, p. 27, 1092486, and Seoul 788 to State, 10 Dec 49, sub: Summary of Political Affairs of the Republic of Korea, November 1949, pp. 14–16, 620368. Both in ID, G–2, RG 319, NARA.

[12] Quote from Rpt, Army G–2, 19 Jan 50, sub: General Survey of Guerrilla Activity in South Korea, p. 6, Historians files, CMH. USAFIK G–2 Periodic Rpt 1093, 23 Mar 49, p. 2, ID, G–2, RG 319, NARA; Merrill, "Internal Warfare in Korea," pp. 257, 357–59; Incl 1 to Despatch 720, Seoul to State, 12 Nov 49, sub: Guerrilla Raid on Chinju; Governor Submits Resignation, 612082, ID, G–2, RG 319, NARA; Cumings, *Origins of the Korean War*, 2:289; Memo, HQ, Korean Army, for All Commanders, 27 Apr 51, sub: Military Conduct Toward Civilians, KMAG, RG 338, NARA.

[13] Roberts had lobbied for heavier equipment once the possibility became clear that the ROK Army would have to be prepared to fight North Korea's conventional forces, but Washington denied his request fearing Rhee might invade the North. Cumings, *Origins of the Korean War*, 2:264, 397–98, 400; Sawyer, *Military Advisors in Korea*, p. 186; Memo, Roberts for All American Advisers with Units in the Field, 24 Aug 49, and Ltr, Roberts to Lt Col Walden J. Alexander, Senior Adviser, ROK 5th Division, 3 Sep 49, both in 333, KMAG, RG 338, NARA; KMAG, Advisers' Handbook, 1949, p. 3. Mil Hist Ofc, HQ, U.S. Army, Japan, United States Military Advisory Group to the Republic of Korea, pt. 4, KMAG's Wartime Experiences, 11 July 1951 to 27 July 1953, n.d., pp. 339–40, CMH (hereafter cited as KMAG's Wartime Experiences).

[14] Cumings, *Origins of the Korean War*, 2:286–88, 389, 573. For Japanese counter-guerrilla techniques, see Lincoln Lee, *The Japanese Army in North China, 1937–1941* (New York: Oxford University Press, 1975); Gene Hanrahan, Japanese Operations Against Guerrilla Forces, ORO–T–268 (Chevy Chase, Md.: Operations Research Office, Johns Hopkins University, 1954); U.S. Army Forces, Far East, Military Studies on Manchuria, bk. 4, Historical Observations of Various Operations in Manchuria, ch. 9, Bandits and Inhabitants (1955), CMH.

[15] Quote from Despatch, Seoul 788 to State, 10 Dec 49, sub: Summary of Political Affairs of the Republic of Korea, November 1949, p. 13. Cumings, *Origins of the*

Korean War, 2:244, 247–48, 257, 271, 289; Merrill, "Internal Warfare in Korea," p. 243; FEC Intel Sum 2984, 10 Nov 50, ID, G–2, RG 319, NARA; Pusan 27, Incl 1, pp. 7, 22; Virgil Ney, *Notes on Guerrilla War: Principles and Practices* (Washington, D.C.: Command Publications, 1961), p. 118; HQ, Eighth U.S. Army in Korea (EUSAK), Enemy Tactics, 1951, p. 119, box 73, USARPAC History files, RG 338, NARA (hereafter cited as EUSAK, Enemy Tactics).

[16] Cumings, *Origins of the Korean War*, 2:256; U.S. Army Intelligence Center, History of the Counter Intelligence Corps, n.d., pp. 140–41, CMH; Memo, Roberts for All American Advisers with Units in the Field, 24 Aug 49; Merrill, "Internal Warfare in Korea," pp. 243, 353; Pusan 27, Incl 1, p. 20; Despatch 720, Seoul to State, 12 Nov 49, sub: Guerrilla Raid on Chinju; Governor Submits Resignation; Rpt, KMAG, Weekly Intel Sum, 13 Feb 52, p. 3, 950126, ID, G–2, RG 319, NARA.

[17] Rpt, PMAG, 22 Nov 48, sub: Weekly Activities of PMAG, KMAG, RG 338, NARA; Merrill, "Internal Warfare in Korea," p. 127.

[18] First quoted words from Merrill, "Internal Warfare in Korea," p. 351. Second quoted words from Cumings, *Origins of the Korean War*, 2:399. For other examples of "search and destroy" phraseology, see FEC, History of U.S. Army Forces in Korea, vol. 3, pt. 3, p. 17; KMAG's Wartime Experiences, p. 367; Special Activities Gp Command Rpt, Jan 51, Infantry School Library, Fort Benning, Ga.

[19] Quote from Merrill, "Internal Warfare in Korea," pp. 253–54. Even during RATKILLER, perhaps the most effective encirclement of the war, as many as 60 percent of the guerrillas were thought to have escaped. Pusan 27, Incl 1, p. 22.

[20] Walter Hermes, *Truce Tent and Fighting Front*, United States Army in the Korean War (Washington, D.C.: U.S. Army Center of Military History, 1966), p. 347; KMAG's Wartime Experiences, pp. 367–69; Guerrilla Warfare and Airpower, p. 56.

[21] Sunderland and Andrews, Guerrilla Operations in South Korea, pp. 257–58; MFR, 23 Jul 48, sub: Opinion of the Settlement of the Cheju Situation: 23 Jul 48, at Cheju-do by Koh Pyung Uk, Superintendent of National Police Department, box 83, USAFIK, RG 332, NARA.

[22] Despatch, Seoul 389 to State, 15 Apr 50, sub: Guerrilla Strength and Activity; Rpt, USAFIK G–2, 23 Mar 49, sub: Military Estimate of Situation in Korea, p. 14, 543752, ID, G–2, RG 319, NARA.

[23] Sawyer, *Military Advisors in Korea*, p. 76; Merrill, "Internal Warfare in Korea," pp. 362, 413–14.

[24] Quote from Office, Chief, Army Field Forces, Training Bulletin 2, 9 Nov 50, p. 7, in 350.9 AFF Training Bulletins, CMH. Allan David, ed., *Battleground Korea, the Story of the Twenty-fifth Infantry Division* (1951); EUSAK, Enemy Tactics, pp. 113–14; "Guerrilla Warfare and Airpower," pp. 34–47; John Beebe, "Beating the Guerrilla," *Military Review* 35 (December 1955): 10; HQ, Far East Command, Issue 9, Supplement, Enemy Documents Korean Operations, 10 Apr 51, Historians files, CMH; Barton, Operational Aspects, pp. 19, 26–27; Paul Hughes, Battle in the Rear: Lessons from Korea (Student paper, U.S. Army School of Advanced Military Studies, CGSC, 1988), pp. 7–8.

[25] Lord, Rear Area Security, p. 118.

[26] Roy Appleman, *South to the Naktong, North to the Yalu*, United States Army in the Korean War (Washington, D.C.: U.S. Army Center of Military History, 1961), pp. 722–28; Halliday and Cumings, *Unknown War*, p. 146; FEC Intel Sum 3001, 27 Nov 50, p. 2-b, ID, G–2, RG 319, NARA.

[27] FEC Intel Sum 3071, 5 Feb 51, p. M-3; Pusan 27, Incl 1, pp. 2, 15; Lord, Rear Area Security, p. 121.

[28] In Operation RATKILLER, Van Fleet took advantage of winter weather and a relative lull at the front to launch a major counterguerrilla drive in southwest Korea. The operation, which lasted from December 1951 to March 1952, was multiphased and involved several encirclements and repeated sweeps using approximately 30,000 South Korean Army, police, and paramilitary soldiers. Paik Sun Yup, *From Pusan to Panmunjom* (Washington, D.C.: Brassey's, 1992), p. 183.

[29] Guerrilla Warfare and Airpower, pp. 42–43; Paik, *From Pusan to Panmunjom*, p. 184. The UN allocated ten fighter-bomber sorties per day for RATKILLER. William Dodds, "Anti-Guerrilla Warfare" (Student thesis, AWC, 1955), pp. 26–27; DeWitt Smith, Counterguerrilla Operations: Can We Learn from Task Force Paik? (Student paper, AWC, 1966).

[30] Richard Weinert, The U.S. Army and Military Assistance in Korea Since 1951, CMH–132, U.S. Army Center of Military History, n.d., p. III-9, CMH; "KMAG's Wartime Experiences," pp. 110–13, 367–70; Pusan 27, Incl 1, p. 5.

[31] Most of the 10,000 prisoners taken during RATKILLER were civilians, 60 percent of whom were eventually classed as guerrilla sympathizers. Rpt, KMAG, Weekly Intel Sums, 19 Dec 51, p. 1, and 10 Jan 52, p. 2, both in 950126, ID, G–2, RG 319, NARA; Pusan 27, Incl 1, pp. 7, 14; Merrill, "Internal Warfare in Korea," pp. 352–56; Appleman, *South to the Naktong*, p. 478; Despatch, Pusan 177 to State, 25 May 51, sub: Anti-Guerrilla Activities of ROK 8th Division in the South Kyongsang and Cholla Provinces, 812113, ID, G–2, RG 319, NARA; Rpt, KMAG, Guerrilla Activity for the Period Ending 14 Nov 51, p. 4, KMAG, RG 338, NARA.

[32] David, *Battleground Korea*.

[33] Hughes, Battle in the Rear, pp. 9–11; William Hacker, G–2 Section, Logistical Command (Student paper, IOAC, Infantry School, 1952–53); HQ, EUSAK, Special Problems in the Korean Conflict, 1952, pp. 98, 106–07, CMH; History of the Korean Communications Zone, n.d., USARPAC History file, box 339, RG 338, NARA; 772d Military Police Battalion, SOP [Standing Operating Procedure] for Railway Security, 1953, Infantry School Library.

[34] Robert Rigg, "Get Guerrilla-Wise," *U.S. Army Combat Forces Journal* 1 (September 1950): 11.

[35] X Corps Command Rpt, Jan 51, pp. 24–25, box 33, USARPAC History file, RG 338, NARA; Appleman, *South to the Naktong*, pp.721–28, 740.

[36] Quoted words from X Corps, Big X in Korea, 1954, p. 19, and see also pp. 20–21, copy in CMH. MFR, HQ, IX Corps, 30 Oct 50, sub: Resume of Operations, IX Corps War Diary, Oct 50, box 1766; 25th Inf Div History, Oct 50, bk. 1, pp. 1–14, 23; IX Corps War Diary, 1–31 Oct 50, bk. 1, p. 3, box 1761; 2d Inf Div G–3 Opns Rpt, Sep–Dec 50. All in RG 407, NARA. Richard Harris et al., Rear Area Operations, Korean Conflict, Rear Area Security, October 1950 (Staff Group B, Section 1, Division A, CGSC course, May 1984), CGSC–N–20326.15, CGSC Library, Fort Leavenworth, Kans.; Richard Pullen, ed., *25th Infantry Division, Tropic Lightning in Korea* (Atlanta, Ga.: Albert Love, n.d.); Max Dolcater, ed., *3d Infantry Division in Korea* (Tokyo: Toppan Printing Co., 1953), pp. 67–86.

[37] Harris, Rear Area Operations.

[38] Ross Barrett, The Role of the Ground Liaison Officer with a Tactical Control Group and Close Air Support (Student paper, IOAC, Infantry School, 1952–53), pp.

11–12; Harris, Rear Area Operations; David, *Battleground Korea*; Appleman, *South to the Naktong*, p. 721.

[39] EUSAK, Special Problems, p. 98.

[40] Quote from 25th Inf Div History, Oct 50, bk. 1, p. 45. Agenda Prepared by Army Field Forces Observer Team 5, FECOM, Aug 51, p. 171, 319.1, Army Field Force Reports, CMH.

[41] Quote from Jean Moenk, Training During the Korean Conflict, 1950–1954, Office of the Historian, U.S. Army Transportation Command, 1962, p. 22, and see also pp. 9–10, 23, copy in CMH. EUSAK, Special Problems, pp. 57–58; Hughes, Battle in the Rear, pp. 18–19.

[42] Lynn Montross, *Cavalry of the Sky: The Story of Marine Corps Combat Helicopters* (New York: Harper & Bros., 1954), pp. 172–73, 178; Homer Wright, Ambush Tactics as Applied by the Chinese and North Korean Forces Against U.S. Troops in Korea (Student paper, IOAC, Infantry School, 1952–53), pp. 13–15.

[43] Waller Booth, "The Pattern That Got Lost," *Army* 31 (April 1981): 62–64; David Gray, "Black and Gold Warriors: United States Army Rangers During the Korean War" (Ph.D. diss., Ohio State University, 1992), pp. 35, 43, 94–95; John Provost, "Nomads of the Battlefield: Ranger Companies in the Korean War, 1950–1951" (Master's thesis, CGSC, 1989), pp. 3–5, 20–21, 31, 35–38; David Hogan, *Raiders or Elite Infantry? The Changing Role of the U.S. Army Rangers from Dieppe to Grenada* (Westport, Conn.: Greenwood Press, 1992), p. 112.

[44] X Corps, G–2, Enemy Tactics, Bulletin 2, c. Spring 1951, USARPAC History, box 79, RG 338, NARA; James Olson, Organization and Use of an Anti-Guerrilla Unit in Korea During the Period November 1950 to March 1951 (Student paper, IOAC, Infantry School, 1952–53); EUSAK, Special Problems, p. 106; X Corps Command Rpts, Jan 51, p. 25, and Apr 51, p. 57, both in box 33, USARPAC History file, RG 338, NARA; Special Activities Gp, Command Rpts for Dec 50 and Jan, Feb, and Mar 51, Infantry School Library.

[45] Hogan, *Raiders or Elite Infantry*, pp. 122–32; EUSAK, Special Problems, pp. 81–87.

[46] Quote from HQ, EUSAK, Enemy Tactics, 1951, p. 118. Memo, HQ, EUSAK, for Distribution, 24 Jun 51, sub: Criminal Offenses, KMAG, RG 338, NARA; Cumings, *Origins of the Korean War*, 2:690–96; Harris, Rear Area Operations; Hughes, Battle in the Rear, pp. 13–14; Office, Chief, Army Field Forces, Training Bulletin 1, 8 Sep 50, p. 6, 350.9 AFF Training Bulletins, CMH; Appleman, *South to the Naktong*, p. 478; Memo, Lt Col Leon F. Lavoie, Comdr, 92d Armd Field Arty Bn, for Comdr, X Corps Arty, 22 Nov 50, sub: Report, Special Operation 'Sunshine,' X Corps War Diary, Nov 50; Ltr, Maj Gen Laurence R. Keiser, CG, 2d Inf Div, to CG, 2d Inf Div Arty, et al., 2 Oct 50, G–3 Operations Orders, 2d Inf Div, Sep–Oct 50; 25th Inf Div History, Oct 50, bk. 1, p. 14. Last three in RG 407, NARA.

[47] First quote from Barton, Operational Aspects, p. 64. Second quote from Memo, FEC for Adj Gen, 17 Nov 52, sub: Technical Memorandum Paramilitary Warfare in South Korea (FEC), "Operational Aspects of Paramilitary Warfare in South Korea," p. 3, in 040 ORO, 1952, RG 319, NARA. Cumings, *Origins of the Korean War*, 2:687, 690, 706; Carl Peterson, The 1st Battalion, 187th Airborne Regimental Combat Team, in Anti-Guerrilla Operations in the Mountains East of Pyongyang, North Korea, November 1950 (Student paper, IOAC, Infantry School, 1952–53), p. 8; Despatch, Seoul 389 to State, 15 Apr 50, sub: Guerrilla Strength and Activity.

48 Alfred Hausrath, Civil Affairs in the Cold War, ORO–SP–151 (Bethesda, Md.: Operations Research Office, Johns Hopkins University, 1961), pp. 59–60; Daugherty and Andrews, Historical Experience with Civil Affairs, pp. 446–47; Thomas Teraji, History of the Korean War, vol. 3, pt. 5, Civil Affairs/Civil Assistance Problems (Military History Section, UN Command and HQ, Far East Command, c. 1951), pp. 1–8, CMH; "The Second Year in Korea," Army Information Digest 7 (November 1952): 27; James Mrazek, "The Fifth Staff Officer," Military Review 36 (March 1957): 47–51. Coordinating a multinational civil affairs and relief effort in a sovereign country during a period of intense disruption was no easy task, and the American-UN effort experienced many difficulties. Carlton Wood et al., Civil Affairs Relations in Korea, ORO–T–2464 (Baltimore, Md.: Operations Research Office, Johns Hopkins University, 1954); Darwin Stolzenbach and Henry Kissinger, Civil Affairs in Korea, 1950–1951, ORO–T–184 (Baltimore, Md.: Operations Research Office, Johns Hopkins University, 1952).

49 Rpt, HQ, EUSAK, 8 Jan 51, sub: Conference Notes, box 20, Matthew Ridgway Papers, MHI.

50 Quoted words from Agenda Prepared by Army Field Forces Observer Team 5, FECOM, Aug 51, p. 1. Pusan 27, p. 3; CINCFE Directive, 5 Jul 50, reissued as Admin Order 12, HQ, Korean Army, 18 Nov 50, KMAG, RG 338, NARA.

51 Quote from Memo, Ridgway for CGs, I, IX, X Corps and Republic of Korea Army, 2 Jan 51, box 17, Ridgway Papers. Memo for Ridgway, 5 Jan 51, sub: Notes of Conference at HQ EUSAK, box 20, Ridgway Papers; Special Activities Group, Command Rpt, Jan 51; 25th Inf Div History, Oct 50, bk. 1, p. 44, RG 407, NARA; Summary for 1000 Hour Briefing, 26 Jan 51, 1 Feb 51, and 4 Feb 51, in KMAG, RG 338, NARA.

52 First quote from Ltr, Almond to Ridgway, 16 Jan 51. Second and third quotes from Ltr, Almond to Ridgway, 25 Jan 51. Both in box 17, Ridgway Papers, MHI.

53 Msg, Barr to Almond, 18 Jan 51, Miscellaneous Radios CG X Corps, Korean War General files, X Corps, Edward M. Almond Papers, MHI.

54 First two quotes from Msg, Almond to Barr, 19 Jan 51, Miscellaneous Radios CG X Corps, Korean War General files, X Corps, Almond Papers. Third and fourth quotes from Robert Black, Rangers in Korea (New York: Ivy Books, 1989), pp. 46–48.

55 Quote from Cumings, Origins of the Korean War, 2:755. Montross, Cavalry of the Sky, p. 173.

56 Barton, Operational Aspects, pp. 12–14.

57 Rpt, Ofc, Chief of Psychological Warfare, 10 Nov 53, sub: Psychological Warfare Operations Deficiencies Noted in Korea—A Study, p. 72, 091 Korea, Office, Chief of Special Warfare, 1951–54, RG 319, NARA; Sunderland and Andrews, Guerrilla Operations in South Korea, pp. 257–58, 263.

58 FEC Intel Sum 2246, 28 Oct 48, p. 3, 504233, ID, G–2, RG 319, NARA; Handwritten Note, 1 Feb 50, atch to Memo, Hussey for G–2, KMAG, 28 Jan 50, sub: G–2 Report, 319.1, KMAG, RG 338, NARA; Pusan 27, Incl 1, p. 5; Despatch, Pusan 177 to State, 25 May 51, sub: Anti-Guerrilla Activities of ROK 8th Division in the South Kyongsang and Cholla Provinces.

59 First quote from Rpt, Army G–2, 19 Jan 50, sub: General Survey of Guerrilla Activity in South Korea, p. 6. Second quote from Rpt, Army G–2, 18 Jan 52, sub: Weekly Intel Rpt 152, p. 39, and see also p. 37, Historians files, CMH.

60 In addition to the 300 guerrillas who surrendered due to UN propaganda during RATKILLER, another 1,400 other prisoners (roughly 10 percent of the total number of prisoners taken during the operation) acknowledged that the leaflets lowered their

morale. Dodds, "Anti-Guerrilla Warfare," p. 11; Rpt, KMAG, Weekly Intel Sums, 6 Feb 52, p. 1, and 13 Feb 52, p. 3, 950126, ID, G–2, RG 319, NARA; Paik, *From Pusan to Panmunjom*, pp. 188–89; Sunderland and Andrews, Guerrilla Operations in South Korea, pp. 259–60.

[61] For example, propaganda during Operation TRAMPLE (December 1953–July 1954) focused squarely on the people: only 3.75 million propaganda leaflets and a portion of the 1,700 hours of loudspeaker broadcasts were aimed at the guerrillas, while 8.95 million leaflets, 10.6 million news sheets, 15 motion picture shows, and the remaining broadcast hours were directed at the population. Qtrly Hist Rpt, KMAG, Jan–Mar 54, 26 Jul 54, p. 13; Qtrly Hist Rpt, KMAG, Apr–Jun 54, 5 Oct 54, pp. 6–7, 9. Both in KMAG, RG 338, NARA.

[62] Quote from Dodds, "Anti-Guerrilla Warfare," p. 10, and see also p. 11. Beebe, "Beating the Guerrilla," p. 16. Communist guerrillas sometimes welcomed American leaflet drops, using the sheets either as toilet paper or as supplies for their own propaganda machine, printing Communist slogans on the back of allied leaflets and issuing them to villagers. Such activity compelled the allies to print two-sided leaflets. Rpt, HQ, Korean Communications Zone, Intel Sum 75, 31 Jan 54, p. 4, 950794, ID, G–2, RG 319, NARA; Barton, Operational Aspects, pp. 29, 40; Rpt, Ofc, Chief of Psychological Warfare, 10 Nov 53, sub: Psychological Warfare Operations Deficiencies Noted in Korea—A Study, pp. 71–72.

[63] Of South Korea's 21.5 million population, 2.5 million were refugees and 5 million more were indigent. *FRUS, 1952–54*, 15:1245–49.

[64] Quotes from *FRUS, 1952–54*, 15:1680, and see also 1245–49, 1797–98. When a 1952 study commissioned by the Army criticized the allies for trying to defeat the insurgency by military measures alone, Far East Command conceded the advantages of a combined political, economic, and military approach but noted that the massive socioeconomic dislocation caused by the war, when coupled with inadequate financial resources and incomplete cooperation on the part of the Rhee government, limited what could be done. Memo, FEC for Adj Gen, 17 Nov 52, sub: Technical Memorandum Paramilitary Warfare in South Korea (FEC), "Operational Aspects of Paramilitary Warfare in South Korea," p. 2; Barton, Operational Aspects, pp. 4–5; Rpt, HQ, Korean Communications Zone, Intel Sum 81, 16 Mar 54, pp. 1–2, 6950794, ID, G–2, RG 319, NARA; Donald Howard, "Anti-Guerrilla Operations in Asia" (Student thesis, AWC, 1956), p. 41; Lord, Rear Area Security, p. 135.

[65] For background, see Andrew Birtle, *U.S. Army Counterinsurgency and Contingency Operations Doctrine, 1860–1941* (Washington, D.C.: U.S. Army Center of Military History, 1998), pp. 249–54.

[66] American support was never unconditional, as Fulgencio Batista found to his detriment when in 1959 the United States stood by and permitted Fidel Castro to overthrow the Cuban dictator. Shafer, *Deadly Paradigms*, p. 226.

[67] Quote from Shafer, *Deadly Paradigms*, p. 229. Merrill, "Internal Warfare in Korea," p. 175.

[68] FM 27–5, *United States Army and Navy Manual of Civil Affairs Military Government*, 1947, pp. 9–10.

[69] Bohannan, "Antiguerrilla Operations," p. 20; Dodds, "Anti-Guerrilla Warfare," pp. 1, 32–33. Compare the modern concept with Lt. Gen. Nelson A. Miles' formula for counter-Indian warfare, as found in Birtle, *Counterinsurgency Doctrine*, p. 69.

4

THE DEVELOPMENT OF
COUNTERINSURGENCY DOCTRINE
1945-1960

While American soldiers abroad cobbled together impromptu measures to fight the spate of insurgencies that erupted after 1945, back home the U.S. Army took its first steps toward developing a formal counterguerrilla doctrine. Finding a way to defeat the ongoing insurgencies was not the primary impulse for the effort. Rather, the driving force behind this, as well as most other defense initiatives during the early years of the Cold War, was the prospect of a major war with the Soviet Union. Since the Soviets had successfully employed partisans against Germany during World War II, U.S. Army planners fully expected that they would do so in any future conflict with the United States. Prudence dictated that the Army prepare for such a possibility.

In the late 1940s Army Field Forces was in charge of generating doctrine, but there was no fixed system for its development. Sometimes Army Field Forces assigned particularly knowledgeable individuals to write doctrine in their area of expertise. In other cases, it formed boards or committees. Most of the work was performed at Army branch schools, with each school writing manuals applicable to its branch of service. In the case of guerrilla warfare, the Army chose to assign the job of writing initial doctrine to a single individual, Lt. Col. Russell W. Volckmann.

Russell Volckmann was well qualified to write about irregular operations. A 1934 Military Academy graduate, Volckmann had been stationed in the Philippines when the Japanese invaded in December 1941. Rather than surrender with the rest of the Filipino-American forces in the spring of 1942, he escaped from Bataan and made his way to the mountains of northern Luzon. Over the next three years he fought behind the lines, organizing a large guerrilla force that eventually helped liberate the Philippines. Consequently, when Army Field Forces decided that it needed someone to develop doctrine on irregular warfare, Volckmann seemed a logical choice. In 1949 the Army sent him to the Infantry School at Fort Benning to write a pair of manuals on guerrilla and counterguerrilla warfare—the first U.S. Army manuals devoted entirely to these subjects. Published in 1951, these manuals arrived too late to influence the Chinese and Greek civil wars but were employed during the later stages of the Korean and Philippine conflicts. They became the basis of all future Army counterguerrilla doctrine.[1]

Sources of Doctrine

In formulating counterguerrilla doctrine during the late 1940s and early 1950s, Volckmann and subsequent doctrinal writers drew from several sources. Past American experience in counterguerrilla operations played a role, although in a general way, because few soldiers had any detailed knowledge of these events in the Army's history. Occupation duties during and immediately after World War II were perhaps more influential, and many of the principles that eventually emerged in the new manuals reflected the Army's recent experiences with military government. Perhaps most influential, however, were the precedents established by the Axis powers in combating Allied resistance movements.

Axis experience, and the lessons derived therefrom, reached American doctrine writers in a variety of ways. Some, like Volckmann, had experienced Axis countermeasures firsthand as members of Allied partisan units. A more indirect method of transmission occurred as a result of America's involvement in the postwar insurgencies. Most of the countries afflicted with Communist rebellions after 1945 had been occupied by the Axis during the war, and their newly reconstituted armies were staffed by men who had served either in Axis collaborationist units or in wartime resistance movements. Not surprisingly, these men applied their knowledge of Axis methods during the post-1945 civil wars, and American observers picked up on their example.[2]

To such personal and indirect modes of transmission the Army added deliberate and direct study of Axis methods, most notably those of Nazi Germany. During the war the Allies had collected and

Colonel Volckmann in the Philippines at the end of World War II

disseminated much information about German antipartisan techniques. This effort had not been a mere academic exercise, for the Allies believed that Germany might resort to guerrilla warfare to resist an Allied occupation. Since the Allies did not have any immediate experience in counterguerrilla warfare themselves, they published doctrinal pamphlets prescribing German counterguerrilla techniques should Adolf Hitler's threatened "Werewolf" guerrilla movement come to life. This approach continued into the postwar era when, in November 1947, an Army report specifically called for the study of German counterguerrilla methods as a vehicle for the development of American doctrine. Volckmann adopted this methodology, using not only the Allied pamphlets, but a U.S. Army translation of the German Army's basic counterguerrilla treatise, the 1944 manual *Fighting the Guerrilla Bands*.[3]

The postwar Army added to this body of knowledge through an intensive historical program. By 1949 U.S. Army, Europe, had sponsored 721 historical studies written by German officers about their wartime experiences. Twenty-one of these monographs were devoted entirely to partisan and antipartisan warfare, while another forty-four touched on these subjects in varying degrees. After the outbreak of the Korean War, the chief of Army Field Forces, with the help of the chief of military history, immediately distributed all of this information to help commanders develop techniques to use against Korean guerrillas.[4] The Army followed up this release by producing a special series of sixteen German-derived pamphlets that it distributed to every unit down to the battalion level. Two of the sixteen were devoted to antiguerrilla operations, while another five touched on the subject. The distribution of these reports, coupled with their distillation in Army journals and curricular materials, ensured that the lessons of Germany's counterguerrilla operations during World War II would exert a profound influence over American doctrine for many years.[5]

FM 31–20, Operations Against Guerrilla Forces

Based largely on this distillation of World War II experience, Volckmann produced a draft counterguerrilla manual in May 1950. The relevance of this document became immediately apparent when, the following month, the Army found itself pitted against Communist guerrillas and infiltrators in South Korea. Because the Army's doctrinal system would take some time to publish the urgently needed manual, the Infantry School rushed the manuscript into print in September 1950 as Special Text (ST) 31–20–1, "Operations Against Guerrilla Forces." The Army formally published Volckmann's work as FM 31–20, *Operations Against Guerrilla Forces*, five months later, in February 1951.

Recognizing that guerrilla warfare could take various forms, from partisan activities during an otherwise conventional conflict to "a people's war or revolution against existing authority," Volckmann decided to focus the manual on two types of situations. The first was conflicts "conducted by irregular forces (supported by an external power) to bring about a change in the social-political order of a country without engaging it in a formal, declared war," as had occurred in Greece and South Korea prior to 1950. The second was operations conducted by irregulars in conjunction with regular forces as part of a conventional war, as had been practiced by the Soviet Union during World War II. In both situations, Volckmann believed guerrillas required a secure base or cross-border sanctuary, external material aid, and an extensive clandestine network of intelligence agents, propagandists, organizers, and support personnel. He also expressed the traditional view that guerrillas were rarely capable of achieving victory without the support of regularly trained and equipped forces. Finally, he acknowledged that guerrilla warfare had significant political and economic components and that a guerrilla movement could not survive unless it had the support of the population, upon which it depended for recruits, labor, food, shelter, and intelligence. This recognition played an important part in FM 31–20's counterguerrilla strategy.[6]

Volckmann asserted that preventing the formation of a guerrilla movement was easier than destroying it. Consequently, the manual advocated the creation of proactive political, economic, security, and intelligence measures to redress the causes of discontent or, should this fail, to suppress potential resistance before it could evolve into a full-scale insurgency. The first step in any counterinsurgency program was to formulate "a broad, realistic" politico-military plan that was "based on a detailed analysis of a country, the national characteristics, and the customs, beliefs, cares, hopes, and desires of the people."

Such a plan, the manual stated, offered "the best solution to prevent, minimize and combat guerrilla warfare," for "political, administrative, economic, and military policies, intelligently conceived, wisely executed, and supported by appropriate propaganda, will minimize the possibility of a massive resistance movement." This prescription was one of the major lessons of Germany's failed Russian campaign, as Hitler's oppressive and exploitative polices had fomented, rather than quelled, resistance. FM 31–20 specifically enjoined its readers not to make the same mistake.[7]

While acknowledging the importance of politics in guerrilla warfare, the manual refrained from prescribing a set political program for counterinsurgency, both because Volckmann understood that each situation was unique and because the formulation of policy was largely outside the Army's purview. The manual therefore confined its suggestions to general themes that had guided past American occupation, pacification, and nation-building operations. Specifically, it enjoined commanders to foster trust and goodwill between the Army and the people by restoring law, order, and socioeconomic stability; by providing humanitarian relief; and by initiating programs to alleviate some of the grievances that might fuel resistance movements.[8]

Although political measures were important, Volckmann maintained that intelligence, propaganda, and military force were equally necessary. Good intelligence was fundamental to the formulation of both pacification and military plans. FM 31–20 therefore advocated giving commanders more intelligence and counterintelligence personnel than would normally be allocated for conventional operations. Psychological warfare specialists were equally important to win over the population against the irregulars, while military force provided the fuel that propelled the entire campaign forward. Volckmann also believed that commanders should employ sufficiently large and capable forces, both to maximize the chance of a quick battlefield victory and to overawe the opposition and avoid any perception of weakness that might encourage further resistance.[9]

Armed with a comprehensive, coordinated politico-military plan backed by adequate intelligence, psychological, and military resources, a commander was ready to undertake pacification operations. For analytical purposes, Volckmann introduced the concept of dividing the theater of operations into three zones: areas controlled by the guerrillas, areas controlled by the government, and the contested areas that usually lay between the first two zones. Under the normal sequence of events prescribed by the manual, a commander would move his troops into a contested or guerrilla-controlled zone, establish bases, and inaugurate necessary security measures. He would next erect a military government according to standard American doctrine, enacting political, economic, financial, and propaganda measures designed to restore an atmosphere of normalcy and redress certain grievances. If appropriate, commanders could also institute an amnesty program.[10]

Throughout this process, the manual stressed the importance of maintaining continuity in both policy and personnel. Continuity of policy was important lest frequent shifts confuse or unsettle the inhabitants. Continuity in personnel was necessary so that the soldiers would become fully acclimated to the local political and military situation. Rotating troops before they had a chance to gain and utilize this knowledge would be self-defeating, a lesson the Germans had learned in Europe and that Volckmann himself had observed when, as a guerrilla commander in the Philippines, he had profited from Japanese troop rotations. Also drawing from personal experience, Volckmann noted how guerrillas benefited when regional commanders failed to coordinate their actions, and he urged his readers not to create situations in which guerrillas could evade counterguerrilla operations in one sector simply by crossing an administrative boundary into another.[11]

Once the army had occupied an area and established politico-military measures to assert government authority, the stage was set for undertaking military operations. FM 31–20 set three objectives for all counterguerrilla operations. The first was to isolate the guerrillas from the civilian population from which they drew their support. While sound policies and propaganda wooed the population, military and police operations would break up the guerrilla bands and drive them away from populated areas. Acknowledging that people were often reluctant to assist authorities unless they were protected from guerrilla retaliation, the manual urged the formation of village self-defense groups. It also called for the imposition of controls over human and materiel resources. Included in the commander's arsenal were the issuance of civilian identity cards; the imposition of restrictions on movement, assembly, communications, and speech; curfews; village searches; and regulations governing the possession and transportation of certain commodities, most notably food, weapons, and medicines. FM 31–20 also authorized commanders to evacuate entire areas to sever the links between the local population and the guerrillas.[12]

Although Volckmann hoped that commanders would exercise intelligence and restraint in imposing these measures, he did not shrink from advocating more drastic actions, noting that "a firm, and if necessary harsh, attitude is necessary in dealing with the guerrillas and their civilian supporters. . . . Rigid military government control and stern administrative measures are imposed on a populace collaborating with hostile guerrilla forces."[13] While eschewing Axis barbarity and cautioning against excessive punishments that might drive previously uncommitted civilians into the enemy camp, the manual insisted that "the rules of land warfare place upon the civilian population of an occupied area the obligation to take no part whatsoever in hostilities and authorize the occupier to demand and enforce compliance." Among the more severe actions FM 31–20 permitted were the taking of hostages, the placement of hostages on trains and in convoys to deter attack, and retaliatory measures, including "reprisals against civilians living near" the site of an ambush.[14]

None of these measures were new. The United States and many other nations had availed themselves of these tools prior to 1939, though this had not stopped the Allies from labeling similar Axis acts as evidence of "totalitarianism." Indeed, an article written to disseminate FM 31–20's precepts during the Korean War ruefully admitted that "we find ourselves somewhat embarrassed by our criticism of such measures used by our enemies during World War II." The uneasy juxtaposition of severity and moderation in the manual created the possibility of confusion among readers, yet it also reflected a fundamental truth about the nature of guerrilla warfare—that, no matter how distasteful, repressive actions under certain circumstances could be effective and, consequently, had to remain in the counterinsurgent's arsenal. FM 31–20's mixed message with regard to the treatment of a population under conditions of irregular warfare thus reflected the symbiotic relationship that benevolence and repression had long enjoyed in American military thought and practice.[15]

The second major counterinsurgent objective after isolating the guerrillas from the population was to deny them access to external support. The manual did not offer any suggestions on how this goal could be achieved, since the elimination of external aid was largely a function of diplomatic, military, and geographical conditions specific to the conflict. Consequently, the manual proceeded to the third major objective of a counterinsurgency campaign, destroying the guerrillas.

Operationally, FM 31–20 called for continuous, aggressive, offensive action and vigorous combat patrolling to break up, harass, and ultimately destroy the guerrillas. It advised commanders to regard lulls in guerrilla activity with suspicion, lest the enemy be given time to rest and recover. It particularly cautioned against suspending operations too early, advocating that areas be thoroughly cleansed before moving troops on to the next sector targeted for pacification. Although FM

31–20 copied German security techniques for the protection of installations and lines of communications, it also embraced the German view that purely defensive measures sapped Army morale and ceded the initiative to the enemy, thereby allowing a guerrilla movement to grow. Maintaining the offensive, in contrast, not only compelled the guerrillas to look to their own survival, but enhanced the Army's image among the population, as experience had shown that people frequently sided with whoever seemed to have the upper hand. The object of offensive action in counterguerrilla warfare was thus not only the destruction of the enemy's combat forces, but also of his will and the will of his civilian supporters. The mere capture of terrain, on the other hand, was not an objective, as guerrillas rarely accepted set-piece battles and easily reinfiltrated areas captured by government forces once the regulars had departed. Only by targeting the guerrillas and the elements that sustained them—their command and control system, their sources of food and supply, and their clandestine network among the people—could the counterinsurgent gain decisive results.[16]

Volckmann believed that basic military principles applied to irregular warfare much as they did to conventional conflicts but that doctrine and tactics had to be adapted to the circumstances at hand. He further warned that "the scope and nature of a commander's mission may include political and administrative aspects seldom encountered in normal operations. The methods and technique of combat that commanders have been trained to apply within their parent organizations may have to be modified or even disregarded." Since these adaptations would necessarily be situation specific, he did not lay down fixed procedures, preferring instead to confine his discussion to general principles. He advocated obtaining mobility through initiative, improvisation, and intelligent tailoring of forces, noting the special advantages of airborne units and the great potential offered by a newfangled machine, the helicopter. He advised commanders to inculcate a spirit of alertness and observation in their men for intelligence, counterintelligence, and force protection purposes. He also recommended the use of cover plans, deception, and security restrictions to prevent the enemy from learning about upcoming actions. He suggested that counterinsurgents conduct operations at night, in inclement weather, or along unanticipated avenues of approach for similar reasons. Finally, he noted that in the search for mobility and surprise, emphasis would naturally shift from large formations to small, highly mobile units capable of operating with the dexterity, speed, and stealth necessary to hunt elusive guerrilla bands across varied terrain.[17]

Although conventional infantry units would doubtlessly form the backbone of any counterguerrilla campaign, Volckmann believed that elite antiguerrilla units would often prove more effective, and FM 31–20 urged commanders to supplement their regular infantry with such formations. Inspired by Germany's antipartisan *Jagdkommando* units of World War II, the manual described the organization, training, and functions of a prototype counterguerrilla unit of roughly platoon size. Designed to operate independently for prolonged periods, specially trained antiguerrilla units were to be devoid of impedimenta, armed with light, automatic weapons, and outfitted with plenty of radios in order to coordinate dispersed operations, report enemy sightings, and request assistance. Volckmann envisioned that these units would operate largely at night, employing guerrilla tactics to raid, ambush, and harass the enemy. The manual also suggested that antipartisan units occasionally masquerade as guerrillas to deceive the irregulars and their civilian supporters.[18]

A second category of troops endorsed by the manual was the indigenous unit. FM 31–20 encouraged U.S. commanders to use local civilians as intelligence agents, propagandists, administrators, guides, policemen, and special antiguerrilla troops. Care was required to screen such personnel for enemy infiltrators and spies, but once trustworthy natives had been found, they were invaluable, not only because they freed U.S. troops for other duties, but because their familiarity with the population, language, and terrain endowed them with a unique ability to uncover enemy guerrillas and their civilian supporters. Friendly guerrillas were also useful, while the manual advised that clever policies and propaganda could be used to divide the population and pit rival enemy bands against each other.[19]

With regard to the other combat arms, FM 31–20 had little to say. Armor was useful in securing roads and convoys and in supporting offensive operations when terrain conditions permitted. Although tanks might prove particularly demoralizing to untrained irregulars, FM 31–20 cautioned that they must be accompanied by infantry, as guerrillas often were adept at devising makeshift antitank devices. The manual deemed reconnaissance and ground attack aircraft to be especially valuable but stated that conventional methods for orchestrating air support would not be flexible enough to meet the demands of counterguerrilla warfare, and it suggested ways in which the existing air control system could be modified for counterguerrilla work. Finally, FM 31–20 noted that the dispersed nature of guerrilla warfare and the rugged terrain in which irregulars usually operated greatly limited the usefulness of artillery in antiguerrilla operations. Flexibility, ingenuity, and resourcefulness were required to overcome these obstacles. The manual suggested that covert reconnaissance teams scout out possible artillery positions so that the guns could deploy rapidly just prior to an attack. Once established, artillery positions were to be laid out for all-round defense, using fortifications and attached infantry to secure their perimeters. Because of the limitations and hazards of ground movement and the problems that rough terrain posed to communications, aircraft would be used to supply firing positions, to relay messages between ground observers and artillery units, and to serve as airborne fire direction centers.[20]

In addition to frequent small-unit patrolling, Volckmann envisioned three types of offensive action—encirclement, attack, and pursuit. On this subject he most closely followed the precepts laid down by the German 1944 manual, copying not only the form and substance of *Wehrmacht* tactical doctrine, but the illustrative diagrams as well. The Germans had deemed encirclements—often executed on a large scale—to be the best single method of bringing the guerrillas to battle, and the U.S. Army agreed. Detailed planning, secrecy, and deception; efficient communications; rapid movements; and adequate forces were required if the Army was to surround the targeted area before the enemy learned of the operation and fled. Encirclements were to be made in depth to prevent enemy exfiltration, with the lead troops establishing defensive positions immediately upon arrival on the line of encirclement to repel breakout attempts.[21]

Once an area had been sealed, FM 31–20 offered commanders four different ways to reduce the pocket, all of which were derived from German practice. The first method, labeled "tightening the encirclement" (or "tightening the noose"), was to be used when the encircled area was small and the enemy weak and consisted of a simultaneous advance around the entire perimeter. The second, or "hammer and anvil," technique involved an advance by only a portion of the encircling forces, while the remaining elements waited for the guerrillas to be driven upon their defensive positions, which were often established along some barrier or obstacle. The third approach consisted of sending one or more forces into the encircled area, splitting it into two or more smaller pockets, which were then reduced piecemeal. Finally, the fourth tactic, which was to be used when the guerrillas had established a strong fortified position, employed a powerful assault force to overrun the main guerrilla bastion. Once this had been achieved, the encircling forces would advance to mop up the remaining resistance.[22]

Regardless of the means employed, once the encirclement had been cast the subsequent reduction was to be performed methodically and without haste. The Army would arrest and interrogate all civilians found inside the targeted area. Successive waves of troops would comb every possible hiding place for fugitives and hidden supplies. Meanwhile, small patrols would keep the remaining guerrillas on the run, wearing them down and increasing their vulnerability to psychological warfare initiatives. Volckmann believed that prolonged, in-depth area control measures such as these would ultimately produce more casualties on the guerrillas than those inflicted by the front-line troops during the initial encirclement, and consequently he deemed them critical to the ultimate outcome of any operation.

While he considered encirclement to be the most effective tactic in the counterguerrilla's arsenal, Volckmann acknowledged that guerrilla elusiveness, difficult terrain, and shortages of time and manpower often made encirclements impossible. He therefore offered the surprise attack as a secondary tactic. Achieving surprise against wary guerrillas was admittedly difficult, and Volckmann advocated using small parties of scouts and native guides to locate and shadow the enemy, with the remainder of the column moving up rapidly, usually at night, to launch a surprise dawn assault. If possible, a single or double envelopment would be used, as the goal was to destroy the guerrillas, not to disperse them or to capture ground. Since irregulars usually lacked supporting weapons, Volckmann directed the attacker to close with the enemy more rapidly than would be customary against regular forces in conventional combat.[23]

Should any guerrillas escape from either an encirclement or an attack, FM 31–20 called for pursuit, the third form of offensive operations. Antiguerrilla formations and small units of regulars linked by radio to mobile reserves and aerial and artillery support were to hound the guerrillas relentlessly. Contact, once gained, was never to be lost, until such time as the guerrillas had been run to earth. Only in this manner could the Army achieve the ultimate destruction of an irregular opponent.[24]

Having presented a broad operational framework and suggested some specific techniques, Volckmann offered some cautionary advice. He warned that guerrillas often scavenged supplies from their enemies, and he urged soldiers to police their camps and to exercise strict supply discipline to prevent materiel from falling into guerrilla hands. He also alerted commanders about the unusual morale problems associated with guerrilla warfare. Counterguerrilla service was especially enervating because it involved placing small detachments of soldiers in relatively isolated locations for prolonged periods amid a population with whom the soldiers could neither readily communicate nor fully trust. Frustrated by their inability to come to grips with an elusive opponent and discouraged by the seemingly endless routine of garrison duty and fruitless patrols, soldiers might become abusive toward civilians or lose the aggressive, offensive edge called for by doctrine. To avoid these pitfalls, Volckmann urged commanders to inculcate strong leadership traits among their junior leaders and to initiate troop indoctrination programs. He also recommended that commanders adopt policies that kept troops in one location long enough for the soldiers to operate with intelligence, skill, and confidence.[25]

Operations Against Guerrilla Forces represented a major milestone in the evolution of U.S. Army doctrine. By blending traditional American concepts with German military practices, World War II lessons, and some fresh insights, the manual filled an important gap in official doctrinal literature. Although it made no reference to Mao Tse-tung or the rising tide of third world insurgencies in which U.S. Army personnel were increasingly engaged, FM 31–20 (1951) related enduring principles relevant to a wide range of counterguerrilla situations. Among the manual's most salient concepts were its emphasis on flexibility, adaptability, mobility, security, and surprise; its recognition that prevention and early action were better than a massive, but belated, military response; and its call for careful politico-military planning and coordination. Although it did not elaborate on exactly how one could achieve the complicated integration of political and military measures, the thrust of this strategy was sound, as was the doctrine's central goal of cutting the guerrilla off both physically and spiritually from all sources of assistance. Together with the operational, tactical, and training advice contained in its pages, the manual gave officers a solid basis on which to craft situation-specific counterguerrilla campaigns.

The Evolution of Army Doctrinal Literature, 1951–1958

FM 31–20's precepts were widely disseminated during the early 1950s, thanks largely to the Korean War. Not only had the Army distributed a pre-publication version of the manual (ST 31–20–1) in late 1950, but it immediately followed up the publication of the manual in February 1951 by printing a digested version of the doctrine in *Officer's Call*, an official publication that brought important subjects to the attention of the officer corps. The extensive circulation of several studies on German counterguerrilla methods during World War II—studies that Volckmann had used in preparing the manual—reinforced the new doctrine, as did the publication of a number of articles examining post-1940 guerrilla conflicts.[26]

While the publication of FM 31–20 in 1951 represented both the first and most important step by the Army in the field of irregular warfare doctrine, it was not the final step. Although much of the urgency behind the dissemination of counterguerrilla doctrine faded after the conclusion of the Korean War, third world instability and the potential threat of a war with the Soviet Union mandated continued interest, albeit at a lower level of intensity.

The first manual to discuss issues related to counterguerrilla warfare after the publication of FM 31–20 (1951) was FM 31–21, *Organization and Conduct of Guerrilla Warfare*. Published eight months after FM 31–20, FM 31–21 was Volckmann's companion piece to the counterguerrilla manual. Based like its counterpart on World War II experience, FM 31–21 described the nature, organization, and methods of guerrilla warfare with an eye toward the use of such techniques by U.S. forces during a conventional war. Though the manual did not prescribe counterguerrilla tactics, it served as a useful adjunct to counterinsurgent planners, for whom understanding the enemy was the first step toward defeating him.

Of equal interest to soldiers charged with counterguerrilla duties was a formal "change" made by the Department of the Army in July 1952 to the 1949 edition of FM 100–5.[27] The update, which represented the first modification to the Army's basic combat manual since the outbreak of the Korean War, added a new section on "Security Against Airborne Attack, Guerrilla Action, and Infiltration." The ten-page addendum reflected the Army's growing concern over the threat that guerrillas and partisans posed to Army rear areas during a conventional war. It focused on ways to protect rear areas without having to divert too many combat forces from the battlefront. Among the measures recommended were the establishment of comprehensive warning and communications systems, the use of convoys, air and ground patrols, and guards to keep lines of communications open, and the creation of self-defending service and supply installations reinforced, when necessary, by mobile reaction forces. Although largely defensive in nature, the addendum also elevated into FM 100–5 certain key concepts from FM 31–20 concerning the nature of guerrilla and counterguerrilla action. Included among these were the necessity of good intelligence and the utility of local civilians in obtaining it; the importance of maintaining continuity in command, policy, and personnel; the value of security, mobility, and surprise; the use of encirclement tactics aided by airborne or heliborne troops; the merits of forming special antiguerrilla units; and the necessity of isolating guerrillas from the civilian population. While this last point could be achieved partly through military and security measures, "more important," the insert explained, "is the necessity for winning the support of the indigenous population away from the guerrillas and infiltrators. This can best be accomplished by the establishment of cooperation and good will between the civil population and the military forces. . . . Adherence to basic military government principles will do much toward diverting the civil population from activities designed to prevent the maintenance of good order and public safety. Propaganda plays an important part in winning the good will and trust of the local populace."[28]

By incorporating some of the principles contained in FM 31–20 into FM 100–5—one of the Army's most widely read manuals—the Department of the Army further ensured their dissemination throughout the force as a whole. Still, the Army believed that doctrinal gaps remained, not so much in terms of the overall concept of counterirregular warfare, but in the specifics of rear area defense. Consequently, in 1953 the Army published FM 31–15, *Operations Against Airborne Attack, Guerrilla Action, and Infiltration*. Designed to flesh out the general concepts expressed in the 1952 change to FM 100–5, FM 31–15 focused on the organizational and operational details involved in orchestrating the defense of a rear area during a conventional war. Its coverage of counterguerrilla warfare was truncated and incomplete, not because the subject was unimportant, but because counterirregular operations had already been covered in FM 31–20. FM 31–15 was thus not meant to replace FM 31–20, but rather to supplement it, and the new manual frequently referred readers to FM 31–20 and FM 31–21 for more specific information about guerrilla and counterguerrilla warfare. Nevertheless, the 1953 manual was careful to reiterate many of the themes contained in earlier doctrine. It repeatedly noted the important role the population played in supporting enemy irregulars and the necessity of severing this relationship through a combination of military, police, intelligence, psychological, resource-control, and political measures. Thus FM 31–15 stated that "the scope of rear area defense involves consideration of matters that are not purely military in nature, but may exert tremendous influence on the military operations to be conducted," and it repeated FM 31–20's call for the careful coordination of the "purely military effort with the political, administrative, and economic aspects of the over-all plan." "Failure to recognize and apply necessary nonmilitary measures," the manual continued, "may render military operations ineffective, regardless of how well these operations are planned and conducted."[29]

Despite these warnings, FM 31–15 did not discuss the nonmilitary aspects of rear area security in detail, partly because these were covered to an extent in the Army's civil affairs manuals and partly because the Army believed that the formulation of policies pertaining to the internal affairs of foreign countries was beyond its bailiwick. Though the manual endorsed the close coordination of political and military measures, it specifically stated that "the conduct of political and economic warfare is not a function of the armed forces," and it limited the Army's participation in the execution of such programs to "auxiliary action." Apparently, the Army felt uncomfortable with such a flat renunciation of responsibility because the following year it changed the wording to state that the conduct of political and economic warfare was not a *"primary"* function of the armed forces, thereby opening the door to its participation in such matters.[30]

No sooner had the Army published FM 31–15 than it began again revising FM 100–5, *Field Service Regulations, Operations*. The revision had two goals: to incorporate the lessons of the Korean conflict and to help prepare the Army for the defense of Western Europe against a Soviet invasion, a mission that had evolved in earnest only after the publication of the last full edition of FM 100–5 in 1949. As part of this effort, the Army commissioned six German officers led by Franz Halder, the former chief of the German General Staff, to critique the 1949 edition of FM 100–5 in light of their experience fighting the Russians. Halder's report, which was distributed to Army doctrine writers in the spring of 1953, concluded that

as an army manual, FM 100–5, just as did our own pre-war service regulations, overlooks the presence of the civilian population inhabiting the combat area. . . . However, the population of an area touched by war, whether friendly or hostile, will frequently confront not only the higher command but also the combat forces with problems which affect even tactics and which must not find them unprepared. Aside from such hindrances as the mass flight of civilians, problems of supply, and similar considerations, the main problem is that of coping with partisan warfare. Today a service manual must cover this aspect fully.[31]

In the opinion of the German commentators, the 1949 version of FM 100–5 fell short in this regard, so much so that they took the trouble of writing an entirely new partisan warfare section that they recommended be included in FM 100–5. In actuality, the Halder report had no influence over the treatment of irregular warfare in the new edition of FM 100–5, not because the Army did not value the Germans' opinions, but because it had already incorporated them into official doctrine, both in FM 31–20 (1951), and in the 1952 change to FM 100–5, neither of which had been provided to the German analysts. The report did, however, serve as additional confirmation of the direction in which the Army was already moving, as demonstrated by the remarkable similarity between the ideas expressed by Halder's group and those that had already been incorporated into U.S. doctrine based on the Army's previous study of the German experience.[32]

The new edition of FM 100–5 that appeared in 1954 thus broke no new ground with regard to antiguerrilla warfare. Central to its approach was the notion that

Guerrilla forces cannot exist without civilian support. Consequently, every effort should be made to prevent them from receiving this support. Such an effort consists of physically isolating guerrilla forces from each other and both physically and psychologically separating them from the civilian population. This requires gaining and maintaining the support of the indigenous population. This can best be accomplished by the establishment of goodwill between the civil population and the military forces; and rewards for friendly assistance, and punishment for collaboration with guerrillas. In those instances where control of the indigenous government is vested in the commander adherence to principles of good military government will do much toward accomplishing the above. Propaganda, followed by implementation of promises, plays an important part in winning the goodwill and trust of the local populace.[33]

For the most part, the manual limited its coverage of irregular warfare to broad, yet important, statements of principle, referring its readers to FMs 31–20 (1951), 31–21 (1951), and 31–15 (1953) for details. It did, however, include several additional points that touched, albeit indirectly, on the issue of counterguerrilla operations. Among these were its assertion that the doctrines, tactics, and techniques contained in its pages were merely guidelines that commanders were expected to modify as circumstances warranted, and its recognition that, since "war is a political act," military means and objectives had to be tailored to meet political ends. Both of these points, if taken to heart, had significant implications for counterguerrilla and pacification operations.[34]

Following the publication of FM 100–5 in 1954, the Army moved to revise many of its other manuals during the mid-1950s. In 1955 it updated the 1949 edition of FM 33–5, *Psychological Warfare Operations*. The new edition mentioned counterguerrilla operations only briefly and was bereft of information on Communist insurgent movements, a significant failing. On the other hand, it was the first Army psychological warfare (psywar) manual to include a discussion of consolidation psychological warfare, that branch of the persuasive arts directed toward friendly and occupied populations. The manual recognized the advantages of providing food, shelter, and economic rehabilitation to help win public support but also warned against making promises that one could not keep. It understood the psychological importance of military success and personal security, noting that civilians who believed that the enemy might return would be reluctant to cooperate with friendly forces in fear of retaliation, while those who were convinced that their security was assured would be more willing to cooperate with the Army.[35]

Of potentially greater import for counterinsurgency was FM 27–10, *The Law of Land Warfare*, published in 1956. This manual officially incorporated the results of the 1949 Geneva Convention into Army doctrine. Yet, other than extending some of the protections afforded to civilians and prisoners in international conflicts to conflicts "not of an international character," the new rules changed very little with regard to American doctrine. Hostage taking, long accepted in Army regulations, was now banned, and the manual repeated traditional proscriptions against cruelty, torture, pillage, and personal misconduct.[36] The manual frowned on devastation, unless there was "some reasonably close connection between the destruction of property and the overcoming of the enemy's army," a caveat that counterinsurgents could use to justify the destruction of food and shelter in guerrilla-dominated areas.[37] It also repeated international law's long-standing refusal to accord captured guerrillas prisoner-of-war status unless they were organized under a responsible command, wore distinctive insignia, bore their arms openly, and conducted themselves in accordance with the laws of war. Individuals who violated these rules by concealing their weapons or otherwise masking their identity as combatants could be put on trial and punished, possibly by death. Finally, FM 27–10 (1956) noted that the Geneva Convention permitted armed forces to "undertake total or partial evacuation of a given area if the security of the population or imperative military reasons so demanded," a precept that sanctioned the counterinsurgent tactic of population removal.[38]

Having set the legal parameters under which U.S. soldiers would conduct counterguerrilla and pacification operations, the Army proceeded to update its doctrine governing its relationship with foreign and occupied populations—the first such revision since 1947. Like most Army manuals, FM 41–10, *Civil Affairs Military Government Operations* (1957), had a distinctly conventional focus, yet it was profoundly relevant for counterguerrilla warfare because the Army would apply the manual's principles to all of the Army's dealings with civilian populations, regardless of the nature of the conflict. Moreover, since a major war with the Soviet Union might involve the occupation of enemy territory, American civil affairs planners were well aware that they needed to be prepared to neutralize the lingering vestiges of the

Communist political, military, and social apparatus—problems akin to those that would materialize in a counterinsurgency situation not associated with a major war. Consequently, the 1957 edition of FM 41–10 became the first civil affairs and military government manual to include a section specifically devoted to civil affairs' role in counter-guerrilla warfare.[39]

Like its predecessors, FM 41–10 (1957) prescribed a blend of prag-matic and humanitarian measures. Believing that guerrillas flourished under conditions of disorder and socioeconomic hardship, the manual called for the early restoration of law, order, and stability through the establishment of police and judicial services, the resumption of local government, the revitalization of economic and agricultural produc-tion, and the provision of humanitarian relief. Mobile clinics would treat the sick and demonstrate child care and sanitation techniques, military engineers would improve public infrastructures, and agricul-tural specialists would test soils and offer advice on animal husbandry. Such projects would be carefully planned and closely coordinated with local officials to ensure that they would meet the genuine needs and desires of the local population. Meanwhile, information, education, and propaganda programs would provide maximum publicity for these and other initiatives to ensure that the policies were understood and that the government received credit for its efforts. Finally, commanders were to encourage their subordinates to respect local beliefs and customs, to cultivate personal relationships with the population, and to exhibit proper behavior at all times to win public support for the government and the Army.[40]

While benevolence was by far the preferred policy, the manual called for sterner measures should the population respond to these overtures with continued resistance. Punishments were to be propor-tional to the offense, explained to the population, and crafted so as to minimize undue injury to innocent parties. Among the Army's more punitive weapons were censorship, population registration, restrictions on the movement of people and goods, licensing, fines, imprisonment, and reparations. Like FM 31–20 (1951), the manual deemed strict controls over the distribution of food, clothing, and medicines to be especially important in counterguerrilla warfare.

Although coercion had an important, if distasteful, role to play, FM 41–10 echoed other manuals in recognizing that the military had an obligation to protect the population from guerrilla coercion and exploitation. It likewise reiterated Army doctrine with respect to the use of natives in police, administrative, self-defense, reconnaissance, and intelligence capacities. On the other hand, while the manual declared that the military had the right to relocate civilians, it generally discouraged such actions. Forced evacuations disturbed social order; imposed significant burdens on the government for the transportation, resettlement, and care of the affected populations; and created resentment that was readily exploited by the enemy's propaganda machine.[41]

FM 41–10's uneasiness concerning population relocation highlighted an ambiguous doctrinal area. Although both the Axis powers and several Western nations, including the United States, had relocated populations during past counterguerrilla operations, Americans sometimes found such measures distasteful. Recent experiences in Korea and Greece, where removal schemes had proved effective but enormously disruptive and expensive, probably gave Americans further pause. Thus, while removal remained in the Army's official doctrinal repertoire during the 1950s, it was always regarded as merely one tool among many, and one that had to be handled carefully at that. Not until the end of the decade, when recent French and British experience seemed to demonstrate the virtues of relocation, did American writers begin to warm noticeably toward this technique.[42]

Although FM 41–10's consideration of guerrilla warfare was brief, the manual complemented earlier manuals that had focused more exclusively on the military aspects of counterinsurgency. Unfortunately, by the time it was published several changes had occurred that seriously eroded counterinsurgency's place in Army doctrine. The decline had begun in 1954, when Army Field Forces directed that doctrinal responsibility for counterguerrilla warfare be shifted from the Infantry School at Fort Benning, where Volckmann had written the doctrine, to the Psychological Warfare Center at Fort Bragg, North Carolina. It further ordered that FM 31–20 and FM 31–21 be merged into a single manual covering both guerrilla and counterguerrilla warfare. The transfer from Benning to Bragg was well intentioned and made a certain amount of sense. The Psychological Warfare Center was responsible for both psychological warfare and the Army's budding Special Forces organization, which was charged with conducting guerrilla warfare behind enemy lines. Since counterguerrilla warfare required some familiarity with both psychological and guerrilla warfare activities, Army Field Forces reckoned that Fort Bragg was the logical place to focus all of the Army's unconventional warfare endeavors. Besides, during the early 1950s the special warfare community, under the leadership of chief of Psychological Warfare Brig. Gen. Robert A. McClure, had been one of the leading proponents within the Army for studying counterguerrilla warfare.

There were, however, several countervailing factors. To begin with, the failure of enemy irregulars to play a decisive role in the now concluded Korean War had taken some of the urgency out of the Army's interest in counterguerrilla warfare. This decline in interest was noticeable not only in the Army as a whole, but in the special warfare community as well, which, after McClure's departure for another assignment in 1954, ranked counterguerrilla and consolidation psychological warfare at the very bottom of its list of priorities for unconventional warfare research. Indeed, the Psychological Warfare Center argued vigorously against Army Field Forces' decision to give it doctrinal responsibility for counterinsurgency on the grounds that "the tactics, doctrine and the conduct of anti-guerrilla operations is not the responsibility or mission of special forces." Army Field Forces overruled the objection, however, and counterinsurgency became the unwanted stepchild of the special warfare community.[43]

The inevitable result of this unhappy arrangement was that counterinsurgency doctrine suffered a slow death at the hands of its mentors at Fort Bragg, who gave little more than lip service to it during the remainder of the decade. The first step in this process occurred in 1955 when, at the direction of Army Field Forces, the Psychological Warfare Center released two new guerrilla warfare manuals. The first, *U.S. Army Special Forces Group (Airborne)*, bore the designation FM 31–20 but differed dramatically from the FM 31–20 of 1951 in that it was devoted exclusively to the tactics and techniques of American-sponsored guerrilla warfare. The second manual, *Guerrilla Warfare*, merged the two original Volckmann manuals of 1951—*Operations Against Guerrilla Forces* (FM 31–20) and *Organization and Conduct of Guerrilla Warfare* (FM 31–21)—into a single volume, designated FM 31–21.[44]

The intellectual thrust of the new FM 31–21 differed little from its 1951 progenitors. It reiterated most of the themes and much of the language of the earlier manuals, albeit in a reorganized and less verbose fashion. The 1955 manual was also a bit more reticent about employing stern tactics, as it shunned hostage taking and reprisals and dropped the word *harsh* from its description of acceptable control measures. Technology also played a somewhat greater role in the new doctrine, as FM 31–21 (1955) described small-unit heliborne operations that foreshadowed the "eagle flight" technique employed by American forces a decade later in Vietnam.[45]

Yet not all of the changes were positive, for in the process of distilling two manuals into one, the writers at Fort Bragg deleted some valuable information contained in the original FM 31–20. Gone were most of the historical examples as well as some of the useful insights, like the original manual's precautionary advice for soldiers to police their bivouacs to prevent guerrillas from salvaging supplies. The new manual curtailed much of its predecessor's discussion about the employment of artillery, armor, close air support, and special antiguerrilla units, and even gave less attention to the role of the population. Moreover, while the authors of *Guerrilla Warfare* had preserved many of the principles found in FM 31–20 (1951), in their quest to consolidate the Volckmann manuals they eliminated much of the explanatory material that had given these principles meaning. The result was a doctrinal product that, while more succinct, was less robust.

Matters were soon to become worse, however, for in 1958, the Army implemented a second consolidation that virtually eliminated counterguerrilla theory from U.S. Army doctrine altogether. The consolidation merged the 1955 versions of FM 31–20 and FM 31–21 into a single manual—FM 31–21, *Guerrilla Warfare and Special Forces Operations*. This new manual focused exclusively on guerrilla warfare and eliminated entirely the 1955 edition's counterguerrilla section. In a single stroke, the Army lost its most important source of information on counterguerrilla warfare. True, FM 31–15, *Operations Against Airborne Attack, Guerrilla Action, and Infiltration* (1953), remained in force, while FM 100–5 (1954), FM 41–10 (1957), and a few branch-level manuals contained small counterguerrilla sections. But the treatment of counterguerrilla warfare in these manuals was incomplete, in part because they had been written with the assumption that readers could always turn to either the original FM 31–20 (1951) or FM 31–21 (1955) for background. Indeed, they explicitly instructed their readers to do so. After 1958, however, detailed doctrine for counterguerrilla operations no longer existed in the family of Army manuals, leaving manuals like FMs 31–15 and 100–5 adrift, without the intellectual and conceptual moorings necessary for the formulation of a well-grounded understanding of the principal aspects of counterguerrilla warfare. Thus, after promising beginnings in 1951, by decade's end counterinsurgency doctrine had fallen into disarray.[46]

Counterinsurgency in the Educational and Training Systems

While manuals were the primary source of doctrine, soldiers also received exposure to counterinsurgency concepts in the classroom and on the training field. In 1948 the U.S. Army Command and General Staff College (CGSC) at Fort Leavenworth, Kansas, had become the first Army school after World War II to cover counterguerrilla warfare. The coverage was infinitesimal, consisting of just two pages out of a lecture devoted to the employment of partisans by U.S. forces during a

conventional war. The first real examination of counterguerrilla operations occurred at the Infantry School, which introduced the subject,
together with ST 31–20–1, in the fall of 1950 in reaction to the Korean
War. Thereafter, students enrolled in the infantry officer's advanced
course at Fort Benning received three hours of antiguerrilla warfare
instruction and one hour on the employment of friendly guerrillas.
Other institutions, including the Command and General Staff College
and the Armor, Engineer, Transportation, and Army General schools,
offered similar courses tailored to their particular specialties.[47]

Attention to counterguerrilla warfare quickly faded after the
Korean War. The Army War College at Carlisle Barracks, Pennsylvania,
which had virtually ignored the subject even during the height of the
war, continued to neglect it, preferring to devote what little time the
college spent on irregular conflict to the employment of friendly partisans in Eastern Europe. The Command and General Staff College
likewise refocused its partisan operations course exclusively on guerrilla, as opposed to counterguerrilla, warfare. Most other Army schools
omitted the subject entirely. Even the Infantry School cut its coverage
of counterguerrilla warfare in half after 1955.[48]

The disappearance of counterguerrilla studies from most military
curriculums during the second half of the 1950s, when coupled with
the subject's declining fortunes in Army manuals, meant that the number of officers exposed to the subject steadily diminished after 1955.
This is not to say, however, that the educational system completely
ignored counterinsurgency issues. To begin with, after 1954 all Reserve
Officers' Training Corps (ROTC) cadets received a brief introduction
to counterguerrilla warfare through ROTC manual 145–60, *Small Unit
Tactics, Including Communications.*[49] Moreover, there were many subjects taught in Army schools that were applicable in varying degrees to
a counterinsurgency environment. Among these were civil affairs and
military government, refugee control, military law and the laws of war,
mountain and jungle warfare, small-unit infantry tactics, riot control,
Special Forces operations, consolidation psychological warfare, and rear
area defense, not to mention basic intelligence, reconnaissance, and staff
techniques. Courses in civil affairs and rear area defense, as taught at the
Civil Affairs and Provost Marshal General's schools at Camp Gordon,
Georgia, and the Adjutant General's School at Camp Lee, Virginia,
were particularly relevant, especially since these courses continued to
be based on the original series of counterguerrilla works of 1950–1952,
thereby perpetuating some concepts that had faded from subsequent
doctrinal works. Finally, during the latter half of the 1950s, a new course
of instruction began to emerge, most notably at the Command and

General Staff College, on "situations short of war," a subject that was closely related to counterguerrilla and pacification issues.[50]

In addition to developing and disseminating course material, the Army education system encouraged the examination of doctrine through two other media—articles in the Army's professional journals and student papers. Between 1950 and 1960, Army professional journals published over forty articles that dealt to some degree with subjects related to counterguerrilla warfare and pacification. These articles, some of which were written by school instructors, represented a blend of historical studies, operational accounts, commentaries, and synopses of current doctrine which, taken collectively, furthered the dissemination of counterguerrilla doctrine to the Army as a whole.

Student papers received significantly less dissemination but provided valuable insights into the state of Army thinking, especially since some of them were explicitly written for the purpose of evaluating doctrine in response to school initiatives. Although World War II examples remained of enduring interest to students throughout the 1950s, by mid-decade student papers increasingly made reference to Maoist concepts and more contemporary foreign experiences, a trend that indicated that at least some officers were delving beyond the initial sources of American doctrine to examine new concepts.[51]

For the most part, the articles and student essays written by officers during the 1950s endorsed the principles expressed in FM 31–20 (1951) and its successors, concluding as had CGSC instructor and counterguerrilla veteran Lt. Col. John Beebe, that U.S. Army doctrine was "sound and adequate." Themes that received special attention included the importance of comprehensive politico-military planning and the necessity for separating the guerrillas from the population through a mixture of military action, propaganda, restrictive measures, and progressive social, political, and economic programs. Continuous offensive action remained the key to the military side of the equation, but nearly every writer during the 1950s appreciated the importance of nonmilitary factors in counterinsurgency operations. When disagreements emerged, they usually occurred over such topics as the wisdom of creating special counterinsurgency units or the relative merits of saturation patrolling versus large-scale encirclement operations. More pointedly, while most authors endorsed the general outline of existing doctrine, they fretted that it was not well understood within the officer corps as a whole, given the limited amount of time devoted to counterguerrilla subjects in the Army's pedagogical system.[52]

Officers who were dissatisfied with the amount of attention allocated to counterguerrilla subjects in Army classrooms were likewise

*U.S. Army cavalrymen playing the role of mounted guerrillas
during a counterguerrilla training exercise*

critical of the scant attention devoted to these areas in training. The
Army training system had virtually ignored counterguerrilla warfare
during the late 1940s. The seriousness of this omission was demonstrated in March 1950, when the 3d Infantry Division participated in a
Caribbean training exercise that included an "enemy" guerrilla force.
Organized by an OSS veteran, the "guerrillas" consisted of Puerto
Rican soldiers from the U.S. 65th Infantry, and a network of civilian
spies. The exercise proved somewhat embarrassing for the 3d Infantry
Division after the insurgents "killed" the division's entire command
element, "blew up" supply depots, and "ambushed" several troop columns, all without loss to themselves. The division protested the simulation as unfair, but several months later, both it and the 65th Infantry
were performing counterguerrilla duty in Korea against an opponent
who was deaf to cries of foul play.[53]

By the fall of 1950 Communist guerrillas had become sufficiently
bothersome to U.S. forces in Korea that the Army ordered that greater
attention be paid to antiguerrilla warfare throughout the training system. Indeed, the Korean experience and the threat that it would be
repeated in any war with the Soviet Union was sufficient to persuade
the Army to continue providing a modicum of counterguerrilla training throughout the remainder of the decade. Exposure to counterguerrilla warfare began in basic training, as all Army recruits during
the 1950s received four hours of antiguerrilla instruction. Training

regulations governing rifle companies required that antiguerrilla patrolling situations be included in advanced individual training for infantrymen, while in 1956 the Army published guidelines for an eight-hour block of anti-infiltration and antiguerrilla instruction as part of unit-level training. Throughout the decade the Army repeatedly directed commanders to integrate counterguerrilla subjects into all phases of training and instruction, including field exercises. Special Forces or other Army personnel sometimes played the role of hostile guerrillas in these exercises, while manuals and private publications by interested officers offered advice on how counterguerrilla training could best be accomplished. Most of this training revolved around individual soldier skills and defensive measures, such as the protection of march columns, convoys, bivouacs, and installations—subjects that were applicable to all forms of irregular combat but which reflected the Army's particular preoccupation with rear area security during a conventional conflict. Offensive antiguerrilla operations, when included in training, were almost always restricted to squad-, platoon-, and company-level patrols, raids, and ambushes.[54]

Other areas of training that occasionally touched on subjects related to irregular warfare and pacification included civil affairs, "population control," and Ranger training. Of these, Ranger training was particularly important. Senior Army leaders were enamored with the Ranger concept during the 1950s, and, after the abortive experiment with Ranger units during the early stages of the Korean War, the Department of the Army directed that all newly commissioned Regular Army infantry, armor, artillery, engineer, military police, and signal corps officers receive either Ranger or airborne training. The five- to seven-week course at Fort Benning focused on individual combat and survival skills, physical conditioning, fieldcraft, mountain, jungle, swamp, and amphibious operations, patrolling, and small-unit tactics—exactly the type of knowledge that was at a premium in counterguerrilla warfare. The Army's goal was to have at least one Ranger-trained officer in each rifle company and one Ranger-qualified noncommissioned officer in each rifle platoon who would then spread their knowledge throughout the infantry force. The effort proved so popular that several divisions began Ranger training for entire units, and in 1957 the Army published FM 21–50, *Ranger Training*, to help commanders establish such courses. Not only was the manual devoted to subjects that were useful in combating guerrillas, like ambush and counterambush techniques, but it also contained a brief concept for counterguerrilla operations. According to this concept, a liberal use of troop-carrying aircraft and helicopters would permit a relatively small number of highly trained

"Guerrillas" ambush an unsuspecting soldier during a training exercise.

infantrymen to control large areas through airmobile reconnaissance, strike, and patrol actions.[55]

A final genre of training applicable to irregular warfare was night combat. The basic infantry officers course at Fort Benning included thirty hours of training in nighttime guerrilla and counterguerrilla operations, while Army regulations required that at least one-third of all applicatory stages of tactical and movement training be conducted at night. Such an edict, if obeyed, would have greatly improved the ability of U.S. soldiers to operate during the guerrillas' favorite time of day. Unfortunately, the regulation was not always observed because commanders considered night training difficult and burdensome.[56]

The Army's failure to train aggressively at night illustrates the difficulty of evaluating the state of counterguerrilla training during the 1950s. Unlike night training that, in theory at least, was mandatory, most counterguerrilla training was optional, to be integrated into a unit's normal training regimen at the discretion of the commander. Consequently, proficiency varied widely from unit to unit. Given the diminishing attention devoted to counterguerrilla subjects in Army manuals and schools during the mid-1950s, the Army's repeated exhortations that counterguerrilla subjects be treated as a normal part of training were not likely taken to heart during the second half of the decade. Moreover, the Army sent out conflicting signals. While it encouraged the integration of irregular warfare into exercises, it cautioned that "guerrilla operations must be carefully planned and controlled in order

156

to prevent undue interference with the planned progress of the maneuver and the accomplishment of other maneuver objectives." Concerns over safety and controllability similarly limited the involvement of civilians in exercises, as well as the wearing of civilian clothing by the "guerrillas," restrictions that further compromised the realism of Army maneuvers. The result was that many counterguerrilla exercises were of limited value, consisting largely of road-bound patrols and disappointing sweeps.[57]

This was not, however, universally the case. For example, during Exercise DEVILSTRIKE in Germany in 1959, an infantry battalion augmented by scout and psychological warfare teams successfully established a system of area control in which each of its companies extensively patrolled an assigned sector while an airmobile strike force waited in reserve to exploit potential contacts. Meanwhile, on the other side of the globe, the Hawaii-based 25th Infantry Division conducted what was perhaps the Army's most sustained program of counterguerrilla training. Beginning in 1956, the division, which was earmarked for contingency operations in Asia where potential adversaries were likely to resort to irregular warfare, required all its personnel to cycle through the division's Jungle and Guerrilla Warfare Center for a minimum of five and a half days per year. Such exercises, together with the general interest in Ranger training, ensured that at least some soldiers and units would gain proficiency in the type of individual and small-unit skills required in a counterguerrilla environment.[58]

The Resurgence of Counterinsurgency Doctrine, 1958–1960

One factor that contributed to the Army's inattention to irregular warfare was its preoccupation with nuclear weapons. By the early 1950s a debate was raging within the Army as to how it should adjust to the nuclear age. Nuclear weapons made their first appearance in the Army's basic combat manual, FM 100–5, in 1954, nine years after the development of the atomic bomb. The following year, the Army published its first manual devoted exclusively to the use of nuclear devices in combat—FM 100–31, *Tactical Use of Atomic Weapons*—and initiated a major overhaul of its educational system. At the Command and General Staff College, nuclear combat became the standard model for future warfare while nonnuclear situations were depicted as deviations from that norm. By 1956 Fort Leavenworth was devoting approximately 50 percent of its curriculum to nuclear warfare scenarios, and the strain of having to cover both nuclear and conventional combat without extending the length of the course left little time for the study of unconventional warfare.

Moreover, between 1956 and 1958, the Army completely restructured its combat divisions to create new formations—called "pentomic" divisions—specifically tailored for nuclear warfare conditions. Under such circumstances, the Army had neither the time nor the intellectual energy to devote to counterguerrilla issues.[59]

Nor could it readily justify such a diversion given the policies of Truman's successor in the White House, retired General of the Army Dwight D. Eisenhower. Convinced that the United States could not afford to match the Soviet Union's massive conventional forces and that nuclear weapons had made such forces virtually obsolete in any case, the Eisenhower administration (1953–1961) sharply limited resources for ground combat forces. Eisenhower was equally outspoken in his determination not to embroil U.S. ground forces in small wars or insurgencies on the grounds that such conflicts were difficult to win and placed undue burdens on American resources. Better to arm and train our allies to fight for themselves under the general protection of America's nuclear umbrella than to commit U.S. ground forces to secure them from local Communist aggression. Such a policy gave the Army little incentive to devote its already scarce resources to preparing for third world conflicts. Rather, the Army's neglect of counterinsurgency during most of the Eisenhower years was in full consonance with U.S. national security policy.[60]

Not everyone, however, was happy with Eisenhower's policies. Opposition arose both from within the Army, which felt it suffered unduly from the president's nuclear orientation, and from the growing community of national security strategists. In 1957 two leading civilian theorists, Robert Osgood and Henry Kissinger, published books criticizing the Eisenhower administration's policy of massive retaliation, which they regarded as dangerous, inflexible, and ultimately unbelievable as a deterrent to local conflicts. They argued the United States needed to develop the political and military capability to conduct limited wars below the threshold of an all-out nuclear confrontation. Although limited war theory eventually included much theorizing about conflict management and the use of graduated responses to deter aggression that many soldiers neither fully understood nor embraced, the Army recognized in the limited war advocates a welcome ally in the struggle to save ground forces from irrelevancy.[61]

While neither the limited war theoreticians nor the Army's senior leadership had much interest in or understanding of guerrilla warfare, both agreed that the United States needed to be able to combat irregulars without resorting to atomic weapons. In his bid to win greater resources for the Army, Chief of Staff General Maxwell D. Taylor frequently cited "the increasing danger of so-called small wars" as justification for the development of "flexible, proportioned strength" capable of coping with "small wars as well as big wars, with wars in jungle or mountains as well as in Europe," and with "brush fires."[62] Under his aegis, in 1957 the Command and General Staff College drafted a strategy for combating Communist insurgencies. The "think piece" called for the provision of economic, financial, and technical aid to threatened societies to promote stability and economic development, the construction of communication and transportation infrastructures in those same countries to facilitate American intervention, and the creation of a U.S. Army intervention force endowed with "both a military capability and a political capability" and trained in antiguerrilla warfare, civil disturbances, and small-unit operations.[63]

Eisenhower's aversion for brush fire wars notwithstanding, he was already moving toward embracing elements of the CGSC's proposed strategy. Mirroring the philosophy exhibited by the Marshall Plan and the policies pursued by the Truman administration in combating the postwar insurgencies, President Eisenhower announced in 1956 that poverty was the primary facilitator for the spread of communism throughout the less developed areas of the world, and he vowed to increase the amount of economic, military, and ideological warfare assistance given to such areas. In addition to deploying eighty-five counterguerrilla mobile training teams to fourteen countries between 1955 and 1960, Eisenhower initiated a police aid program that he thought would prove both more economical and more effective than military assistance in addressing the problems of internal insecurity. Managed largely by the International Cooperation Agency, with occasional participation by the Department of Defense and the Central Intelligence Agency (CIA), this program had by 1958 provided training in police administration, countersubversion, and community relations to 690,000 policemen in twenty-one countries.[64] As will be discussed more fully in the following chapter, President Eisenhower even saw merit in Taylor's call for an intervention force, and in 1958 he authorized the creation of a Strategic Army Corps whose mission included preparing for overseas contingencies.

Still, concerns over the threat of Communist insurgencies in the less developed world continued to grow, and in November 1958 Eisenhower initiated a major review of the military assistance program. Chaired by William H. Draper, the President's Committee To Study the U.S. Military Assistance Program issued a report in August 1959 that called for several programmatic reforms. Among these were improvements in the selection and preparation of advisory personnel and a greater emphasis on countering subversion by providing counterintelligence, psychological warfare, and civil affairs assistance.[65]

The Draper committee also subscribed to an idea, recently proposed by the Army's civil affairs community, that the United States encourage foreign armies to promote socioeconomic development in their home countries. In this the committee was particularly influenced by two of its members—retired Army Brig. Gen. Don G. Shingler, an engineer who wrote the committee's civil affairs annex, and Col. Robert H. Slover, the committee's secretary, who was a civil affairs officer and a veteran of the Army's civil assistance program in Korea, AFAK. Also influential on this score were Army Chief of Staff Taylor, founder of AFAK, and Air Force Colonel Lansdale, who submitted a report on his Philippine activities to the Draper committee. In the committee's view, military organizations were often the most efficient and modern institutions in underdeveloped countries, and consequently could act as "transmission belts" of administrative and technological skills to their parent societies. Moreover, by taking an active part in promoting socio-economic progress, foreign armies could help redress the causes of internal unrest and win popular approval for both themselves and their governments. The committee adopted Lansdale's term *civic action* to describe military involvement in social, political, and economic reform programs of this kind.

Not everyone was comfortable with civic action. Some soldiers feared that it would undermine readiness by diverting manpower and resources to nonmilitary functions, while State Department officials disliked the prospect of soldiers meddling in political affairs. Nor was there any true agreement as to exactly what civic action entailed. Was it nation building writ large or merely a collection of piecemeal projects? Did it aim to achieve long-term development or short-term changes of less lasting but more immediate impact? These and other questions were never fully answered, but the committee did establish some guide-lines. It stated that the performance of civic action activities should not be allowed to distract from an army's primary, military duties; that civic action projects should not be carried out to the detriment of private enterprise or for the benefit of special interest groups; and that such programs should not exceed the capacity of the local society to absorb and maintain them. Within these parameters, the Draper committee strongly endorsed military civic action.[66]

The Eisenhower administration quickly embraced the committee's recommendations. After incorporating language into the Mutual Security Act of 1959 that encouraged military involvement in nation building, in May 1960 it gave the Army limited authority to promote civic action programs overseas. The Departments of State and Defense reaffirmed this decision by informing all U.S. embassies, unified commands, and military assistance groups that U.S. policy was to encourage foreign military and paramilitary organizations to promote economic development. The United States likewise offered to send mobile training teams to help foreign governments plan and organize such efforts. The response was hardly overwhelming. Only two countries—Guatemala and Iran—responded positively to the offer, in part because the United States intended to confine its civic action assistance to providing advice, rather than money and materiel. Unless the United States financed such endeavors, few countries were interested in having American military emissaries pontificate about the benefits of civic action. Undeterred by the lackluster response, in November 1960 the U.S. Army dispatched its first mobile civic action team to Guatemala, thereby setting in motion what would become one of America's major weapons against Communist subversion in the third world.[67]

Meanwhile, back in Washington, the pace of activity quickened. Spurred by the triumph of Fidel Castro's insurgency in Cuba, the Joint Chiefs endorsed the administration's growing concern over third world revolutions, noting that "the growth of nationalism and the desire for an improved lot among backward and dependent people" meant that "a major prize in the continuing conflict [with communism] . . . will be the adherence of wavering peoples to the Soviet or Western democratic cause." General Taylor concurred, and he initiated a review of the Army's ability to combat guerrilla warfare. The review reached the rather dubious conclusion that the amount of attention devoted to counterguerrilla warfare in the Army's training and doctrinal systems was "adequate and in balance with other training objectives." Nevertheless, change was in the offing, and by 1960 the Joint Chiefs were freely admitting that at least one component of the military's training system, the military assistance program, had not done an adequate job of preparing foreign soldiers to suppress insurgencies. Consequently, the Joint Chiefs directed the Army to begin posting a limited number of Special Forces, civil affairs, psychological warfare, and intelligence personnel in countries threatened by insurgency. It likewise instructed the Army to establish a special counterguerrilla operations course for both American and foreign personnel. This directive led to the establishment of a six-week "Counter-Guerrilla Operations and Tactics" course at the Special Warfare School at Fort Bragg on 26 January 1961, the first course in Army history entirely devoted to the subject. Finally, in October 1960 the National Security Council directed the Defense Department to develop a new doctrine for counterinsurgency, a task that the department delegated to the Army. Reflecting the growing consensus that "we need to improve our capabilities and those of our allies to conduct anti-guerrilla warfare," Taylor's successor as Army chief of staff, General Lyman L. Lemnitzer, immediately put his staff to work crafting new doctrinal materials.[68]

In undertaking this task, Army personnel examined not only past American doctrine, but the recent experiences of others. As early as October 1950 the National Security Council had called for the United States to lead a multinational effort to gather information about the free world's experiences in countering Communist guerrillas. In practice, this effort had had little if any impact on Army doctrine because the basic doctrine (FM 31–20 of 1951) had already been written and subsequent Army manuals had done little more than convey distilled versions of this material. Nevertheless, the Army had not ignored the contemporary experiences of others. Throughout the decade, military attaches and intelligence officers had gathered foreign works pertaining to counterinsurgency, while a small number of officers had analyzed and disseminated this information through journal articles and student papers.[69]

For the most part, Americans focused their attention on the British and French. As early as 1951, one of the Army's foremost experts on psychological warfare, Maj. Paul Linebarger, had declared Britain's methods in countering Communist guerrillas in Malaya to be "one of our most valuable codes of military training and doctrine." Although interest in Malaya remained modest for most of the decade, by 1960 the Army had distributed copies of the British manual *Conduct of Anti-terrorist Operations in Malaya* to all its service schools for use in formulating doctrine.[70]

The Army also gathered information on French operations in Indochina and Algeria during the 1950s, but U.S. soldiers did not show much interest in the French experience until the end of the decade. The language barrier and political tensions between the United States and France impeded the acquisition of information, while France's defeat in Indochina further discouraged analysis, as Americans looking for examples to emulate naturally gravitated toward winners, like the British, rather than losers. Those who examined the Indochina War echoed the conclusions drawn by U.S. political and military officials at the time. They roundly criticized France for failing to initiate sound political policies to win Vietnamese popular favor, while dismissing French military operations as being too passive and defensively oriented. Such criticisms fully reflected U.S. Army preference for positive programs and aggressive action.[71]

While the Indochina experience was largely dismissed, Army analysts of the late 1950s paid somewhat more attention to the civil war in Algeria (1954–1962), partly because it was more recent and therefore offered a window into the latest French thinking and partly because the French seemed more successful there. American interest in French thought also intensified when, after several years of soul searching, the French began to distill the lessons of their Indochina and Algerian experiences into a new counterinsurgency doctrine, which they called *guerre revolutionnaire* ("revolutionary war"). The Army acquired and translated several tracts on *guerre revolutionnaire*, republishing excerpts in military journals, while individual officers occasionally analyzed the new doctrine through articles and essays. Although U.S. commentators found certain aspects of the French Army's behavior disturbing—most notably its willingness to resort to torture, heavy-handed propaganda, and antidemocratic activities—they were drawn by the doctrine's modern feel. Unlike existing American and British doctrine, which addressed guerrilla warfare from the perspectives of rear area security and colonial administration, *guerre revolutionnaire* placed irregular conflict firmly in the context of the Cold War. Modern guerrilla warfare, according to *guerre revolutionnaire* theorists, was the product of an international Communist conspiracy that attacked the West by exploiting third world conditions. *Guerre revolutionnaire*'s relevance to contemporary issues was further amplified by its explicitly Maoist focus. Unlike American manuals, which made no mention at all of Mao's theories, the French were fascinated by contemporary Communist organizational, political, and manipulative techniques, insisting that counterinsurgents develop Western equivalents to counteract each Communist initiative. French theory also elevated political, social, and psychological countermeasures to positions coequal with that of traditional military action—a perspective that many U.S. politicians, civilian strategists, and unconventional warfare specialists found appealing, not only because it magnified the roles they would play in managing future conflicts, but because the doctrine dovetailed with their own perceptions. Consequently, though still new and only partially understood, *guerre revolutionnaire* added momentum to the reevaluation of U.S. doctrine.[72]

The Army's promotion of civic action and its growing interest in Mao and *guerre revolutionnaire* also reflected broader trends in the academic and political community. During the 1950s the continuous political, social, and economic upheaval experienced by many of the world's poorer and post-colonial societies had drawn the attention of academics and policy makers alike. They sought to understand the nature of political and economic development in the hope of discovering a way to stop the spread of communism and encourage the growth of open, democratic, and capitalistic societies. Leading the academic effort was Walt W. Rostow whose 1960 book, *The Stages of Economic Growth: A Non-Communist Manifesto*, had an immediate and far-ranging impact.

Rostow theorized that every society went through five fairly comparable stages of economic development. Of these, the transition to modernity was the most destabilizing, as traditional values and institutions clashed with more modern ones, creating confusion, strife, and upheaval in every aspect of political, social, and economic life. Rapid population growth, urbanization, and technological change complicated the transition, as did the competing forces of colonialism, nationalism, and regionalism. Rostow hypothesized that a "revolution of rising expectations" existed that, if long unfulfilled, might tempt the peoples of the underdeveloped world to embrace communism as a shortcut to modernization. Indeed, in his estimation, communism was a disease that thrived during this transitional stage, shamelessly exploiting and subverting the aspirations of the masses for its own ends. But just as a doctor could use medical science to defeat disease, Rostow believed that skilled practitioners of the social sciences—politics, economics, and sociology—could defeat communism by administering carefully crafted programs in a way that would allow emerging societies to "take off" on their journey toward achieving Western-style democratic capitalism.[73]

While the theory was new, the prescription—enlightened political, social, and economic reforms implemented under the guidance of a benevolent American patron—echoed long-established themes in America's liberal and progressive tradition, not to mention general Western conceptions of the "white man's burden." As such, Rostow's blending of state of the art social science with traditional American themes struck a cord among many policy makers who, like Truman and Eisenhower, regarded economic rehabilitation and modernization as vaccines against communism. One politician who was particularly enamored with Rostow's theories was the presidential candidate and senator from Massachusetts, John F. Kennedy, who had long believed that aggressive political, psychological, and economic measures—rather than mere military force—were the surest way to defeat Communist insurgencies in the developing world.[74]

During the 1960 presidential contest, Kennedy charged that President Eisenhower's frugality had allowed the Soviet Union to surpass the United States in nearly every field of strategic endeavor—nuclear missile construction, conventional force modernization, political and psychological warfare, and economic aid to developing countries. The only way to address these "gaps," Kennedy argued, was to lavish economic, social, and technical assistance on developing countries, while creating military organizations capable of defeating Communist forces in both conventional and third world conflicts.

Kennedy's platform appealed to Army leaders. Like much of official Washington, the Army accepted Rostow's developmental theory at face value. Kennedy's call for the creation of more robust and "flexible" conventional military forces likewise paralleled the Army's own critique of Eisenhower's defense policies, as expressed in two books written by retired Army generals—*The Uncertain Trumpet*, by Maxwell Taylor, and *War and Peace in the Space Age*, by James M. Gavin. The result was that a multiplicity of factors—previous Army thinking about counterguerrilla warfare and pacification, emerging academic theories about politico-economic development and limited war, the continued threat of Communist-backed insurgencies, and contemporary European experience in colonial conflicts—all converged to influence Army planners and doctrine writers in the waning days of the Eisenhower administration.[75]

During the closing months of 1960 the Army produced a number of documents that reflected the prevailing trends. The first such document was a new edition of FM 7–100, *The Infantry Division*, published in November. The manual incorporated for the first time a seven-page section on counterguerrilla warfare that provided a condensed version of some of the principles first developed by Colonel Volckmann nine years earlier. Although the manual made no reference to Maoist revolutionary warfare, the resurrection of old, but still valid, doctrinal principles signaled the Army's rising interest in irregular warfare.[76]

A more forward-looking document appeared the following month in the guise of "Strategic Army Study, 1970" (STARS–70). This report offered a blueprint for how the Army might exploit the opportunity offered by the presidential election to win a greater share of defense resources. Army Chief of Staff General George H. Decker believed that President-elect Kennedy would be receptive to constructive proposals on how the United States could shed itself of the "political straight jacket" created by Eisenhower's policies in favor of a more "active forward military strategy" in which the United States could, with flexibility and precision, either deter, meet, or defeat every form of Communist aggression. Decker maintained that the U.S. Army was "uniquely fitted for and must take the lead in meeting the Communists face-to-face in the struggle for freedom of the less developed countries."[77] Following Rostow's precepts, the study stated that a "revolution of rising expectations" was sweeping the third world. To meet the legitimate aspira-

165

tions of underdeveloped nations for prosperity while preventing any drift toward communism, Decker argued that the United States should "expand the role of the armed forces in contributing to political and economic growth in underdeveloped countries."[78] Refocusing the military assistance program on internal security and utilizing American military resources to implement civic action and public welfare programs would, the Army asserted, "have the effect of insinuating the political power of the United States into these countries," thereby helping to stem any untoward radicalism that might derail progress toward achieving democratic, capitalistic institutions.[79]

In practical terms, STARS–70 called for Army officers to broaden their horizons and embrace a more activist role in world affairs. It also recommended that the Army recruit more Special Forces personnel, raise three new divisions, and create two Cold War task forces. One task force would be oriented toward Africa and the Middle East while the other concentrated on Southeast Asia. Each would contain 9,000 men split among a reinforced airborne brigade, a Special Forces group, an aviation element, and a logistical command. In addition to providing training assistance in conventional, unconventional, and counterguerrilla warfare, the airborne and Special Forces elements would be able to undertake independent operations should the United States choose to intervene directly in another nation's affairs, while the civil affairs, engineer, medical, and psychological warfare components provided humanitarian, socioeconomic development, and reconstructive assistance. Such task forces would spearhead the Army's efforts to shape the destiny of the underdeveloped world.[80]

About the time General Decker approved the STARS–70 report, the Special Warfare Division of the Office of the Deputy Chief of Staff for Military Operations (ODCSOPS) produced a paper on counterinsurgency operations that fully reflected the new policy thrust. The study, "Counter Insurgency Operations: A Handbook for the Suppression of Communist Guerrilla/Terrorist Operations," represented a blend of American, British, and to a lesser extent, French, influences.[81] Although the handbook could be used by U.S. troops in a foreign insurgency, the authors really intended the study as a guide for U.S. advisory and assistance personnel, since they believed that "it is neither politically feasible or operationally practicable to entertain the use of U.S. conventional forces in any intervention role within these numerous and widespread areas." This reflected both Eisenhower administration policy and an awareness of public antipathy for directly intervening in the internal affairs of foreign countries. The handbook also asserted that

The use of major elements of foreign . . . troops to suppress such guerrilla/terrorist operations is neither practical from a military viewpoint nor psychologically feasible. These forces are generally unfamiliar with the customs, geography, language, and people of the area and have not been trained in the specific techniques and tactics necessary for successful operations. The presence of major bodies of foreign troops is unpalatable to the indigenous population and discredits the government in power as a 'puppet' or 'tool' of the foreign imperialists incapable of ruling without the support of foreign troops.[82]

Consequently, the study advocated that the United States work primarily through its military assistance groups and small teams of specialists, such as the task forces called for in STARS–70.

The ODCSOPS handbook stated that counterinsurgency was unlike conventional war in that conventional war was largely destructive while counterinsurgency revolved around mainly constructive actions designed to redress whatever societal problems were causing unrest. It further asserted that military force alone "cannot win the conflict without extensive changes and reforms to eliminate the causes of the dissension and revolt," and it criticized most past counterinsurgency efforts for focusing too narrowly on conventional military solutions while failing both to redress grievances and to protect people from guerrilla influence and intimidation. Consequently, the handbook, echoing established American doctrine, called for the formulation of a national politico-military plan that coordinated the actions of every branch of government. To further such coordination, the handbook took a page from the British in Malaya by advocating the establishment of joint civil-military commands and pacification committees at every layer of government down to the village level.[83]

Having established an overall strategy and the mechanisms needed to execute it, the handbook offered a four-phase plan of operations. During the first phase, government forces would enter a region slated for pacification and establish local governments, pacification committees, and paramilitary self-defense militias. The government would also create an elaborate intelligence and propaganda system, initiate economic rehabilitation programs, and impose a variety of population- and resources-control measures, including a stringent food rationing system. Although reforms designed to eliminate government corruption and stimulate economic recovery would begin at the outset of the campaign, the plan placed most of its emphasis on organizational and security measures and on short-term, high-impact programs rather than long-term development projects as it believed that the latter were generally ineffective in a revolutionary environment. Phase two consisted of offensive operations to break up and destroy large guerrilla concentrations and drive them away from populated areas. Other measures, including forc-ibly relocating people and creating "sanitary zones" cleared of human habitation, would likewise serve to isolate the guerrillas. Military operations during the third phase were similar, but targeted smaller guerrilla bands and the enemy's clandestine support structure, with "stringent punishment" being meted out to persons harboring guerrillas. Meanwhile, every effort would be made to continue to harass the guer-rillas and make their situation untenable, especially by destroying "small garden plots, fields and cattle stock held or used by guerrilla elements in remote or sparsely populated regions." These measures, coupled with a strong propaganda campaign and offers of amnesty and rehabilitation, would, the handbook authors hoped, break the back of the insurgent movement. Once the military had cleared an area of guerrillas and their politico-military apparatus, the government would initiate major socio-economic reform programs during the fourth and final phase. The Army would transfer most of the regular troops to pacify other areas, while those who remained, together with local police and paramilitary forces, would actively assist in the economic restoration effort.[84]

Operationally, the handbook called for continuous, aggressive action, warning against passivity and overdispersion. Perhaps reflect-ing British experience in Malaya, the authors departed from previous American doctrine by discouraging the use of large-scale operations, which they believed were frequently ineffective. In the view of the Special Warfare Division, operations of battalion size or larger should be rare, with most actions being undertaken by infantry companies, pla-toons, and squads augmented by specially trained hunter-killer teams and units of police, militia, and "galvanized guerrillas." Heliborne operations also played a critical role in official thinking, and, although the paper declined to recommend specific tactics in recognition of the need for flexibility, it endorsed the Army's traditional formulation of finding, fixing, fighting, and finishing the enemy.[85]

The ODCSOPS handbook heralded counterinsurgency's resurgence in official American military thought. On 8 December 1960, just one week after the ODCSOPS had completed the handbook, the Department of the Army elevated many similar ideas into official doctrine when it approved for publication a new chapter to FM 100–1, *Doctrinal Guidance*. Developed at the Command and General Staff College in response to the National Security Council (NSC) directive requiring the formulation of new doctrine, the chapter mirrored the handbook in reflecting a mix of traditional American principles with the gleanings of foreign experience. Titled "Military Operations Against Irregular Forces," the chapter differed from previously published doctrine in that it placed guerrilla warfare firmly in the context of contemporary third world insurgency, describing the social, political, and economic conditions that generally gave rise to revolutionary movements.[86]

Because FM 100–1 was devoted to propounding basic doctrinal statements, the new chapter did not delve into the type of detail found in the ODCSOPS handbook. Like the ODCSOPS piece, it stressed the political aspects of counterinsurgency, stating that "military units employed against irregular forces normally operate in an environment which is inherently sensitive, both politically and militarily. The scope and nature of missions assigned will frequently include political and administrative aspects and objectives not usually considered normal to military operations."[87] Cognizant of the fact that guerrilla movements were usually the product, not the cause, of civil unrest, and that popular support was vital to the success of insurgent and counterinsurgent alike, the manual stressed that "the local government being supported by the U.S., as well as U.S. forces, must present a concrete program which will win popular support." Such a program entailed a mixture of good troop conduct and discipline, psychological warfare, political and administrative reform, relief and rehabilitation, and civic action, which the manual defined as "any action performed by the military forces utilizing available human and material resources for the well-being and improvement of the community." The manual also reiterated civil affairs doctrine in recommending that restrictions on civilian activity be as limited as conditions would allow so as not to alienate the population, though it permitted the imposition of sanctions if necessary.[88]

Operationally, the new chapter called for the conduct of a coordinated military, psychological, and intelligence campaign in terms that were similar to the ODCSOPS handbook. The first step of any campaign was to isolate the guerrilla from all sources of internal and external support, including civilian supporters and the members of the covert apparatus, whom the manual stated were often more dangerous than the armed insurgents themselves. The military would seal the nation's borders, blockade guerrilla base areas, and clear areas sympathetic to the insurgency by removing the inhabitants. Population- and resource-control measures, including stringent controls over the production and distribution of food, weapons, and medical supplies, would further deny the guerrillas access to these vital commodities, as would "extensive ground and air search for and destruction of irregular force supply caches and installations."[89]

Because allied forces would not likely have enough manpower to conduct pacification operations everywhere simultaneously, the manual recommended that counterinsurgents divide the operational area into subareas, each of which would be sealed, scoured, and pacified in turn before moving to the next. This prescription was reminiscent of allied operations during the Greek Civil War as well as the old French *tache d'huile* system in which government control gradually spread across the countryside like a drop of oil on water. Once an area had been selected for pacification, security forces would seal the region's perimeter while other forces established strongpoints for the area control operations that were to follow. In addition to reestablishing government authority and quelling civil disturbances, the security forces would initiate an extensive psychological warfare and counterintelligence effort to sway opinion and attack the enemy's covert apparatus. The military would also conduct extensive ground and heliborne patrols, raids, and ambushes to keep the enemy off-balance and on the move. Those enemy forces willing to fight in open battle were to be surrounded and annihilated. Smaller groups would be perpetually hounded by patrols composed of regular soldiers, police, paramilitary, and special antiguerrilla formations. Operations would continue, supplemented by civil initiatives, until the area had been fairly well cleared, at which time the bulk of the regulars would move on to a new district, leaving behind enough troops and paramilitary forces to provide security and assist the government's reconstructive efforts.[90]

Having described the general course of a campaign, the chapter made several peripheral suggestions as to the conduct of counterirregular operations. It recommended maximum use of indigenous manpower as soldiers, policemen, and village militiamen. The manual likewise recommended that troops be kept in the same general area as much as possible so as to reap the benefits that came with familiarity with a locality's political and military topography. In terms of training, the manual indicated that troops slated for counterguerrilla service receive an intensive course in small-unit tactics, long-range patrolling, night movements, raids, ambushes, security, civil affairs, intelligence, and police operations. Troop indoctrination courses, as well as country-specific language, cultural, and environmental training, were also desirable. Finally, the chapter concluded with general remarks on the logistical, intelligence, and civil affairs aspects of counterguerrilla operations.[91]

Published on 10 January 1961 as Change 1 to FM 100–1, *Doctrinal Guidance*, "Military Operations Against Irregular Forces" was an important document. Together with the ODCSOPS handbook, it marked a dramatic shift from the generic counterguerrilla and rear area security focus of previous doctrine to a new paradigm of third world revolution and Maoist-style "people's wars." Both documents were consistent with current trends in American political, strategic, and developmental theory and with contemporary foreign thinking. As such they represented the first steps toward the gradual reorientation of doctrine to better meet the threats and challenges of the contemporary world. And yet, while these documents introduced some new terms, concepts, and techniques, what is perhaps most striking about the new literature was how little of it was actually "new." Many of the ideas, concepts, and methods touted in the ODCSOPS handbook and the insert to FM 100–1 had appeared ten years earlier in the now defunct FM 31–20 of 1951 and were still represented to an extent in manuals like FM 31–15 (1953), 100–5 (1954), and 41–10 (1957). Rather than discard the lessons of previous experience, American doctrinal writers had merely reframed them into a more contemporary context. Change 1 to FM 100–1 thus marked not just the birth of new ideas, but the resurrection of old ones.

"Military Operations Against Irregular Forces" was the last doctrinal initiative to come to fruition under the Eisenhower administration. Ten days after its publication, John F. Kennedy was sworn into office as the thirty-fifth president of the United States. His elevation to the presidency buoyed the spirits of many of the Army's senior leaders who believed that he would lift the Army out of the doldrums of the Eisenhower years into a new place of bureaucratic and strategic prominence. In this, they would not be disappointed, and yet senior officers would soon have cause to appreciate the old adage "be careful what you wish for." The vigorous new president and his civilian aides would soon initiate a torrent of new programs and initiatives with regard to the organization, administration, and doctrine of America's armed forces that would leave Army leaders scrambling to catch up. Although many of Kennedy's initiatives would be beneficial, they also included decisions that would ultimately lead to war in Vietnam. U.S. Army counterinsurgency doctrine would be at the very center of the coming vortex.

Notes

¹ Ltrs, Russell Volckmann to Maj Tommy King, John F. Kennedy Center for Military Assistance, 1 Aug 75, and to Beverly Lindsey, 21 Mar 69. Both in the History Office, John F. Kennedy Special Warfare Center, Fort Bragg, N.C. (hereafter cited as JFKSWC/ HO). Rod Paschall, "Low-Intensity Conflict Doctrine: Who Needs It?" *Parameters* 15 (Autumn 1985): 42, 45; Johnny Stevens, "Russell William Volckmann," *Assembly* 47 (April 1988): 148–49. After completing the drafts of the two manuals, Volckmann helped organize guerrilla and counterguerrilla operations during the Korean War. In 1952 he returned to the United States where he became one of the founding fathers of the U.S. Army's Special Forces. He retired as a brigadier general in 1957.

² For example, FM 31–20 contained several passages lifted virtually verbatim from Greek counterguerrilla doctrine—doctrine that was itself based on German techniques. Compare Greek General Staff, Suppression of Irregular Bandit Operations, c. 1947–1948, pp. 15–16, Historians files, CMH, with FM 31–20, *Operations Against Guerrilla Forces*, 1951, p. 108.

³ McClintock, *Instruments of Statecraft*, pp. 59–60; "German Tactics of Combating Guerrillas," *Military Review* 24 (June 1944): 104–06; Allied Force Headquarters, "German Measures in Combating the Partisans," *Intelligence Notes* 62 (6 June 1944): C-4 to C-6; Allied Force Headquarters, "German Instructions for Operations Against Partisans," *Intelligence Notes* 72 (5 September 1944): C-6 to C-7; Allied Force Headquarters, "German Methods in Anti-partisan Warfare," *Intelligence Notes* 78 (17 October 1944): C-7 to C-8; Great Britain, Imperial General Staff, *Notes from Theatres of War*, no. 21, *Partisans* (War Office, 1945), pp. 9–30; Supreme Headquarters, Allied Expeditionary Force, *Combating the Guerrilla* (1945); Translation, U.S. Army Intelligence Division, Fighting the Guerrilla Bands, 1944.

⁴ For a listing of German monographs, see Historical Division, U.S. Army Europe, Guide to Foreign Military Studies, 1945–54, Catalog and Index (HQ, U.S. Army, Europe, 1954). Ofc, Ch, Army Field Forces, Training Bulletin 1, 8 Sep 50, p. 15, in 350.9 AFF Training Bulletins, CMH.

⁵ Kevin Soutor, "To Stem the Red Tide: The German Report Series and Its Effects on American Defense Doctrine, 1948–1954," *Journal of Military History* 57 (October 1993): 653–88; Memo, Brig Gen Robert McClure for Ch of Military History, 15 Mar 51, sub: Generation and Character of Guerrilla Resistance, 370.64, Office of Chief of Special Warfare, 1951–54, RG 319, NARA. The two antiguerrilla pamphlets were Department of the Army Pamphlet (DA Pam) 20–240, "Rear Area Security in Russia," distributed in manuscript form in July 1950 in response to the Korean situation but not formally published until July 1951, and DA Pam 20–243, "German Antiguerrilla Operations in the Balkans," by Robert Kennedy, originally produced as a monograph before being published as a pamphlet in August 1954. That Volckmann had access to these monographs before their formal publication can be seen by comparing DA Pam 20–240, pp. 34, 36, 39, with FM 31–20, 1951, pp. 71–72. Some of the more important German monographs produced by the Historical Division, U.S. Army, Europe, can be found in the section of the select bibliography titled "Foreign Military Studies and Monographs." For examples of articles that derived lessons from German experience, see Lloyd Marr, "Rear Area Security," *Military Review* 31 (May 1951): 57–62; Hellmuth

Kreidel, "Agents and Propaganda in Partisan Warfare," *Military Review* 39 (November 1959): 102–05; Thomas Collier, "Partisans, the Forgotten Force," *Infantry School Quarterly* (August–September 1960): 4–8; Joseph Bourdow, "Big War Guerrillas and Counter-Guerrillas," *Army* 13 (August 1962): 66–69. Other studies concerning the Axis experience produced by either the Office of the Chief of Military History, the Army, or some other Department of Defense agency can be found in the section of the select bibliography titled "Studies and Monographs." Privately published books available to Army officers in the early 1950s included Heilbrunn, *Partisan Warfare*, and Laqueur, *Guerrilla*.

[6] Quotes from FM 31–20, *Operations Against Guerrilla Forces*, 1951, p. iii, and see also pp. 1, 12, 24, 27–30, 37, 41, 49–51.

[7] Quotes from ibid., p. 63, and see also pp. 61, 64, 66.

[8] Ibid., p. 65.

[9] Ibid., pp. 61, 66–72, 74, 78–83.

[10] Ibid., pp. 44–45.

[11] Ibid., pp. 62, 65, 75–76.

[12] Ibid., pp. 55, 71, 86, 93. The manual's population- and resources-control measures were in accord with international law. Compare, for example, the measures listed in FM 31–20, 1951, pp. 84–85, with the standards applied during the Nuremberg war crimes trials as found in *Trials of War Criminals Before the Nuremberg Military Tribunals Under Control Law Number 10* (Washington, D.C.: Government Printing Office, 1950), 11:1249–50.

[13] First quote from FM 31–20, *Operations Against Guerrilla Forces*, 1951, p. 61. Second quote from ibid., p. 83.

[14] First quote from ibid., p. 28. Second quote from ibid., p. 99, and see also pp. 52, 93.

[15] Quote from Arthur Murphy, "Principles of Anti-Guerrilla Warfare," *Infantry School Quarterly* 39 (July 1951): 59. Even Volckmann admitted that Japan's retaliatory measures, while generally counterproductive, had occasionally succeeded in turning the Filipino population against his guerrillas. Volckmann, *We Remained*, pp. 151, 234. As late as 1977 the U.S. government objected to efforts to amend the 1949 Geneva Conventions so as to completely ban reprisals on the grounds that such measures were indispensable in counterguerrilla warfare. Donald Wells, *The Laws of Land Warfare: A Guide to Army Manuals* (Westport, Conn.: Greenwood Press, 1992), p. 44. A similar dichotomy existed in doctrine written in 1951 for use by American guerrillas which, while encouraging good conduct and the initiation of measures designed to win popular support, also permitted the guerrillas to use reprisals, destruction, terror, and assassination to impose their will on the population. FM 31–21, *Organization and Conduct of Guerrilla Warfare*, 1951, pp. 113–17.

[16] FM 31–20, *Operations Against Guerrilla Forces*, 1951, pp. 37, 62, 71–74, 102–03. Compare security techniques as presented in the Army's translation of *Fighting the Guerrilla Bands*, pp. 36–46, with FM 31–20, 1951, pp. 85–91.

[17] Quote from FM 31–20, *Operations Against Guerrilla Forces*, 1951, p. 126, and see also pp. 62–63, 78, 104–05, 124, 130, 134–35.

[18] Ibid., pp. 83, 104, 117–24. Many of the ideas used to describe the special antiguerrilla units were drawn directly from *Fighting the Guerrilla Bands*, pp. 34–36.

[19] FM 31–20, *Operations Against Guerrilla Forces*, 1951, pp. 76–77.

[20] Ibid., pp. 127–34.

[21] Compare *Fighting the Guerrilla Bands*, pp. 11–12, 28–34, 63–65, with FM 31–20, 1951, pp. 105–17. Compare also Greek General Staff, Suppression of Irregular Bandit Operations, c. 1947–1948, pp. 15–16, with FM 31–20, 1951, p. 108.

[22] FM 31–20, *Operations Against Guerrilla Forces*, 1951, pp. 109–13.

[23] Ibid., pp. 113–17.

[24] Ibid., pp. 103–04, 117.

[25] Ibid., pp. 26, 86, 125–26.

[26] AWC, Report of Conference of Commandants of Army Service Schools, 29 January–1 February 1951, p. 21; "Antiguerrilla Operations," *Officer's Call* 3 (March 1951): 1–15.

[27] A "change" document alters, amends, or supplements an existing manual. The Army issues a change when it believes that a modification is necessary but does not warrant the printing of an entirely new manual. The substance of a change can vary from minor editorial corrections to significant doctrinal statements. Though sometimes ignored by historians, changes represent official doctrine and by regulation must be incorporated immediately into all existing manuals.

[28] Quote from FM 100–5, *Field Service Regulations, Operations*, chg 1, 25 Jul 52, p. 9, and see also pp. 1–8.

[29] First quote from FM 31–15, *Operations Against Airborne Attack, Guerrilla Action, and Infiltration*, 1953, p. 43. Remaining quotes from ibid., p. 6, and see also pp. 12–13, 44–45.

[30] First and second quotes from ibid., p. 6. Third quote from FM 31–15, *Operations Against Airborne Attack, Guerrilla Action, and Infiltration*, chg 1, 5 Nov 54, p. 2. See also Study, Lt Col Russell Volckmann, Ofc, Ch of Psychological Warfare, Rear Area Defense, 27 Aug 51, Historians files, CMH; AWC, Report of Conference of Commandants of Army Service Schools, 29 January–1 February 1951, p. 31.

[31] Quote from Franz Halder et al., Analysis of U.S. Field Service Regulations, P–133 (Historical Division, U.S. Army, Europe, 1953), pp. 9–10, Foreign Military Studies Collection, MHI. Soutor, "Stem the Red Tide," pp. 676–77.

[32] The Army probably did not give Halder FM 31–20 because it lay outside his narrow focus on FM 100–5. Halder's group began working in February 1952, five months before the Army published Change 1 to FM 100–5. The Army probably never gave a copy of the change to the Germans, and their final report, submitted in April 1953, does not reflect any awareness of its existence.

[33] Quote from FM 100–5, *Field Service Regulations, Operations*, 1954, p. 133, and see also pp. 58–59, 132.

[34] Quote from ibid., p. 7, and see also pp. 4–6. Worth noting is that of the six missions the manual stated the Army was uniquely suited to perform, three—combating guerrilla forces and suppressing revolutions, preventing enemy infiltration of friendly areas, and occupying and controlling enemy territory and the populations therein— were directly related to counterguerrilla and pacification operations. Although this declaration did not imply that the Army actually devoted half of its time preparing for such missions, their enumeration as fundamental Army tasks at least guaranteed them some consideration. The Army's other three tasks, all of which were listed before the three "unconventional" missions, were defending against enemy land forces, attriting enemy land forces through sustained pressure, and compelling the enemy's ground forces to mass, thereby enhancing their vulnerability to nuclear attack.

[35] The Army had developed the concept of consolidation psywar during World War II and included its techniques in its postwar training curriculums, but prior to 1955 the Army had not actually included it in an official field manual. FM 33–5, *Psychological Warfare Operations*, 1955, pp. 223, 229, 239.

[36] Quote FM 27–10, *The Law of Land Warfare*, 1956, p. 9, and see also p. 19.

[37] Quote from ibid., p. 23.

[38] Quote from ibid., p. 145. The regulation further pointed out that according to American law, any citizen who provided an enemy with weapons, money, supplies, or intelligence could be tried and executed, a precedent that other countries could apply against their own nationals who supported indigenous insurgent movements. Ibid., pp. 25–28, 31, 33–34.

[39] Strom Thurmond, "CAMG Combat Support Axioms," *Military Review* 38 (January 1959): 1, 7.

[40] FM 41–10, *Civil Affairs Military Government Operations*, 1957, pp. 4–5, 7, 17–18, 66–67, 93–96.

[41] Ibid., pp. 67, 72–73, 97–99, 109.

[42] For American attitudes toward population relocation prior to 1941, see Birtle, *Counterinsurgency Doctrine*. As illustrated in the preceding chapters, American military and political officials had exhibited mixed feelings toward population relocation during the Greek, Philippine, and Korean civil wars. FM 31–20, 1951, p. 85, had listed population evacuation as a possible tool but had assigned it no special significance, and officers continued to be divided over its utility. Evidence for this can be seen in reactions to a 1953 Operations Research Office study of counterguerrilla operations in Korea, the Philippines, and Malaya. The study had recommended that "as far as possible, local citizens should be concentrated and employed in emergency governmental programs in an effort to occupy them gainfully and reduce the danger of continuous Communist agitation." Maj. Gen. Harry M. Roper, the Deputy Assistant Chief of Staff, G–3, for Research, Requirements, and Special Weapons, wrote that, while Army doctrine recognized the salutary effects of promoting employment, "this recommendation appears to establish a basic principle of wholesale evacuation of the civilian population to concentration camps and the impressment into labor units. This is not acceptable as doctrine." See Memo, Maj Gen Harry M. Roper, Dep Assistant Chief of Staff (ACS), G–3, for Research, Requirements, and Special Weapons, for Ch of Military History, 13 Sep 54, sub: Technical Memorandum ORO–T–228, "Salient Operational Aspects of Paramilitary Warfare in the Three Asian Areas," Incl to Fred Barton, Salient Operational Aspects of Paramilitary Warfare in Three Asian Areas, ORO T–228 (Chevy Chase, Md.: Operations Research Office, 1953), copy in CMH. On the other hand, Col. Wendell W. Perham, of the Office of Civil Affairs and Military Government, while sharing General Roper's concerns that morale "within the enclosure may become that of a *captive* rather than of a *protected* population," believed that the benefits derived from providing economic and social relief in a controlled atmosphere outweighed the disadvantages of relocation and resettlement, citing the Economic Development Corps as one such example. Memo, Col Wendell W. Perham, Dep Ch, Ofc of Civil Affairs and Military Government, for ACS, G–3, 15 Dec 54, sub: Technical Memorandum ORO–T–228, 040 ORO, G–3, 1954, RG 319, NARA.

[43] Quote from Memo, Commandant, Psychological Warfare School, for Ch, Army Field Forces, 17 Feb 54, sub: Transfer of FMs 31–20 and 31–21 to the Psychological Warfare School. Memo, Ch, Army Field Forces, for Commandant, Psychological

Warfare School, 4 Mar 54, sub: Transfer of FMs 31–20 and 31–21 to the Psychological Warfare School. Both in 300.7 manuals, Office of Chief of Special Warfare, 1951–58, RG 319, NARA. Memo, Joint Subsidiary Plans Div, JCS, for Ch, Psychological Warfare, et al., 17 Jan 54, sub: Operational Requirements for Psychological and Unconventional Warfare, 370.64, Office of Chief of Special Warfare, 1951–54, RG 319, NARA.

[44] Alfred Paddock, *U.S. Army Special Warfare: Its Origins—Psychological and Unconventional Warfare, 1941–1952* (Washington, D.C.: Government Printing Office, 1982), p. 120.

[45] FM 31–21, *Guerrilla Warfare*, 1955, p. 63.

[46] Discussions of counterguerrilla operations in branch-level manuals during the 1950s were brief, consisting of little more than excerpts from either FM 31–20 (1951) or FM 31–21 (1955). See, for example, FM 7–17, *The Armored Infantry Company and Battalion*, 1951, pp. 545–51; FM 17–1, *Armor Operations—Small Units*, 1957, p. 318; FM 17–100, *The Armored Division and Combat Command*, 1958, pp. 186, 220.

[47] "Partisan Operations," CGSC lecture 3362, 1949–1950, pp. 7–8; "Partisan Operations," CGSC lecture 3303, 1948–1949; "Partisan Operations," CGSC lecture 64008/1, 1950–1951. All in the Combined Arms Research Library (CARL), Fort Leavenworth, Kans. George Metcalf, "Offensive Partisan Warfare," *Military Review* 32 (April 1952): 53; Report on Infantry School Instruction in Special Forces Operations, atch to Memo, Lt Col Russell Volckmann, Special Opns Div, Ofc, Ch of Psychological Warfare, for Brig Gen Robert A. McClure, Ch of Psychological Warfare, 24 Apr 51, sub: Findings and Recommendations Regarding Special Operations Training, Fort Benning, Ga., 370.64, Office of Chief of Special Warfare, 1951–54, RG 319, NARA; Infiltration and Guerrilla Warfare, T–7800, 16 Dec 50 [Army General School, Course Material]; Combating Guerrilla Operations, 1951 [Engineer School, Course Material]; Security and Defense Measures in Rear Areas, 1953 [Transportation School, Course Material]; Security of the Trains of Armored Units Against Guerrilla-type Activity, Committee 12, Armored Officer Advanced Course, Armored School, 1951–1952, p. 56. All in Historians files, CMH.

[48] Stephen Bowman, "The Evolution of United States Army Doctrine for Counterinsurgency Warfare: From World War II to the Commitment of Combat Units in Vietnam" (Ph.D. diss., Duke University, 1985), p. 78; AWC curriculum pamphlets, 1950–1960, MHI; Military Doctrines and Technique, General Directive and Problem Directives for Courses Five, Six, and Seven, Phase 2, AWC, 1950–1951 curriculum, 4 Jan 51, pp. 48–54, MHI; Daniel Graham, Let's Get Acquainted with Guerrillas (Student paper, IOAC, Infantry School, 1955–1956), p. 3.

[49] Ironically, during the late 1950s ROTCM 145–60 provided some of the best coverage of counterinsurgency in Army manuals, since it had been based largely on the original FM 31–20 of 1951, rather than the less inspiring manuals of the later years. See Reserve Officers' Training Corps Manual (ROTCM) 145–60, *Small Unit Tactics, Including Communications*, 1954, pp. 414–18, and republished in 1958, pp. 402–16.

[50] See, for example, Program of Instruction (POI), Military Government Advanced Course, Provost Marshal General's School, Camp Gordon, Ga., Nov 54; Rear Area Defense, Lesson Plan MG 1783, Provost Marshal General's School, 1954; Unit and Team Tactics, Lesson Plan 1210, Civil Affairs and Military Government School, 1958; German and Japanese CAMG in World War Two, Lesson Plan 1103, Civil Affairs and Military Government School, 1958; Defense of Rear Areas, Adjutant General's School,

Special Text (ST) 12–170, 1958; Defense of Rear Areas, U.S. Army, ST 55–190, 1958. All in Historians files, CMH.

[51] Research sponsored by the Army and other Department of Defense agencies produced a number of studies regarding Communist Chinese theories of guerrilla warfare during the 1950s. See the "Studies and Monographs" section of the select bibliography for examples. Other discussions of Communist tactics include Robert Rigg, *Red Chinese Fighting Hordes* (Harrisburg, Pa.: Military Service Publishing Co., 1952), pp. 58, 180–82, 187–90, 224–27; Robert Rigg, "Red Parallel: The Tactics of Ho and Mao," *U.S. Army Combat Forces Journal* 5 (January 1955): 28–31; S. J. Watson, "A Study of Revolution," *Military Review* 35 (May 1955): 7–14; Gene Hanrahan, "The Chinese Red Army and Guerrilla Warfare," *U.S. Army Combat Forces Journal* 1 (February 1951): 10–13; Edward Downey, "Theory of Guerrilla Warfare," *Military Review* 39 (May 1959): 53–54; George Jordan, "Objectives and Methods of Communist Warfare," *Military Review* 39 (January 1960): 50–59.

[52] Quoted words from Beebe, "Beating the Guerrilla," p. 18. For examples of articles and student papers that related these themes, see "War Against Partisans," *Military Review* 38 (June 1958): 88; Samuel B. Griffith, "Guerrilla," *Antiaircraft Journal* 93 (September–October 1950): 15–18, and (November–December 1950): 50–53; Murphy, "Principles of Anti-Guerrilla Warfare"; "Guerrilla Warfare," *Military Review* 37 (September 1957): 95–101; Virgil Ney, "Guerrilla War and Modern Strategy," *Orbis* (Spring 1958): 66–83; Bashore, "Dual Strategy"; Collier, "Partisans"; Bruce Palmer, Jr., The Modern Role of Unconventional Warfare (Student paper, AWC, 1952), 370.64, Office of Chief of Special Warfare, RG 319, NARA; John Roddy, "Anti-Guerrilla Warfare" (Student thesis, AWC, 1955); Thomas Williams, Critique of Mao's 'On the Protracted War' (Student paper, AWC, 1959); Robert Mathe, "Revolutionary War" (Student thesis, AWC, 1959); Edgar McGee, Small Unit Defense Against Guerrilla Forces (Student paper, IOAC, Infantry School, 1955–56); William Tausch, What Should Be the Anti-guerrilla Warfare Doctrine for the Battle Group? (Student paper, IOAC, Infantry School, 1958); Lloyd Van Court, "Counterguerrilla Operations with Intelligence Support" (Student thesis, AWC, 1957); William Dodds, "Anti-Guerrilla Warfare" (Student thesis, AWC, 1955).

[53] Booth, "The Pattern That Got Lost," pp. 62–63; Waller Booth, "Operation Swamprat," *U.S. Army Combat Forces Journal* 1 (October 1950): 23–26. For another example of the early use of guerrillas in an Army exercise, see Robert Rigg, "The Guerrilla: A Factor in War," *Armored Cavalry Journal* 58 (November 1949): 4. For an early proposal regarding counterguerrilla training, see Memo, Lt Col Adams for Adj Gen, 3 Jul 50, sub: Proposed Anti-guerrilla Training, with atch, 4th Ind, HQ, Infantry Center, for Ch, Army Field Forces, 12 Sep 50, sub: Proposed Anti-guerrilla Training, Historians files, CMH.

[54] Memos, Ofc, Ch of Psychological Warfare, for ACS, G–3, 2 Mar 55, sub: Adequacy of Antiguerrilla Training in the Army, and ACS, G–3, for CG, CONARC, 14 Mar 55, sub: Anti-guerrilla Training. Both in 040 ORO, G–3, 1955, RG 319, NARA. Atch to Memo, Lt Gen James E. Moore, Deputy Chief of Staff for Military Operations (DCSOPS), for CSA, 31 Jul 58, sub: U.S. Army Guerrilla Warfare Activities, 370.64, CSA, 1948–62, RG 319, NARA; Army Training Program (ATP) 7–200, Army Training Program for Infantry Rifle Company and Airborne Infantry Rifle Company, 21 Apr 54, p. 25; Army Subject Schedule (ASubjScd) 21–26, Squad Patrolling, 5 Jul 55; ASubjScd 7–2, Rifle Squad Tactical Training, 22 Aug 55; ASubjScd 7–2, Rifle Squad Tactical Training, 20 Mar 59; ASubjScd 21–16, Anti-infiltration and Antiguerrilla Warfare

Training, 29 Sep 55; ASubjScd 33–11, Anti-infiltration and Antiguerrilla Training, 22 Jun 56; Richard Rogers, Small Unit Defense Against Guerrillas (Student paper, IOAC, Infantry School, 1955–56), pp. 10–11; Memo, Col Frank W. Norris, Secretary of the General Staff (SGS), for Col Robert G. Fergusson, Naval War College, 29 Nov 60, 370.64, CSA, 1955–62, RG 319, NARA.

[55] ASubjScd 30–38, Population Control, 1956; McClintock, *Instruments of Statecraft*, p. 51; Hogan, *Raiders or Elite Infantry*, pp. 139–40; FM 21–50, *Ranger Training*, 1957, pp. 6–7; An. B, Brief History of Ranger Course, atch to Rpt, Infantry School, 16 Feb 70, sub: Mandatory Ranger Training, CONARC, RG 338, NARA. Counterguerrilla training advice could be found in such publications as FM 31–20, *Operations Against Guerrilla Forces*, 1951, pp. 122–24, 139–41; FM 31–15, *Operations Against Airborne Attack, Guerrilla Action, and Infiltration*, 1953, pp. 76–78; Collier, "Partisans," pp. 7–8; FM 30–101, *Aggressor, The Maneuver Enemy*, 1959, pp. 82–84; FM 30–104, *Aggressor Representation*, 1953, pp. 3–5, 42–43; FM 30–102, *Handbook on Aggressor Military Forces*, chg 1, Jul 48, and subsequent editions of this manual: Aug 50, p. 137; Mar 51, p. 137; Feb 59, p. 150–54; and Jun 60, pp. 164–69.

[56] Douglas Stickley, Jr., Are We Giving Just 'Lip Service' to Night Training? (Student paper, IOAC, Infantry School, 1955–56).

[57] Quote from FM 30–104, *Aggressor Representation*, 1953, p. 42. Lloyd Norman and John Spore, "Big Push in Guerrilla Warfare," *Army* 12 (March 1962): 36.

[58] Charles Simpson, *Inside the Green Berets: The First Thirty Years* (Novato, Calif.: Presidio, 1983), pp. 44–46; Dillon, Concept for Antiguerrilla Operations, pp. 3–4; *Tropic Lightning, 1 Oct 41–1 Oct 66, 25th Infantry Division* (n.p., n.d.), pp. 148–54.

[59] Donald Carter, "From G.I. to Atomic Soldier: The Development of U.S. Army Tactical Doctrine, 1945–1956" (Ph.D. diss., Ohio State University, 1987), pp. 55, 121–24, 135–38, 159, 188; W. W. Culp, "Resident Courses of Instruction," *Military Review* 36 (May 1956): 17, 20. In 1956 special operations instruction accounted for 42 of the 1,219 hours in Leavenworth's regular course. This should not be minimized because it represented a sixfold increase over prior years and placed special operations ninth out of the twenty-six subjects covered at Leavenworth in terms of total course time. On the other hand, the special operations course virtually ignored counterguerrilla warfare.

[60] Carter, "G.I. to Atomic Soldier," pp. 170–78; Bowman, "Evolution of Army Doctrine," p. 74. One of the reasons that Assistant Chief of Staff, G–3, Maj. Gen. James M. Gavin, gave for rejecting proposals in 1954 for creating special counterguerrilla units in the Army's force structure was that the Army was already heavily engaged in restructuring for atomic war and did not have the resources to create additional specialized formations. Other reasons included a belief that conventional troops could effectively combat guerrillas, especially if they were properly trained and organized for theater conditions, and America's policy of relying on indigenous forces as the first line of defense against Communist irregulars. Memos, G–3 for G–2, 2 Apr 54, sub: Guerrilla Type Warfare, and G–2 for G–3, c. 1954, sub: Guerrilla Type Warfare; MFR, G–3, c. Apr 54, sub: Guerrilla Type Warfare. All in 370.64, G–3, 1954, RG 319, NARA. Memo, Col Fitzhugh H. Chandler, Chairman, Project Advisory Gp Parabel, for the ACS, G–3, 20 Oct 54, sub: Periodic Report on Project Parabel, 040, G–3, 1954, RG 319, NARA.

[61] George Lincoln and Amos Jordan, Jr., "Limited War and the Scholars," *Military Review* 37 (January 1958): 50–60; William Olson, "The Concept of Small Wars," *Small Wars and Insurgencies* 1 (April 1990): 39–46; Michael Cannon, "The Development of the American Theory of Limited War, 1945–63," *Armed Forces and Society* 9 (Fall

1992): 78–80; Harry Coles, "Strategic Studies Since 1945, the Era of Overthink," *Military Review* 53 (April 1973): 6. The two books were Robert Osgood, *Limited War: The Challenge to American Strategy* (Chicago, Ill.: University of Chicago Press, 1957), and Henry Kissinger, *Nuclear Weapons and Foreign Policy* (New York: Harper & Bros., 1957).

[62] First quote from "Readiness for the Little War, Optimum Integrated Strategy," *Military Review* 37 (April 1957): 23. Other quotes from ibid., p. 26. Osgood, *Limited War*, p. 237.

[63] Quote from "Readiness for the Little War," p. 25, and see also pp. 20–21.

[64] Donald Howard, "Anti-Guerrilla Operations in Asia" (Student thesis, AWC, 1956), p. 27. Harold Clem, *Collective Defense and Foreign Assistance* (Washington, D.C.: Industrial College of the Armed Forces, 1968), p. 117; Rpt, JCS, Sep 63, sub: Development Status of Military Counterinsurgency Programs, Including Counterguerrilla Forces, as of 1 August 1963, p. V-157; Shafer, *Deadly Paradigms*, pp. 86, 88; McClintock, *Instruments of Statecraft*, pp. 188–89; Memo, Special Gp, Counterinsurgency, for the President, 20 Jul 62, sub: Report of the Committee on Police Assistance Programs, p. 1, Historians files, CMH.

[65] *United States President's Committee To Study the United States Military Assistance Program*, vol. 2, *Supplement to the Committee Report* (Washington, D.C: Government Printing Office, 1959), pp. 56–58.

[66] Willard Barber and C. Neale Ronning, *Internal Security and Military Power, Counterinsurgency and Civic Action in Latin America* (Columbus: Ohio State University Press, 1966), pp. 65–66, 71, 74, 78–84; John DePauw and George Luz, eds., *Winning the Peace: The Strategic Implications of Military Civic Action* (Carlisle Barracks, Pa.: Strategic Studies Institute, 1990), p. 10; Kyre and Kyre, *Military Occupation*, pp. 14–15; Edward Glick, *Peaceful Conflict: The Non-Military Use of the Military* (Harrisburg, Pa.: Stackpole Books, 1967), pp. 68–69.

[67] Special Operations Research Office (SORO), Symposium Proceedings. The U.S. Army's Limited-War Mission and Social Science Research (Washington, D.C.: American University, 1962), p. 74; Msg, DEF 976945 to U.S. Commander in Chief, Europe (USCINCEUR), et al., 11 May 60, 370.64, CSA, 1955–62, RG 319, NARA; Harry Walterhouse, *A Time to Build: Military Civic Action—Medium for Economic Development and Social Reform* (Columbia: University of South Carolina Press, 1964), p. 116.

[68] First quote from Shafer, *Deadly Paradigms*, p. 19. Second quote from Memo, SGS for General Lemnitzer, 9 Sep 58, sub: Army Guerrilla Warfare Activities, 370.64, CSA, 1948–62, RG 319, NARA. Third quote from Christopher Cheng, *Airmobility: The Development of a Doctrine* (Westport, Conn.: Frederick A. Praeger, 1994), p. 72. Memo, Brig Gen Charles H. Bonesteel, SGS, for DCSOPS, 10 Jul 58, sub: U.S. Army Guerrilla Warfare Activities, 370.64, 1955–62, RG 319, NARA; Ltr, George H. Roderick, Actg Secy of the Army, to Secy of Def, 30 Dec 60, sub: Counter-Guerrilla Training Under the Military Assistance Program, 370.64, CSA, 1955–62, RG 319, NARA; Memo, Assistant Secretary of Defense (ASD), Internal Security Affairs (ISA), for Chairman, JCS, 5 May 60, sub: Counterguerrilla Training Provided Under the MAP; Briefing Paper for Chairman, JCS, on a Report by the J–5 Operations Deputies Meeting, Tuesday, 13 September 1960, agenda item 3. Both in 3360, JCS, RG 218, NARA. Previous Army instruction on counterguerrilla operations and small wars had been given as subsets of other courses.

[69] Schafer, *Deadly Paradigm*, p. 17; NSC 90, A Report to the National Security Council by the Secretary of State on Collaboration with Friendly Governments on Operations Against Guerrillas, 26 Oct 50, 370.64, G–3, 1950–55, RG 319, NARA.

[70] Quote from Paul Linebarger, "They Call 'Em Bandits in Malaya," *U.S. Army Combat Forces Journal* 1 (January 1951): 29. Memo, Maj Gen John Williams, ACS for Intelligence, 4 Mar 60, sub: U.S. Military Forces Benefits Resulting from British Anti-guerrilla Warfare in Malaya, Historians files, CMH. About a half-dozen articles on Malaya appeared in Army journals during the 1950s, while other articles made reference to it. A few students in Army schools wrote papers on the British experience, and the Army either commissioned or had access to a number of other studies on Malaya. For examples of studies, see the "Studies and Monographs" section of the select bibliography.

[71] For examples of Army-sponsored translations, studies, or lectures on Indochina, see Translation, Army G–2, Combat Methods of the Viet Minh in Villages, 1952; Translation, Army G–2, Tactics and Combat Methods of the Viet Minh, 1953; Translation, Army G–2, Practical Guide for Pacification, 1959; Translation, Army G–2, Special Training in Counterguerrilla Warfare, 1959; George Tanham, "The Likely Nature of Enemy Operational Concepts in Asia," AWC lecture, 1958. All at MHI. See also George Tanham, Doctrine and Tactics of Revolutionary Warfare: The Viet Minh in Indochina, RM 2395 (Santa Monica, Calif.: RAND, 1959); Andre Souyris, "An Effective Counterguerrilla Procedure," *Military Review* 36 (March 1957): 86–90; Lamar Prosser, "The Bloody Lessons of Indochina," *U.S. Army Combat Forces Journal* 5 (June 1955): 23–30; Paul Linebarger, "Indochina: The Bleeding War," in *Modern Guerrilla Warfare*, ed. Osanka, pp. 245–52; Bernard Fall, "Communist Organization and Tactics," *Military Review* 36 (October 1956): 1–11; idem, "Indochina, The Last Year of the War, The Navarre Plan," *Military Review* 36 (December 1956): 48–56.

[72] Considering that the doctrine of *guerre revolutionnaire* only gradually emerged in French publications between 1956 and 1961, the U.S. Army moved quickly to acquire and translate these texts. The Army even translated the entire February–March 1957 issue of the *Revue Militaire d'Information*, which was devoted to *guerre revolutionnaire*. See Translation, Army G–2, Revolutionary Warfare, 1958, MHI; Ximenes, "Revolutionary Warfare," *Military Review* 37 (August 1957): 103–08; Colonel Nemo, "The Place of Guerrilla Action in War," *Military Review* 37 (November 1957): 99–107. American analyses of French doctrine included Robert Rigg, "Twilight War," *Military Review* 40 (November 1960): 28–32; George Kelly, "Revolutionary War and Psychological Action," *Military Review* 40 (October 1960): 4–13; Mathe, "Revolutionary War"; SORO, Insurgents and Counterinsurgent Strengths and Tactics in Tunisia, 1952–1956 (Washington, D.C.: SORO, 1956). For a general discussion of French doctrine, see Shafer, *Deadly Paradigm*, pp. 138–65, and Chester Cooper, The American Experience with Pacification in Vietnam, 3 vols. (Institute for Defense Analyses, 1972), 3:95–113.

[73] First quote from Max Millikin and Walt Rostow, *A Proposal: Key to an Effective Foreign Policy* (New York: Harper & Bros., 1957), p. 6. Second quoted words from Walt Rostow, *The Stages of Economic Growth: A Non-Communist Manifesto* (New York: Cambridge University Press, 1960), p. 7. Geoffrey Fairbairn, "Approaches to Counter-Insurgency Thinking Since 1947," *South-East Asian Spectrum* 2 (January 1974): 27. For a general discussion and critique of American theories of political development, see Packenham, *Liberal America*; Shafer, *Deadly Paradigm*, pp. 48–85.

[74] John F. Kennedy, *The Strategy of Peace* (New York: Harper & Bros., 1960), pp. 60–64; Latham, *Modernization as Ideology*, pp. 1–8, 30–45, 56–66.

[75] Maxwell Taylor, *The Uncertain Trumpet* (New York: Harper & Bros., 1960); James Gavin, *War and Peace in the Space Age* (New York: Harper & Bros., 1958); Russell Weigley, *History of the United States Army* (Bloomington: Indiana University Press, 1984), p. 526; Coles, "Strategic Studies," pp. 8–9.

[76] FM 7–100, *The Infantry Division*, 1960, pp. 247–54.

[77] First quote from Presentation, General Decker to General Staff Council, 25 Nov 60, sub: The U.S. Army and National Security, 1960–70, p. 11, DCSOPS, 1960, RG 319, NARA (hereafter cited as Decker Presentation). Other quotes from ibid., p. ii.

[78] First quote from Rpt, U.S. Army, 7 Dec 60, sub: Strategic Army Study (STARS–70), the U.S. Army and National Security, 1960–70, p. 32, DCSOPS, 1961, RG 319, NARA (hereafter cited as STARS–70). Second quote from Decker Presentation, p. 13.

[79] Quote from STARS–70, p. 116.

[80] Decker Presentation, pp. ii, 16–18; STARS–70, pp. 129–31, 143–44.

[81] French influence was apparent in a general way in the depiction of the problem as a revolutionary, largely unconventional struggle against international communism. British influence was more discernable, as certain terms employed in the manuscript, like *special police*, *special constables*, and *special intelligence personnel* were all terms employed by the British. McClintock, *Instruments of Statecraft*, p. 215.

[82] Quotes from Special Warfare Division, ODCSOPS, Counter Insurgency Operations: A Handbook for the Suppression of Communist Guerrilla/Terrorist Operations, 1 Dec 60, pp. 2–3, and see also p. 25, Historians files, CMH.

[83] Quote from ibid., p. 21, and see also pp. 2, 22, 40–41.

[84] Quotes from ibid., p. 40, and see also pp. 22–26, 38–41.

[85] Quote from ibid., p. 30, and see also pp. 22–26, 31–34, 45.

[86] Memo, Lt Gen John C. Oakes, DCSOPS, for ASD, Financial Management (FM), 29 Nov 60, sub: Counter-Guerrilla Activities; Memo, Brig Gen Edward G. Lansdale, Dep Asst to the Secy of Def (Special Opns), for Asst Secy of the Army George H. Roderick, 21 Oct 60, sub: Counter-Guerrilla Activities; Memo, Lt Gen John C. Oakes, DCSOPS, for ASD (FM), 21 Dec 60, sub: Counter-Guerrilla Activities. All in 370.64, CSA, RG 319, NARA. Talking Paper, Unconventional Warfare Br, J–5, JCS, 21 Feb 61, sub: Service Guerrilla Warfare and Counterguerrilla Warfare Capabilities and Training, 031.1, Nov 60–Dec 61, Chairman Lemnitzer file, JCS, RG 218, NARA; FM 100–1, *Doctrinal Guidance*, chg 1, 10 Jan 61, p. 23-102.

[87] Quote from FM 100–1, *Doctrinal Guidance*, chg 1, 10 Jan 61, p. 23-101.

[88] First quote from ibid., p. 23-103. Second quote from ibid., p. 23-902, and see also pp. 23-104, 23-901.

[89] Quote from ibid., p. 23-105, and see also pp. 23-103, 23-104.

[90] Ibid., pp. 23-105, 23-106, 23-701.

[91] Ibid., pp. 23-103, 23-104, 23-501, 23-502.

5

COLD WAR CONTINGENCY
OPERATIONS, 1958-1965

President Eisenhower may not have wanted to involve U.S. ground forces in foreign imbroglios, but neither he nor his successors could ignore the utility of military power in conducting foreign policy. Nor could the Army, as both history and prudence dictated that it be prepared to undertake limited contingency operations in support of American diplomacy. After the Korean War the Army tried to improve its capability for performing contingency missions, at least to the extent permitted by the limited budgets of the Eisenhower years. Most of these arrangements were of a conventional nature and were undertaken to facilitate the Army's capacity either to wage war or to reinforce forward-deployed forces in Germany and Korea. Yet any improvements in the Army's ability to project power also made it a more capable body for performing missions of a diplomatic or constabulary nature. These initiatives were still in their infancy when President Eisenhower put the Army's skills in coercive diplomacy to the test by sending it to intervene in the Lebanese Civil War.

Lebanon, 1958

America's involvement in the Lebanese Civil War stemmed from President Eisenhower's desire to prevent the wave of radical, anti-Western nationalism that was sweeping through the Middle East in the mid-1950s from engulfing Lebanon, a nation riven by deep political, factional, and religious conflicts. Concerned that the Soviet Union was exploiting Arab nationalism to cover Communist activity in the region, in 1957 Eisenhower declared that the United States would provide military assistance to any Middle Eastern nation threatened by international communism. Camille Chamoun, the pro-Western, Christian president of Lebanon, was the only Arab leader to embrace the Eisenhower Doctrine. This action, however, inflamed Lebanon's Muslim community, which accused Chamoun of violating the country's neutralist policies that had kept that deeply divided country at peace. (*Map 8*)

Charges of fraud in Lebanon's 1957 legislative elections and Chamoun's ambition to be reelected for a second term in 1958 despite constitutional prohibitions heightened tensions within Lebanon. So too did the announcement in February 1958 by Egypt, Syria, and Yemen that they were forming a United Arab Republic (UAR), an entity that both Eisenhower and Chamoun regarded with suspicion, but which was warmly received by proponents of pan-Arabism in Lebanon. The situation came to a head in May when one of Chamoun's critics was assassinated. Rioting erupted in the Lebanese capital of Beirut that quickly took on the trappings of a civil war. The Lebanese Army under the command of General Fuad Shihab adopted a neutral stance, guarding government buildings but otherwise standing aside as Chamoun's supporters and opponents battled in the streets. Chamoun accused the United Arab Republic of arming his opponents and inflaming Muslim sentiments with radio broadcasts calling for Lebanon's absorption into the new pan-Arab state, and when UAR sympathizers overthrew the pro-Western ruler of Iraq, Chamoun used the incident to request American intervention on 14 July. Fearing that a similar coup might occur in Lebanon, Eisenhower immediately ordered U.S. troops to Beirut, despite Joint Chiefs Chairman Air Force General Nathan F. Twining's warning that "we may be there for ten years or longer."[1]

The celerity with which the president acted caught the armed forces only partially prepared. Consequently, U.S. troops entered Lebanon in piecemeal fashion, a dangerous maneuver given the fact that the Lebanese Army might well have chosen to defend Lebanon's territorial sovereignty despite Chamoun's plea for intervention. Fortunately, the first troops to wade ashore on 15 July—the 2d Battalion, 2d Marines—faced nothing more dangerous than bikini-clad women and boys aggressively hawking bottles of soda pop. After securing a beachhead that included the national airport, the marines peacefully entered Beirut the following day escorted by the Lebanese Army, a development made possible only by last-minute negotiations between the expedition commander, Admiral James L. Holloway, Jr.; U.S. Ambassador Robert M. McClintock; and General Shihab that narrowly averted a clash between American and Lebanese forces. Meanwhile, more marines streamed into Lebanon, followed on 19

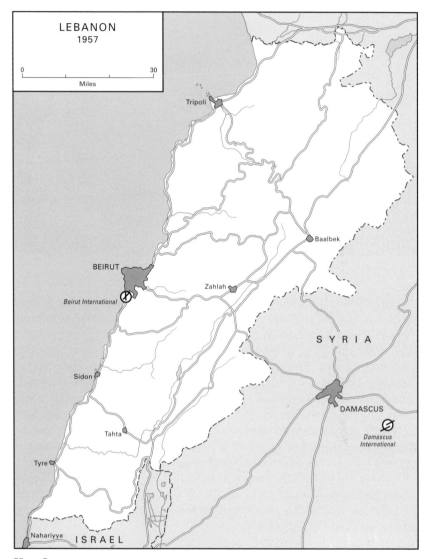

MAP 8

July by soldiers from the 24th Infantry Division's 187th Airborne Battle Group. Additional 24th Division units arrived in ensuing days until the United States had approximately 14,000 men on the ground—over 8,000 soldiers and nearly 6,000 marines—not counting air units and the U.S. Sixth Fleet offshore.[2]

Soldiers gain their bearings in Lebanon.

Eisenhower gave the military a threefold mission. The first task, to protect American life and property, was concrete and easily achieved. Thanks to the cooperation of Lebanese authorities, the United States had no trouble placing guards at American facilities as well as other vital installations. The second goal, to dissuade either the United Arab Republic or the Soviet Union from meddling in Lebanon's internal affairs, was more nebulous but readily achieved, since neither entity made any overt moves to intervene. The president's final objective, to thwart any attempt to overthrow the Lebanese government, proved the thorniest. Eisenhower hoped to achieve stability without having to commit U.S. forces in direct support of any particular political faction. Of course, by using U.S. forces to protect the government, the United States had already meddled in Lebanon's internal affairs. Nevertheless, Eisenhower maintained some room for maneuver by refusing to endorse Chamoun's bid for a second term.[3]

Although Marine patrols occasionally traveled as far as 32 kilometers inland, for the most part U.S. forces operated in a narrow area 20 kilometers wide and 16 kilometers deep that included Beirut, the international airport, and the landing beaches. By mutual agreement, most Americans remained outside of the city and confined their activities to garrisoning key facilities and conducting combined patrols with the Lebanese Army along roads the Americans used to maintain communications between their outposts. The Lebanese Army assumed positions between the Americans and those sections of Beirut controlled by radical Muslim elements, thereby minimizing the danger of a clash. Although the situation was sometimes tense and always unpredictable, the soldiers soon settled into a fairly uneventful routine of patrol and sentry duty. Snipers frequently menaced the troops, but no conflict of any size developed, thanks to Shihab's buffer forces and to strict rules of engagement. These rules prohibited U.S. soldiers from shooting unless they were fired upon, and then only if they could clearly identify the source of the fire and respond without unduly risking innocent lives.[4]

An American and Lebanese soldier man a joint checkpoint.

The expeditionary force also tried to discourage confrontation by overawing potential adversaries. Heavily armored patrols, live-fire exhibitions, and choreographed training exercises all served to demonstrate American power. Strict codes of conduct that demanded good behavior, neat uniforms, and correct martial bearing likewise helped impress the population. U.S. efforts to influence the Lebanese Army were less successful, as the Lebanese politely declined most offers of U.S. training assistance.[5]

Two weeks after the intervention began, Lebanon held presidential elections. Under American pressure, Chamoun did not run and instead supported Shihab, who won the election and quickly set about creating a compromise cabinet. Shihab's reputation for neutrality and his efforts to reach out to all sides mollified most, though not all, of the opposition. Unrest continued, albeit at increasingly lower levels, until September when pro-UAR elements inside Beirut finally disbanded. By the end of the month the United States withdrew all of the marines from Lebanon. The Army contingent soldiered on for another month before completing the withdrawal on 25 October. Shortly thereafter, Shihab renounced the Eisenhower Doctrine.[6]

In the words of Ambassador McClintock, the Lebanon intervention proved to be "that rarest of military miracles: the making of an omelet without breaking the eggs." In just 102 days the United States had stopped the fighting and paved the way for peaceful elections and a constitutional resolution to the crisis. The price of success was $200 million, not counting millions more in economic and military aid, and one American life. As far as was known, U.S. forces did not cause a single casualty. A wise policy of not backing Chamoun's bid for a second term, capable negotiating on the part of American diplomatic personnel, a cautious employment of U.S. ground forces, and the indispensable support provided by the Lebanese Army under General Shihab had, along with a good deal of luck, facilitated the positive outcome. The brief intervention had not resolved Lebanon's deep social and sectarian problems, fissures that would eventually erupt into renewed civil war and foreign intervention in the 1970s and 1980s. But for the present, the intervention had achieved its purpose.[7]

Although the Army had performed well, the operation nevertheless revealed many weaknesses in conception and execution. Many of the troubles that plagued the intervention were recurring problems that pertained to all forms of contingency operations. Included among the lessons learned in Lebanon were the need for more detailed, yet flexible, plans; the necessity of adhering to proper regimens governing the loading and shipping of equipment; and the benefits to be gained by frequently practicing for contingency operations. Interservice coordination, though it improved over the course of the operation, had been weak at the outset, particularly since the plans had failed to provide for an overall ground force commander. Rather, the Marine force commander, Brig. Gen. Sidney S. Wade, and the Army contingent commander, Brig. Gen. David W. Gray, had operated independently under the loose coordination of Admiral Holloway until 24 July, nine days into the operation, when the Joint Chiefs of Staff finally sent Army Maj. Gen. Paul D. Adams to oversee the land effort.[8]

The command oversight mirrored other problems that, taken together, had seriously compromised the ability of the armed forces to act as an effective instrument of national policy during the early days of the intervention. To begin with, there had been virtually no direct communication between the Navy and Ambassador McClintock during the initial hours of the operation. The communication breakdown made adjusting military plans to changing political realities difficult and could easily have produced grave consequences. The eventual establishment of a single ground commander in the person of General Adams and the creation of a Lebanese-American Civil Affairs Commission with representatives from the Lebanese government, the embassy, and the American military greatly facilitated coordination, as did the arrival of Deputy Under Secretary of State Robert Murphy as President Eisenhower's special representative. Billed as a "five-star diplomat" in a theater in which the highest-ranking military officer

A U.S. tank clears away an insurgent roadblock.

(Admiral Holloway) was of four-star rank, Murphy was in a position to oversee both the ambassador and the armed forces, thereby unifying the politico-military effort.[9]

Though the command structure functioned adequately in the end, logistical issues were an enduring problem. The Army's logistical system was geared toward pushing large quantities of supplies forward in support of combat operations on hostile shores, and it proved too cumbersome and inflexible for a limited contingency in which there was virtually no fighting. Indeed, zealous logisticians soon buried the small intervention force under nearly 50,000 tons of supplies. Storing and handling this vast mountain of equipment was a major headache, as was the task of protecting it against enterprising Lebanese pilferers. Because of the paucity of combat troops in Lebanon, General Gray required supply and service personnel to protect the depots, with unhappy results. Despite the fact that doctrine had long required that support troops be prepared to defend themselves against infiltrators and irregulars, the service elements loudly protested security details, which they performed with indifference.

Unimaginative thinking with regard to security also manifested itself in the initial plans for the defense of the Army's main base in Lebanon, the international airport. General Gray's staff wanted to disperse U.S. paratroopers in company-size packets around the airport as called for in conventional doctrine for the defense of an airfield. When he learned of this, Gray immediately redrew the plans to create a much tighter perimeter designed to stop snipers, fanatics, and small bands of infiltrators—the type of threat he believed posed the greatest danger to his forces. The alteration was a wise one, though it illustrated the lack of forethought Gray's planners had given to the unconventional aspects of their mission.

Planning was most inadequate in the realms of civil affairs and intelligence. The Army entered Lebanon without either a status of forces agreement between the United States and Lebanon—a major impediment to smooth relations when operating inside a sovereign country—or any detailed information as to the political and military situation on the ground. Fortunately, the U.S. embassy in Beirut was still functioning and was able to provide the military with a great deal of assistance on political and intelligence matters, without which the expedition would have faced grave difficulties. Although the Army successfully implemented its traditional creed of good conduct by enforcing troop discipline, by providing humanitarian assistance, and by compensating Lebanese property owners for damages and inconveniences, it concluded from the experience that future intervention forces must be given larger civil affairs staffs and more detailed politico-military intelligence.[10]

Perhaps the most embarrassing failure occurred in public relations. Although the United States Information Service (USIS) was in charge of the overall public information effort, each of the military services was to provide its own public affairs staff to help manage the information "war" in Lebanon. Unfortunately, General Gray had decided not to include his public information staff in the initial contingent that deployed to Lebanon since none of his public affairs personnel were parachute qualified. This left him without anyone during the initial days of the operation to handle the pack of newsmen who had descended on Lebanon. The consequences were not long in coming. Soon after the landing, the *Washington Post* published photos depicting U.S. forces in Lebanon—one of a battle-hardened marine charging across a beach with a fixed bayonet, the other of a soldier sitting on a donkey drinking a soda. Army Chief of Staff General Maxwell D. Taylor was so upset that he immediately flew a special public affairs team from Washington to Beirut to perform the important task of managing press relations—and shaping public perceptions—for the remainder of this sensitive politico-military operation.[11]

The Emergence of Doctrine for "Situations Short of War"

The Lebanon experience demonstrated that the Defense Department needed to be better prepared for limited overseas contingency operations. While most of the military's remedial efforts focused on relatively

190

General Taylor believed this photo of a U.S. soldier riding a burro created adverse publicity for the Army.

conventional issues of joint planning, command and control, logistics, and interoperability, the Army did in fact examine issues peculiar to operations of a constabulary nature. Although the 1954 edition of FM 100–5, *Field Service Regulations, Operations*, had first broached the subjects of limited warfare and the subordination of military action to political and diplomatic purposes, the Army took several years to flesh out some basic concepts regarding peacetime contingencies. These ideas were just entering Army doctrinal literature at the time of the Lebanese crisis under the designation "situations short of war."

As the Army defined them, situations short of war were "military operations which lie in the area between normal peaceful relations and open hostilities between nations." According to Army manuals, the United States undertook such operations to bolster a faltering government, to stabilize a restless area, to deter aggression, and to maintain order. Missions that the Army believed it might have to perform during a situation short of war included making a show of force, enforcing a truce, serving as an international police force, and undertaking a legally sanctioned occupation—in short, missions largely of a diplomatic and constabulary nature.[12]

For the most part, Army texts during the 1950s confined their discussion of situations short of war to broad principles. In part, this reflected a recognition by doctrine writers that such operations were too varied to be easily codified into rules and regulations. Moreover, the Army believed that many of the particulars of constabulary service—like riot control, civil affairs, military policing, and small-unit patrolling—were already adequately covered in existing doctrine. The proper execution of these and other functions during an overseas contingency was less a matter of developing new doctrine than of intelligently adapting existing procedures to the exigencies of the moment.

Because peacetime contingency operations were "inherently delicate," Army manuals emphasized that all personnel regardless of rank had to be thoroughly familiar with American policy and the implications of that policy when performing their duties. Recognizing that "sound troop discipline" was indispensable for a successful outcome, Army doctrine recommended that troops assigned to contingency duty be instructed on local laws and customs, personal conduct, and the proper treatment of women. Smart dress and the maintenance of a courteous, yet martial, bearing were integral to winning the respect of the local population. Army texts during the mid-1950s also counseled commanders to prepare their men for some of the frustrations typically associated with politico-military operations, including long tours, enervating sentry duty, and shadowy foes who might employ terrorism and other irregular methods against U.S. forces. Strong discipline, troop indoctrination, and inspired leadership would help counteract corrosive influences on troop morale and behavior. Restraint was also a watchword, for in the words of one manual, "the excessive use of force can never be justified; it can only lead to the need to apply ever-increasing force to maintain the same degree of order, and to the loss of the sympathy and support of the local populace. If efforts to win over the local populace are not to be defeated, the enemy dead and wounded must be treated with respect and humanity, no matter how despicable the acts."[13]

Unlike the pre-1939 Army, which had generally resented civilian interference in military operations and had sought to insulate commanders from external meddling, the post–World War II Army accepted the premise that "in most cases, political considerations are overriding." It acceded to the State Department's primacy on policy issues in short-of-war operations. It further enjoined expeditionary commanders to establish sound, collaborative relationships with the many entities that would inevitably be involved in a contingency operation, starting with the various service components and extending to the local representatives of the State Department and other U.S. civilian agencies, the armed forces of allied contingents (if present), and the civil and military officials of the country in which the operation was being undertaken. Still, a jealous regard for professional autonomy led the Army to endorse the use of mission-type orders that would give an expedition commander "considerable latitude in determining how to accomplish his assigned mission." It likewise argued that "the commander on the spot alone is in a position to establish the degree of force that must be used." Command relationships between Washington and the field and between civil and military authorities thus defied easy categorization and remained a delicate doctrinal issue.[14]

The Army believed that the division would be the basic element employed in contingency operations, as smaller formations would lack both the manpower and the administrative apparatus needed to operate effectively as an autonomous force. Recognizing the inherently political nature of the contingency environment, doctrine writers recommended that the State Department assign an adviser to the expedition if a U.S. embassy was not functioning in the area of operations. A division operating in a situation short of war was also to receive additional civil affairs personnel so that it could adequately prepare civil and economic plans in conjunction with other U.S. agencies. Division engineers and service personnel would support these plans by providing humanitarian and construction assistance to benighted areas. Official doctrine also recognized the need to augment the division's intelligence capability. Unlike conventional warfare, in which military intelligence tended to focus on the terrain and the enemy's war-making assets, situations short of war required a much broader effort, to include political, historical, and social factors; personalities; and the causes of unrest. All sources, including U.S. civilian agencies and indigenous institutions, were to be tapped in the pursuit of information, perhaps to include the establishment by the Army of its own police and clandestine intelligence networks. Safeguarding information, personnel, and supplies from the machinations of hostile agents, guerrillas, and black marketeers likewise required extra vigilance in the shadowy world of constabulary operations, where front lines and clearly defined enemies would be rare. These circumstances, together with the inherent sensitivity of politico-military operations, also raised the specter of adverse media relations, as the photo incident in Lebanon demonstrated. To address this problem, doctrine writers recommended that "within sensible security limitations, a cordial and straightforward treatment of correspondents will go far toward public understanding of the issues and it will facilitate accomplishment of the mission."[15]

Because doctrine for situations short of war was just being drafted around the time of the Lebanon intervention, few officers were familiar with it.[16] Nevertheless, the Lebanon experience confirmed many of the new doctrine's tenets, and consequently the Army expended little effort in revising its manuals after the Lebanon intervention. Change 1 to FM 17–100, *The Armored Division and Combat Command*, which appeared in June 1959, greatly increased that manual's coverage of situations short of war but introduced little that was new. Perhaps based on the Lebanese experience, the manual warned that political considerations might restrict a commander's freedom of action, even to the degree of seriously impairing the effectiveness of the operation. Such obstacles could be alleviated only by time-consuming negotiation. The manual likewise noted that "the general requirement for application of minimum necessary force to avoid unwarranted alienation of local populations can seriously reduce the availability of normal fire support to the maneuver elements. The division commander will often find it necessary to limit or even prohibit the use of field artillery, primary tank guns, mortars, and rocket launchers except under specific emergency conditions." Finally, the manual emphasized the positive role civil affairs officers could play in minimizing these adverse conditions by forming civilian-military liaison agencies as had been done in Lebanon. Yet beyond this the manual did not go, stating that the "unusual conditions posed by a situation short of war" precluded any attempt to prescribe more definitive procedures.[17]

Other manuals published after the Lebanese incursion likewise failed to break new ground. This fact drew criticism from a small number of officers who believed that the Army was not doing enough to prepare for overseas constabulary duty. Chief among the critics was General Gray, who in 1960 wrote an article outlining operational concepts for what he described as situations "short of Small War." Although he admitted that the Army already had relevant doctrinal and training materials and that some units were indeed training for such missions, Gray believed that the Army needed to devote greater attention to constabulary subjects. The best way to do this, he felt, was to amplify the existing materials and publish them in a single manual devoted exclusively to situations short of war. Conceptually, the principles that Gray espoused differed little from published doctrine, though his article did contain useful descriptions of some of the special tactics and techniques he had recently used in Lebanon. These included roadblocks, area sweeps, town searches, urban combat, population screening, and show-of-force operations.[18]

The Army did not answer Gray's call for a manual on situations short of war, although it continued to expand its coverage of the subject in Army texts. This movement received a significant boost in 1962, when the Army began publishing a new family of manuals in response to President Kennedy's drive to create flexible military forces capable of responding to any contingency. Toward this end, the 1962 edition of FM 100–5, *Field Service Regulations, Operations*, formally adopted Robert Osgood's conceptual paradigm of a "spectrum of war," a sliding scale on the employment of military force to achieve national ends. All-out nuclear warfare lay at the most extreme end of the spectrum, from which point the degree of violence gradually declined along a continuum through general war, limited war, and finally to the least violent category of conflict, cold war. The manual defined *cold war* as the sum total of political, military, economic, and psychological measures, short of waging general or limited war, which could be used in a power struggle between contending nations or coalitions. Situations short of war represented a subset of the cold war, "in which military force is moved to an area directly and is employed to attain national objectives in operations not involving formal open hostilities between nations," but which might include combat, most probably against irregular forces like rioters, subversives, and guerrillas.[19]

FM 100–5 (1962) also expounded on the notion, first introduced in the 1954 edition, that military force must be tailored to fit the political objectives for which it was being employed, asserting that an operation was "futile unless it is directed toward the attainment of the objective set for it." Broad political objectives circumscribed strategy and tactics alike, although the Army maintained that operations always needed to be conducted with sufficient strength and vigor to obtain the desired result. This caveat, which the manual argued did not contradict the primacy of national objectives, nonetheless highlighted the dynamic tension over ends and means that inevitably accompanies the use of force, especially in limited wars and contingencies. The manual further noted that commanders had to demonstrate ingenuity in wrestling with the complex web of political, military, and geographical factors that gave each operation a unique cast.[20]

Having established a general context for military operations in the mid-twentieth century, FM 100–5 (1962) included two new chapters related to cold war operations: "Military Operations Against Irregular Forces," which will be discussed in Chapter 6, and "Situations Short of War." While the inclusion of an eight-page chapter on situations short of war in the Army's prime combat manual elevated the visibility of the subject throughout the Army, the content of that chapter differed little from the doctrine propounded in earlier manuals. Both the precepts and the wording remained virtually unchanged. The manual envisioned that commanders would be subordinated to the State Department in all matters pertaining to political and civil affairs and that they would have to be prepared to coordinate their actions with a host of American and indigenous bureaucratic institutions. It reaffirmed the advisability of tailoring forces and procedures to the situation and of issuing "mission-type orders" in which the commander would "be given necessary latitude in determining how to accomplish his assigned mission." The manual highlighted the important roles that civil affairs, psychological warfare, and intelligence personnel played in such operations. It also endorsed the application of minimum force and emphasized the necessity of winning the support of the local population. Finally, FM 100–5 (1962) reiterated earlier calls that, to the extent possible, contingency troops receive special tactical, environmental, linguistic, and cultural training for the specific mission in which they were to be employed.[21]

Lower-level manuals published in 1962 also expanded their coverage of situations short of war. Most significantly, both FM 41–10, *Civil Affairs Operations*, and FM 33–5, *Psychological Operations*, added new sections on the application of their particular arts in cold war environments. Reflecting the Lebanon experience, the civil affairs manual noted the importance of negotiating a favorable status of forces agreement at the earliest opportunity and endorsed using civil affairs personnel in a wide variety of liaison, training, and civic action roles. According to FM 33–5, the main function of psychological operations (psyops) during situations short of war was to convince the indigenous population that America's actions were legal, that its intentions were benevolent, and that its presence would be temporary. Psychological operations personnel were expected to win popular support for intervention forces, to counter hostile propaganda, and to undermine the popularity of enemy irregulars. The manual also discussed the relationship between military and civilian information organizations, stating that Army psyops units would have to be prepared to operate in close coordination with and under the supervision of embassy personnel. Neither manual, however, described many tactics or techniques specifically designed for contingency operations. This was in keeping with the premise that conventional methods, intelligently modified to the conditions at hand, would prove adequate.[22]

If the thrust of Army doctrine changed little between 1955 and 1965, the Army continued to take actions to improve its cold war capabilities. A number of schools introduced cold war operations into their curriculums, including the Command and General Staff College, whose mission to teach mid-level staff procedures and to develop combined operations doctrine at the division and corps level made it the natural locus for contingency operations education in the Army. In 1957 the CGSC introduced three new courses into its curriculum: "Infantry

Division in a Situation Short of War," "Airborne Division in Situations Short of War," and "Airborne Corps in Independent Police Action." By the late 1950s instruction in situations short of war constituted about 7 percent of the Fort Leavenworth curriculum. By 1962 cold war operations, including situations short of war and counterinsurgency, had grown to encompass about 13 percent of the school's instruction. Still, while Leavenworth related a great deal of information relevant for planning, organizing, transporting, and supporting overseas expeditions, it did not delve too deeply into the conduct of military interventions beyond the general principles contained in the manuals.

The school's cold war and limited war operations courses did serve, however, as a vehicle for reinvigorating counterguerrilla studies at the college. This trend reflected the fact that Army planners believed that irregular warfare was the most likely threat U.S. soldiers would face in conducting short-of-war operations. Consequently, beginning in 1958 and for nearly every year thereafter during the period covered by this volume, the Command and General Staff College included either a cold war or limited war counterguerrilla exercise in its curriculum. In 1958, for example, CGSC students reviewed a variety of sources (including historical treatises on World War II partisan movements and the 1944 German manual *Fighting the Guerrilla Bands*) to craft plans for a hypothetical American intervention in Iran to combat a Soviet-inspired tribal uprising. The scenario called for the "maximum use of psychological warfare to separate the guerrillas and the civilians ideologically," and an active civil affairs program in which U.S. troops would "go out of their way" to "gain the support of the civilians by doing so-called good works where possible by such means as lending medical assistance to civilians," distributing food, and undertaking other "beneficial projects to consolidate popular support." According to the school, these and other nation-building activities were "an important adjunct to military operations." In the meantime, the United States would arm village self-defense groups to insulate the population from guerrilla intimidation while sealing the border to prevent external aid from reaching the insurgents. Having denied the rebels both external and internal support, the plan mimicked established doctrine in seeking to destroy them through a combination of aggressive, highly mobile small-unit actions and encirclements in which artillery and tanks took a backseat to light infantry tactics and heliborne operations.[23]

Scenarios employed in subsequent years quoted heavily from the now defunct FM 31–20 (1951) in considering counterguerrilla campaigns under a variety of circumstances, from situations where the United States restricted its role to providing military advice, to more direct interventions, to operations conducted in the course of a limited war in some third world country. All of these exercises stressed the synergistic effect of political, economic, and psychological action, population and resources security, clandestine intelligence, and vigorous, small-unit operations to isolate a guerrilla force from its sources of support and ultimately destroy it. Such were the tactics the United States would employ if its intervention forces were confronted by an irregular opponent.[24]

While students at the Command and General Staff College practiced planning interventions designed to suppress local insurgencies, the Army moved ahead during the late 1950s and early 1960s to create the tools necessary to execute such contingencies. In 1958 the Army formed the Strategic Army Corps (STRAC), whose four divisions—the 82d and 101st Airborne Divisions and 1st and 4th Infantry Divisions—were to act as a ready reserve, either to reinforce forward-deployed units in a general war or to provide the initial forces for a limited war or lesser contingency. In 1961 the Pentagon merged the STRAC into a new joint entity, Strike Command (STRICOM), under the command of General Adams, the former joint land force commander during the Lebanon intervention. The Strike Command drafted contingency plans, developed doctrine for executing contingency missions, and imposed training programs to ensure that the Army and Air Force units under its command were capable of implementing those plans and doctrines.[25]

If the creation of STRAC and STRICOM, together with upgrades to the Air Force's transportation fleet, improved the Army's ability to conduct contingency operations in general, the Army also began to look at creating contingency forces specifically for situations short of war. Army Chief of Staff General George H. Decker's suggestion in December 1960 that the United States create two regionally oriented Cold War task forces, each composed of an airborne brigade and a Special Forces group, would have created organizations specifically designed for taking direct action in the lower end of the spectrum of war. The following year, however, Decker eliminated the airborne brigades from the proposed task forces, recasting them from direct action forces into organizations intended primarily to advise and assist foreign countries "in low intensity cold war situations." The revised concept eventually came to fruition in 1962 in the form of Special Action Forces (SAFs). Each SAF consisted of a Special Forces group augmented by engineer, civil affairs, psychological warfare, military police, medical, and intelligence detachments. Although theoretically capable of deploying in toto during a contingency, the SAF's primary mission was to provide mobile teams of area-oriented, linguistically trained experts who would supplement more conventionally oriented military assistance advisory groups in helping foreign armies perform unconventional warfare, counterinsurgency, civic action, and nation-building activities.[26]

Ultimately, the Army formed six SAFs, one each for Europe, Latin America, Asia, Africa, and the Middle East, plus a reserve. Supporting the Latin American, Asian, African, and Middle Eastern SAFs were four "backup" brigades drawn from each of the four divisions in the STRAC. In addition to providing added personnel from whom the SAFs could draw training assistance teams, the brigades were to be the initial spearheads for direct American action in any situation short of war that the supported SAF and the indigenous military could not handle. The backup brigades were capable of operating independently for up to five weeks but required significant augmentation and reinforcement for longer or larger operations. Their personnel received some language and cultural orientation relevant to their assigned regions, plus at least six weeks of counterinsurgency training every year. The SAF-backup brigade arrangement reflected a recognition on the part of the Army of the benefits of having a body of linguistically capable, culturally sensitive, and specially trained troops available for delicate cold war operations. The backup brigade concept remained in force throughout the period considered by this study.[27]

Over the next few years the SAFs would send hundreds of training teams to dozens of countries to help redress socioeconomic ills and suppress internal unrest. In the meantime, conventional Army forces put their cold war training and doctrine to the test on two occasions—in Thailand in 1962 and the Dominican Republic in 1965.

Doctrine at Work: Thailand and the Dominican Republic

The 1962 deployment to Thailand had its origins in the Indochina War and subsequent turmoil in Thailand's northern neighbor, Laos. The 1954 Geneva agreement that terminated the Indochina War had created a nonaligned kingdom in Laos. The newly independent state was deeply divided between Communist, anti-Communist, and neutralist factions—a situation that eventually led to civil war in 1959. The United States, which had been secretly providing the Royal Laotian Army with materiel since 1957, backed the anti-Communists by covertly detailing Special Forces personnel to train the Laotian Army. This operation continued on a clandestine basis until the United States formally created a military assistance group and White Star Mobile Training Teams in Laos in 1961. The Communists countered these moves by sending Soviet advisers and North Vietnamese soldiers to support the Laotian Communists, the Pathet Lao. Weakened by political infighting, corruption, logistical shortfalls, and inexperience, the Royal Laotian Army performed poorly. Even America's newest cold war weapon, civic action, which U.S. Army Special Forces and civil affairs personnel introduced to Laos in 1957 based on Philippine precedents, failed to stem Communist momentum. Consequently, in 1961 the Laotian government agreed to a shaky truce with the Pathet Lao and its allies in the neutralist camp. The truce, however, proved short-lived, for in May 1962 the Pathet Lao renewed the war by seizing the strategic town of Nam Tha in northwestern Laos.[28]

President Kennedy feared that the Communists might conquer Laos and use that country as a springboard to subvert the pro-Western government in neighboring Thailand. He was also reluctant to commit U.S. forces to a remote and ineffectively governed country. Having come to the conclusion that the restoration of a truly neutral, non-aligned Laos was the best he could hope for, the president decided to use military power to achieve that result. Rather than sending intervention troops directly into Laos, Kennedy opted to deploy U.S. forces to neighboring Thailand in what amounted to a show-of-force operation. The deployment would signal the Communists that the United States would not permit Laos to fall under communism. It would also boost the morale of anti-Communist forces in Laos and reassure Thailand, a Southeast Asia Treaty Organization (SEATO) ally, that the United States would not abandon it to the approaching Communist tide. Yet by stopping short of direct intervention, Kennedy would also put pressure on the pro-Western forces in Laos to seek an accommodation with the neutralist faction.[29]

To these ends and with the consent of the Thai government, Kennedy ordered U.S. troops to Thailand in May 1962. Col. William A. McKean's 1st Battle Group, 27th Infantry, 25th Infantry Division, was already in Thailand on a SEATO exercise and formed the nucleus of the force. It was soon joined by additional 25th Division troops, a Marine brigade, an air squadron, and token allied contingents from Great Britain, Australia, and New Zealand—approximately 5,000 men in all, of whom 2,300 were U.S. Army personnel. Washington appointed the 25th Infantry Division's commander, Maj. Gen. James L. Richardson, to lead the expedition, which was designated Joint Task Force 116.

The deployment proved uneventful. Whether influenced by the demonstration of force or not, the warring factions inside Laos quickly reached an accord in which they agreed to set aside their weapons and create a coalition government committed to a nonaligned foreign

U.S. soldiers undergo live-fire counterguerrilla training in Thailand.

policy. The international community lent its support to the settlement by agreeing at Geneva that all foreign military personnel should depart from Laos, thereby transforming Laos—at least on paper—from battleground to neutral ground in the ongoing Cold War. By July the crisis was over.

With no enemy to fight, the Americans spent most of their time building camps and airfields, conducting training, and participating in exercises with the Thai armed forces. They also reconnoitered much of northern Thailand in case they had to undertake more active operations on the Laotian border. Meanwhile, General Richardson kept a keen eye on the public relations aspects of the deployment. Soldiers of the 25th Division repaired roads and bridges, cleared fields for farmers, treated the sick, hosted sporting events, and formed an amateur band that performed daily concerts. These and other civic actions kept Joint Task Force 116 in good standing with the general population during its sojourn in Thailand.[30]

Washington recalled the marines in August, and the following month Richardson replaced the original Army contingent with Col. John A. Olson's 1st Battle Group, 35th Infantry. Olson's men remained in Thailand until December, when the Pentagon withdrew the task force altogether. The withdrawal did not, however, terminate America's military presence in Thailand, as the United States replaced the infantrymen with engineers who over the next decade revamped Thailand's logistical and transportation systems to facilitate U.S. military operations

Soldiers from the 27th Infantry patrol the Thai-Laotian border.

in support of the growing conflict in Vietnam. Nor had the operation succeeded in resolving the Laotian conflict, for in 1963 the precarious agreement fell apart and the civil war resumed in earnest, fueled by the presence of thousands of North Vietnamese combat troops who remained in Laos in violation of the 1962 accords. Not wishing to violate the Geneva agreement openly, the United States confined itself to providing covert aid to the Laotian Army in the guise of training, materiel, and Special Forces personnel, who, under the control of the CIA, organized guerrilla resistance to the Communists. Ultimately, none of these measures were sufficient, and after a long and bitter struggle the Pathet Lao and their North Vietnamese allies finally swept into power in 1975. Joint Task Force 116 thus proved a momentarily successful use of force in support of what otherwise turned out to be a failed effort to keep communism at bay in Laos.[31]

President Kennedy's modest deployment to Thailand had proceeded peacefully. Such was not the case when his successor, Lyndon B. Johnson, returned to coercive diplomacy several years later, this time in the Dominican Republic. The Dominican Republic was an impoverished nation burdened by a political culture in which individuals battled as much for personal gain as they did for ideological reasons. In 1961 it entered a particularly unstable period when an assassin killed the country's long-time right-wing dictator, Rafael Leonidas Trujillo Molina. The following year, the United States compelled Trujillo's ally and successor, Joaquin Balaguer, to resign, a move that paved the way for free elections and the elevation to the presidency in 1963 of Juan Bosch, leader of the left-leaning reform party, Partido Revolucionario Dominicano (PRD). Bosch's tenure proved short-lived, as military conservatives rebelled and installed Donald Reid Cabral in his place.

Reid might have been able to survive his unpopularity with the people had his efforts at reducing corruption and military spending not alienated his erstwhile patrons in the armed forces, some of whom formed a loose cabal with other anti-Reid elements and staged a coup on 24 April 1965. The coup received strong support from the people of Santo Domingo, the nation's capital. Urged into action by the PRD and other leftist organizations, including the island's three Communist parties, the city's residents took to the streets in support of Reid's ouster, thrusting the city into chaos. After capturing Reid, the Constitutionalists, as the rebels called themselves, installed a provisional government under PRD politician Jose Rafael Molina Urena. The situation quickly unraveled as the victors began to squabble among themselves over the ultimate disposition of the government. Although many hoped that Bosch would return from exile and resume the presidency, others championed Balaguer or favored establishing a military junta. The anti-Bosch elements began to defect from the Constitutionalists' cause when units of the armed forces hostile to Bosch, dubbed Loyalists, staged a counterattack that caused Molina Urena to flee the country. Constitutionalist forces under the command of Col. Francisco Caamano, however, managed to stall the Loyalist offensive, and the country gradually slipped toward civil war. Unable to retake Santo Domingo on their own, the Loyalists changed tactics, pledging to hold elections if the United States would intervene on their behalf. After evacuating many foreigners from Santo Domingo on 27 April and deploying 500 marines on the twenty-eighth to provide additional security, President Johnson decided to intervene directly in the Dominican Civil War.[32]

Johnson's motives for launching the intervention were complex. Although American authorities were unenthusiastic about Bosch, the United States did not oppose his return. Moreover, Johnson truly wished to promote democracy in the Dominican Republic and had no desire to return the country to the dictatorships and juntas of the past. But reports from Santo Domingo seemed to indicate that the Communists were behind much of the unrest inside the city and that they were using the rebellion to mask their own plans to seize control of the country. In reality, U.S. intelligence greatly overestimated the influence of the Communists within the Constitutionalist camp. But the prospect of allowing the revolution to take its course, only to find out

*Residents of Santo Domingo express confusion over
the arrival of U.S. troops.*

at the end of the day that it was indeed controlled by the Communists, frightened Johnson. Just a few years before President Eisenhower had stood by as Fidel Castro had overthrown Cuba's dictator Fulgencio Batista, only to learn too late of Castro's Communist loyalties. Johnson was determined that there should be no more Castros in Latin America, and, rather than take a chance, he chose to intervene against just such an eventuality.[33]

The first reinforcements for the 500 marines already ashore came in the form of 1,500 additional marines on 29 April. They met no resistance as they took up positions in the western part of the city around the U.S. embassy and the Embajador Hotel, where foreign nationals had gathered for evacuation. Early the following morning airplanes carrying lead elements of the 82d Airborne Division, the STRAC unit earmarked for Latin American contingencies, touched down at San Isidro airport about eighteen kilometers east of the capital. Officially, the deployment was billed as a neutral interposition to protect American lives and property. Privately, Joint Chiefs Chairman Army General Earle G. Wheeler informed Army Lt. Gen. Bruce Palmer, Jr., the ultimate commander of U.S. Forces, Dominican Republic, that his "unstated mission" was to prevent a Communist takeover.

U.S. military authorities immediately effected a close collaboration with the Loyalists. Not only had the Loyalists allowed the paratroopers to land at San Isidro, but they turned over to the 82d Airborne Division the vital Duarte Bridge, the only access point to the capital from San Isidro. The Americans in turn gave the Loyalists supplies and advice, hoping that the Dominican military would be able to quash the rebellion on its own. Palmer even developed a plan in which Loyalist forces would drive into Santo Domingo to capture several key installations and link the two American positions. If successful, the move would have trapped the bulk of the Constitutionalists in the southeastern corner of the city along the banks of the Ozama River, thereby preventing them from escaping into the countryside. Loyalist military forces proved unequal to the task, and U.S. diplomats, without consulting Palmer, agreed to a cease-fire that left the two American lodgments isolated from each other.[34]

Palmer believed the resulting situation was both militarily untenable and injurious to America's ultimate goal of suppressing the uprising. After some negotiation he managed to persuade the diplomats to allow him to link his two positions. On the night of 3 May, the marines expanded their security zone in western Santo Domingo while three battalions of paratroopers leapfrogged over each other to cut a corridor through the city along a route chosen to avoid key Constitutionalist installations and minimize the danger of conflict. The night operation took the Constitutionalists by surprise, and in just a little over an hour the soldiers secured the desired link up with minimal casualties. Over the next few days the Americans gradually expanded the corridor, variously dubbed Battle Alley and the All American Expressway, into a relatively secure line of communications that trapped 80 percent of the Constitutionalists in the southeastern corner of the capital. Although Palmer permitted people to travel freely between the two halves of the city, his roadblocks gave the Americans a stranglehold over the movement of arms into the rebel bastion, notwithstanding the ingenious efforts of Dominican smugglers.[35] (*Map 9*)

With the rebels isolated, Palmer sought authority to close in for the kill, but to no avail. President Johnson wished to avoid both the spectacle of U.S. soldiers crushing a popularly supported revolution as well as the prospect of increased U.S. casualties. Moreover, the intervention had already sparked a tremendous outcry among Latin American nations that deeply resented anything that smacked of old-fashioned Yankee gunboat diplomacy. Having already agreed to a call by the Organization of American States (OAS) for a cease-fire, Johnson was reluctant to do anything further to inflame hemispheric sensibilities. Consequently, like President Woodrow Wilson a half-century before, Johnson refrained from authorizing blunt force and endeavored instead to wield military power in a somewhat more delicate, if not entirely subtle, way to pressure the

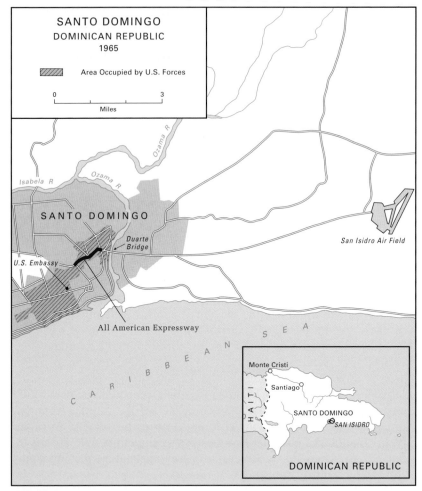

MAP 9

Dominicans into accepting his ultimate will. He ordered the 24,000 U.S. soldiers and marines in Santo Domingo to interpose themselves between the two warring parties while American diplomats capitalized on the leverage provided by the military's presence to persuade the Dominicans to accept a negotiated settlement. His decision to refrain from applying additional force, while admirable, placed a heavy burden on those charged with implementing this policy.[36]

Although Army doctrine accepted the preeminence of civilian policy makers and diplomatic concerns during situations short of war,

An American checkpoint controls the movement of people through Santo Domingo.

General Palmer resented some of the restraints placed on his freedom of action. Likewise, while doctrine fully endorsed the principle of minimum force, U.S. troops in Santo Domingo soon began to chafe at the many restrictions placed upon them by senior officials. According to the rules of engagement, U.S. tankers could return fire with their .45-caliber pistols if fired upon but needed clearance from their company commander to fire their carbines. To fire the coaxial .30-caliber machine gun mounted on their tanks, the tankers had to get the permission of General Palmer. To fire their tank's larger .50-caliber machine gun, U.S. tankers had to get the approval of the theater commander. A tank crew could not fire its 90-mm. main gun without first receiving authorization from the Pentagon in Washington. Eventually, so many restrictions were added, deleted, qualified, or changed that the troops became confused as to what the rules actually were at any given moment. One restriction, which prevented soldiers from firing unless their position was in imminent danger of being overrun, proved both demoralizing and hazardous, as Constitutionalist snipers learned that they could fire with impunity knowing that the Americans would not fire back.[37]

These problems notwithstanding, the soldiers endeavored to execute faithfully their difficult and sometimes murky assignment. Palmer collocated his headquarters with the embassy to effect closer politico-military coordination, frequently voicing his opinion on policy questions. His sensitivity to the delicate aspects of his mission and his insistence that his men exhibit decorum contributed greatly to the ultimate success of the intervention.[38]

Over the next few months U.S. troops labored to maintain the fragile and oft-violated truce while enduring frequent harassment from Constitutionalist snipers. Yet the soldiers were not truly neutral peacekeepers, for they were always ready to apply coercive measures in the interest of furthering U.S. national objectives. Army Special Forces teams, for example, assaulted Constitutionalist-controlled radio transmitters throughout the country to prevent them from disseminating revolutionary and anti-

A U.S. soldier watches a manhole to prevent the Constitutionalists from moving men and supplies through the sewer system.

American propaganda. Then, when the Constitutionalists refused to exile several Castroite leaders, Palmer helped plan a Loyalist attack that seized the country's central broadcast facilities, thereby knocking the rebels off the airwaves for good. The following month, Maj. Gen. Robert H. York, commander of the 82d Airborne Division, retaliated against the heavy Constitutionalist fire by attacking the main rebel quarter of the city. In a few hours York's men had seized approximately thirty square blocks of Constitutionalist territory and were poised to overrun the entire enclave before Palmer, on orders from Washington, reluctantly reined in his subordinate. A military solution, no matter how quick and easy to achieve, was not what President Johnson desired, yet there was no doubt in whose direction U.S. guns were pointed.[39]

The July fight proved a sobering one for the Constitutionalists, who realized that their military weakness undermined their overall negotiating position. In August they agreed to a settlement brokered by the Organization of American States. The agreement created a new provisional government under a moderate, Hector Garcia-Godoy, who pledged to hold new elections in nine months.

Although the marines had withdrawn in June, a portion of the 82d Airborne Division remained in the Dominican Republic to help implement the pact as part of an Inter-American Peacekeeping Force (IAPF). The Organization of American States had created the peace-keeping force in May at the request of the United States, which sought refuge from international condemnation by cloaking its heretofore unilateral intervention in the mantle of a multinational initiative. Ultimately, six countries—Brazil, Honduras, Paraguay, Nicaragua, Costa Rica, and El Salvador—participated by sending 1,600 soldiers and policemen. As part of its price for creating the peacekeeping force, the Organization of American States demanded that a Latin American be given command of the force, including the U.S. contingent. Palmer argued vigorously against placing U.S. troops under foreign command on the grounds that such an arrangement would undermine America's ability to use its armed forces in pursuit of national interests, but Washington acceded to the OAS' demand.

In practice, the experiment in international peacekeeping worked well. The commander of the Inter-American Peacekeeping Force, Brazilian Lt. Gen. Hugo Panasco Alvim, established a good relationship with Palmer, who by arrangement was made Alvim's deputy and retained exclusive control over the approximately 6,200 U.S. paratroopers who made up the American contingent. The United States provided nearly all of the IAPF's logistical and combat capabilities and posted Spanish-speaking officers to the staff, which was run according to American procedures. The fact that most of the Latin officers assigned to the peacekeeping force had attended U.S. military schools further smoothed operations. Nevertheless, Palmer never wavered in his opinion that placing U.S. combat troops under the field command of a foreign officer had been a "serious error" that should never be repeated.[40]

Over the course of the next year, the American contingent of the peacekeeping force protected the provisional government from subversion from both the right and the left. It demilitarized the Constitutionalist quarter of the city when rebel elements refused to disarm, while also blocking several attempted coups by military units. Meanwhile, the Americans conducted an aggressive psychological and civic action campaign. Most airborne officers in the Dominican Republic had been exposed to the concept of civic action in Army schools and readily initiated such programs from the beginning of the intervention. While Army bands serenaded the residents of Santo Domingo, Army engineers restored municipal services, repaired roads, and built schools; Army doctors provided free medical care to 58,000 people; and Army paratroopers organized youth baseball teams, hosted Christmas parties, and assisted civilian aid agencies in distributing 30 million pounds of food and 15,000 pounds of clothing. Army psyops specialists supported

A soldier distributes milk to civilians.

these activities through millions of printed propaganda items and thousands of hours of loudspeaker and radio broadcasts.

Sometimes American generosity backfired, as civilians reacted with indignation when their demands for money and helicopter rides were not met. Other complications arose when the Army chose not to reopen Santo Domingo's schools due to faculty shortages and intelligence reports that the city's schools were havens for Communist agitators. Nevertheless, while there is no objective evidence as to the effectiveness of military civil and psychological operations in the Dominican Republic, the Army's endeavors in these areas doubtlessly helped reduce civilian suffering and sped restoration of normality in the capital.[41]

In June 1966 Balaguer defeated Bosch in the presidential elections. With a new democratically elected government in place, the last Army paratroopers departed the Dominican Republic on 21 September 1966. Twenty-seven Americans had lost their lives and another 172 had been wounded during the seventeen-month intervention.

Like the Army's previous forays into situations short of war in Lebanon and Thailand, the Dominican intervention must be considered a success. A Communist takeover, if it had ever been in the cards, was forestalled and a more democratic and stable regime had been installed. On the negative side, the intervention had cost the United States the trust of its Latin neighbors, while the new Dominican government, though less oppressive than those heretofore, retained certain unsavory characteristics. The Dominican military, while somewhat chastened,

210

showed little interest in absorbing American proposals for reform and civic action, ideals which even the United States prioritized behind the maintenance of order and stability. Moreover, little progress had been made in redressing the deep-seated social and economic problems that underlay the island's political instability. But no one could reasonably expect a relatively short military intervention to achieve such lofty, yet difficult, goals. In the end, U.S. military forces did a commendable job in navigating the treacherous course laid down for them by civilian policy makers.[42]

From an operational standpoint, many of the deficiencies that had occurred in Lebanon reappeared during the Dominican expedition, notwithstanding the six years the Pentagon had had to correct them. As in Lebanon, military forces deployed to the Dominican Republic without reliable or timely intelligence on the political and military situation in the country. Although the 82d Airborne Division was the Army's contingency force for Latin America, it had not had time prior to the operation to adjust its plans to recent changes in Army organization and joint-level plans. Nor had the backup brigade concept measured up to expectations. Not only had a single brigade proved far too meager a force to send to even a small country like the Dominican Republic, but when the initial call came, General York had sent his 3d Brigade to the Caribbean rather than the designated Latin American backup force, the 1st Brigade. He had done so because elements of the 3d Brigade were currently pulling alert duty while the language-qualified and counterinsurgency-trained men of the 1st Brigade had rotated into a stand-down mode and were not immediately available for action. The 1st Brigade eventually arrived in the Dominican Republic with the rest of the division but not in its envisioned role as the highly specialized, culturally sensitive advance element for situations short of war. Even then, scheduling problems and personnel rotations left the 82d Airborne Division far short of the number of language-qualified men it could have used on the streets of Santo Domingo.[43]

While the Dominican experience pointed up some shortcomings in Army planning, the operation also illustrated other problems. Though designated for contingency duty, a mission that Army doctrine recognized required careful tailoring of forces, the 82d Airborne Division had failed to develop austere tables of organization for less than a full combat load. Once in command, General Palmer tried to limit logistical shipments to only those supplies he actually needed. This proved difficult, for as in Lebanon, the Army's logisticians were incredibly efficient at moving vast quantities of unneeded materiel to the scene of operations.[44]

Parallels to the Lebanon experience also existed in the realm of command and control. Given the complexity and sensitivity of the mission, command arrangements needed to be as clear as possible, yet during the early days of the operation three major changes in command structure occurred, and violations of the chain of command were frequent. Moreover, the communication gear the 82d Airborne Division initially brought to the island lacked the range to effect direct communication with the United States, a severe handicap in a delicate operation in which Washington strove to control every move.[45]

Just as disturbing as these flaws in command, control, and logistics was the low priority Army planners had again given to the deployment of noncombat personnel, such as civil affairs, psychological warfare, medical, and police specialists. The Army unwisely denied requests by brigade commanders for experienced civil affairs officers to be posted to their staffs, thereby forcing the commanders to create civil affairs positions from their own assets. It likewise failed to program any medical units to minister to the population and limited the number of psychological warfare and police personnel to be deployed. Experience soon showed these arrangements inadequate. Unlike Lebanon, where the United States Information Service had handled virtually the entire propaganda and public information burden using its in-country resources, in the Dominican Republic the rebels had seized USIS' physical plant, and the agency was unable to disseminate information. Caught unprepared, the Army had to increase its psychological warfare contingent from a small detachment to an entire battalion. A similar situation existed with regard to military policemen, whom Palmer found were "literally worth their weight in gold." Eventually military policemen arrived in battalion strength. A greater application of doctrinal principles by Army planners would have redressed these shortcomings and resulted in a smoother operation from the beginning.[46]

Doctrine in the Aftermath of the Dominican Intervention

The military made extensive efforts to learn from the Dominican experience. The Joint Chiefs and the three services all initiated lessons learned programs. Both U.S. Forces, Dominican Republic, and the 82d Airborne Division compiled multivolume reports, while the Army established a special center that debriefed returning soldiers and distilled their recollections into precepts to be applied in future Cold War operations. These reports were distributed to appropriate officials for planning and training considerations, as well as to the Army War College, whose students would study the Dominican crisis for the next five years.

Although many of the lessons derived from these efforts pertained to technical matters relevant to almost any contingency operation or deployment, some did indeed focus on the distinctive aspects of overseas constabulary and intervention service. One lesson widely derived by Army commentators was the need to use overwhelming force early in an intervention to overawe one's opponents. Many officers believed that the rapid deployment of a large and capable force had helped minimize the fighting in the Dominican Republic, and they roundly criticized initial plans that had envisioned employing only three battalions.

A corollary to this argument was that the best time to intervene was early in a crisis, before the opposition had time to marshal its forces. While this made sense from a combat standpoint, Army officers also favored the rapid application of overwhelming force as a way of avoiding what they regarded as undue political interference in military operations. The 82d Airborne Division report, for example, stated that the division could have easily defeated the Constitutionalists and brought the crisis to a rapid conclusion had it not been reined in by the diplomats and forced to obey a truce that initially placed U.S. military forces at a disadvantage. The report thus highlighted the continuing, and perhaps unresolvable, conflict between military and political needs and objectives in situations short of war. Had the Army dealt with the operation its way, it could have ended the conflict quicker and on a much sounder military basis, but at a much higher cost in lives and political capital and without the opportunity for obtaining the relatively peaceful resolution that was ultimately achieved, all of which were of great concern to civilian policy makers. Palmer understood this, but ultimately both York and Alvim were relieved from duty when their military and ideological preferences clashed with those of civilian policy makers.[47]

The exasperation that some soldiers voiced with regard to the degree of political interference they had endured during the Dominican intervention did not mean that Army officers objected to civilian control. Indeed, all post-operation analyses emphasized the need for continuous and close coordination between civilian and military agencies during situations short of war. Such cooperation would help ensure that military force would serve political goals under difficult and often rapidly changing circumstances. But the Army also advocated closer coordination as a way of ensuring that politicians would have to take military considerations into account in formulating their policies, something many officers believed had not been adequately achieved during the Dominican crisis. Moreover, while acceding to the principle of ultimate civilian control, Palmer and his subordinates urged a return to the principles of decentralized execution and mission-type orders, arguing that the people on the ground—the intervention commander and the ambassador—and not military and civilian officials in Washington, should be the ones making day-to-day tactical decisions.[48]

Other lessons learned, or relearned, as a result of the Dominican experience included the need for mental and organizational flexibility, the inevitability of public controversy during foreign interventions, the critical importance of acquiring and rapidly disseminating intelligence (especially information regarding political and social conditions), and the need for restraint in employing firepower and handling the population. The operation also served to drive home to the Army at large the importance of limited contingency missions and the need to be prepared for them, a message Army Chief of Staff General Harold K. Johnson had been pushing for several months prior to the intervention.

General Johnson believed that America's strategy of combating communism in third world countries through political, social, and economic programs would fail unless those programs were protected from subversive forces. Affording that security—either through military assistance programs or by direct intervention—was, in Johnson's opinion, the most important contribution the Army could make toward winning the Cold War. In 1964 General Johnson had coined the phrase "stability operations" to describe such activities, which he asserted were the "third principal mission of the Army," along with waging general and limited warfare.[49]

General Palmer fully embraced the chief of staff's philosophy, and during the Dominican intervention he frequently referred to the stability operation concept, stating that the goal of such operations was neither "to maintain the status quo, . . . nor to support any particular faction or political group, but rather to establish a climate of order in which political, psychological, economic, sociological and other forces can work in a peaceful environment." His experience in the Dominican Republic, however, led him to concede that these goals were difficult to achieve, and consequently he concluded in his official report that the United States should carefully weigh any intervention decision before committing its forces to what might prove to be a "bottomless pit."[50]

The Dominican intervention thus bequeathed the Army many valuable insights into the intricate and sometimes treacherous nature of situations short of war. Yet the Army incorporated relatively few of these lessons into its official manuals. Firsthand experience on the part of participants and the ideas derived from the many reports that followed the intervention certainly had an impact, especially at the planning and technical levels, but other lessons either remained unlearned or were not applied, just as had been the case after Lebanon. Human and bureaucratic inertia partially accounted for this situation, but other factors contributed as well.

To begin with, many of the technical and tactical lessons derived from the Dominican experience were not new at all but were already expressed in Army literature. Thus the lack of attention to civil affairs and psychological warfare concerns in Army intervention plans represented less a doctrinal gap than a failure to apply already existent doctrine. Moreover, the very nature of overseas contingency and constabulary operations continued to defy the formulation of more detailed doctrine. While the Army undoubtedly would have benefited had it given the lessons of the Dominican intervention more attention in its doctrinal literature, ultimately many problems characteristic of stability operations could not be reduced to pat answers and fixed procedures. Even General Palmer, who fully appreciated the unique challenges posed by situations short of war, puzzled over how best to prepare for such contingencies. "How do you forewarn troops, trained to be aggressive, hard hitting, and tough, for such missions requiring great restraint?" wondered Palmer. "I don't know the answer. But I do know that it takes superbly disciplined, intelligent, and alert troops." These were qualities expected of all U.S. soldiers, and consequently he doubted that troops needed special training for stability operations, noting that "peacekeeping demands the same disciplined, skilled troops as does combat." Rather than special training, Palmer believed that preparing troops for constabulary duties was more a matter of indoctrination—that is, of acquainting them with the political objectives of their mission, acculturating them to the local scene, and teaching them to be open minded enough to adapt to the exigencies of the moment.[51] These principles were already incorporated into Army doctrine, and consequently, Army manuals published after the Dominican intervention differed in neither scope nor substance from those published before the operation.

The Army also did not develop a doctrine specific to peacekeeping operations. With the exception of a few minor adjustments in wording, the 1968 edition of FM 100–5, *Operations of Army Forces in the Field,* contained concepts virtually unchanged from those that had first emerged a decade before, a situation that continued until 1976, when the Army deleted stability operations from FM 100–5 altogether. The same situation obtained in other Army manuals of the late 1960s and early 1970s, which not only did not update their doctrine, but gradually phased out all coverage of situations short of war, cold war operations, and stability operations.[52]

The apparent willingness of the United States to intervene directly in the internal troubles of other nations during the mid-1960s, as exhibited by the deployment of U.S. troops to the Dominican Republic and

South Vietnam in 1965, did, however, cause the Army to reevaluate its organizational approach to stability operations. Noting that the Special Action Forces suffered from a number of organizational and administrative deficiencies, in October 1965 General Johnson approved a proposal to replace them with Regional Assistance Commands (RACs) in each overseas unified theater command. Although designed to perform the same advisory functions as the SAF, the RAC differed fundamentally from the Special Action Force in that it substituted a combat brigade for the SAF's Special Forces group, thereby giving RACs the ability to spearhead an intervention operation. The Regional Assistance Command thus reflected a reversion to the more activist posture contained in the original proposal for Cold War task forces.

Because of personnel shortages associated with mobilizing for the Vietnam War, General Johnson decided to phase the RACs in gradually, beginning with U.S. Southern Command, the Panama-based unified command devoted to Latin America. The proposed Latin American Regional Assistance Command, however, quickly ran afoul of political considerations. Senior officials in the Departments of State and Defense balked at stationing a Regional Assistance Command in Panama on the grounds that Latin Americans would react negatively to the prospect of having an intervention corps based in their midst. As the conflict in Vietnam continued to escalate, the Army placed the RAC concept on hold until the end of the war, at which point it scrapped the idea altogether due to force reductions and a clear recognition of the public's dwindling interest in overseas adventures. Meanwhile, the ostensibly less threatening, advisory-oriented SAFs remained in place, reinforced as before by backup brigades drawn from the Strategic Army Corps. After Vietnam, however, the Army drastically reduced both the number of Special Forces personnel and the amount of counterinsurgency and constabulary training given to the backup brigades. By the early 1980s students at the Command and General Staff College refused to take seriously exercises that called for employing backup brigades in independent intervention roles, noting that the United States had never used these units in such a capacity in the past. By then, whatever claims the backup brigades could have made to being culturally attuned, specially trained "short-of-war" formations had clearly fallen by the wayside.[53]

The stagnation and ultimate demise of overseas constabulary doctrine should not lead one to conclude that the Army ignored subjects pertinent to situations short of war after the Dominican intervention. Instead, the Army's attention was absorbed by events in Vietnam and the doctrinal behemoth of the 1960s—counterinsurgency. So obsessed were U.S. civil and military officials with the need to combat

Communist-inspired insurgencies during the 1960s that this one form of Cold War activity eventually absorbed the broader subject of situations short of war. Although this development meant that some aspects of situations short of war—such as peacekeeping and international truce enforcement—never had a chance to develop doctrinally, many of the basic principles contained in Army doctrine for situations short of war did find expression in the burgeoning counterinsurgency literature of the 1960s.

Notes

[1] Barry Blechman and Stephen Kaplan, *Force Without War: U.S. Armed Forces as a Political Instrument* (Washington, D.C.: Brookings Institution, 1978), pp. 226–33. Quote from Margaret Bodron, "U.S. Intervention in Lebanon—1958," *Military Review* 56 (February 1976): 72. Roger Spiller, *'Not War But Like War': The American Intervention in Lebanon* (Fort Leavenworth, Kans.: Combat Studies Institute, 1981), pp. 14–18; U.S. Army, Europe (USAREUR), The U.S. Army Task Force in Lebanon, 1959, p. 2, copy in CMH; Charles Koburger, "Morning Coats and Brass Hats," *Military Review* 45 (April 1965): 68.

[2] Spiller, *Not War But Like War*, pp. 12, 18, 25; Koburger, "Morning Coats," p. 70; Blechman and Kaplan, *Force Without War*, p. 237; USAREUR, Task Force in Lebanon, p. 32.

[3] Blechman and Kaplan, *Force Without War*, pp. 232–33; USAREUR, Task Force in Lebanon, p. 42.

[4] Bodron, "Intervention in Lebanon," p. 74; Lynn Smith, "Lebanon—Professionalism at Its Best," *Military Review* 39 (June 1959): 39; Spiller, *Not War But Like War*, p. 41.

[5] Smith, "Lebanon," p. 43; USAREUR, Task Force in Lebanon, pp. 42, 44, 47–48; David Gray, *The U.S. Intervention in Lebanon, 1958: A Commander's Reminiscence* (Fort Leavenworth, Kans.: Combat Studies Institute, 1984), p. 39.

[6] Koburger, "Morning Coats," p. 73; USAREUR, Task Force in Lebanon, pp. 36–37.

[7] Quote from Smith, "Lebanon," p. 40, and see also p. 46. Bodron, "Intervention in Lebanon," pp. 74–75; Blechman and Kaplan, *Force Without War*, pp. 239, 247–48, 254–55.

[8] Spiller, *Not War But Like War*, pp. 37–38, 44; Gary Wade, *Rapid Deployment Logistics: Lebanon, 1958* (Fort Leavenworth, Kans.: Combat Studies Institute, 1984), p. 81; USAREUR, Task Force in Lebanon, p. 40.

[9] Quoted words from Koburger, "Morning Coats," p. 73, and see also p. 71. USAREUR, Task Force in Lebanon, pp. 61–62; Wade, *Rapid Deployment Logistics*, pp. 66–67.

[10] Status of forces agreements explain the rights and obligations of American forces stationed overseas and of the foreign government that is hosting them. They typically cover issues like troop movements, basing privileges, labor relations, legal jurisdictions, and compensation for property damage. USAREUR, Task Force in Lebanon, pp. 62, 70, 74–75; Wade, *Rapid Deployment Logistics*, pp. 5–6, 66–69, 72, 75; Spiller, *Not War But Like War*, pp. 38–39; Smith, "Lebanon," p. 45.

[11] Gray, *U.S. Intervention in Lebanon*, pp. 25–26.

[12] Quote from FM 7–100, *The Infantry Division*, 1958, p. 202, and see also p. 203.

[13] First and second quoted words from ibid., pp. 203 and 205, respectively. Third quote from ibid., p. 207.

[14] First, second, and third quotes from ibid., pp. 204, 203, and 207, respectively.

[15] Quote from ibid., p. 207, and see also pp. 204–05, 209.

[16] Doctrine for situations short of war was developed in 1956 and first appeared in the initial draft manuscript for FM 7–100, The Infantry Division, in January 1957. Continental Army Command (CONARC) published the draft manual as Training Text

7–100–2, "The Infantry Division," in March 1957. The material did not find formal expression in an officially approved manual, however, until May 1958—two months before the Lebanon intervention—with the publication of FM 17–100, *The Armored Division and Combat Command*. FM 17–100 offered only cursory treatment of the subject, which did not receive a full official airing until the publication of the final version of FM 7–100 in October 1958, just as the Lebanon intervention was ending.

[17] First and second quotes from FM 17–100, *The Armored Division and Combat Command*, chg 1, Jun 59, pp. 23 and 22, respectively, and see also p. 21.

[18] FM 30–5, *Combat Intelligence*, 1960, pp. 9–10; FM 7–100, *The Infantry Division*, 1960, pp. 240–42; David Gray, "When We Fight a Small War," *Army* 10 (July 1960): 27–34; William Kelly, Situations Short of War (Student paper, IOAC, Infantry School, 1960).

[19] First and second quotes from FM 100–5, *Field Service Regulations, Operations*, 1962, pp. 5 and 155, respectively, and see also pp. 11–12. Osgood, *Limited War*, p. 20.

[20] Quote from FM 100–5, *Field Service Regulations, Operations*, 1962, p. 8, and see also pp. 9, 15–17.

[21] Quotes from ibid., p. 156, and see also pp. 45, 56, 155–62.

[22] FM 41–10, *Civil Affairs Operations*, 1962, pp. 85–99; USAREUR, Task Force in Lebanon, pp. 75–76; FM 33–5, *Psychological Operations*, 1962, pp. 107–10; FM 61–100, *The Division*, 1962, pp. 4–5, 235–40.

[23] First four quotes from Lesson Plan A4600/9, CGSC, Antiguerrilla Operations in a Local War, 1958–1959, p. I-4-1. Last quote from ibid., p. V-1. CGSC, The Military History of the Command and General Staff School, c. 1963, p. 60; Clyde Eddleman, The Report of Educational Survey Commission of the United States Army Command and General Staff College, November 1962, p. 12. All at CARL, Fort Leavenworth, Kans.

[24] Lesson Plans 4600/60, CGSC, Anti-Guerrilla Operations in a Limited War, 1959–1960; 4600/1, CGSC, Anti-Guerrilla Operations in a Limited War, 1960–1961; 4112–3/1, CGSC, 1960–1961; 2015/1, CGSC, Infantry Division, Part of a Strategic Army Strike Force, Deployment in a Situation Short of War, 1960–1961; 4112–3/2, CGSC, 1961–1962; and R2310–1, CGSC, 1962–1963. All at CARL.

[25] Paul Adams, "Strike Command," *Military Review* 42 (May 1962): 2–10.

[26] Quote from Speech, "The Military Aspects of the Cold War," Decker to the National Security Seminar, AWC, 8 Jun 61, p. 9, Historians files, CMH.

[27] Lesson Plan R2310/5, CGSC, 1964–1965, app. II to an. M to USCONARC Training Directive, Counterinsurgency Training, Special Action Force Backup Force Training, pp. LP 2-3 to LP 2-8, CARL; Addendum to Summary Sheet, DCSOPS to CSA, 8 Sep 61, sub: U.S. Free World Liaison and Assistance Group (US FLAG), with atchs, in 380, DCSOPS, 1961, RG 319, NARA.

[28] For Laos' civic action program, see Harry Walterhouse, *A Time To Build: Military Civic Action—Medium for Economic Development and Social Reform* (Columbia: University of South Carolina Press, 1964), pp. 95–98; Martin Massoglia et al., Military Civic Action, Evaluation of Military Techniques, 2 vols. (Research Triangle Institute, 1971), 2:vii–18; Oudone Sananikone, "Laos: Case Study in Civic Action, The Royal Lao Program," *Military Review* 43 (December 1963): 44–54; Charles Stockell, "Laos, Case Study in Civic Action, The Military Program," *Military Review* 43 (December 1963): 55–63; Memo, Commander in Chief, Pacific (CINCPAC), for JCS, 21 Feb 63, sub: Lessons Learned, MAAG and Special Forces Activities in Laos, pp. 13–14, Geog V Laos, 350.05 Lessons Learned, CMH.

[29] Timothy Castle, *At War in the Shadow of Vietnam: U.S. Military Aid to the Royal Lao Government, 1955–1975* (New York: Columbia University Press, 1993), pp. 7–46; Blechman and Kaplan, *Force Without War*, pp. 136–41.

[30] "Thailand Album," *Army Information Digest* 18 (January 1963): 8–11; William Burr, "The Use of U.S. Army Power in Nonviolent Support of Political Objectives (The Role of the Army in the Cold War)" (Student thesis, AWC, 1963), p. 16; Burton Lesh, "Lessons Learned: Thailand," *Infantry* 54 (March–April 1964): 59.

[31] For the war in Laos, see Castle, *War in the Shadow of Vietnam*; Douglas Blaufarb, Organizing and Managing Unconventional Warfare in Laos, 1962–1970, RAND–R–919–ARPA (Santa Monica, Calif.: RAND, 1972); Ben Baldwin et al., Case Study of United States Counterinsurgency Operations in Laos, 1955–1962, RAC–T–435, Research Analysis Corporation, 1964; Roger Warner, *Back Fire: The CIA's Secret War in Laos and Its Link to the War in Vietnam* (New York: Simon & Schuster, 1995); Oudone Sananikone, *The Royal Lao Army and U.S. Army Advice and Support*, Indochina Monographs (Washington, D.C.: U.S. Army Center of Military History, 1981).

[32] Lawrence Yates, *Power Pack: U.S. Intervention in the Dominican Republic* (Fort Leavenworth, Kans.: Combat Studies Institute, 1988), pp. 14–66; Blechman and Kaplan, *Force Without War*, pp. 291–93, 303–08; Lawrence Greenberg, *U.S. Army Unilateral and Coalition Operations in the 1965 Dominican Republic Intervention* (Washington, D.C.: U.S. Army Center of Military History, 1987), pp. 13–16.

[33] Jerome Slater, *Intervention and Negotiation: The United States and the Dominican Republic* (New York: Harper & Row, 1970), pp. 199–200; Blechman and Kaplan, *Force Without War*, pp. 308–10.

[34] Quoted words from Yates, *Power Pack*, p. 86.

[35] Ibid., pp. 79, 93–95; Abraham Lowenthall, *The Dominican Intervention* (Cambridge, Mass.: Harvard University Press, 1972), pp. 100, 108, 119–20, 125; Bruce Palmer, "The Army in the Dominican Republic," *Army* 15 (November 1965): 44; William Klein, "Stability Operations in Santo Domingo," *Infantry* 56 (May–June 1966): 36; Rpt, United States Forces, Dominican Republic (USFORDR), 1965, Stability Operations, Dominican Republic, pt. 1, vol. 1, pp. 7–10, copy in CMH (hereafter cited as USFORDR Rpt).

[36] Birtle, *Counterinsurgency Doctrine*, pp. 191–231; P. Haley, "Comparative Intervention: Mexico in 1914 and Dominica in 1965," in Robin Higham, ed., *Intervention or Abstention: The Dilemma of American Foreign Policy* (Lexington: University of Kentucky, 1975), pp. 41, 49; Yates, *Power Pack*, pp. 77, 96, 98; Blechman and Kaplan, *Force Without War*, p. 310.

[37] Yates, *Power Pack*, pp. 142–43; Mark Gillespie et al., *The Sergeants Major of the Army* (Washington, D.C.: U.S. Army Center of Military History, 1995), p. 117.

[38] Yates, *Power Pack*, pp. 73–74, 96, 119, 140–43, 177; CONARC, The Role of the U.S. Continental Army Command in Operations in the Dominican Republic, 1965, 1966, pp. 109–10, 136, copy in CMH.

[39] Yates, *Power Pack*, pp. 158–59; Blechman and Kaplan, *Force Without War*, pp. 324–25.

[40] Quoted words from Yates, *Power Pack*, p. 156, and see also pp. 49–50, 146–55; Frederick Turner, "Experiment in Inter-American Peace-Keeping," *Army* 17 (June 1967): 34–39.

[41] Yates, *Power Pack*, pp. 133, 139, 163, 169; Blechman and Kaplan, *Force Without War*, pp. 327–28; Study of Civil Affairs Organization, atch to Memo, U.S. Army

Combat Developments Command (USACDC) Institute of Strategic Studies Stability Operations (Prov) for the CG, Combat Developments Command (CDC), 17 Apr 69, sub: Evaluation of Civil Affairs Organization, p. 3, Historians files, CMH; James Clingham, "'All American' Team Work," *Army Information Digest* 22 (January 1967): 21; USFORDR Rpt, pt. 4, vol. 1, pp. vi-3 to vi-4, vi-9 to vi-10, vi-20-1 to vi-20-12; Wallace Moulis and Richard Brown, "Key to a Crisis," *Military Review* 46 (February 1966): 13.

[42] Bruce Palmer, Jr., *Intervention in the Caribbean: The Dominican Crisis of 1965* (Lexington: University of Kentucky Press, 1989), pp. 142, 148, 153; Greenberg, *U.S. Army Unilateral and Coalition Operations*, pp. 95–96; Slater, *Intervention and Negotiation*, p. 205; Yates, *Power Pack*, pp. 171–73; Blechman and Kaplan, *Force Without War*, p. 340.

[43] Wade, *Rapid Deployment Logistics*, p. 80; Yates, *Power Pack*, pp. viii, 56, 65, 176; Rpt, Office of the Director of Defense Research and Engineering, Weapon System Evaluation Group (WSEG), 16 Aug 66, sub: The Dominican Republic Crisis of 1965, pp. 254–55, in 091 Dominican Republic, CMH (hereafter cited as WSEG Rpt).

[44] Yates, *Power Pack*, p. 99; Lawrence Greenberg, "The U.S. Dominican Intervention: Success Story," *Parameters* 17 (December 1987): 19; WSEG Rpt, p. 269.

[45] Yates, *Power Pack*, pp. 56–59; Palmer, *Intervention in the Caribbean*, pp. 148–52, 156; WSEG Rpt, pp. 266–67.

[46] Quote from USFORDR Rpt, pt. 1, vol. 1, p. 19. Case Study 5–01, Dominican Republic, Course 5, AWC, 1968, p. 20, MHI; Disposition Form (DF), A. K. Marttinen, OPS SOOP to OPS ODWH, 26 Jul 65, sub: United States Army Psychological Operations During DomRep Crisis, p. 3, Historians files, CMH; Yates, *Power Pack*, pp. 136–39; John Kallunki, Operations of the 1st Psychological Warfare Battalion (Broadcast and Leaflet), in Support of Counterinsurgency Operations in the Dominican Republic, 3 May 1965 to 10 May 1965 (personal experience of graphics and printing team leader) (Student paper, IOAC, Infantry School, 1968).

[47] CONARC, Role of U.S. Continental Army Command in Operations in the Dominican Republic, pp. 136, 205; Klein, "Stability Operations," pp. 38–39; Yates, *Power Pack*, pp. 120, 124, 142, 169, 177; USFORDR Rpt, pt. 1, vol. 1, pp. 2, 7–10, 20; Palmer, *Intervention in the Caribbean*, pp. 80, 158; Harold Johnson, "Subversion and Insurgency: Search for a Doctrine," *Army* 15 (November 1965): 41; Slater, *Intervention and Negotiation*, pp. 194–95; Rpt, 82d Airborne Division, 1965, Stability Operations in the Dominican Republic, pt. 1, vol. 4, ch. 17, p. 2, CARL (hereafter cited as 82d Abn Div Rpt); Frank Galati, "Military Intervention in Latin America: Analysis of the 1965 Crisis in the Dominican Republic" (Master of Military Arts and Sciences (MMAS) thesis, CGSC, 1983), pp. 114–18.

[48] 82d Abn Div Rpt, pt. 1, vol. 4, ch. 17, p. 1; Palmer, *Intervention in the Caribbean*, pp. 155–56; USFORDR Rpt, pt. 1, vol. 1, pp. 19–20.

[49] Quotes from Harold Johnson, "Landpower Missions Unlimited," *Army* 14 (November 1964): 41–42; Harold Johnson, "The Army's Role in Nation Building and Preserving Stability," *Army Information Digest* 20 (November 1965): 6–13; Stephen Bowman, "The Evolution of United States Army Doctrine for Counterinsurgency Warfare: From World War II to the Commitment of Combat Units in Vietnam" (Ph.D. diss., Duke University, 1985), pp. 129–30; Palmer, *Intervention in the Caribbean*, pp. 156–57; 82d Abn Div Rpt, pt. 1, vol. 2, p. 14; Yates, *Power Pack*, pp. 178–79; USFORDR Rpt, pt. 1, vol. 1, pp. 19–20.

[50] First quote from Yates, *Power Pack*, p. 73. Second quote from USFORDR Rpt, pt. 1, vol. 1, p. 2. Greenberg, "Dominican Intervention," p. 27; Palmer, *Intervention in the Caribbean*, p. 158.

[51] First quote from Bruce Palmer, "Lessons from the Dominican Stability Operation," *Army* 16 (November 1966): 41. Second quote from Palmer, *Intervention in the Caribbean*, p. 159.

[52] Ralph Hinrichs, "U.S. Involvement in Low Intensity Conflict Since World War II: Three Case Studies—Greece, Dominican Republic, and Vietnam" (Master's thesis, CGSC, 1984), pp. 4–16; FM 100–5, *Operations of Army Forces in the Field*, 1968, pp. 1–2, 12-1 to 12-5. See also FM 100–5, *Operations*, 1976; FM 41–10, *Civil Affairs Operations*, 1967 and 1969 editions; FM 33–5, *Psychological Operations—Techniques and Procedures*, 1966; FM 61–100, *The Division*, 1965 and 1968 editions.

[53] Peter Kafkalas, "Low Intensity Conflict and Today's U.S. Army: An Assessment" (Master's thesis, Harvard University, 1984), pp. 97–102; CDC, Analysis of the Validity of Special Action Forces (SAF), 1965, 73A2677, CDC, RG 338, NARA; Summary Sheet, Assistant Chief of Staff for Force Development (ACSFOR) to CSA, 16 Oct 65, sub: Planning and Programming Forces for Stability Operations, 68A2344, RG 319, NARA; Fact Sheet, DSDC, 6 Jan 67, sub: U.S. Army Regional Assistance Command (RAC) Concept, with atchs, in 73A2677, CDC, RG 338, NARA.

6

THE COUNTERINSURGENCY FERMENT, 1961-1965

On 6 January 1961, four days before the Army published its new doctrinal guidance on counterguerrilla warfare in FM 100–1, Soviet Premier Nikita Khrushchev declared his nation's support of wars of national liberation. With several dozen insurgencies already percolating around the globe, Khrushchev's words signaled an escalation of what appeared to be a deliberate strategy to undermine Western institutions where they were weakest, in the emerging nations of the third world. Not one to let a challenge go unmet, President John F. Kennedy announced in his 20 January inaugural address that America would "pay any price, bear any burden, meet any hardship, support any friend, oppose any foe, to assure the survival and success of liberty."[1]

Kennedy and the Army

Kennedy's strategy for rescuing the underdeveloped world from communism rested on three pillars—economic development, political reform, and military assistance. Of these, military action was the least important. As Kennedy explained in a May 1961 address to Congress, insurgency was really more of a "battle for minds and souls" rather than of weapons, for "no amount of arms and armies can help stabilize those governments which are unable or unwilling to achieve social and economic reform and development. Military pacts cannot help nations whose social injustice and economic chaos invite insurgency and penetration and subversion. The most skillful counter-guerrilla efforts cannot succeed where the local population is too caught up in its own misery to be concerned about the advance of communism."[2]

Kennedy's approach differed from that of prior administrations less in substance than in style. A charismatic leader, Kennedy turned the fight against communism into a national crusade. He rallied public support, expanded foreign aid programs, and created the Peace Corps to spread American ideas to the peoples of the world. To guide this effort, the president recruited to his administration the "best and the brightest" America's universities and corporations had to offer, including the leading proponent of economic development and nation-building theory, Walt Rostow. These "action intellectuals" preached a creed of social engineering that proved quite popular, resonating as it did with several deeply ingrained aspects of the American psyche, including liberal progressivism, Christian evangelicalism, and cultural chauvinism, not to mention the nation's growing acceptance of government activism as a remedy for social ills. Together, Rostow's theory about the revolution of rising expectations, and Kennedy's proposed solution—sociopolitical reforms that would win the "hearts and minds" of disaffected peoples the world over—created an "ideology of modernization" that would dominate American strategic policy for the next decade.[3]

While the president considered political reform and economic development to be the key weapons against communism, he did not neglect the Cold War's military aspects. He abandoned Eisenhower's nuclear-oriented doctrine in favor of a strategy of "flexible response" designed to meet every form of Communist aggression without having to use nuclear weapons. He initiated a major buildup that by 1965 had added five new divisions and nearly $10 billion worth of new materiel to the U.S. Army. He also authorized the Army to recast its combat divisions into a new organization, the Reorganization Objective Army Division (ROAD), whose conventionally oriented, flexible structure was much more adaptable to the president's purposes than the nuclear-oriented pentomic division of the Eisenhower era.[4]

But improving America's ability to wage wars without resorting to nuclear weapons was only part of the president's program. More important in his mind were initiatives designed to meet the threat posed by "sub-limited" war—guerrilla action, insurgency, and subversion. Kennedy shared the view voiced by fellow politician Hubert H. Humphrey that Maoist revolutionary warfare represented nothing less than "a bold new form of aggression which could rank in military importance with the invention of gunpowder." The politicians were not alone in this assessment, as many social scientists, strategists, and commentators also propounded this view. In answer to the president's call to arms, the nation's intellectuals rushed to put forward various theories about the insurgency threat, creating in the process an atmosphere of "overthink" similar to that which had prevailed in the 1950s with regard to nuclear warfare. Fascinated by the black arts of guerrilla warfare, espionage, and propaganda and convinced that Maoist revolutionary warfare was qualitatively different than anything heretofore known, Kennedy insisted that "it is nonsense to think that regular forces trained for conventional war can handle jungle guerrillas adequately." Consequently, he demanded that the Army devise "a wholly new kind of strategy; a wholly different kind of force and therefore a new and different kind of military training" to meet what he considered to be the preeminent threat of the day.[5]

For the most part, the Army responded positively to President Kennedy's security initiatives. It strongly supported the new doctrine of flexible response, accepted the necessity of developing countermeasures to Communist insurgent warfare, and readily embraced both Rostow's theory about the revolution of rising expectations and the president's nation-building counterstrategy. Although many officers felt uncomfortable with suggestions that they be transformed from warriors into social engineers, they challenged neither the importance of political considerations in counterinsurgency nor the notion that specialists were required to deal with insurgency's many political and social facets. As Army Chief of Staff General George H. Decker himself conceded,

our splendid field armies in Europe and Korea and in reserve in the United States . . . are designed for conventional and tactical nuclear warfare. Their purpose is to meet clearly-defined, large-scale military threats. Obviously these units are not the proper response to a band of guerrillas which in a flash will transform itself into a scattering of "farmers." Neither are they best geared to move into a weak country and help it move up the development ladder by training local forces to improve the people's health, transportation, and building program.[6]

Moreover, the Army maintained that introducing large ground forces into a highly charged nationalistic environment could well prove to be the "kiss of death" for the government the United States was trying to aid. Consequently, it shared the president's interest in creating small, specialist formations and of improving the nation's advisory and assistance programs. This was evidenced by Decker's 1960 recommendations to increase the size of Special Forces and to create Cold War task forces, proposals that eventually bore fruit in the form of the Special Action Forces and the SAF backup brigades. But at this point, Decker and the president parted company. For Kennedy was not content

Army Chief of Staff General Decker chats with soldiers who were playing the role of villagers during a counterguerrilla training exercise.

with making minor adjustments around the edges of American defense policy. Rather, he wanted to transform the entire U.S. Army, both mentally and structurally, into the type of politically astute, socially conscious, and guerrilla-savvy force that he believed was necessary to combat Maoist-style revolutions—and General Decker did not.[7]

To begin with, Decker questioned the wisdom of overhauling the military to meet third world contingencies on the grounds that "our primary interest must be in Europe. With the exception of Japan, the areas of the East have nothing to contribute toward our survival. Therefore we could lose in Asia without losing everything, but to lose in Europe would be fatal." Indeed, the Army had a very practical dilemma—the president insisted that it restructure itself without jeopardizing its other missions, including the defense of Europe and Korea. Lacking the time, money, and manpower to create different armies for different types of warfare, the Army favored a more gradual introduction of counterinsurgency than the president was willing to tolerate.[8]

Although he did not doubt that the United States needed to be able to fight guerrillas effectively, Decker also challenged Kennedy's assertion that conventional soldiers were incapable of defeating irregulars. He regarded such talk as excessive and ahistorical, believing instead that, with proper preparation, "any good soldier can handle guerrillas." He was not alone, as many other military leaders, including Joint Chiefs Chairman General Lyman L. Lemnitzer; the president's personal military adviser and future chairman of the Joint Chiefs, General Maxwell D. Taylor; and Marine Corps Maj. Gen. Victor H. Krulak, the Joint Chiefs' point man for counterinsurgency, shared Decker's opinion.[9]

Kennedy regarded such sentiments as heresy and attempted to quash them. During his three-year tenure the president issued no fewer than twenty-three National Security Action Memorandums pertaining to counterinsurgency—formal ukases that demanded immediate compliance. He peppered his military advisers with questions, scrutinized their answers closely, and requested periodic updates on the state of the counterinsurgency program. He let everyone know that he considered counterinsurgency experience to be an important factor in determining promotions, and many believed that he did not renew Generals Decker's and Lemnitzer's tenures on the grounds that they had failed to demonstrate sufficient enthusiasm for his counterinsurgency initiatives. Finally, in January 1962 Kennedy formed an interagency task force, the Special Group (Counterinsurgency), with the mission of ensuring "proper recognition throughout the United States government that subversive insurgency ('wars of liberation') is a major form of politico-military conflict equal in importance to conventional warfare," and "that such recognition is reflected in the organization, training, equipment and doctrine of the United States armed forces and other United States agencies."[10]

In pressing his agenda the president was not without allies within the Army, including Brig. Gen. William P. Yarborough, commander of the Special Warfare Center at Fort Bragg, and Brig. Gen. William B. Rosson, the special assistant to the chief of staff for special warfare activities. Together with elements drawn largely from the Special Forces, psyops, and civil affairs communities, these "young moderns" advanced Kennedy's agenda from within with some success. But this success came at a price, for like all bureaucratic institutions, the Army cherished its institutional autonomy, and many soldiers resented Kennedy's interference in what they believed were internal matters that were best left to professionals.[11]

The Army was not alone in opposing aspects of the president's counterinsurgency initiative. The State Department flatly resisted the more operational role that the president expected it to play in orchestrating the counterinsurgency effort. There also existed in the State Department a core of officials who "appeared to consider problems of internal conflict a diversion from their main interest of foreign policy and diplomacy, and something that would, if played

*President Kennedy talks with General Yarborough at
Fort Bragg, North Carolina.*

down long enough, eventually be resolved in the normal course of
international relations." Similar sentiments existed within the Agency
for International Development (AID), which resisted suggestions that
it abandon its traditional long-term development projects for more
short-term, civic action-type activities—activities that the agency
tended to dismiss as gimmickry. AID showed equal disinterest in
improving indigenous police forces, a key counterinsurgency program that it controlled but which seemed out of step with its primary
socioeconomic mission. Finally, all civilian agencies feared that the
counterinsurgency movement represented a militarization of policy
that would give military men influence in areas that had previously
been the exclusive domain of civilians, a fear that further impeded
interagency coordination. In fact, Kennedy created the Special Group
in 1962 largely due to frustration over the unwillingness of civilian
agencies to jump on the counterinsurgency bandwagon.[12]

Nevertheless, foot dragging—perceived or real—on the part of
the Army usually brought the strongest reaction from the president.
Given the innate tendency of bureaucracies to resist outside interference, the president believed that he had to keep the pressure on if he
was to have any hope of seeing the government adopt his programs
in a speedy fashion. But deep down, many soldiers continued to feel
uncomfortable with a process that they believed had politicized military doctrine.[13]

Sources of Doctrine

Misgivings aside, the Army moved with due diligence in formulating a doctrine for defeating wars of national liberation. In the process, its doctrine writers cast a wide net. They consulted outside experts, examined published works, and sponsored research. They read the works of Mao Tse-tung and the Cuban revolutionary Ernesto "Che" Guevara, whose 1960 book, *On Guerrilla Warfare*, the Army rushed to translate. Military doctrine writers also mined recent counterinsurgency operations for nuggets of useful information. Because of the covert nature of American activities in Laos, relatively little emerged from that conflict into the broader doctrinal world. On the other hand, the Army made a concerted effort to acquire, digest, and disseminate the latest lessons generated by the growing insurgency in South Vietnam. In addition to circulating pertinent reports produced by the Military Assistance Command, Vietnam (MACV), the Army established the Army Concept Team in Vietnam, which used the burgeoning insurgency as a laboratory to test new organizations, equipment, and techniques. Still, in the early 1960s Vietnam experiences worked mainly along the edges of doctrine, adding a technique here or a bit of emphasis there but not changing doctrine's core principles.[14]

Compared with America's ongoing and as yet inconclusive advisory operations in Southeast Asia, the lessons of conflicts already concluded seemed both clearer and more readily available, and consequently the Army took great pains to study the many irregular conflicts that had occurred over the previous twenty years. Although the Army continued to examine *Wehrmacht* techniques, it focused most of its historical inquiries on more recent conflicts.[15] The two the Army studied most were the Malayan emergency and the Huk rebellion. The popularity of these events stemmed both from a desire to emulate success and from the fact that information pertaining to them was readily available in English. As in the late 1950s the Army turned to the British for examples of civil-military coordination and administration, jungle tactics, and population-control techniques. From the Philippines, the Army derived examples of the roles that intelligence, psychological warfare, and civic action played in suppressing unrest. Unfortunately, the overwhelming popularity of the Malayan and the Philippine cases led to a relatively uncritical acceptance of the alleged lessons of these conflicts. All too often Americans saw only what they wanted to see in these two episodes. They tended to overestimate the ease and extent to which resettlement programs and political reforms had won the hearts and minds of the people while ignoring contradictory evidence and minimizing the role that coercion had contributed to the success of these campaigns.[16] Not until they had had some direct experiences of their own would Americans begin to question some of their earlier Malayan- and Philippine-based assumptions.

The Army's infatuation with Malaya and the Philippines notwithstanding, the service did not ignore the French experience. As it had done during the previous decade, the Army monitored ongoing operations in Algeria and continued to translate and distribute French texts to instructors and doctrine writers.[17] Most Army schools examined either the Indochinese or Algerian civil wars in their curriculums, assisted in some cases by French liaison officers like Lt. Col. Paul Aussaresses, who visited both the Infantry and Special Warfare schools in the early 1960s. Interested officers could further their studies by consulting a variety of books and articles that appeared on these two conflicts in the early 1960s, including the works of journalist/political scientist Bernard Fall, who was a popular speaker at Army institutions despite his criticism of American methods in South Vietnam.[18] Such study was not idle curiosity, for according to General Yarborough, special warfare doctrine writers consciously employed *guerre revolutionnaire* theory when fashioning doctrinal tracts.[19] Though Americans admired aspects of French doctrine, most continued to treat French operations in Indochina as a paradigm for how not to wage a counterinsurgency.

As in the 1950s, Army analysts believed France had lost the Indochina War due to its shortsighted colonial policies that neither recognized the legitimacy of Vietnamese nationalism nor introduced any significant political, social, or economic reforms to win the support of the Vietnamese people. Army commentators also noted that France had not committed sufficient forces to win the war, in part due to a lack of public support back home, which had put the French military in the unenviable position of trying "to maintain a position of strength from which some sort of 'honorable' settlement might be negotiated." Militarily, Army documents criticized the French for fighting conventionally, for moving in road-bound columns, and for dispersing their forces in a myriad of small, static posts that robbed them of the initiative. Although U.S. soldiers conceded that there were not always easy solutions to the problems the French had faced, many of them believed that the reform-oriented, offensive doctrine they were crafting would allow the United States to avoid many of the mistakes France had made in Indochina.[20]

While the Army examined recent foreign experiences with insurgency, it generally ignored its own rich heritage in irregular warfare. True, Army leaders liked to brag about legendary guerrilla fighters of yesteryear—Robert Rogers and his Rangers during the French and Indian War, George Crook in Apacheria, J. Franklin Bell in the Philippines, and John J. Pershing, who fought bandits from Moroland to Mexico. The exploits of such men may have been relevant had the Army actually made a determined effort to remember and document them. In fact, most soldiers had only the vaguest impressions about the old Army's counterinsurgency and constabulary operations. Nor did the Army make much of an effort to correct this deficiency, since it shared the popular belief that distant wars involving obsolescent technologies and pre-Communist organizations could not possibly be relevant to understanding modern insurgency.[21]

If the Army ignored its own past, there was one source of American knowledge of which the manual writers of the 1960s did take full advantage—the Army's own doctrine as developed in the 1950s. In word, thought, and concept, the U.S. Army's response in the 1960s to the threat of Communist revolutionary warfare ultimately rested in large part on recycling the lessons Colonel Volckmann had derived a decade earlier from his study of partisan warfare in World War II. Thus, while examinations of recent foreign experiences would add richness and depth to the Army's understanding of insurgency, they would not fundamentally alter it.

The Doctrine Development System

Doctrine may be about ideas, but like so many other human endeavors its final form is frequently influenced as much by the process through which it is created as the ideas themselves. In the case of counterinsurgency, the development of doctrine was complicated both by the nature of the subject and the organization of the Army's doctrinal development system.

Between 1942 and 1962 a succession of major Army commands—Army Ground Forces (1942–1948), Army Field Forces (1948–1955), and Continental Army Command (1955–1962)—had overseen the Army's doctrinal, educational, and training activities. Under their supervision, school faculties, select committees, or specially chosen individuals like Volckmann had drafted Army manuals. For the most part, Army schools wrote and disseminated doctrine pertaining to their particular branch of service, while the Command and General Staff College prepared upper-level combined arms doctrine. By the early 1960s, however, the Army had decided that the fast pace of technological change had made the task of developing and inculcating doctrine too difficult for one agency. Consequently, in 1962 General Decker split these functions between Continental Army Command (CONARC) at Fort Monroe, Virginia, and a new entity, Combat Developments Command (CDC), at Fort Leavenworth, Kansas.

According to the arrangement, Combat Developments Command was responsible for determining the Army's future needs and developing broad policies and concepts to meet them. It was then to publish these overarching concepts in doctrinal manuals. The Continental Army Command, on the other hand, retained control of the Army's educational and training system. It was responsible for teaching CDC doctrine as well as for developing the tactics, techniques, and procedures necessary to implement the broad concepts contained in CDC manuals. Continental Army Command published these applicatory techniques in what the Army termed training manuals. To facilitate coordination and communication between the two commands, CDC collocated a doctrine development agency at each CONARC school. Thus the CDC Infantry Agency at Fort Benning, Georgia, developed infantry doctrine, while CONARC's Infantry School, also at Fort Benning, developed tactics and techniques to implement that doctrine while teaching the combined CDC-CONARC material to its students.

After a CDC field agency had drafted a manual, it would forward the draft to an intermediary CDC group headquarters for review. Once other CDC field-level agencies had had a chance to comment on the proposed manual, the manual would next be sent up through CDC headquarters to a newly created entity on the Pentagon's Army Staff—the Office of the Assistant Chief of Staff for Force Development (OACSFOR)—which in 1963 assumed from the deputy chief of staff for military operations responsibility for doctrinal development and manual production within the Army. After coordinating the proposed doctrine within the Army Staff, OACSFOR would either return the manual to Combat Developments Command for revision or forward it to the Office of the Adjutant General for publication.

Although Decker had created Combat Developments Command to improve the Army's ability to adapt to a fast changing world, the process proved cumbersome. CONARC and CDC did not always coordinate their actions as closely as they should, and for the Army to take up to three years to produce a manual under the new system was not unusual. This was clearly an impediment given the urgency for developing and disseminating new doctrine for counterinsurgency. The fact that the counterinsurgency wave hit the Army at a time when it was in the midst of reorganizing its doctrinal system merely exacerbated the already difficult task of developing and integrating new concepts.[22]

Anxious that counterinsurgency not become lost in the organizational shuffle, General Decker created a temporary Remote Area Conflict Office to expedite the development of counterinsurgency doctrine. Once Combat Developments Command was up and running, the Army replaced the office in October 1962 with a permanent CDC group-level headquarters, the Special Doctrine and Equipment Group. Located at Fort Belvoir, Virginia, the group (which the Army renamed the Special Warfare Group in 1963) worked to ensure that counterinsurgency doctrine was properly incorporated into all applicable manuals. Much of the group's day-to-day work in this regard fell upon its subordinate field element, the CDC Special Warfare Agency at Fort Bragg, North Carolina. In addition to writing doctrine for Special Forces, psychological operations, and military advisory activities, the Special Warfare Agency developed basic counterinsurgency doctrine and reviewed manuals developed by other Army agencies for counterinsurgency content.[23] This was not a simple task.

To begin with, the Army had several hundred field manuals in its inventory, many of which the Special Warfare Agency would have to review periodically for possible inclusion of counterinsurgency material. In addition to the heavy work load this created for the Special Warfare Agency, the fact that counterinsurgency cut across branch and functional lines created a certain degree of conceptual and bureaucratic friction between it and other CDC entities. The parent agencies for the Army's numerous branch and functional manuals did not always concur with the special warfare community about the degree to which their manuals needed to incorporate counterinsurgency-related material. Moreover, some confusion existed between the Special Warfare Agency and other agencies over proponency for certain aspects of counterinsurgency doctrine. For example, the Civil Affairs Agency at Fort Gordon, Georgia, believed that the Special Warfare Agency did not pay it proper deference with regard to counterinsurgency's many civil aspects for which Fort Gordon held proponency.

The Army tried to improve the coordination between these two agencies in 1964 by transferring control of the Civil Affairs Agency from the Combat Service Support Group to the Special Warfare Group, which the Army redesignated the Special Warfare and Civil Affairs Group. However, other tensions simmered between the Special Warfare Agency and the Infantry Agency, which developed tactical counterguerrilla doctrine, as well as the Institute for Advanced Studies at Carlisle Barracks, Pennsylvania, which formulated broad, Army-wide concepts, and the Command and General Staff College and its associated CDC agency, the Combined Warfare Agency, which held proponency for all doctrinal matters at the army, corps, and division level. Ultimately, all of these agencies and their related CONARC institutions would at one time or another hold proponency for some aspects of counterinsurgency doctrine, and the friction that sometimes developed between them adversely affected the formulation of doctrine.[24]

The Evolution of Doctrine, 1961–1964

The Army published its first response to the president's counterinsurgency drive—FM 31–15, *Operations Against Irregular Forces*—just four months after Kennedy assumed office. The rapid appearance of this manual stemmed from the fact that the Command and General Staff College had written the bulk of it prior to Kennedy's election. The manual, which replaced FM 31–15, *Operations Against Airborne Attack, Guerrilla Action, and Infiltration* (1953), provided broad guidance concerning the conduct of counterguerrilla operations, repeating and amplifying the doctrine that had just been published a few months before in FM 100–1.

Operations Against Irregular Forces opened with the premise that guerrilla warfare was merely the "outward manifestation" of public disenchantment with certain political, social, and economic conditions. This premise led to two conclusions: first, that a guerrilla movement required at least some degree of public support to flourish, and second, that the only permanent solution to an insurgency was to rectify the conditions that had given rise to it in the first place. Military action, unaccompanied by meaningful reforms, could at best suppress, but never completely eradicate, a heartfelt revolutionary movement.[25]

FM 31–15 (1961) followed the 1960 ODCSOPS handbook in identifying four tasks that had to be achieved to defeat guerrillas and prevent their resurgence. First and foremost, government authorities had to establish an effective intelligence system. Second, through a combination of military and police measures, the Army had to separate the irregulars both physically and psychologically from the population and all sources of support—internal and external. Third, the Army had to destroy the guerrillas as a military force. Finally, the government would have to reeducate the dissidents, rebuild damaged institutions, and redress the causes of discontent.

To help commanders accomplish these tasks the manual offered five operational principles. The first principle was unity of command, as it recommended that a single person be placed in charge of all civil and military counterinsurgency programs at each level of command. Corollaries to this principle included the need to develop an integrated politico-military campaign plan, the desirability of maintaining continuity of personnel in a particular area to promote regional expertise, and the utility of creating a combined command to coordinate the activities of U.S. and indigenous military forces. The remaining principles also stressed concepts that had appeared in previous American doctrine—respect for human rights, offensive operations, and the creation of mobile task forces. Finally, the manual reiterated that police, combat, and political operations all had to be conducted simultaneously throughout the course of a campaign, despite the fact that in any particular stage one of those methods might predominate over the others.[26]

Like earlier writings, FM 31–15 (1961) adopted a strategy of progressive area clearance. The force commander would establish regional commands, normally along existing political boundaries, in order to facilitate civil-military coordination. Within each region, subareas would be created, with each being cleared in turn according to government priorities and troop availability. Once an area was cleared, the commander would leave behind a sufficient number of troops, backed by a large number of police, paramilitary, and village defense forces, to prevent a guerrilla resurgence, while the bulk of the soldiers moved on to the next area to be cleared.

The manual enumerated four types of military operations that were to be conducted during a counterguerrilla campaign: *reaction operations*, in which mobile reserves responded to guerrilla sightings or actions; *harassment operations*, in which small patrols and raiding parties beleaguered the enemy, keeping him fragmented and on the move; *denial operations* that sought to block guerrilla access to external sources of supply; and *elimination operations* that were offensive actions designed to destroy guerrilla units once intelligence or reconnaissance forces had "definitely located" them. The manual repeated earlier doctrine in making the destruction of the enemy, not the capture of ground, the primary objective, prescribing encirclement as the most effective, if admittedly difficult, means of achieving this end.[27]

While military operations broke up the irregulars and drove them away from populated areas, FM 31–15 (1961) prescribed a variety of intelligence, psychological warfare, civic action, and police measures to complete the separation of the guerrillas from the people. In line with previous doctrine, the manual required that commanders achieve a delicate balance between benevolence and repression. Thus, the manual advised that "persons whose property is searched and whose goods are seized should be irritated and frightened to such an extent that they will neither harbor irregular force members nor support them in the future. Conversely, the action must not be so harsh as to drive them to collaboration with the irregular force because of resentment." Humane treatment of prisoners, correct behavior toward inhabitants, and civic actions were, when necessary, to be supplemented by strict controls over assembly, movement, and the possession of food, arms, and medicine. The manual authorized commanders to relocate populations from insecure areas to places where they could be more readily monitored and protected and recommended instituting a *pao chia*–style system in which villagers spied on their neighbors.[28]

FM 31–15 (1961) recommended several modifications that might be necessary in conducting a counterguerrilla war. It listed planning factors to be considered and highlighted the important roles civic action and intelligence operations would play. It recommended that commanders augment standard infantry battalions with additional rifle companies, an artillery battery, aviation, and detachments of intelligence, psychological warfare, civil affairs, and military police personnel, not unlike the battalion combat teams that U.S. advisers had developed during the Huk rebellion. Finally, the manual echoed earlier doctrine in pointing out the unique moral and psychological aspects associated with guerrilla warfare. Among these were frustration born from an inability to achieve tangible results against an elusive foe, disenchantment derived from prolonged service under primitive living conditions among an alien population, and fear of guerrilla atrocities. FM 31–15 (1961) also noted the corrosive effects of several conflicting emotions: the desire to retaliate against civilians for guerrilla misdeeds, "the ingrained reluctance of the soldier to take repressive measures against women, children, and old men who usually are active in both overt and covert irregular activities or who must be resettled or concentrated for security reasons," and "the sympathy of some soldiers with certain stated objectives of the resistance movement such as relief from oppression." For these and other dilemmas the manual offered no solutions other than those prescribed a decade earlier by Volckmann—intensive training, troop indoctrination, and dynamic leadership.[29]

Operations Against Irregular Forces established the basic outline of Army counterinsurgency doctrine for the next few years. Subsequent manuals would amplify and clarify it, adding a few new concepts and updating its language, but truly substantive changes would be few. FM 31–15 (1961) was not, however, meant to be the Army's final word on the subject. Two major areas remained to be addressed. First, the broad themes contained in the manual needed to be fleshed out with applicatory methods and techniques. Conversely, the Army believed that FM 31–15 (1961) needed to be placed in a broader strategic context. This was especially important given counterinsurgency's many political aspects and the administration's professed desire to approach the problem on an interagency basis. But such a doctrine was not the Army's to make, as it required policy decisions at the highest levels of government. Still, as the first agency to have published a counterguerrilla doctrine of any sort, the Army was well positioned to influence events as they unfolded.

The first step on the road to formulating a national counterinsurgency doctrine occurred nearly a year after the Army had published FM 31–15. In April 1962 the Joint Chiefs of Staff issued a document titled "Joint Counterinsurgency Concept and Doctrinal Guidance." Based chiefly on input from the Army Staff, the joint concept established broad guidelines for the military services as they developed organizations and doctrines to meet the threat of Communist insurgency. The document called for unified action by all government agencies—U.S. and foreign alike—to create a "fully integrated, mutually supporting and concurrently applied" mesh of political, military, and socioeconomic programs. Such an approach was essential, "since economic and political progress are dependent upon reasonable internal security, and internal security cannot be permanently effective without complementing non-military action."[30]

The Joint Chiefs established three roles for the U.S. military as part of the national counterinsurgency program: providing advice and assistance in nation building, furnishing advice and assistance in counterguerrilla operations, and undertaking direct combat action. The extent of military activity in each of these areas was pegged to the three stages of a Maoist insurgency. In the first phase, when insurgency was still latent, U.S. military advisers were to concentrate their efforts on improving the indigenous military's civic action, security, and counterguerrilla capabilities. In phase two, under conditions of active guerrilla warfare, the Americans would continue and intensify these efforts. Finally, should the insurgency escalate into a full-blown phase three conflict, the United States as a last resort might intervene. Should it do so, the joint concept called for the commitment of soldiers trained in the military, social, and psychological aspects of insurgency, as well as the language and culture of the afflicted area. The Joint Chiefs also directed that "U.S. military units employed in any counterinsurgency role will be tailored to the conditions where insurgency exists. Use of large combat units will be avoided." Such stipulations, together with the injunction that military agencies were to develop individuals for counterinsurgency duty, indicated that the Pentagon envisioned its role largely as an advisory one—an approach that reflected administration policy.[31]

In the joint concept the Joint Chiefs of Staff assigned to the Army the task of developing counterinsurgency tactics, techniques, and doctrine for both itself and the Marine Corps. However, the Joint Staff established a broad conceptual framework within which Army doctrine would have to operate. Thus the joint concept asserted that the basic function of military forces was to "insulate the people from the insurgents both physically and psychologically; win and maintain popular respect, support, and confidence." To achieve these ends, military forces were to seal populated areas, clear them of guerrillas, and hold them against the possibility of a guerrilla resurgence. Operations were to be continuous, aggressive, and varied, using ruses and deception to keep the enemy off-balance. Meanwhile, the military would assist police and government officials in eliminating the last vestiges of civilian support for the insurgents through a combination of civic and psychological actions, counterintelligence activities, security operations, and "appropriate reprisals."[32]

The importance of the joint concept stemmed from the fact that it imposed on the military services a doctrinal vision that was virtually identical to the views already held by the Army. It could not, however, definitively address the larger issues of national policy and the interaction of civil-military agencies. Such policies required higher-level action—action that occurred in September 1962 when the National Security Council formally published a government-wide counterinsurgency doctrine, known as the Overseas Internal Defense Policy (OIDP).

The OIDP made Rostow's nation-building theory the official policy of the United States government. It enunciated in a formal way Kennedy's threefold strategy of applying sociopolitical reforms, economic stimuli, and military assistance as both prophylactics and remedies for the disease of Communist insurgency. Like the joint concept, the OIDP embraced the Maoist model of revolutionary warfare, using it as a framework around which to build American countermeasures. The policy asserted that political, social, and economic reform, not repression, were the keys to defeating subversion. The OIDP also established as policy the notion that the job of defeating an insurgency rested primarily upon the indigenous government, not the United States. Finally, the OIDP called for the creation of a well-integrated, seamless counterinsurgency effort on the part of all elements of the federal government, assigning particular roles to the Departments of State and Defense, the CIA, AID, and the U.S. Information Agency (USIA).[33]

Although the OIDP fulfilled the Army's desire for a formal enunciation of national policy, the document had several weaknesses. First, it was, in the words of one of its principal architects, a "somewhat simplistic document," whose broad prescriptions were inadequate to meet what was in reality a highly complex world. Second, while the OIDP had assigned roles and missions, it had not detailed how the actions of the various agencies would be integrated into a cohesive whole other than through the coordinative powers of the Special Group (Counterinsurgency) in Washington and, at the country level, through the ambassador. Since both entities were given only the power to monitor and coordinate, rather than direct and control, there was in fact very little to ensure the necessary integration of effort. The Army would complain for several years that the absence of a well-integrated system for executing the national counterinsurgency program greatly impeded its efforts, both doctrinally and operationally.[34]

Finally, the OIDP suffered from a third major weakness, one that its authors recognized but for which they did not have an answer. For if, as the doctrine asserted, insurgency was the product of social, economic, and political inequities that were not being addressed by indigenous authorities, what confidence could the United States have that it would be able to persuade these very same people to adopt American-proffered reforms? While the OIDP proudly showcased Ramon Magsaysay as an example of what could be achieved when an able leader listened to American advice, there was little guarantee that the United States would always be so fortunate. Indeed, the OIDP conceded that U.S. officials would be confronted with indigenous elites who benefited from the status quo and who would exhibit "deep-seated emotional, cultural, and proprietary resistance to any change that diminishes power and privilege, regardless of how unrealistic and short-sighted this stubbornness may seem objectively."[35]

Given America's reluctance to intervene directly, the OIDP saw only two options when confronted by a recalcitrant regime. Either the United States could threaten to withhold aid until the indigenous government implemented reforms, or it could employ covert means to change the political landscape of the country in question, possibly resulting in the removal of particularly obstinate leaders. Neither option was very palatable, and thus the old dilemma of leverage would continue to bedevil any counterinsurgency action undertaken by the United States.[36]

Like the joint concept, the OIDP was of great importance to the Army because it established the basic policy positions that Army doctrine would have to reflect. Nevertheless, it had very little effect on the shape of Army doctrine, largely because the document echoed positions that had already been adopted by both the Army and the Pentagon. In fact, the National Security Council had relied heavily on the Joint Chief's joint concept when it had written the OIDP.[37]

While national authorities spent most of 1962 crafting overarching policies, the Army did not remain idle. Due to both the newness of the subject and its perceived importance, the Army adopted a two-pronged approach in developing counterinsurgency doctrine. The first approach involved integrating broad counterinsurgency principles into as many manuals as possible, folding the material in whenever a manual came up for routine review and revision. Perhaps the most important example of this approach occurred in February 1962, when the Army published a new edition of FM 100–5, *Operations*, that included new chapters on situations short of war, guerrilla warfare, counterguerrilla warfare, and airmobile operations. All told, Cold War– and counterinsurgency-related subjects accounted for about 20 percent of this widely read manual. In actuality, the manual contained little that was new, as it merely summarized the basic principles already established in FM 31–15 the year before. Still, the increased visibility that the manual afforded counterinsurgency and contingency operations represented a major milestone that helped solidify their places as important missions within the Army.[38]

While the integration of counterinsurgency principles into existing manuals proceeded, the Army also advanced on a second track, developing new tactics and techniques to help soldiers implement FM 31–15's broad principles. Perhaps the best examples of this approach in 1962 were FM 33–5, *Psychological Operations*, and FM 41–10, *Civil Affairs Operations*. Of the two, *Psychological Operations*, written at Fort Bragg, was the more progressive. It revised the 1955 edition of FM 33–5 by adding new chapters on the important role psychological operations played in insurgencies and situations short of war. It was also the first manual to employ such cutting edge terms as *counterinsurgency* and *nation building*. The manual impressed upon its readers that "no tactical counterinsurgency program can be effective without major nation building programs. The causes for unrest must be in the process of reduction for the successful counterinsurgency operation. This implies extensive political, economic, and social reform."[39]

FM 41–10 (1962), prepared by the Civil Affairs School at Fort Gordon, agreed with this philosophy. Although the bulk of this manual was dedicated to conventional operations, it strongly endorsed civic action, defined as "any function performed by military forces in cooperation with civil authorities, agencies, or groups through the use of military manpower and material resources for the socio-economic well-being and improvement of the civil community with a goal of building or reinforcing mutual respect and fellowship between the civil and military communities." Based on recent experience, FM 41–10

(1962) examined the organization and function of civic action advisory teams and related lessons regarding the implementation of a civic action program. It stated that projects originated by the local population were more likely to succeed than those imposed from above by well-meaning, but often ignorant and ethnocentric advisers. The manual concluded that a project must have a fairly short completion time, both because military units moved frequently and because the government needed to win public support in the present, rather than in the distant future. Finally, FM 41–10 (1962) advised soldiers to coordinate all of their civic action projects with civilian agencies to ensure that those activities would complement, and not compete, with the efforts of other government elements.[40]

While FMs 33–5 and 41–10 added depth to the Army's understanding of its role in an insurgency, the Army pressed ahead with the development of counterguerrilla tactics and techniques. This effort had begun in December 1961, when the Army had directed the Command and General Staff College to flesh out the principles established in FM 31–15 (1961). After completing an initial draft in early 1962, CGSC handed the project over to the Infantry School. The effort came to fruition in February 1963 as FM 31–16, *Counterguerrilla Operations*.[41]

Counterguerrilla Operations added detail to the multiphased and multifaceted area control strategy called for in FM 31–15 (1961). Reflecting an appreciation for counterinsurgency's uniquely local and decentralized nature, as well as the belief that deployments larger than a division were unlikely, FM 31–16 established the brigade as the basic operational and command element. The manual envisioned that a brigade would be assigned to control a geographical area. Upon arrival, it would establish a main base camp and subsidiary installations, further subdividing the region into battalion and company operating areas, with each level of command retaining a mobile (preferably airmobile) reserve reaction force. Like FM 31–15 (1961), *Counterguerrilla Operations* placed special emphasis on accumulating intelligence, for "in counterguerrilla operations, the commander is even more deeply dependent upon intelligence and counterintelligence than in conventional warfare situations." Noting that, "the unit which conducts counterguerrilla operations without sound intelligence wastes time, materiel, and troop effort," the manual urged commanders to tap every conceivable resource to acquire a coherent picture of a region's political, social, and military topography.[42]

Included among the seven pages the manual devoted to intelligence matters were suggestions concerning methods and techniques appropriate for insurgency situations. The manual recommended maintaining personality files on guerrilla leaders and asserted that friends and family of known guerrillas were "valuable as sources of information, as hostages, and as bait for traps that can be laid for guerrillas visiting them." Conversely, the manual recognized that insurgents usually had excellent intelligence sources of their own, a fact that demanded that military forces exercise the utmost secrecy if they were ever to have a hope of catching the irregulars. To help even the odds, FM 31–16 recommended that commanders leak false information, manipulate suspected enemy agents, and employ cover operations and deception plans to outfox the enemy as to the Army's true intentions.[43]

Having established itself in a region, the brigade's next step was to separate the irregulars from the population. Off the battlefield, the government would achieve this goal through police and security measures, intelligence operations, civic actions, and propaganda. The manual described each of these in turn, stressing the necessity of weaving them together into a seamless whole with the help of Malayan-style civil-military pacification committees in each brigade and battalion sector. Recognizing that the task of securing the population "should never be deemphasized," FM 31–16 called for the creation of large police and village defense forces and the imposition of effective measures to control the behavior and resources of the civilian population.[44]

While never minimizing the importance of positive measures, FM 31–16 paralleled British manuals of the day by dwelling upon pacification's more restrictive aspects, reminding its readers that "counterguerrilla operations must include appropriate action against the civilian and underground support of the guerrilla force without which it cannot operate." The manual reviewed the usual list of control measures—curfews, travel restrictions, and the like—describing several in more detail than had appeared in previous manuals. Throughout, FM 31–16 tried to balance the desirability of winning popular support with the less palatable requirements of military necessity. Following American tradition, the manual advised commanders to apply a judicious mixture of moderation and fairness on the one hand, and "vigorous enforcement and stern punishment" on the other, warning that "half-heartedness or any other sign of laxness will breed contempt and defiance."[45]

Although *Counterguerrilla Operations* focused on the internal aspects of insurgency, it conceded that past experience had shown that insurrections rarely achieved their full potential without access to external sanctuaries and sustenance. Consequently, the manual included a short section on border control operations. The section was of necessity vague since actual measures would depend on the military, diplomatic, and topographical features of the conflict. Nevertheless, FM 31–16 prescribed a vigorous surveillance program involving observation posts, intelligence agents, electronic listening and sensing devices, and ground, air, and waterborne patrols. Crop destruction and defoliation measures were recommended for eliminating food and cover in guerrilla base areas. The manual also endorsed the creation of restricted zones, in which the Army would remove the entire population so as to create a no-man's land along the border, and buffer zones, in which the military removed only the disloyal while permitting trusted individuals to stay on to create a hostile environment for guerrilla infiltrators. The manual recognized the significant human and materiel cost of such methods, and consequently it recommended that relocation and resettlement schemes be employed only when absolutely necessary and in close coordination with civil authorities.[46]

As civil, military, and police officials secured the country's resources, regular military units would provide the necessary cover, keeping the enemy off-balance and away from populated areas through a continuous harassment campaign. Because guerrillas were usually difficult to locate, *Counterguerrilla Operations* stated that harassment campaigns could proceed for months before they had an appreciable effect in clearing the enemy out of a targeted area. The primary weapon in this campaign was the patrol. Ranging in size from a squad to a reinforced company, patrols would continuously scour their assigned areas, searching villages, establishing ambushes, and launching raids. Generally, these patrols would employ conventional small-unit tactics, though the manual did add a new technique, the area ambush, based on British counterguerrilla experience. Night marches, frequent relocations of patrol bases, and movements by circuitous or unexpected routes were all advised to ensure security and secrecy. Aircraft would provide crucial assistance by conducting surveillance, ferrying troops and supplies, and supporting airmobile hunter-killer teams, an idea which had first appeared in the mid-1950s and was currently being employed in Vietnam. Indeed, noting the difficulty conventional forces normally experienced in trying to catch irregulars, FM 31–16 asserted that "the imaginative, extensive, and sustained use of the airmobile forces offers the most effective challenge available today to this mobility differential of the enemy guerrilla force. It is imperative that, whenever possible, the concept of counterguerrilla operations be based on the maximum employment of this type of force."[47]

While decentralized, small-unit harassment operations backed by airmobile reaction forces constituted the bulk of the Army's daily operational routine, *Counterguerrilla Operations* advised that offensive operations be undertaken whenever a sizable force or installation had been located. Although linear tactics might be appropriate if the enemy fielded large, conventional units and endeavored to hold ground, FM 31–16 believed the most effective counterguerrilla tactic was encirclement. Because of the difficulties posed by terrain and the guerrillas' proclivity for avoiding combat, the manual repeated earlier warnings that encirclements were difficult to execute. To be effective such operations had to be carefully planned, flawlessly executed, and backed by a considerably larger force than that of the enemy to prevent him from escaping the trap. As a guide, FM 31–16 prescribed three of the four *Wehrmacht* encirclement tactics initially introduced by the 1951 Volckmann manual: "tightening the noose," "fragmenting the disc," and "hammer and anvil."[48]

When conditions prohibited using encirclement, FM 31–16 offered five other methods for conducting offensive operations. Two of these—surprise attack and pursuit—had appeared in Volckmann's manual. However, FM 31–16 slightly modified Volckmann's pursuit operation—which it subtitled a "sweep"—by adding airmobile encircling forces that would attempt to block the enemy as he fell back in front of the pursuing ground forces. The manual also provided additional information on a technique that had first appeared in FM 31–15 (1961), the urban cordon and sweep. As FM 31–16 explained it, political considerations were the primary feature that differentiated urban counterguerrilla operations from their conventional counterparts. Included among the factors to be considered were the desirability of minimizing civilian casualties and property destruction, the utility of waging an aggressive propaganda campaign to mollify the population and entice the irregulars to surrender, and the necessity of quickly retaking lost urban areas to prevent the appearance of a guerrilla victory.[49]

Finally, the manual added two new maneuvers, both partly derived from British doctrine. The first, the "rabbit hunt," was a cordon-and-sweep, encirclement tactic that the manual stated was "a very effective technique for finding and destroying elements of a guerrilla force known or suspected to be in a relatively small area." It involved nothing more than establishing blocking forces around three sides of a designated area while a line of beaters advanced from the fourth, scouring the area and driving the guerrillas into ambush teams deployed around the perimeter. The second new technique, the fire flush, used troops to surround an area approximately 1,000 meters square that was then subjected to concentrated air and artillery fire—fire so severe that it would either destroy the enemy or drive him into the arms of the encircling troops.[50]

The appearance of the fire flush tactic in FM 31–16 marked a subtle but important development in Army counterguerrilla doctrine. Although the Army had occasionally employed similar tactics in Korea, historically artillery had played a minor role in the Army's approach to counterguerrilla warfare. This had been true not only before World War II, but thereafter as well, as Army counterguerrilla advisers repeatedly criticized America's Chinese, Greek, Korean, Filipino, and Vietnamese allies for employing artillery as a substitute for mobile, aggressive infantry action. While recognizing the utility of artillery, tanks, and tactical airpower under certain conditions, Army doctrine writers had always doubted that heavy firepower could be applied effectively against guerrillas, whose elusive nature and penchant for deep swamps, thick forests, and rugged mountains were well known. Thus Army texts of the early 1960s had asserted that infantry battalions would rarely receive fire support beyond their own organic weapons and that when such support was provided, it would be limited to "a section or a platoon and will seldom require units of more than battery size." To extend at least token support to dispersed patrols and outposts, Army doctrine writers had even overcome traditional prejudices against dispersing artillery and accepted the unorthodox Franco-Vietnamese practice of distributing artillery in one- and two-tube positions.[51]

Counterguerrilla Operations adhered to these themes. It pointed out the many impediments to effectively employing artillery and limited the amount of artillery support a brigade could expect to a single battalion of 105-mm. howitzers. Yet the manual also talked about artillery in more positive terms than the past, a change that seems to have been based on British doctrine, from which the writers of FM 31–16 lifted not only the fire flush technique, but also the idea of using artillery fire to harass and interdict the movement of enemy irregulars. From these beginnings, Army doctrine would move inextricably toward a more expansive view of firepower, perhaps as a result of the growing availability of helicopters to transport guns into remote areas, as well as the escalating conflict in Vietnam, where enemy firepower increasingly approximated that of government forces. Though never abandoning its faith in the bayonet, by 1965 Army texts were conceding that "it is often more economical in terms of manpower to maneuver the guerrilla force into a killing area by fire, rather than by hand-to-hand combat. It is easier to maneuver artillery fire across the battle areas than it is to maneuver personnel."[52]

A similar, though less dramatic shift in Army doctrine occurred vis-a-vis the role of armor in an insurgency, as doctrine writers began to assert more positive roles for armored and armored cavalry formations. Interestingly, however, the movement to embrace heavier forms of weaponry did not extend to airpower. Perhaps based on the lessons of the Indochina War, FM 31–15 (1961) had questioned the utility of tactical aircraft on the basis of the guerrilla's "tactics of clinging to his enemy or of mingling with the populace." FM 31–16 (1963) retained this skepticism, noting that adverse terrain and weather, difficulties in air-ground coordination, and the guerrillas' habit of operating dispersed and at night all reduced the effectiveness of airpower.[53]

Regardless of the weapons and tactics employed, *Counterguerrilla Operations* pointed out that "counterguerrilla warfare is a contest of imagination, ingenuity, and improvisation by the opposing commanders. Commanders must be ever alert to change or adapt their tactics, techniques, and procedures to meet the specific situation at hand. Once the routine operations of a counterguerrilla force becomes stereotyped, surprise (a major ingredient of success) has been lost." The manual enjoined commanders to be continuously on the offensive and to focus their efforts on destroying the guerrillas rather than on capturing ground. It likewise understood that units would have to be tailored to the mission and environment, deleting unneeded and burdensome equipment, restructuring superfluous elements—like antitank units—to more useful functions, and adding other resources, such as man-portable radios, helicopters, and additional intelligence, signal, fire control, civil affairs, and psychological warfare personnel.[54]

Continuous, aggressive small-unit operations punctuated by larger offensive strikes as part of a wider, coordinated politico-military–police campaign were thus FM 31–16's prescription for how the U.S. Army would defeat contemporary Communist insurgencies. If this sounded familiar, it was. Very little of it was new. In addition to following the lead charted by the most recent doctrinal works, like the 1960 ODCSOPS handbook and FM 31–15 (1961), *Counterguerrilla Operations* had relied heavily on the Army's premier counterguerrilla work—FM 31–20 (1951). Not only had doctrine writers adopted many of FM 31–20's principles, but they had lifted significant portions, sometimes virtually verbatim, from the original Volckmann manual. In the process, they not only preserved concepts initially introduced in 1951—like *Wehrmacht* encirclement tactics—but resurrected ideas that had long since fallen out of Army manuals, like Volckmann's analytical division of an operational area into guerrilla-controlled, Army-controlled, and disputed zones. Even FM 31–16's description of guerrilla warfare was drawn from the 1951 manual, a description that, while still serviceable, had been based on a study of World War

II partisans, not Vietnamese irregulars. Thus three years after the inauguration of the great counterinsurgency drive, the Army's response to the threat posed by Maoist third world insurgencies remained firmly rooted in the past.

Counterguerrilla Operations may well have represented a repackaging of old wine in a new bottle, but it was good wine, one that embodied principles that had generally stood the test of time. Nevertheless, the Army recognized the need to supplement and refine it. Two important examples of this emerged at the end of 1963. The first, the "Counterinsurgency Planning Guide," was issued by the Special Warfare School in October 1963 as a guidebook for soldiers charged with planning and implementing counterinsurgency campaigns. The booklet was filled with practical tips, worksheets, and checklists to help the practitioner apply current doctrinal concepts. It was also a virtual primer on social engineering, blending modern developmental theory with a host of suggestions on what U.S. soldiers could do to bring prosperity and democracy to foreign lands. Finally, the booklet introduced some modest refinements to doctrine, dividing the pacification committees into two entities—civil-military advisory committees that served as liaison bodies between the military and the civilian community, and security coordination centers, which focused more narrowly on the integration of military, police, and intelligence matters. It also assigned a new label, clear and hold, to the area control concept espoused by FM 31–16.[55]

The last doctrinal product of 1963 was FM 31–22, *U.S. Army Counterinsurgency Forces*, published by the Special Warfare Agency in November. While FM 31–16 (1963) had outlined what U.S. forces would do when directly engaged in counterguerrilla warfare, FM 31–22 focused on the earlier stages of an insurgency, when American participation would be limited to providing advice and support. Consequently, while the manual reiterated the broad tenets of national and Army counterinsurgency doctrine, it was dedicated more narrowly to what the Army in 1961 had termed *counterinsurgency forces*. Counterinsurgency forces were those elements of the Army specifically designated to help third world countries combat Communist subversion, primarily by providing advice and support, rather than direct action. FM 31–22 (1963) divided such forces into three tiers according to the order in which they were to be committed. Military assistance advisory group (MAAG) personnel and mobile advisory teams drawn mainly from SAFs made up the first tier. SAF backup brigades composed the second, while any other individual, combat support, or combat service support units drawn from the Army at large made up the third tier.

FM 31–22 (1963) examined in depth the organization and function of the Special Action Forces and the SAF backup brigades. Because of its advisory focus, FM 31–22 also discussed the organization, operation, and training of indigenous paramilitary forces in greater detail than had heretofore appeared in official manuals. The manual noted that people who joined paramilitary forces did so at great risk to themselves and their families and that consequently the government had a moral obligation to reward and protect them. The manual also suggested establishing village radio systems that could be used for both security and administrative purposes.[56]

FM 31–22 (1963) assigned two major functions to indigenous paramilitaries. First, paramilitaries protected villages—a function that yielded immense political, morale, and intelligence benefits. Second, and equally important, paramilitary forces performed static security missions "in order that the national army may be relieved of these tasks to concentrate on offensive operations." This view not only reflected the advice the Army had given insurgency-torn countries since 1945, but mirrored British doctrine as well, which asserted that "the primary role of the army is to seek out and destroy CT [Communist terrorists] in the jungle and on its fringes. . . . The secondary role of the Army is that of supporting the . . . police in the populated areas by helping to enforce food denial measures, curfews, etc." American doctrine writers in the 1960s thoroughly agreed with this approach. Although FM 31–16 acknowledged that military units would have to perform police and population- and resources-control functions to one degree or another, American texts repeatedly assigned primary responsibility for such missions to indigenous forces in general and to police and paramilitary formations in particular. Such a division of labor made the best use of the indigenous forces' local knowledge and linguistic skills; minimized the involvement of foreign troops in politically sensitive, population-oriented operations; and freed the more heavily armed regulars for the mission for which they were best suited—offensive combat.[57]

Throughout its pages, FM 31–22 dispensed additional observations with regard to implementing Army counterinsurgency doctrine. It recommended maintaining high stock levels at all bases so that sudden increases in supply activities at a particular base would not tip off the enemy about upcoming operations. It cautioned that the intermingling of guerrillas and civilians would restrict the application of firepower, except in declared "free zones" where artillery could be employed "indiscriminately." It warned, however, that "the amount of such fire must be well controlled to prevent wasting ammunition."[58]

FM 31–22 also repeated injunctions to the effect that counterinsurgency was a "war for men's minds" in which every soldier was a "grass roots ambassador." Still, while socioeconomic action programs were vital to winning public support, the manual advised commanders not to allow civic action programs to interfere with their units' primary mission of engaging the enemy in combat. Finally, based on the Army's many advisory experiences over the past decade, FM 31–22 (1963) reviewed some of the problems that typically impeded advisory missions, offering several pages of suggestions on how advisers might overcome these difficulties before concluding with a series of appendixes outlining paramilitary training, village defense, civic action, and resettlement programs.[59]

FM 31–22 was the last counterinsurgency manual published during President Kennedy's three-year administration. Ten days after its publication, Kennedy fell victim to an assassin's bullet. During the first year of his successor's administration, the Army published only one major counterinsurgency work—FM 100–20, *Field Service Regulations, Counterinsurgency*. Prepared by the Army's Institute for Advanced Studies, FM 100–20 was intended to be the highest-level statement of counterinsurgency doctrine in the family of Army manuals. The manual described the current world situation in Rostowian terms, explaining how communism endeavored to exploit the revolution of rising expectations for its own ends. It related U.S. national policy as found in the OIDP and summarized the part each U.S. government agency was to play in implementing this program before focusing on the Army's particular role during each stage of a Maoist-style insurgency. In the process, it reiterated the fact that U.S. national policy generally restricted American overseas involvements to providing advice and assistance to avoid exposing the United States "unnecessarily to charges of intervention and colonialism." The manual concluded by reviewing some operational and planning factors for counterinsurgency actions.[60]

Much of the information contained in FM 100–20 had already appeared in earlier texts. Nevertheless, the publication of FM 100–20 in April 1964 marked an important milestone in the development of Army counterinsurgency literature, as the Army now had a fairly complete family of counterinsurgency manuals. FM 100–20 (1964) put the Army's role in counterinsurgency in a national context and provided information useful for high-level planners. FM 31–22 (1963) explained the role of Army forces in more depth, particularly during the preliminary stages of an insurrection when the Army's role would be confined to providing advisers, while FM 31–15 (1961) described what the Army would do once the United States directly intervened in an irregular conflict. Finally, FM 31–16 (1963) described in even more detail how infantry brigades and battalions would go about the business of fighting guerrillas.

The Development of Doctrine, 1964–1965

The publication of the Army's capstone counterinsurgency manual three years into the national counterinsurgency campaign reflected some underlying problems in the Army's doctrinal effort. Ideally, the Army would have preferred to publish its highest-level manual first, followed by an orderly progression of derivative manuals, each describing in greater detail exactly how the concepts contained in the preceding manuals were to be implemented. In practice, the Army had not been able to adhere to this scheme. Definitive national-level doctrine, in the form of the OIDP, had not been available until the fall of 1962, and, although the Army had immediately drafted a manual incorporating that policy, cumbersome internal review procedures and the need to coordinate the manuscript with outside agencies had delayed the publication of FM 100–20 until after Kennedy's death. Consequently, the Army ended up publishing lower-level operational doctrine, like FM 31–16, before higher-level manuals, like FM 100–20. Since the service's fundamental philosophy with regard to counterinsurgency did not alter during this period, the ill effects of the delay were perhaps minimal. On the other hand, the language of counterinsurgency was changing so rapidly during the 1960s due to intense military and public interest in the subject that manuals published at different times employed different, and somewhat conflicting, terms. The confusion was exacerbated by the Army's decision, taken in deference to the importance assigned to counterinsurgency, to incorporate new ideas into existing doctrine as soon as they were available rather than waiting for the development of a complete doctrinal base.[61]

Meanwhile, the inclusion of counterinsurgency in branch-level, how-to-do-it manuals had proceeded unevenly for a variety of reasons. To begin with, few doctrine writers had the type of knowledge needed to write detailed implementing-level doctrine for counterinsurgency. Army efforts to rectify this situation were only marginally effective until America's growing involvement in Vietnam eventually generated a surplus of such individuals. The fact that the branches introduced counterinsurgency material into their manuals at different times, depending on when particular manuals were due for review, added to the doctrinal unevenness. Turf battles between agencies over proponency for certain aspects of doctrine, as well as philosophical differences as to the degree to which counterinsurgency needed to be integrated into functional manuals, further complicated matters. A few branches—including Special Forces—argued that standard branch techniques were entirely adequate to meet counterinsurgency needs and hence there was no need to develop special tactics for counterguerrilla operations. Some doctrinal writers also objected to including counterguerrilla information in lower-level manuals on the grounds that higher-level manuals had already covered the subject adequately, citing regulations that discouraged redundancy. In fact, the Army's counterinsurgency literature was exceedingly redundant despite these regulations. This was not entirely bad, given the president's desire that the Army rapidly immerse itself in what was for many an unfamiliar subject. The redundancy, however, muddied doctrinal clarity and added to the confusion as to exactly what each manual was supposed to achieve.[62]

Army Chief of Staff General Johnson was particularly dissatisfied with the state of counterinsurgency doctrine and training in the Army. He felt that while the Army had made significant progress on the counterinsurgency front over the past few years, it had still not fully come to grips with the issue. He was disturbed by uneven treatment of the subject in Army manuals and wanted the technical and operational aspects of waging a counterinsurgency campaign developed in more detail. Johnson also thought that civil affairs doctrine had not yet made the adjustment from conventional occupation duty to the more varied demands of the contemporary world. Finally, he suspected that a belief existed "in many parts of the government and within the army as well that counterinsurgency and Special Forces are synonymous." Until this notion was put to rest once and for all, Johnson believed he would not be successful at integrating counterinsurgency into the mainstream of the Army.[63]

To correct these deficiencies, General Johnson launched two major initiatives in the latter half of 1964. The first focused on convincing the Army that counterinsurgency was not just for advisers and Special Forces personnel anymore, but a mission affecting the whole Army. To help sell this notion, Johnson coined a new term, *stability operations*, that broadly encompassed the entire range of activities that the Army might perform in support of national policy in the third world—constabulary operations, situations short of war, counterinsurgency, and nation building. From his perspective, the common denominator to all of these missions was that they required that the Army establish a level of stability and security sufficient to allow political, social, and economic measures—the true instruments of change—to work. Some observers criticized the term, saying it implied a status quo policy, but

251

Johnson denied such an inference, arguing that *stability operations* was far preferable to the other terms of the day—*counterinsurgency*, which he believed had negative connotations, and *special warfare*, which he felt implied that such operations were not a normal military function. After declaring in the fall of 1964 that stability operations represented the "third principal mission" of the Army, coequal with general and limited warfare, Johnson waged an aggressive campaign to make sure that everyone in the Army understood the new paradigm and took it seriously.[64]

Meanwhile, General Johnson launched the second prong of his offensive by ordering Combat Developments Command to review the entire counterinsurgency doctrinal program. The command responded to Johnson's request in August 1964 with a "Program for Analysis and Development of U.S. Counterinsurgency Doctrine and Organization." The program proposed a two-track approach. On the one hand, CDC would quickly redress some of Johnson's most urgent concerns. Meanwhile, it would proceed in a more systematic fashion to examine, refine, and revise the entire corpus of counterinsurgency literature.[65]

The fast track part of the CDC program required that the special warfare community publish a new handbook for advisory personnel and revise existing psyops and Special Forces manuals by the end of 1965. Although the psyops manual did not reach print until early 1966, Combat Developments Command did publish new versions of FM 31–21, *Special Forces Operations*, and FM 31–20, *Special Forces Operational Techniques*, in 1965. These manuals explained the techniques Special Forces personnel were to use in combating insurgencies and reflected to a large degree current practices in Southeast Asia. Of more importance to the Army as a whole, however, was the new advisory text, FM 31–73, *Advisor Handbook for Counterinsurgency*, released in April 1965.

FM 31–73 was the first manual published by the Army devoted exclusively to advisory issues. Although intended for general use, it was clearly written with an eye to Vietnam, where the United States already had over 30,000 military personnel. In addition to discussing advisory duty in general, the manual offered detailed coverage of the conduct of a counterinsurgency campaign in a way that was useful for advisers and operators alike. FM 31–73 endorsed civic action but cautioned from experience that "rural traditions are resistant to change and often will work against the project." It discussed the practical aspects of building defended hamlets, relocating populations, and conducting clear-and-hold operations, noting that such operations might take several years to succeed. The handbook also warned advisers that they would likely find that indigenous forces treated captured guerrillas much more harshly than would be tolerated in the U.S. Army. It instructed advisers to avoid becoming involved in atrocities and to encourage their counterparts to abide by the 1949 Geneva Convention. Finally, the manual reminded readers that they should apply "the minimum destruction concept in view of the overriding requirements to minimize alienating the population. (Bringing artillery or air power to bear on a village from which sniper fire was received may neutralize guerrilla action but will alienate the civilian population as a result of casualties among noncombatants.)"[66]

While Combat Developments Command proceeded to meet General Johnson's most urgent concerns, it initiated concurrently its broader doctrinal review. This effort called for the accomplishment of twenty-four tasks in an orderly, multiphased process of data collection, analysis, and publication. The desired result was a new family of manuals that covered the entire range of counterinsurgency issues, from national policy to the most technical procedure, with minimum redundancy in a clear, coherent, and linguistically consistent fashion. The command also planned to use the revision process to reinforce Johnson's campaign to integrate stability operations into the Army and to reorient the officer corps "from the purely military aspects of warfare to a recognition that every military move must be weighed with regard to both its political effects and military effects."[67]

General Johnson insisted that the conceptual aspects of the program be completed by November 1965, although he recognized that integrating the results of this review into Army literature would take much longer. Of the twenty-four tasks, perhaps the most important was task five, a study prepared by the CDC's Special Warfare and Civil Affairs Group in July 1965 titled "Concepts and General Doctrine for Counterinsurgency." Combat Developments Command intended this study to be the conceptual mainspring for the development of all future doctrine. What was most notable about the study, however, was how little it differed from existing doctrine. Although the report acknowledged problems in application, it fully embraced the social engineer's creed, stating that America's job was to change "the basic attitudes and value scales of the people to conform to that needed by the new nation that is being built to replace the former structure." Such measures were to go forward despite the fact that a majority of the population might object to the American-inspired changes.[68]

The study also did not challenge the U.S. government's basic strategy of relating American actions to the three phases of Maoist revolutionary warfare. Nation building still took precedence when insurgency was in a latent or incipient stage (phase one). Once guerrilla warfare had emerged (phase two), these efforts would share center stage with police, intelligence, and population- and resources-control programs. Military activities throughout these two phases remained of secondary importance in the minds of Army doctrine writers, who insisted on limiting the armed forces to performing clear-and-hold–type operations. But the study's tone changed dramatically when it came to considering appropriate policies for a full-blown, phase three war. In the opinion of the Special Warfare and Civil Affairs Group, "in a phase three insurgency, the survival of the government is predicated upon its ability to successfully undertake combat operations. . . . The government must concentrate its resources to completely defeat the guerrilla forces." Under these circumstances, nation-building and reform efforts, though never completely halted, were to take a backseat to more violent measures.[69]

The study's view of phase three warfare, while consistent with earlier Army writings, represented one of the strongest assertions to date that military considerations should take priority over political ones once major warfare had broken out. It was not an opinion universally held, as some soldiers believed that political and economic reforms should never be subordinated to military action. It was, nevertheless, consistent with past experience, where time after time counterinsurgents had found that political and economic programs could not advance without adequate security.

While the CDC study asserted the importance of military action during a full-scale war, it was less confident as to what that action should be. In the authors' opinion, the Army faced a difficult situation once an insurgency had reached its final stage.

If the guerrilla forces organize for conventional military operations, the problem for the government forces is resolved to that of defeating the insurgents, using standard military operations. . . . On the other hand, if the guerrillas remain dispersed to avoid battle but concentrate sufficiently to cause severe government attrition, the government faces a dilemma. Concentration of government forces permits the spread of insurgent control to those areas where government strength has been reduced. Conversely, failure to concentrate invites piecemeal destruction.[70]

The Special Warfare and Civil Affairs Group did not have a pat solution for such an eventuality. The group recommended that the government first secure those areas of the country that it needed for its own survival, such as major population centers and regions containing important resources, while applying vigorous population, resources, and border controls to deny the enemy sustenance. Meanwhile, the military would maintain pressure on the insurgents by inflicting casualties and destroying their supplies and equipment. "The resulting insurgent attrition combined with the requirement for the guerrillas to react to government operations contributes to the loss of insurgent operational initiative. . . . Where the government has gained the initiative, combat operations to destroy guerrilla units and to harass their safe areas should be extended."[71] Large units, employing massed artillery fires when appropriate, would conduct major operations, striking at guerrilla bases and gradually extending the government's zone of control, while small units kept up a constant pressure around populated areas through patrols and raids. Such was the advice of CDC's counterinsurgency experts for combating a phase three insurgency.

The Special Warfare and Civil Affairs Group's three-phase approach to insurgency betrayed several weaknesses. From the beginning, national policy and Army doctrine alike had tended to treat the differences between the phases in a Maoist revolutionary war as ones of scale and intensity, not method. Consequently, the United States had adopted the view that the only response to an escalating insurgency was to do more of the same—more reforms, more police controls, more combat operations—seemingly oblivious to the implication that if such measures had failed to arrest an insurgency in its earlier stages, they would be unlikely to do so after it had escalated to mobile warfare. Army doctrine also reflected national policy in depicting the enemy primarily in terms of small guerrilla bands. Its proposed countermeasures—decentralized area operations conducted by battalions and brigades operating on an independent or semi-independent basis—seemed to presuppose such a scenario. Army manuals never discussed division-level operations in an insurgency environment, adhering stubbornly to the independent brigade-battalion-company model. Some soldiers dismissed the whole question with an intellectual slight of hand, maintaining that any conflict in which the United States committed troops in division strength was, by definition, outside the bounds of counterinsurgency doctrine. Nonetheless, when forced to confront the question as to what was to be done once an enemy fielded large, conventional-type units, the Army's general response had been that conventional offensive and defensive tactics would suffice. In fact, as late as January 1965, CDC's Special Warfare Agency had asserted that "major combined arms operations per se are not visualized for counterinsurgency," and, in the unlikely event that they were required, "the doctrine will be essentially that of general war or limited war." Although a few soldiers warned that such assumptions were inaccurate, the Army gave little thought to the possibility that the enemy's large conventional formations might be able to continue to operate on a semiguerrilla basis, coalescing to strike, then dispersing to avoid retaliation, all the while maintaining the relatively fluid aspects characteristic of lower-level insurgencies.[72]

The Army's failure to consider the problems associated with conventional warfare in phase three represented one of the most significant flaws in its counterinsurgency doctrine. The CDC's failure to rectify the omission was not, however, the only area where the doctrinal review effort came up short. For example, the CDC's effort to identify techniques that would help the Army motivate indigenous populations to support a counterinsurgency campaign hit a snag when the organization tasked with preparing the study, the Special Operations Research Office, conceded that social science was still an "infant science" that had not yet progressed to the stage where it could provide the type of concrete solutions so desperately needed by doctrine writers. This admission should not have come as a surprise. As early as 1962, the academician Lucian W. Pye had warned that "the disturbing truth" was that the social science community had yet to develop a practical "doctrine about how to go about nation building."[73] That such a doctrine still did not exist three years later illustrated the difficulties doctrine writers would have in trying to produce more definitive guidance pertaining to counterinsurgency's complex social aspects.

General Johnson did not receive any better news from Deputy Chief of Staff for Military Operations General Palmer, who at Johnson's request prepared a paper on the nature of conflict in the "lower spectrum of war" in early 1965. After examining thirty-seven past insurgencies, Palmer concluded that Army doctrine was sound in its broad outlines but that any attempt to produce a definitive counterinsurgency doctrine would be like looking for a "Will-O-The-Wisp," since every insurgency was a unique event, the product of distinct political, social, topographical, and military factors. "This particularization," Palmer concluded, "calls into serious question the validity of current U.S. Army attempts to devise a universal doctrine for counterinsurgency comparable to our conventional war doctrine."[74]

Palmer's words of caution notwithstanding, Johnson still pressed ahead with the quest for a more perfect doctrine, even if it had to be acknowledged that no doctrine could ever fully address counterinsurgent warfare. By the end of 1965 Combat Developments Command had accomplished some important preliminary work toward revising the Army's counterinsurgency literature. Yet much remained to be done, and the revision program would take several more years before it was fully in place.

Disseminating Doctrine: The Education System

All of the Army's efforts at writing and revising doctrine would go for naught unless that doctrine was inculcated into the Army at large. This was no small task. Introducing new ideas is always time consuming. Counterinsurgency's heavy emphasis on political affairs posed special difficulties for an institution that, while it had long performed civil functions, had never felt comfortable doing so. The fact that soldiers had to master counterinsurgency while still maintaining proficiency in nuclear and conventional warfare added to the complexity of the task. Kennedy's determination that soldiers absorb the new style of warfare as quickly as possible, and the Army's reluctance to increase the amount of time its already busy soldiers spent in classrooms, merely exacerbated the problem.[75]

Because national policy placed the primary burden for countering third world revolutions on indigenous armies and their U.S. advisers, the military initially concentrated its educational initiatives on these two groups. The Army's first educational effort—the counterguerrilla operations and tactics course that opened at Fort Bragg in January 1961—was just such a course, as a significant portion of its student body consisted of foreign officers and Americans slated for overseas advisory duty. This class, which the Special Warfare School eventually expanded from six to ten weeks and renamed the counterinsurgency operations course, offered the most comprehensive treatment of counterinsurgency in the military education system. It covered everything from national policy to tactics and techniques. The course's central theme was that an insurgency could not be defeated unless significant progress was made in raising living standards, improving production, and achieving social and political equality. By 1962 the Army had established similar courses in Okinawa, Germany, and the Panama Canal Zone. Like the parent course at Fort Bragg, these courses primarily taught foreign officers, although the commander of U.S. Army, Europe, cycled enough men through the school in Germany to post at least one graduate in each brigade and battalion headquarters in Europe.[76]

Meanwhile, the Army introduced a number of other advisory-oriented initiatives. The service assisted the Pentagon's Military Assistance Institute in integrating counterinsurgency into its advisory training program and sent some of the Army's most senior adviser-designates to the Department of State's counterinsurgency-oriented National Interdepartmental Seminar. General Decker also initiated a Senior Officer Orientation Tour program, in which selected senior

Classroom instruction as part of the military assistance
training adviser course

officers spent up to six weeks in a troubled third world country to experience insurgency-related problems. Over two hundred senior officers participated in this program during its two-year existence. Last but not least, the Army developed a number of adviser-preparation courses. The most notable of these was the military assistance training adviser (MATA) course at Fort Bragg, established in early 1962. The four-week (later six-week) course was oriented exclusively to preparing advisers for the burgeoning conflict in Vietnam. Only a portion of all personnel going to Vietnam took the course, which experienced some growing pains. Nevertheless, the Special Warfare School continuously adjusted and improved the class based on feedback from Vietnam. The course reviewed doctrine, related Vietnam-specific tactics, and provided an orientation to Vietnamese language and culture.[77]

Based on the premise that a purely military solution was not possible in Vietnam, the original MATA course devoted roughly 25 percent of its time to civic action. In 1963 the Civil Affairs School reinforced this effort by initiating a six-week civic action course that taught nation-building theory to civil affairs personnel slated for duty overseas. Other schools eventually added adviser-oriented courses as well, so that by the end of 1965 perhaps 7,000 officers had graduated from the Army's most intensive counterinsurgency-related courses. While this number represented just a small fraction of the officer corps, it was an important one, as these individuals composed the front line of America's overseas counterinsurgency effort.[78]

The Army did not, however, limit its educational efforts to future advisers. From the beginning of the national counterinsurgency campaign, the Army committed itself to the goal of indoctrinating the entire officer corps in counterinsurgency. At the president's urging, the Pentagon established counterinsurgency libraries at many installations and published bibliographies and reading lists containing hundreds of counterinsurgency-related titles.[79] The Army's professional journals helped spread the counterinsurgency gospel as well, publishing hundreds of articles between 1961 and 1965. Some of these articles presented distillations of the latest doctrine, while others offered critiques, reviewed historical examples, or related tactics and techniques. A significant percentage of these articles emphasized the importance of good troop behavior and civic actions in the battle for the hearts and minds of the afflicted population.[80] The Army also integrated counterinsurgency studies into a number of short familiarization and refresher courses, the most notable of which was the senior officer counterinsurgency and special warfare course at Fort Bragg, a one-week intensive course that by 1964 was graduating about 450 colonels and generals a year.[81]

Meanwhile, in early 1961 Continental Army Command ordered that counterinsurgency be introduced into every level of officer education. Initially, it left the question of how much time schools should devote to counterinsurgency up to the individual school commandants. One consequence of this approach was that coverage varied widely from school to school in 1961, ranging from twelve hours given to Infantry officers to a mere two hours presented to Special Forces officers.[82] In September Continental Army Command attempted to impose some uniformity by mandating minimum hours of instruction for each level of schooling in the Army. However, rather than creating an entirely new block of instruction separate from the rest of a school's curriculum, CONARC directed that most counterinsurgency instruction be integrated into existing courses. To help meet these new requirements, the Special Warfare School drafted a series of common subject courses that service schools were to use as the basis of their instruction. These courses focused heavily on the political, social, and psychological aspects of counterinsurgency theory. For example, the three-hour common course for newly commissioned second lieutenants devoted no more than ninety seconds to tactics, while the twelve-hour branch career course contained just four hours on military tactics and techniques, still only a third of the total program. Using these lectures as a starting point, the schools were then free to add additional hours of instruction tailored more directly to their particular missions, a method that still allowed a great deal of flexibility. By January 1962 the average branch orientation course (given to all newly commissioned second lieutenants) devoted 6.2 hours to "pure" counterinsurgency and 73.4 hours to "related" subjects, while career courses (for first lieutenants and captains) contained, on average, 35 pure and 182 related hours.[83]

The significance of these statistics is difficult to judge, as school officials, eager to demonstrate their responsiveness to the president, used somewhat questionable criteria as to what constituted counterinsurgency and counterinsurgency-related course hours. The absence of any formal definition of these terms, together with CONARC's preference that most counterinsurgency instruction be integrated into preexisting courses, lent further confusion. Skeptics rightly scoffed at the Infantry School's claim that by January 1962 the school was devoting over 400 hours to counterinsurgency-related subjects. On the other hand, there was a certain legitimacy to the view that many conventional subjects were relevant to performing counterinsurgency missions, especially if instructors integrated appropriate counterinsurgency observations into their standard lectures. For example, the Commandant of Cadets at West Point in 1962, Brig. Gen. Richard G. Stilwell, claimed that an English course titled "Evolution of American Ideals as Reflected in American Literature from 1607 to the Present" was counterinsurgency-related because it helped "the cadet in realizing and understanding the American way of life. Such background training is considered valuable in working with peoples of underdeveloped nations." He similarly argued that the activities of the judo and debate clubs bore "some relationship" to counterinsurgency. While his reasoning was not without merit, statements such as these illustrate the difficulty one experiences in trying to quantify counterinsurgency education in the Army.[84]

What is incontrovertible is that Army leaders were dissatisfied with the way the schools were handling counterinsurgency, as evidenced by a number of internal reports generated in 1961 and 1962. Nor was President Kennedy satisfied, and in March 1962 he directed that all government agencies involved in counterinsurgency, including the Departments of State and Defense, USIA, AID, and the CIA, establish counterinsurgency education programs. According to National Security Action Memorandum 131, all civil and military officers in the aforementioned agencies were to receive a basic orientation in the history and nature of insurgency, to include Communist tactics and America's counterstrategy. In addition, junior- and mid-grade officers were to study counterinsurgency tactics and techniques applicable to their branches and departments, while staff-level officers received instruction in planning and conducting counterinsurgency campaigns. Finally, the memorandum required that all mid- and senior-grade officers slated for overseas service in developing countries receive both general counterinsurgency instruction as well as more specific information about the country to which they were about to be posted.[85]

Spurred by this directive, Continental Army Command redoubled its efforts to improve the quantity and quality of instruction given in its schools, directing that all officer orientation and career courses contain between twenty and twenty-seven hours of pure counterinsurgency instruction. This was rapidly achieved, and between 1963 and 1965 the average branch officer career course included about twenty-eight hours of pure counterinsurgency instruction, of which about eight hours were devoted to theory and twenty to branch-oriented tactics and techniques. All schools also continued to report many additional hours of counterinsurgency-related instruction.[86]

Exposure to counterinsurgency began at the very beginning of officer education, in ROTC and at the United States Military Academy at West Point, New York. Counterinsurgency proved quite popular on college campuses, where students, inspired by Kennedy's somewhat romantic portrayal of guerrilla warfare, began forming volunteer counterguerrilla units. CONARC quickly tapped into the fad, and by 1965 nearly half of all college ROTC programs sported counterguerrilla units that practiced patrol, survival, and fieldcraft skills. In the meantime, the command ensured that all ROTC students were exposed to the idea that "subversive insurgency is a battle for the hearts and minds of men" in a six-hour required course.[87]

Cadets at the Military Academy received an even heavier dose of counterinsurgency theory. The works of Communist theoreticians Mao Tse-tung, Vo Nguyen Giap, and Truong Chinh were required reading at the academy beginning in 1962, as were histories of past revolutionary struggles in Malaya, Indochina, and the Philippines. Also mandatory for cadets were lectures on the current war in Vietnam. By 1963 West Point's curriculum included sixty-six mandatory lessons in counterinsurgency plus twenty-six hours of Ranger-style counterguerrilla training in summer camp. Seniors were also required to write a paper chosen from a list of twenty-nine topics developed by the academy, eight of which (28 percent) were counterinsurgency related. The academy further identified another 136 required lessons and 45 hours of field training as being counterinsurgency related, while the school offered an additional 226 counterinsurgency lessons in such elective courses as "National Security Problems," "Military History of Insurgency and Counterinsurgency," and "Revolutionary Warfare."[88]

Upon commissioning, the Army sent its young second lieutenants to branch schools for roughly nine weeks of orientation training in their new duties. They then went to operational assignments, only to return a few years later as first lieutenants and captains to receive six to nine months of branch career instruction. While the amount of counterinsurgency instruction offered in Army branch schools varied widely, one school that played a pivotal role in disseminating doctrine was the Infantry School, both because of the large number of officers who passed through its doors each year and because of the central role the Army assigned to Infantry units in counterguerrilla doctrine.

Like all of its sister institutions, the Infantry School found the task of integrating a complex subject like counterinsurgency into an already cramped curriculum to be no easy matter. School instructor Maj. Harold D. Yow explained the school's dilemma and the rationale behind its ultimate solution.

We cannot give a complete course in geography, political science, applied psychology, comparative religions, ethnology, aesthetics, economics, and the tactics and techniques of counterguerrilla operations—it just cannot be done. Yet knowledge in all of these areas is vital to success in counterinsurgency operations and as you know we have a multitude of prophets about us, each setting forth, what in his own best judgment, is the one facet of these operations to be most emphasized. In all probability they are all right to a degree, for above all else, counterinsurgency operations must have a "total" approach, prepared to attack every deficiency which can present obstacles in a country to the rapid development of human capabilities, with a concomitant development of an environment of individual freedom necessary for their exercise. . . . We realize that the infantryman must have an acute awareness of the totality of the successful counterinsurgency formula. He must be aware of the importance of psychological operations, economics, politics, etc.—in fact, at the individual level he must become directly involved in many of these activities within his own means—in the program of activities which are called "military civic actions." But, first, last, and foremost, the business of the infantry officer in counterinsurgency operations is most properly the beating of the overt armed guerrilla force, whether by an American unit he is leading, or by an indigenous unit he is advising.[89]

Guided by this philosophy, the Infantry School proceeded to integrate counterinsurgency instruction into its curriculum. At the start of the Kennedy administration the orientation course for newly commissioned infantry lieutenants included a mere two hours of counterinsurgency instruction, while the longer branch career course offered twelve hours. This was clearly insufficient. In fact, only 32 percent of the students expressed satisfaction with the school's treatment of counterguerrilla warfare, while only 25 percent believed they had sufficient knowledge to train a unit effectively for antiguerrilla operations. From these meager beginnings the school's coverage of counterinsurgency matters expanded rapidly, so that by 1965 the orientation course included 29 hours of pure and 195 hours of integrated counterinsurgency instruction. The career course was even more impressive, devoting about sixty-seven hours to pure counterinsurgency instruction by 1965.[90]

Throughout the 1960s, Infantry School curricular materials stressed the idea that soldiers who blindly adhered to conventional methods, without taking into account a conflict's unique political, military, and topographical facets, were bound to fail. To outfox the guerrilla, the school advocated that soldiers employ ruses and deceptions, operate at night and in inclement weather, and leave ambush parties behind to catch unsuspecting enemies as they investigated abandoned positions. It also recommended using small, seemingly vulnerable units as bait to tempt the irregulars into attacking, thereby exposing themselves to a powerful riposte by reaction forces. In fact, the school stressed the importance of maintaining ready reaction forces at all levels, for "this is the crux of our tactical doctrine: use minimum forces to find the guerrilla and maintain maximum forces, preferably airborne or airmobile, in an advanced state of readiness to react to any located guerrilla force."[91]

Emulating principles that the old Indian fighting Army would have well understood, Army schools preached continuous, aggressive action, for in the words of one text, "if the guerrilla is kept running, fighting and hiding long enough, attrition from casualties, desertions and the loss of contact with the civilian population can cause the guerrilla band to break up to a point where they could be effectively controlled by police." Reflecting the small-unit focus of Army doctrine, the Infantry School's career course spent only four hours considering division and larger operations, compared to forty-one hours on brigade, battalion, and company operations. Clear-and-hold–type pacification operations were the infantry battalion's bread and butter, for according to the school, "no large coordinated action in the conventional sense will take place . . . until there is a requirement for offensive action against a located guerrilla force. The majority of the day-by-day activity . . . will be small-unit action to locate guerrilla forces, secure the population, installations, and lines of communication, train and assist the indigenous paramilitary forces, and conduct military civic action."[92]

Notwithstanding the requirement that the Infantry School produce combat leaders, the school in no way ignored counterinsurgency's many political facets. "The important thing," it reminded its pupils, "is to realize that from the very start you are fighting an ideology. And, since shooting guerrillas is a very ineffective way to destroy an ideology . . . actions on the counterinsurgency battlefield at all levels of command must be a total military-civilian effort to both destroy the armed guerrilla of an insurgency and attack this ideological root of the resistance." In fact, the school devoted approximately twelve hours of instruction to civic action, during which instructors explained to their students that "the guerrilla force is only a symptom of the over-all problem in the area which caused the resistance movement to arise in the first place. Prior to, during, and following the successful completion of counterguerrilla operations, a positive program of civil assistance to the area must be conducted to eliminate the original cause of the resistance movement."[93]

Curricular materials also reviewed counterinfrastructure and police-style population- and resource-control measures. While preaching an overall policy of enlightened moderation, the school conceded that "if it cannot be determined which portion of the civilian population is actively supporting the irregular force, harsh measures may have to be used with the entire population until such a determination can be made." While the Army clearly discouraged severity, such statements were not unusual, and other schools flirted with equally distasteful practices, including the Special Warfare School, which advised its students that the "children of known guerrillas should be separated from their parents to prevent further subversion and act as a deterrent to association with the guerrillas." The destruction of crops and foodstuffs, the creation of forbidden zones "where *anyone* in the area will be shot on sight," and the resettlement of populations were also to be included in the counterinsurgent's arsenal, although Army schools cautioned that such actions were measures of last resort and had to be implemented with care lest they cause undue hardship and fan the flames of resistance.[94]

While most instruction given at Fort Benning was generic in nature, neither it nor its sister institutions could ignore the growing conflagration in Vietnam. The Infantry School began presenting information about Vietnam in 1962, as the Kennedy administration dramatically increased America's presence there. The school related information based on reports from the field and occasionally employed Vietnam scenarios in its tests and exercises. In 1963 the school modified its traditional small arms instruction, which had focused on long-range marksmanship, to include "quick fire" techniques designed to allow soldiers to respond rapidly and effectively to the type of close-in, surprise targets often encountered in jungle ambushes. The Infantry School also introduced in 1963 a voluntary forty-hour course on Vietnam for students who were slated to go there upon graduation. A mixture of U.S. soldiers who had recently returned from Vietnam and South Vietnamese who were currently students at the school taught the class. The following year the assistant commandant, Brig. Gen. John Norton, initiated a "Win in Vietnam" program. He formed committees that considered various aspects of the war and recommended doctrinal, training, and organizational improvements. The school reviewed the curriculum to ensure that it was as effective as possible in preparing officers for duty in Vietnam. The Infantry School also launched a variety of initiatives that included inviting Vietnam veterans as guest speakers, publishing articles, assembling special reading materials, and organizing displays and demonstrations. As the United States moved toward intervention, the school redoubled its efforts. By 1965 it was operating two mock South Vietnamese villages, complete with female inhabitants drawn from the Women's Army Corps, who were used to teach search and seizure techniques.[95]

Students who passed through the Infantry or other branch-level schools in the early 1960s would have found much of their course material repeated at the Command and General Staff College. This represented a deliberate policy, as the college was well aware that many of its students might have attended branch schools prior to the introduction of counterinsurgency into those curriculums. To ensure a common base of understanding, the school reviewed the entire sweep of counterinsurgency doctrine, from national policy and nation-building theory to tactics. The college naturally focused, however, on organizational, operational, and planning issues in accordance with its overall mission of producing mid-level commanders and staff officers.

Like all Army schools, the college steadily increased the amount of time devoted to counterinsurgency issues throughout the early 1960s. By 1964 the Command and General Staff College provided 42 hours of direct counterinsurgency instruction, with another 171 hours of related material scattered throughout the 38-week course. Students studied case histories from Greece, Algeria, Malaya, and the Philippines, with about 18 percent of the student body writing theses on counterinsurgency-related subjects. As part of the training, the college put students to work drafting hypothetical counterinsurgency plans, advisory procedures, and intervention deployments for a variety of countries, real and imagined, all in accordance with current national policies and doctrines.

Although school exercises occasionally depicted division-size encircle-ment operations, for the most part the school's curriculum emphasized the type of brigade, battalion, and small-unit area control techniques that lay at the heart of U.S. doctrine. Civic and psychological actions also featured prominently in school exercises, as did questions relating to the formation of paramilitary defense organizations, the imposition of population and resource controls, and, when necessary, the resettle-ment of populations.[96]

Those officers who were fortunate enough to be selected to attend the Army's highest educational institution, the Army War College, concentrated their studies on such subjects as national policy, strategy, and interagency coordination. The school introduced irregular warfare in 1961 when the "Concepts of Future Land Warfare" course dedicated twelve of its sixteen study committees to counterinsurgency questions. The following year coverage of low intensity conflict grew to about 12 percent of the curriculum, with about 10 percent of the students writing counterinsurgency theses. In 1962 the college also hosted two senior officer counterinsurgency courses, each of three weeks' duration. Although these courses were designed to immerse a select group of nonstudent officers in counterinsurgency issues, the college permitted the general student body to attend a number of the lectures as well.[97]

In 1963 the college introduced a 3 ½-week course on the developing world. The course focused on the problems of modernization, the nature and causes of insurgency, and the U.S. response. By 1965 the college had expanded this course to five weeks. In addition, the school required that all students write papers on some aspect of low intensity warfare. Meanwhile the college kept abreast of the latest developments by hold-ing special seminars and panel discussions on Vietnam. Thus by 1965 the Army's school system had assembled a creditable, though by no means flawless, program of instruction that sought to ensure that all officers, from cadets to generals, were exposed to counterinsurgency doctrine.[98]

Disseminating Doctrine: The Training System

While the Army transmitted counterinsurgency theory to its officers through lectures and readings, training provided the best means to test students' understanding, reinforce doctrinal precepts, and refine tactics and techniques. It was also the Army's primary means of acquainting rank-and-file soldiers with the counterguerrilla mission.

At the outset of the Kennedy administration Army regulations required that every recruit receive four hours of antiguerrilla instruc-tion as part of basic combat training, with an additional eight hours for rifle companies. Army leaders evinced little enthusiasm for imposing additional hours of mandatory counterguerrilla training at the expense of conventional combat capability. They also considered that most of the conventional skills taught to individuals and small units were fully applicable to counterguerrilla warfare. True, tactics might have to be modified to meet local conditions, and soldiers would undoubtedly have to demonstrate a higher degree of aptitude in certain individual skills, but the Army believed that it could accommodate these requirements with only minor changes to conventional training programs. Given the fact that military training schedules were already heavily burdened to meet the diverse requirements of nuclear, chemical, airmobile, and conventional warfare, the Army initially decided against imposing a separate counterinsurgency training program. Rather, as with officer education, it opted to integrate counterguerrilla instruction into the normal training regimen.[99]

The Continental Army Command officially affirmed this policy in May 1961, when it issued its first training directive of the Kennedy era. The directive encouraged training officers to integrate counterinsurgency into routine training, asserting that this could easily be done as 918 of the 1,443 hours that made up the Army's core training programs concerned subjects that had some counterinsurgency application. It also recommended that rifle companies incorporate counterguerrilla situations into exercises and that major unit commanders designate portions of their commands for more intensive irregular warfare training. But beyond this it did not go, specifying neither the quantity nor content of such training.[100]

By focusing on the training of individuals and small groups of specialists rather than units, the May 1961 directive clearly reflected the Army's belief that the United States intended to follow an advisory, rather than interventionist, approach to the counterinsurgency problem. Unfortunately, the individual training approach, when coupled with the Army's initial categorization of counterinsurgency as a subset of special warfare, created an impression among many soldiers that counterinsurgency was really only something that Special Forces had to be concerned with. This, of course, was not the true position of either the administration or the Army. To drive home this point, CONARC issued a new training directive in September 1961 that clearly stated that the "task of improving the capability of the Army to cope with counterinsurgency/counterguerrilla warfare now involves the entire army and not special forces alone. All combat forces must develop a broad base of knowledge. . . . Counterinsurgency and counterguerrilla operations are the entire army's business and all elements must become familiar with their respective roles and develop the required proficiency in this type of warfare." The directive mandated that all Army personnel receive training in the nature, causes, prevention, and elimination of third world insurgency, to include the employment of intelligence, medical, civil affairs, and psychological assets. Individuals or units assigned to counterinsurgency missions were to receive specialized training beyond this, including appropriate language and cultural skills. The September regulations also directed that certain divisions, most notably those in the Strategic Army Corps, provide intensive counterguerrilla training to at least some of their component units. Meanwhile, CONARC began revising many of its Army training programs (ATPs) and Army training tests (ATTs) to include suggestions as to how counterinsurgency subjects might be integrated into conventional training regimens.[101]

Even these measures fell short. A survey of officers enrolled in the infantry officer career course at Fort Benning in 1961 found that while 47 percent of them had conducted counterguerrilla training in their units prior to coming to the school, only 22 percent believed that training had been adequate. A subsequent study in January 1962 led by Lt. Gen. Hamilton H. Howze concurred in this assessment and advised that all eight Regular Army divisions based in the continental United States be given counterguerrilla training. Continental Army Command responded to these criticisms in March 1962 by revising the counterguerrilla training directive yet again.[102]

The new directive made a distinction between "counterinsurgency" and "counterguerrilla" training. Counterinsurgency training included the whole range of insurgency-related issues, from the nature of Maoist insurgency and the revolution of rising expectations to America's national strategy, nation building, and Army roles and missions. Counterguerrilla training focused more narrowly on the actions military units would take when operating against irregular forces. According to the directive, all soldiers were to be trained for counterguerrilla warfare, and all soldiers were to receive familiarization training in counterinsurgency. However, only designated "counterinsurgency forces"—primarily Special Forces and other elements assigned to what would eventually become the SAFs and SAF backup brigades—were to receive intensive training in both counterinsurgency and counterguerrilla warfare, to include an annual six-week training cycle for the backup brigades.

The March 1962 directive reiterated CONARC's policy that commanders integrate counterguerrilla subjects into all phases of training to the maximum extent possible, including training tests, exercises, and maneuvers. To assist in this task, the directive enumerated subjects that lent themselves to counterguerrilla training. It also required that all active duty infantry, armor, combat engineer, military police, and cannon artillery units conduct two three-day counterguerrilla exercises every year. Administrative and technical units were required to devote ninety-two hours a year to counterguerrilla training and to partake in semiannual counterguerrilla field exercises. The regulation specifically directed that civil affairs and civic action, psychological operations, and intelligence issues be integrated into all phases of counterguerrilla training. Continental Army Command further ordered that training at all levels focus on the formation and operation of small, mobile task forces, from squad to battle group, capable of undertaking independent or semi-independent action. Patrol, reaction, police, and clear-and-hold–type activities, rather than large-scale operations, were to be the order of the day.[103]

This directive represented a significant step forward over the first regulation issued less than a year earlier. Nevertheless, the Army's adherence to a strategy of integrated instruction and decentralized execution created a situation in which the amount and quality of instruction inevitably varied from unit to unit. Moreover, although CONARC encouraged commanders to modify standard Army training tests for use in counterguerrilla training, it never issued an Army-wide test for counterguerrilla operations. Since military trainers, like most educators operating under a regime of standardized exams, tended to focus their efforts on preparing their charges for what was on the tests, the lack of an official test for counterguerrilla warfare undermined the Army's efforts to persuade commanders to devote precious training time to the subject.[104]

Commanders' reluctance to deviate from conventional norms was particularly troublesome in the area of small-unit leadership, which the Army understood was critical in conducting highly dispersed operations. Conventional training regimens generally did not accord junior officers and noncommissioned officers at the fire team, squad, and platoon levels much opportunity to plan and direct independent operations. A 1962 survey of students at the Infantry School found that 61 percent of the respondents could not recall having received any counterguerrilla leadership training in their units, while 19 percent stated that their units engaged in such training only occasionally. On the other hand, 20 percent of the students reported that their parent brigades and divisions had indeed established special counterguerrilla leadership academies, some of which offered courses of up to three weeks' duration. Such institutions became more common as the decade progressed, as commanders became ever more aware of the need to improve their

"Guerrillas" maneuver during a 1962 counterguerrilla exercise at Fort Carson, Colorado.

units' counterguerrilla proficiency. In fact, while some units did little more than the minimum expected of them, others well exceeded Army standards. Weaknesses remained, however, even in crack outfits like the 173d Airborne Brigade, which prior to its deployment to Vietnam in May 1965 had seldom given its junior noncommissioned officers the opportunity to lead independent patrols, a skill that would soon be in high demand.[105]

Technically, CONARC's regulations only applied to units in the continental United States, but overseas Army commands generally followed CONARC's lead. This was especially true in Asia, where U.S. Army, Pacific, imposed mandatory counterguerrilla training for all combat and combat support units. By the spring of 1962 its three major units—the 7th and 25th Infantry Divisions and 1st Cavalry Division—were all operating special counterinsurgency schools, while the U.S. Eighth Army had a counterinsurgency study group as well.[106]

Meanwhile, back home Continental Army Command introduced a special lecture program for all incoming recruits. It consisted of two hours of counterinsurgency and one hour of counterguerrilla orientation in basic training, with the two-hour counterinsurgency lecture repeated in advanced individual training, supplemented by a three-hour course on communism. These courses reviewed Maoist principles, endorsed land reform and economic growth as tools to eliminate the causes of disaffection, and cited historical examples

*"Guerrilla" mortarmen emerge from concealment
during Vietnam-oriented training.*

of counterinsurgency operations. The orientation programs also reviewed Communist tactics based on Viet Minh manuals and warned soldiers that they would have to modify conventional tactics if they were to defeat such an opponent.[107]

By the end of 1962 CONARC had erected special counterguerrilla reaction and testing courses at each of its major recruit training facilities, with the command claiming that 25 percent of all recruit training was now directly related to counterinsurgency. It had also begun encouraging commanders to integrate Vietnam experience into their training programs, assisting them by periodically disseminating the latest lessons learned from that part of the world. Finally, in November, in the most important training development of the year, Continental Army Command mandated that all regular combat units in the United States conduct six weeks of counterguerrilla training annually. The new program was identical to that established in March for the backup brigades and consisted of three phases, each of two weeks' duration. The first phase focused on individual and Ranger-type training. The second phase consisted of small-unit counterguerrilla tactics, while the third phase was devoted entirely to field training, culminating in a battalion-level exercise.[108]

The six-week counterguerrilla training program represented the single largest block of mandatory training imposed by the Continental Army Command. Many commanders disliked the requirement, believing that it was too restrictive and that it contravened the latitude the Army customarily accorded commanders in managing their training time. Although the command refused to budge on this issue, it did eventually reduce the number of hours of counterinsurgency lectures given to recruits on the grounds that many of the subjects were too abstract for young soldiers to absorb. Still, by 1963 all of the elements of the Army's counterinsurgency and counterguerrilla training program were in place. All soldiers were expected to be familiar with the general precepts of American counterinsurgency doctrine, and all underwent some form of mandatory counterguerrilla training each year, with combat units receiving the most intense training. Although training increasingly took on a Vietnam focus as the decade wore on, officially training was to be generic in nature. Only after receiving notification of a possible overseas deployment were units to begin training for a specific theater of operations during a short, intensive program that would include both general counterguerrilla and country-specific environmental and cultural training. Such an approach was essential due to the impossibility of predicting where units might be called upon to serve.[109]

CONARC assisted officers in crafting their training programs with an extensive catalog of all available counterinsurgency training materials. Several manuals were also particularly useful to the trainer, including FM 30–102, *Aggressor Forces* (1963), which provided advice on integrating guerrillas into training exercises; FM 31–30, *Jungle Operations* (1960); FM 31–30, *Jungle Training and Operations* (1965); and FM 57–35, *Airmobile Operations* (1960 and 1963). Other manuals of special utility were FM 31–18, *Long Range Patrols* (1962 and 1965); FM 21–75, *Combat Training of the Individual Soldier and Patrolling* (1962); and FM 21–50, *Ranger Training and Ranger Operations* (1962).

FM 31–18, *Long Range Patrols*, described the organization, function, and operation of long-range reconnaissance patrols (LRRPs). These were small teams of highly trained soldiers whose primary mission was to gather intelligence and acquire targets deep in enemy territory—a concept the Army would shortly put to the test in Vietnam. FM 21–75, *Combat Training of the Individual Soldier and Patrolling*, not only covered ambush, patrol, and airmobile techniques applicable to counterguerrilla warfare, but also impressed upon each soldier the importance of proper behavior toward civilians, noting that

practicing self-discipline is an extremely important part of combating the guerrilla. Almost every man is proud of the spiritual values, culture, and customs of his country. If you ignore or neglect the importance of these items,

Soldiers search "dead" insurgents that they have just ambushed during training.

hatred of you and sympathy for the guerrilla will result. The guerrilla desires to spread resentment against you and your country. Disregarding these considerations will aid his effort. Self-discipline, combined with a firm, just, and understanding policy in dealing with civilians, will reduce chances of guerrilla success.[110]

The 1962 edition of FM 21–50, *Ranger Training and Ranger Operations*, further reinforced the Army's efforts to develop the type of highly skilled infantrymen so necessary in counterguerrilla warfare. The Ranger movement of the 1950s continued to flourish into the 1960s, with concomitant benefits for counterguerrilla proficiency as a whole. Not only did Army regulations require that all rifle companies undergo annual Ranger training, but by 1962, 80 percent of all Regular Army second lieutenants had already taken the Ranger course at Fort Benning. In 1964 the Army directed that all Regular Army officers should take either Ranger or airborne training, and the following year the Infantry School revised the Ranger curriculum to include an eighteen-day counterguerrilla phase. Ultimately, in 1966 the Army would make Ranger training mandatory for all newly commissioned Regular Army officers.[111]

Commanders put all of their training efforts to the test through exercises. Initially, most counterguerrilla exercises were merely small phases of larger conventional exercises. Such exercises usually had a

Helicopter shortages meant that soldiers sometimes had to practice airmobile operations using mock-ups.

rear area flavor and were of limited utility. However, as time passed all-guerrilla exercises became more common, as did the use of "live" guerrillas played by combinations of regular soldiers and Special Forces teams. The vast majority of these exercises emphasized small-unit operations, patrolling, camp and march security, ambush and counterambush situations, raids, and night and aerial movements. Exercises involving entire brigades or divisions in a counterguerrilla role were rare. Artillery and tactical airpower were also seldom employed in training exercises. More important, the small inventory of helicopters meant that few units had any opportunity to practice the airmobile tactics espoused by doctrine.[112]

Perhaps the most difficult aspect for Army trainers to simulate was the complex interrelationship between soldiers, civilians, and a covert insurgent apparatus. Although many exercises included civil, psychological, and intelligence aspects, there was never enough time and resources to depict the twilight struggle that occurred in the villages. The Army recognized this problem. FM 31–16 (1963) declared that "it is impossible to conduct a three- or four-day exercise and expect elements of a large unit to realistically locate, harass, consolidate, and eliminate a guerrilla force in its area during the available time. Such an operation may take weeks or months in actual combat. By the same token, it is impossible in a short-term exercise to conduct extensive civic action or police operations concurrently with combat operations and receive any significant proficiency in the skills involved."[113]

The fact of the matter was that counterinsurgency just did not lend itself very well to customary exercise schedules. Although the Army never resolved this problem, it did come up with some partial solutions. As in the 1950s, one of the leaders in pacification simulation was the 25th Infantry Division. The division used mock villages to train its soldiers in the full range of pacification strategies, from civic action to more severe methods, in which soldiers were instructed to "move the people out of the area and then destroy their crops, put the area off limits, and shoot anyone who goes into this area."[114] Still, there was always an air of artificiality about such undertakings.

A more promising method was available when maneuvers were held off military reservations because in these areas the Army was able to incorporate local inhabitants into exercise play. The usual technique was to have the "guerrillas" enter the maneuver area first to give them a chance to familiarize themselves with the terrain and cultivate the friendship of the local populace. Then, once the exercise began, the counterinsurgents would try to woo the population away from the guerrillas. Typically, the counterinsurgents attempted to achieve this goal by issuing propaganda, distributing candy, hosting concerts and sporting events, providing free medical care, and performing civil works. Sometimes these measures paid off, as occurred during one exercise in Germany, where villagers promptly turned in a German Army "guerrilla" force after the Americans built the village a soccer field. More often than not, the allure of being on the side of the underdog proved too great. In exercise after exercise, civilians freely provided guerrillas with food, shelter, and information, while giving a cold shoulder to counterinsurgents. During Exercise HELPING HAND II, held in Washington state, townspeople flew revolutionary flags while children posed for guerrilla propaganda photos that purported to show U.S. soldiers killing innocent boys and girls. During Exercise SHERWOOD FOREST, also held in Washington, businesses temporarily "hired" guerrillas as cover for their espionage activities, while a school let the irregulars use its mimeograph machine to churn out anti-American pamphlets. During another exercise, the inhabitants of a North Carolina town hosted a "guerrilla appreciation night" that featured a potluck supper and country music.

Civilian enthusiasm for the guerrillas was sometimes so intense that it became hard to control. In one case, a group of college students formed their own partisan unit. In another, a sheriff fired an employee who had provided information to counterguerrilla forces, while a seven-year-old boy attacked and bit soldiers who had captured a guerrilla who

*Soldiers enter a mock village during counterguerrilla training in
Hawaii in 1962.*

had befriended him. Sometimes the guerrillas too became unmanageable, committing acts of vandalism or establishing bases outside the authorized exercise area, a real-life tactic that infuriated counterinsurgent players. Ultimately, most counterinsurgents shared the experience of the 2d Infantry Division, which ruefully reported after one 1964 exercise that "civic affairs productions were well-attended and politely applauded, but they did not change the basic loyalty of anyone."[115]

The State of Affairs, 1965

In January 1962, one year after he had initiated the counterinsurgency drive, President Kennedy told Secretary of Defense Robert S. McNamara that he was "not satisfied that the Department of Defense, and in particular the Army, is according the necessary degree of attention and effort to the threat of insurgency and guerrilla war." Just a few months later, as General Decker's new education and training initiatives began to take root, the president evinced a more favorable attitude, remarking that "they're beginning to recognize the nature of the problem, and what they're doing at Fort Bragg is really good."[116] Whether the president would have been satisfied with the state of affairs as they emerged by 1965 is impossible to say. Certainly he would have recognized that his strategy for defeating wars of national liberation continued to be bedeviled by a number of conceptual,

With the help of an interpreter and friendly village officials, an Army patrol interrogates captured "guerrillas" during training.

organizational, and programmatic weaknesses. Nevertheless, much had been achieved.

In just a few short years the Army had completely restructured its divisions into a new configuration more capable of executing the flexible response strategy. It had developed an entirely new dimension of warfare—airmobility—and elevated that concept to a prominent place in its approach to counterguerrilla warfare. It had improved both the quantity and quality of the advice it gave to nations threatened by insurgencies by adjusting military assistance programs, expanding Special Forces, and creating new entities, like the Special Action Forces, which spread American counterinsurgency methods around the globe. It had absorbed the thrust of popular counterinsurgency and developmental theory and blended these with traditional Army counterguerrilla and civil affairs precepts to produce an extensive body of doctrinal literature. It had also made significant efforts to see that this doctrine was understood and practiced by all echelons. While Army leaders had not always agreed with the full scope of Kennedy's policies, they had made a creditable effort to implement them.[117]

Such at least was the finding of a special commission established by President Johnson in 1965 to review the state of the national counterinsurgency program. The panel, which consisted of representatives of every federal agency involved in the counterinsurgency effort, reported that the Army was the only agency that had developed a cogent, written doctrine for counterinsurgency and that only it and the Marine Corps had comprehensive training programs to disseminate that doctrine to all ranks. Given the government's stance that counterinsurgency was primarily a political and not a military phenomenon, the failure of the government's civilian agencies to match the Army's efforts in developing and disseminating doctrine did not bode well for a program that required a high degree of civil-military coordination.[118]

Still, the Army could take pride in its achievements, for after a somewhat slow start in 1961, it had by 1965 succeeded in integrating counterinsurgency and counterguerrilla warfare in substantive ways into its doctrinal, educational, and training systems. At no other time in its history had the Army been better prepared to wage a counterinsurgency campaign, if preparedness is measured in the amount of manual pages, classroom time, and training exercises specifically devoted to counterinsurgent warfare. The question was, would it be enough to meet Khrushchev's challenge?

Notes

[1] Inaugural Address, 20 Jan 61, in *Public Papers of the Presidents of the United States: John F. Kennedy, 1961* (Washington, D.C.: Government Printing Office, 1962), p. 1.

[2] Quotes from Special Message on Urgent National Needs to Congress, 25 May 61, in ibid., pp. 397, 399, respectively. Lawrence Grinter, "How They Lost: Doctrines, Strategies and Outcomes of the Vietnam War," *Asian Survey* 15 (December 1975): 1112.

[3] First quote from David Halberstam, *The Best and the Brightest* (New York: Random House, 1972), p. i (title page). Second quote from Packenham, *Liberal America*, p. 61, and see also pp. 6, 18–21, 62–63, 253. Sir Henry Gurney, British high commissioner for Malaya, coined the phrase "hearts and minds" in 1951 to describe efforts to defeat Communist guerrillas through political and social action during the Malayan emergency. Americans in the 1960s adopted the phrase to describe their own politically oriented approach to counterinsurgency. Third quote from CGSC, *Counterinsurgency Case History, Malaya: 1948–60*, RB 31–2 (Fort Leavenworth, Kans.: CGSC, 1965), p. 6. Shafer, *Deadly Paradigms*, pp. 9–13, 21, 49–50, 79, 104, 111, 135; DePauw and Luz, *Winning the Peace*, pp. 133–34; Howard Wiarda, *Ethnocentrism in Foreign Policy: Can We Understand the Third World?* (Washington, D.C.: American Enterprise Institute for Public Policy Research, 1985), pp. 1–4; Charles Maechling, "Insurgency and Counterinsurgency: The Role of Strategic Theory," *Parameters* 14 (Autumn 1984): 33. Fourth quote from Latham, *Modernization as Ideology*, p. 71, and see also pp. 1–8, 50, 56–68, 166–67.

[4] Quote from Maurice Matloff, ed., *American Military History*, Army Historical Series (Washington, D.C.: U.S. Army Center of Military History, 1989), p. 623. Department of Defense, *Annual Report for Fiscal Year 1965*, p. 21; Weigley, *History of the United States Army*, pp. 527–28; Doughty, *Army Tactical Doctrine*, pp. 19–22; Donald Carter, "From G.I. to Atomic Soldier: The Development of U.S. Army Tactical Doctrine, 1945–1956" (Ph.D. diss., Ohio State University, 1987), pp. 210, 219; Myles Marken, "The Atomic Age Divisions," *Army Information Digest* 20 (September 1965): 58–64.

[5] First quoted word from Seymour Deitchman, *Limited War and American Defense Policy* (Cambridge: Massachusetts Institute of Technology Press, 1964), p. 4. Second quote from Andrew Kauffman, "On 'Wars of National Liberation,'" *Military Review* 48 (October 1968): 33. Third quoted word from Harry Coles, "Strategic Studies Since 1945, the Era of Overthink," *Military Review* 53 (April 1973): 3. Fourth quote from W. Bruce Weinrod, "Counterinsurgency: Its Role in Defense Policy," *Strategic Review* 2 (Fall 1974): 37. Fifth quote from Richard Schultz et al., *Guerrilla Warfare and Counterinsurgency: United States–Soviet Policy in the Third World* (Lexington, Mass.: Lexington Books, 1989), p. 10. For criticisms of the counterinsurgency "fad," see Laqueur, *Guerrilla*, pp. ix–x, 101, 374, 384–87, 391–96; Bell, *Myth of the Guerrilla*, p. 64; Shy and Collier, "Revolutionary War," in *Makers of Modern Strategy*, ed. Peter Paret (Princeton, N.J.: Princeton University Press, 1986), pp. 818–19; 840–42, 857–58.

[6] Quote from Department of the Army (DA), *Special Warfare: An Army Specialty* (1962), pp. 15–16. Memo, Decker for the President, 15 Feb 61, sub: U.S. Army Role

in Guerrilla and Anti-Guerrilla Operations, in 385, Secretary of the Army (Secy of the Army), 1961–64, RG 335, NARA; Rpt, CSA, n.d., sub: A Compilation of U.S. Army Cold War Activities, 1 Jan 61 to 26 Jan 62, p. II-14, Historians files, CMH (hereafter cited as CSA, Cold War Activities).

[7] Quoted words from Rpt, DCSOPS, 2 Jan 62, sub: Concept of Employment of U.S. Army Forces in Paramilitary Operations, p. 2, Historians files, CMH. CSA, Cold War Activities, pp. I-3, I-4; Jonathan Ladd, "Some Reflections on Counterinsurgency," *Military Review* 44 (October 1964): 75.

[8] Quote from Stephen Bowman, "The Evolution of United States Army Doctrine for Counterinsurgency Warfare: From World War II to the Commitment of Combat Units in Vietnam" (Ph.D. diss., Duke University, 1985), p. 134, and see also pp. 5–6. Lloyd Norman and John Spore, "Big Push in Guerrilla Warfare," *Army* 12 (March 1962): 34–35.

[9] Quote from Blaufarb, *Counterinsurgency Era*, p. 80. Richard Betts, *Soldiers, Statesmen, and Cold War Crises* (Cambridge, Mass.: Harvard University Press, 1977), p. 130; Ricky Waddell, "The Army and Peacetime Low Intensity Conflict, 1961–1993: The Process of Peripheral and Fundamental Military Change" (Ph.D. diss., Columbia University, 1994), p. 141; Bowman, "Evolution of Army Doctrine," p. 85; Andrew Krepinevich, The U.S. Army and Vietnam: Counterinsurgency Doctrine and the Army Concept of War (Fort Bragg, N.C.: U.S. Army John F. Kennedy Special Warfare Center, 1984), pp. 25–26; Memos, Krulak for Chair, JCS, 10 Apr 62, sub: Special Group (Counterinsurgency), Establishment of Special Group (Counterinsurgency), Wheeler files, RG 218, NARA, and Krulak for Lansdale, Rosson, 22 May 62, sub: Counter-guerrilla Tactics, 370.64, CSA, 1962, RG 319, NARA.

[10] Quote from Bowman, "Evolution of Army Doctrine," p. 85, and see also pp. 113–14. David Petraeus, "The American Military and the Lessons of Vietnam: A Study of Military Influence and the Use of Force in the Post-Vietnam Era" (Ph.D. diss., Woodrow Wilson School of Public and International Affairs, 1987), p. 96.

[11] Quoted words from William Yarborough, "'Young Moderns' Are Impetus Behind Army's Special Forces," *Army* 12 (March 1962): 38. Betts, *Soldiers, Statesmen*, pp. 10–13; Bowman, "Evolution of Army Doctrine," p. 179; Thomas Adams, "Military Doctrine and the Organization Culture of the U.S. Army" (Ph.D. diss., Syracuse University, 1990), pp. 5–6, 68.

[12] Quote from Corr and Sloan, *Low-Intensity Conflict*, p. 21. Charles Maechling, "Counterinsurgency: The First Ordeal by Fire," in *Low-Intensity Warfare*, ed. Michael Klare and Peter Kornbluh (New York: Pantheon, 1988), pp. 26–27; Michael Hennessy, *Strategy in Vietnam: The Marines and Revolutionary Warfare in I Corps, 1965–1972* (Westport, Conn.: Frederick A. Praeger, 1997), p. 18; George Tanham, *War Without Guns* (New York: Frederick A. Praeger, 1966), pp. 7, 24; Memo, Special Group, Counterinsurgency, for the President, 20 Jul 62, sub: Report of the Committee on Police Assistance Programs, p. 1, Historians files, CMH.

[13] Doughty, *Army Tactical Doctrine*, pp. 46–48.

[14] Memo, Lt Gen Earle Wheeler, Dir, Joint Staff, for Chair, JCS, 9 Feb 61, sub: Review of Lieutenant General McGarr's Papers, in 3360, JCS 1961, RG 218, NARA.

[15] Special Warfare School, ST 31–180, Readings in Guerrilla Warfare, 1960 and 1961 editions, and ST 31–170, Tactics and Techniques in Counter-Guerrilla Operations, c. 1963. Both at Special Warfare School. Lesson Plan C3.A1408, C6.A1408, Special Warfare School, Fundamentals of Counterguerrilla Operations, 1964, pp. LP-61 to

LP-64, MHI; Infantry School, Selected Readings, 1962 and 1965 editions, Infantry School; T. A. McCarry, Report on the Burma Counterinsurgency Campaign, 1961, N–18745.10, CARL; Lesson Plan A2310–1, CGSC, 1965–1966, CARL. As late as 1965 the Command and General Staff College still employed the German Army's 1944 manual, *Fighting the Guerrilla Bands*, as well as other derivative materials, as course reading materials. Lesson Plan A2300, CGSC, 1964–1965 , p. L4-1, CARL.

[16] Veterans of the Philippine and Malayan conflicts, including Air Force Maj. Gen. Edward G. Lansdale, Army Lt. Col. Charles T. R. Bohannan, and Britain's liaison officer at the CGSC, Col. Richard L. Clutterbuck, frequently spoke at American educational institutions in the early 1960s. Examples of publications discussing Malaya and the Philippines include G. C. Phipps, "Guerrillas in Malaya," *Infantry* 51 (May–June 1961): 36–40; William Long, "Counterinsurgency: Some Antecedents for Success," *Military Review* 43 (October 1963): 90–97; CGSC, Reference Book (RB) 31–3, Counterinsurgency Case History, the Philippines, 1946–54, 1965, CGSC.

[17] For examples of Army translations and studies, see Translation, Army G–2, Counter Guerrilla Training in the Scope of Maintenance in the A.F.N., n.d.; Translation, Army G–2, Special Training in Counter Guerrilla Warfare, n.d.; Translation, Army G–2, Guerrilla and Counterguerrilla Operations, 1962. All in MHI. Donn Starry, La Guerre Revolutionnaire: Some Comments on a Theory of Counterinsurgency Operations (Student paper, AWC, 1966); William Malone, Unconventional Warfare: A Look at French "Psychological Action" in Algeria (Student paper, AWC, 1962).

[18] Interv, Andrew Birtle with Carl Bernard, 28 Jan 03, and CONARC, Counterinsurgency Conference Report, 23–24 March 1962, p. A-16-1, both in Historians files, CMH; Bowman, "Evolution of Army Doctrine," pp. 139–40; AWC, U.S. Army War College Curriculum Coverage of Counterinsurgency, 1961–62, 1962, p. 18, MHI; Bernard Fall, "Counterinsurgency: the French Experience," Industrial College of the Armed Forces lecture, 1962.

[19] CONARC, Counterinsurgency Conference Report, 23–24 March 1962, p. A-5-1; Program of Instruction (POI) 33–G–F6, Special Warfare School (SWS) Counterinsurgency Operations, 1964; Memo, Maj Gen Yarborough for CG, CONARC, 20 Dec 64, sub: Counterinsurgency Training, with atchs, Historians files, CMH; Ltr, Maj Gen Lawrence J. Lincoln, Commandant, U.S. Army Engineer School, to Gen Herbert Powell, CG, CONARC, c. 1962, 71A3439, CONARC, RG 338, NARA; Clyde Eddleman, The Report of Educational Survey Commission of the United States Army Command and General Staff College, November 1962, p. 55, CARL.

[20] Quote from Addendum to Lesson IV–50, History of Military Art Course, U.S. Military Academy (USMA), 1962–1963, p. 9. Lesson Plan, USMA 1963–1964, History of Military Art, pp. 27, 30–33. Both from the Department of Military Arts and Engineering, Organizational History, POI files, USMA, West Point, N.Y. French Operations in Indo-China, pp. 1–4, 7, atch to Memo, Commander in Chief, Pacific, for Distribution, 16 Oct 61, sub: Lessons from Limited War Operations, with atchs, Historians files, CMH; Charles Biggio, "Let's Learn from the French," *Military Review* 46 (October 1966): 28–34; David Foster, Irregular Warfare—Challenge to the Free World (Student paper, AWC, 1962), pp. iii, 26, 36; Lesson Plan 112A, SWS, Insurgency Movement, Indochina, 1965, pp. LP-1, LP-48, LP-49, LP-65, MHI; Memos, DCSOPS War Plans Div for OPS-PI, n.d., sub: Phase III Warfare in Indochina, and Johnson for DCSOPS, 27 Mar 65, both in Geog v Indochina, 380 Warfare, CMH; "Phase III Warfare Indochina 1951–1954. Vietnam 1965?" *Weekly Intelligence Digest*, WID 18–65 (1965): 14–15.

[21] Kevin Sheehan, "Preparing for an Imaginary War? Examining Peacetime Functions and Changes of Army Doctrine" (Ph.D. diss., Harvard University, 1988), pp. 376–77; DA, *Special Warfare: An Army Specialty* (1962); Donald Rattan, "Antiguerrilla Operations: A Case Study from History," *Military Review* 40 (May 1960): 23–27.

[22] Bowman, "Evolution of Army Doctrine," pp. 49–56; "ACSFOR Comes of Age," *Army Information Digest* 20 (February 1965): 34–37; CONARC, Historical Background of USCONARC Participation in Combat and Materiel Development Activities, Dec 63, pp. 1–9, 23–24, 32; John Daley, "U.S. Army Combat Developments Command," *Army Information Digest* 17 (September 1962): 13–18.

[23] CDC Planning Group, Preliminary Implementation Plan, vol. 3, Field Agencies, CDC, 16 Apr 62, ans. A, B, pts. 2 to 7, p. A-iv-A-1; Ltrs, Lt Gen John Daley, CDC Planning Group to Director, Reorganization Project Office, 11 May 62, sub: Activation of Remote Area Conflict Office, and Decker to Gen Herbert Powell, 8 Mar 62, with atched Staff Summary Sheet, Lt Gen Barksdale Hamlett, DCSOPS, to CSA, 26 Feb 62, sub: Remote Area Conflict Office. All in 69–0630, CDC, RG 338, NARA.

[24] CONARC, Historical Background of USCONARC Participation in Combat and Materiel Development Activities, Dec 63, p. 37; CDC Cir 10–2, 11 Sep 64, 73A2678, RG 338, NARA.

[25] FM 31–15, *Operations Against Irregular Forces*, 1961, pp. 3–4. For criticism of FM 31–15's view of insurgency, see Laqueur, *Guerrilla*, p. 377.

[26] FM 31–15, *Operations Against Irregular Forces*, 1961, pp. 4, 5, 12–14, 25, 32.

[27] Quoted words from ibid., p. 27, and see also pp. 25–26, 28, 34.

[28] Quote from ibid., p. 21, and see also pp. 17–22, 24, 36–39, 48.

[29] Quotes from ibid., p. 47, and see also pp. 15–18, 33, 36–39. FM 31–20, *Operations Against Guerrilla Forces*, 1951, p. 125.

[30] Quotes from JCS, SM–797–62, 18 Jul 62, sub: Military Accomplishments in the Counterinsurgency Field Since 20 January 1961, p. I-11, and see also pp. I-1 to I-12, Historians files, CMH (hereafter cited as Joint Concept).

[31] Quote from ibid., p. I-20, and see also pp. I-14 to I-19. Blaufarb, *Counterinsurgency Era*, p. 78.

[32] Quotes from Joint Concept, p. I-29, and see also p. I-24.

[33] Overseas Internal Defense Policy, atch to National Security Action Memorandum 182, Counterinsurgency Doctrine, 1 Sep 62 (hereafter cited as OIDP).

[34] Quote from Maechling, "Insurgency and Counterinsurgency," p. 34. Maechling, "Counterinsurgency," p. 25; Hennessy, *Strategy in Vietnam*, p. 18; Schultz, *Guerrilla Warfare*, p. 103; Memo, Maj Gen William R. Peers for Gen Taylor, 15 Dec 65, sub: Review of the Committee I Report, Historians files, CMH; CDC Special Warfare Agency, Operational, Organizational, and Material Concepts for U.S. Army Counterinsurgency Operations During the Period 1970–80, Aug 64, pp. 55, 64–66, 76–77.

[35] Quote from OIDP, p. 17.

[36] Ibid., pp. 17–18; Shafer, *Deadly Paradigms*, pp. 112, 119.

[37] Memo, Decker for Secy of the Army, 14 Sep 62, sub: Army Responsibilities for Counterinsurgency, 385, Secy of the Army, RG 335, NARA.

[38] Rod Paschall, "Low-Intensity Conflict Doctrine: Who Needs It?" *Parameters* 15 (Autumn 1985): 42; FM 100–5, *Field Service Regulations—Operations*, 1962, pp. 136–62.

[39] Quote from FM 33–5, *Psychological Operations*, 1962, p. 124.

[40] Quote from FM 41–10, *Civil Affairs Operations*, 1962, p. 83, and see also pp. 88–99.

[41] Memo, Lt Gen Barksdale Hamlett, DCSOPS, for CG, CONARC, 7 Dec 61, sub: Improvement of U.S. Army Capability To Meet Limited and Cold War Requirements, with atchs, 250/12, DCSOPS 1961, RG 319, NARA; CGSC, A Detailed Concept for Employment of U.S. Army Combat Units in Military Operations Against Irregular Forces, 1962, CARL.

[42] Quotes from FM 31–16, *Counterguerrilla Operations*, 1963, p. 92, and see also pp. 31–32, 93–98.

[43] Quote from ibid., p. 96, and see also p. 98.

[44] Quote from ibid., p. 37, and see also pp. 24, 38.

[45] First quote from ibid., p. 20. Remaining quotes from ibid., p. 40, and see also pp. 7, 22, 38–42, 111.

[46] Ibid., pp. 8, 40, 71, 73.

[47] Quote from ibid., p. 31, and see also pp. 21, 32–35, 49, 53, 55–56. FM 31–21, *Guerrilla Warfare*, 1955, p. 63. For airmobile issues, see FM 1–100, *Army Aviation*, 1959 and 1963; FM 57–35, *Airmobile Operations*, 1960 and 1963; Cheng, *Airmobility*, pp. 125–30, 175–79, 184–87; Marquis Hilbert and Everett Murray, "Use of Army Aviation in Counterinsurgency Operations," *U.S. Army Aviation Digest* 8 (October 1962): 3–9; Rpt, CDC, War Game Evaluation of the Air Assault Division in Counterinsurgency Operations in Southeast Asia, Dec 63, C–1895634, CARL; William Griffin, "Army Aviation in Support of Counterguerrilla Operations," *U.S. Army Aviation Digest* 8 (September 1962): 9–14.

[48] Quotes from FM 31–16, *Counterguerrilla Operations*, 1963, p. 60, and see also pp. 31, 49, 61–70.

[49] FM 31–15, *Operations Against Irregular Forces*, 1961, pp. 29–31; FM 31–16, *Counterguerrilla Operations*, 1963, pp. 61–63, 67.

[50] Quote from FM 31–16, *Counterguerrilla Operations*, 1963, p. 67, and see also pp. 69–72.

[51] Quote from FM 6–20–2, *Field Artillery Techniques*, 1962, p. 81. Infantry School, Infantry Battalion Operations Against Irregular Forces, 1962, p. 15; FM 100–5, *Field Service Regulations—Operations*, 1962, pp. 140, 144; Neal Grimland, "The Formidable Guerrilla," *Army* 12 (February 1962): 66; FM 31–20, *Operations Against Guerrilla Forces*, 1951, p. 127; FM 31–15, *Operations Against Irregular Forces*, 1961, pp. 14-15; FM 61–100, *The Division*, 1962, pp. 243–44.

[52] Quote from Counterinsurgency III, Infantry Career Subcourse 497, Infantry School, 1965, p. 38. Infantry School, Report of the Infantry Instructors' Conference, 15–19 July 1963, p. 119. Compare Great Britain, Ministry of Defence, *The Conduct of Anti-Terrorist Operations in Malaya* (London: Ministry of Defence, 1958), pp. XVIII-1 to XVIII-4, with FM 31–16, *Counterguerrilla Operations*, 1963, pp. 83, 89.

[53] Quote from FM 31–15, *Operations Against Irregular Forces*, 1961, p. 44, and see also p. 15; George Tanham, Doctrine and Tactics of Revolutionary Warfare: The Viet Minh in Indochina, RM 2395 (Santa Monica, Calif.: RAND, 1959), p. 135; FM 31–16, *Counterguerrilla Operations*, 1963, pp. 84–91; FM 31–22, *U.S. Army Counterinsurgency Forces*, 1963, p. 56; FM 61–100, *The Division*, 1962, pp. 243–44.

[54] Quote from FM 31–16, *Counterguerrilla Operations*, 1963, p. 2, and see also pp. 20, 75–76, 79–83, 103–11.

[55] Special Warfare School, ST 31–176, Counterinsurgency Planning Guide, 2d ed., 1964, pp. 39–46, 77, 80–87, 94–113.

[56] FM 31–22, *U.S. Army Counterinsurgency Forces*, 1963, pp. 20–45, 75–76.

[57] First quote from ibid., p. 84. Second quote from Great Britain, *Conduct of Anti-Terrorist Operations*, p. III-11. FM 31–16, *Counterguerrilla Operations*, 1963, p. 37; Boyd Bashore, "Organization for Frontless War," *Military Review* 44 (May 1964): 10, 16; Special Warfare School, ST 31–176, Counterinsurgency Planning Guide, 2d ed., 1964, p. 70; FM 31–73, *Advisor Handbook for Counterinsurgency*, 1965, p. 28; Infantry School, Report of the Infantry Instructors' Conference, 15–19 July 1963, p. 118; John McCuen, *The Art of Counter-Revolutionary War* (Harrisburg, Pa.: Stackpole Books, 1966), p. 327.

[58] Quotes from FM 31–22, *U.S. Army Counterinsurgency Forces*, 1963, p. 55, and see also pp. 70–71.

[59] Quotes from ibid., pp. 61, 81, respectively, and see also pp. 4–5, 9, 60, 77, 96–97, 110–17.

[60] Quote from FM 100–20, *Field Service Regulations, Counterinsurgency*, 1964, p. 20, and see also pp. 1–10.

[61] CONARC, CONARC World Wide Combat Arms Conference II, vol. 3, 25–29 Jun 62, p. 56; Annual Hist Sum, Office of the Assistant Chief of Staff for Force Development (OACSFOR), 1 Jul 63 to 30 Jun 64, pp. E-I-1, E-I-2; Rpt, HQDA, U.S. Army Special Warfare Study and Program, Fiscal Years (FYs) 63–68, 1962, pp. 76–77, DCSOPS, RG 319, NARA.

[62] FM 31–20, *Special Forces Operational Techniques*, 1965, pp. 47, 49–50, 68–69; Special Warfare Agency, Doctrinal Literature for Special Warfare, 1964, pp. 1, 4–6, 26–31, and an. B, pp. 1–7, 73A2677, CDC, RG 338, NARA.

[63] Quote from Ltr, Gen Johnson to Lt Gen Dwight Beach, CG, CDC, 24 Aug 64, 73–2678, CDC, RG 338, NARA. Bowman, "Evolution of Army Doctrine," pp. 127–31; Memos, Col Darnell, CDC, for Maj Gen Harry L. Hillyard, 13 Apr 64, sub: Aftermath of General H. K. Johnson's Vietnam Visit, 73A2677, CDC, RG 338, NARA; Lt Gen Harold K. Johnson, DCSOPS, for Dir of Special Warfare, 14 Apr 64, sub: Special Warfare Doctrine, p. 2, Historians files, CMH; and Johnson for ACSFOR, 29 Jun 64, sub: Doctrine, Training and Organization for Counter Insurgency, Historians files, CMH.

[64] Ltr, Gen Johnson to Gen Hugh Harris, CG, CONARC, 29 Oct 64, 71A2333, RG 338, NARA.

[65] Bowman, "Evolution of Army Doctrine," pp. 128–31; Rpt, CDC, Nov 64, sub: Program for Analysis and Development of U.S. Counterinsurgency Doctrine and Organization, p. B-3, 73A2677, CDC, RG 338, NARA (hereafter cited as CDC, Program for Analysis).

[66] Quotes from FM 31–73, *Advisor Handbook for Counterinsurgency*, 1965, pp. 22, 87, respectively, and see also pp. 58–63, 67, 180–81. Other texts also cautioned against indiscriminate fire. See, for example, FM 6–20–1, *Field Artillery Tactics*, 1965, p. 48; Infantry School, Infantry Battalion Operations Against Irregular Forces, 1962, p. 15.

[67] Quote from CDC, Program for Analysis, p. 3, and see also pp. 1, 4. Briefing, CDC Special Warfare and Civil Affairs Group to Gen Ben Harrell, CG, CDC, 5 May 66, CDC, 73A2677, RG 338, NARA.

[68] Quote from CDC, Special Warfare and Civil Affairs Group, Concepts and General Doctrine for Counterinsurgency, Jul 65, pp. 56–57. Memo, Lt Gen Dwight Beach, CG,

CDC, for Distribution, 8 Dec 64, sub: Counterinsurgency Doctrinal Review Program; Fact Sheet, CDC, 4 Jan 66, sub: Program for Analysis and Development of US Counterinsurgency Doctrine and Organization. All in 73A2677, CDC, RG 338, NARA. Ltr, Johnson to Beach, 29 Oct 64, 71A3439, CONARC, RG 338, NARA.

[69] Quote from CDC, Special Warfare and Civil Affairs Group, Concepts and General Doctrine for Counterinsurgency, Jul 65, p. 98, and see also pp. 26–27, 73–74, 79, 83.

[70] Ibid., p. 98.

[71] Ibid., p. 99.

[72] Quotes from Special Warfare Agency, Doctrinal Literature for Counterinsurgency, 1965, pp. 35, 56, respectively, 73A2677, CDC, RG 338, NARA. Bashore, "Organization for Frontless War," pp. 10, 16; FM 61–100, *The Division*, 1965, p. 149; Gustav Gillert, "Counterinsurgency," *Military Review* 45 (April 1965): 31; FM 31–16, *Counterguerrilla Operations*, 1963, pp. 47, 69; Henry Emerson, Can We Out-Guerrilla the Communist Guerrillas? (Student paper, AWC, 1965), pp. 45–52.

[73] First quote from SORO, Motivating Populations To Support Counterinsurgency, 1965, p. 9, and see also pp. 111, 169, 23A2677, CDC, RG 338, NARA. Remaining quotes from Special Operations Research Office, Symposium Proceedings. The U.S. Army's Limited-War Mission and Social Science Research (Washington, D.C.: American University, 1962), p. 163.

[74] First two quotes from Memo, Lt Gen Palmer for CSA, c. 1965, sub: Study on Lower Spectrum Conflict—WINS-II. Third quote from Study, DCSOPS, 1965, sub: A Worldwide Integral National Strategy for 1970, pt. II, p. 21. Both in 68A2344, RG 319, NARA.

[75] Rpt, Counter-insurgency Operations Instruction and Related Matters, pp. 9–10, atch to Memo, Brig Gen Richard Stilwell for Secy of the Army, 6 Oct 61, sub: Report on the Counter-insurgency Operations Course and Related Matters, 319.1, CSA, RG 319, NARA. Rpt, Brig Gen Stilwell, 13 Oct 61, sub: Army Activities in Underdeveloped Areas Short of Declared War, pp. 47–48, atch to Memo, Stilwell for Secy of the Army, 13 Oct 61, sub: Army Activities in Underdeveloped Areas Short of Declaring War, and Rpt, CONARC, 28 Jan 62, sub: Special Warfare Board, Final Report, p. 5, both in Historians files, CMH.

[76] SWS, A Summary of Counter Guerrilla Operational Concepts, 1961, pp. 1–3, 12; POI, SWS, Counter-Guerrilla Operations, Oct 60, Historians files, CMH; Rpt, Counterinsurgency Training for Officers in Military Schools, p. 13, atch to Memo, Special Assistant to the Chief of Staff for Special Warfare Activities (SACSA) for Dep Secy of Defense, 14 May 62, sub: Training Objectives for Counterinsurgency, 3360, JCS 1961, RG 218, NARA.

[77] Rpt, JCS, n.d., sub: Development Status of Military Counterinsurgency Programs, Including Counterguerrilla Forces, as of 1 August 1965, p. III-106, C–15361.90, CARL.

[78] POI 41–G–F7, Civil Affairs School, Civic Action, 1963, Historians files, CMH; Barber and Ronning, *Internal Security*, pp. 152–54; Civil Affairs School, ST 41–10–90, Command and Staff Guidelines for Civic Action, 1964.

[79] By 1962 the Infantry School had accumulated 202 publications on counterinsurgency. D. M. Condit et al., *A Counterinsurgency Bibliography* (Washington, D.C.: American University, Special Operations Research Office, 1963); Infantry School, Military Operations Against Irregular Forces: A Bibliography of Works Available in the U.S. Army Infantry School Library, 1962, Infantry School.

[80] The *Infantry* journal alone published over seventy articles pertaining to unconventional and counterinsurgency warfare between 1961 and 1965. Memo, Lemnitzer for Maj Gen Clifton, 23 Jan 62, sub: Coverage on Guerrilla and Counter-Guerrilla War in Professional Military Journals, 370.64, Lemnitzer, RG 218, NARA.

[81] POI 33–G–F8, SWS, Senior Officer Counterinsurgency and Special Warfare Orientation Course, 1962; William Peers, "Meeting the Challenge of Subversion," *Army* 15 (November 1964): 97; Rpt, JCS 1969/212, 1 Jun 61, sub: Status of Development of Counterguerrilla Forces, p. 1867, C–15361.90–A, CARL.

[82] The statistics are for the Infantry and Special Forces branch career courses as of July 1961. Hours Programmed for Instruction in Counterguerrilla Warfare in U.S. Army Service Schools, 28 Jul 61, Incl 2 to Memo, DCSOPS for Dir, Joint Staff, 28 Jul 61, sub: Status of Development of Counter Guerrilla Forces, 250/15, DCSOPS 1961, RG 319, NARA; CONARC, Counterinsurgency Conference Report, 23–24 March 1962, pp. A-10-3 and A-10-11; Rpt, JCS, n.d., sub: Development Status of Military Counterinsurgency Programs, Including Counterguerrilla Forces, as of August 1965, p. II-4.

[83] Rpt, JCS 1969/330, 9 Apr 62, sub: Status of Development of Counterguerrilla Forces, pp. 6, 16–17, C–15361.90–A, CARL; Memo, SWS to CG, CONARC, 19 Mar 62, sub: Common Subject "Counterinsurgency Operations," N–18517.50, CARL; Rpt, Counterinsurgency Training for Officers in Military Schools, p. 12, atch to Memo, SACSA for Dep Secy of Defense, 14 May 62, sub: Training Objectives for Counterinsurgency.

[84] Quotes from Ltr, Stilwell to DCSOPS, 7 Mar 62, sub: Counterinsurgency Instruction at USMA. Memo, Stilwell for Superintendent, USMA, 10 May 62, sub: Interim Report of the Counterinsurgency Committee. Both in 10002–02, Training (Counterinsurgency Committee), Training Operations files, USMA. Krepinevich, The U.S. Army and Vietnam: Counterinsurgency Doctrine and the Army Concept of War, pp. 61–62; Bowman, "Evolution of Army Doctrine," p. 110.

[85] National Security Action Memorandum 131, Training Objectives to Combat Subversive Insurgency, 13 Mar 62, 3360, JCS 1961, RG 218, NARA. Rpts, DA, c. 62, sub: U.S. Army Special Warfare Study and Program, FY 63–68, pp. 55, 75–76; Brig Gen Stillwell, 13 Oct 61, sub: Army Activities in Underdeveloped Areas Short of Declared War; and CONARC, 28 Jan 62, sub: Special Warfare Board, Final Report, pp. 4, 12, 52. All in Historians files, CMH. Bowman, "Evolution of Army Doctrine," pp. 93–97.

[86] Rpt, Counterinsurgency Training for Officers in Military Schools, pp. 12–13, atch to Memo, SACSA for Dep Secy of Defense, 14 May 62, sub: Training Objectives for Counterinsurgency; Ltr, Powell, CG, CONARC, to Distribution, 15 Aug 62, 71A2333, RG 338, NARA. Rpts, HQDA, U.S. Army Special Warfare Study and Program, FY 63–68, 1962, p. 70; JCS, n.d., sub: Development Status of Military Counterinsurgency Programs, Including Counterguerrilla Forces, as of 1 August 1963, p. II-4, C–15361.90, CARL; and JCS, n.d., sub: Development Status of Military Counterinsurgency Programs, Including Counterguerrilla Forces, as of February 1964, p. II-4, C–15361.90, CARL. Briefing, CGSC to Maj Gen Peers, 11 Oct 65, sub: Individual Counterinsurgency Training, p. 5, Historians files, CMH.

[87] Quote from CONARC SubjScd 444, Reserve Officers' Training Corps Military Science II and III, Introduction to Counterinsurgency Operations, 1963, p. 8. "Counterguerrilla Units Flourish in ROTC," *Army Reservist* 9 (April 1963): 15; David

The Counterinsurgency Ferment, 1961–1965

Blackledge, "ROTC Counterguerrillas," *Infantry* 53 (January–February 1963): 49–50; Rpt, JCS, n.d., sub: Development Status of Military Counterinsurgency Programs, Including Counterguerrilla Forces, as of 1 August 1965, pp. II-2 to II-4.

[88] First Class Staff Study, USMA, Office of Military Instruction, Department of Tactics, 1963, p. 3, 1011–03, Course Publication files, Curriculum—Tactics; POI, USMA, History of Military Art Course 401–402, Department of Military Art and Engineering, Organizational History, POI files; The Combined Arms Team (Company), USMA, Office of Military Instruction, Department of Tactics, 1963; Memo, Brig Gen Michael S. Davison, Commandant of Cadets, for Superintendent, USMA, 8 Jul 63, sub: Report of Counterinsurgency Committee, p. 5, and atched paper, Regular Counterinsurgency Instruction, 1963–64, 10002–02, Training (Counterinsurgency Committee), Training Operations files; Program of Military Instruction, 1963–64, Dept. of Tactics, 1011–03, Course Pub. files, Curriculum—Tactics; The Combined Arms Team (Battalion), USMA, Office of Military Instruction, Department of Tactics, 1963. All at USMA.

[89] Quote from Infantry School, Report of the Infantry Instructors' Conference, 15–19 July 1963, pp. 105–06, and see also pp. 108–09.

[90] Ibid., p. 127; Bobby Boyd, Does the Infantry Officer Career Course Counter-Guerrilla Instruction Meet the Needs of the Infantry Officer? (Student paper, Infantry Officers Career Course (IOCC), Infantry School, 1961); Peter Andre, Counter Guerrilla Warfare (Student paper, IOCC, Infantry School, 1960–61); POI 7–A–C20, Infantry School, Infantry Officer Basic Course, 1963; Memo, W. Hamilton, CDC Special Warfare Group, for Col Marr, 31 Aug 64, sub: Counterinsurgency Courses, 73A2677, CDC, RG 338, NARA; POI 2–7–C20, Infantry School, Infantry Officer Basic Course, 1965.

[91] Quote from Infantry School, Report of the Infantry Instructors' Conference, 15–19 July 1963, p. 123, and see also p. 109. Counterinsurgency II, Infantry Career Subcourse 497, Infantry School, Apr 65, p. 3; Counterinsurgency III, Infantry Career Subcourse 497, Infantry School, Apr 65, p. 76.

[92] First quote from SWS, ST 31–170, Counter-Guerrilla Operations, p. 38. Second quote from Infantry School, Report of the Infantry Instructors' Conference, 15–19 July 1963, p. 118. Infantry School, Military Operations Against Irregular Forces, 1962, p. 39; POI 7–A–C22, Infantry School, Infantry Officer Career Course, 1963.

[93] First quote from Infantry School, Report of the Infantry Instructors' Conference, 15–19 July 1963, p. 107. Second quote from Lesson Plan 6062, Infantry School, 1962, Fundamentals of Counterguerrilla Operations, p. 27.

[94] First quote from Infantry School, Military Operations Against Irregular Forces, 1962, p. 38, and see also pp. 21, 37–38, 68–69. Second and third quotes from Lesson Plan 6405, SWS, 1964, p. LP-28, and see also pp. LP-29 to 36. Infantry School, Report of the Infantry Instructors' Conference, 15–19 July 1963, p. 126; Counterinsurgency III, Infantry Career Subcourse 497, Infantry School, Apr 65, p. 71.

[95] Advance Sheet 6063, 6064, Infantry School, Fundamentals of Counterinsurgency Operations, 1962; Infantry School, Report of the Infantry Instructors' Conference, 15–19 July 1963, pp. 38–39, 110; POI 7–A–C22, Infantry School 1963, Infantry Officer Career Course; Thomas Block, "Quick Fire," *Infantry* 54 (January–February 1964): 18–19; Infantry School, Infantry Instructors' Workshop, Report of Conference, 17–20 August 1965, pp. 59–60; Historical Supplement, 1965, U.S. Army Infantry School, 1966, pp. 8, 11–12, 17–18, 22–23.

[96] Lesson Plan 4112–3/2, CGSC, 1961–1962, pp. LP-III-2, LP-III-3; Briefing, CGSC, Oct 65, sub: Committee II (Training), President's Review of Counterinsurgency, pp. D-1, D-5, N–13423.355–B–3, CARL; Eddleman, "Report of Educational Survey Commission," pp. 12, 55–57; Memo, Hamilton for Marr, 31 Aug 64, sub: Counterinsurgency Courses; Lesson Plans R2310/5, CGSC, 1964–1965; M 2300–1, CGSC, 1964–1965, p. L1-AS-1-2, and see also p. L1-AS-1-4; M2300–3, CGSC, 1964–1965; R2310–1, CGSC, Combined Operations in Tropical Africa Counterinsurgency, 1962–1963; R5170, CGSC, Corps Operations in Tropical Africa, 1964–1965; 4112–3/2, CGSC, 1961–1962, p. LP-III-17; M2300–1 and M2300–2, CGSC, Introduction to Unconventional Warfare and Counterinsurgency Operations—Operations Against Irregular Forces, 1962–1963; and A2300, CGSC, 1964–1965.

[97] AWC, U.S. Army War College Curriculum Coverage of Counterinsurgency, 1961–62, 1962; AWC, AWC Curriculum Pamphlet, 1962–63, pp. 8–11; AWC, U.S. Army War College Curriculum Coverage of Counterinsurgency, 1962–63, p. 22; Memo, Col R. Dalrymple, c. 1963, sub: Counterinsurgency Education, p. 2, Industrial College of the Armed Forces, Military Education Coordination Conference, tab G, box II-C-I, Service War Colleges Annual Meetings, 1961–63. All in AWC Curricular Archives, MHI.

[98] AWC, AWC Curriculum Pamphlet for 1963–64, pp. 11, 16; AWC, AWC Curriculum Pamphlet for 1964–65, p. 8; AWC, AWC Curriculum Pamphlet for 1965–66, pp. 10–11; AWC, Positions for the Department of the Army Board to Review Army Officers Schools, 21 Sep 65, pp. 21–24, 53. All in AWC Curricular Archives, MHI.

[99] Bowman, "Evolution of Army Doctrine," p. 121; CONARC, CONARC World Wide Combat Arms Conference II, vol. 3, 25–29 Jun 62, pp. 201–02; Sheehan, "Preparing for an Imaginary War?" p. 293.

[100] William Rosson, "Accent on Cold War Capabilities," *Army Information Digest* 17 (May 1962): 5; Memo, DCSOPS for Dir, Joint Staff, 28 Jul 61, sub: Status of Development of Counter Guerrilla Forces; Heath Twichell, Counter Guerrilla Warfare Training (Student paper, Infantry School, 1961), p. 2.

[101] Quote from Stanton Smith, Counterinsurgency Training for the Infantry Platoon Leader (Student paper, Infantry School, 1961), p. 1, and see also p. 2. CONARC, Annex N to USCONARC Training Directive, Counter Guerrilla Training, 30 Sep 61, Historians files, CMH; Memo, Maj Gen John L. Throckmorton, SGS, for Dep CSs et al., 21 Nov 61, sub: Special Warfare Activities, Historians files, CMH; Bowman, "Evolution of Army Doctrine," pp. 92, 179; Army Training Programs, Training Tests and Subject Schedules To Be Published or Revised To Increase Emphasis on Counterguerrilla Warfare Training, 28 Jul 61, Incl 4 to Memo, DCSOPS for Dir, Joint Staff, 28 Jul 61, sub: Status of Development of Counter Guerrilla Forces; ATP 7–18–1, Rifle Company, Infantry, Airborne and Mechanized Infantry Battalions, Dec 61.

[102] Boyd, Infantry Officer Course, an. A; Norman and Spore, "Big Push," p. 28; Schultz, *Guerrilla Warfare*, p. 105; Rpt, CONARC, 28 Jan 62, sub: Special Warfare Board, Final Report, pp. 19–20.

[103] CONARC, Annex N to USCONARC Training Directive, Counterinsurgency/Counterguerrilla Warfare Training, 30 Mar 62, pp. N-4, N-5, N-IV-1; FM 31–22, *U.S. Army Counterinsurgency Forces*, 1963, pp. 87–92; Memo, CONARC for CG, 3d Army, 17 Apr 62, sub: Counterguerrilla Warfare Training, N–18668.39, CARL; Rpt, HQDA, U.S. Army Special Warfare Study and Program, FY 63–68, 1962, an. V; Memo, Lt Gen Barksdale Hamlett, DCSOPS, for CG, CONARC, c. Mar 62, sub: U.S. Continental Army Command Special Warfare Board, with atch, Historians files, CMH.

[104] David Pemberton, Battalion Counterguerrilla/Insurgency Training for Specific World Areas (Annex A) (Student paper, Infantry School, 1962), p. 1; Wilford Warren, Antiguerrilla Operations (Student paper, IOAC, Infantry School, 1961); J. A. Wallace, "Counterinsurgency ATT," *Army* 16 (August 1966): 76–77; Ben Walton, Army Training Program To Train the Infantry Company for Both Conventional and Unconventional Combat (Student paper, IOAC, Infantry School, 1962).

[105] Richard Scott, Training of the Junior Leader for Counter Guerrilla Warfare (Student paper, Infantry School, 1962), an. B; William Olds, Predeployment Training of B Company, 2d Battalion, 503d Infantry, 173d Airborne Brigade (Sep) on Okinawa During the Period February Through April 1965 (Personal Experience of a Platoon Leader) (Student paper, Infantry School, 1965), p. 23; Smith, Counterinsurgency Training, an. D; Rpt, JCS, n.d., sub: Development Status of Military Counterinsurgency Programs, Including Counterguerrilla Forces, as of 1 August 1965, p. IV-16; Harry Trigg, "A New ATT," *Army* 13 (February 1963): 35–39.

[106] Memo, CINCPAC for JCS, 4 May 62, sub: Status of Development of Counter-Guerrilla Forces, p. 15, Historians files, CMH.

[107] Rpt, HQDA, U.S. Army Special Warfare Study and Program, FY 63–68, 1962, p. 70; CONARC Pam 515–2, Counterinsurgency, 1962; CONARC Pam 516–2, Counterinsurgency Operations, Counterinsurgency—An Orientation for Basic and Advanced Trainees, 1963.

[108] CONARC, CONARC World Wide Combat Arms Conference II, vol. 3, 25–29 Jun 62, pp. 199, 202–03; Rpt, JCS, sub: Development Status of Military Counterinsurgency Programs, Including Counterguerrilla Forces, as of 1 August 1963, p. IV-7; "USCONARC Uses Viet Nam Lessons in Counterinsurgency," *Army Reservist* 8 (November 1962): 11; CONARC, Appendix VII to Annex of CONARC Training Directive, Nov 62.

[109] CONARC, Annex N to USCONARC Training Directive, Counter Guerrilla Warfare Training, 22 Apr 64; Army Regulation (AR) 220–55, *Field Organizations, Field and Command Post Exercises*, 18 Jun 64, p. 3; Memo, CONARC for Distribution, 26 Aug 63, sub: Revised Infantry AIT Program, Historians files, CMH; Ltr, Maj Gen Hugh M. Exton, Dep CS for Unit Training and Readiness, CONARC, to ACSFOR, 3 Oct 63, sub: Mandatory Training Requirements, and Fact Sheet, 5 Feb 64, sub: Training Subjects and the Extent of Their Impact on Total Available Training Time, both in 71A2333, CONARC, RG 338, NARA; Rpt, CONARC, Mar 63, sub: Army Training Center Conference, 71A1562, CONARC, RG 338, NARA.

[110] Quote from FM 21–73, *Combat Training of the Individual Soldier and Patrolling*, 1962, p. 113. CONARC Pam 515–3, Counterinsurgency, Counterinsurgency Instructional/Training Material, 1962; FM 31–15, *Operations Against Irregular Forces*, 1961, pp. 46–47; FM 31–16, *Counterguerrilla Operations*, 1963, pp. 105, 112–16.

[111] Infantry School, Ranger Training, 1961, pp. 12, 34, 73, 116 ; Hogan, *Raiders or Elite Infantry*, pp. 147–48, 156–57; Historical Supplement, 1965, U.S. Army Infantry School, 1966, pp. 9–10; Rpt, JCS 1969/212, 1 Jun 61, sub: Status of Development of Counterguerrilla Forces, p. 1870.

[112] 25th Inf Div, Clear and Hold Operations, an. E, Army Troop Test ROAD Brigade in Counterinsurgency Operations, 1965, pp. E-2 to E-4, Historians files, CMH; Rpt, HQDA, U.S. Army Special Warfare Study and Program, FY 63–68, 1962, an. V; Scott, Training of the Junior Leader, an. B. For examples of training, see Rpt, JCS 1969/330, 9 Apr 62, sub: Status of Development of Counterguerrilla Forces, pp. 37–39; "Exercise Swamp Fox," *Infantry* 54 (May–June 1964): 50–51; Bruce Palmer, Jr., and Roy Flint,

"Counter-Insurgency Training," *Army* 12 (June 1962): 32–39; Memo, Lt Col A. Aakkula for Commandant, CGSC, 24 May 62, sub: Trip Report, Yakima Washington (Exercise MESA DRIVE), p. 8. After Action Reports (AARs), Exercise MESA DRIVE, Jun 62, p. 22; Exercise SHERWOOD FOREST, 32d Inf Div, 17 Jul 62, pp. 26–27, and see also pp. 3–4, 25–28, 43–44; and Exercise SENECA SPEAR, 2d Inf Div, 1962, pp. 1, 5, 14–15. Last three at MHI. Annual Hist Sums, 1st Bn, 8th Inf, 1964 and 1965; Memo, 4th Inf Div for CG, 6th Army, 6 Nov 64, sub: Exercise EASTWIND, 71A3439, RG 338, NARA.

[113] Quote from FM 31–16, *Counterguerrilla Operations*, 1963, p. 116. 25th Inf Div, Clear and Hold Operations, an. E, Army Troop Test ROAD Brigade in Counterinsurgency Operations, 1965, pp. E-2 to E-4; Richard Terry, Guerrilla Warfare in Army Maneuvers (Student paper, Infantry School, 1961).

[114] Quote from 25th Inf Div, Twenty-fifth Division Jungle and Guerrilla Warfare Training Center, 1962, n.p., CARL. Ernest Easterbrook, "Realism in Counterinsurgency Training," *Army Information Digest* 17 (October 1962): 12–21; 25th Inf Div, Training Memo 9, Brigade Jungle Exercise 10–23 January 1962, 29 Dec 61, 17526.59A, CARL.

[115] Quote from James Rast, "Highland Fox: The 2d Division's Off-Post Counterinsurgency Exercise," *Infantry* 55 (May–June 1965): 49. Erik Villard, "Guerrillas in the Mist: 4th Division Counterinsurgency Training Exercises in the Olympic National Forest, 1963–65," paper presented at American Military Experience in Asia Conference, Madison, Wisc., Oct 98, pp. 5, 12, Historians files, CMH; Annual Hist Sum, 4th Inf Div, 1963, pp. 10–12, CMH; Jean Moenk, *A History of Large-Scale Maneuvers in the United States, 1935–1964* (Fort Monroe, Va.: Historical Branch, HQ, CONARC, 1969), p. 289; Joint Exercise COULEE CREST, Final Report, 30 April–20 May 1963, p. 10, MHI; Hal Lyon, "If the Cause Is Right," *Infantry* 54 (March–April 1964): 52–53.

[116] First quote from Andrew Krepinevich, *The Army and Vietnam* (Baltimore, Md.: Johns Hopkins University Press, 1986), p. 31. Second quote from Barber and Ronning, *Internal Security*, p. 81.

[117] Bowman, "Evolution of Army Doctrine," p. 125; Doughty, *Army Tactical Doctrine*, p. 29.

[118] Memo, CDC Special Warfare and Civil Affairs Group for Chief of Staff, CDC, 18 Oct 65, sub: National Counterinsurgency Review, 73A2677, CDC, RG 338, NARA; Maxwell Taylor, "The U.S. Government and Counterinsurgency," AWC lecture, 11 Jan 66, p. 8, MHI; Rpt, Counterinsurgency Review Board, 1 Dec 65, sub: Report of Committee II (Training), Counterinsurgency Review Board, 1 December 1965, Counterinsurgency Training in U.S. Government Agencies, pp. II-1 to II-9, A-3 to A-9, A-18, A-21, Maxwell D. Taylor Papers, National Defense University, Fort McNair, Washington, D.C.

7

PUTTING DOCTRINE TO THE TEST
THE ADVISORY EXPERIENCE
1955-1975

During the third quarter of the twentieth century, the U.S. Army helped dozens of countries combat subversive movements. With the exception of South Vietnam and, to a lesser extent, Laos, the Army confined its activities to providing materiel and advice. Although U.S. soldiers often found the task of working through others frustrating, they could claim a considerable measure of success, for during this period not a single U.S. ally—again with the exceptions of South Vietnam, Laos, and Cambodia—fell to Communist insurgents. The experience gave the Army ample opportunity to test its counterinsurgency and nation-building doctrines.[1]

The Latin American Experience

Although the battle against communism was global, Latin America was a prime area of U.S. concern. In 1959 Fidel Castro, a rebel who later proved to be a Communist, overthrew a weak dictatorship in Cuba. Stung by a Communist triumph so close to home and concerned that Castro might make good on his pledge to spread the revolutionary virus to the rest of the hemisphere, President Eisenhower initiated a counterinsurgency program for Latin America. Reflecting the traditional notion that socioeconomic distress provided the breeding ground for Communist agitation, Eisenhower allocated $500 million in 1960 to promote improvements in health, education, and agrarian conditions

throughout Latin America. He attempted to supplement these civil programs with $96.5 million in military assistance, but Congress rejected
the military aid package. Latin American militaries had a long history
of antidemocratic behavior, and Congress was loath to strengthen their
coercive powers.[2]

When Kennedy succeeded Eisenhower in January 1961, he shared
Eisenhower's and Castro's belief that Latin America was ripe for revolution. The new administration also believed the region was ready to
participate in Rostow's takeoff toward modernization. Consequently,
Kennedy followed Eisenhower's lead in seeking political and economic,
rather than military, solutions to the problem of regional instability. In August 1961 representatives of the United States and nineteen
Latin American countries signed the Charter of Punta del Este, which
launched an ambitious hemispheric initiative called the Alliance for
Progress. The plan committed the signatories to investing $100 billion
in development projects over the next ten years, with $20 billion com-
ing from the United States. The charter established specific goals in the
areas of economic growth, health, housing, and literacy. It also sought
to promote land reform, social justice, and democracy. In short, the
Alliance for Progress was a kind of Marshall Plan, a highly ambitious
program of economic growth and social engineering founded on a faith
in the ability of centralized planners and enlightened experts to remold
a continent. Certain of the outcome, the U.S. government confidently
predicted that the 1960s would be a "historic decade of democratic
progress."[3] (*Map 10*)

During the ten-year life of the Alliance for Progress the United
States dedicated roughly 92 percent of the aid it gave Latin America to
economic programs. Yet, like Eisenhower, Kennedy also believed that
military assistance had a positive role to play, and he urged legislators
to rescind the ban on providing internal security assistance to Latin
America. As Secretary of Defense McNamara explained, "the essential
role of the Latin American military as a stabilizing force outweighs
any risks involved in providing military assistance for internal security
purposes." The administration found support for its position from a
growing number of academics led by Samuel P. Huntington, Morris
Janowitz, and John L. Johnson, who asserted that military establishments were prime vehicles for promoting modernization in third world
societies. Armed with such arguments, Kennedy succeeded in persuading Congress to allow the Pentagon to provide counterinsurgency training and equipment to Latin America.[4]

In November 1961 the Joint Chiefs of Staff gave President Kennedy
twenty-seven recommendations on how the U.S. military could support

MEXICO
BRITISH HONDURAS
HONDURAS
GUATEMALA
NICARAGUA
EL SALVADOR
COSTA RICA
PANAMA
West Indies
VENEZUELA
BRITISH GUIANA
DUTCH GUIANA
FRENCH GUIANA
COLOMBIA
Galapagos Is
ECUADOR
B R A Z I L
PERU
BOLIVIA
PARAGUAY
C H I L E
ARGENTINA
URUGUAY
Falkland Is

15°
15°
0°
0°
15°
15°
30°
30°
45°
45°
60°
60°
45°
60°
90°
105°
75°
90°
45°
60°

CENTRAL AND SOUTH AMERICA
1961

0   1000   2000
Miles

MAP 10

the Alliance for Progress, twenty-three of which had been put forth by the Army. The thrust of the Army's plan was to expand military, police, psychological, and intelligence assistance while simultaneously encouraging Latin American militaries to undertake significant civic action programs. The Army also hoped to promote democratic and constitutional behavior on the part of area militaries by bringing young officers to the United States where they could observe how a modern, professional, apolitical military organization functioned in a democracy. Kennedy enthusiastically endorsed the proposals, directing that the Pentagon implement them on an accelerated basis.[5]

Not everyone was sanguine about the shift in U.S. policy. Many civilians doubted the wisdom of strengthening the repressive powers of Latin American governments, while the Agency for International Development resented the infusion of military considerations into developmental matters. The Pentagon's Director of Military Assistance, General Williston B. Palmer, also had reservations. He openly challenged the idea that the U.S. military should attempt to indoctrinate foreign soldiers in democracy, economics, or even civic action. He argued that such matters were beyond the Army's professional competence and would merely expose it to charges of meddling in politics. McNamara dismissed such reservations, yet in practice the military aid program limited political training to civic action issues in deference to foreign governments that objected to potential U.S. interference in their domestic affairs.[6]

Although Latin America enthusiastically embraced the Alliance for Progress, U.S. officials were frustrated by the fact that many area governments seemed ambivalent about the threat of Communist subversion. Latin American skepticism, however, was not unwarranted. True, unrest existed in various forms and active insurgencies existed in about a dozen Latin American states. But in evaluating these threats, Americans often underestimated the institutional strengths of area governments and the many social, political, and cultural barriers to revolutionary change.

Fortunately for U.S. interests, many Latin American revolutionaries also underestimated these barriers. Inspired by the apparent ease with which Castro had overthrown an unpopular and inept Cuban government, many revolutionaries adopted unrealistic expectations about their ability to duplicate Castro's accomplishment. Their misapprehension was fueled by the Cubans themselves, most notably Castro's lieutenant, Che Guevara. Guevara's 1960 book *On Guerrilla Warfare* asserted that a small military cell, or *foco*, could spark a wider revolution without waiting for optimum political conditions. His *foco* theory, which

American and Ecuadorian engineers discuss a road-building project in 1962 as part of the Alliance for Progress; below, *Ecuadorian villagers try out a new water pump built for them by U.S. Army and Ecuadorian Army engineers.*

received further amplification and dissemination throughout Latin America thanks to the literary efforts of the French Communist Regis Debray, maintained that area Communists could jump-start the revolutionary process by moving directly into guerrilla warfare without first engaging in the long and arduous task of building party organizations and mobilizing public support. By subordinating the party and political considerations to military action, the *foco* theory essentially stood Marxist-Leninist theory on its head.

Latin American leftists formed approximately two dozen *foco*-type movements during the 1960s. In practice, the theory proved unworkable. Undertaking military action without having first mobilized at least a portion of the population exposed insurgents to military countermeasures when they were relatively weak. Compounding the tenuousness of the guerrillas' links to the people was the fact that many insurgent leaders were urbanites who were neither acclimated to the hardships of campaign life nor attuned to the needs, aspirations, and character of the rural population. More at home in university classrooms and smoky cafes than in the bush, Latin American guerrilla leaders were particularly prone to endless squabbles over ideology, strategy, and personality that badly fractured their movements. Consequently, most insurgent groups fielded no more than a few hundred guerrillas, and not one came remotely close to success. The futility of the *foco* method was finally demonstrated in 1967, when Che himself was killed in a farcical attempt to spark a revolution in Bolivia.[7]

Che's demise marked a turning point in the nature of Latin American insurgency. External support for Latin American revolutionaries began to fade as first the Soviet Union and then Cuba progressively disassociated themselves from the region's floundering insurgent movements. Moreover, while a few *focos* sputtered on into the 1970s, the Latin Americans themselves began to change their tactics. Some, disheartened by their failure to rouse the countryside, returned to the cities where they resorted to a new form of revolutionary warfare, urban terrorism. Guided by the writings of Abraham Guillen and Carlos Marighella, a new breed of radicals attempted to keep the revolutionary dream alive through assassinations, bombings, kidnappings, and robberies. These urban *focos* enjoyed some success, but by the early 1970s they too had largely collapsed, partly because their terroristic acts alienated local populations and partly because the urban *foco*ists were frequently no more interested in long-term political work than their rural cousins had been.[8]

More successful than the urban terrorists were a few groups that ultimately rejected all forms of *foco*ism in favor of a more balanced

Nicaraguan soldiers take part in a U.S.-assisted urban counterterrorism exercise in 1969; below, *a U.S. Army adviser* (center) *observes Guatemalan soldiers practice riot control techniques.*

politico-military approach. These movements ultimately posed the greatest challenge to Latin American counterinsurgents, and in 1979 they produced the only successful Marxist insurgency in Latin America outside of Cuba—Nicaragua's Sandinista Revolution. Such movements were still in their infancy during the period covered by this book, however, and did not pose serious threats to most states. Indeed, the Sandinista Revolution, like the Cuban, proved to be the exception rather than the rule. By the end of the twentieth century no other Latin American country had fallen to a Marxist-Maoist assault, while the Sandinista regime itself had given way to a democratic government.

The languid performance of most Latin American revolutionaries notwithstanding, they still created significant problems in the 1960s and early 1970s, most notably in Colombia, Guatemala, Venezuela, Brazil, Uruguay, and Peru. They could have proved much more dangerous but for the countervailing effect of U.S. security assistance. Between 1950 and 1975, the United States trained over 28,000 Latin American military personnel in the United States and at the U.S. Army School of the Americas in the Panama Canal Zone. The latter school was especially important, as it eventually dedicated approximately 70 percent of its Spanish-based curriculum to counterinsurgency-related subjects. Meanwhile, the Agency for International Development trained several thousand Latin American police officers either in the Canal Zone or at the International Police Academy in Washington, D.C., while the CIA provided intelligence assistance. The U.S. Army complemented these efforts through a small number of military advisers backed over the years by several hundred mobile training teams, many of whose members were drawn from the Canal Zone–based 8th Special Forces Group that formed the nucleus of the Army's Latin American Special Action Force.[9]

The advice proffered by U.S. soldiers during the 1960s and 1970s closely followed the precepts laid out in U.S. manuals, many of which the Army translated into Spanish. Army advisers urged area governments to develop cogent politico-military plans that attacked both the guerrillas in the field and the socioeconomic conditions that spawned them. They also recommended the establishment of bureaucratic mechanisms to better coordinate and integrate the efforts of various government agencies. Included among such devices were joint coordination centers that orchestrated the activities of police, military, and intelligence agencies. First introduced in Venezuela by an Army training team, the joint center concept proved so successful that the United States created a demonstration unit that marketed the idea to several other countries.[10]

Representative of America's approach to Latin American insurgency were the programs the United States developed to counter instability in Colombia. In 1959 President Eisenhower responded to an epidemic of social and political violence in Colombia by dispatching a special mission to that troubled nation. The mission recommended that the Colombian government initiate the full panoply of U.S. Army counterinsurgency measures, from increased psychological, civil affairs, and intelligence activities to intensified counterguerrilla training. It likewise suggested an array of programs to restore public trust in the government by reducing corruption, improving troop conduct, and enhancing government services. Based on these recommendations, the Colombian government revamped its counterinsurgency effort, initiating economic reforms and instituting a Council of National Defense that coordinated the activities of the military high command with those civilian ministries charged with promoting economic development and social order. Still, many shortcomings remained, and in 1962 the United States provided additional recommendations, first through a special study group led by General Yarborough, and later by a two-man Special Forces team that helped the Colombian military craft a comprehensive three-year program called Plan Lazo.[11]

The Lazo plan closely followed the precepts of Army counterinsurgency doctrine. It called for tightened command and control over all public security forces to ensure unified action, expanded psychological and civic action activities to win popular support, and improved intelligence operations to ferret out the guerrillas and their clandestine agents amid the people. To facilitate this last objective, the Colombian Army created networks of paid informants and offered rewards for information. It also established mobile intelligence groups that integrated military, police, and civilian intelligence activities at the local level and special hunter-killer teams that exploited the correlated information to kill or capture insurgent leaders.

True to U.S. Army doctrine, Plan Lazo assigned Colombian infantry brigades to geographical zones with the mission of clearing those areas of an insurgent presence. Operating out of widely scattered bases, small infantry units were to scour the countryside day and night to keep the guerrillas on the run. Once one of these patrols had located an irregular unit, Plan Lazo called for unrelenting pursuit to capture or destroy the enemy, most likely by some form of encirclement. To facilitate the execution of such highly dispersed yet aggressive actions, the advisory mission pledged to help improve the Colombian military's performance, most notably through the provision of communications gear and vehicular transport, including twelve heli-copters. Meanwhile, rigorous population- and resource-control mea-sures, sweetened by civic action programs, would facilitate the return of government authority to unruly regions. Helping to solidify these gains would be newly raised police and paramilitary formations whose pres-ence would both enhance local security and free the regular forces for additional offensive operations. A series of U.S.-funded radio networks that linked farms and villages to military reaction forces rounded out the local security system. Though by no means perfect, the Lazo plan provided Colombia with its comprehensive blueprint for an integrated counterinsurgency campaign. By 1965 Colombia had greatly reduced the amount of territory controlled by antigovernment forces.[12]

Not every country received as detailed assistance as Colombia, but throughout the hemisphere U.S. Army advice was generally cut from the same cloth—aggressive, light infantry operations to hunt the guer-rillas, paramilitary formations to protect and control the population, and intelligence, propaganda, and civic action measures to solidify government gains. Guatemala applied such a formula to defeat leftist guerrillas in the mid-1960s, while Peru successfully destroyed several guerrilla base areas in 1965 by employing a series of phased encircle-ments reminiscent of those conducted in Greece and Korea. The U.S. Army helped these and other nations develop a variety of special coun-terguerrilla formations that frequently spearheaded operations. One such unit, a Bolivian ranger battalion, earned the distinction of killing Che Guevara. Conversely, large-unit, conventional operations; heavy artillery concentrations; and ponderous, road-bound formations played little part in the Army's program for Latin America.[13]

While American-style counterinsurgency methods succeeded in keeping the hemisphere's rural insurgents at bay, both the Americans and their allies were unprepared to meet the shift to urban terrorism that occurred in the later 1960s. Although the Army had procedures for conducting combat, riot control, and cordon-and-search operations in urban environments, U.S. doctrine had largely mirrored Maoist revolu-tionary thought by focusing on the countryside rather than the cities. The criminal nature of urban insurgency, however, did not lend itself to a military solution. Consequently, assistance in this area focused on intelligence and police operations—areas that fell more under AID's Office of Public Safety and the CIA than the Army.[14]

Although several Latin American countries had developed civic action concepts independently of the United States, America's strong endorsement of civic action proved influential in persuading them to expand such programs. Guatemala was the first Latin American

A U.S. Army Special Forces adviser discusses tactics with Bolivian troops prior to a counterguerrilla operation in 1967.

nation to accept a U.S. Army civic action advisory team in 1960, with a full-time civic action adviser following in 1962. During the 1960s civic action programs accounted for nearly a quarter of U.S. military aid to Guatemala, and U.S. influence over the program was strong. Guatemala's leading counterinsurgency commander, Col. Carlos Arana Osorio, attributed 70 percent of his success to civic action programs that purportedly won the allegiance of local peasants by building roads and feeding school children hot lunches.[15]

News of the Guatemalan program spread rapidly through the hemisphere, but not until the United States agreed to pay the majority of the bills did the Latin American states show any real enthusiasm for enrolling in U.S. civic action programs. By 1965 thirteen Latin American countries sported U.S.-funded civic action projects. In Ecuador U.S. Army engineers helped supervise the construction of farm-to-market roads. In Bolivia U.S.-financed engineer battalions built dozens of schools, while in Colombia the military established health clinics. Across the length and breadth of the continent, armies cleared jungles, installed sewage systems, and inoculated children. In addition to helping to plan, provision, and execute such undertakings, the U.S. Army distributed thousands of pamphlets describing improved agricultural and health techniques. Advisory missions complemented these good works by encouraging indigenous soldiers to treat civilians in a courteous manner.[16]

Armed with reams of statistics about the number of pamphlets distributed, roads built, and teeth cleaned, U.S. Army officials in the early 1960s concluded that the civic action program in Latin America had "unquestionably been successful." In fact, the situation was murky. Much good had been achieved, but the resources applied paled in comparison with the hemisphere's socioeconomic ills. Confusion and disagreement over whether civic action projects should be substantive or mere palliatives of a temporary and largely propagandistic nature divided administrators and defused the program's impact. Some AID officials disdained military participation in developmental activities and hindered the effort, while budgeting impediments and a shortage of language-qualified specialists hampered effective execution.[17]

Problems on the American side were matched by shortcomings in the recipient nations. Corruption and mismanagement plagued the execution of programs throughout the hemisphere. Moreover, U.S. advisers quickly learned that while giving a foreign soldier a bulldozer and having him build a road with it was fairly easy, changing the way the soldier thought and acted was much more difficult. American protestations notwithstanding, many area military and police establishments insisted on employing torture, terror, and brutality to suppress political and social unrest. The situation actually worsened as the decade progressed, as countries responded to the rise of urban terrorism with terror campaigns of their own. One of the ironies of the period was that Guatemala, which had won acclaim from U.S. officials for its pioneering civic action program, also amassed one of the region's worst records on human rights.[18]

Even when the philosophy of civic action was taken to heart, it sometimes had unforeseen consequences. The most notable example of this occurred in Peru, where military officers who were genuinely committed to civic action precepts overthrew the civilian government on the grounds that the military was the only institution in Peruvian society with the moral virtues and organizational skills capable of enacting reforms. Other Latin American soldiers less sincere in their devotion to civic action adopted similar justifications for meddling in domestic politics, with the result that what had initially been billed as a "historic decade of democratic progress" ended up being an era of heightened military activism in regional politics. Between 1962 and 1973 no fewer than sixteen coups rocked Latin America, and by 1974 more than half of all Latin American countries were under military rule.

The wave of coups that swept the Western hemisphere was not the product of U.S. internal security doctrine. Ultimately, indigenous factors played a far more important role in shaping the course of Latin

A U.S. Army adviser (second from left) *accompanies El Salvadoran Army medics on a medical civic action initiative;* below, *an American soldier distributes propaganda in comic book form to Bolivian children in 1966.*

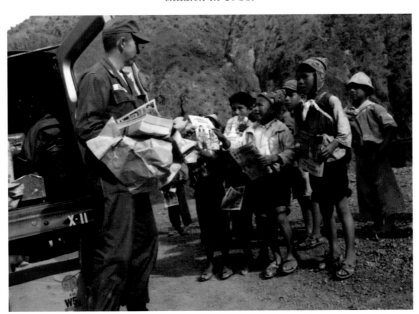

America's political development during the 1960s and 1970s than a few hours of counterinsurgency instruction at the School of the Americas. Nevertheless, U.S. military assistance clearly had not prevented area militaries from adopting unpalatable practices. This fact, when combined with the aforementioned difficulties experienced in the civic action program, led an independent study group commissioned by the Army in 1970 to conclude that "there are no records of specific achievement of any one of the objectives of the Alliance for Progress by the Latin American armed forces through civic action or other programs."[19]

The study group's findings were undoubtedly disappointing to the Army, yet they should not have been surprising, for the Alliance for Progress also fell far short of its goals. Ten years and tens of billions of dollars worth of aid and investment had not yielded the results that U.S. social engineers had so confidently predicted would occur. True, most Latin American economies had grown, life expectancy had increased, and many other positive achievements had been recorded. Yet little or no change had taken place in the overall structure of Latin America's troubled socioeconomic and political systems. For the most part the problems that might spark unrest—poverty, social immobility, racial and ethnic prejudice, unrepresentative government, corruption, and oppression—continued to flourish throughout the hemisphere.

The failure of the Alliance of Progress and its military component—civic action—to remedy Latin America's many social and political ills muddied the doctrinal assertion that an insurgency could not be defeated without development and reform. From one point of view, the experience had validated this tenet, for the failure of area governments to redress the underlying causes of discontent meant that unrest would continue to percolate throughout Latin America for years to come. Yet the fact that Latin American governments had succeeded in quashing one guerrilla movement after another without making significant structural changes indicated that some counterinsurgency theorists had gone too far in their assertions about the necessity of winning hearts and minds. While reform was desirable and coercion only dealt with the symptoms of a deeper social disease, the fact was that coercion could indeed achieve the immediate goals of the counterinsurgent.[20]

Advice and Support in Vietnam

Although keeping the Western hemisphere free of communism was a primary goal of American foreign policy, Latin America was a relative backwater for the U.S. Army compared to Southeast Asia. Here the United States expended vast sums in a futile effort to stop Communist insurgents in three countries—South Vietnam, Laos, and Cambodia. The Army's involvement in each of these wars varied greatly, but nowhere in Southeast Asia—or the world, for that matter—did the United States expend more blood and treasure in the name of counter-insurgency than in the ill-starred state of South Vietnam.

South Vietnam was the product of the 1954 Geneva Accords that terminated the Indochina War. The accords had split Vietnam along the 17th Parallel into a Communist-controlled north and non-Communist south. The partition was meant to be temporary pending a vote on reunification, but the elections were never held. Instead, what emerged were two sovereign, antithetical states.

After a few years of relative peace, Viet Minh agents, dubbed Viet Cong by South Vietnamese authorities, initiated an insurgency designed to bring down the southern government and reunify the country under Communist rule. Building upon the teachings of Mao Tse-tung as well as their own experiences in the French Indochina War, the Viet Cong created a parallel government, or infrastructure, that exercised de facto control over large areas of rural South Vietnam. Through this organization, the Viet Cong intimidated opponents, collected taxes, and raised recruits for guerrilla bands that over the course of several years matured into a three-tiered system of hamlet militias, regional guerrilla units, and quasi-regular "main force" battalions, regiments, and divisions. Together, these forces waged an enervating war of terror, raid, and ambush that severely challenged the southern government's control over the countryside. North Vietnam directed the effort, providing cadres, supplies, and eventually soldiers that it infiltrated into the South through Laos and Cambodia, weak neutral states that offered ready sanctuaries for Communist forces.

President Ngo Dinh Diem's Republic of Vietnam (South Vietnam) was poorly positioned to parry the threat. Years of colonial domination had bequeathed it a languid economy and a weak administrative system that barely extended into the countryside. Unlike the Communists, whose highly motivated, locally recruited cadres lived and worked among the people, South Vietnam was dominated by men drawn from the country's urban and educated classes who often had little sympathy for the peasantry and generally opposed any reforms that might undermine their power. Instead, corruption, nepotism, and inefficiency hampered the government, while deep social, ethnic, and religious fissures plagued the countryside.[21] (*Map 11*)

Overcoming these obstacles was a daunting task, but over the years Diem succeeded in creating a personal political machine that held his rivals in check. With the help of American largess, Diem kept South

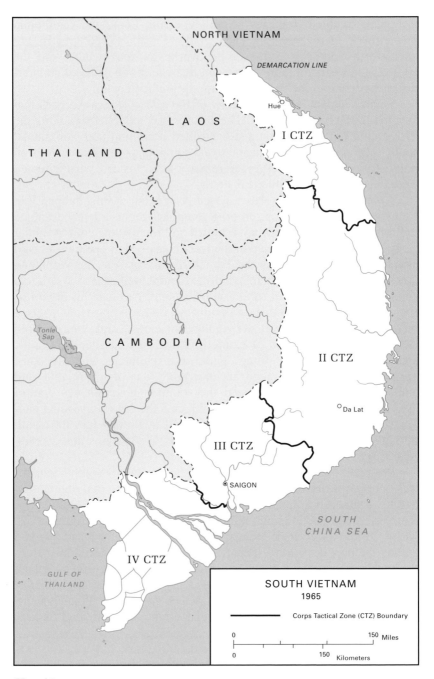

NORTH VIETNAM

DEMARCATION LINE

Hue

I CTZ

LAOS

THAILAND

CAMBODIA

Tonle
Sap

II CTZ

Da Lat

III CTZ

SAIGON

SOUTH
CHINA SEA

IV CTZ

GULF OF
THAILAND

SOUTH VIETNAM
1965

━━━━━ Corps Tactical Zone (CTZ) Boundary

0   150 Miles

0   150 Kilometers

MAP 11

Vietnam afloat and even managed to initiate a few reforms, including a modest land redistribution initiative. Meanwhile, he moved to destroy Communist influence in the countryside. He replaced local officials with government appointees, established *pao chia*–style neighborhood watch and reporting systems, relocated populations, and hunted down Communist cadres with a special intelligence organization that used torture to achieve its ends.[22]

Diem's state-building efforts scored some successes during the mid-1950s. Yet they fell far short of effecting permanent change. Likewise, Diem's occasional use of Draconian measures, when combined with his imposition of officials chosen for their loyalty rather than their talent, alienated the very people over whom he was trying to gain control.

If the regime's bungling retarded the nation-building process, so too did the Viet Cong, who worked assiduously to thwart the government at every turn. Communist agitators and spies penetrated virtually every town, hamlet, and government agency in South Vietnam. When they could not achieve their ends peacefully, they did not hesitate to kidnap or kill anyone who stood in their way. By 1961 the Viet Cong had assassinated thousands of people and forced the government to abandon over 600 rural schools, thereby stripping the fledgling regime of what little presence it had in the countryside. Meanwhile, thanks to its ability to inspire and intimidate the rural population, the Viet Cong gradually escalated its terror campaign to include attacks on isolated garrisons, military convoys, and pro-government villages. In 1959 the Communist Party of Vietnam formally initiated the second, or guerrilla, phase of its Maoist-style insurgency, and, by the time of Kennedy's election in November 1960, South Vietnam's security forces were beginning to crack under the strain of an accelerating guerrilla campaign.[23]

The job of pacifying the countryside fell to the security forces Diem had inherited from the French, an assortment of military and paramilitary organizations bereft of any overarching command or administrative structure. With the French rapidly phasing out their presence in Vietnam following the Geneva Accords, Eisenhower decided to undertake the job of transforming this motley assemblage into an effective fighting force. He did so despite warnings from Army Chief of Staff General Ridgway and the rest of the Joint Chiefs that such an undertaking would be "hopeless" unless "a reasonably strong, stable, civil government" existed first.[24]

The first chief of the U.S. military aid mission to Vietnam, Lt. Gen. John W. O'Daniel (1954–1955), charted a course that was not dissimilar to that followed by other U.S. advisory groups during the 1940s and 1950s. Like his counterparts, O'Daniel was faced with the dual task of

South Vietnamese troops search for insurgents.

preparing South Vietnam to meet both conventional and unconventional threats—namely an invasion from the North and internal instability in the South. As his contemporaries had done in other countries, O'Daniel adopted the existing array of military and paramilitary organizations as the basis upon which to build a multilayered security system. Security began at home with the Self-Defense Corps, a part-time militia that mobilized civilians to defend their villages against guerrilla raiders and Communist cadres. Backing the local militia was the Civil Guard, which consisted of company-size units deployed on a provincial basis to perform rural constabulary and security functions. Finally, at the top of the security system was the Army of the Republic of Vietnam, a loose collection of military units inherited from the French that O'Daniel proposed to transform into ten infantry divisions, thirteen independent territorial regiments, and an airborne regiment backed by an array of administrative, logistical, and combat support elements.

Though based on American precepts, the South Vietnamese Army was not a carbon copy of the U.S. Army. Unlike the U.S. Army, whose organizational structure focused almost exclusively on the conduct of conventional warfare, only four of South Vietnam's ten divisions were conventional "field" divisions. The remaining six divisions were "light" divisions that, together with the territorial regiments, were designed primarily for internal security work. Moreover, U.S. planners deliberately created a relatively austere force in deference to South Vietnam's difficult topography, limited transportation infrastructure, and modest technical and logistical resources. Thus, the field divisions were half the size of a standard U.S. infantry division and included only one battalion of artillery, a stark contrast to the four artillery battalions typically found in a U.S. division. The light divisions were even leaner—merely one-third the size of a U.S. division. These formations had few trucks and no artillery heavier than the 81-mm. mortar. In this way, the advisory group sought to endow the South Vietnamese Army with a structure that was capable of performing both counterguerrilla and limited conventional operations over Vietnam's varied terrain.[25]

O'Daniel recognized the civil aspects of the South Vietnamese Army's mission, and he requested that Colonel Lansdale be detailed to Vietnam to orchestrate the aid mission's civic action and psychological operations advisory programs. As the mission's chief pacification adviser, Lansdale blended local methods with his own experiences in the Huk rebellion to craft a program for the reclamation of Viet Cong–dominated areas. Following Viet Minh and French precedents, he established civic action cadre teams under the control of a Civic Action Directorate. Clad as peasants, the teams accompanied troops into Communist-controlled areas, where they sought to win the allegiance of the population by sponsoring a variety of small-scale socioeconomic programs. The cadres disseminated propaganda, distributed food and medicines, and encouraged the peasants to undertake a variety of self-improvement projects, such as digging wells, repairing roads, and building dispensaries.[26]

When Lt. Gen. Samuel T. Williams became chief of the Military Assistance Advisory Group, Vietnam, in October 1955, he fretted that the light divisions would be unable to contribute effectively to the nation's defense should the North Vietnamese invade, and he did not like the idea of a small country like Vietnam maintaining two different divisional organizations. Therefore, in 1958 he persuaded the South Vietnamese to reorganize their army into seven standardized divisions. Although somewhat larger than the original field divisions and equipped with two artillery battalions, the new divisions remained keyed to the Vietnamese environment.[27]

Despite the fact that the South Vietnamese Army was supposed to be equally adept at regular and irregular warfare, neither O'Daniel nor Williams paid much attention to the special aspects of counterguerrilla warfare. Part of the reason for this was that both men were preoccupied with the Herculean task of creating a viable military organization in a new and unstable country. The fact that the Viet Cong did not initiate serious guerrilla activity until the late 1950s reinforced the advisory group's conventional orientation, as did Williams' view that to teach specialized missions to an army that had yet to master the fundamentals of military organization and operations was pointless. Like many American officers, Williams firmly believed that a thorough inculcation in the basics of individual soldiering and small-unit tactics was the best possible preparation for any type of combat, conventional or unconventional, and consequently during the 1950s the advisory group concentrated on these subjects.[28]

Williams did not, however, completely ignore counterguerrilla warfare. In December 1955 he gave Diem a short paper outlining his thoughts on counterinsurgency. After reviewing the Maoist approach to guerrilla warfare, Williams noted that "military operations alone are not sufficient for success as there are really two objectives: the destruction of the guerrilla force and the elimination of the Communist influence on the civil population. An over-all plan at Government level embracing political, psychological, economic, administrative and military action is necessary for success." The ultimate goal of such a plan was to deny the guerrillas the human and material resources they needed to survive, whether these were drawn from the population or from an external source. While a keen intelligence service and aggressive military action using patrols and encirclement tactics drove the guerrillas away from populated areas toward their eventual disintegration and destruction, Williams called for the intelligent implementation of the "old principle of reward and punishment" to control the behavior of the population. In implementing such a program, he emphasized the importance of proper conduct on the part of civil and military officials, since "harsh, unjust, arbitrary action or mass punishment of innocent people, for the misdeeds of a few, will drive more people into the guerrilla ranks." By executing an aggressive military campaign that was "in harmony with the political, psychological, and economic policies," he believed South Vietnam could eventually slay the Communist dragon.[29]

Williams' 1955 paper was in full accord with U.S. Army doctrine, and he transmitted similar recommendations throughout his tenure as MAAG chief (1955–1960). In 1957 MAAG, Vietnam, translated into Vietnamese all U.S. Army guerrilla and counterguerrilla manuals. The following year Williams circulated additional guidance in the form of a memo titled "Notes on Anti-Guerrilla Operations." This document, which was lifted virtually verbatim from the 1951 edition of FM 31–20, *Operations Against Guerrilla Forces*, succinctly reiterated the basic principles of U.S. Army counterinsurgency doctrine, including the desirability of an integrated politico-military approach and the necessity of cutting the guerrillas off from the population via aggressive military action, restrictive control measures, and counterinfrastructure operations. The memo also encouraged advisers to promote training in subjects conducive to improved counterguerrilla performance. MAAG, Vietnam, reinforced these suggestions by developing counterguerrilla-training curriculums in 1958 and 1959 and by reissuing the "Notes" in 1960.[30]

Although U.S. doctrine acknowledged that small, specially trained units were often more effective in irregular warfare than large, conventional formations, Williams discouraged Diem from creating sizable numbers of elite formations on the grounds that such units would drain army battalions of their best personnel and impede the overall organizational effort. Diem ignored this advice and in 1960 formed special antiguerrilla units called rangers. Faced with a *fait accompli*, the United States agreed to provide Special Forces personnel to train the new units, which Diem formed by stripping each infantry battalion of one of its four companies. The rangers proved effective soldiers but were often misused as garrison and strategic reserve troops. Moreover, by creating the rangers, Diem had reduced the effectiveness of his line battalions, since a battalion with four rifle companies was more effective in non-linear, area-style warfare than one with three. Unfortunately, American recommendations regarding the restoration of the fourth rifle company went unheeded.[31]

Regardless of how the South Vietnamese Army was organized, it could not operate effectively under any circumstances unless it had first been effectively trained. This proved to be a difficult task. Manpower constraints and linguistic and cultural barriers impeded MAAG, Vietnam's efforts, as did the South Vietnamese Army's tendency to assign mediocre personnel as instructors. Compounding these difficulties was the lackadaisical attitude that some Vietnamese officers displayed toward professionalism in general and training in particular. Many had served in the French Army and dismissed American advice as coming from ignorant and pushy newcomers. Others were political appointees who believed that their careers depended more on political alignments than military performance. Caution, intrigue, and plodding staff work, not initiative and combat experience, were the tickets to promotion, and, under such circumstances, U.S. advisers had difficulty convincing Vietnamese officers to take training seriously. Finally, even the most diligent officer could claim with some justification that the press of operational requirements prevented effective training. Dispersed among innumerable small outposts, South Vietnamese units often lacked the time and manpower to devote to training, and as the guerrilla menace grew, the situation got worse. By 1959 the government had committed 57 percent of its infantry to either pacification or static security missions. The drain caused by these assignments meant that one-third of all infantry battalions did not undergo any type of training that year. This situation placed grave strains on the army's immature administrative and logistical systems, strains that proved just as disruptive to the development of the South Vietnamese Army as they had to the development of the South Korean military just a few years before.[32]

The comparison was not lost on Williams. In Korea, the Communists had used guerrilla warfare to sap the strength of their opponents before staging a major conventional invasion to reunify that divided country. The parallels to Vietnam appeared all too menacing to neglect, and consequently Williams attempted, as his predecessors had in Korea, to minimize the army's involvement in internal security functions. Only by giving the army a respite from enervating garrison and pacification duty could it truly develop the professional competence it needed to become an effective organization. Thus Williams opposed suggestions that South Vietnamese troops perform civic action work, not because he failed to recognize the importance of winning popular support, but because he felt that the conscript's twelve-month tour of duty was barely enough time to train and utilize him in his military functions. Diverting the conscript to perform manual labor would merely exacerbate the army's serious training deficiencies.[33]

To free the South Vietnamese Army for additional training, Williams hoped to rely on the paramilitary forces to shoulder the lion's share of the internal security burden. In this his actions mirrored those taken by U.S. military advisers in Greece and Korea, but he was doomed to frustration. A tight ceiling limiting the number of U.S. military advisers and a philosophical decision on the part of the U.S. government that police forces were a civil, not military, concern meant that MAAG, Vietnam, had little influence over South Vietnam's police and paramilitary forces. Instead, the United States contracted out the paramilitary advisory function to Michigan State University. The Michigan group was oriented primarily toward traditional police functions and generally neglected the quasi-military aspects of internal security. Moreover, the group proved unequal to the difficult job of improving the image of the nation's police forces, whose ineffectiveness, brutality, and corruption alienated them from the people.[34]

In 1957 U.S. Ambassador to South Vietnam Elbridge Durbrow rebuffed Williams' offer to extend military assistance to the Civil Guard and Self-Defense Corps, choosing instead to withhold material assistance from the paramilitaries altogether until Diem agreed to make certain concessions regarding their organization. The three-way donnybrook between Diem, Durbrow, and Williams over the paramilitary forces meant that those forces languished unattended during the first critical years of the insurgency. The inability of the civilian security apparatus to protect the nation's people and resources from the Viet Cong thus created a vicious and downward-pulling spiral. Growing instability compelled the South Vietnamese Army to devote an ever-increasing share of its resources to internal security functions. This diversion impeded its professional development, which in turn made it less capable of combating the Viet Cong, hence leading to even greater instability.[35]

In 1960 Williams' successor, Lt. Gen. Lionel C. McGarr, attempted to reverse this sequence of events. McGarr came to Vietnam from the Command and General Staff College, where, as the school's commandant, he had played an active role in reviving Army counterinsurgency doctrine, an effort that would soon come to fruition in the 1961 editions of FM 100–1 and FM 31–15. Shortly after arriving in the South Vietnamese capital of Saigon, McGarr committed his thoughts on counterguerrilla warfare to paper in two memos—"The Anti-Guerrilla Guerrilla" and "Implementing Actions for Anti-Guerrilla Operations."

In these widely distributed tracts, McGarr reiterated Williams' call for an integrated politico-military campaign, as well as for the imaginative adaptation of conventional techniques to Vietnamese conditions. He also reminded his readers that counterguerrilla warfare was just as much an ideological struggle as it was a military one, and he particularly stressed the importance of protecting the population from Viet Cong intimidation because unless people felt secure they would never provide the type of intelligence the government needed to root out the insurgents. Finally, McGarr used the papers to outline a strategy for countering the insurgency problem.

To cut the Viet Cong off from their North Vietnamese brethren, McGarr proposed the creation of a *cordon sanitaire*, or "firebreak," along Vietnam's borders, where the entire population would be evacuated and anyone found inside the restricted zones could be killed. Meanwhile, in the interior, he advocated a strategy of progressive area clearance on the "oil spot" model. To implement this strategy, McGarr developed an operational concept that he labeled the net and spear. Under this concept, the South Vietnamese government would assign infantry units to specific operational areas where they would soon gain an intimate knowledge of the local military and political topography. Once established, these units would break down into innumerable small patrols that would act like a "net" to catch and destroy any small enemy units operating in the area. Should the "net" catch a large guerrilla formation, the patrols would shadow their quarry until larger reaction forces—the "spear"—could strike and destroy the ensnared guerrilla band, most likely through some form of encirclement action. After the army had succeeded in clearing a sector of guerrillas using the net-and-spear method, it would turn the defense of the area over to the paramilitaries and move on to clear another area, repeating the process until all of South Vietnam was free of guerrilla activity.[36]

After publishing these ideas in November 1960, McGarr formed a combined U.S.-Vietnamese team to expand them into a more robust document. The resulting product was a handbook titled *Tactics and Techniques of Counterinsurgent Operations*. Continuously revised and updated by the allies, the handbook provided comprehensive guidance on the insurgency in South Vietnam. Included among its pages were background information on the land and its people, a review of Viet Cong tactics, and suggestions to advisers on how they could best perform their functions. Although certain sections were lifted from the British manual *Conduct of Anti-terrorist Operations in Malaya*, the majority of the manual related standard U.S. doctrine, augmented by insights derived by advisers and their Vietnamese counterparts.

The handbook encouraged its readers to be flexible and to remember that what worked in one situation might not be appropriate in another. It recommended that commanders employ ruses and deceptions to beat the guerrilla at his own game. Among the tricks suggested by the manual were employing pseudo-guerrillas to masquerade as Viet Cong, concealing troops in seemingly innocuous vehicles, and using small outposts and patrols to bait the insurgents into launching an attack, while nearby reserves lay in wait to pounce on the unsuspecting enemy.

By 1963 new editions of the handbook had begun to use the phrase *clear and hold* to describe pacification operations. The manual's authors likewise kept abreast of new techniques as they were developed, including the "eagle flight," a type of heliborne patrol and strike operation. While terms and tactics might change, the handbook continued to adhere to the underlying concept of progressive area clearance. It likewise retained statements regarding the importance of political factors. Thus the manual called for the humane treatment of prisoners and civilians, as well as for remedial actions to redress the causes of dissent, reminding its readers that "at all times the requirement to ultimately separate the people from the insurgents, and induce them to support the local government must dominate every action."[37]

During his tenure as MAAG chief (1960–1962), McGarr supported the establishment of an overarching Counterinsurgency Plan as a means of bringing greater cohesiveness to allied activities. The plan, which President Kennedy approved shortly after his inauguration, called for a carefully integrated political, military, economic, paramilitary, and police campaign to eliminate the Viet Cong and establish firm government control. To achieve this end, the plan recommended that the South Vietnamese government establish a National Security Council, with parallel councils at every level of administration. The Counterinsurgency Plan also endorsed more functional command and control arrangements and laid the groundwork for revitalizing Vietnam's paramilitary forces by transferring U.S. funding and advisory functions for those formations from American civilian agencies to the Pentagon.[38]

While U.S. authorities prodded Diem to energize his counterinsurgency apparatus at the national level, they also undertook to create an ever more elaborate scaffold of military and civilian advisers with which to prop up the tottering regime. During his first year in office, Kennedy tripled the number of military advisers in Vietnam, from 900 to over 3,000. Still this seemed insufficient, and a special study team headed by General Taylor and Walt Rostow recommended in November 1961 that the president commit 8,000 combat troops to Vietnam. Kennedy balked at sending combat formations but accepted Taylor's recommendation that the United States provide not only more advisers, but entire units of combat support personnel. This represented a major escalation of U.S. involvement in the Vietnamese civil war.[39]

In December 1961 the first major U.S. Army units arrived in South Vietnam in the guise of the 8th and 57th Transportation Companies, whose thirty-two helicopters were intended to give the South Vietnamese new mobility. Their arrival, together with the infusion of a growing number of other operational units, necessitated a change in command arrangements in Vietnam. On 8 February 1962, the Pentagon created a new entity, the Military Assistance Command, Vietnam, to supervise the activities of MAAG, Vietnam (which MACV eventually absorbed), and the growing number of support units sent to bolster the South Vietnamese. By the time of Kennedy's death in 1963, the United States had deployed approximately 16,000 military personnel to Vietnam.

One group of U.S. soldiers not initially under MACV control were small teams of Special Forces personnel sent into Vietnam's hinterlands to rally ethnic minorities to the anti-Communist cause. Operating initially under the CIA, the Special Forces teams worked primarily with South Vietnam's Montagnard population, conducting civic actions, building fortified villages, and raising a paramilitary defense force— the Civilian Irregular Defense Group—to protect the Montagnards from the Viet Cong. By the time MACV assumed control over the program in 1963, Special Forces had raised 51,000 paramilitary troops.[40]

As Special Forces expanded its presence among the Montagnards, so too did the Army increase its support of the rest of South Vietnam's security establishment. In 1961 MAAG, Vietnam, finally began to rearm and train the heretofore neglected Civil Guard and Self-Defense Corps—soon to be renamed Regional Forces and Popular Forces, respectively. It also authorized advisers to accompany Vietnamese units into combat, although it did not begin assigning advisers to South Vietnamese infantry battalions until 1962. Efforts to strengthen the government's ability to secure its people from Communist intimidation received an added boost in 1962, when Saigon announced the formation of a National Police force to be advised and trained by AID and the CIA. Meanwhile, the United States pressed the Vietnamese to accept a greater American presence in the countryside through the guise of military advisory detachments at the province (1962) and district (1964) levels. These advisers involved themselves in the full panoply of counterinsurgency endeavors. They correlated and disseminated information in province and district intelligence coordination centers, drew up operational plans and pacification schemes, assisted local paramilitary forces, and provided advice on a wide range of civil matters, from agronomy to digging wells. Indeed, in contrast to advisers posted to military units, the Army's provincial and district advisers spent about 50 percent of their time on civil issues.[41]

While the advisory framework kept the South Vietnamese government intact, MACV worked to improve the performance of combat units. By 1962 Army advisers had reoriented all of the South Vietnamese Army's training programs to counterguerrilla warfare. As had been the case during the 1950s, FM 31–20 (1951) and subsequent U.S. Army manuals heavily influenced the new training materials.[42]

In these materials and in their conversations with their counterparts, the Americans urged the South Vietnamese to abandon the "Maginot-type defensive attitude" inherited from the French and to employ fire and maneuver to find, fix, fight, and finish the enemy. Having learned from experience that linear sweeps by large formations rarely succeeded in bringing the enemy to battle, the Americans recommended that the South Vietnamese limit such undertakings to situations where intelligence was poor or a known base area needed to be combed. Otherwise, the Army preferred that the South Vietnamese employ extensive small-unit patrols as part of a wider clear-and-hold strategy. Such operations, the Army believed, offered the best way of keeping an area clear of enemy forces for a prolonged period. Small-unit infantry tactics, ambush and counterambush drills, march and camp security, patrolling, raiding, and village search techniques thus formed the core of the training program. American training materials also taught the South Vietnamese to employ traditional encirclement tactics to effect the enemy's destruction, supplemented by the new techniques of air-mobile warfare. U.S. advisers particularly emphasized night operations, and thanks to their efforts South Vietnamese regulations required that 50 percent of all tactical training be conducted at night. Conversely, advisory personnel also believed that the nature of the terrain and the enemy largely negated the value of large armored formations and heavy air and artillery bombardments, and therefore such tactics received subsidiary treatment in American-drafted training materials.[43]

While the training program focused on tactical issues, U.S. advisers were also careful to stress that the "most delicate and important job" of counterguerrilla warfare was isolating the guerrillas from the people, a task that the Americans believed required that the South Vietnamese Army gain the "trust, confidence and support of the people by showing in deeds as well as words that military forces do, in fact, help support and defend the people." Consequently, training materials emphasized the importance of good troop behavior and civic actions while discouraging uncompensated foraging, looting, and indiscriminate shooting. In fact, advisers warned the Vietnamese that "fire power is a double-edged weapon in a 'peoples' war,'" and that it must be carefully controlled to avoid undue harm to the population. For this reason, MACV recommended that unobserved artillery fire only be employed in areas that either were devoid of friendly civilians or were known to support the Viet Cong.[44]

Although General Williams had not been enthusiastic about diverting South Vietnamese soldiers to civic action work, his successors made it an increasing priority. The Army started sending civic action teams to Vietnam shortly after Eisenhower authorized the concept in 1960, and by 1962 these teams, together with a newly established civil affairs adviser within MAAG, Vietnam, had persuaded the Saigon government to reinvigorate its sagging civic action program. In 1963 the Army reinforced this effort by posting civic action and psyops advisers down to the division and province level. It also initiated what was perhaps the most popular combined civic action program of the war—the medical civic action program (MEDCAP). Under MEDCAP, teams of American and Vietnamese medical personnel traveled the countryside providing free services to civilians. By 1965 MEDCAP teams had dispensed over 4.5 million treatments in their effort to win over the Vietnamese people by treating their illnesses.[45]

Few soldiers believed that communism could be defeated by inoculations alone, and therefore the Army also communicated less benevolent ways of controlling the behavior of Vietnamese civilians. These ranged from relatively passive measures, like taking a census, to more intrusive restrictions over the movement of people and goods. When such measures were insufficient, South Vietnamese doctrine also permitted soldiers to destroy villages, livestock, and crops, heavy-handed techniques that could well backfire if not exercised with care.[46]

By the early 1960s America's prescription for South Vietnam was fairly well in place. At the national level, U.S. civil representatives pressed for reforms and economic development backed by more efficient administrative

A U.S. Army medic treats a Vietnamese child as part of the medical civic action program.

mechanisms to produce a well-integrated politico-military campaign. U.S. military advisers supported these efforts and sought to reinforce them by encouraging proper troop behavior and civic actions. Operationally, the Army counseled an aggressive campaign in which military units, freed from garrison work by the development of more efficient police and paramilitary forces, would take to the field to drive the guerrillas away from the population, thereby laying the basis for the gradual expansion of government control throughout the country. Over the years, both the Vietnamese and the Americans would tinker with this formula, adopting new organizational structures, dropping failed initiatives, and generally adjusting their activities to the ebb and flow of the war. Yet the core goals would remain fundamentally unchanged. Perhaps the best example of this continuity of purpose despite outward changes in organization and nomenclature had to do with the village security program, a program that lay at the core of all South Vietnamese pacification initiatives.[47]

Following precedents established by both sides during the Indochina War, the South Vietnamese government had always favored the idea of using traveling teams of officials to extend its control over the countryside. Lansdale's civic action teams were just the first example of numerous cadre schemes employed by the government over the years. Although the organization, composition, and mission of these teams varied, in general they all sought to organize local governments, form paramilitary defense groups, and otherwise rally the people to the government's cause through a combination of propaganda and civic action programs. Since the government lacked sufficient military forces to be everywhere at once and since many Vietnamese villages were not readily defensible, the government also adopted early on the idea of relocating people to places more readily controlled by the government. Such relocation and fortification schemes served the dual purpose of enhancing the security of the Vietnamese people while draining the countryside of the human sea on whom the guerrillas depended for their survival.

Although U.S. military advisers recognized the desirability of increasing the security of the population, the Vietnamese themselves took the lead on this issue. Based on French colonial precedents, Diem, without consulting the United States, began organizing defended hamlets, dubbed "agrovilles," in 1959. Three years later he launched an even more ambitious scheme when, inspired by British activities in Malaya, he initiated the Strategic Hamlet Program. Like the agrovilles, the primary purpose of the strategic hamlets was to separate the people from the guerrillas, although the program also paid lip service to the notion that the new hamlets would become vehicles for introducing improved amenities like schools and dispensaries. In theory, the strategic hamlets were to be constructed in an orderly fashion in accordance with an expanding oil-spot area security approach, though this was not observed in practice. The program lasted until 1964, only to be replaced by a succession of similar programs under different names, all of which sought to bring greater security, control, and public services to the countryside through the fortification of old villages and the establishment of new, more defensible ones.[48]

None of the many military and pacification initiatives launched by South Vietnam in the early 1960s succeeded in stemming the Communist tide. Saigon continued to resist American-proffered reforms, while corruption, incompetence, and a general lack of leadership at all levels impeded the execution of those programs the government attempted to undertake. Insufficiently trained cadres, inadequate resources, and poorly executed security measures likewise combined to undermine the various village defense schemes, many of which were unpopular as they imposed hardships and moved people away from ancestral lands. What gains were made were largely wiped out in late 1963 with the assassination of Diem, whose death initiated a year and a half of political turmoil that severely undermined most pacification programs. Even in the best of times, rivalry and poor communication between government ministries greatly impeded the prosecution of the counterinsurgency campaign. The magnitude of the problem was shown by the

South Vietnamese civilians build fortifications around their hamlet.

fact that by 1965 the government was fielding twenty-seven different types of pacification cadres and fifteen different armed forces, few of which were inclined to cooperate with the others.[49]

Meanwhile, the bureaucratic wrangling within the South Vietnamese government was complicated by similar divisions within the U.S. government. The result was that various U.S. agencies ended up pushing upon the South Vietnamese a plethora of competing initiatives that diffused the counterinsurgency effort, overburdened South Vietnam's already strained administrative apparatus, and reinforced the innate parochialism exhibited by Vietnamese institutions. Moreover, while most U.S. officials broadly accepted the basic tenets of counterinsurgency theory, they differed sharply on how best to implement them. The differences were myriad, but the divisions were not always drawn along bureaucratic lines. Indeed, one could usually find soldiers and civilians on each side of any particular issue.[50]

Perhaps the debate that had the most serious consequences for the prosecution of the war was that over the relative priority to be accorded to military versus political action. Civilian agencies tended to emphasize nation building and reform as the *sine qua non* of pacification, sometimes going so far as to assert that it should take precedence over the military campaign. This had been Ambassador Durbrow's philosophy, and many others shared this belief. MACV and most of the military establishment, on the other hand, tended to place military issues first. While acknowledging the ultimate importance of political affairs, the military argued that most civil initiatives would go for naught until some semblance of security had been achieved. As General Williams explained, "the truth is the population of South Vietnam, like any other, is more responsive to fear and force than to an improved standard of living. The conclusion is clear: the paramount consideration is to gain and maintain a superiority of force in all parts of the country. This is done by developing the military and police potential as the most urgent objective of our national program in Vietnam." McGarr agreed, stating that "while this is a Politico-Military situation, it has reached the stage where it must be recognized that a military solution must come before the political can be meaningful." Subsequent advisory chiefs adopted similar positions, as did some prominent civilians, including Ambassador Henry Cabot Lodge and senior pacification official Robert W. Komer. Nevertheless, the argument over whether political or military issues should receive the most emphasis was never fully resolved. When coupled with bureaucratic rivalries and personal jealousies, the debate impeded American efforts to put forward a coherent program. It also resulted in much wasted effort, as overly optimistic expectations as to the seductive power of material goods and internal improvements led allied agencies to dispense aid indiscriminately among the Vietnamese people. All too often the recipients were no more loyal after they had received American largess than they had been before, either because their loyalty could not be bought or because the government's inability to secure them from Viet Cong retaliation made risking one's life in exchange for a free medical exam impolitic.[51]

The dissipation of America's sizable nation-building effort on fallow or insecure ground was not the only factor impeding the effectiveness of the government's civic action program. Just as important were impediments embedded within South Vietnamese society. Many South Vietnamese officials found civic action work demeaning. Enlisted men were equally uninterested in performing civic action, in part because the army's poorly housed and paid soldiers saw little virtue in doing good deeds for people who in many cases were not only better off than they, but were actively helping the enemy as well. Ultimately, too many bureaucrats exhibited haughty and self-aggrandizing behavior, too many soldiers shot and foraged indiscriminately, and too many policemen engaged in extortion for the government's American-financed civic action programs to make a significant difference in the course of the war.[52]

These shortcomings in pacification might have been overcome by effective military action, for, although the government had failed to win the support of the population at large, a growing number of people were

As in many insurgencies, war and peace shared an uneasy coexistence in South Vietnam.

also becoming disenchanted by the Viet Cong's seemingly unquenchable thirst for food, money, and recruits. The military was, however, unable to stamp out the insurgency.

In the opinion of U.S. soldiers, the South Vietnamese Army's inability to contain the Viet Cong stemmed not from weaknesses in U.S. doctrine, but from the army's failure to implement American advice. There was much to substantiate such a view, as the Vietnamese diluted or ignored many American recommendations. Regulations notwithstanding, Vietnamese officers seldom trained or operated at night. They generally did not feel inclined to embrace calls for vigorous, offensive action, preferring instead the relative safety of their cantonments. Their passivity—exacerbated by heavy security commitments—dissipated the army's strength, sapped its morale, and ceded the initiative to the enemy.[53]

When they did act, South Vietnamese commanders favored caution over initiative and imagination. They clung to roads rather than delve into the bush and habitually returned to their bases each evening rather than remain in the field, thereby violating the principles of continuous contact and relentless pursuit. Vietnamese commanders also generally ignored admonitions that they saturate the countryside with small-unit patrols, preferring instead to operate in battalion or larger groups. These large-unit formations typically undertook ponderous linear sweeps toward fixed terrain objectives that the nimble guerrillas easily avoided. Once such an operation was completed—and 65 percent of South Vietnamese operations of battalion-size or larger lasted no more than one day—the troops would depart, leaving the Viet Cong to reassert their control over the recently "cleared" countryside and its inhabitants.[54]

Encirclement operations likewise usually failed to catch the enemy due to inadequacies of execution, the exigencies of terrain, and the excellence of the enemy's espionage service. Similarly, when the Vietnamese did make contact with the enemy, they usually failed to apply effectively American combined arms, fire, and maneuver concepts. Rather than closing aggressively with the enemy in the Fort Benning tradition, Vietnamese commanders preferred to sit back and let supporting air and artillery fires do the work of the infantryman. This might have worked had the South Vietnamese employed such tactics effectively, but all too often poorly executed operations allowed the enemy to escape potential firetraps. Moreover, government artillery resources were so limited and widely dispersed that they were rarely in a position to deal the enemy a decisive blow. In fact, a 1965 study indicated that the South Vietnamese Army rarely employed more than two artillery pieces at a time, with approximately half of all fire missions expending six or fewer rounds of ammunition. Under such circumstances, government artillery strikes served more as warning shots than as agents of destruction.[55]

While the government floundered, the Viet Cong prospered. From 3,000 guerrillas in 1959, the Viet Cong grew to 30,000 full-time regulars and 80,000 militiamen by 1965. To these, North Vietnam was rapidly adding thousands of regular soldiers and tons of military supplies. Thanks to the infusion of modern Soviet and Chinese materiel, by the mid-1960s Communist main force troops had more firepower at their disposal than the average South Vietnamese infantryman, let alone the more poorly equipped paramilitary soldier.[56]

Outfoxed, outmaneuvered, and increasingly outgunned, by the spring of 1965 the South Vietnamese government was losing the equivalent of one battalion and one district capital a week. With about half of South Vietnam already in Communist hands and with no end to the deterioration in sight, MACV Commander General William C. Westmoreland concluded reluctantly that the United States had no choice "other than to put our finger in the dike." President Lyndon B.

Johnson concurred, and in March 1965 he deployed the first ground combat units to Vietnam. Four years later, U.S. troop strength in theater would peak at 543,000 men.[57]

America's direct military involvement succeeded in stopping the hemorrhage and in inflicting significant losses on the enemy. Yet the war continued as the North Vietnamese offset allied deployments with troop infusions of their own. Then, in early 1968, the Communists struck back with a major offensive that, while initially successful, was ultimately repulsed with heavy casualties. The failed Tet offensive proved to be a turning point in the war. As had occurred in Korea in 1950, many southern cadres had come out of hiding to assist the general offensive, and when that effort collapsed, they became vulnerable to allied countermeasures. Moreover, local Viet Cong forces bore the brunt of the offensive, and their high casualties left the village Communist apparatus dangerously exposed. The resulting weakness of the local Communist infrastructure, when combined with the increasing reluctance of a war-weary population to support a cause whose chances for victory now seemed much diminished, meant that the Communists had to rely increasingly on force and intimidation to obtain men and sustenance from the population, a situation that further eroded their popularity with the people.[58]

The United States recognized the opportunity and moved to exploit it. Assisted by the shock that the 1968 offensive had given senior South Vietnamese leaders, the United States succeeded in coaxing the government to make some significant reforms. Included among these were a more effective manpower mobilization system and a major land reform initiative that by 1973 had distributed roughly 2.5 million acres of land to previously landless peasants. Meanwhile, MACV redoubled its efforts at improving the security situation. With the Viet Cong reeling from their defeat, MACV was able to shift the weight of the allied military effort into operations that directly supported pacification. The result was that government control over the countryside steadily grew after 1968, with the Communists receiving a concomitant decline in support.[59]

One element that contributed to the government's improved performance after 1968 was a series of measures undertaken between 1964 and 1967 to reduce the bureaucratic wrangling that had often undermined allied pacification efforts. After the government consolidated its many cadre and village fortification schemes into a coordinated Revolutionary Development program in 1965, the United States put its own house in order by placing MACV in charge of most U.S. pacification support activities.[60] This step, which was in full accord with the Army's long-established view that unity of command and politico-military coordination were essential in counterinsurgency, was fiercely resisted by civilian agencies as an unwarranted erosion of their institutional autonomy. Nevertheless, the establishment of a single manager for pacification in the guise of the Office of the Assistant Chief of Staff for Civil Operations and Revolutionary Development Support (CORDS) improved the orchestration and presentation of U.S. advice and assistance on pacification-related programs. Headed by a civilian who served as a deputy to the MACV commander, CORDS' military-heavy staff applied itself to nearly every aspect of pacification, from civic action and propaganda to amnesty programs and paramilitary defense.[61]

CORDS particularly championed MACV's traditional viewpoint that security was essential to pacification, and it devoted the vast majority of its resources toward improving the day-to-day safety of Vietnamese civilians through a variety of police, paramilitary, village defense, and counterintelligence programs. Through its auspices, the government's paramilitary forces, which usually equaled or exceeded the South Vietnamese Army in numbers, grew in capability, eventually achieving parity with the Viet Cong in terms of weaponry. In conjunction with AID and the CIA, CORDS also redoubled U.S. efforts at inducing South Vietnam's police and intelligence agencies to ferret out the Communist infrastructure through an initiative called the Phoenix program. The resilience of the Viet Cong underground and continued disarray in the government's police, judicial, and intelligence systems limited the Phoenix program's achievements. Nevertheless, through the cumulative weight of military and counterinfrastructure activities, the South Vietnamese and their U.S. allies gradually whittled away the strength of the Viet Cong. By 1973 U.S. analysts estimated that southerners constituted only about 17 percent of all Communist combat troops and 50 percent of all enemy administrative and service personnel in South Vietnam. What had once been a flourishing southern-based insurgency had given way to a faltering war effort whose continued prosecution was possible only by the infusion of men and materiel from North Vietnam.[62]

While South Vietnam had made significant headway in squelching the insurgency after 1968, its achievements were not without serious blemishes. To begin with, many of the reforms proffered by the South Vietnamese government proved to be hollow. Despite decades of prodding, South Vietnam's leaders were no more effective in 1974 than they had been in 1954. With the exception of the belated land reform law, the government had made little progress in alleviating the nation's

A South Vietnamese Army cultural drama group woos villagers as part of the battle for the hearts and minds of the population.

many social ills. What progress had been made was largely offset by ravaging inflation fueled by U.S. military spending. Meanwhile, military actions on both sides had killed and maimed over a million civilians and dislocated millions more. Some of these refugees had willingly fled their homes to escape the Communists. The allies had forcibly relocated others—several hundred thousand over the course of the war—to separate them from the guerrillas. The vast majority of refugees, however, were people who left their homes to avoid the hazards posed by military operations. Ultimately, over half of South Vietnam's population left their homes at some point during the conflict, a situation that imposed enormous burdens on the country and compelled the allies to divert much of their nation-building resources to humanitarian relief.[63]

Problems pertaining to the civil side of the war were matched by deficits on the security side, where once again ostensible gains proved superficial. Sixteen thousand advisers and vast quantities of materiel could not easily correct the harmful effects of continued maladministration within the ranks of South Vietnam's security services. More often than not, the government's military victories after 1965 had been achieved as the result of the application of American combat power, rather than through the actions of the government's security apparatus. Even the improved level of security enjoyed by a growing number of civilians was not all that it seemed. For despite the allies' stated goal of bringing security to the people, in reality a large proportion of the people added to the rolls of those living in "secured" areas were refugees who had relocated—either voluntarily or otherwise—from Viet Cong areas into government-controlled enclaves. Many of these people were impoverished, so that while their ability to aid the enemy was restricted, few could be counted as enthusiastic subjects of the government. Senior U.S. and Vietnamese officials were cognizant of this fact and attempted to direct psychological and humanitarian programs to relieve suffering and build greater support for the government among the people, but all too often the resources were inadequate and the government's administrative machinery too frail, corrupt, or uncaring to carry out this policy effectively.[64]

All of these shortcomings might not have been important had the allies been able to cut the insurgents off from their northern benefactor. Isolated from external support, the southern insurgents could no more have survived allied military and security programs than the guerrillas of South Korea or Greece before them. Such isolation was not achieved, however, with the result that the South Vietnamese government was never able to secure large sections of the countryside. The decision by the United States and South Vietnam's other allies to withdraw their combat forces in the early 1970s without having first evicted the North Vietnamese from South Vietnam thus left the Saigon government in an extremely precarious position. From an all-time high of twenty-two allied divisions, by 1973 South Vietnam had only its own thirteen divisions left to face the eleven divisions and twenty-four regiments North Vietnam still maintained in the South.[65]

Had the government made better use of two decades worth of American support it might have been able to survive. Instead, the proficiency of nearly all South Vietnamese military, paramilitary, police, and intelligence services declined noticeably with the withdrawal of U.S. advisers and support units. Crash efforts by MACV prior to the withdrawal to improve South Vietnam's military capability so that it could stand up to the North Vietnamese Army likewise fell short, in part because, as General Williams had feared, years of relatively static and disjointed territorial security duty had kept the South Vietnamese Army from developing the type of command, control, and administrative apparatus needed to conduct large-scale conventional operations on a sustained basis. Once the United States began to curtail its financial and material assistance, South Vietnam's days were numbered. The final blow came in 1975, when the North Vietnamese Army overran South Vietnam in a lightning offensive led by tanks and heavy artillery, an offensive not unlike the one which had almost extinguished South Korea a quarter-century before. Williams' nightmare had finally come true.[66]

The Asian Experience Outside Indochina

The triumphal entry of North Vietnamese troops into Saigon in April 1975 was the last act of the thirty-year civil war that had racked Indochina since 1945. Shortly before South Vietnam's denouement, the two other non-Communist states that had emerged from the old French colony—Laos and Cambodia—also fell to indigenous guerrillas backed by North Vietnamese regulars. Although the civil wars in Indochina accounted for the lion's share of America's overseas counterinsurgency expenditures between 1955 and 1975, the United States had also worked to staunch the flow of revolution throughout the rest of Asia. The degree of American activity and the methods used varied from country to country, but for the most part U.S. soldiers acted in accordance with the basic principles embodied in U.S. doctrine.

Throughout Asia, U.S. officials preached a creed of social and economic modernization, military civic action, and, when necessary, counterguerrilla warfare. In Southwest Asia, Army advisers enthusiastically supported Turkey's use of its armed forces as a school of the nation. Under this program, the Turkish military taught conscripts how to read and write as well as technical skills, like typing and automotive mechanics, that they could use after completing their military service. Even more impressive was the Iranian military's civic action program. Initiated by U.S. advisers in the 1950s, the program represented a broad-spectrum use of the military as a nation-building agent. In addition to constructing roads and providing disaster relief, the Iranian military strove to improve its public image by eliminating corruption and brutality from within its ranks. It also posted civic action officers to every battalion in the army and created three special organizations—the Literacy, Sanitary and Health, and Rural Development Corps—that worked to improve the life of the ordinary Iranian. Together with the counterguerrilla tactics taught by U.S. military advisers, the Iranian civic action program helped the shah pacify rebellious tribes and push forward an ambitious program of land reform, industrialization, and modernization. So effective was the Iranian program that the U.S. Army considered it a textbook example of American principles in action.[67]

Unfortunately, the actual results of American-sponsored civic action programs were less notable. In Turkey, discharged conscripts trained as typists frequently returned to villages devoid of typewriters. Meanwhile, the shah of Iran's strenuous efforts to transform his country into a modern, industrialized, and Westernized society eventually created a cultural and religious backlash that resulted in his overthrow in 1979 and the establishment of a radical Islamic republic that was extremely hostile to the United States. Much to the chagrin of U.S. theorists, neither the shah's ambitious land reform program nor his patronage of a rising middle class saved him from the violent social forces unleashed by the modernization process.[68]

The situation in East Asia was equally mixed. American-backed developmental programs frequently succeeded in promoting modernization, but all too often failed to redress the underlying factors that might spawn unrest. U.S. social engineers were particularly unsuccessful in promoting democracy, social equality, and apolitical military institutions. Ruthless action rather than reform crushed Indonesia's Communists, while the hollowness of Magsaysay's reforms and the corruption of his successors led to a renewed Communist insurgency and ethnic rebellions in the Philippines in the late 1960s, conflicts that continue to the present day.[69]

The circumstances in South Korea were somewhat different. There, rapid modernization engendered social dislocations that, when coupled with festering tensions between rightists, leftists, and proponents of greater democratization, seemed to create fertile ground for Communist activity. On the other hand, the nation's growing prosperity, when linked with the effects of a land reform program that by 1966 had virtually eliminated tenant farming, produced a mixture of complacency and pride that dampened revolutionary sentiment.

Although an indigenous Communist underground movement persisted in South Korea, it had never recovered from the defeats of 1948–1953 and lacked the ability to overthrow the government on its own. Recognizing this fact, North Korea's Kim Il Sung had continued to send agitators into the South, either by sea or by land across the heavily defended Demilitarized Zone (DMZ) that separated the two Koreas. By the mid-1960s these actions had failed to undermine the Seoul government, and consequently Kim decided to press the issue further. He escalated military activity along the inter-Korean border and increased the infiltration, not just of individual agents, but of entire units of saboteurs and guerrillas, into the South. In addition to taking direct action against the U.S.-led United Nations contingent that guarded the DMZ, Kim hoped the infiltrators would form the nucleus of a renewed insurgency that would drive the Americans out of Korea, undermine the staunchly anti-Communist government of President Park Chung Hee, and pave the way for the reunification of the peninsula under

Communist control. With the United States increasingly distracted by the war in Vietnam, the time seemed opportune.[70] (*Map 12*)

After thirteen years of relative quiet guarding the inter-Korean border, the U.S. Eighth Army received a rude introduction to Kim's revived ambitions on 2 November 1966, when North Korean troops ambushed a U.S. patrol south of the Demilitarized Zone, killing six Americans. As the infiltrations escalated, additional clashes occurred in the spring of 1967. While northern infiltrators ambushed U.S. and South Korean patrols, mined roads, and bombed an American barracks near the DMZ, others moved farther south in an effort to link up with indigenous Communists and spark renewed peasant uprisings.

Although UN defenses along the border were well suited to blunting a conventional attack, South Korea's rugged terrain and long coastline made stopping small bands of infiltrators exceedingly difficult. On the other hand, the commander of UN forces in Korea, U.S. Army General Charles H. Bonesteel III, enjoyed several advantages over General Westmoreland in Vietnam. South Korea's border with the North, while mountainous, was well mapped, heavily guarded, and only about 243 kilometers long. Moreover, thanks to a system worked out during the Korean War, Bonesteel had operational control over the South Korean Army. This arrangement gave him much more latitude and authority than Westmoreland in shaping indigenous actions. Although not without its problems, South Korea was also a much more homogenous nation than South Vietnam, with an abler military, a stronger governmental apparatus, and a history of successful counterinsurgency operations. These factors, when coupled with the overall weakness exhibited by the South's indigenous insurgent movement, would place South Korea on a very different course from its sister Asian republic.

Bonesteel adopted a twofold approach to the irregular threat. The first element was to tighten security along South Korea's borders. In addition to stepping up patrol, ambush, and counterinfiltration training, he erected a new defensive barrier just behind the DMZ. The new barrier consisted of a chain link fence topped with barbed wire, behind which lay a dirt strip to reveal footprints and a defoliated zone to provide improved observation and fields of fire. High tech sensors, minefields, observation posts, and regular patrols backed by rapid reaction forces rounded out the system. Although it could not stop every enemy incursion, the barrier presented hostile intruders with a daunting, multilayered gauntlet that greatly increased the ability of UN forces to thwart infiltrators.

While Bonesteel was fairly successful in sealing South Korea's border, he was less successful in stopping infiltration by sea. Twenty-eight

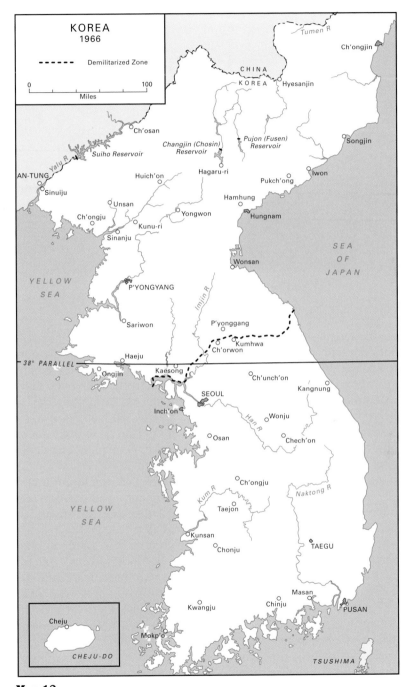

KOREA
1966

- - - Demilitarized Zone

0 ———————— 100
Miles

Tumen R.
Ch'ongjin
CHINA
KOREA
Hyesanjin
Songjin
Ch'osan
Changjin (Chosin) Reservoir
Pujon (Fusen) Reservoir
Suiho Reservoir
AN-TUNG
Yalu R.
Iwon
Huich'on
Hagaru-ri
Pukch'ong
Sinuiju
Unsan
Hamhung
Ch'ongju
Yongwon
Hungnam
Kunu-ri
Sinanju
YELLOW SEA
P'YONGYANG
Wonsan
SEA OF JAPAN
Imjin R.
Sariwon
P'yonggang
Kumhwa
Ch'orwon
Haeju
38° PARALLEL
Kaesong
Ch'unch'on
Ongjin
Kangnung
SEOUL
Inch'on
Wonju
Han R.
Osan
Chech'on
Ch'ongju
Kum R.
Naktong R.
Taejon
YELLOW SEA
Kunsan
TAEGU
Chonju
Masan
Kwangju
Chinju
PUSAN
Cheju
Mokp'o
CHEJU-DO
TSUSHIMA

MAP 12

U.S. soldiers patrol the barrier fence bordering the Korean Demilitarized Zone.

times the length of its land frontier, South Korea's coastline presented infiltrators with many havens. A barrier system was out of the question, and the small South Korean Navy did not have the means to patrol Korea's heavily trafficked coastal waters effectively. Moreover, unlike the Demilitarized Zone, which was essentially an Army preserve, the protection of Korea's coasts was complicated by the fact that it was of necessity an interagency affair, in which South Korean military, police, intelligence, and political entities all needed to cooperate. Such cooperation took time to achieve. Eventually South Korea would develop a multilayered coastal anti-infiltration system that employed aircraft, ships, radar, coast watchers, village defense units, and military reaction forces. Though increasingly successful at detecting infiltrators, this system was never as tight as that developed along the DMZ.[71]

Side by side with efforts to stop infiltrators was a second major element, a counterinsurgency campaign in South Korea's interior. Here Bonesteel's influence was less direct. Although his position as UN commander gave him operational control over the Korean armed forces during periods of conflict, Bonesteel generally confined himself to providing advice when managing Korea's internal war. Such a stance reflected both respect for Korean sovereignty and American reticence about becoming directly involved in the internal affairs of other nations. It likewise mirrored command arrangements during the first Korean insurgency of 1948–1954, as well as similar arrangements

South Korean troops debark from a U.S. Army helicopter during a counterguerrilla operation in South Korea in 1968.

in South Vietnam, where the United States devoted the majority of U.S. military might to the conventional battle while letting the indigenous government bear the burden of pacification. With the exception of KMAG advisers and a few Special Forces training teams, Bonesteel would keep the U.S. Army in Korea firmly fixed along the DMZ to face the external threat posed by the North Korean Army and its special infiltration units.[72]

Many of the problems South Korea experienced during the initial phases of the insurgency mirrored those from the 1948–1954 period. As in the 1940s and 1950s, the Korean police bore primary responsibility for the counterguerrilla war, as the bulk of South Korea's Army was deployed along the border. And, as in that first conflict, rival police, intelligence, and military bureaucracies initially waged an uncoordinated campaign in which ad hoc task forces chased after guerrillas on a piecemeal basis. Drawing on both their own experiences as well as American advice, the Koreans gradually moved to correct these deficiencies. They mobilized rear area security divisions from the reserves and created special counterinfiltration battalions to assist in maintaining security in the interior. In 1969 the Koreans added two ranger brigades to their force structure, deploying one each to the two traditional hotbeds of insurgent activity in South Korea, the Taebaek and Chiri mountains. Meanwhile, the government resurrected two institutions from the first guerrilla war—the combat police and the civilian paramilitary forces. South Korea's paramilitary forces consisted of 200,000 unarmed coast watchers and an armed element known as the Homeland Defense Reserve. Built around a core of ex-servicemen, the homeland defense force numbered approximately two million men and women. The force guarded villages, provided intelligence, and mobilized the citizenry in support of the government. Finally, Park created mechanisms to ensure greater cooperation among his disparate security elements. The United States supported these endeavors with advice, training, and an infusion of new equipment, to include radios for paramilitary units.[73]

While Bonesteel worked to strengthen South Korea's security apparatus, he did not neglect the softer side of counterinsurgency work—pacification. With American assistance, the South Korean Army revitalized its long-standing civic action program. Government troops dug wells, constructed schools, and undertook other actions to win the favor of the rural populace. Of particular note were the "medical/enlightenment teams," which traveled the countryside dispensing pills and propaganda in an effort to inoculate the population against communism. Meanwhile, in 1968 the South Korean government began building a series of "reconstruction villages" south of the Demilitarized Zone. Populated by armed ex-soldiers and their families on the model of Israeli kibbutzim, these settlements created yet another obstacle through which would-be infiltrators would have to move before they could attack Korean society at large. The United States also supplemented the venerable Armed Forces Assistance to Korea program with new initiatives designed to foster friendship between Koreans and U.S. servicemen.[74]

By the end of 1969 the war against Kim Il Sung's second major attempt to subvert the government of South Korea had been won. Progressively fewer infiltrators succeeded in penetrating South Korea's land and sea barriers, while Korea's intelligence agencies, backed by a widespread network of military and police patrols, civilian informers, and paramilitary groups, snagged many of the remaining interlopers. Although the North had scored some stinging blows against the United States, ambushing some patrols, capturing the U.S. Navy intelligence ship *Pueblo* in 1968, and downing a U.S. Navy aircraft in 1969, it had failed to destabilize the Park regime. In a campaign that had largely followed the basic precepts of U.S. counterinsurgency doctrine, the United States and South Korea successfully thwarted Kim Il Sung's attempt to turn the Republic of Korea into a second Vietnam.

While U.S. advice must be credited with a win in South Korea, the situation was murkier in Thailand. As one of the few nations in Asia to have escaped colonial rule and the ravages of world war, Thailand did not appear to be a strong candidate for Communist subversion. Thai culture was not conducive to revolutionary activism, and Thailand's Communist Party had little mass appeal. Nevertheless, Thailand was neither exempt from the stresses of modernization nor devoid of social problems. Economic disparities, oligarchic rule, limited opportunities for social mobility, and ethnic tensions offered conditions suitable for exploitation. Of these, the last was especially important. The Communist Party Thailand (CPT) was itself dominated by people of Chinese extraction, while many of the social and economic injustices that existed in Thailand fell most heavily upon the ethnic minorities who lived along Thailand's borders. Indeed, in many respects the insurgent threat in Thailand was not so much a national movement as it was a collection of several loosely connected, regionally centered insurgencies composed primarily of ethnic minorities, most notably Meo tribesmen in the north, Laotians and Vietnamese in the northeast, and Muslims and Malays in the south. The limited appeal of revolutionary propaganda among ethnic Thais would ultimately prove to be one of the insurgency's greatest weaknesses.[75] (*Map 13*)

Inspired by the revolutionary philosophy of Mao and Ho Chi Minh, the Thai Communist Party moved progressively in the early 1960s toward launching a revolutionary struggle. With the help of China and North Vietnam, which provided training and arms, the CPT officially embraced a strategy of rural revolutionary warfare in 1961. In 1962 the Communist Party established a remote jungle headquarters in northeastern Thailand and stepped up efforts to create a united front with other dissident groups against the government.

Anxious to prevent the Communist contagion that was sweeping Indochina from engulfing Thailand, the United States urged the Thai government to take prophylactic measures against the nascent insurrection. Although few Thai officials shared America's sense of urgency, they were favorably disposed to Anglo-American counterinsurgency theories that emphasized socioeconomic development and improved security. Labeled Civilian-Police-Military, the Thai program recognized the importance of crafting a well-integrated national response to the threat of insurgency. As the order of the words implied, the Thais believed that civilian and police measures took precedence over military action, with economic development playing the preeminent role as both prophylactic and cure for the Communist malaise.[76]

In 1962 Thailand created a National Security Command to coordinate and direct government-wide counterinsurgency efforts. The command's primary instruments in the emerging battle for the hearts

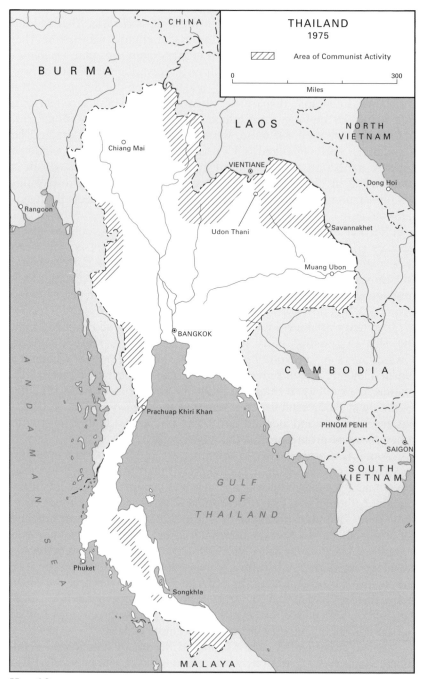

MAP 13

and minds of the Thai peasantry were several American-funded Mobile Development Units. Each unit consisted of about 120 civilian and military technicians who brought social, economic, and construction services to insurgency-prone areas. Thailand also created a civilian Department of Community Development in 1962 that sent government workers into the countryside to address local needs. Other civilian agencies soon joined the outreach program, as did the Royal Thai Army, which in 1963 established the first of several Special Operations Centers, 84-man units that supplemented their border patrol work with civic and psychological actions. Still, the focus of U.S.-Thai efforts remained firmly in the civil sphere, with AID and the CIA lavishing considerable attention on the Thai National Police and its elite sub-element, the Border Patrol Police, which like the Special Operations Centers sought to gain control over the nation's fractious borders through a combination of intelligence, security, and civic activities. In 1965 the United States reinforced these efforts by funding an Accelerated Rural Development program. The program's primary focus was road building, but it also supported a variety of other initiatives, including farmer co-ops, youth activities, mobile medical teams, and potable water projects.[77]

Unfortunately, none of these measures succeeded in preventing the development of an insurgency in Thailand. In 1965 Thai Communists declared a people's war of liberation and initiated guerrilla attacks on security forces. The outbreak of violence shocked both the Thais, who had downplayed the threat of an overt insurgency, and the Americans, who had believed that the prescribed civil-police approach was working. Disturbed, the allies redoubled their efforts. The government created a Communist Suppression Operations Command to coordinate civilian, police, and military activities at the national level, while subordinate regional and provincial organizations performed similar functions in areas of active insurgency. It organized Joint Security Centers to coordinate the collection and analysis of intelligence. With the help of American largess, Thai security forces continued to expand their nation-building activities, building 150 schools, 463 kilometers of road, 101 bridges, 49 irrigation canals, 21 wells, 2 regional development centers, and scores of medical aid stations by 1968. Finally, at American urging, the Thais greatly increased efforts to provide security to the population living in insurgent areas. In some cases this meant encouraging people to leave guerrilla-infested regions. In others, particularly in the north, the government forcibly resettled civilians. Most importantly, AID and the CIA worked to expand the number and capability of Thai police and paramilitary forces.

A Thai Mobile Development Unit accompanied by an
American adviser visits a village.

Initially, the government relied primarily on the police rather than the military to combat the insurgents. The police arrested suspects, established stations in remote villages, and conducted short-duration sweeps. Still the insurgency grew, and by 1967 the army was playing a more active role. In the northeast, the Thais attempted to surround guerrilla base areas with paramilitary-secured villages backed by rapid reaction forces. In the north, the military adopted a more punitive approach, attacking villages and burning crops. In all guerrilla areas the army conducted occasional search-and-destroy operations, usually on a small scale but occasionally in division strength. These activities frequently failed to produce decisive results. A lack of aggressiveness hampered operations, as did the Thai government's distaste for suffering casualties. When fighting the Meo, whom the Thais regarded as savages, the military was also prone to engage in heavy-handed tactics that alienated the population. Moreover, the army's interest in the counterguerrilla war was spasmodic, as the military still preferred to let the police and civic action programs carry most of the burden. Conventional defense duties, coupled with the fact that Thai authorities kept much of the army tied down around Bangkok as counter-coup troops, further constrained military activities, as did financial considerations that limited the amount of time Thailand could afford to put its soldiers in the field. The result was that prior to the early 1970s, the army never committed more than 25 percent of its strength to counterinsurgency activities. Most military operations were of short duration and failed to establish an effective government presence in guerrilla regions.[78]

In 1973 student and labor unrest in Bangkok introduced a period of greater democracy in Thailand. The experiment was turbulent, however, and failed to produce any reduction in the insurgent movement that had grown steadily from a few hundred guerrillas in 1965 to around 6,500 combatants by 1974. Thanks to Chinese aid, the guerrillas were well led, well trained, and frequently better armed than government troops. The situation took a further turn for the worse in 1976, when a coup ushered in a reactionary regime that reversed Thailand's tentative steps toward a more democratic system. Thousands of leftist and prodemocracy students fled to the bush, swelling insurgent ranks to over 12,000 guerrillas. Though the government remained in control throughout most of the country, the war was clearly not going well.[79]

The United States provided military assistance to Thailand through the Joint U.S. Military Assistance Group, which in 1962 was subordinated to the Military Assistance Command, Thailand (MACTHAI). By the late 1960s the American presence in Thailand had grown to about 49,000 military personnel, the vast majority of whom provided logistical and air support for the wars in Laos and Vietnam. Other than performing limited civic action activities around their bases, most Americans played no role in Thailand's internal disorders. The U.S. Army's contribution to Thailand's internal defenses included an engineer battalion that built roads, a psychological operations company that performed propaganda work, and about 130 advisers who helped train the Royal Thai Army for both conventional and counterguerrilla missions. In 1966 the Army also posted a Special Forces company in Thailand to provide counterinsurgency training to army and police personnel. Although U.S. advisers were permitted to accompany Thai units during field operations at the battalion level, they did so as observers only, and except for a brief period in 1966–1967 when U.S. Army helicopter pilots flew transport missions, U.S. military personnel did not participate in internal security operations.[80]

The advice American military officials gave Thailand generally conformed to both U.S. national counterinsurgency policy and U.S. Army doctrine. Mirroring the tenets of contemporary counterinsurgency philosophy, U.S. military officers accepted the notion that the best way to respond to Thailand's incipient insurgency was through a coordinated, government-wide program of socioeconomic development backed by improved police, paramilitary, intelligence, and military systems. Thailand's conventionally oriented officer corps initially

A U.S. adviser instructs Thai soldiers in counterguerrilla warfare.

showed little interest in counterinsurgency, but with JUSMAG's help the Thais established a counterguerrilla training program based on American models. Recognizing that "machines of war can conquer land, but communist ideology aims at conquering people," JUSMAG emphasized the importance of integrated politico-military operations, in which police, military, and intelligence activities would be blended with population-control and civil improvement measures to separate the population from the guerrillas. Small-unit patrols, ambushes, deception, and night operations formed the backbone of JUSMAG's tactical precepts. On the other hand, JUSMAG warned in 1961 that "massive uses of firepower . . . large armored formations and air bombardment; and massive logistical support to include heavy wheeled, track and air transportation" were "not useable in anti-guerrilla warfare."[81]

The Army's influence was limited, however. Graham Martin, the U.S. ambassador to Thailand from 1963 to 1967, was anxious to avoid an over militarization of American policy in Thailand, a phenomenon that he and many other civilians believed had occurred in Vietnam. Consequently, Martin made the CIA the lead agency in most counterinsurgency matters. Moreover, unlike many other ambassadors in the 1960s, Martin moved beyond the rather loose coordinative efforts of most country teams and imposed a single manager for American counterinsurgency programs in Thailand. Although the Army traditionally supported greater unity of effort, in this case the arrangement worked to limit its influence. Martin appointed a veteran CIA official with experience in Vietnam, Peer de Silva, as his special assistant for counterinsurgency, and together they kept a tight rein over American military activities in Thailand. They severely limited contact between U.S. officers and senior Thai officials and restricted MACTHAI's involvement in Thai counterinsurgency programs. Thus, while U.S. Army personnel acquainted the Thai Army with American doctrine, they had comparatively little direct influence on the broader course of the counterinsurgency campaign.[82]

Many embassy civilians considered the tethering of the U.S. military establishment in Thailand to have been a bureaucratic triumph. It did not, however, spare the counterinsurgency effort from discord. Civilian agencies were just as jealous of their bureaucratic prerogatives as the military, and their deep resentment of the single manager concept eventually led to the abolishment of the special assistant for counterinsurgency post after only a few years. Furthermore, in Thailand as elsewhere, U.S. officials soon found that the national consensus over counterinsurgency was broad but not deep, and throughout the 1960s U.S. diplomatic, intelligence, economic, and police personnel were constantly at loggerheads with each other over the details of the Thai campaign.

Bureaucratic rivalries among U.S. officials were matched by similar tensions among the Thais. The creation of coordinative bodies notwithstanding, Thai government agencies frequently expended more energy maneuvering for power and prestige than they did fighting the enemy. The resultant discord between competing political, philosophical, and bureaucratic agendas produced a confusing medley of overlapping and competing programs. By 1974 the Thai government had launched approximately 120 different socioeconomic development programs, initiated 12 major security initiatives, and organized 20 different types of paramilitary forces. As in South Vietnam, such a cacophony of programs merely dissipated the impact of U.S. aid.[83]

Continuous infighting was not the only problem. As in all advisory experiences, U.S. soldiers and diplomats were often frustrated by the unwillingness of Thai officials to take their recommendations to heart. Despite American advice and their own doctrine, Thai security forces occasionally abused civilians, fired indiscriminately, and demonstrated other undesirable behaviors. Inertia, funding limitations, and programmatic problems likewise had adverse roles to play. Yet the lackluster performance of the Thai campaign also revealed some defects in U.S. policy.

If the U.S. government's inability to impose discipline over its counterinsurgency programs was one aspect of the problem, America's efforts in Thailand also suffered from the opposite defect, a tendency of many officials to apply a single, universal formula regardless of local circumstances. In Thailand, efforts by U.S. civilians to impose their view that insurgency was largely a civil and police, not a military, problem ran headlong into the hard realities of Thai politics, which demanded the careful balancing of rival bureaucratic interests, particularly between the army and police. Failure to adjust to this reality caused many U.S.-backed programs to wither on the vine.[84]

Many of the assumptions of U.S. social engineers also proved false. Contrary to theory, Thai efforts to expand the government's presence in the countryside failed to stop the spread of Communist influence. In part this was because the $223.8 million the United States and Thailand spent on development programs between 1960 and 1974 was insufficient to address Thailand's socioeconomic needs. At times the concentration of aid on a few model villages encouraged feelings of jealousy and discontent among neighboring towns that did not receive such attention. Yet even villages that received aid did not always respond in a positive manner. This was because development administrators, anxious to accomplish something, often ignored doctrinal precepts about the importance of winning community collaboration and imposed projects without taking into consideration the needs, desires, or capabilities of people themselves. Villagers did not necessarily enjoy the greater attention lavished upon them by officials either. Indeed, one of the ironies of the Thai program is that government outreach efforts actually created more dissent than had existed before, both by increasing contact between the rural population and inept officials and by making the peasants more aware of their socioeconomic backwardness, thereby creating a revolution of rising expectations where none had previously existed.[85]

Although beyond the chronological scope of this book, Thailand eventually defeated the insurgency in the early 1980s. The Thais would take great pride that they defeated the insurgents after the United States withdrew virtually all of its military and police personnel in the mid-1970s. Many Thais believed that their victory resulted from their abandoning U.S. doctrine, with one story claiming that the high command burned all its U.S. textbooks. While the Thais had a right to be proud of their accomplishment, the fact was that they continued to embrace the counterinsurgency concept that Americans had helped fashion in the 1960s and early 1970s. Nor did they ever free themselves from the influence of U.S. doctrine, as U.S. Army manuals continued to be standard fare in Thailand's military schools, most of which were themselves closely patterned on their U.S. counterparts.

Despite the apocryphal book burning, Thai success was not so much due to the development of completely new ideas than to the fact that the Thais eventually became more proficient at executing the old

U.S. Army engineers build a school in Thailand.

ones. Over time the Thais initiated a more effective village government and self-defense program that expanded the government's presence in disaffected areas in an oil-spot fashion. The Army became more circumspect in using firepower, the paramilitaries became more effective, and government coordination of the total counterinsurgency effort improved. Although the government cracked down hard on dissidents, it also offered the insurgents amnesty, stepped up its propaganda initiatives, and undertook measures to improve the quality of the officials that it sent into dissident areas. None of these endeavors were flawless, and many of the old problems continued to plague Thai efforts. Nevertheless, the Thais eventually became sufficiently proficient at implementing the doctrinal concepts of the 1960s to achieve a significant, if belated, victory over the insurgents.[86]

While socioeconomic development remained an integral part of post-1975 Thai counterinsurgency efforts, it was not in itself the cause of victory. Thailand was ultimately much more successful in improving rural security through military and paramilitary measures than it was in improving rural administration and development. The Thais also recognized that many U.S. aid programs had been misguided in that they had spent millions of dollars trying to correct economic ills that, while real, were not always the true cause of unrest. Instead, the Thais decided that political and social issues were more important factors than mere poverty alone. Ultimately, their success rested not on the introduction of significant socioeconomic reforms, but on political measures designed to rebuild a consensus within the country (which continued to be dominated by military men who rejected Western-style democracy), limited civic actions, and extensive security and population-control activities.[87]

There was, however, one other factor in the government's eventual success—perhaps the most important. In an odd twist of fate, America's defeat in Vietnam and the simultaneous triumph of Communist forces in Cambodia and Laos undermined the insurgency in Thailand. The fall of Thailand's neighbors to communism finally galvanized the government to take its own insurgency seriously. The genocide campaign that the Communists instituted in Cambodia particularly aided the Thai government in that it discredited communism in the eyes of many Thais. Finally, squabbles among Thailand's Communist neighbors fatally weakened the Thai Communist movement. Vietnam's 1978 invasion of Cambodia and China's subsequent falling out with Vietnam led to a serious division in Communist ranks. The war in Cambodia—which at times spilled over the border into Thailand itself—stirred Thai nationalism and reinforced the government's claim that the Thai Communist Party was the tool of foreign aggressors. The turmoil in Cambodia also cut the guerrillas off from one of their traditional external sanctuaries. Meanwhile, China and Laos, anxious to find allies against Vietnamese expansionism, courted the Thai government by terminating their aid to Thailand's Communist Party.

The loss of external aid and sanctuaries proved just as catastrophic for Thai Communists as it had for the Greek Communists in 1949. Divided internally between rival Leninist and Maoist camps, increasingly perceived by the population as being foreign puppets, and cut off from outside assistance, the Communists withered under the government's suppression campaign. Discouraged and disillusioned, many of the students who had joined the insurgency in the mid-1970s took advantage of government amnesty offers and surrendered. Population security efforts, backed by civic and psychological actions, increasingly cut the guerrillas off from the inhabitants, while a series of major offensives in the late 1970s and early 1980s overran one guerrilla base area after another. With no place left to run, guerrilla numbers plummeted, and by the mid-1980s there were only a few hundred armed dissidents left in the bush.[88]

The Advisory Experience in Retrospect

The unsatisfactory results achieved in Thailand by 1975, together with the fall of Cambodia, Laos, and South Vietnam to communism in that same year, led many commentators to conclude that U.S. policy in general, and Army doctrine in particular, was fatally flawed. Yet the three unfortunate stepchildren of French Indochina were also the only U.S. allies between 1950 and 1975 to fall to Communist revolutions, a fact that would seem to indicate that America's defeat in Indochina was the result of factors unique to that region rather than to U.S. doctrine in general. In truth, both interpretations have merit, for while the Indochina states suffered from an unusually unfavorable set of circumstances, many of the difficulties experienced there were also present to different degrees in the majority of successful counterinsurgencies. Thus the Army's experience in Vietnam, while exceptional in many respects, also reflected problems inherent in the United States' approach to counterinsurgency.

America's experience in overseas counterinsurgency during the 1960s and 1970s revealed that many of the tenets of nation-building theory were somewhat tenuous. First among these was the assumption that improved economic conditions would inevitably foster stability. In practice, economic development programs often failed to redress popular grievances. In fact, they sometimes aggravated them, either by unduly raising expectations, by accentuating disparities in wealth between regions or classes, or by accelerating unsettling socioeconomic changes. Poorly executed programs that brought uncaring or incompetent government representatives into closer contact with the people also turned out to be worse than no programs at all. The formation of middle classes likewise failed to promote the spread of democratic values. Thus many members of the middle class in Latin America adopted the interests and attitudes of the old aristocracy, while in Iran, the middle class joined with the majority of the people in rejecting modernization in favor of more traditional cultural values. Ultimately, even Rostow had to admit that "as for the linkage between economic development and the emergence of stable political democracies, we may, in retrospect, have been a bit too hopeful."[89]

A second assumption that appeared misguided was that American-style democracy was both an exportable commodity and a necessary and effective weapon against insurgency. In many cases America's allies had defeated communism without instituting substantially more democratic political systems. On the other hand, programs designed to promote American-style political pluralism could backfire if they detracted from the type of unity of effort and control essential for the survival of a besieged government. American concepts of governance also did not often translate well into other cultures. Historian Daniel Boorstin had warned of this phenomenon in 1953, arguing that "if we rely on the 'philosophy of American democracy' as a weapon in the world-wide struggle, we are relying on a weapon which may prove to be a dud." According to Boorstin, this was because democratic institutions "always grow out-of-doors in a particular climate and cannot be carried about in a flower pot." Time and again, U.S. policy makers would discover the truth in Boorstin's words, as American-style values and institutions withered after being transplanted to the infertile soils and inhospitable climates that characterized many countries. If democracy is to flourish, it must be carefully cultivated and nourished over a long period of time under appropriate conditions, not hastily imposed in the midst of a crisis.[90]

A related assumption that proved questionable was that outsiders could properly diagnose the ills of a foreign society. Often U.S. social engineers approached their tasks with a dangerous mixture of naivete, ethnocentrism, and hubris that hampered their activities. Ambassador Ellsworth Bunker's advice to South Vietnamese Prime Minister Nguyen Cao Ky that "people are drifting toward communism because they are poor. If you give the people everything they want—television sets, automobiles, and so on—none of them will go over to communism," reflected the type of simplistic and materialistic philosophy that all too many nation builders applied to their work.[91] Unfortunately, the issues were usually more complicated than televisions and automobiles. In fact, many U.S. nation builders were surprised to find that the peoples of the world were not as eager for the fruits of Western-style modernity as the creed of rising expectations had led them to believe. After many disappointing experiences, Army doctrine writers eventually had to admit that one of the greatest obstacles to "progress" was indigenous people's "satisfaction with the existing way of life." The revolution of rising expectations thus proved to be as much myth as reality, a projection of modern Western values onto a non-Western, tradition-minded world. With expectations lagging, U.S. soldiers primed with the notion that development was the key to dampening revolutionary ardor were placed in the dubious position of having to impose projects on people for their own good, a tricky proposition given doctrine's insistence that nation builders respect the values and desires of the population.[92]

More training in the social sciences might have helped U.S. civil and military officials negotiate the complexities of social engineering, but this was not practical for the vast majority of soldiers charged with nation-building responsibilities. Besides, social scientists themselves were divided as to the best nation-building methods, and their varied and sometimes conflicting theories usually failed to provide adequate road maps for practitioners in the field. All too often, American nation builders—civilian and military alike—ended up like so many sorcerer's apprentices, vainly struggling to direct vast and mysterious forces that they could neither fully comprehend nor control.[93]

Even when U.S. personnel were fairly sure of their methods, they often ran into yet another intractable problem—their inability to compel foreign governments to take their advice. Time after time, indigenous authorities ignored American prescriptions. U.S. officials had always recognized that the indigenous elites that controlled many foreign governments would have a vested interest in opposing change, yet no one could come up with a sure way to overcome such resistance. Better-trained advisory personnel with more language and cultural skills might have helped increase U.S. influence, as could longer tours of duty. This was especially true in Vietnam, where the Army insisted on limiting most advisory tours to one year, with many personnel serving no more than six months in any given post. The rotation policy was based on the premise that shorter tours were more equitable and healthier (both physically and emotionally) than long assignments. Unfortunately, the policy also disrupted continuity, impeded the development of perspective and understanding, and weakened interpersonal relationships with Vietnamese counterparts. On the other hand, agencies that used longer tours of duty, like the State Department, AID, and the CIA, often had just as much trouble as the Army in convincing foreign officials to follow their advice, so longer tours alone were not the answer.[94]

One potential solution was leverage—using threats of unfavorable action, or even the suspension of aid, to prod a reluctant ally into action. Sometimes leverage worked, sometimes not. Moreover, U.S. officials were frequently divided over how far they should push a sovereign, independent government over matters that pertained to its internal affairs. By the time of the Vietnam War the Army had embraced the view that its advisory personnel should avoid adopting uncompromising tones when proffering advice. Many individuals would later criticize this policy as being ineffective, and certainly it exacted a high price, as when General Westmoreland decided to sacrifice desperately needed cohesiveness by not pressing the South Vietnamese to accept a combined military command under U.S. control. Yet there were limits both as to how far the United States could pressure a proud people like the Vietnamese, as well as to how much responsibility the United States was willing to assume over the affairs of another country. Ironically, U.S. officials soon learned that the more involved they became in keeping a foreign government afloat, the less leverage they had, as the receiving state often assumed that the United States would not do anything that might jeopardize the survival of the allied government. This assumption did not always prove correct, as South Vietnam ultimately discovered, yet it paid off enough times to encourage recalcitrant regimes to resist unpalatable American initiatives.[95]

The frustration that U.S. diplomatic and military personnel experienced over their inability to influence indigenous governments sometimes produced pressure for a quick fix, usually in the guise of a change of leadership. This had been the lesson Secretary of State Dean Acheson had drawn from the China debacle, and favorable command changes in Greece and the Philippines had indeed helped pave the road to success in those countries. Seeking progress through a change of leadership was not an unreasonable proposition, and consequently the Kennedy administration had incorporated the notion into the Overseas Internal Defense Policy. But such changes were not always possible. They were not a panacea either, as was demonstrated when Diem's assassination plunged South Vietnam into a lengthy period of instability.

If a reluctance on the part of many governments to heed U.S. advice was a weakness, so too was the difficulty that the United States had in giving that advice in a clear and consistent manner. Part of the difficulty was the age-old problem of coordinating the activities of multiple, independent bureaucracies, each with its own mission and agenda. The United States never developed an effective way to integrate and direct counterinsurgency activities at the national level. At the country level, several integrative mechanisms were tried, but none turned out to be entirely satisfactory. The result was that the doctrinal ideal of a closely integrated politico-military program was often difficult to obtain.

Another aspect of this problem was the vagueness inherent in U.S. counterinsurgency doctrine itself. The official statement of national doctrine, the OIDP, had done little more than establish overarching concepts. It left the implementing details to the agencies themselves. Some agencies, like the Army, had expended much effort in developing and disseminating doctrinal materials to their members. Other agencies had not. Moreover, no single agency could impose its precepts on the others, while the single national-level coordinative body, the Special Group (Counterinsurgency), had proved a weak vessel. Since everyone accepted the broad tenets associated with the nation-building doctrine, the perils of this situation had not been truly apparent until U.S. policy was put to the test in the field, at which point the fissures became evident as agency feuded with agency and individuals within agencies argued with each other over exactly how to apply the broad precepts established by the OIDP and various manuals.

More definitive organizational arrangements and doctrinal materials at both the national and agency level would have helped alleviate the confusion. Yet there were also advantages to be gained by vagueness, as it encouraged experimentation and flexibility. Dogmatic adherence to stated principles could just as well lead to problems as a lack of doctrinal clarity. Such a situation occurred in several countries where U.S. officials had pressed their indigenous counterparts to assign key counterinsurgency roles to civilian (police and paramilitary) organizations on the premise that counterinsurgency was primarily a political and civil—not military—affair. Unfortunately, what sounded good in theory was unsatisfactory in practice, as a combination of historical and institutional factors often made such an arrangement either impolitic or unfeasible. This was particularly true in states where military organizations were more powerful than civilian ones. The result in Thailand, South Vietnam, and some Latin American countries was that vital pacification, population security, and counterinfrastructure functions were poorly accomplished because the assigned civilian agencies lacked the talent, resources, or bureaucratic clout to perform them effectively. Ultimately, American counterinsurgents of the 1960s and 1970s found that counterinsurgency was more art than science. No one formulation could fit all circumstances, and any attempt to force local conditions to conform to preconceived doctrinal or philosophical notions was bound for trouble.[96]

Another critical assumption that frequently proved incorrect was that recipients of aid would necessarily behave more favorably toward their benefactors. As General Williams had suggested, guerrilla intimidation certainly dissuaded many potentially friendly people from helping the government, yet other forces also played a role. Thus a combination of political, cultural, and nationalistic factors caused America's popularity to decline in Iran and Latin America during the 1960s and 1970s despite the disbursement of billions of dollars to those regions. As diplomat George Kennan had observed in 1954, "even benevolence, when addressed to a foreign people, represents a form of intervention into their internal affairs, and always receives, at best, a divided reception." Unfortunately, unqualified assertions by some hearts-and-minds enthusiasts about the virtues of civic action had not prepared U.S. soldiers for this reality.[97]

The frequent inability of nation-building activities to effect measurable structural or behavioral change, as well as the difficulty which U.S. officials had in persuading indigenous governments to implement meaningful reforms, meant that coercion would play the predominant role in most U.S.-backed counterinsurgency efforts. This certainly was true in Vietnam, where the government's many failings rendered force the only effective tool. Indeed, virtually all of the government's gains in terms of pacification, security, and population control after 1967 were directly attributable to the application of military might, not political and social action. Eventually, increasing numbers of people sided with the government not because they loved it, but because it was increasingly dangerous not to do so, because the luster had worn off the enemy's image of invincibility, and because they were simply tired of the war and wanted to side with the apparent winner.[98]

This phenomenon was repeated in many other countries around the world. From Thailand to Guatemala, "positive programs" of civic action, nation building, and reform had failed to win the day. True structural reforms were too difficult to effect under most third world insurgency conditions, while most civic actions were too superficial to have anything other than a transitory effect. No credible evidence emerged from the 1960s and 1970s to suggest that military civic action had significantly contributed to American nation-building goals, not just in Latin America, but anywhere in the world. All this did not mean that carefully crafted psychological and civic action programs could not influence perceptions and behavior by alleviating suffering, introducing modest improvements, and generally demonstrating government goodwill. But the expansive claims made by modernization theorists as to the ability of social reforms to quell an insurgency had proved exaggerated. Even the vaunted MEDCAP program had failed to generate widespread conversions to the Saigon government's cause.[99]

The nation's experiences during the 1960s and 1970s in assisting foreign governments in countering internal disorder thus bequeathed the Army a complex legacy. On the one hand, civilian theorists and Army doctrine writers alike had been correct in asserting that military means needed to be subordinated to political ends and that some manner of reform was usually necessary to guarantee peace and stability into the future. General Ridgway's warnings as to the potential hazards of trying to save a hopelessly disorganized and unpopular regime through military power had also been prophetic. Yet American theorists had fallen short on two fronts. First, they had never truly come to grips with the fact that the modernization process was itself destabilizing and that policies designed to promote change were not always compatible with the maintenance of internal order and stability. More often than not, the United States would resolve this contradiction by choosing stability over reform, for when push came to shove, U.S. policy makers generally found a friendly repressive government to be preferable to a Communist one. Second, many American theorists had asserted a far too expansive view of the ability of civil measures to combat an active insurgency. Although some soldiers had adopted this view, mainstream Army doctrine had been correct in portraying civic action as an important, yet ancillary, weapon.[100] Traditional Army doctrine had also been correct in postulating that significant social progress could be achieved only after military and police operations had succeeded in establishing effective control over the countryside. Ultimately, experience demonstrated that military success was just as necessary in counterinsurgency as in conventional warfare.

Notes

[1] Cuba also fell during this period to a revolutionary movement that the United States did not initially perceive as communistic. The Cuban government received little U.S. support.

[2] Stephen Rabe, *Eisenhower and Latin America* (Chapel Hill: University of North Carolina Press, 1988), pp. 141–49.

[3] Quote from State Department, *Foreign Relations of the United States [FRUS], 1961–63*, vol. 12, *American Republics* (Washington, D.C.: Government Publishing Office, 1996), p. 174. Tony Smith, "The Alliance for Progress: The 1960s," in *Exporting Democracy, the United States and Latin America*, ed. Abraham Lowenthal (Baltimore, Md.: Johns Hopkins University Press, 1991), p. 72; Howard Wiarda, "Did the Alliance 'Lose Its Way,' or Were Its Assumptions All Wrong from the Beginning and Are Those Assumptions Still with Us?" in *The Alliance for Progress: A Retrospective*, ed. L. Ronald Scheman (New York: Frederick A. Praeger, 1988), pp. 97–99; Stephen Rabe, *The Most Dangerous Area in the World: John F. Kennedy Confronts Communist Revolution in Latin America* (Chapel Hill: University of North Carolina Press, 1999), p. 151.

[4] Quote from Barber and Ronning, *Internal Security*, p. 45, and see also pp. 37, 44. *FRUS, 1961–63*, 12:231; Cole Blasier, *The Hovering Giant: U.S. Responses to Revolutionary Change in Latin America, 1910–1985* (Pittsburgh, Pa.: University of Pittsburgh Press, 1985), table 11; Frank Pancake, "Military Assistance as an Element of United States Foreign Policy in Latin America, 1950–68" (Ph.D. diss., University of Virginia, 1969), pp. 109–13, 131; Brian Smith, "United States–Latin American Military Relations Since World War II: Implications for Human Rights," in *Human Rights and Basic Needs in the Americas*, ed. Margaret Crahan (Washington, D.C.: Georgetown University Press, 1982), pp. 265–66.

[5] *FRUS, 1961–63*, 12:197–202, 215; Rpt, HQDA, Feb 62, sub: Cold War Activities, pp. V-3 to V-5, Historians files, CMH; Rabe, *Most Dangerous*, p. 133.

[6] Ltr, Gen Palmer to D. Sprague, 29 Apr 60, Historians files, CMH; Pancake, "Military Assistance," p. 154; *FRUS, 1961–63*, 12:215–16; Miles Wolpin, *Military Aid and Counterrevolution in the Third World* (Lexington, Mass.: Lexington Books, 1972), pp. 60–61.

[7] Laqueur, *Guerrilla*, pp. 316–19, 330–31, 340–41; Georges Fauriol, ed., *Latin American Insurgencies* (Washington, D.C.: National Defense University Press, 1985), pp. 13–16; Timothy Wickham-Crowley, *Guerrillas and Revolution in Latin America* (Princeton, N.J.: Princeton University Press, 1992), pp. 20–30.

[8] Fauriol, *Latin American Insurgencies*, pp. 16, 134, 172; James Kohl and John Litt, *Urban Guerrilla Warfare in Latin America* (Cambridge: Massachusetts Institute of Technology Press, 1974), pp. 10, 15–27; Enrique Codo, "The Urban Guerrilla," *Military Review* 51 (August 1971): 3–10; Laqueur, *Guerrilla*, pp. 343–44.

[9] Gary Arnold, "IMET in Latin America," *Military Review* 67 (February 1987): 33; Smith, "United States–Latin American Military Relations," pp. 269–70, 292ns29, 30, 32; "U.S. Army School of the Americas," *Military Review* 50 (April 1970): 88–93.

[10] Rpt, Col Joy K. Vallery, c. 1965, sub: Debriefing Report, pp. 21–22, 39, 49, 400.318 U.S. Assistance, Geo G Colombia, CMH; McClintock, *Instruments of Statecraft*, pp. 223, 527n31; Pancake, "Military Assistance," pp. 162–63.

[11] Dennis Rempe, "Guerrillas, Bandits, and Independent Republics: United States Counter-Insurgency Efforts in Colombia, 1959–1965," *Small Wars and Insurgencies* 6 (Winter 1995): 305–11; Richard Maullin, *Soldiers, Guerrillas, and Politics in Colombia* (Lexington, Mass.: D. C. Heath, 1973), p. 68; Memo, JCS for Special Group (Counterinsurgency), 12 Mar 62, sub: Report of Visit to Colombia, South America, by a Team from Special Warfare Center, Fort Bragg, N.C., with atch Memo, Brig Gen Yarborough for Distribution, 26 Feb 62, sub: Visit to Colombia, South America, by a Team from Special Warfare Center, LIC, National Security Archives, Washington, D.C.

[12] Maullin, *Soldiers, Guerrillas, and Politics in Colombia*, pp. 69–75; Rempe, "Guerrillas, Bandits, and Independent Republics," pp. 313–21; Rpt, Vallery, c. 1965, sub: Debriefing Report, pp. 18, 52, 57; Keith Nusbaum, "Bandidos," *Military Review* 43 (July 1963): 23–25; Clark Irving, "Internal Defense Operations in Colombia—a Success Story" (Student thesis, AWC, 1967), p. 15.

[13] Blaufarb and Tanham, *Who Will Win?* pp. 97–99; Caesar Sereseres, "Military Development and the United States Military Assistance Program for Latin America: The Case of Guatemala, 1961–69" (Ph.D. diss., University of California, Riverside, 1971), pp. 238–43; Wayne Kirkbride, *Special Forces in Latin America: from Bull Simons to Just Cause* (Wayne Kirkbride, 1991), pp. 60–61, 84; Thomas Rogers, "The Military and Nation Building in Guatemala" (Student thesis, AWC, 1967), p. 6; Luigi Einaudi and Alfred Stepan, Latin American Institutional Development: Changing Military Perspectives in Peru and Brazil, R–586–DOS (Santa Monica, Calif.: RAND, 1971), pp. 25–26; Luis Vega, *Guerrillas in Latin America*, trans. Daniel Weissbort (New York: Frederick A. Praeger, 1969), pp. 84–85, 173–87; Lloyd Picou, "The Effectiveness of Stability Operations in Eliminating Insurgency in Peru" (Student thesis, AWC, 1968), pp. 23–24, 29–33; Gen Andrew O'Meara, "CINCSOUTH Plans and Problems," AWC lecture, 13 Dec 63, pp. 7–8, MHI.

[14] Vincent Lopez, "What the U.S. Army Should Do About Urban Guerrilla Warfare" (Student thesis, AWC, 1975), p. 24; Blaufarb and Tanham, *Who Will Win?* pp. 101–02.

[15] Maullin, *Soldiers, Guerrillas, and Politics in Colombia*, pp. 55, 60–68; Einaudi and Stepan, Latin American Institutional Development, pp. 22–25, 81–85; Smith, "United States–Latin American Military Relations," pp. 266–67; J. Bina Machado, "The Making of Brazilian Staff Officers," *Military Review* 50 (April 1970): 75–81; Anthony Auletta, "Ten-Nation Progress Report," *Army* 13 (July 1963): 53; Brian Jenkins and Caesar Sereseres, "United States Military Assistance and the Guatemalan Armed Forces," *Armed Forces and Society* 3 (Summer 1977): 580; Rogers, "Military and Nation Building," pp. 7–11; Walterhouse, *A Time To Build*, pp. 99–102.

[16] *FRUS, 1961–63*, 12:205; Memo, SGS for Gen Eddleman, 27 Apr 61, sub: Plan To Step Up Latin American Attendance in Counter-guerrilla Training Activities, 370.64, CSA, 1955–62, RG 319, NARA; Jerome Levinson and Juan de Onis, *The Alliance That Lost Its Way* (Chicago: Quadrangle Books, 1970), pp. 241–42; Rpt, U.S. Southern Command, c. 1965, sub: Civic Action Projects Report, 1 March 1964–1 January 1965, History Office, U.S. Army Special Operations Command, Fort Bragg, N.C. (hereafter as USASOC/HO).

[17] Quote from U.S. Southern Command Historical Report, Calendar Year (CY) 63, p. v-20, copy in CMH. Memo, Gen George Lincoln, 8 Nov 65, sub: Memorandum of Notes Concerning "Internal Security," pp. 1–7, Historians files, CMH.

[18] Maullin, *Soldiers, Guerrillas, and Politics in Colombia*, pp. 69, 70–79; U.S. Southern Command Annual History, 1964, pp. v-22, v-23, viii-3, copy in CMH; Rpt,

DCSOPS, 31 Dec 63, sub: A Review of the Civic Action Program, pp. 5–6, Historians files, CMH; Edward Glick, "Military Civic Action: Thorny Art of the Peace Keepers," *Army* 17 (September 1967): 70; Liza Gross, *Handbook of Leftist Guerrilla Groups in Latin America and the Caribbean* (Boulder, Colo.: Westview Press, 1995), pp. 29, 145–49; Memo, Dir of Intelligence and Research, State Department, for Secy of State, 23 Oct 67, sub: Guatemala: A Counter-Insurgency Running Wild? National Security Archives, Washington, D.C.; Kenneth Johnson, *Guatemala: From Terrorism to Terror* (London: Institute for the Study of Conflict, 1972), pp. 14, 17.

[19] First quote from *FRUS, 1961–63*, 12:174. Second quote from Martin Massoglia, Military Civic Action, Evaluation of Military Techniques, 2 vols. (Research Triangle Institute, 1971), 2:iv-4. Abraham Lowenthal and J. Samuel Fitch, eds., *Armies and Politics in Latin America* (New York: Holmes and Meier, 1986), pp. 3–4; David Hughes, "The Myth of Military Coups and Military Assistance," *Military Review* 47 (December 1967): 3–9; Rabe, *Most Dangerous*, pp. 141–44.

[20] Martin Needler, *The United States and the Latin American Revolution* (Los Angeles: University of California, 1977), pp. 48, 51; Frances Foland, "Agrarian Reform in Latin America," *Foreign Affairs* 48 (October 1969): 97–112; Lowenthal, *Exporting Democracy*, pp. 79–80. For varying assessments of the role of force and political action in Latin insurgencies, see David Ronfeldt and Luigi Einaudi, Internal Security and Military Assistance to Latin America in the 1970s: A First Statement, R–924–ISA (Santa Monica, Calif.: RAND, 1971), pp. 16, 18, 24–30; Laqueur, *Guerrilla*, p. 318; Barber and Ronning, *Internal Security*, pp. viii–ix; Rabe, *Most Dangerous*, pp. 148–72.

[21] Jeffrey Clarke, *Advice and Support: The Final Years, 1965–1973*, United States Army in Vietnam (Washington, D.C.: U.S. Army Center of Military History, 1988), pp. 213, 251; Spector, *Early Years*, pp. 353, 371; Eric Bergerud, *The Dynamics of Defeat: The Vietnam War in Hau Nghia Province* (Boulder, Colo.: Westview Press, 1991), pp. 3, 327.

[22] Dale Andrade, *Ashes to Ashes: The Phoenix Program and the Vietnam War* (Lexington, Mass.: Lexington Books, 1990), pp. 38–41; Boyd Bashore, "Diem's Counterinsurgency Strategy for Vietnam: Right or Wrong?" (Student thesis, AWC, 1968), pp. 4–7.

[23] MacDonald, Outline History, pp. 23–24; William Duiker, *The Communist Road to Power in Vietnam* (Boulder, Colo.: Westview Press, 1981), p. 198; Spector, *Early Years*, pp. 308–11, 326.

[24] Quote from Spector, *Early Years*, p. 224, and see also pp. 223, 228.

[25] *U.S.-Vietnam Relations*, bk. 2, ch. IV.A, pp. 4, 17–20; Spector, *Early Years*, pp. 264, 272–73; Frederick Schneider, "Advising the ARVN: Lieutenant General Samuel T. Williams in Vietnam, 1955–60" (M.A. thesis, University of North Texas, 1990), pp. 21–22, 37–38; Hoang Ngoc Lung, *Strategy and Tactics*, Indochina Monographs (Washington, D.C.: U.S. Army Center of Military History, 1980), p. 15.

[26] Chester Cooper, The American Experience with Pacification in Vietnam, R–185, 3 vols., Institute for Defense Analyses, 1972, 3:17–18, 120–21, MHI; Lansdale, *In the Midst of Wars*, pp. 126–27, 138–39, 216; Richard Hunt, *Pacification: The American Struggle for Vietnam's Hearts and Minds* (Boulder, Colo.: Westview Press, 1995), pp. 11, 21; William Nighswonger, *Rural Pacification in Vietnam* (New York: Frederick A. Praeger, 1966), pp. 35–36.

[27] Arnold, *First Domino*, pp. 306–08, 320–21, 359–60; *FRUS, 1958–60*, 1:471–74; Spector, *Early Years*, pp. 296–300.

[28] *FRUS, 1958–60*, 1:291, 475–76.

[29] Quotes from *FRUS, 1955–57*, 1:608, and see also pp. 606–07, 609–10.

[30] Spector, *Early Years*, p. 351; Memo, Military Assistance Advisory Group, Vietnam (MAAG, Vietnam), n.d., sub: Notes on Anti-Guerrilla Operations, atch to Msg, CINCPAC to JCS, 18 Mar 60, sub: Notes on Anti-Guerrilla Operations, forwarding of, 3360, 1960, RG 218, NARA; *FRUS, 1958–60*, 1:291–92.

[31] *FRUS, 1958–60*, 1:353–54, 358, 477; Spector, *Early Years*, pp. 350, 352; Memo, Col Richard Comstock, Army Attache, Saigon, for Assistant Chief of Staff for Intelligence (ACSI), 25 Apr 60, sub: Conversation Regarding Vietnamese Army Problems, Historians files, CMH.

[32] James Collins, *The Development and Training of the South Vietnamese Army, 1950–1972*, Vietnam Studies (Washington, D.C.: Department of the Army, 1975), pp. 123–24; Cooper, American Experience with Pacification, 1:65–67; *FRUS, 1958–60*, 1:479.

[33] Spector, *Early Years*, pp. 274, 326; *FRUS, 1958–60*, 1:131–33.

[34] Spector, *Early Years*, pp. 273, 320.

[35] Collins, *Development and Training*, p. 8; Spector, *Early Years*, pp. 321–24, 378; *U.S.-Vietnam Relations*, bk. 2, ch. IV, pp. 22–23.

[36] MAAG, Vietnam, Anti-Guerrilla Guerrilla, 10 Nov 60; MAAG, Vietnam, Implementing Actions for Anti-Guerrilla Operations, 15 Nov 60. Both in Black Memos, CJCS Lemnitzer, RG 218, NARA. Cooper, American Experience with Pacification, 3:150–51.

[37] Quote from MAAG, Vietnam, Tactics and Techniques of Counterinsurgent Operations, 1963, p. V F-1, and see also pp. ix–xiv, III C-1 and C-2, III E-1, IV A-1, IV B-1 to IV B-16, V L-2, VI A-1 to VI B-5.

[38] Spector, *Early Years*, pp. 361–62, 371–72; *FRUS, 1958–60*, 1:613–20; Memo, CINCPAC, 26 Apr 60, sub: Counter-Insurgency Operations in South Vietnam and Laos, Historians files, CMH.

[39] Michael Clodfelter, *Vietnam in Military Statistics: A History of the Indochina Wars, 1772–1991* (Jefferson, N.C.: McFarland, 1995), pp. 44, 57; Stanley Karnow, *Vietnam, a History* (New York: Viking Press, 1983), pp. 251–53.

[40] Francis Kelly, *U.S. Army Special Forces, 1961–1971*, Vietnam Studies (Washington, D.C.: Department of the Army, 1973), p. 37.

[41] Richard Hunt and Richard Shultz, eds., *Lessons from an Unconventional War: Reassessing U.S. Strategies for Future Conflicts* (New York: Pergamon Press, 1982), pp. 6, 13; Nighswonger, *Rural Pacification*, pp. 47–48; MACV, Guide for Subsector Advisers, 1966, p. 1, Historians files, CMH.

[42] Stephen Bowman, "The Evolution of United States Army Doctrine for Counterinsurgency Warfare: From World War II to the Commitment of Combat Units in Vietnam" (Ph.D. diss., Duke University, 1985), p. 69; Collins, *Development and Training*, pp. 17–18, 33; MAAG, Vietnam, Training Tips (Small Unit Tactics), Oct 62; Memo, Brig Gen Howard K. Eggleston, Ch, Army Section, MAAG, Vietnam, for Distribution, 13 Mar 63, sub: Counterinsurgent Orientation of POI's and ATP's. Both in Historians files, CMH.

[43] Quote from Ltr, McGarr to Brig Gen William Cunningham III, Asst Commandant, CGSC, 13 Apr 61, Historians files, CMH. MAAG, Vietnam, Tactics and Techniques of Counterinsurgent Operations, 1963, pp. III D-1 to III D-5; Memos, U.S. Army, Pacific, for Distribution, 2 Nov 62, sub: USARPAC Counterinsurgency Summary Number 1, pp. 2–5, N–16082.21, CARL, and McGarr for MAAG Advisers, 15 Nov 60,

sub: Implementing Actions for Anti-Guerrilla Operations, p. 3, Black Memos, CJCS Lemnitzer, RG 218, NARA. Memo, MAAG, Vietnam, for Distribution, 19 Jun 62, sub: Lessons Learned [LL] Number 16, pp. 1–4, Historians files, CMH (lessons learned reports will be hereafter cited as MAAG, Vietnam, LL number, and the date); MAAG, Vietnam, LL 35, 10 Jan 64, pp. 1–7, and LL 36, 4 Feb 64, pp. 1–3. Compare FM 31–20, 1951, with Army of the Republic of Vietnam (ARVN) training materials as found in Translations, Army G–2, Counter Insurgency Training Lesson Plans, 27 Mar 62, MHI, and Counter Insurgency Training Material, 4 Apr 62, C–18745.17–B, CARL.

⁴⁴ First quote from Translation, Army G–2, Counter Insurgency Training Material, 4 Apr 62, p. 4, and see also pp. 5–7. Memos, MAAG, Vietnam, for Distribution, 6 Dec 62, sub: Search Techniques Training, pp. 14, 35, 37, N–18745.28–a, CARL, and U.S. Army, Pacific, for Distribution, 2 Nov 62, sub: USARPAC Counterinsurgency Summary Number 1, pp. 11–12. Second quote from Memo, Col Frank Lee, Ch, CA-MTT, for Ch of Civil Affairs, 20 Oct 60, sub: Report of Civil Affairs MTT in Vietnam During Period 19 July–5 October 1960, USASOC/HO. Third quote from MAAG, Vietnam, Tactics and Techniques of Counterinsurgent Operations, 1963, p. III I-1, and see also p. III I-3. MAAG, Vietnam, LL 16, 19 Jun 62, p. 4; LL 20, 27 Aug 62, pp. 1–2; LL 25, 17 Dec 62, pp. 2, 5, 7–8; LL 30, 19 Aug 63, pp. 1–7; and LL 35, 10 Jan 64, p. 5.

⁴⁵ Collins, *Development and Training*, pp. 43–46.

⁴⁶ Rpt, Brig Gen John Finn, Mar 64, sub: Report to the Chief of Staff United States Army on the U.S.-GVN Effort, p. I-a-6, 68–3306, RG 319, NARA (hereafter cited as Finn Rpt); Louis Wiesner, *Victims and Survivors: Displaced Persons and Other War Victims in Viet-Nam, 1954–1975* (New York: Greenwood Press, 1988), p. 32; MAAG, Vietnam, Tactics and Techniques of Counterinsurgent Operations, 1963, pp. IV B-13 to IV B-15.

⁴⁷ Clarke, *Final Years*, p. 12; *FRUS, 1958–60*, 1:310–11, 322–24, 550–51, 555; William Westmoreland, "The Fight for Freedom in Viet Nam," *Army Information Digest* 20 (February 1965): 10; *The Pentagon Papers: The Defense Department History of United States Decisionmaking on Vietnam*, Senator Gravel ed., 4 vols. (Boston: Beacon Press, 1971–1972), 2:752–56.

⁴⁸ Nighswonger, *Rural Pacification*, p. 46; Spector, *Early Years*, p. 332; Hunt, *Pacification*, pp. 20–28, 42–44; Cooper, American Experience with Pacification, 2:49–50, and 3:139–43, 204–05, 235–36; William Westmoreland, *A Soldier Reports* (Garden City, N.Y.: Doubleday, 1976), pp. 82–88, 99–100.

⁴⁹ Bergerud, *Dynamics of Defeat*, p. 144; Nighswonger, *Rural Pacification*, p. 224.

⁵⁰ Clarke, *Final Years*, pp. 515–16; Robert Komer, *Bureaucracy at War: U.S. Performance in the Vietnam Conflict* (Boulder, Colo.: Westview Press, 1986), p. 82; Cooper, American Experience with Pacification, 1:18–20, and 2:114–18, 148.

⁵¹ First quote from Spector, *Early Years*, p. 335, and see also, p. 368. Second quote from Outline for Chief MAAG, Vietnam, 24 Apr 61, p. 1. Memo, McGarr, c. Apr 61, sub: Anti-Guerrilla Warfare—Vietnam Style—Part I, p. 10. Both in Black Memos, CJCS Lemnitzer, RG 218, NARA. Ltr, McGarr, MAAG, Vietnam, to Lemnitzer, Chairman, Joint Chiefs of Staff (CJCS), 20 Jan 61, pp. 2–3, Historians files, CMH; Shafer, *Deadly Paradigms*, pp. 263–64; Blaufarb, *Counterinsurgency Era*, pp. 218–19.

⁵² Hunt, *Pacification*, p. 75.

⁵³ Finn Rpt, pp. D-2, D-3, D-4, I-a-2, I-a-4, I-a-5, I-a-7, I-a-34, I-B-10, V-G-5, VI-a-1; Rpt, DCSOPS, 1 Apr 65, sub: Analysis of the Military Effort in South Vietnam, pp. 61, 67, 68A2344, RG 319, NARA; Collins, *Development and Training*, pp. 35, 123–26.

[54] DCSOPS, A Program for the Pacification and Long-Term Development of South Vietnam, Mar 66, pp. 5–37 (hereafter cited as PROVN); Army Concept Team in Vietnam (ACTIV), Armor Operations for Counterinsurgency in Vietnam, 9 Feb 66, p. 25; MAAG, Vietnam, LL 16, 19 Jun 62, pp. 1–4, and LL 35, 10 Jan 64, pp. 1–2, 6.

[55] ACTIV, Armor Operations, pp. 24–25; Finn Rpt, pp. D-5, D-6, I-a-7 to I-a-10, I-B-10, I-B-11; Memo, MAAG, Vietnam, n.d., sub: Notes on Anti-Guerrilla Operations; William Miller, ARVN Infantry Tactics Before 1965 (Research Report, Air War College, 1970), pp. 4, 23–24; Rpts, Brig Gen Harvey Jablonsky et al., to DCSOPS, Mar 62, sub: Report of Orientation Tour to South Vietnam, p. 4, Historians files, CMH, and DCSOPS, 1 Apr 65, sub: Analysis of the Military Effort in South Vietnam, p. 22; ACTIV, Employment of Artillery in Counterinsurgency Operations, 1965, pp. xiii, xiv, 64, D-4, E-4; MAAG, Vietnam, LL 36, 4 Feb 64, pp. 1–3.

[56] Miller, ARVN Infantry, pp. 4, 23–24; Lung, *Strategy and Tactics*, pp. 53–54, 73.

[57] Quote from George Herring, *America's Longest War: The United States and Vietnam, 1950–1975* (New York: John Wiley and Sons, 1979), p. 132. HQDA, Final Report of the Research Project: Conduct of the War, May 71, p. 5, CMH.

[58] Cooper, American Experience with Pacification, 2:17 and 3:230; Duiker, *Road to Power*, pp. 245–49, 261–62; Andrade, *Ashes to Ashes*, pp. 71–72, 81.

[59] Cooper, American Experience with Pacification, 1:58.

[60] Hunt, *Pacification*, p. 36; Blaufarb, *Counterinsurgency Era*, pp. 227–29.

[61] Finn Rpt, p. I-F-6; Rpt, DCSOPS, 1 Apr 65, sub: Analysis of the Military Effort in South Vietnam, p. 93; PROVN, pp. 1, 53, 58–59; CDC, Special Warfare and Civil Affairs Group, Concepts and General Doctrine for Counterinsurgency, Jul 65, pp. 3–4, 47, 73A2677, CDC, RG 338, NARA; Komer, *Bureaucracy at War*, pp. 89–92, 119; Hunt, *Pacification*, pp. 36, 76, 90–93; Cooper, American Experience with Pacification, 2:266–71.

[62] John Gates, "Peoples' War in Vietnam," *Journal of Military History* 54 (July 1990): 338; Komer, *Bureaucracy at War*, p. 119.

[63] According to one scholar, forcible relocations accounted for only about 10 percent of all people displaced during the war. Tran Dinh Tho, *Pacification*, Indochina Monographs (Washington, D.C.: U.S. Army Center of Military History, 1980), p. 155; Gunther Lewy, *America in Vietnam* (New York: Oxford University Press, 1978), p. 445; Thomas Thayer, "How To Analyze a War Without Fronts, Vietnam 1965–72," *Journal of Defense Research*, Series B, Tactical Warfare 7B (Fall 1975): 924–25; Seymour Melman, ed., *In the Name of America* (Annandale, Va.: Turnpike Press, 1968), pp. 328, 365–66; Wiesner, *Victims and Survivors*, pp. 73–75, 90, 168–69, 210, 229–52, 353; Southeast Asia Analysis Rpt, The Refugee Problem, Magnitude and Measures, Sep 67, p. 16, Historians files, CMH.

[64] John Forrest, "The Civic Action Advisory Effort: Republic of Vietnam" (Master's thesis, Massachusetts Institute of Technology, 1969), pp. 69, 93, 107–08, 128–30; Tho, *Pacification*, p. 188; Lung, *Strategy and Tactics*, p. 95.

[65] In addition, North Vietnam had several divisions outside of South Vietnam, while both sides still fielded large paramilitary and local force units. Charles Timmes, "Vietnam Summary: Military Operations After the Cease-Fire Agreement, pt. 1," *Military Review* 56 (August 1976): 65–66; Tho, *Pacification*, pp. 167, 184–85.

[66] Blaufarb and Tanham, *Who Will Win?* pp. 83–84; Cooper, American Experience with Pacification, 2:42; Blaufarb, *Counterinsurgency Era*, p. 216; Andrade, *Ashes to*

Ashes, pp. 158–64, 185, 240–42, 276, 284; Lung, *Strategy and Tactics*, pp. 39–40; Clarke, *Final Years*, p. 254; Tho, *Pacification*, p. 188.

[67] Clifton Fox, "Turkish Army's Role in Nation Building," *Military Review* 47 (April 1967): 68–74; Auletta, "Ten-Nation," pp. 55–56; Robert Peters, "So This Is Civic Action," *Army Information Digest* 22 (April 1967): 14; Civil Affairs School, ST 41–1094, Civic Action Plan for the Imperial Iranian Armed Forces, 1963, Historians files, CMH; Rpts, Brig Gen Richard Whitney, Debriefing of Senior and Key Officers, 1964, pp. 5–7, 14–28, and Maj Gen George Eckhardt, Debriefing of Senior and Key Officers, 1965, pp. 10–15, both in 314.82, CMH.

[68] Irving Heymont, "The U.S. Army and Foreign National Development," *Military Review* 51 (November 1971): 22; Jack Miklos, *The Iranian Revolution and Modernization: Way Station to Anarchy* (Washington, D.C.: National Defense University Press, 1983), pp. 16, 21, 25–26, 29, 39–42, 62–63.

[69] Lachica, *The Huks*, pp. 187–88, 230–48; Kessler, *Rebellion and Repression*, pp. 136–56.

[70] Daniel Bolger, *Scenes from an Unfinished War: Low-Intensity Conflict in Korea, 1966–1969* (Fort Leavenworth, Kans.: Combat Studies Institute, 1991), pp. 1–4, 24.

[71] Ibid., pp. 49–51, 55–57, 77–78; Wesley Pruden, "Asia's Other War," *Army* 17 (November 1967): 26–31; Robert Davenport, "Barrier Along the Korean DMZ," *Infantry* 57 (May–June 1967): 40–42; William Guthrie, "Korea: The Other DMZ," *Infantry* 60 (March–April 1970): 17–22; James Wroth, "Korea: Our Next Vietnam?" *Military Review* 48 (November 1968): 34–40.

[72] Bolger, *Unfinished War*, pp. 45–46, 57.

[73] Ibid., pp. 30, 56–59, 83; Charles Bonesteel, "U.S.–South Korean Partnership Holds a Truculent North at Bay," *Army* 19 (October 1969): 59–63.

[74] Bolger, *Unfinished War*, pp. 83–85, 97.

[75] Robert Zimmerman, "Thailand: The Domino That Did Not Fall," in Edwin Corr and Stephen Sloan, *Low-Intensity Conflict: Old Threats in a New World* (Boulder, Colo.: Westview Press, 1992), pp. 77–79; Robert Zimmerman, "Insurgency in Thailand," *Problems of Communism* 25 (May–June 1976): 18–26, 30–33.

[76] Saiyud Kerdphol, *The Struggle for Thailand: Counterinsurgency, 1965–1985* (Bangkok: S. Research Center, 1986), pp. 2, 5; Muthiah Alagappa, *The National Security of Developing States, Lessons from Thailand* (Dover, Mass.: Auburn House, 1987), pp. 150–58, 168–69, 188; *FRUS, 1961–63*, vol. 23, *Southeast Asia*, pp. 917, 973–86, 992–93; Rpt, DCSOPS, 1 Apr 65, sub: Counterinsurgency: Operations and Planning in Thailand, MHI.

[77] George Tanham, *Trial in Thailand* (New York: Crane, Russak and Co., 1974), pp. 71–89; Chaiyo Krasin, "Military Civic Action in Thailand," *Military Review* 48 (January 1968): 73–77; Thomas Lobe, *U.S. National Security Policy and Aid to the Thailand Police* (Denver, Colo.: University of Denver, 1977), pp. 19–25, 28–30, 37–45; Robert Muscat, *Thailand and the United States: Development, Security, and Foreign Aid* (New York: Columbia University Press, 1990), pp. 160–65; J. Alexander Caldwell, *American Economic Aid to Thailand* (Lexington, Mass.: D. C. Heath, 1974), pp. 55, 58.

[78] Tanham, *Trial in Thailand*, pp. 78–80, 85–87, 91, 97–100.

[79] Zimmerman, "The Domino That Did Not Fall," in Corr and Sloan, *Low-Intensity Conflict*, p. 87; Thomas Marks, *Thailand—the Threatened Kingdom* (London:

Institute for Conflict Study, 1980), pp. 8–13; Kerdphol, *Struggle for Thailand*, pp. 228–29.

[80] Caldwell, *American Economic Aid*, p. 16; Tanham, *Trial in Thailand*, pp. 124–25.

[81] First quote from Memo, JUSMAG, Thailand, c. 1961, sub: Small Unit Tactics— Anti-guerrilla Warfare, p. 2, atch to Memo, JUSMAG, Thailand, c. 1962, sub: Thailand Guerrilla Warfare, CARL. Second quote from ibid, p. 1. Memo, CINCPAC for JCS, 4 May 62, sub: Status of Development of Counter-guerrilla Forces, p. 14, Historians files, CMH; *FRUS, 1961–63*, 23:52, 874–75, 913–14, 917, 973–74.

[82] Blaufarb, *Counterinsurgency Era*, p. 187; Tanham, *Trial in Thailand*, pp. 123–25, 130–50.

[83] Kerdphol, *Struggle for Thailand*, pp. 82, 130; Caldwell, *American Economic Aid*, p. 15; Lobe, *Thailand Police*, pp. 46, 65, 67; Zimmerman, "The Domino That Did Not Fall," in Corr and Sloan, *Low-Intensity Conflict*, pp. 83–84.

[84] Tanham, *Trial in Thailand*, pp. 72, 92, 149; Lobe, *Thailand Police*, pp. 6, 37, 75–77, 104–06.

[85] Tanham, *Trial in Thailand*, pp. 80, 101–04; Kerdphol, *Struggle for Thailand*, pp. 90–94, 129–31, 153–54; David Wyatt, *Thailand, a Short History* (New Haven, Conn.: Yale University Press, 1984), pp. 289–90; Caldwell, *American Economic Aid*, pp. 57–58, 62, 68–69, 140–43; Muscat, *Thailand and the United States*, pp. 168–71, 315.

[86] Memo, Col Aaron Walker, Ch, JUSMAG, Thailand, for CINCPAC, 27 Oct 78, sub: End of Tour Report, Historians files, CMH; Stuart Slade, "Successful Counter-insurgency: How Thais Burnt the Books and Beat the Guerrillas," *International Defense Review, Editorial Supplement to October 1998 Issue, Internal Security and CO-IN* (October 1989): 21–25; Kerdphol, *Struggle for Thailand*, pp. 84–87; Jennifer Taw, Thailand and the Philippines, Case Studies in U.S. IMET Training and Its Role in Internal Defense and Development (Santa Monica, Calif.: RAND, 1994), pp. xi, 16–17, 26–29; Alagappa, *Lessons from Thailand*, pp. 170–71, 175–78.

[87] Kerdphol, *Struggle for Thailand*, pp. 87, 153, 167, 177; Caldwell, *American Economic Aid*, pp. 148, 158; Alagappa, *Lessons from Thailand*, pp. 151, 192–93, 244.

[88] Barbara LePoer, *Thailand: A Country Study*, Area Handbook Series (Washington, D.C.: Library of Congress, 1989), pp. 231–33; Kerdphol, *Struggle for Thailand*, pp. 166–67; John Esterline and Mae Esterline, *"How the Dominoes Fall": Southeast Asia in Perspective* (New York: University Press of America, 1990), p. 276; Zimmerman, "The Domino That Did Not Fall," in Corr and Sloan, *Low-Intensity Conflict*, pp. 89, 95; Alagappa, *Lessons from Thailand*, pp. 166, 171, 177–78, 190–92.

[89] Quote from Walt Rostow, *Eisenhower, Kennedy, and Foreign Aid: Ideas and Actions* (Austin: University of Texas Press, 1985), p. 50. Rabe, *Most Dangerous*, pp. 155–59; Massoglia, Military Civic Action, pp. viii-1 to viii-11; Raymond Barrett, "The Development Process and Stability Operations," *Military Review* 52 (November 1972): 58–63; Hennessy, *Strategy in Vietnam*, pp. 150–51; Clarke, *Final Years*, pp. 501–02; Kerdphol, *Struggle for Thailand*, pp. 129, 153–54; Smith, "Alliance for Progress," in Lowenthal, *Exporting Democracy*, pp. 78–79; Wiarda, *Ethnocentrism in Foreign Policy*, pp. 1–6; Miklos, *Iranian Revolution*, pp. 16, 21, 25–26, 29, 39–42, 62–63.

[90] Quotes from Packenham, *Liberal America*, p. 190.

[91] Quote from Richard Sutter, "The Strategic Implications of Military Civic Action," in DePauw and Luz, *Winning the Peace*, p. 143.

[92] Ibid., pp. 133–38. Quotes from 300th Civil Affairs Group, A Guide to Military Civic Action, 1969, p. 55, and see also pp. 53–62, copy in CMH. Wiarda, *Ethnocentrism*

in Foreign Policy, pp. 9–10, 23, 27–30; Lawrence Harrison, *Underdevelopment Is a State of Mind* (Lanham, Md.: University Press of America, 1985), p. xv; U.S. Congress, Senate, Committee on Foreign Relations, Subcommittee on Western Hemisphere Affairs, *U.S. Military Policies and Programs in Latin America*, 91st Cong., 1st sess., 1969, pp. 1–31; Solomon Silver, Counter-Insurgency and Nation Building: A Study with Emphasis on South East Asia (Washington, D.C.: U.S. Agency for International Development, 1967), p. 46; Latham, *Modernization as Ideology*, pp. 66, 204, 211.

[93] Miklos, *Iranian Revolution*, p. 1; Thomas Adams, "Military Doctrine and the Organization Culture of the U.S. Army" (Ph.D. diss., Syracuse University, 1990), p. 576.

[94] Cooper, American Experience with Pacification, 1:73; Finn Rpt, 2:H-17, H-18.

[95] Collins, *Development and Training*, pp. 52, 129–30; Clarke, *Final Years*, p. 245; Komer, *Bureaucracy at War*, pp. 25–37, 127; Nighswonger, *Rural Pacification*, pp. 199–203; Blaufarb, *Counterinsurgency Era*, pp. 73, 86–87; Rabe, *Most Dangerous*, pp. 160–61.

[96] Lobe, *Thailand Police*, p. 6; Andrade, *Ashes to Ashes*, p. 85.

[97] Quote from David Greenberg, "The United States Response to Philippine Insurgency" (Ph.D. diss., Fletcher School of Law and Diplomacy, Tufts University, 1994), p. 3.

[98] Rpt, Vietnam Special Studies Group, 16 Mar 70, sub: The Situation in the Countryside, Quang Nam Province, pp. 7–8, 10, 14, 16, 38–40, 48, 51–52; Rpt, Vietnam Special Studies Group, The Situation in the Countryside, 10 Jan 70, pp. 2–4, 7, 90, 92–93. Both in Historians files, CMH. Hunt, *Pacification*, p. 247; Blaufarb, *Counterinsurgency Era*, pp. 118–19, 207, 271, 277; Bergerud, *Dynamics of Defeat*, pp. 5, 328, 333.

[99] Raymond Bishop, Medical Support of Stability Operations: a Vietnam Case Study (Student paper, Army War College, 1969), pp. 6–13, 23; Maullin, *Soldiers, Guerrillas, and Politics in Colombia*, pp. 69, 76–78; Barber and Ronning, *Internal Security*, pp. 197–206, 230; Glick, *Peaceful Conflict*, pp. 176–82; Packenham, *Liberal America*, pp. 174–81; Miklos, *Iranian Revolution*, pp. 12, 64–65; Heymont, "U.S. Army and Foreign National Development," pp. 20–23; Hennessy, *Strategy in Vietnam*, pp. 147–48, 166, 182.

[100] Hoyt Livingston and Francis Watson, "Civic Action: Purpose and Pitfalls," *Military Review* 47 (December 1967): 21–22.

8

DOCTRINE APPLIED: THE U.S. ARMY IN VIETNAM, 1965-1973

The deployment of U.S. combat forces to Vietnam in 1965 gave the Army the opportunity to apply directly its counterinsurgency concepts in a major conflict for the first time since the Korean War. U.S. soldiers soon realized that giving advice was easier than combating an insurgency themselves. The deployment also forced the Army to confront a significant conceptual oversight—the tendency of most counterinsurgency literature to focus on the political and guerrilla aspects of an insurgency (phases I and II) at the expense of the quasi-conventional third phase.

Despite the fact that the crowning piece of Mao's three stages of revolutionary warfare was the "war of movement," most theorists had ignored this phase in favor of the more uniquely "revolutionary" aspects of insurgent warfare. Unfortunately, phase III insurgencies were exactly the type most likely to result in the commitment of U.S. ground troops, for as Vietnam demonstrated, a natural reluctance on the part of politicians to embroil the United States in foreign wars tended to limit U.S. participation to advisory activities in anything less than the most dire circumstances. Thus when U.S. combat troops arrived in 1965 they faced a situation more akin to the later stages of the Chinese Civil War, in which the counterinsurgents were whipsawed by a dual guerrilla-conventional threat, than a purely guerrilla conflict like the Malayan and Philippine insurgencies. Ironically, while Army counterguerrilla doctrine was rooted in the lessons of irregular combat fought within a conventional war context, these roots had become overshadowed during the early 1960s by a somewhat romanticized view of people's wars, in which motley bands of ill-armed peasants under the inspired leadership of Communist Party organizers overthrew governments with little assistance from outside powers and conventional armies. While such eventualities were possible, this was not the situation in Vietnam. Consequently, the Army was compelled to rely more heavily on conventional forms of power than many theorists had envisioned.[1] Many of the most perplexing problems faced by the Army in Vietnam would revolve around the inherent tensions between fighting a large, conventional war on the one hand while attempting to pacify the countryside on the other.

Strategy

The insertion of U.S. combat forces into the Vietnamese civil war in 1965 dramatically altered the course of that conflict, but it did not significantly change American conceptions about how the war should be fought. American national and military doctrine maintained that the best way to defeat an insurgency was through a deft combination of political, economic, and military measures that would remove the underlying causes of unrest while suppressing the overt, military manifestations of discontent. This had been the policy the United States had pursued in Vietnam without success over the previous decade, and it remained U.S. policy for the remainder of the war. Central to America's strategy was the ubiquitous oil-spot theory that blended military operations, population-control measures, and civil programs into a cohesive tapestry of gradually expanding government control.[2]

While most Americans embraced this formula, they differed profoundly over the means to be used and the relative priority of those means with regard to each other. Many believed that socioeconomic and political issues had to receive priority at every step of the counterinsurgency process. Westmoreland and other senior officers disagreed. Hard experience had already demonstrated that socioeconomic betterment programs could not survive in an insecure climate, no matter how well intentioned they might be. Thus, while he did not question the need to address political issues, Westmoreland believed that military concerns had to take precedence in many cases, with genuine reform being relegated to the later stages once a sufficient measure of security had been achieved through military operations.[3]

A second strategic choice that engendered controversy concerned the role that U.S. troops were to play in the upcoming campaign. Experience indicated the importance that foreign aid and safe havens played in successful insurgent movements, and consequently Army

General Westmoreland inspects Viet Cong prisoners.

doctrine had made the isolation of the guerrillas from external assistance one of the three principal objectives of counterguerrilla warfare, along with isolating the guerrillas from internal support and effecting their destruction. Civilian policy makers, however, fearing a widening of the conflict into a regional conflagration, refused to use ground troops to drive the enemy from his cross-border bases. Consequently, Westmoreland had little choice but to rely on air power and covert operations to interdict the Viet Cong's external lifelines. Not until 1970 would Washington lift its self-imposed ban on cross-border operations and then only briefly. This policy, coupled with the failure of American military, diplomatic, and unconventional warfare efforts to deny the enemy the use of Laos and Cambodia, meant that the allies were never able to isolate the battlefield. This predicament would ultimately prove fatal, for despite romantic talk about guerrillas living off the land, the reality was that Communist forces in South Vietnam depended heavily on outside sources for weapons, ammunition, and manpower. Unlike in Greece and Korea, where successful border interdiction caused indigenous guerrillas to wither on the vine, in South Vietnam Communist forces enjoyed the benefit of an endless influx of men and materiel from the North that significantly offset Free World assistance to the Saigon government.[4]

If Westmoreland found the idea of isolating South Vietnam from northern infiltration an attractive—if difficult—objective, he found little merit in an alternative proposal to confine U.S. operations to coastal enclaves. This concept, championed by the U.S. ambassador to South Vietnam, retired Army General Maxwell Taylor, called for U.S. troops to guard vital air bases and population centers while the Army of the Republic of Vietnam took to the field. Such a deployment would limit America's involvement in the conflict and position the United States for an easy exit should the situation deteriorate. Generals Westmoreland and Johnson, however, rejected the enclave concept. The South Vietnamese Army had already proved that it was unable to defeat the enemy in the field, and the situation was becoming more critical every day. A strategy of defensive enclaves would also forfeit the initiative to the enemy—a violation of the offensive spirit that permeated U.S. doctrine. Moreover, Westmoreland believed that maximizing the Army's strength—its fighting power—made better sense than restricting the Army to a defensive role. Eventually, Taylor conceded that South Vietnam could not be saved by passive measures, and the enclave strategy gave way to a more aggressive approach.[5]

The final plan determined by Westmoreland attempted to achieve a delicate balance between several important counterinsurgency objectives. To detect and intercept the steady stream of enemy reinforcements crossing South Vietnam's porous borders, Westmoreland would employ a screen of American-led CIDG irregulars backed by special reconnaissance elements and a relatively small number of regular combat troops. While these forces patrolled the hinterlands, he would base the majority of his men closer to the coast and around Saigon. From such locations, U.S. forces would be positioned to protect the South Vietnamese people from attack and to isolate the guerrillas from the majority of the nation's resources, much as the enclave strategy had envisioned. Yet unlike the enclave strategy, Westmoreland also planned to use these bases to launch offensives into Communist-controlled territory, breaking up and destroying enemy concentrations and laying the groundwork for the eventual expansion of government control throughout South Vietnam via the oil-spot method.

Westmoreland explained the complicated offensive-defensive role allied military forces would play with the analogy of a boxer.

His right hand stays in close to secure his jaw, his mid-section, his vulnerable areas. His left stays out, punching, to keep the initiative on the enemy. If there is an opening he can uncork his right, to reinforce the left and knock the opponent out. But he must always bring it back. When it is out he is vulnerable. Sometimes he brings the punch hand back to help cover the vital areas; then the opponent has the initiative.

The right hand is the forces we need to secure the population, to be employed on pacification and revolutionary development missions. These concentrate on killing the guerrillas who harass the people and are the eyes and ears of the enemy.

The punch hand carries the fight to the Main Force and keeps the initiative on him. "Right hand" troops are moved occasionally if the opportunity arises, but they can't be gone long. They must provide security. If we pull our punch hand in, then like the boxer, we lose the initiative. So our fundamental strategy is a balance between the right and left-hand forces. We can reinforce the left, but we must never pull it in and button up. This is the enclave concept. . . . The art of command in this environment consists in achieving the proper balance between the two hands.[6]

Having settled on this concept, the next step was to establish a division of labor between the Vietnamese and the newly arriving Americans. For the past twenty years U.S. foreign policy had consistently maintained that indigenous governments bore primary responsibility for their own defense, especially in matters of internal security. This policy reflected the fact that indigenous governments were usually quite sensitive about foreigners meddling in their internal affairs, not to mention the aversion the American public typically exhibited toward becoming embroiled in overseas conflicts. U.S. officers had likewise recognized the merits of relegating internal security issues to local troops. Native soldiers were the logical instruments for enforcing the internal policies of indigenous governments. They not only had a legitimacy that no foreign soldier could possess in the post-colonial era, but also their inherent language skills, cultural affinity, and regional knowledge gave them great advantages over foreign soldiers when they undertook constabulary operations. On the other hand, the military power of most third world nations paled in comparison to that of the United States. Thus creating a rough division of labor between the allies made sense. The militarily weak South Vietnamese would shoulder the primary burden of the internal war—fighting village guerrillas, establishing control over the nation's population and resources, and building new social institutions capable of withstanding the Communist onslaught. Conversely, the United States, while assisting in all of these endeavors, would play to its own strengths to wage the big battles against the enemy's main force units. In so doing, U.S. forces would provide the necessary umbrella of security so desperately needed if Saigon's pacification and nation-building endeavors were to have any chance of success. This approach was entirely consistent with Anglo-American doctrine and mirrored the way the United States had divided responsibilities fifteen years earlier in the Korean War. As Westmoreland explained, "we can carry the major share of the punch, while the weight of their [the South Vietnamese] effort goes into securing."[7]

The allies incorporated Westmoreland's division of labor into their annual combined campaign plans. The bifurcation, however, was never absolute. Throughout the war the South Vietnamese Army participated in major offensive operations. Conversely, U.S. units were always performing security and pacification support missions akin to the "right hand" in Westmoreland's analogy. Thus the relationship between U.S. and Vietnamese roles, as well as the relative "weight" given to each of the two "fists," would remain dynamic throughout the war.[8]

In envisioning how the war would be fought, Westmoreland postulated that he first needed to "stem the tide" of Communist aggression by employing the few U.S. troops initially available to him in 1965 and 1966 in a series of raids and spoiling attacks to keep the enemy off-balance. Once the situation had stabilized, he planned to switch from harassment to sustained offensive operations, exploiting the steady growth of American combat and logistical power to destroy the enemy's major forces and bases. Meanwhile, the Vietnamese, under the cover of American operations and with some direct American help, would undertake pacification operations in selected areas. Finally, after the enemy's main forces had been broken and dispersed, the allies would mop up the remaining insurgent infrastructure and solidify the government's presence in the countryside, introducing more permanent political and socioeconomic reforms to strengthen the government's presence and redress the causes of discontent.

This formulation mirrored Army doctrinal precepts, and to an extent the war played out as Westmoreland had envisioned. After passing through the initial defensive stage, MACV was able to transition to division- and even corps-size offensive operations by 1967. These operations imposed significant human and material losses on the enemy, but they neither dampened his determination nor sufficiently weakened his offensive capability, thanks in large measure to the continued infusion of troops from North Vietnam. The result was a bloody stalemate.

At this point in January 1968 the Communists launched their massive Tet offensive. Tet proved a political coup for the North Vietnamese. The sheer size and power of the offensive shocked and demoralized many Americans who were beginning to tire after three years of war. As the conflict became increasingly unpopular at home, America's new president, Richard M. Nixon, initiated a gradual withdrawal of U.S. troops while continuing the peace talks his predecessor had initiated with North Vietnam. This dual process eventually led to a tenuous cease-fire and the final removal of U.S. forces in 1973.

Although the Tet offensive ultimately proved to be a political victory for the Communists, militarily it was a disaster. Heavy losses led the Communists to withdraw some of their major units to remote base camps and cross-border sanctuaries far from South Vietnam's population centers. Communist main force activity dropped precipitously, from an annual average of seventy battalion-size assaults between 1965 and 1968 to an annual rate of twenty battalion-size attacks during 1969 and 1970. Ironically, the Communist offensive had achieved what MACV had only imperfectly accomplished after three years of effort—it had driven the main force units back and weakened the remaining guerrillas to the extent that pacification could finally move forward.[9]

General Creighton W. Abrams, who replaced Westmoreland as MACV commander in June 1968, was determined to exploit the opportunity. He championed the notion that the conflict in Vietnam should be treated as "one war," in which military and pacification operations blended into a seamless tapestry. Consequently, Army units began paying greater attention to the type of area security and pacification support missions that had always been central to Army doctrine, but that had frequently assumed a backseat prior to 1968 due to the threat posed by the enemy's main forces.[10]

The new tack taken by U.S. forces in the wake of Tet was fairly successful in increasing population security and reducing, though never eliminating, the presence of Communist guerrillas and political cadres among the population. Still, Abrams' one-war campaign differed from Westmoreland's activities more in emphasis than in substance. As MACV admitted in 1970, "the basic concept and objectives of pacification, to defeat the VC/NVA [Viet Cong/North Vietnamese Army] and to provide the people with economic and social benefits, have changed little since the first comprehensive GVN [government of Vietnam] plan was published in 1964." This was equally true with regard to operational and tactical methods, which did not differ substantially from those developed during Westmoreland's tenure. Although the military situation after Tet permitted the Army to undertake more pacification operations than had been the case prior to 1968, the counterforce mission remained a central feature of Army operational life after Tet, as the enemy's main forces remained poised to strike whenever the opportunity arose.[11] Indeed, in 1970 MACV's office of Civil Operations and Revolutionary Development Support admitted that U.S. combat units continued to "have the primary mission of locating and neutralizing enemy main force units, base areas, and liaison, communications, and logistical systems in clearing zones and border surveillance zones," a mission that, in its opinion, was "perfectly consistent with the principles of area security."[12] As Lt. Gen. Julian J. Ewell, one of the more successful commanders during the Abrams years, explained, "I had two rules. One is that you would try to get a very close meshing of pacification . . . and military operations. The other rule is the military operations would be given first priority in every case. That doesn't mean you didn't do pacification, but this gets at what you might call winning the hearts and minds of the people. I'm all for that. It's a nice concept, but in fighting the Viet Cong and the NVA, if you don't break their military machine you might as well forget winning the hearts and minds of the people."[13]

Thus, under Abrams as under Westmoreland, defeating the enemy remained "the single best way of achieving security." The means employed differed somewhat, only because the situation differed. The gradual evolution of American operations from major offensives to a more balanced, area control and pacification approach represented little more than the natural progression envisioned by Westmoreland and Army doctrine. That this transformation remained incomplete had more to do with the ultimate failure of the Army to win the main force war and isolate the battlefield than a dogmatic adherence to large-unit operations.[14]

Operational Concepts

Army doctrine recognized that insurgencies were multifaceted phenomena requiring a multifaceted response. When applying this precept to Vietnam, General Westmoreland crafted three broad categories of military operations, each designed to meet a particular aspect of the overall mission.

The first category, "search-and-destroy" operations, included offensive thrusts undertaken to attack the enemy's major combat formations and base areas. Search-and-destroy operations were a mainstay of the main force war and ranged in duration from a day to several weeks. They were not designed to hold ground or establish any type of permanent presence, though they could be used in conjunction with pacification operations, either to protect an already pacified sector or to prepare an area for future pacification by driving off the enemy's main combat units. The amount of force employed in a search-and-destroy operation varied from corps to companies, depending on the strength of the enemy and the size and nature of the operational area. Tactically, they usually involved the execution of some manner of sweep or encirclement.[15]

Westmoreland labeled the second type of operation "clearing," or "clear and hold." The Army used clearing operations to break up the enemy's guerrilla forces in an area slated for pacification. Following doctrine, an Army brigade would move to the targeted area, establish base camps, and create a liaison with indigenous civil, military, and intelligence agencies. The brigade commander would then divide the area among his subordinate battalions. Depending upon the terrain and the strength of the enemy, MACV estimated that a battalion could clear an area up to 373 square kilometers in size. Once established, the battalions would subdivide their assigned territory among their component companies, being careful to keep a reserve for rapid reaction operations. The companies would saturate their areas of responsibility with frequent day and night patrols, raids, and ambushes ranging in size from squads to companies. Army units during clearing operations continuously operated on the offensive, eschewing static garrison duty. When a patrol detected guerrillas, reinforcements would be rushed to the scene to destroy them in a fashion not unlike the net-and-spear tactics U.S. advisers had introduced to the South Vietnamese in the early 1960s. The troops would also assist in an array of population- and resources-control measures designed to strengthen the government's presence in the area. As the enemy's hold over the territory weakened, allied units would break down into progressively smaller units, laying the way for the third, and final, "securing" operation.[16]

Securing operations differed little from the later phases of clearing operations. Rather, they represented the final stage in the solidification of government control over an area. Continuous patrols would reduce the guerrillas to a level manageable by paramilitary and police forces, who assumed increasing responsibility for local defense. As the paramilitaries and police uprooted the last vestiges of the Communist apparatus, increased civil, economic, and psychological measures would cement the government's hold over the region's people and resources, thereby allowing the military to initiate the process in another area.[17]

MACV's three operational categories corresponded with the general phases of progressive area clearance outlined in Army doctrine. Since politico-military conditions varied widely across Vietnam, the allies ran all three operations concurrently, applying the appropriate remedy to meet local circumstances. In keeping with the division of labor Westmoreland had formulated in 1965, U.S. combat forces generally concentrated their efforts on conducting search-and-destroy and clearing missions, while the South Vietnamese performed most of the securing operations.[18]

Westmoreland's decision to focus U.S. energy initially on search-and-destroy rather than clearing and securing operations drew criticism not only from individuals who believed politically oriented pacification programs should receive top priority, but also from those who shared

Westmoreland's "security first" philosophy, but who differed with him over how best to achieve it. The debate reflected ambiguities within Army doctrine, which had never specifically embraced any particular level of military activity. Rather, doctrine had endorsed a wide range of operations—large and small, conventional and unconventional—that could be executed in different combinations to meet the situation at hand. Such an approach, while offering maximum flexibility, inevitably gave rise to differing interpretations as to what the best type of operation might be.[19]

One school maintained that Army doctrine was too biased toward large-unit operations, holding as an example the central place counter-guerrilla doctrine gave encirclements—operations that were not only difficult to execute, but which often required large numbers of men to conduct successfully. Advocates of small-unit warfare argued that the best way to destroy guerrillas was by saturating an area with innumerable small patrols that would relentlessly hound the enemy until he was destroyed. They likewise believed that small-unit operations offered the best method of protecting the people and separating them from the guerrillas. There was, however, a second school of thought—one composed of officers who chose to dwell on a different facet of revolutionary theory: the guerrilla base. While not denying the importance of small-unit actions, the alternate opinion maintained that under Maoist doctrine guerrillas must have a secure base if they were to succeed in transforming their petty harassing tactics into a movement capable of overthrowing a government. This point led people of the second school of thought to conclude that "we must not be diverted by fighting every small, scattered band that may be encountered. These actions are only incidental to the primary objective of locating, surrounding, and destroying the guerrilla's base of operations."[20]

Westmoreland embraced both points of view. Like many senior generals, he readily acknowledged that saturation patrols were the single best method for locating the enemy and rooting out Communist cadres. Indeed, from the start of the war MACV repeatedly urged commanders to undertake such operations whenever and wherever possible. Yet Westmoreland also appreciated the importance of the enemy's base areas. All armies—including Ho Chi Minh's *People's Army of Vietnam* (*PAVN*)—march on their stomachs, and, without their prestocked caches of food and arms, Communist main forces would be unable to mount major offensives. Moreover, by 1965–1966 the enemy had already developed the ability to operate in regimental and division strength. Until he had succeeded in neutralizing the main force threat, Westmoreland felt he had no choice but to keep a significant portion of his command concentrated for offensive strikes and counterstrikes against major Communist units and the bases that sustained them.[21]

Most senior officers agreed with Westmoreland as to the importance of destroying the enemy's major forces. As Chief of Staff Johnson explained, "The enemy's larger military formations must be driven away from the population. . . . If we were to adopt a strategy which emphasizes only clear and hold operations, enemy base areas would become reasonably secure again. Any change in emphasis away from search-and-destroy operations would free the enemy to operate with relative impunity around and between the peripheries of our enclaves."[22] Lt. Gen. Richard G. Stilwell agreed, stating that "Large-unit operations are thus the precondition for and shield behind which proceed all other actions to bring security to the people. With the [enemy's] big battalions isolated, the remaining and smaller elements of the total communist structure can be subjected to widespread attack by something approaching saturation tactics." Large-unit operations were therefore "the number one mission of the U.S. units" according to Maj. Gen. Frederick C. Weyand.[23] Even those who criticized some aspects of the Army's operations in Vietnam generally agreed that Westmoreland's prioritization made sense. This was the conclusion of a major study that General Johnson commissioned to critique the Army's policies in Vietnam titled "A Program for the Pacification and Long-Term Development of South Vietnam" (or "PROVN" for short). Although the 1966 report expressed concern that the United States was not doing enough to win the allegiance of the Vietnamese people, it repeatedly stressed that the "bulk" of allied regular forces should be directed against the enemy's main forces while the "remainder" guarded the people, since "the primary role" of U.S. armed forces in Vietnam was "'to isolate the battlefield' by curtailing significant infiltration, demolishing the key war zones, and fully engaging PAVN–main force VC units wherever and whenever they are located. Unrelenting pressure must be imposed upon these major enemy combat forces."[24]

None of this meant that clearing operations and the small-unit saturation tactics associated with them did not have an important place in MACV's thinking. At no time did Westmoreland or any of his senior lieutenants ever advocate the exclusive use of either large-unit or small-unit operations. Both had their place. In fact, from the beginning of Westmoreland's tenure, small-unit operations vastly outnumbered large-unit operations. Moreover, the tendency of some analysts to equate small-unit operations with pacification and large-unit operations with the big-unit war was misleading. When one considers that a battalion was generally needed to surround a single village and that two battalions were required to effect the average encirclement, the necessity of using large units during pacification operations becomes apparent.[25]

Operational Practices

The keys to bringing peace and security to Vietnam, wrote General Johnson in 1965, were finding the enemy, fixing him in place, and fighting and finishing him. General Johnson's prescription was hardly new, as it mirrored a formulation identified by Lt. Gen. Nelson A. Miles during the Indian wars of the nineteenth century and applied by generations of U.S. soldiers in virtually every war thereafter.[26]

Whether combating Native American irregulars on the Great Plains or Asian guerrillas in the jungles of Vietnam, the first requirement—to find the enemy—posed the most difficult challenge to Army soldiers. Following classic guerrilla doctrine, the Communists generally fought only when it served their purposes. They made their homes in terrain that was difficult to penetrate, and they did not hesitate to burrow elaborate underground complexes to further elude detection. The cover provided by earth and leaf, when coupled with the guerrillas' caginess and the shelter they received from the population, made them a most difficult quarry.

The enemy's ability to fight, run, or hide at his discretion meant that the insurgent, and not the Americans, most often determined the tempo of the war. This fact both surprised and frustrated senior commanders who sought to wrest the initiative from the enemy.[27]

The key to finding the enemy was intelligence, and MACV employed every possible means to obtain it. In its endless pursuit of information, MACV supplemented traditional methods with new devices hurried into production—sensors to detect heat, sound, pressure, and movement; side-looking airborne radar; and night vision equipment. As doctrine had predicted, U.S. soldiers learned that they needed to consider more political, social, and economic factors in planning and executing operations than was normally the case in conventional warfare. MACV also decided that it needed to increase the size of its intelligence staffs down to the brigade level in response to the complexities of a frontless war. Interpreters were in especially short supply, and the Army quickly found that indigenous personnel were invaluable adjuncts to the conduct of any pacification operation. When government personnel were not available, some units resorted to expedients, like the 1st Battalion, 50th Infantry, which "adopted" Vietnamese boys of nine to fourteen years of age to use as interpreters and intelligence agents.[28]

A Viet Cong prisoner, wearing a mask to hide his identity, helps U.S. troops locate his former colleagues.

The existence of two coequal but independent armies caused many problems for allied intelligence. While local Vietnamese authorities frequently had good information, that information had to be sent up the South Vietnamese chain of command, then passed over to MACV, before wending its way back down to an American unit for action—a process that took so long that the information lost much of its utility. To overcome this obstacle, Army units formed combined intelligence centers with their Vietnamese provincial and military counterparts. The 25th Infantry Division was one of the first U.S. units to establish such centers in 1966, and as time passed the collocation of South Vietnamese and U.S. intelligence and headquarters elements became common practice.[29]

Through the various means available to it, American intelligence was often able to narrow the location of an enemy unit to an area of fifty square kilometers or less. At that point ground operations generally assumed the job of actually finding the enemy. One way of doing so was through the use of large-unit sweeps. As the name implied, search-and-destroy operations were often launched without firm knowledge of the enemy's whereabouts. The maneuver entailed having one or more battalions line up and sweep through an area looking for the enemy. Sometimes these operations were undertaken with the assistance of blocking or encircling units, and sometimes not. In December 1965 Westmoreland expressed doubts about the ability of large-unit sweeps to locate an enemy who did not want to be found, lamenting that "we have learned through long and unhappy experience that preplanned schemes of maneuver, with successive objectives, by a force moving in one direction, will nearly always fail to make significant contact unless that contact is at the choosing of the VC at a time and place chosen by him when he thinks he has all the advantage."[30]

Westmoreland's concerns were unsurprising, as U.S. advisers had long criticized the South Vietnamese for making the very same mistakes. The Army persisted in using sweeps to find the enemy, in part

Vietnam's terrain posed significant challenges to counterguerrilla operations.

because there were situations in which the enemy seemed too strong to employ smaller patrols. Moreover, MACV hoped that, with greater ingenuity and skill, U.S. troops could eventually improve the effectiveness of such expeditions. The command counseled subordinates to encircle the suspect area completely before launching a sweep and to be more diligent in executing the search, taking as much as three weeks to scour the targeted area. It likewise adopted the policy of having troops return to suspect areas in the hope that multiple operations would gradually wear down the enemy's infrastructure. These and other modifications did indeed improve the performance of allied operations. Still, manpower shortages frequently interfered with such undertakings, while the enemy continued to display an uncanny ability to evade even the most meticulous sweep. More often than not, sweeps uncovered Communist supplies and killed enemy troops but rarely generated decisive battles.[31]

Many officers expressed dissatisfaction with large sweep operations. "I hope that we have conducted our last 'search and destroy' operation," wrote Brig. Gen. Ellis W. Williamson, the commander of the 173d Airborne Brigade in September 1965. "I am thoroughly convinced that running into the jungle with a lot of people without a fixed target is a lot of effort, a lot of physical energy expended. A major portion of our effort evaporates into the air." Frustrated at the enemy's ability to sidestep major expeditions, a growing number of officers began to look for alternative ways to find the enemy. Two such officers were Brig. Gen. Willard Pearson, commander of the 101st Airborne Division's 1st Brigade in 1966, and Col. David H. Hackworth, his one-time subordinate.[32]

Rather than sending out entire brigades in a vain attempt to locate the enemy, Pearson suggested that the Army adopt subtler methods, an approach he called semi-guerrilla tactics. Among the techniques he advocated were the extensive use of small reconnaissance and ambush patrols, night operations, deception activities, and informer networks. His views received wide distribution through the efforts of the outspoken Colonel Hackworth, a successful practitioner of Pearson's method and prolific publicist.[33]

Hackworth's declaration that "to defeat the guerrilla we must become guerrillas. Every insurgent tactic must be employed against the insurgent," became a rallying cry for those who believed that the Army had failed to adapt to modern revolutionary war. Nevertheless, neither officer advocated a radical departure from Army doctrine. They accepted both the Army's basic tactics and the important place that technology played in them. They also believed that large-unit sweeps and search-and-destroy operations had a legitimate function to play in counterguerrilla warfare. The emphasis in Pearson's phrase *semi-guerrilla tactics* was squarely on the prefix *semi*, for as one 1st Brigade publication explained, "once contact is made remove the cloak of being a guerrilla and operate conventionally using all available firepower, mobility, and reserves." Even Hackworth's guerrilla tactics were based on the full exploitation of what he called America's "two aces in the hole—firepower and helicopter mobility"—neither of which were available to true guerrillas. Thus, rather than embracing guerrilla warfare, Pearson and Hackworth were merely trying to augment the Army's existing capabilities with some guerrilla-style techniques. This approach was fully within the bounds of doctrinal thought. Indeed, in seeking to find an appropriate balance between conventional and unconventional techniques, Pearson and Hackworth were acting in the finest tradition of American counterguerrilla warfare, a tradition that reached back to Dennis Hart Mahan's teachings at the U.S. Military Academy during the 1830s, if not to the colonial frontier. MACV recognized this and encouraged subordinate commanders to employ schemes akin to Pearson's semi-guerrilla methods that, while never replacing the sweep, became increasingly common as the war progressed.[34]

Regardless of whether a unit was performing a search-and-destroy, clearing, or semi-guerrilla mission, patrolling was essential to finding the enemy. During the war, unit commanders developed a variety of patrol procedures, each tailored to a particular need or environment. Among these were such exotically named methods as the cloverleaf, the checkerboard, bushmaster patrols, eagle flights, thunder runs, and the jitterbug.[35]

Although all infantry units conducted patrols on a daily basis, the need for skilled reconnaissance personnel was so great that commanders turned to a number of expedients. In 1965 Westmoreland encouraged his brigade and division commanders to raise specially trained recon-naissance elements patterned on the Army's long-range reconnaissance patrol units. The Army had first created these units in the 1950s as special teams for conducting reconnaissance, intelligence, rescue, and target acquisition missions behind enemy lines. Though originally envi-sioned for use during a conventional or nuclear war, the missions they were designed to fulfill were at a premium in Vietnam. However, since the Department of the Army had not authorized the manpower needed to form such organizations, commanders had to create them on an ad hoc basis by reallocating personnel organic to their units.[36]

The first Army brigade to deploy to Vietnam, the 173d Airborne Brigade, was also the first to create a long-range reconnaissance patrol from organic assets in October 1965. In 1966 Westmoreland estab-lished a reconnaissance and commando school in Vietnam to provide training for all such special detachments, and by the fall of 1967 every division and most separate brigades had provisional LRRPs. MACV issued a doctrinal pamphlet governing the use of these special assets in late 1967, but the units remained provisional until the Army belatedly authorized them in 1969 under the designation of Rangers. Ultimately, thirteen Ranger companies served in Vietnam.[37]

Most LRRP and Ranger outfits consisted solely of Americans, but the Army also created mixed formations of American and indigenous troops. These units blended the combat power of U.S. soldiers with the invaluable local knowledge of Vietnamese personnel. One such forma-tion was the Combined Reconnaissance Intelligence Platoon developed by the 25th Infantry Division in 1966. Divided equally between U.S. and South Vietnamese soldiers, the unit was especially useful in ferret-ing out the enemy's clandestine infrastructure, and eventually several other divisions formed similar organizations.

Another potential source of intelligence was the thousands of enemy personnel who defected to the allies every year. A number of U.S. units recruited defectors and formed them into combined U.S.-Vietnamese detachments designated Kit Carson Scouts. In the 9th Infantry Division, the program was so successful that the division

A member of a long-range reconnaissance patrol

eventually assigned defectors, called Tiger Scouts, to every rifle squad in the division.

The vast majority of Vietnamese who served as scouts and auxiliaries for American forces did so in units either controlled or advised by U.S. Army Special Forces soldiers. Included among these were the Civilian Irregular Defense Groups, the Mobile Guerrilla Forces, and the Delta, Sigma, Omega, Gamma, and Apache Forces. Some of these units were technically part of the South Vietnamese armed forces, while others were essentially mercenaries recruited from South Vietnam's ethnic and religious minorities. Each had a unique structure and different, though somewhat overlapping, missions, including border patrol, population security in remote areas, deep reconnaissance, target acquisition, rapid reaction, and special strike missions.

Overall, the United States had mixed success with special reconnaissance units. At times these organizations were truly a thorn in the side of the enemy. At others they were less than successful due to resource shortages, personnel problems, and inadequate training.[38]

Once U.S. forces had located the enemy, the next task, fixing him in place, was likewise complicated by the terrain and the enemy's evasive ways. Historically, encirclement had been an effective means of bringing opponents bent on evasion to battle, and this was no less true in Vietnam. In concept, language, and execution, U.S. battle plans in Vietnam closely mirrored the *Wehrmacht*-based encirclement techniques that had graced the pages of Army manuals since 1950. The only major difference between U.S. encirclement operations and their *Wehrmacht* predecessors was America's use of the helicopter, which gave the Americans an enveloping capability undreamed of by past counterinsurgents.[39]

Still, doctrinal admonitions about the inherent difficulties of encirclement operations remained as true in 1970 as they had been twenty years earlier. Troop shortages and rugged, heavily forested terrain often meant that encirclements were rather porous, a fact that the enemy fully exploited. Even the helicopter, despite its many invaluable services, proved to be less of a panacea than some had anticipated. Helicopters were initially in short supply and were expensive to operate and maintain, while Vietnam's seasonal monsoons further impeded operations. The noise of approaching helicopters frequently tipped the enemy off to American intentions, as did the scarcity of suitable landing zones in certain areas. Helicopters were also vulnerable to ground fire, a fact that led most commanders to precede their airmobile descents with a bombardment that again disclosed allied intentions to the enemy. Moreover, the helicopter's vulnerability to ground fire also made redeploying troops during a firefight hard. Consequently, airmobile infantrymen, once deployed, were no more mobile than their foes. Nevertheless, trapping the enemy with some form of ground or heliborne encirclement remained the single best method available to the Army to compel a reluctant enemy to accept battle.[40]

Having found the enemy through a combination of intelligence and reconnaissance and fixed him in place through some manner of envelopment, the job remained to destroy him. Historically, fighting an irregular enemy had been the least difficult of the counterinsurgents' three tasks. In Vietnam, however, Viet Cong and North Vietnamese regulars were particularly formidable adversaries. By the time U.S. infantry arrived in Vietnam in 1965, most Communist units were well trained, motivated, and led by seasoned veterans. Though it could not match the allies in terms of air power, artillery, and ammunition supply, the average Communist main force infantry battalion with its typical attachments had approximately as much firepower as a U.S. infantry battalion. Just as troublesome was the enemy's penchant for fortifications. During 1966, for example, Communist forces employed fortifications in 63 percent of all their combat actions with U.S. forces. Many enemy bunkers were impervious to anything other than a direct hit by bomb, rocket, or artillery. Studies indicated that a 750-pound bomb had less than a 50 percent chance of inflicting a casualty on an entrenched enemy unit, while the probability that a single 105-mm. artillery round would cause a casualty under the same circumstances

*Airmobile infantry played a central role in U.S.
counterguerrilla operations.*

was estimated at less than 1 percent. Triple canopy forests and dense
vegetation provided additional cover from bomb blasts and prying eyes
alike. So well concealed was the enemy that most contacts occurred at
less than forty-six meters, a range that made both maneuver and the
employment of fire support exceedingly difficult, especially given the
enemy's habit of "hugging" U.S. units so as to avoid the worst effects
of an allied bombardment.[41]

The enemy's many strengths caused the Army to adjust its standard
combat methods. Perhaps no one better represented this transformation
than Maj. Gen. William E. DePuy, one of the Army's leading tacticians during the war. As MACV's chief of operations in 1965, DePuy
had developed MACV's operational "bible," a directive titled "Tactics
and Techniques for Employment of U.S. Forces in the Republic of
Vietnam." Shortly after promulgating this work, DePuy left MACV to
become commander of the 1st Infantry Division, a position from which
he would be able to put his thoughts into practice.

Upon assuming command, DePuy immediately issued detailed
guidance to the division. He reasserted MACV's position that saturation
patrolling offered the best means of locating the enemy. He also strongly advocated the use of defensive works, and the 1st Infantry Division
soon became legendary for the interlocking bunkers that sprang up at
each evening's campsite. Most importantly, DePuy reminded his subordinates that in modern warfare firepower killed, and he urged them to

379

use as much firepower as they could obtain to destroy the enemy. Yet he also adhered to traditional fire and maneuver tactics, stating that closing with the enemy was the true climax of battle. Consequently, upon making contact with the enemy, DePuy instructed his men to establish a base of fire to pin the enemy while maneuvering a portion of the command to outflank or encircle him. Once fire superiority had been achieved, the infantry was to advance—by crawling if necessary—until it had closed with the enemy. Reflecting the doctrinal principle that guerrillas, once contacted, should never be allowed to escape, the general ordered that "under NO circumstances, repeat, NO circumstances will forward elements in contact withdraw in order to bring artillery fire on the VC." Similarly, he insisted that his infantry maintain contact throughout the night, rather than withdrawing to nighttime laagers.[42]

Experience soon forced some pragmatic modifications to traditional fire and maneuver doctrine. The enemy's bunkers were too strong, his firepower too deadly, and jungle engagement ranges too short to permit maneuver in the face of the enemy. Time after time, the Viet Cong and the North Vietnamese bloodily repulsed American ground assaults led by young, gung-ho officers. Consequently, by mid-1966 DePuy had modified his initial statements to the extent of permitting officers who found themselves confronted by Communist fortifications to pull their units back and allow artillery to pummel the enemy's position. Still, he insisted that "nothing that is said above is to be construed as eliminating the necessity, eventually, to close with the position, destroy the remaining defenders and achieve the objective, by infantry elements. This should be done after sufficient ordnance has been expended to soften the position and, ideally, to kill all or most of the defenders." Infantry assault, while thus still an integral part of combat tactics, had begun to take a backseat to the application of heavy firepower.[43]

DePuy's experience was replicated throughout the Army in Vietnam in 1965 and 1966 and became the basis for U.S. tactics for the rest of the war. "The trick of jungle fighting," DePuy summarized, "is to find the enemy with the fewest possible men and to destroy him with the maximum amount of firepower." According to the new "pile on" tactics, the infantry would locate the enemy with small patrols, fix and encircle him with airmobile reinforcements, and then bury him under an avalanche of air- and artillery-delivered ordnance.[44]

The change in American tactics—from one that balanced fire and maneuver to one in which fire held overwhelming precedence—was logical given the realities of Vietnam. In a war in which capturing ground was less important than destroying the enemy, using bullets rather than bodies made sense. Such tactics also coincided with the political constraints that came with fighting an increasingly unpopular war and made the most of America's technological and logistical strengths. On the other hand, pile-on tactics were not easy to use, as they required commanders to choreograph the activities of fixed-wing aircraft, helicopter gunships, artillery, and naval gunfire with the movement of troops on the ground and transport helicopters in the air. Such operations required detailed planning, precise timing, rapid communications, and flawless coordination if they were to be executed in a manner that both prevented the enemy's escape and minimized U.S. casualties.

Not every commander could effect such coordination successfully. Moreover, old ways died hard, and veteran officers had to stress repeatedly to their less-experienced colleagues the importance of using firepower rather than infantry to take most enemy positions. In fact, the officer corps remained at odds throughout the war as to what the exact mix of fire and maneuver should be. A 1969 survey of over two hundred officers revealed that 56 percent felt that decisively closing with the enemy still represented a better tactic than simply sitting back and allowing artillery to do the infantry's work for it. Westmoreland himself complained that an overreliance on fire support was sapping soldiers' offensive spirit and creating a "firebase psychosis" in which the smallest tactical task could not be performed without intensive artillery preparation. The plethora of firepower available to the average platoon and company commander led to frequent abuses of that power, with one study finding fifteen instances of ground commanders firing up to a hundred rounds of artillery fire to dislodge a single Communist sniper.[45]

As the war progressed the Army began to exhibit some of the behaviors for which U.S. advisers had criticized the South Vietnamese for years. Not only did the Army demonstrate an increasing reliance on artillery, but in practice many officers ignored DePuy's initial admonitions and broke contact with the enemy to "maneuver to the rear," either to call in fire support or to establish nighttime laagers. While there were practical reasons for breaking contact, disengaging robbed battles of their decisiveness and weakened already porous encirclements, notwithstanding the best efforts by artillery blocking fires to prevent the enemy from escaping during the night. The Communists appreciated this fact and frequently timed their attacks so that night would fall before the Americans could effectively react and seal the battlefield.[46]

In addition to the allegedly corrosive effects abundant firepower had on tactical efficiency and initiative, it also had serious ramifications for the political side of the war. While air and artillery strikes minimized American casualties, they killed and maimed civilians, destroyed homes and businesses, and potentially alienated the very people the United States was fighting to protect. Particularly galling to the population was harassment and interdiction (H&I) fire. H&I fire was used to disrupt suspected enemy concentrations and lines of communications. It was often preplanned and executed at night, with little or no direct observation of the target. Born out of frustration with the Army's inability to come to grips with the enemy and made possible by America's incredible wealth, H&I fire eventually came to represent about half of all fire missions in Vietnam. Some of this fire was undoubtedly effective and necessary, and every soldier manning some remote outpost slept a little easier knowing that U.S. artillery enveloped him in a protective blanket of steel and shrapnel. But it was also an extremely wasteful practice.

As the war progressed an increasing number of soldiers expressed unease at the Army's vast ammunition expenditures. Efforts by Westmoreland, Abrams, and others to reduce the volume of H&I fire were only modestly successful, however, as these went against the grain of the Army's growing dependence on fire. In fact, a postwar survey of 110 generals found that only about 30 percent believed that the United States had employed too much air and artillery firepower in Vietnam.[47]

While not minimizing the ill effects of the Army's growing dependence on fire support, firepower kept casualties down, a principal factor of morale both at home and in the field. The fact that the high ammunition expenditures had little to do with the use of search-and-destroy operations or conventional battle tactics is also worth noting. Regardless of the size or type of forces involved or the mission they were on—whether village security, long-range reconnaissance, saturation patrolling, or major offensive operations—allied troops depended to a large degree on air and artillery support for their survival. The enemy may have had less ammunition to burn and fewer pieces of artillery, but his weaponry was not inconsequential and no less deadly than American ordnance. Indeed, if not for the devastating effect of U.S. fire support, many a battle large and small would have been lost. Thus supporting fires, though abused, were a vital component of warfare in Vietnam.[48]

Organizational and Tactical Adaptations

The shift from a balanced fire and maneuver philosophy to one that was increasingly firepower oriented represented just one of the many changes that occurred during the war. Army doctrine had always encouraged commanders to adapt to the situation rather than to apply dogmatically textbook solutions that might not fit the vagaries of war. Not everyone had the mental agility to make such adjustments. On the whole, however, U.S. soldiers exhibited the ability to learn and adapt during the Vietnam conflict.

Though not created for counterguerrilla duty, the Army had developed the ROAD division in such a way as to facilitate tailoring. This was fortunate, for no sooner had units begun to arrive in Vietnam than their commanders began to clamor for a host of adjustments to meet the demands of area warfare. Chief among these was the need for more troops—more staff to man headquarters elements for round-the-clock operations, more fire control specialists to accommodate the highly dispersed and firepower-intense nature of Vietnam combat, and more intelligence, psychological warfare, and civil affairs officers to deal with the particularly heavy work load that revolutionary warfare posed for each of these disciplines. For the most part, Army theoreticians had anticipated these needs, but the stateside bureaucracy often moved slowly in making the necessary adjustments. This situation compelled many units to resort to ad hoc arrangements in the interim.

While the Army reacted gradually to irregular warfare's manpower needs, it tried to anticipate materiel challenges. The military entered Vietnam convinced that its formations needed to be light and mobile, unencumbered by some of the heavier trappings required for conventional warfare. Consequently, in 1965 the Army undertook a number of steps toward streamlining its formations for Southeast Asian service. In the case of the 1st Infantry Division, the first full infantry division sent to Vietnam, the Army reorganized the division's five infantry, two mechanized, and two armor battalions into nine infantry battalions. The Army deleted the division's nuclear-capable rocket systems, removed most of its tanks, and stripped the division of 90 trucks and 120 trailers. Brig. Gen. Arthur L. West, the deputy assistant chief of staff for force development, wanted to make even deeper cuts, but Chief of Staff Johnson resisted further streamlining until the Army had gained some practical experience in Vietnam.[49]

Other units made similar modifications before deploying to Vietnam. Once in country, the shakedown process continued, as commanders mothballed unnecessary, ineffective, or overly burdensome equipment. Conversely, by hook or by crook they acquired additional items that had proved indispensable, like portable field radios, light machine guns, and M79 grenade launchers.[50]

Although the general trend was toward lightness, streamlining was not always appropriate. Thus the 1st Infantry Division was soon begging to have the trucks and trailers that the Army had stripped from the division returned to it, since the highly dispersed nature of the division's operations placed great strains on its reduced transportation resources. After studying the situation Combat Developments Command concluded that some of the Army's streamlining measures had been misguided—trucks and trailers were just as necessary in low intensity conflict as in conventional warfare.[51]

A similar reversal occurred with respect to armored vehicles. Army doctrine had always stated that tanks and armored personnel carriers would be of limited utility in counterguerrilla warfare. Westmoreland initially shared this philosophy, stating in 1965 that "Vietnam is no place for either tank or mechanized infantry units." This view, together with an apprehension that "the presence of tank formations" would tend "to create a psychological atmosphere of conventional combat," had led Generals Johnson, Westmoreland, and Taylor to resist the deployment of armor to Vietnam. The only armored vehicles the Army had permitted the 1st Infantry Division to bring to Vietnam had been those assigned to the division's armored cavalry squadron. Only with the greatest reluctance did Westmoreland yield to General Weyand's insistence that he be allowed to bring three armored battalions (one battalion each of tanks and armored personnel carriers plus an armored cavalry squadron) with him when the 25th Infantry Division deployed to Vietnam in early 1966. The heavy vehicles demonstrated their worth as convoy escorts, raiders, rapid reaction forces, and as integral parts of many sweep, search-and-destroy, and assault operations. They were especially useful in minimizing casualties from mines, booby traps, and bunkers. Seeing the results, Westmoreland dropped his preconceived notions and increased the level of armor in Vietnam until it accounted for 24 percent of all Army maneuver battalions deployed during the war. This reversal, as in the case of the 1st Infantry Division's trucks, further illustrated that a dogmatic adherence to traditional counterguerrilla precepts could be just as debilitating as a refusal to adjust conventional formations to unconventional situations.[52]

As more troops deployed to Vietnam and the Army gained more experience in the conditions under which the war was being fought, the service continued to modify its organizational structure. Many platoon leaders, for example, reordered their platoons from three rifle squads and one weapons squad into a more balanced force of four rifle squads, each carrying one machine gun. Similarly, many battalion commanders came to appreciate the benefits of having four rifle companies rather than the normal three found in the standard ROAD infantry battalion.

Three companies—typically two up front and one in reserve—had served the Army well in linear warfare in World War II and Korea, and the Army had preserved this structure when it created the ROAD division in the early 1960s. But in Vietnam, area warfare placed such heavy demands on rifle strength that most battalions found that they needed an extra maneuver element. Westmoreland began petitioning Washington to authorize a fourth rifle company for his infantry battalions in 1965, but the Army bureaucracy moved slowly on his requests. Consequently, unit commanders had to resort to realigning manpower within their organizations. Battalion headquarters and headquarters companies, battalion reconnaissance and antitank platoons, company antitank sections, and battalion ground surveillance sections were the most frequent entities tapped to create ad hoc fourth rifle companies. These expedients continued until 1967, when the Army finally shipped additional rifle companies to Vietnam.[53]

The addition of a fourth rifle company, together with the addition of a fourth maneuver battalion to certain brigades, led some divisions to add a fourth firing battery to their artillery battalions so as to support the additional maneuver elements better. The Army also created a new formation—the light infantry brigade—for counterinsurgency and contingency operations service. Meanwhile, inspired by French and Vietnamese experience, the Army restructured part of the 9th Infantry Division for riverine duty in the Mekong Delta. The riverine force worked in conjunction with a Navy task force replete with gunboats and special troop ferrying rivercraft. With all this experimentation, the Army's seven divisions and five separate brigades in Vietnam did not reach their final configurations until 1969, at which point no two were alike, as the Army had allowed each to evolve individually to fit the unique conditions in which it operated.[54]

While the Army modified its organizational and logistical structures to meet the exigencies of Vietnam, commanders continued to tinker with tactics and techniques. They developed new methods and revised old ones, constantly seeking to improve their performance. Artillery units learned how to decentralize their operations and deploy their guns to ensure 360-degree coverage in a frontless war. Infantry units developed techniques to meet some of the unique challenges posed by the enemy's tactics, including mine, tunnel, and fortification warfare. Armored cavalry and mechanized infantry units learned to execute tank-like roles, while tank units created special formations for forest and ambush warfare.[55]

Finding some way to surprise the elusive and cautious enemy lay at the heart of many American adaptations. Following prescriptions contained in prewar manuals and training texts, U.S. commanders leaked misleading information to the enemy, prestocked depots so as not to give away impending operations with big logistical buildups, and kept their plans secret from subordinates and, more particularly, the spy-ridden South Vietnamese government. They employed feints, ruses, and other stratagems, like sending out a seemingly vulnerable unit to tempt the enemy into attacking what, in reality, was a well-supported formation. They also deployed stay-behind forces to ambush Communist scavengers who inevitably showed up at abandoned American campsites. To confuse the enemy further about American intentions, units launched decoy operations and bombarded multiple potential landing sites during airmobile operations. Some units even opted to forgo preliminary bombardments altogether during airmobile operations, a risky tactic given the vulnerability of troops during the landing process. Finally, many commanders sought to take the night back from the enemy.[56]

Achieving this last goal was not easy. Not only were nighttime heliborne actions hazardous, but U.S. soldiers inherently disliked nocturnal operations, despite repeated training and command emphasis. Fatigue engendered from round-the-clock operations likewise worked against the efficiency of night activities. Moreover, portions of Vietnam's terrain were so difficult as to preclude any type of maneuver at night. This was no less true for the Viet Cong and North Vietnamese as for the Americans, with the exception that the enemy generally knew where he was going and the Americans did not. Consequently, most U.S. night operations consisted of relatively short troop movements and static ambushes. Still, as the war progressed U.S. units invested ever greater effort to make the night inhospitable to the enemy, with the 1st Infantry Division laying an average of 1,200 night ambushes a month by 1968.[57]

MACV actively encouraged night operations as well as virtually every other conceivable innovation. Throughout the war it permitted unit commanders to fit their tactics and techniques to the conditions in which they found themselves, rather than to adhere slavishly to what might appear in manuals. To improve performance and help overcome the continuous loss of experience caused by casualties and personnel rotation policies, virtually every unit developed extensive rules and guidelines known as standing operating procedures (SOPs). Many unit SOPs were similar, but much variety existed as well. Such diversity allowed commanders to adjust to Vietnam's many different challenges.

Units backed these SOPs with continuous training programs, while MACV instituted a comprehensive reporting system to capture and disseminate the war's lessons. Taken together, these actions reflected an atmosphere of experimentation that was highly beneficial.[58]

Over the course of the war the Army made hundreds if not thousands of adjustments to prescribed prewar methods. For the most part these changes were compatible with existing doctrine and represented relatively slight adjustments to technique rather than fundamental deviations from the overarching concepts and principles contained in manuals. On the other hand, there were many cases where the exigencies of the situation prevented the Army from implementing doctrinal precepts that, if followed, might well have been beneficial.

Many officers recognized that the Army was not meeting doctrinal standards, but they were not always able to rectify the situation. Thus, while manuals clearly warned against the ill effects of soldiers littering the countryside with supplies and equipment that the enemy could use, MACV's repeated attempts to correct such transgressions were only marginally effective. Similar problems existed in the areas of camp and march security. Habitual shortcomings in these and other areas weakened the effectiveness of U.S. operations in Vietnam. Still, U.S. troops demonstrated remarkable ingenuity in adapting their tactics and techniques to conditions in Vietnam. Unfortunately, the enemy proved equally resourceful, with the result that the war took on a seesaw quality, as each side adapted to its adversary's latest innovation and countered with one of its own.[59]

Pacification

While the Army directed much of its energy toward finding, fixing, and fighting the enemy, MACV readily acknowledged that "the war in Vietnam cannot be won by offensive military operations alone."[60] From the start, Westmoreland and other senior commanders repeatedly emphasized the importance of the struggle to win control over, and hopefully the support of, the Vietnamese people. MACV termed the process by which the allies achieved this objective *pacification*, which it defined as "the military, political, economic, and social process of establishing or re-establishing local government responsive to and involving the participation of the people." In the military's opinion, pacification was the necessary precursor for achieving the type of systematic socioeconomic and political reforms that Americans generally thought were necessary to redress the underlying causes of revolutionary ferment, a process that MACV termed *nation building*.[61]

Soldiers teach English as part of the Army's outreach efforts in Vietnam.

Following national policy and Army doctrine, MACV maintained that responsibility for both short-term pacification and long-term nation building lay primarily with the South Vietnamese and the U.S. civilian agencies assigned to assist them. Thus MACV left the destruction of the enemy's covert apparatus largely to the indigenous police and paramilitaries to accomplish. Similarly, South Vietnam bore primary responsibility for measures related to politics, civil administration, socioeconomic betterment, village defense, and population and resources control. Nevertheless, MACV recognized that it had a major role to play in the pacification effort, and from the start Westmoreland directed his subordinates to assist the Republic of Vietnam's pacification programs.[62]

Several factors impeded the Army's ability to support pacification effectively. To begin with, military requirements limited the amount of time frontline units could devote to pacification. Although there were exceptions, most pacification support operations lasted only a few weeks or months. Often this was an insufficient amount of time to do the job thoroughly. Moreover, the fruits of even the most successful pacification endeavor tended to be short lived, as South Vietnamese officials frequently proved incapable of maintaining the gains achieved by the departing Americans.[63]

Maintaining politico-military connectivity was a second major problem. Pacification's multifaceted nature required the close coordination of a host of U.S. and South Vietnamese civil and security agencies.

All too often these agencies worked at cross-purposes. This was partly the result of bureaucratic infighting in Saigon and Washington, but more fundamentally, there were just too many people charged with stirring the pacification pot, each with his own agenda and chain of command. The centralization of most pacification programs under MACV in 1967 helped but did not fully resolve this problem.[64]

Inadequacies in the Army's personnel and force structure systems also hindered the Army's participation in pacification. Although Army schools had familiarized many officers and noncommissioned officers with the pacification concept, relatively few had had any direct experience in performing pacification-type functions. Ironically, the people with the most training in conducting civil-military operations—the Army's civil affairs specialists—were not deployed to Vietnam in any numbers. In fact, only 1 percent of the Army's total civil affairs assets ever saw service in Vietnam. There were two reasons for this. First, in 1965 Ambassador Taylor, backed by the State Department and the Agency for International Development, blocked an Army plan to send civil affairs teams into the countryside because he feared that such an action would militarize what he believed should be a civilian matter. Second, the Army had placed most of its civil affairs structure in the reserves in the belief that a war that was large enough to require substantial civil affairs activities would inevitably involve a general mobilization. President Johnson's decision against mobilizing the reserves thus left the Army in a quandary, and ultimately only three civil affairs companies saw service in Vietnam.[65]

A final factor that interfered with the effective performance of pacification operations stemmed from a lack of clarity in doctrine. Army doctrine had always recognized the important role that civilian populations played in influencing the outcome of counterguerrilla and constabulary operations. During the 1960s, however, two schools of thought had emerged over civil affairs issues. The traditional school depicted civil affairs as an important, yet distinctly auxiliary weapon whose utility lay in facilitating military operations. The second school adopted a more expansive view, in which soldiers would don the mantle of social engineers to implement the latest nation-building theories. Since both philosophies found expression in Army texts, confusion inevitably arose as to the proper aims and boundaries of Army civil activities.[66]

A related divergence of thought existed with regard to population-control matters. Army doctrine traditionally asserted that commanders should adopt a firm-but-fair attitude toward civilians, treating them as benevolently as possible and as sternly as necessary (within the confines of international law). On the other hand, some of the more extreme disciples of the hearts-and-minds philosophy opposed virtually any measure that might inconvenience or annoy the population. Westmoreland strove to find a middle course between positive programs and repression. Such a course was not easy to execute and naturally resulted in confusion and criticism, as commanders wrestled with the inherent ambiguity of politico-military operations.

The most frequent way in which U.S. combat formations participated in pacification was through clearing operations. Following doctrine, MACV assigned divisions and brigades to relatively permanent tactical areas of responsibility in the belief that "only by remaining in an area for a protracted period can a close relationship with the populace be developed. This in turn engenders confidence. When the local people no longer live in fear that the VC will return, they will inform on them because it is in the interest of their own security and welfare to do so."[67]

The amount of effort U.S. units were able to put into pacification support operations varied considerably from province to province, season to season, and unit to unit. Some units spent the overwhelming majority of their time performing search-and-destroy, encirclement, and other offensive operations typical of the main force war. Others, situated in locales less threatened by large enemy units, were able to focus their energies on area clearance and pacification support missions. One statistical snapshot taken in the fall of 1966 revealed that 22 percent of American combat units were currently assigned to support the revolutionary development program, compared to 10.1 percent of South Vietnamese Army units and 91.1 percent of the Regional and Popular Forces. One year later, Westmoreland reported that the proportion of U.S. units assigned to area security missions had nearly doubled, to 40 percent. A second study performed around the same time noted that while U.S. forces were responsible for about 70 percent of the search-and-destroy effort, they also spent about 52 percent of their time performing tasks associated with improving local security. Attention to pacification increased after Tet, while even operations that were not specifically pacification-oriented furthered the process by weakening the enemy's overall military position. Thus pacification support represented a significant activity for the U.S. Army throughout the war.[68]

Brigades and battalions performed most area clearance operations. In addition to conducting many small-unit patrols and ambushes, the most common mission assigned to units during pacification operations was the village search. The typical search involved establishing a

U.S. infantrymen search a village.

cordon around a village—preferably in the predawn hours—with helicopters, airmobile reserves, and artillery fire covering areas that could not be readily sealed by infantry. Once the cordon was established, troops would enter the village to search house-to-house for contraband, deserters, and Communist agents. The preferred method was to use Vietnamese police and soldiers for all the work inside the hamlets, but when this was not possible, the Americans did it themselves. Often the allies would round up all of the males and take them to an off-site location for interrogation, a method the Army had employed in the Philippine War of 1899–1902.[69]

Most searches were conducted as a part of wider military operations and were necessarily limited to a day or less. Brief forays such as these often failed to uncover the enemy's most important personnel, many of whom retreated to underground complexes stocked with several days' worth of supplies. Moreover, many villagers were reluctant to help the visiting troops for fear of Communist retaliation. MACV recognized these facts and recommended that troops remain in a village for ten to fourteen days, a goal that was rarely achieved.

By capturing Viet Cong sympathizers and disrupting the enemy's political and logistical infrastructure, village cordon-and-search operations materially assisted the restoration of government authority in the countryside. Cordoned villages provided captive audiences for government propaganda and, if sufficiently cleared, represented potentially fertile ground for the assertion of greater government control. Search operations were, on the other hand, inherently unpleasant. Few civilians enjoyed being turned out of their homes and having their possessions searched. The military's method of foiling booby traps by compelling villagers to precede soldiers down streets and into buildings also won few friends.[70]

Doctrine stated that searches should be sufficiently discomforting to the civilian population so as to discourage future cooperation with the guerrillas, while not being so severe as to convert the populace into revolutionaries. This was a fine line to walk, and not one that could always be done successfully from either the Army's or the population's point of view. Early in the war some commanders complained that their men had not been sufficiently trained in search techniques. Rather than being overly aggressive, these officers believed their men were so squeamish about discomforting civilians that they were ineffective in conducting searches. Time and experience soon remedied this shortcoming, but figuring out a way to avoid alienating people was a tougher problem to solve.[71]

One solution to the public relations problem posed by search operations was to sugarcoat the unpleasantries with more palliative fare. Thus, when U.S. soldiers arrived to search a village, they often brought with them food, medicine, and entertainment ranging from military bands to theater troops. While some soldiers searched houses and interviewed villagers, others curried the favor of the inhabitants by distributing candy to children, conducting lotteries, and performing small civic action projects. Meanwhile, American psychological warfare personnel joined with representatives of the Saigon government in proselytizing the peasants over hot dog and ice cream luncheons. The idea was to create a carnival-like atmosphere that would make the villagers forget and forgive the difficulties visited upon them by government forces.

Early in the war Army and Marine commanders claimed great success from such activities, which they dubbed "county fairs" and "hamlet festivals." Over time, however, more sober appraisals took hold. Hershey bars and musical serenades were inadequate distractions for women worried about the fate of sons and husbands carted off for interrogation. Similarly, minor kindnesses could not overcome the mixture of loyalty and fear many people held for the enemy. Consequently, by 1967 the Army began to tone down its expectations for the county fair technique which, while never entirely discarded, assumed a less important role as the war progressed. Cordon and searches, without the frills, continued apace, however, as necessary vehicles for asserting control over the countryside.[72]

Soldiers round up civilians as part of a village search.

In addition to searching villages, U.S. soldiers helped implement the government's population- and resources-control program by conducting patrols and manning checkpoints. The allies also sought to sever the enemy's logistical ties to the people by controlling the production and distribution of food in those parts of the country where it was feasible to do so. In addition to spraying herbicides in Communist-controlled areas, MACV regularly launched operations during rice harvest season to prevent the peasants from passing the fruits of their labors to the enemy. Sometimes these missions simply involved increased patrolling of farming regions. In others, the Army would round up all the peasants of a particular area and evacuate them to a temporary compound where it could both protect and watch the people. Each day the farmers would sally forth to harvest their crops, and each evening the Army would truck the peasants and their produce back to the compound for safekeeping. Such operations imposed hardships on civilians, but they increased the government's control over the harvest and, conversely, reduced the Communists' take, so much so that enemy forces were sometimes seriously short of food.[73]

Although the allies' goal was to bring greater security and government services to the people where they lived, this objective was difficult to achieve given the size of the country, the remoteness of many rural habitations, and the strength of the enemy's forces. In addition to temporarily evacuating people during harvest season, the allies sometimes found that the only way to cut the guerrillas' umbilical link with

Population and resources control: a Vietnamese policeman and an American soldier check identities and look for contraband at a joint checkpoint.

the people was to remove the population from Communist-dominated areas. For the most part, the Army undertook forcible removals only at the behest of and in coordination with government officials. This fact, however, did not necessarily result in an amelioration of refugee conditions. Public criticism slowed, but never entirely stopped, forced evacuations, and over the course of the war allied forces removed hundreds of thousands of Vietnamese civilians—a powerful, though double-edged, weapon.[74]

Once government troops evacuated an area, they typically put it to the torch to ensure that nothing was left behind for enemy use. Homes, livestock, or crops—anything that could sustain life—were destroyed. "I was reminded of Sherman's march to the sea," remarked a U.S. soldier who participated in one such devastation mission in 1966, and the comparison was apt, for the Army destroyed civilian property in the 1960s for the same reason it had in the 1860s—to deny the enemy resources and break the spirit of rebellion.[75]

While Americans wielded the torch fairly liberally in evacuated areas, they needed to exercise more discretion in locales where the population was allowed to remain. This was a difficult task given the intertwining of guerrilla and civilian infrastructures in many Vietnamese villages. U.S. commanders frequently left hamlets alone despite suspicions that the inhabitants were colluding with the enemy. In other cases,

U.S. soldiers forcibly relocate civilians from their village.

they targeted only those buildings most associated with the Viet Cong. However, if a hamlet showed signs of a significant and long-standing enemy presence, then commanders might well put the entire community to the torch. While the primary reason for burning hamlets was to destroy enemy installations and deny the enemy resources, destruction also played a punitive role. As one Marine Corps pamphlet distributed in Quang Ngai Province explained,

Many Vietnamese have paid with their lives and their homes have been destroyed because they helped the Vietcong in an attempt to enslave the Vietnamese people. Many hamlets have been destroyed because these villages harbored the Vietcong.

The hamlets of Hai Mon, Hai Tan, Sa Binh, Tan Binh, and many others have been destroyed because of this. We will not hesitate to destroy every hamlet that helps the Vietcong who are powerless to stop the combined might of the G.V.N. and its allies.

The U.S. Marines issue this warning: The U.S. Marines will not hesitate to destroy, immediately, any village or hamlet harboring the Vietcong. We will not hesitate to destroy, immediately, any village or hamlet used as a Vietcong stronghold to fire at our troops or aircraft.

The choice is yours. If you refuse to let the Vietcong use your villages and hamlets as their battlefield, your homes and your lives will be saved.[76]

The Army issued similar warnings, disavowing responsibility for the consequences should villagers allow Communist forces to live and fight among them.

A U.S. patrol destroys buildings used by the Viet Cong in the Boi Loi Woods, a major Viet Cong base area outside of Saigon.

While devastation certainly denied the enemy succor, it came at a price. Americans watching the war from their living rooms cringed at seeing GIs burn civilian homes. Reactions among the Vietnamese were more complex. Sometimes civilians blamed the allies for the death and destruction that resulted from allied military actions. In other cases, the villagers blamed the Viet Cong and North Vietnamese for their suffering, just as allied propagandists hoped they would.[77] Still, adverse public reaction to seeing U.S. soldiers setting the houses of seemingly innocent villagers afire led MACV to issue orders recommending that commanders exercise more discretion in selecting targets for devastation. When possible, the Army also preferred to have the South Vietnamese do the actual destruction. Nevertheless, MACV continued to insist that destruction remain a legitimate weapon of counterguerrilla warfare.[78]

The Army tried to ameliorate some of the war's rougher edges through a dizzying array of humanitarian programs. Within four months of its arrival in Vietnam, the 173d Airborne Brigade had established a coordinated civil affairs/psychological operations program whose primary goals were to build goodwill and gather intelligence. During the first seven months of this program, the 173d either built, refurbished, or began work on 14 schools, a laundry facility, 3 latrines, 5 wells, a refugee settlement, 2 playgrounds, 29 bridges, about 43 kilometers of roads, a church, and 2 medical facilities. It also administered 51,400 medical treatments, distributed 182 tons of food and clothing, donated nearly 200,000 piasters to local charities, and hosted 10 parties for Vietnamese civilians.[79]

Such deeds were just the beginning. As more American units arrived they enacted similar programs. In 1967 alone the U.S. military either built or repaired 31,000 houses, 83 hospitals, 180 kilometers of irrigation systems, 200 churches, 380 dispensaries, 225 market places, 72 orphanages, 1,052 schools, and over 2,000 wells, while dispensing 10,286,677 medical treatments and 41,573 tons of food and commodities. So eager were U.S. troop commanders to perform good works that some observers complained that the Army's activities were proving counterproductive. Contrary to doctrine, commanders did not always tie their actions to larger pacification plans, nor did they always take the wishes and culture of the population into account, either out of ignorance, misplaced idealism, or just plain "can do" enthusiasm to get things done. Finally, as MACV had feared, American energy tended to make the South Vietnamese government look bad in the eyes of its people, since the authorities had neither the resources—nor in many cases the inclination—to shower gifts upon its own people.[80]

Perhaps the most highly touted of all of the Army's many civic activities were medical initiatives. Since 1963, American military medical personnel had been traveling the countryside with their Vietnamese counterparts providing free medical and dental services through the medical civic action program. The deployment of Army combat

Dental services as civic action

formations in 1965 allowed for the expansion of this program, designated MEDCAP II. Between 1965 and 1968 American medical personnel dispensed over twenty-seven million medical treatments through MEDCAP II, a number that exceeded the entire population of South Vietnam. Other U.S. military programs, such as the Civilian War Casualty Program and the Military Provincial Hospital Program, provided improved care to thousands of civilians as well.[81]

A U.S. soldier helps Vietnamese civilians build a school.

Building schools and inoculating children won the Army many accolades, garnered some intelligence, and undoubtedly strengthened the government's position in the countryside. Yet the Army soon discovered that civic action programs, even when managed directly by the United States, were not as powerful as some had hoped. Just as had occurred in America's many advisory experiences, U.S. beneficence more often than not failed to turn the tide against the insurgents, and generally for the same reasons. Many Vietnamese were genuinely loyal to the Viet Cong and could not be bought with a few trinkets. Others were more inclined to submit to government authority but were unwilling to act on this inclination until they felt secure from guerrilla retaliation. Moreover, while the program generated impressive statistics in terms of money spent and projects accomplished, these paled in comparison with Vietnam's deep socioeconomic needs—needs that merely deepened due to the hardships imposed by the war itself.[82]

Still, the sheer size of U.S. civic action and psychological warfare efforts was bound to have some effect, and tens of thousands of enemy soldiers and cadres surrendered over the years. Yet in Vietnam, as in many other insurgencies, relatively few guerrillas abandoned their cause because of allied civic actions or cleverly worded propaganda leaflets. Offers of amnesty and humane treatment did help guerrillas reconcile themselves to surrender, but in the end most enemy soldiers surrendered because they had grown tired of the war, doubted that they would prevail, and feared for their lives and the lives of their families—factors generated primarily through military action rather than uplifting social programs.[83]

If military action was the key to pacification, then some argued the Army should extend its military efforts beyond clearing operations and into the securing stage. One of the leading advocates of this approach was the U.S. Marine Corps, whose Combined Action Platoon (CAP) program inserted marines directly into the securing process.

Marine Corps counterinsurgency doctrine was modeled on Army doctrine and did not differ materially from it. However, the marines' initial mission of protecting several coastal enclaves in northern South Vietnam lent itself to a more intensive pacification effort than that of the Army units Westmoreland was using in mobile reaction roles in 1965. In an effort to improve local security, the marines experimented with marrying a Marine squad with a Regional or Popular Forces platoon. The combined force, or CAP, lived, worked, and fought in a designated village until such time as the Vietnamese were capable of providing for their own protection. Once this had been achieved, the plan called for the marines to deploy to a new village where they would repeat the process, slowly extending government control over a wider area. Meanwhile, regular Marine battalions stationed in the region lent support by conducting small-unit patrols and search-and-destroy operations. Thus, while Westmoreland's soldiers tried to achieve pacification from the "top down" by destroying the enemy's large units first, the CAP marines worked from the "bottom up," at the village level.[84]

Westmoreland acknowledged the merits of the Marine concept, but he refused to allow Army units to join in the practice. The South Vietnamese government was not keen on the idea of stationing U.S. soldiers inside Vietnamese villages, and Westmoreland, ever sensitive to accusations of colonialism, was not inclined to push the issue. Dispersing U.S. soldiers in penny packets across the countryside also raised the specter of piecemeal defeats at the hands of Communist main forces unencumbered by the threat of U.S. offensive strikes. Finally, Westmoreland, Secretary of Defense Robert S. McNamara, and CORDS Chief Robert W. Komer all doubted that the United States had the will and resources to engage in an all-out CAP strategy. A nationwide CAP program not only would absorb more manpower than the United States could afford, but it would also tightly bind the fate of the government's local security and pacification efforts to the long-term presence of U.S. military forces. This contradicted America's overall policy of promoting Vietnamese self-reliance and seemed particularly unwise given President Johnson's 1966 offer to withdraw U.S. forces if North Vietnam did the same.[85]

In the end, the CAP program realized neither the loftiest hopes of its proponents nor the darkest fears of its detractors. On the one hand, the CAPs materially improved the security of the villages in which they were based. On the other, Westmoreland had been correct in predicting that pacifying the countryside would be difficult until the enemy's big battalions were checked. In 1966 increasing North Vietnamese infiltration into Marine Corps sectors led the marines to devote 35 percent of their time to large-unit operations, up from 11 percent the year before. By 1967 the increasing North Vietnamese threat compelled the marines to curtail most of their pacification support activities, and the CAP program fell seriously behind in its goals. By the end of 1968 not a single CAP village had progressed to the point where the marines could withdraw their men.

The defeat of the Communist's Tet offensive by allied conventional forces opened the door for greater pacification progress, and by 1970 ninety-three CAPs had achieved their goals. Still, the program remained small. At no time did the U.S. Marine Corps allocate more than 3 percent of its total in-country manpower to the program, and only about 20 percent of all villages in the Marine Corps area ever received a CAP. While some CAPs had prospered, Marine Corps selection and training procedures had not always generated suitable personnel for this very delicate assignment. Moreover, as in every other pacification initiative, success or failure ultimately came down to the South Vietnamese, who often fell short. Not only did the South Vietnamese fail to provide the necessary manpower to implement the program fully, but many Popular Forces soldiers assigned to CAP units preferred "to sit back and let the Marines do the work," much as Westmoreland and Komer had feared they would. The fact that CAP marines suffered 2 ½ times the number of casualties as their Popular Forces counterparts indicated that the Americans were truly shouldering most of the burden. Thus, while a worthy endeavor, the CAP program did not meet expectations.[86]

Although the Army generally refrained from becoming directly involved in the securing business, it did in fact lend a hand. Army efforts to secure the areas around military bases through patrol and civic action programs differed little from Marine practices. Over the course of the war the Army also experimented with a variety of approaches for improving the local security climate upon which pacification was so dependent. Beginning in 1966, Westmoreland arranged for several U.S. Army units to provide operational and training assistance to counterpart organizations in the South Vietnamese Army and the paramilitaries. Westmoreland's successor, General Abrams, especially favored such initiatives, and by the late 1960s combined operations, cross-attachments, and buddy systems that linked U.S. and South Vietnamese units flourished.[87]

The Army also employed a multiplicity of advisory mechanisms to assist the paramilitaries, from permanent territorial advisory teams to mobile training groups of various sorts. One such program, run by the 4th Infantry Division in 1968, utilized twenty-seven five-man Civic Action Teams. Team members—90 percent of whom were volunteers—lived in the hamlets to which they were assigned. They provided assistance in economic self-help and security projects and helped train local Popular Forces units. The following year the 173d Airborne Brigade created Security Training Assistance Group teams that trained and conducted combined operations with People's Self-Defense Force units.[88]

In the end, Army efforts to bolster village security differed from Marine activities more in style than in substance. Over time, the Army provided ever greater support to local paramilitaries through mobile training teams and combined operations, while the marines stopped stationing troops in villages and began operating their CAPs from mobile patrol bases, so that in practice the differences between the Army and the Marine approaches diminished even further. Ultimately, neither service was any more successful than the other in promoting village security.[89]

Next to security, probably the single greatest way in which the Army influenced pacification was through the conduct of its troops. Since the publication of General Orders 100 a century earlier, the U.S. Army had maintained that ethical and military considerations demanded that soldiers treat civilians with dignity and humanity. Contemporary counterinsurgency doctrine amplified this precept, and when the Army deployed to Vietnam Westmoreland did not hesitate to make such policies a central theme.[90]

Essentially, there were two components to the issue of troop conduct—battlefield behavior and civil-military relations. Noncombatant deaths and collateral damage are as inevitable as they are regrettable in war, but Westmoreland believed that the political nature of the conflict required that he do everything possible to minimize the war's unpleasant byproducts. As U.S. combat troops began to arrive in the spring and summer of 1965, he directed that "the application of U.S. military force in Vietnam and the conduct of U.S. troops must be carefully controlled at all times . . . a conscious effort must be made to minimize battle casualties among those non-combatants who must be brought back into the fold in the course of time. This requires an extremely high caliber of leadership plus the exercise of judgment and restraint not formerly expected of soldiers." MACV emphasized this point by promulgating special rules of engagement. The rules dictated when and how troops, aircraft, and warships could employ their weaponry so as to cause the least amount of collateral damage. So important did Westmoreland consider this subject that during his tenure as MACV commander (1964–1968) he issued no fewer than forty directives regarding battlefield conduct.[91]

As the war evolved so too did the rules of engagement, with the trend being toward ever stricter controls. So strict did the rules become that they frequently delayed or prevented the application of effective air and artillery support, much to the disgruntlement of troops under fire. On the other hand, Westmoreland also believed that no set of rules could entirely replace the judgment of the man on the ground, nor was he willing to tie the hands of his subordinates so as to risk unduly the lives of U.S. soldiers. Consequently, rather than produce an exhaustive document covering every conceivable situation, MACV preferred to establish the basic parameters, leaving local commanders free to deal with individual circumstances. Over time many units developed their own rules of engagement that, while falling broadly within the framework set by MACV, did not necessarily fully coincide with each other.[92]

Although the spirit of the rules was widely understood, not everyone comprehended all of the details as they evolved. Moreover, there were always some soldiers who chose to play fast and loose with the rules to serve their own purposes. Thus, while the rules of engagement did not allow U.S. forces to fire on unarmed civilians even if they were in a free fire zone, many soldiers and airmen adopted the unofficial rule of shooting anyone who ran at their approach on the theory that evasion signified guilt. Ultimately, the rules proved an imperfect response to a complex problem, but they were better than nothing and undoubtedly did reduce civilian suffering. While exact data are not available, some statistics indicate that allied forces were responsible for about half of all civilian casualties in Vietnam, a modest number given the preponderance of American firepower.[93]

Closely allied with the rules of engagement was the issue of troop behavior. In late 1965 MACV directed that all soldiers entering Vietnam receive a lecture on the importance of winning popular support. The course stated that the conflict in Vietnam was "in many ways a new *kind* of war for Americans, a struggle in which the decisive battles must be won not only in the field, but ultimately and finally in the hearts and in the minds of the *people* of South Vietnam." Although admitting that civilian casualties were inevitable, the lecture urged soldiers to exercise care and discretion to avoid the "*needless*" destruction of civilian life and property. "Wild and indiscriminate firing against populated places, or vengeful burning of houses and hamlets as blind and wholesale reprisal for VC sniper fire, is not only wrong in and of itself; but if there is anything that could cause us to lose this new kind of struggle we're in, this kind of thing is it." The course appealed to the men's notions of justice and fair play, stating that "throughout our history, American fighting men have fought clean. American fighting men don't kill noncombatants, if they can possibly help it. American fighting men don't kill women and children, either in the heat of battle or in cold-blooded reprisal against enemy sniper fire. American fighting men don't molest or insult the women. American fighting men don't deliberately destroy the houses and private property of innocent civilians, unless it's absolutely necessary to the accomplishment of their tactical mission."[94]

Westmoreland amplified these points by distributing four pocket-size cards to every soldier entering Vietnam: "Code of Conduct," "Geneva Conventions," "The Enemy in Your Hands," and "Nine Rules." The first two reviewed general policies and legal requirements, while the third encouraged soldiers to treat captured guerrillas humanely as prisoners of war, even if the irregulars did not qualify for such treatment under international law. The Army hoped benevolent treatment would encourage defections, produce more intelligence, appease civilians who might have friends and relatives among the insurgent ranks, and break the cycle of brutality and retaliation that accompany most guerrilla wars. Finally, the "Nine Rules" laid out some basic rules of conduct in a fashion copied directly from Mao.[95]

The Army mandated that soldiers receive refresher training in the Geneva Conventions annually, while many commanders incorporated MACV's troop conduct precepts into their unit SOPs and training curriculums. All of this came on top of routine instruction in international law, military law and discipline, and counterinsurgency principles given to all U.S. soldiers in stateside training centers and schools before they departed for Vietnam. Most divisions also established community councils and other forums with which to improve relations between themselves and the indigenous population, while MACV provided compensation to civilians for property damaged by American actions.[96]

Unfortunately, the tremendous effort MACV expended in trying to maintain proper relations with the civilian population did not prevent soldier misconduct. Reckless driving, indiscriminate firing, and unprofessional behavior were just some of the many forms of deleterious conduct that tarnished the image of the U.S. soldier in the eyes of the Vietnamese citizenry. Racism, ethnocentrism, haughtiness, and callousness all reared their ugly heads in Vietnam as well. Many soldiers had difficulty relating to the Vietnamese, whose non-Western culture, alien language, and comparatively primitive standard of living made them appear inferior in the minds of some soldiers. Furthermore, the very nature of the war—the tension of living under the constant threat of ambush and the gnawing suspicion that arose from being unable to distinguish friend from foe—inevitably ate away at the morale and morals of U.S. soldiers.

Army efforts to counteract this problem were hampered by the fact that jaded veterans did their best to disabuse newly arriving replacements of any lofty conceptions they might have had about nation building and multicultural comity. "Trust no one" was the refrain, a mantra that the Army itself was compelled to repeat because such an attitude saved American lives, yet it did not help build confidence between soldiers and civilians. Helping villagers dig a well while watching for the child that might be carrying a grenade took mental and emotional agility. Some soldiers had it and some did not. Consequently, units tended to adopt the age-old attitude of holding the population responsible for whatever should befall it. Thus, if an enemy sniper should cause the Army to fight back in a way that damaged a village, the destruction was the villagers' fault for not informing on the sniper.[97]

While insults, petty abuses, and criminal behavior represented the bulk of American misdeeds toward the Vietnamese population, there were genuine incidents of atrocities and war crimes perpetrated by U.S. servicemen, the most famous of which was the massacre of civilians at Son My village (commonly referred to as My Lai) in 1968. Although only a few soldiers were convicted of committing war crimes, the total number of such incidents is unknown, as there were undoubtedly cases that went undiscovered.

The scale of the My Lai massacre caught the military in a whirlwind of public criticism and compelled it to revamp its troop training programs. Soldiers received additional instruction in the laws of war, instruction made more pointed by directives that soldiers disobey "illegal" orders to torture or kill civilians. "Our purpose is not to lay waste to the country as the Romans did to Carthage, and bury its people forever beneath the salted earth," stated the new training materials, which emphasized the notion that humane conduct was both necessary and "consistent with the effective conduct of hostilities." Still, the new materials, while perhaps more provocative, differed little from the principles established repeatedly in various Army, MACV, and unit directives over the years. Additional efforts to better prepare young soldiers for the culture shock they frequently experienced might well have been beneficial. But there were limits to the effectiveness of such training, and little time in which to provide it given the short enlistments (draftees only served two years) and the Army's twelve-month rotation policy. Ultimately, Army doctrine was correct in forecasting that all the theoretical training in the laws of war was of no consequence without leadership, for as Army training materials reminded unit leaders, "your men, scared, tired and having their comrades killed, may not respond entirely rationally unless you, by your bearing and conduct, have previously established the control essential to assure their proper response at the moment of testing."[98]

Despite the damage done to the Army's image at home and abroad from soldier misconduct, the injury was not necessarily fatal. Civic actions, humanitarian relief programs, and damage compensation procedures ameliorated some of the harm, as did the exemplary behavior of tens of thousands of U.S. soldiers who through correct military bearing and simple acts of kindness helped erase the misdeeds of others. Blemishes notwithstanding, many Vietnamese preferred U.S. soldiers to their own security forces, whose record with regard to human rights, honesty, and efficiency was less than enviable. American misdeeds also paled in comparison to the behavior of Communist forces, which did not hesitate to employ terror, forced labor, or extortion. Thus, while U.S. misconduct undoubtedly harmed the allied cause, the behavior of the two Vietnamese antagonists cast a much wider pall. Caught in the middle, the people of South Vietnam, like civilians in so many other civil wars, suffered egregiously at the hands of all parties to the conflict. As the war dragged on, many peasants wished only for the war to end and were probably willing to accept whoever had the strength to protect them and bring the conflict to a close.[99]

All the King's Horses: The Army Experience in Vietnam

During the Vietnam War the U.S. Army made a concerted effort to implement contemporary counterinsurgency doctrine. At virtually every level, from the conceptual to the tactical, Army actions in Vietnam mirrored the concepts and methods contained in Army manuals. The failure of the Army to prevent a Communist takeover of South Vietnam, therefore, would seem to indicate that Army doctrine was fatally flawed. And flaws there were.

In putting doctrine into practice, Army commanders frequently found that they had either to modify or discard many technical, tactical, and operational precepts to meet the conditions they found in Vietnam. There is no evidence, however, that this phenomenon was any more prevalent in Vietnam than it had been in major conventional wars like

World War II. Despite claims that Vietnam was a new kind of war, most of the changes the Army made to its tactical precepts represented adjustments rather than fundamental revisions. By and large, basic small-unit infantry and jungle warfare tactics adequately met the challenges of Vietnam. And when they did not, the Army did not hesitate to change them, demonstrating a pragmatic approach to the application of doctrine. More often than not, serious failings in tactics and techniques stemmed from insufficient training, inadequate planning, and faulty execution rather than major flaws in prescribed doctrine.[100]

Although Army doctrine fared fairly well at the tactical level, it evidenced more significant weaknesses at higher levels. While the basic operational concepts contained in Army manuals were generally sound, the texts were not always sufficiently detailed to guide operators. This vagueness was partly by design, as general statements are more conducive to adaptation. Nevertheless, more definitive explanations as to the relative roles to be played by large-unit, small-unit, population security, civil affairs, and psychological operations might have reduced uncertainty and argument, even if exact relationships still needed to be formulated on a case-by-case basis.

The fact that most counterinsurgency literature had focused on the first two phases of Mao's revolutionary program was unfortunate since what the Army faced after 1965 was a civil war in which the "guerrillas" were able to field divisions armed and directed by an external power whose regular combat formations played a central role in the conflict. The myopia with which many theorists had approached the problems of advanced revolutionary warfare stemmed in part from a penchant for analytical constructs that compartmentalized the military continuum into mutually exclusive categories. Thus wars were either limited or not, conventional or unconventional, internal insurgencies or external invasions. Once defined, the problem could be addressed with measures suitable for that category of conflict. Unfortunately, the war in Vietnam did not fit neatly into these intellectual stereotypes. It was at once limited (for the United States) and unlimited (for the Vietnamese). It was both conventional and unconventional, high-tech and low-tech, a civil war and an international war. This untidiness did not settle well with either theoreticians or practitioners, who tended to focus on one aspect of the conflict while ignoring the others. Intellectual rigidity and doctrinaire behavior were sometimes the result.

In the case of Army doctrine, what had occurred in the 1960s was that the Army had placed a layer of "new" counterinsurgency theory on top of older, established counterguerrilla tactics and techniques. The resulting doctrine was more comprehensive and robust, yet experience would demonstrate that the new theory also had some shortcomings. Among these were unrealistic expectations as to the power of sociopolitical reforms to defeat an implacable foe, an overly optimistic faith in the ability of foreign nation builders to transform an ailing society in the throes of war, and a lack of appreciation for the central role force plays in revolutionary warfare.

In considering the role Army doctrine played in America's defeat in Vietnam, one should remember that failure in war is not necessarily due to failure in doctrine. Doctrine is only one of a host of factors—strategic, political, personal, organizational, and economic—that determines the fate of military operations. In fact, the U.S. Army has a long history of copying the military doctrines of nations that ultimately failed in war, such as Napoleonic France and Nazi Germany, because it believed that those doctrines contained valuable insights into the conduct of war despite the ultimate demise of their parent states. A similar situation existed in Vietnam: flaws in tactical and operational doctrine contributed to America's defeat, but they were not in themselves responsible for the outcome.[101]

In Vietnam, America's most egregious errors lay in the realms of policy and strategy rather than military doctrine. The United States seriously overestimated its ability to bend North Vietnam to its will. Contrary to the theory of limited war that guided the actions of the Johnson administration, U.S. posturing and incremental escalations did not deter North Vietnam from pursuing a patently unlimited goal—the obliteration of the Republic of Vietnam. The failure of U.S. military and diplomatic efforts to prevent North Vietnamese infiltration, unrealistic expectations about America's capacity to transform South Vietnamese institutions, and chronic disunity were also fatal flaws.[102] Ultimately, these and other factors created adverse circumstances that neither the writers of doctrine nor the soldiers called upon to implement that doctrine were able to overcome.

Notes

[1] Westmoreland, *A Soldier Reports*, p. 414; Henry Emerson, "Can We Out-Guerrilla the Communist Guerrillas?" (Student thesis, AWC, 1965), pp. 50–53.

[2] MACV Directive 525–4, 17 Sep 65, sub: Tactics and Techniques for Employment of US Forces in the Republic of Vietnam, p. 2, Westmoreland History files, CMH; FM 31–15, *Operations Against Irregular Forces*, 1961, pp. 14–15, 18–19; FM 100–5, *Field Service Regulations—Operations*, 1962, pp. 88, 153.

[3] DCSOPS, A Program for the Pacification and Long-Term Development of South Vietnam, Mar 66, pp. 4-14, 5-18 (hereafter cited as PROVN), Historians files, CMH; Blaufarb, *Counterinsurgency Era*, pp. 118–19, 207; Westmoreland, *A Soldier Reports*, p. 211; FM 31–16, *Counterguerrilla Operations*, 1963, p. 31; CDC, Special Warfare and Civil Affairs Group, Concepts and General Doctrine for Counterinsurgency, Jul 65, p. 98, 73A2677, CDC, RG 338, NARA.

[4] FM 31–16, *Counterguerrilla Operations*, 1963, pp. 8, 71; Bergerud, *Dynamics of Defeat*, pp. 328–29; W. Scott Thompson and Donaldson Frizzell, eds., *The Lessons of Vietnam* (New York: Crane, Russak and Co., 1977), p. 91.

[5] FM 100–5, *Field Service Regulations—Operations*, 1962, pp. 141–42; FM 31–16, *Counterguerrilla Operations*, 1963, pp. 21, 49; Herring, *America's Longest War*, pp. 132–33, 139–40; PROVN, p. 70.

[6] MFR, MACV, 3 Oct 66, sub: MACV Commanders' Conference, 28 Aug 66, p. 28, Historians files, CMH.

[7] Quote from ibid., p. 29. FM 31–15, *Operations Against Irregular Forces*, 1961, pp. 10, 32, 34–36; FM 31–16, *Counterguerrilla Operations*, 1963, pp. 37–38, 101.

[8] The division of labor was implied in the combined campaign plan for 1966 and more formally stated in the plan for 1967, which assigned the South Vietnamese Army "the primary mission of supporting Revolutionary Development activities. . . . The primary mission of U.S. and FWMAF [Free World Military Assistance Forces] will be to destroy the VC/NVA main forces, base areas, and resources and/or drive the enemy into the sparsely populated and food scarce areas." Joint General Staff/MACV Combined Campaign Plan for Military Operations in the Republic of Vietnam, 1967, 7 Nov 66, AB 142, pp. 4–6, Historians files, CMH; John Carland, *Combat Operations: Stemming the Tide, May 1965 to October 1966*, United States Army in Vietnam (Washington, D.C.: U.S. Army Center of Military History, 2000), p. 152.

[9] HQDA, Final Report of the Research Project: Conduct of the War, May 71, pp. 15–16, CMH.

[10] Bergerud, *Dynamics of Defeat*, pp. 268–69; FM 31–73, *Advisor Handbook for Counterinsurgency*, 1965, pp. 58–63; FM 31–16, *Counterguerrilla Operations*, 1963, pp. 30–31.

[11] Quote from MACV Lesson Learned 80, U.S. Combat Forces in Support of Pacification, 1970, p. 1, and see also p. i, Historians files, CMH. Study, MACV, c. 1968, sub: Area Security Principles and Application, pp. 4, 32, Historians files, CMH; Rpt, CDC, 15 Aug 69, sub: Dynamics of Fire and Maneuver, vol. 1, p. II-29, MHI; Richard Prillaman, "Vietnam Update," *Infantry* 59 (May–June 1969): 18–19; Clarke, *Final Years*, pp. 391–93; Hunt, *Pacification*, pp. 212–13, 222, 233.

[12] Rpt, Pacification Studies Group, CORDS, c. 1970, sub: The Area Security Concept, pp. 5–6, Historians files, CMH.

[13] Quote from Krepinevich, *Army and Vietnam*, p. 222. Hunt, *Pacification*, p. 189.

[14] Quote from Mark Boatner, What Have We Failed To Learn from History About Counterinsurgency? (Student paper, IR, CRS–4, AWC, 1966), p. 60. Richard Stilwell, "Evolution of Tactics—The Vietnam Experience," *Army* 20 (February 1970): 19, 23; Julian Ewell and Ira Hunt, *Sharpening the Combat Edge: The Use of Analysis To Reinforce Military Judgment*, Vietnam Studies (Washington, D.C.: Department of the Army, 1974), pp. 76, 78, 80–82; Thompson and Frizzell, *Lessons of Vietnam*, pp. 64–65, 214–15, 223, 238. The transition to small-unit operations began early but moved at an uneven pace depending upon local circumstances. Nationwide, the number of U.S. large-unit operations dropped from 655 in 1966 to 464 in 1967. Meanwhile, the number of U.S. small-unit operations rose, from 172,499 in 1966 to 428,250 in 1967. Rpts, Office of the Asst Secy of Defense, Southeast Asia Programs (OASD [SA]), Sep 67, sub: Southeast Asia Analysis Report, pp. 10–12; Nov 67, sub: Southeast Asia Analysis Report, pp. 54–56; and Jan 68, sub: Southeast Asia Statistical Tables Through December 1967, tables 4d, 5b, and 5d, copies in CMH.

[15] 9th Div Advisory Det, MACV, Standing Operating Procedures for Rural Reconstruction, 31 May 65, pp. A-7, C-18745.184A, CARL.

[16] Operational Report-Lessons Learned (ORLL), 1 May–31 Jul 66, 25th Inf Div, 3 Aug 66, p. 2; Memo, MACV for Distribution, 11 Mar 67, sub: Counterinsurgency Lessons Learned No. 62: Salient Lessons Learned, p. 11. Both in Historians files, CMH. FM 31–16, *Counterguerrilla Operations*, 1963, pp. 24, 30–31; FM 31–73, *Advisor Handbook for Counterinsurgency*, 1965, pp. 58–63.

[17] MACV, Guide for Subsector Advisers, 1966, pp. 2–3, Historians files, CMH.

[18] FM 31–16, *Counterguerrilla Operations*, 1963, pp. 30–31; MACV Directive 525–4, 17 Sep 65, sub: Tactics and Techniques for Employment of US Forces in the Republic of Vietnam, pp. 6–8, 14.

[19] FM 7–20, *Infantry, Airborne Infantry, and Mechanized Infantry Battalions*, 1962, p. 234; FM 61–100, *The Division*, 1962, p. 243; FM 100–5, *Field Service Regulations—Operations*, 1962, p. 140; FM 21–50, *Ranger Training and Ranger Operations*, 1962, pp. 136, 141.

[20] Quote from Neal Grimland, "The Formidable Guerrilla," *Army* 12 (February 1962): 65. McCuen, *Art of Counter-Revolutionary War*, pp. 196, 235; Heilbrunn, *Partisan Warfare*, p. 169; R. L. Schweitzer, Military Tactics for Phase III: Mobile Warfare in Vietnam, 1964–65 (Student paper, CGSC, 1966), pp. 131–32; Emerson, "Can We Out-Guerrilla," pp. iii, 27–28, 47–48.

[21] ORLL, 1 May–31 Jul 66, 1st Inf Div, 15 Aug 66, p. 23; MFR, MACV, 3 Oct 66, sub: MACV Commanders' Conference, 28 Aug 66, p. 29; Memo, MACV for Distribution, 30 Aug 65, sub: MACV Concept of Operations in the Republic of Vietnam, p. 2. All in Historians files, CMH. A Summary of Lessons Learned, pp. I-3, I-4, I-13, atch to Memo, Brig Gen John Norton, Deputy Commanding General, United States Army Vietnam (DCG, USARV), for Distribution, 22 Sep 65, sub: A Summary of Lessons Learned, 68A3306, RG 319, NARA; 9th Div Advisory Det, MACV, Standing Operating Procedures for Rural Reconstruction, 31 May 65, pp. A-2, A-3; MACV Directive 525–4, 17 Sep 65, sub: Tactics and Techniques for Employment of US Forces in the Republic of Vietnam, pp. 2, 5.

[22] Quote from Harold Johnson, "The Chief of Staff on Military Strategy in Vietnam," *Army Information Digest* 23 (April 1968): 9, and see also pp. 7–8. Westmoreland, *A Soldier Reports*, pp. 145, 147, 149.

[23] First quote from Stilwell, "Evolution of Tactics," p. 19, and see also p. 23. Second quote from MFR, 25th Inf Div, 23 Oct 66, sub: Briefing for Senate Preparedness Investigating Subcommittee, Cu Chi, 23 Oct 66, p. 8, Historians files, CMH.

[24] First and second quotes from PROVN, p. 5. Third and fourth quotes from ibid., p. 70, and see also pp. 6, 23–24, 49, 111–12.

[25] Rpts, OASD (SA), Sep 67, sub: Southeast Asia Analysis Report, pp. 10–12; OASD (SA), Nov 67, sub: Southeast Asia Analysis Report, pp. 54–56; and CDC, 15 Aug 69, sub: Dynamics of Fire and Maneuver, vol. 1, p. II-30. William Hauser, "Fire and Maneuver," *Infantry* 60 (September–October 1970): 13–14.

[26] Larry Cable, "Everything Is Perfect and Getting Better: The Myths and Measures of the American Ground War in Indochina, 1965–68," in *Looking Back on the Vietnam War*, ed. William Head and Lawrence Grinter (Westport, Conn.: Frederick A. Praeger, 1993), p. 193.

[27] Pamphlet, 1st Inf Div, Fundamentals of Infantry Tactics, Feb 68, p. 11, MHI; MFR, MACV, 10 Mar 66, sub: MACV Commanders' Conference, 20 Feb 66, p. 1, Historians files, CMH; Romie Brownlee and William Mullen, *Changing an Army: An Oral History of General William E. DePuy, USA Retired* (Washington, D.C.: U.S. Military History Institute and U.S. Army Center of Military History, 1988), p. 160.

[28] Quote from Anthony Neglia, "NVA and VC: Different Enemies, Different Tactics," *Infantry* 60 (September–October 1970): 53. ORLL, 1 Jan–30 Apr 66, II Field Force, Vietnam (II FFV), 15 May 66, p. 3, Historians files, CMH; Rpt, USARV, 1966, sub: Evaluation of U.S. Army Combat Operations in Vietnam (ARCOV), p. II-46 (hereafter cited as ARCOV), Historians files, CMH; FM 31–15, *Operations Against Irregular Forces*, 1961, pp. 4, 15, 17, 20, 22, 36–38.

[29] Mission Council Action Memo 122, 20 Sep 66, sub: Minutes of the Special Mission Council Meeting, Sep 17, 1966, p. 3, Historians files, CMH; FM 31–73, *Advisor Handbook for Counterinsurgency*, 1965, pp. 5, 11, 57, 66.

[30] Memo, MACJ3 for CG, Field Force Vietnam, 10 Dec 65, sub: Tactical Employment of US Forces and Defensive Action, p. 2, Historians files, CMH.

[31] ORLL, 1 Jan–30 Apr 66, I Field Force, Vietnam (I FFV), 15 May 66, p. 3; Memo, MACV for Distribution, 11 Mar 67, sub: Counterinsurgency Lessons Learned No. 62: Salient Lessons Learned, pp. 8–10. Both in Historians files, CMH. MACV Directive 525–4, 17 Sep 65, sub: Tactics and Techniques for Employment of US Forces in the Republic of Vietnam, pp. 2–5; Memo, Westmoreland for DCG, USARV, 10 Dec 65, sub: Tactical Employment of U.S. Forces and Defensive Action, Correspondence 1965–68, William E. DePuy Papers, MHI.

[32] Quote from Lewis Sorley, *Honorable Warrior: General Harold K. Johnson and the Ethics of Command* (Lawrence: University of Kansas, 1998), pp. 218–19. Rpt, MACV, History Branch, 25 May 68, sub: Lessons in Strategy, p. 7, Historians files, CMH; PROVN, pp. G-8, G-35; Carland, *Stemming the Tide*, pp. 250–51.

[33] David Hackworth, "Target Acquisition Vietnam Style," *Military Review* 48 (April 1968): 76–79; Robert Scales, "Firepower and Maneuver in the Second Indochina War," *Field Artillery Journal* 54 (September–October 1986): 53; David Hackworth, "Guerrilla Battalion, U.S. Style," *Infantry* 61 (January–February 1971): 24–25.

[34] First and third quotes from David Hackworth, "Your Mission—Out-Guerrilla the Guerrilla," *Army Information Digest* 23 (July 1968): 61. Second quote from Pamphlet, 1st Bde, 101st Abn Div, Tactical SOP for Counterinsurgency Operations, 1 Dec 66, p. 92, Historians files, CMH. According to one 1st Brigade publication published during Pearson's tenure, "Many officers have the mistaken idea that duty in Vietnam means divorcing oneself from former tactics instruction. This is not true. The peculiarities of the war in Vietnam have resulted in the revision of certain tactics and formulation of new tactics. Basic infantry tactics form a foundation for any operation or action." Pamphlet, 1st Bde, 101st Abn Div, Observations of a Platoon Leader, 11 Nov 66, p. 10, and see also p. 29, Historians files, CMH.

[35] John Hay, *Tactical and Materiel Innovations*, Vietnam Studies (Washington, D.C.: Department of the Army, 1974), p. 45; Albert Garland, ed., *Infantry in Vietnam* (Nashville, Tenn.: Battery Press, 1982), p. 120; Pamphlet, 1st Inf Div, Fundamentals of Infantry Tactics, Feb 68, pp. 17–21; Sidney Berry, "Observations of a Brigade Commander, Part I," *Military Review* 48 (January 1968): 17; Doughty, *Army Tactical Doctrine*, pp. 35–36; Ewell and Hunt, *Sharpening the Combat Edge*, pp. 106–18.

[36] Memo, Westmoreland for DCG, USARV, 10 Dec 65, sub: Tactical Employment of U.S. Forces and Defensive Action, p. 2.

[37] Annual Hist Supplement, 173d Abn Bde (Separate), 1 Jan–31 Dec 65, 1966, p. 39, and Qtrly Cmd Rpt, 1st Inf Div, 31 Dec 65, p. 28, both in Historians files, CMH; Albert Garland, *Combat Notes from Vietnam* (Fort Benning, Ga.: Infantry Magazine, 1968), pp. 65–68; Memo, Lt Gen Bruce Palmer, DCG, for Westmoreland, 22 Oct 67, sub: Long Range Patrol Doctrine and Units, 69A5362, RG 319, NARA.

[38] Ewell and Hunt, *Sharpening the Combat Edge*, pp. 41–42; Simpson, *Inside the Green Berets*, pp. 123–24, 133–34, 143, 153; Hogan, *Rangers or Elite Infantry*, pp. 173–84.

[39] FM 31–16, *Counterguerrilla Operations*, 1963, pp. 63–64; Pamphlet, 9th Inf Div, 9th Infantry Division Field SOP, 1 Jan 68, app. 13, Infantry School Library.

[40] Bob Lenderman, "Airmobile Tactics and Techniques," *U.S. Army Aviation Digest* 11 (January 1965): 2–6; Rpt, USARV, 5 Jul 65, sub: Critique of Counterinsurgency Airmobile Operations, Vietnam, 68A2344, RG 319, NARA.

[41] Study, CDC, 15 Aug 69, sub: Dynamics of Fire and Maneuver, vol. 1, pp. II-12, II-210; Robert Scales, *Firepower in Limited War* (Washington, D.C.: National Defense University, 1990), pp. 51–52, 74, 87–88, 133; ACTIV, Organization and Employment of U.S. Army Field Artillery Units in the Republic of Vietnam, Oct 69, p. II-12, Historians files, CMH; Berry, "Observations of a Brigade Commander, Part I," p. 14.

[42] Quote from Memo, DePuy for Distribution, 27 Mar 66, sub: Commanders Notes #1, p. 1, and see also pp. 2–3. Memo, Maj Gen Stanley Larsen, CG, FFV, for Distribution, 17 Dec 65, sub: Tactical Tips, pp. 2–3. Both in Historians files, CMH. MACV Directive 525–4, 17 Sep 65, sub: Tactics and Techniques for Employment of US Forces in the Republic of Vietnam.

[43] Quote from Commanders Notes #4—Attack on VC Fortified Positions, p. 1, Incl 4 to ORLL, 1 Jul–30 Sep 66, 1st Inf Div, 31 Oct 66, Historians files, CMH. David Hackworth, "Baptism to Command," *Infantry* 57 (November–December 1967): 40; David Hackworth, "Hedgerows of Vietnam," *Infantry* 57 (May–June 1967): 3–7; George Shuffer, "Finish Them with Firepower," *Military Review* 47 (December 1967): 11–15; Boyd Bashore, "The Name of the Game Is Search and Destroy," *Army* 17 (February 1967): 56–59; Hackworth, "Guerrilla Battalion," p. 34.

[44] First quote from "The Men Who Run the War," *Newsweek*, 5 Dec 66, p. 53. Second quote from Brownlee and Mullen, *Changing an Army*, p. 138. Scales, "Firepower and Maneuver," p. 52; Annual Hist Supplement, 173d Abn Bde (Separate), 1 Jan–31 Dec 65, 1966, p. 43; George Livingston, "Attack of a Fortified Position," *Infantry* 59 (September–October 1969): 13–15; Rpt, CDC, 15 Aug 69, sub: Dynamics of Fire and Maneuver, vol. 1, p. II-vi; Bashore, "Name of the Game," p. 59; Pamphlet, 1st Inf Div, Fundamentals of Infantry Tactics, Feb 68, p. 23; ORLL 4–67, Observations of a Battalion Commander [U.S. Army Vietnam], 7 Jun 67, p. 32, MHI; Berry, "Observations of a Brigade Commander, Part I," pp. 17–18.

[45] Quote from Doughty, *Army Tactical Doctrine*, p. 37. As late as 1969, an Army study complained that officers new to Vietnam were frequently unprepared for the true nature of the war, primarily because they were still rooted in infantry traditions of assault and maneuver and lacked the skills needed to effectively control the vast array of fire support at their disposal. For differences of opinion over the allegedly corrosive effects of firepower, see Rpt, CDC, 15 Aug 69, sub: Dynamics of Fire and Maneuver, vol. 1, pp. II-213, II-218; Scales, *Firepower in Limited War*, pp. 78, 80, 143–44; Charles Nulsen, The Use of Firepower in Counterguerrilla Operations (Student paper, AWC, 1968), pp. 2, 10–14; Hauser, "Fire and Maneuver," pp. 13–15; Pamphlet, 1st Inf Div, Fundamentals of Infantry Tactics, Feb 68, p. 23; Hackworth, "Hedgerows of Vietnam," pp. 3–7; Swett, "Tips to Senior Commanders," p. 36; Shuffer, "Finish Them with Firepower," pp. 11–15; Bashore, "Name of the Game," pp. 56–59; ACTIV, Organization and Employment of Field Artillery, Oct 69, p. IV-19; FM 31–73, *Advisor Handbook for Counterinsurgency*, 1965, p. 57; Boyd Dastrup, *King of Battle: A Branch History of the U.S. Army's Field Artillery* (Fort Monroe, Va.: HQ, Training and Doctrine Command, 1993), pp. 284–86.

[46] Quote from Rpt, CDC, 15 Aug 69, sub: Dynamics of Fire and Maneuver, vol. 1, p. II-204, and see also p. II-220, and vol. 2, pp. v, 25–26. Pamphlet, 1st Inf Div, Fundamentals of Infantry Tactics, Feb 68, pp. 22–23; Nulsen, Use of Firepower, p. 14; Berry, "Observations of a Brigade Commander, Part I," p. 17.

[47] Only about 15 percent of all American artillery ordnance and 4 percent of Air Force munitions used in Vietnam were fired in direct support of ground troops while they were actually in combat with the enemy. Most of the rest was expended in H&I fire and other intelligence or interdiction missions. Scales, *Firepower in Limited War*, pp. 80, 93–95, 112, 141–43; Eric Bergerud, *Red Thunder, Tropic Lightning* (Boulder, Colo.: Westview Press, 1993), pp. 84–85; Douglas Kinnard, *The War Managers* (Hanover, N.H.: University Press of New England, 1977), p. 170.

[48] Pamphlet, 1st Bde, 101st Abn Div, Tactical SOP for Counterinsurgency Operations, 1 Dec 66, p. 92; Hay, *Tactical and Materiel Innovations*, p. 123; Hackworth, "Guerrilla Battalion," pp. 36–37.

[49] Summary Sheets, ACSFOR, 18 Aug 65, sub: Review of Study "Organization and Equipment of Army Units," and 31 Aug 65, sub: Organization and Equipment of Army Units, both in 68A2344, RG 319, NARA; John Wilson, *Maneuver and Firepower: The Evolution of Divisions and Separate Brigades*, Army Lineage Series (Washington, D.C.: U.S. Army Center of Military History, 1998), pp. 323–24; Qtrly Cmd Rpt, 1st Inf Div, 31 Dec 65, pp. 4–5; Rpt, Army Study Group, Jul 65, sub: Organization and Equipment of Army Units, 68A3306, RG 319, NARA.

[50] ARCOV, pp. II-23, II-28; Y. Y. Phillips, "The ROAD Battalion in Vietnam," *Army* 16 (September 1966): 54; Qtrly Cmd Rpt, 1st Inf Div, 31 Dec 65, pp. 13, 33; FM 31–16, *Counterguerrilla Operations*, 1963, pp. 75–76.

[51] Rpt, CDC, 30 Apr 66, sub: Review and Analysis of the Evaluation of Army Combat Operations in Vietnam, p. 2-II-18, Historians files, CMH, and see also p. 2-II-19; ARCOV, p. II-44; Qtrly Cmd Rpt, 1st Inf Div, 31 Dec 65, pp. 26–28.

[52] First quote from Msg, Westmoreland MAC 3407 to Johnson, 5 Jul 65, Westmoreland History files, CMH. Second quote from Michael Matheny, "Armor in Low-Intensity Conflict: The U.S. Experience in Vietnam," *Armor* 97 (July–August 1988): 10, and see also p. 9. The armor statistic represents tank, armored cavalry, and mechanized infantry formations. Westmoreland, *A Soldier Reports*, p. 178; Rpt, CDC, 15 Aug 69, sub: Dynamics of Fire and Maneuver, p. II-175.

[53] T. A. Williams and Horace Homesley, Small Unit Combat Experience, Vietnam, 1966–1967, Booz Allen Applied Research, 1 Sep 67, pp. 14–15, 26, Historians files, CMH; ARCOV, pp. II-23, II-34 to II-38; Rpt, Army Study Group, Jul 65, sub: Organization and Equipment of Army Units, p. 12.

[54] ACTIV, Organization and Employment of Field Artillery, Oct 69, pp. G-1, G-2; Wilson, *Maneuver and Firepower*, pp. 325–26, 334, 336; Richard Meyer, "The Ground-Sea Team in River Warfare," *Military Review* 46 (September 1966): 54–61; Pamphlet, 9th Inf Div, 9th Infantry Division Methods of Operation and Tactics Adopted to Operations in the Mekong Delta, 1969, Historians files, CMH.

[55] Frank Grossman, "Artillery in Vietnam," *Ordnance* 52 (November–December 1967): 268–71; David Ott, *Field Artillery, 1954–1973*, Vietnam Studies (Washington, D.C.: Department of the Army, 1975), pp. 235–40; Study, USARV, 28 Mar 67, sub: Mechanized and Armor Combat Operations in Vietnam, p. 93, Historians files, CMH; Pamphlet, 1st Bde, 101st Abn Div, Observations of a Platoon Leader, 11 Nov 66, pp. 11–12; Rpt, USARV, 31 Jan 68, sub: Attack of Fortified Positions in the Jungle, MHI.

[56] Bergerud, *Red Thunder*, p. 139; ORLL, 1 May–31 Jul 66, 25th Inf Div, 3 Aug 66, p. 23; Pamphlet, 1st Bde, 101st Abn Div, Tactical SOP for Counterinsurgency Operations, 1 Dec 66, pp. 92–94.

[57] Briefing, Lt Col Pendleton, 19 May 68, sub: Mobile Training Teams, New Arrival Indoctrination Training, Dissemination and Evaluation of New Ideas, p. 8, Incl 7 to MFR, MACV, 1 Jun 68, sub: MACV Commanders Conference, 19 May 1968, Historians files, CMH; Bergerud, *Dynamics of Defeat*, p. 136; DF, AJTIS-W to Asst Commandant, Infantry School, n.d., sub: RVN Liaison Training Visit, 17–28 Jul 68, p. 15, Infantry School Library; Rpt, CDC, 15 Aug 69, sub: Dynamics of Fire and Maneuver, p. II-203; Pamphlet, 9th Inf Div, 9th Infantry Division Night Tactical Techniques, 9th Inf Div file, MHI.

[58] Doughty, *Army Tactical Doctrine*, p. 35; Kevin Sheehan, "Preparing for an Imaginary War? Examining Peacetime Functions and Changes of Army Doctrine" (Ph.D. diss., Harvard University, 1988), pp. 285–88; Thompson and Frizzell, *Lessons of Vietnam*, p. 81.

[59] Patrick Graves, "Observations of a Platoon Leader, Part I," *Infantry* 57 (May–June 1967): 36–37; FM 31-15, *Operations Against Irregular Forces*, 1961, p. 12; Memo, Maj Gen Willard Pearson, Director of Individual Training, DCSPER, for Gen Westmoreland, CSA, 6 Sep 68, sub: Post Mortem on Vietnam Strategy, p. 4, Westmoreland History files, CMH.

[60] Quote from Briefing, MACV, c. Aug 66, sub: Briefing to Mission Council, p. 1, Historians files, CMH.

[61] Quotes from Pamphlet, MACV, Handbook for Military Support of Pacification, Feb 68, p. 1, MHI, and see also pp. 33, 39. MACV Directive 525–4, 17 Sep 65, sub:

Tactics and Techniques for Employment of US Forces in the Republic of Vietnam, p. 9.

[62] Maxwell Taylor, "The U.S. Government and Counterinsurgency," AWC lecture, 11 Jan 66, question-and-answer period, p. 4, MHI; Speech, Maj Gen George Eckhardt, "Commanding General's Talk to Commanders of the 9th Infantry Division Upon Arrival in Vietnam," c. Dec 66–Jan 67, p. 3, Historians files, CMH; Command Policy 66–1, 1st Cavalry Division (Airmobile), 8 Dec 66, sub: Support of Revolutionary Development, Historians files, CMH; Pamphlet, MACV, Handbook for Military Support of Pacification, Feb 68, pp. 33, 39; MFR, MACV, 3 Oct 66, sub: MACV Commanders' Conference, 28 Aug 66, p. 30.

[63] Memo, DePuy, MACJ3, for Westmoreland, 22 Sep 65, sub: The Techniques of Pacification, folder P and W, Correspondence 1965–68, DePuy Papers, MHI; ORLL, 1 Nov 66–31 Jan 67, 1st Inf Div, 15 Feb 67, p. 50, Historians files, CMH.

[64] Memo, DePuy, CG, 1st Inf Div, for Westmoreland, 18 Oct 66, sub: Control of Revolutionary Development, Correspondence 1965–68, DePuy Papers, MHI; Study, DCSOPS, 1 Apr 65, sub: Analysis of the Military Effort in South Vietnam, pp. 59–60, 65, in 68A2344, RG 319, NARA.

[65] A Summary of Lessons Learned, atch to Memo, Brig Gen John Norton, DCG, USARV, for Distribution, 22 Sep 65, sub: A Summary of Lessons Learned, pp. 1–12; William Berkman, "Civil Affairs in Vietnam" (Student thesis, AWC, 1974), pp. 5–7, 11.

[66] FM 31–15, *Operations Against Guerrilla Forces*, 1961, pp. 3–5, 9–10, 14, 18–19, 21; FM 31–16, *Counterguerrilla Operations*, 1963, pp. 6–7, 20, 38–39, 92; FM 100–5, *Field Service Regulations—Operations*, 1962, pp. 88, 131, 139–40, 154; FM 33–5, *Psychological Operations*, 1962, p. 124.

[67] MACV Directive 525–4, 17 Sep 65, sub: Tactics and Techniques for Employment of US Forces in the Republic of Vietnam, p. 8.

[68] Rpts, OASD (SA), Sep 67, sub: Southeast Asia Analysis Report, pp. 10–12, and Nov 67, sub: Southeast Asia Analysis Report, pp. 54–56; Bergerud, *Dynamics of Defeat*, pp. 5, 332–33.

[69] MACV, Guide for Province and District Advisors, 1968, pp. 13-2 to 13-12, Historians files, CMH.

[70] A Summary of Lessons Learned, Section I, Lessons in Combat, atch to Memo, Norton, DCG, USARV, for Distribution, 22 Sep 65, sub: Summary of Lessons Learned, p. I-9.

[71] Ibid.; FM 31–16, *Counterguerrilla Operations*, 1963, p. 40; FM 31–15, *Operations Against Guerrilla Forces*, 1961, p. 47.

[72] MACV, Guide for Province and District Advisors, 1968, pp. 13-9 to 13-12; Rpt, HQ, Phu Loi Pacification Task Force, 11 Jun 66, sub: Tan Phuoc Khanh Operation Summary, Historians files, CMH; Hay, *Tactical and Materiel Innovations*, pp. 139–42.

[73] Msgs, Westmoreland MAC 5740 to Admiral Sharp, 8 Jul 66, Westmoreland History files, CMH, and Westmoreland to Admiral Sharp, Jan 67, sub: Strategy and Concept of Operations for 1967, Historians files, CMH; Carland, *Stemming the Tide*, pp. 92–94.

[74] Wiesner, *Victims and Survivors*, pp. 62–63, 75, 126–29, 133, 136, 144–45, 147, 168, 210, 229–47; Msg, Commander, U.S. Military Assistance Command, Vietnam (COMUSMACV), to DCG, USARV, et al., 29 Jul 68, sub: Limiting New Refugees, Historians files, CMH.

[75] Unit History, 1st Bn, 28th Inf, 1966, p. 10, Historians files, CMH.

[76] Quote from Jonathan Schell, "A Reporter at Large, Quang Ngai and Quang Tin, Part I," *New Yorker*, Vietnam Roundup, Magazine Supplement, 9 Mar 68, p. 6, and see also p. 7.

[77] Wiesner, *Victims and Survivors*, pp. 60, 63–65; Rpt, MACCORDS-RE, 25 Jun 68, sub: Evaluation Report, Territorial Security in Huong Tra, Huong Thuy, and Phu Vong Districts, Thua Thien Province, I Corps Tactical Zone, pp. 8–9, RD Reports, CMH; Ltr, CINCPAC to POLAD, 23 Mar 68, sub: Reactions to Combat in An My Village, Binh Duong Province, with atch, Report by a Rural Technical Team on Popular Reaction in An My Village, Chau Thanh District, Binh Duong Province, Historians files, CMH.

[78] George Dexter, "Search and Destroy in Vietnam," *Infantry* 56 (July–August 1966): 41; Bergerud, *Red Thunder*, pp. 227, 234–36; Memo, James D. Hataway, Jr., for U.S. Ambassador, 26 Jan 68, sub: Destruction in Quang Ngai and Quang Tin, p. 5, Historians files, CMH; MACV Directive 525–9, 2 Feb 66, sub: Combat Operations, Control, Disposition, and Safeguarding of Vietnamese Property and Food Supplies, Historians files, CMH; Melman, *In the Name of America*, pp. 136–37, 139, 140–52, 155, 166–67; Wiesner, *Victims and Survivors*, pp. 62–63; Schell, "A Reporter at Large, Quang Ngai and Quang Tin, Part I," pp. 6–7, 21, and "Part II," 16 Mar 68, pp. 1–5; Memo, Hataway for Ambassador, 12 Dec 67, sub: House Destruction in Quang Ngai and Quang Tin, Historians files, CMH.

[79] Annual Hist Supplement, 173d Abn Bde (Separate), 1 Jan–31 Dec 65, 1966, pp. 57–63, Historians files, CMH.

[80] Fact Sheet, Lt Col Bullard, 29 Apr 71, sub: U.S. Civil Assistance Programs in SVN, 350 Travel Pack, Geo V Vietnam, CMH; Summary Analyses of Weaknesses in Army Civil Affairs Activities, atch to Summary Sheet, DCSOPS to CSA, 1 Jun 68, sub: Civil Affairs Improvement Program, 72A3468, RG 319, NARA; Pamphlet, 1st Bde, 101st Abn Div, Tactical SOP for Counterinsurgency Operations, 1 Dec 66, pp. 137–45.

[81] Raymond Bishop, Jr., Medical Support of Stability Operations: A Vietnam Case Study (Student paper, AWC, 1969), pp. 15, 22, 25–34; Spurgeon Neel, *Medical Support of the U.S. Army in Vietnam, 1965–1970*, Vietnam Studies (Washington, D.C.: Department of the Army, 1973), pp. 162–68.

[82] Bergerud, *Dynamics of Defeat*, pp. 165, 272; Hunt, *Pacification*, pp. 60–61.

[83] A Summary of Lessons Learned, p. 48, atch to Memo, Norton, DCG, USARV, for Distribution, 22 Sep 65, sub: A Summary of Lessons Learned, p. 48; Ewell and Hunt, *Sharpening the Combat Edge*, pp. 166–67, 214; Bergerud, *Dynamics of Defeat*, p. 158; James O'Brien, "Pacification: Binh Dinh's Season of Change," *Infantry* 60 (November–December 1970): 24; ORLL, 1 Aug–31 Oct 66, 25th Inf Div, pp. 24–25.

[84] Lawrence Yates, "A Feather in Their Cap? The Marines' Combined Action Program in Vietnam," in *New Interpretations in Naval History*, ed. William Roberts and Jack Sweetman (Annapolis, Md.: Naval Institute Press, 1991), p. 309; David Brooks, "U.S. Marines, Miskitos, and the Hunt for Sandino: The Rio Coco Patrol in 1928," *Journal of Latin American Studies* 21 (May 1989): 340n75; Hennessy, *Strategy in Vietnam*, pp. 69, 78.

[85] Briefing, c. 1965, pp. 7–11, 091 Vietnam, Army Chief of Staff, 68A3306, RG 319, NARA; Westmoreland, *A Soldier Reports*, pp. 190–91. According to one Defense Department study done in 1967, extending the CAP system throughout Vietnam would have required 167,000 combat troops and $1.8 billion a year. A more optimistic assessment performed by the RAND Corporation two years later when

conditions were more favorable reduced the estimated troop requirement to only 78,000 men—still wildly unobtainable given the fact that the United States had only 52,000 infantrymen in Vietnam at that time. PROVN, p. 5-18; Hennessy, *Strategy in Vietnam*, pp. 76–77, 127; Southeast Asia Analysis Rpt, USMC Combined Action Platoon Program, Jul 67, p. 33, copy in CMH; S. L. Canby et al., Alternative Strategy and Force Structure in Vietnam, RAND, 7 Jul 69, pp. 7, 20; Yates, "Feather in Their Cap," in *New Interpretations in Naval History*, ed. Roberts and Sweetman, p. 311; Memo, Maj Gen William Peers, ADCSOPS (Special Ops), for Gen Johnson, 8 Oct 65, sub: U.S. Marine Corps Emphasis on Counterinsurgency, 68A2344, RG 319, NARA.

[86] Quote from Hunt, *Pacification*, p. 108. Michael Peterson, *The Combined Action Platoons* (New York: Frederick A. Praeger, 1989), pp. 109–10, 123–24; Yates, "Feather in Their Cap," in *New Interpretations in Naval History*, ed. Roberts and Sweetman, pp. 315–21; Hennessy, *Strategy in Vietnam*, pp. 93–98, 111–13; Gary Telfer, Lane Rogers, and V. Keith Fleming, *U.S. Marines in Vietnam: Fighting the North Vietnamese, 1967* (Washington, D.C.: History and Museums Division, U.S. Marine Corps, 1984), p. 188.

[87] Rpt, MACCORDS-EVAL, 20 Dec 68, sub: Evaluation of Pacification Techniques of the 2d Brigade, US 25th Infantry Division, p. 6, Historians files, CMH; Collins, *Development and Training*, pp. 117–19; Clarke, *Final Years*, pp. 184–87, 392–402, 409–17; Hunt, *Pacification*, pp. 223–27.

[88] DF, XXIV Corps G–3 to Chief of Staff, XXIV Corps, c. 1 Nov 69, sub: Infantry Company Intensive Pacification Program, with atchs; Rpt, MACCORDS-EVAL, 7 Jan 69, sub: Evaluation of U.S. Unit Support of Pacification in II CTZ, pp. 2–3. Both in Historians files, CMH.

[89] MACV Lesson Learned 80, U.S. Combat Forces in Support of Pacification, 1970, pp. 6–12; William Ankley, Civic Action—Marine or Army Style? (Student paper, AWC, 1968), p. 9; Yates, "Feather in Their Cap," in *New Interpretations in Naval History*, ed. Roberts and Sweetman, p. 316.

[90] MACV Directive 525–4, 17 Sep 65, sub: Tactics and Techniques for Employment of US Forces in the Republic of Vietnam, p. 14; Memo, Westmoreland for Distribution, 7 Jul 65, sub: Minimizing Non-Combatant Casualties; MACV Directive 525–3, 14 Oct 66, sub: Combat Operations, Minimizing Non-Combatant Battle Casualties. Memo, CDC Command Liaison Det, USARV, for Directorate of Doctrine, CDC, 23 Jan 67, sub: Civil Affairs Organization and Activities; 25th Infantry Division, p. 3. All in Historians files, CMH.

[91] Quote from MACV Directive 525–4, 17 Sep 65, sub: Tactics and Techniques for Employment of US Forces in the Republic of Vietnam, p. 2, and see also p. 1; HQDA, Final Report of the Research Project: Conduct of the War, May 71, p. 30; Scales, *Firepower in Limited War*, pp. 144–46; Bergerud, *Red Thunder*, p. 236; Ltr, COMUSMACV to Distribution, 7 Jul 65, sub: Minimizing Non-Combatant Casualties, Historians files, CMH.

[92] ACTIV, Organization and Employment of Field Artillery, Oct 69, p. II-12; Bergerud, *Red Thunder*, pp. 84–85; Scales, *Firepower in Limited War*, pp. 51–52, 87–88; Ott, *Field Artillery*, p. 18.

[93] Krepinevich, *Army and Vietnam*, pp. 199–200; Wiesner, *Victims and Survivors*, pp. 60–61, 124–25; Thomas Thayer, "How To Analyze a War Without Fronts, Vietnam 1965–72," *Journal of Defense Research*, Series B, Tactical Warfare 7B (Fall 1975): 863–64.

[94] Quotes from Lesson Outline, Avoidance of Noncombatant Casualties and Property Damage (Suggested title, "Kill Your Enemies—Not Your Friends,"), pp. 1, 11, 4, 5, respectively, atch to HQDA, Final Report of the Research Project: Conduct of the War, May 71.

[95] The nine rules were "1. Remember, we are guests here. We make no demands and seek no special treatment. 2. Join with the people—Understand their life, use phrases from their language and honor their customs and laws. 3. Treat women with politeness and respect. 4. Make personal friends among the soldiers and common people. 5. Always give the Vietnamese the right of way. 6. Be alert to security and ready to react with your military skill. 7. Don't attract attention by loud, rude, or unusual behavior. 8. Avoid separating yourself from the people by a display of wealth or privilege. 9. Above all else, you are members of the U.S. Military Forces on a difficult mission, responsible for all your official and personal actions. Reflect honor upon yourself and the United States of America." Memo, I FFV for Distribution, 13 May 66, sub: Fact Sheet—The Nine Rules, Historians files, CMH; USARV GTA 21–1, Sep 67, The Enemy in Your Hands, Historians files, CMH; Lewy, *America in Vietnam*, p. 366.

[96] George Prugh, *Law at War: Vietnam, 1964–1973*, Vietnam Studies (Washington, D.C.: Department of the Army, 1975), pp. 74–76.

[97] Memo, 25th Inf Div, 8 Sep 68, sub: Commander's Combat Note No. 4, Psychological Impact of U.S. Troops on the Vietnamese, 25th Division Commander's Combat Notes, MHI; Bergerud, *Dynamics of Defeat*, pp. 170–76, 225–26.

[98] Quotes from ASubjScd 27–1, The Geneva Conventions of 1949 and Hague Convention No. IV of 1907, 8 Oct 70, pp. 17–18. Bergerud, *Red Thunder*, pp. 220–21, 225, 227, 230; HQDA, Final Report of the Research Project: Conduct of the War, May 71, pp. 84, 88–91.

[99] Bergerud, *Dynamics of Defeat*, pp.172–73; Nighswonger, *Rural Pacification*, p. 9.

[100] ORLL 4–67, Observations of a Battalion Commander, p. 32; Graves, "Observations of a Platoon Leader, Part I," pp. 36–37; David Hackworth, "No Magic Formula," *Infantry* 57 (January–February 1967): 33.

[101] Paret, *French Revolutionary Warfare*, p. 123.

[102] Doughty, *Army Tactical Doctrine*, p. 40; Bergerud, *Dynamics of Defeat*, p. 335; Komer, *Bureaucracy at War*, pp. 10, 12, 16–17, 21–22; Hennessy, *Strategy in Vietnam*, pp. 8–9; Lawrence Grinter, "Nation Building, Counterinsurgency, and Military Intervention," in *The Limits of Military Intervention*, ed. Ellen Stern (Beverly Hills, Calif.: Sage Publishing, 1977), p. 250; Stephen Rosen, "Vietnam and the American Theory of Limited War," *International Security* 7 (Fall 1982): 84–86, 88–98; William Olson, "The Concept of Small Wars," *Small Wars and Insurgencies* 1 (April 1990): 40–41, 44–45; Michael Cannon, "The Development of the American Theory of Limited War, 1945–1963," *Armed Forces and Society* 9 (Fall 1992): 72, 76–77, 85, 92–93; William Olson, "United States Objectives and Constraints: An Overview," in *Guerrilla Warfare and Counterinsurgency: United States–Soviet Policy in the Third World*, ed. Richard H. Shultz et al. (Lexington, Mass.: Lexington Books, 1989), pp. 23–26; Harry Summers, "Vietnam: Lessons Learned, Unlearned, Relearned," in *Military Strategy: Theory and Application, A Reference Text for the Department of Military Strategy, Planning, and Operations, 1983–1984*, ed. Arthur F. Lykke, Jr. (Carlisle Barracks, Pa.: U.S. Army War College, 1983), pp. 12–38; Raymond Barrett, "Graduated Response and the Lessons of Vietnam," *Military*

Review 52 (May 1972): 80–91; George Herring, "The Johnson Administration's Conduct of Limited War in Vietnam," in *Looking Back*, ed. Head and Grinter, pp. 80–81, 86; Richard Betts, "Misadventure Revisited," in *Vietnam as History*, ed. Peter Braestrup (Washington, D.C.: University Press of America, 1984), pp. 5–8; Herbert Schandler, "America and Vietnam: The Failure of Strategy, 1964–67," in *Vietnam as History*, ed. Braestrup, pp. 23–26.

9

THE EVOLUTION OF DOCTRINE
1965-1975

When American combat troops began deploying to Vietnam in March 1965, Army leaders were in the midst of reviewing counterinsurgency doctrine. Several years of frenetic activity had left the service with a large, but somewhat disjointed body of doctrinal literature. Although the Army judged its doctrine to be adequate, Army Chief of Staff General Johnson believed it could do better. In August 1964 he had launched a "Program for Analysis of U.S. Counterinsurgency Doctrine and Organization," a multiphased effort which he hoped would produce a more comprehensive, more sophisticated, and more tightly written corpus of doctrinal thought. Such an endeavor would take time to bring to fruition, time that the Army did not have. Six months after General Johnson launched the review program, President Johnson deployed marines to Vietnam, with Army combat troops following two months later.

During the early 1960s many Americans had come to regard Vietnam as a laboratory in which America could test its military and social theories from afar. Now the experimenters had become participants. If the effort would ultimately prove to be a failure, it at least generated a tremendous amount of data for the analysts back home. After 1965 information from Southeast Asia inundated the Army. Lessons learned reports, after action reports, quarterly command reports, annual historical reports, MACV directives, and the reports of special study teams—not to mention the anecdotal observations of tens of thousands of returning veterans—all vied for the attention of stateside doctrine writers, instructors, and trainers. At the height of the war Combat Developments Command was reviewing an average of seventy

Vietnam reports per month and identifying approximately forty "lessons" requiring some action by the doctrinal and training systems. So great were the Army's efforts at self-examination—arguably the most extensive in Army history—that critics charged that the service had gone too far, generating more information than it could ever use. While the Army may have gone overboard in trying to capture the lessons of Vietnam, the effort attested to its determination to learn and adapt. The result was a far richer tapestry of materials—from manuals to training films—than would have been produced otherwise.[1]

Words and Organizations

By the time the first U.S. combat units arrived in Vietnam, Combat Developments Command had completed many of the preliminary studies called for in General Johnson's review program. But important tasks still remained to be done. One of the seemingly least important, yet ultimately most troubling, had to do with sorting out the arcane world of counterinsurgency terminology.

The counterinsurgency wave of the early 1960s had left the military awash in buzzwords. Combat Developments Command attempted to untangle the linguistic muddle in July 1965 by drafting a study on "Definitions To Support Counterinsurgency Doctrine." The study received a cold reception at the Pentagon's Office of the Deputy Chief of Staff for Military Operations, which immediately produced a counterproposal—a new family of terms crafted by Maj. David R. Hughes that identified what Hughes believed were the two central tasks in counterinsurgency, internal defense and internal development. When the competing proposals went forward to the chief of staff, Johnson chose a course that, if anything, made matters worse rather than better.[2] Stating that "we need to express what we are for, rather than what we are against," he rejected CDC's recommendation that the Army continue to use the term *counterinsurgency*, embracing instead Hughes' new lexicon. As defined by the Army in 1966, *internal defense* constituted "the full range of measures taken by a government to protect its society from subversion, lawlessness, and insurgency," while *internal development* involved "the strengthening of the roots, functions, and capabilities of government and the viability of its national life toward the end of internal independence and freedom from conditions fostering insurgency." Henceforth, Army doctrinal materials were to use the new phraseology exclusively, erasing all traces of the word *counterinsurgency*.[3]

The chief of staff soon learned, however, that rank was no match for the power of words. Five years of intense salesmanship had emblazoned *counterinsurgency* into the collective consciousness of soldiers and civilians alike, and no ukase could readily change that. Moreover, the rest of the U.S. government continued to use the term. To Johnson's chagrin, therefore, the Army had no choice but to continue to include *counterinsurgency* in its official dictionary despite the systematic removal of the word from Army manuals after 1966.[4]

Although General Johnson had adopted Hughes' internal defense and internal development paradigm, he partly accepted CDC's

Chief of Staff General Johnson

recommendation that the Army replace the old terms *general*, *limited*, and *cold* war with a new set of terms that divided the spectrum of conflict by levels of intensity—*high*, *mid*, and *low*. Henceforth manuals would continue to use the old terms, while doctrinal studies employed the levels of intensity phraseology. This decision added yet another layer of terminology without bringing additional clarity. In practice, the term *low intensity conflict* (LIC) became synonymous with counterinsurgency and internal defense and development. Combat Developments Command further particularized LIC into two subcategories—low intensity conflict type I, which involved the commitment of U.S. combat forces, and low intensity conflict type II, which involved the provision of advice and support short of direct intervention.

The situation became even murkier when General Johnson insisted on introducing his own linguistic invention, *stability operations*. Johnson described stability operations as the "employment of force to maintain, restore, or create a climate of order under which a government under law can function effectively," a task that he argued encompassed the Army's third principal mission. Unfortunately, while Johnson insisted that Army literature use the expression *stability operations*, he opted against including it in the Army dictionary. Thus what had begun as an effort to bring clarity to doctrine by imposing order in Army phraseology had produced the exact opposite effect—more, rather than fewer, terms, with a concomitant increase in confusion.

Because General Johnson did not include *stability operations* in the Army dictionary and because his order to rescind the use of the term *counterinsurgency* had been directed only to CDC and not CONARC, some schools initially refused to use the terminology *stability operations*, citing regulations that required that schools employ only officially defined terms. Moreover, for many soldiers the exact relationship between *cold war, low intensity conflict, counterinsurgency, internal defense and internal development*, and *stability operations* was anything but clear. Some manuals implied that stability operations were synonymous with counterinsurgency and internal defense and development. Others portrayed stability operations as a subset of internal defense dealing primarily with overseas constabulary and intervention-type missions, and thus more akin to the older phrase *situations short of war*, which was gradually falling out of use in favor of the term *cold war*.[5]

A semblance of order began to emerge in 1967 when the Army finally included *stability operations* in its official dictionary. As the new lexicon ultimately emerged, internal defense and internal development referred to all government programs designed to counter instability in a foreign country, while stability operations referred to the military's role in internal defense and development—a thin cover for what otherwise was an unnecessary redundancy. Still, the confusion took some time to dissipate because the Army would take several years to fully incorporate the new terms throughout its family of manuals.[6]

Perhaps the best example of how the spirit of "overthink" corrupted the development of doctrine can be seen in the area of acronyms. During the 1960s the Army demonstrated an unsettling penchant for changing acronyms for little or no reason. The introduction of the internal defense and internal development family of terms likewise meant that many older terms had to be changed to fit the new paradigm, despite the fact that the meaning and function of the entities the expressions described had not changed at all. Thus, the Environmental Improvement Program (EIP) became Internal Development (IDEV), the National Internal Security Committee (NISC) became the National Internal Defense Coordination Center (NIDCC), and the Counterinsurgency Operations Group (CIOG) became the Internal Defense/Development Operations Group (ID/DOG). Worst of all, the Army could not settle on an acronym for its flagship term, *internal defense and internal development*. By 1975 the Army had changed the acronym for internal defense and internal development five times—from IDID to ID/D to IDD to IDAID to IDAD—without any change in the meaning of the phrase itself, a pointless exercise that sowed confusion and cynicism throughout the ranks.

Words were not the only stumbling blocks to the formulation of doctrine. As in the early 1960s, organizational issues continued to impede the smooth development and transmission of doctrine. Although the production of manuals was a major CDC responsibility, it often took a backseat to the command's other missions—material research and the production of long-term studies. So cumbersome was the manual coordination and review process that by 1967 CDC Commander Lt. Gen. Harry W. O. Kinnard complained of "severe turbulence in our doctrinal literature program." The bifurcation of the Army's doctrinal and training functions between Combat Developments Command and Continental Army Command likewise continued to create barriers between doctrine writers and educators. Although the Army made some improvements, difficulties remained, and the doctrinal development, training, and education functions performed by CDC and CONARC would not reunite into a single entity, the Training and Doctrine Command, until 1973.[7]

While shortcomings inherent in the doctrine development process adversely affected all aspects of Army doctrine, counterinsurgency remained a particularly thorny problem. Like nuclear warfare, it did not fit easily into the Army's doctrinal establishment because it created an operational milieu that was significantly different from conventional warfare—one that was specialized on the one hand and yet which also cut across all branch and functional lines. Consequently, Army leaders continued to struggle with the question of whether counterinsurgency doctrine was better concentrated in the hands of a few specialists, or should responsibility for different pieces of the counterinsurgency puzzle be farmed out to nearly every agency in CDC. Ultimately, they vacillated between the two approaches.

In 1966 Combat Developments Command initiated a general reorganization that grouped all of its subordinate agencies into three broad, functional categories—combat, combat support, and combat service support. Reflecting General Johnson's belief that stability operations were a mission for the entire Army and not just Special Forces, CDC broke up the Special Warfare and Civil Affairs Group. The command placed the Special Warfare Agency (which retained responsibility for developing broad counterinsurgency principles for type II low intensity conflicts and for reviewing the manuals developed by other agencies for counterinsurgency content) under the new Combat Arms Group and returned the Civil Affairs Agency to its original parent entity, the Combat Service Support Group. The move disturbed the synergy the Army had attempted to create in 1964 when it had brought these two agencies under the supervision of a single group headquarters. On the other hand, by eliminating the Special Warfare and Civil Affairs Group, CDC was indicating that the command believed that counterinsurgency doctrine had matured to the point where it could take its place as a normal part of the doctrinal system without the support of extraordinary bureaucratic mechanisms.[8]

The new arrangement was short lived. In 1967 the Army reversed course and placed the Civil Affairs Agency under the supervision of the Combat Arms Group. Not only did the switch reunite supervisory control over the development of civil affairs and counterinsurgency doctrine, but it symbolically elevated civil affairs to the status of a combat arm—a clear reflection of the Army's growing appreciation for the importance of political matters in contemporary warfare.[9]

Still, Army leaders remained uncomfortable with the doctrine development process. General Johnson sought to create greater unity in 1968 when he ordered the Civil Affairs Agency to move to Fort Bragg and combine with the Special Warfare Agency under a new umbrella organization, the Institute of Strategic and Stability Operations, an organization that reported directly to CDC headquarters. The establishment of this agency (reorganized as the Institute of Military Assistance in 1973) brought the formulation of doctrine for several stability-related functions—civil affairs, politico-military affairs, nation building, advisory assistance, psychological operations, and special forces—under a single entity at a single location. The institute was also able to wrest proponency for the Army's capstone counterinsurgency manual, FM 100–20, from the Institute of Advanced Studies at Carlisle Barracks.

The formation of the institute at Fort Bragg finally centralized responsibility for the four manuals that established overarching counterinsurgency doctrine in the late 1960s (FM 100–20; FM 31–22; FM 31–23, *Stability Operations: U.S. Army Doctrine* [1967]; and FM 31–73). Nevertheless, control over several other key manuals, including FM 31–16, *Counterguerrilla Operations*, remained under their parent agencies, as did the development of all other branch and functional manuals into which stability operations material needed to be integrated. Turf and philosophical battles between Fort Bragg and these agencies over the amount of counterinsurgency doctrine to be incorporated into the general corpus of Army literature would never be resolved, with the result that coverage of counterinsurgency subjects at the branch level continued to be uneven throughout the Vietnam War.[10]

Doctrinal Developments, 1966–1967

While the Army wrestled with language and organizational questions, CDC's Special Warfare Agency completed a major study titled

"Counterguerrilla Warfare Doctrine" in January 1966. The agency concluded that while Army doctrine was "in the main, sound, up-to-date, and beamed at the right enemy," it suffered from several defects. According to the Army's counterinsurgency experts, current doctrine gave the erroneous impression that phase III counterguerrilla warfare was essentially equivalent to conventional combat. This insight, born out of the difficulties the Army was experiencing in coming to grips with enemy main force units in Vietnam, was somewhat ironic, since this very same agency just a year before had declared that doctrine for large-unit counterinsurgency warfare "will be essentially that of general war or limited war."[11]

To correct their mistake, the doctrine writers at Fort Bragg recommended that future manuals remind their readers of the differences between conventional and guerrilla warfare. The study especially noted that "combat power will have to be applied selectively and its effects modified to preclude harming the population. In many instances, U.S. commanders will be faced with choosing between a course of action which will assure entrance into a given area with minimum U.S. losses, and a course of action which will require him to apply his combat power with less violence, and more selectively so as not to harm the population, but at the same time increasing the probability that more U.S. casualties will accrue." Although this statement accurately portrayed one of the central dilemmas of counterinsurgency operations, opposition from within the officer corps to any suggestion that commanders willingly accept greater casualties led the Army to omit the final clause of this statement in future manuals.[12]

Although the conduct of phase III warfare was of great concern to the authors of the study, they also pointed out other shortcomings in contemporary doctrine. Among the subjects requiring greater treatment were border control; riverine, police, and clear-and-hold operations; intelligence; civil-military and state-to-state relations; and mine, electronic, unconventional, and chemical warfare (to include defoliation and crop destruction). In many cases these were areas that experience in Vietnam had indicated a need for additional doctrinal amplification. The report also reiterated previous CDC studies in advocating greater coverage of counterinsurgency throughout the manual system. On the other hand, the Special Warfare Agency also decried redundancy, recommending that FM 31–15, *Operations Against Irregular Forces* (1961), be scrapped since much of its content duplicated what appeared in later manuals, such as FM 100–20 (1964), FM 31–22 (1963), and FM 31–16 (1963).[13] CDC accepted most of Fort Bragg's recommendations, incorporating them into manuals over the next few years. Still, rifts remained over the extent to which Vietnam-style techniques were appropriate to include in manuals intended for general application.

In 1966 the Army published two manuals that illustrate the state of counterinsurgency doctrine during the Army's first full year of combat in Vietnam—FM 33–5, *Psychological Operations—Techniques and Procedures*, and FM 41–5, *Joint Manual for Civil Affairs*. *Psychological Operations* featured an expanded and rewritten section on insurgency and counterinsurgency. In line with the prevailing currents of doctrinal thought, the manual identified development and modernization as the keys to eliminating insurgency, noting that "no tactical counterinsurgent program can be effective for long without major nation-building programs." It further asserted that the counterinsurgent's ultimate aim must be the creation of a nontotalitarian government worthy of public support. Though recognizing the pitfalls of the modernization process, FM 33–5 (1966) urged nation builders to create societies in which power was shared widely among different social groups, a difficult goal given the nature of most third world societies and the perils of dispersing authority in the midst of a crisis. In addition to adding new sections on insurgent and counterinsurgent psychological methods, the manual reiterated the traditional caution that "a few rash, undisciplined acts will jeopardize popular support and the entire operation," a caution that, the manual lamented, was too seldom heeded because "experience has shown that many commanders give too little emphasis to the psychological aspects of military operations. Too often, long range political objectives are sacrificed for temporary tactical gains."[14]

FM 41–5, *Joint Manual for Civil Affairs*, was important because it represented the first statement of interservice civil affairs doctrine since the advent of the counterinsurgency era. Four years in the making (largely due to coordination problems with the Air Force), FM 41–5 (1966) differed from previous civil affairs doctrine in that it focused not on the government of occupied areas, but on the many civil-military situations that confronted military forces short of a major war. The manual urged commanders to avoid ethnocentric behavior and discussed the many issues that might adversely impinge on the establishment of smooth relations between the Army and a sovereign society. It did not, however, break any new ground. Indeed, its observation that "operations directed against insurgents entail a delicate combination of necessary force and measures taken to relieve sources of unrest," essentially reiterated the same principles of firm, yet fair, treatment that had characterized the Army's approach to pacification for over a century.[15]

While 1966 was a relatively slow year for doctrinal publications, 1967 witnessed the emergence of a second generation of counterinsurgency manuals, bringing to fruition Chief of Staff General Johnson's 1964 reform program. Together these manuals covered the full range of counterinsurgency doctrine, from national policy to small-unit actions. Missing from their number, however, was FM 31–15, which Combat Developments Command rescinded on the grounds of redundancy.

At the top of the doctrinal heap was a new edition of FM 100–20, *Field Service Regulations: Internal Defense and Development*, prepared by the Institute of Advanced Studies. Released in May 1967 after a year's delay caused by confusion over the introduction of the new internal defense and stability operations terminology, this manual fulfilled the same role as its 1964 predecessor in outlining U.S. national policy vis-a-vis third world insurgency. It examined the nature of modernization and insurgency and discussed America's response to these phenomena as contained in the 1962 Overseas Internal Defense Policy. FM 100–20 (1967) also related recent government policy that encouraged U.S. embassies in countries threatened by insurgency to establish an office to coordinate all in-country counterinsurgency efforts, though it declined to establish a fixed title or structure for such an entity, leaving such decisions to the ambassador.

Following General Johnson's direction, FM 100–20 (1967) formally enshrined in official doctrine the policy that stability operations were the Army's third principal mission. In line with CDC study recommendations, the manual also devoted somewhat greater attention to the noncombat side of counterinsurgency warfare—police, intelligence, civil affairs, psyops, advisory, and population- and resources-control matters. Overall, however, FM 100–20 (1967) differed little from the 1964 edition. It had a somewhat more sophisticated view of insurgency, but did not materially alter long-standing doctrine.[16]

Just below FM 100–20 (1967) in the doctrinal pecking order was FM 31–23, *Stability Operations: U.S. Army Doctrine*. FM 31–23 (1967) was an entirely new manual written by the Special Warfare Agency as a partial replacement for FM 31–15 (1961). Although FM 31–23's stated purpose was to elaborate on the Army's own particular role in internal defense and development, it repeated much of the information found in FM 100–20 (1967), thereby undermining the Army's efforts to eliminate redundancy. Nevertheless, it was an excellent manual, providing extensive coverage of America's approach to countering third world instability.

Stability Operations illustrated several trends that increasingly characterized post-1965 doctrine. First, while the manual adhered to

Rostow's thesis of rising expectations, it portrayed modernization in a more sociological context and less in terms of material development. Economic development remained central, but the manual exhibited greater cognizance of the role that values played in shaping societies. According to the manual, the key to modernization (which the manual defined as "striving toward an advanced economy and an efficient, popularly supported government") was to effect a change in the indigenous society's "value system." This entailed breaking down traditional mores and replacing them with new ones, all the while avoiding the "unwarranted application of our own political and cultural values"—tricky business for even the most accomplished social engineer.[17]

Like all previous manuals, FM 31–23 placed great emphasis on winning popular support through a combination of good troop conduct, moderate control measures, discriminate force, and "vital and dynamic" socioeconomic programs. However, the manual differed slightly from FM 33–5, *Psychological Operations—Techniques and Procedures* (1966), in that it had more sober expectations with regard to political reform. Although a "remedial political development program" remained a key aspect of American policy, FM 31–23 refrained from calling for the establishment of democracy, stating that "a general rule cannot be established pinpointing the time at which the population should begin to participate in the governmental process, but procedures which permit the people to bring their problems to the government should be established as early as possible." This view, together with increased warnings against trying to impose American institutions on alien cultures, reflected lessons from Latin America and Asia, where U.S. nation builders had experienced great difficulties in persuading allied governments to live up to American political ideals.[18]

A similar retrenchment was evident in the realm of civic action. Although *Stability Operations* continued to stress the importance of civil considerations in military operations, it acknowledged that recent experience had taught that "'do-goodism' for do-goodism's sake seldom is beneficial, often is costly, and in many instances may provoke and alienate the population rather than win its support." Consequently, FM 31–23 (1967) reiterated earlier doctrine that, to be effective, civic action programs had to be carefully crafted.[19]

Another thrust of the new doctrine, again born from recent experience, was the increased emphasis the manual placed on counterinfrastructure activities. Army doctrine in the 1950s had recognized the importance of eliminating guerrilla leaders and uprooting the underground organizations that sustained insurgent movements, but in the early 1960s these practical considerations had been overshadowed in the minds of some

428

theorists by a somewhat romantic view of insurgency. According to this line of thought, if revolutions were truly popular movements spawned by social injustices, a strategy that focused on eliminating the leaders rather than rectifying underlying social problems was misguided and futile. Practical experience in Vietnam reminded theorists that revolutions, like all human activities, require organization and leadership, no matter how just or popular the cause might be. Consequently, the Army began to take a harder look at the infrastructure question. The manual not only provided greater detail about Communist organizational methods, but it also made the elimination of the insurgent leadership a top priority. It similarly stressed the importance of population security, to be achieved largely through the auspices of village-based police and paramilitary formations.[20]

Reflecting the increased importance assigned to noncombat tasks, FM 31–23 added the appellation "operations" to subject headings covering civil affairs, intelligence, and population and resources control, symbolically elevating their status to a level equal with tactical operations. It reinforced this point by leaving the discussion of combat operations to last, a distinct shift from earlier manuals. Still, coverage of combat operations remained far more extensive than any other subject, and FM 31–23 firmly upheld the service's traditional view that, once the shooting started, military operations had to take priority over civil improvements, with meaningful reforms being postponed until after military requirements had been satisfied and security restored.[21]

In considering military actions, *Stability Operations* introduced a new paradigm by dividing military activities into three types of campaigns: strike, consolidation, and remote area. Strike campaigns consisted of offensive missions designed to find, fix, and destroy the enemy. Consolidation campaigns involved clear-and-hold, oil-spot–style pacification measures, while remote area campaigns corresponded to contemporary Special Forces activities with the Montagnards in Vietnam. The execution of these activities remained largely as they had been explained in earlier manuals. When the enemy was strong—as in phase III—large units and massed artillery would be used to attack the insurgents' major units and bases, compelling them to break down into smaller, less menacing entities. Once this goal had been achieved, government forces would break down into progressively smaller units to wage a relentless war of raid, ambush, and saturation patrolling that would eventually wear the guerrillas down and pave the way for the establishment of effective pacification measures.[22]

As in the first generation of counterinsurgency manuals, the details of how these operations were to be conducted was left to the

Army's premier counterguerrilla manual, FM 31–16, *Counterguerrilla Operations*, which the Army republished in March 1967. Like FM 100–20 (1967), publication of this manual had been delayed for over a year due to confusion over the new terminology, as well as disagreements between the manual's parent organization—the Infantry Agency—and the Special Warfare Agency.[23]

FM 31–16 (1967) reflected the Army's growing appreciation for noncombat issues by elevating civil affairs from an auxiliary to a primary weapon system. Rather than leave civil questions to civil affairs personnel, *Counterguerrilla Operations* emphasized that civil affairs was a command responsibility and that plans at all levels must include civil and psychological considerations. In line with the prevailing philosophy, the manual deliberately dropped earlier advice that soldiers should discomfort civilians during searches so as not to muddle the doctrine's primary theme that "abusive, excessive, or inconsiderate search methods" only served to increase civilian support for the enemy. The manual also included for the first time a small psyops section and repeatedly urged commanders to exercise discretion in employing supporting fires, though it continued to endorse harassment and interdiction fire.[24]

Based on the Special Warfare Agency's concern that earlier manuals had not drawn sufficient distinction between conventional and unconventional warfare, the manual highlighted the differences between rear area security in a conventional war and counterinsurgency. Though the point was neither new nor invalid, the doctrine writers descended into hyperbole when they asserted that "local political activities are normally not a major consideration affecting the activities of counterguerrilla forces in limited and general warfare situations," a dangerously misleading statement that reflected more the determination of counterinsurgency enthusiasts to assert the uniqueness of their field than objective, historical analysis.[25]

FM 31–16 (1967) made a more valid point when discussing the differences between conventional warfare and a phase III insurgency. Following the lead of "Counterguerrilla Warfare Doctrine," the manual reflected contemporary experience in Vietnam by cautioning that even in large-unit mobile warfare,

maneuvers such as envelopments, penetrations, and turning movements may not produce the same effects on guerrilla forces as they would on field army-type tactical forces. Caches, guerrilla safe areas, and populations sympathetic to, or dominated by, the guerrilla may be so dispersed that guerrilla units are not dependent on a few critical logistical bases which they must protect. Under these conditions, a turning movement, for example, launched by counterguerrilla forces to cause the guerrilla force to react to protect a base, may produce movement in entirely different directions than those anticipated.[26]

The inclusion of the term *main forces* in the 1967 edition of FM 31–16 to describe "guerrilla regular armed forces" reflected a movement toward incorporating Vietnam-related material into Army manuals. FM 31–16 (1967) introduced cursory discussions of such Vietnam-oriented subjects as tunnel searches, air base defense, and the construction of patrol bases. Warning that the usual measurements of success—battles won and terrain occupied—were not meaningful in a guerrilla context, the manual counseled soldiers that "protraction and attrition in internal defense and development counterguerrilla operations must be expected and accommodated." FM 31–16 (1967) also reflected experience by altering counterambush procedures, stating that ambushed convoys should continue to move forward, not stop as FM 31–16 (1963) had directed. The manual encouraged units assigned to consolidation operations to devote "maximum effort" to organizing indigenous security and paramilitary forces. Finally, *Counterguerrilla Operations* called for "painstaking training" in night operations, while cautioning that "offensive tactics are not to be emphasized to the detriment of the defense," a clear recognition that while U.S. doctrine was operationally offensive, U.S. troops in Vietnam frequently fought on the tactical defensive.[27]

While *Counterguerrilla Operations* included some of the terms that had sprung from the conflict in Vietnam, it did not do so unreservedly. Thus, while the manual made a passing reference to search-and-destroy operations, it did so only for the purpose of stating that such operations were subsumed under the new, official term *strike operations*. Part of the reason for this was that doctrinal writers were averse to including too many colloquialisms and nonstandard terms into doctrine. However, the phrase *search and destroy* had also accrued some negative connotations in the public mind—images of fruitless searching and seemingly excessive destruction—which the Army was anxious to dispel. Consequently, the term would never achieve doctrinal status, as most manuals preferred to use phrases like *offensive operations*, *strike operations*, or *reconnaissance in force*.[28]

Although *Counterguerrilla Operations*' text embraced the new terminology of *strike* and *consolidation operations*, its discussion of the operational and tactical details of counterguerrilla warfare did not differ materially from prewar doctrine. Nor did the manual endorse any one particular operational method over another. It recommended extensive small-unit patrols to consolidate government gains and harass the enemy when he was weak or when the government lacked the resources to challenge him fully and large-unit offensives employing encirclement tactics and "mass artillery fires" to destroy major enemy formations and bases whenever they were found. These operations were to be undertaken against a backdrop of civil, intelligence, and police measures designed to isolate the guerrilla "physically and psychologically from the civilian support," as the government systematically moved forward with an oil-spot–style campaign of progressive area clearance. All of this sounded distinctly familiar not only because it mirrored prewar doctrine, but also because it reflected how operations were actually being conducted in Vietnam—operations that were themselves firmly rooted in that older body of knowledge.[29]

While FM 31–16 (1967) explained the role of combat brigades in internal defense and development operations, new versions of FM 31–73, *Adviser Handbook for Stability Operations*, and FM 21–75, *Combat Training of the Individual Soldier and Patrolling*, spread the gospel to individual soldiers and advisers. FM 31–73 (1967) differed little from its predecessor and continued to relate valuable information on counterinsurgency and advisory subjects. Though intended for a general audience, it inevitably took on an increasingly Vietnam flavor. FM 21–75 (1967) likewise added much Vietnam-oriented subject matter. The manual greatly expanded its coverage of patrolling, ambush, and counterambush techniques, relating specific tactics to different operational environments, from jungles to rice paddies. The text described Viet Cong tactics and added a new section on methods to be used in search-and-destroy operations. The manual also continued its 1962 predecessor's efforts to draw attention to the political side of counterguerrilla warfare, reminding its readers that "the culture, customs, and spiritual values of the people may be quite different from ours, but they are just as much a source of pride as our own. *You must respect them.* Proper behavior toward the people and any assistance or display of friendship for them will go far toward reducing their support for the guerrillas and securing their help in defeating the guerrillas. . . . Exercise self-discipline at all times and deal with the local population in a firm, just, and understanding manner."[30]

Perhaps one of the most glaring weaknesses of Army doctrine during the first half of the 1960s was the relative paucity of information on the intelligence aspects of counterinsurgency. Every manual spoke of the pivotal importance that intelligence played in stability operations, and a number provided some broad guidance, but few had moved beyond generalities to discuss in detail how intelligence functions were to be conducted. In 1967 the Army Intelligence Agency endeavored to redress this shortcoming by publishing a new edition of FM 30–5, *Combat Intelligence*, that added two pages to the manual's counterinsurgency section. True relief came, however, in the form of FM 30–31, *Stability Operations—Intelligence* (1967). Accompanying this manual was a classified companion text—FM 30–31A, *Stability Operations—Intelligence Collection*—which explored the more arcane aspects of the trade. Together, these manuals integrated the intelligence field into the broader counterinsurgency literature, describing how conventional intelligence techniques could best be applied in an unconventional setting.[31]

Just as the production of FM 30–31 (1967) belatedly addressed the 1964 doctrinal revision program's requirements vis-a-vis intelligence, publication of a new version of FM 41–10, *Civil Affairs Operations*, in 1967 was intended to fulfill the review program's demand for new civil affairs doctrine. Although the civil affairs community had been one of the chief promoters of civic action within the Army, the doctrine and organization of the Army's civil affairs units had remained largely oriented toward the execution of traditional military government operations. FM 41–5 (1966) had heralded a new departure in this regard, but General Johnson was still not satisfied. Declaring "we must sweep the World War II ghost out of the Civil Affairs house and refurnish it with new concepts," General Johnson demanded that the civil affairs community become more relevant to contemporary conditions. *Civil Affairs Operations* (1967) attempted to do just that.[32]

FM 41–10 (1967) reflected the Army's new emphasis on civil-military relations on its very first page when it declared that "the Army lives in an environment of people," a statement not unlike Mao's analogy of the guerrilla existing in a human sea. While the manual noted that political and military issues were always intertwined, it asserted that this was particularly true in stability operations, where every military action had to be executed with an eye toward the paramount goal of winning popular support. Consequently, the manual greatly expanded its coverage of civil affairs in unconventional settings, with one chapter on civil-military relations in the Cold War and two chapters on internal defense and development.[33]

FM 41–10 (1967) downplayed vertical military government organization for a more decentralized system in which civil affairs units were subordinated to local tactical commanders in a fashion conducive to the conduct of integrated civil-military operations in a sovereign, friendly country. Like the other manuals published in 1967, *Civil Affairs Operations* strongly asserted that civil affairs was a command responsibility at every echelon. It further postulated that soldiers should act as social "technicians" and "innovators," blending their administrative skills with "an appreciation of societal microcosms" to "eliminate the insurgent movement at its roots."[34] On the other hand, the manual cautioned that American "civil affairs personnel must have a ready comprehension that what is best in the United States is not necessarily always best in other social, political, and economic circumstances and must also understand that the United States is less concerned with making over other nations in its own image than in helping countries to help themselves."[35]

As in earlier doctrine, FM 41–10 (1967) asserted that civic action represented the single greatest vehicle through which soldiers could influence a developing society. *Civil Affairs Operations* tried to portray civic action in a realistic light. It admitted, for example, that "military civic action cannot by itself produce a satisfied populace in areas where basic discontent centers around long standing political, economic, or social grievances." Similarly, it warned that "mere generosity on the part of U.S. troops is not enough, particularly when that generosity is practiced with an unconscious show of wealth, a disregard for local custom, or is accompanied by loud or unusual behavior." FM 41–10 (1967) reviewed the usual list of criteria for effective civic action projects, stressing that soldiers foster villager participation in both the conceptualization and realization of a project. The manual differed from some previous discussions of civic action, however, by laying down a rather narrow definition of what civic action actually was. According to FM 41–10 (1967), "military civic actions should be designed to make real, lasting improvements to the social, economic, and political environment." Actions intended simply to curry favor or to make superficial changes did not rise to the level of civic actions but were, at best, community relations activities. Thus, building a school was inherently a civic action—even if the act failed to win friends for the government—as it offered the prospect of long-term social change through education. On the other hand, sponsoring an outing for children was not a civic action, even if it had the effect of building better relations with the community. FM 41–10 (1967) took a dim view of all such community relations endeavors, warning that they represented "a misapplication of resources which should be devoted to true military civic action."[36]

The manual's attempt to clarify the nature of civic action highlighted the fact that the concept had never been well defined or universally understood. Most soldiers tended to lump all civilian-related activities—from population evacuation to raising funds for orphanages—under the rubric of civic action, regardless of how meaningful those endeavors might be. On the other hand, the manual's dismissive tone toward community relations activities rubbed many soldiers the wrong way and seemed to contradict other guidance that stressed the short-term, high impact, psychological nature of civic actions. Indeed, Army manuals published after 1967 did not universally accept FM 41–10's views on civic action. Thus, one manual maintained that distributing candy and tobacco were civic actions. Another accepted FM 41–10's narrow definition but argued that "civil-military projects which are undertaken to improve the image of the military forces and foster goodwill with the population may serve to replace or augment military civic action projects. Tactical requirements, time, availability of materiel, or other considerations may make these projects more feasible than the developmental ones of military civic action." Such disagreements perpetuated confusion and prevented the formulation of a more uniform understanding of civic action within the Army as a whole.[37]

Reflections on Nation Building

By the end of 1967 the Army had essentially fulfilled the major goals of the doctrinal revision program set in motion by General Johnson in 1964. Broad, vertically organized doctrine for the execution of the Army's third principal mission existed in the form of FM 100–20, *Field Service Regulations: Internal Defense and Development*; FM 31–23, *Stability Operations: U.S. Army Doctrine*; FM 31–73, *Adviser Handbook for Stability Operations*; FM 30–31, *Stability Operations—Intelligence*; and the as-yet unrevised FM 31–22, *U.S. Army Counterinsurgency Forces*. FM 31–16, *Counterguerrilla Operations*, described brigade-level combined arms counterguerrilla warfare, while a host of branch and functional manuals spread the gospel of counterinsurgency horizontally across the spectrum of Army activity, from infantry and armor to civil affairs. Still, General Johnson was dissatisfied, and under his guidance the service initiated yet another round of doctrinal examination, an effort that soon revolved around a debate over the nature and importance of nation building.

Practical experience over the past few years had taken some of the luster off the more ebullient pronouncements of the early 1960s with regard to America's ability to end third world instability through political, social, and economic reform. Building schools and inoculating children had proved inadequate talismans against guerrilla bullets. Economic aid had not sparked Walt Rostow's anticipated take off toward more stable, socially equitable, and politically democratic societies either. As the war in Vietnam and Alliance for Progress stumbled toward uncertain conclusions, even supporters of nation building were compelled to admit that these endeavors had turned out to be more difficult than many had initially supposed. As a result, a new, more pragmatic school of thought had begun to emerge to challenge the "hearts and minds" school.[38]

One of the leaders of the pragmatic movement was Charles Wolf of the RAND Corporation. Wolf argued that there was no evidence that socioeconomic improvement programs necessarily had the desired effects of winning hearts and minds. Noting that "evil governments may quell virtuous rebellions, and virtuous governments may lose to evil rebellions," Wolf urged Americans to abandon some of the righteousness that had come to color U.S. policy during the early 1960s. For Wolf and other pragmatists, winning a people's loyalty was less important than controlling a population's behavior. This conclusion stemmed from recent experiences as well as an analysis of Communist methods. As another leading pragmatist, Lt. Col. Boyd T. Bashore, explained, the Communists drew their strength less from the appeal of their ideology than through the power of their organization. In a pair of widely noted articles that appeared in the *Infantry Journal* in 1968, Bashore reminded his readers of the extensive efforts the Communists made to mobilize and control the populace. Through a careful blend of propaganda, intimidation, and administration, successful Communist movements created an interlocking web of political, social, and military institutions that allowed them to progressively gain control over a society, beginning at the grass-roots level and working up. Bashore labeled the Communist's system of institutions *parallel hierarchies*, a term he took from French counterinsurgency literature. For Bashore and Wolf, the key to countering Communist revolution lay not so much in instituting reforms than in taking practical steps to destroy the parallel hierarchies while bolstering the government's own ability to control the behavior of the population.[39]

Noting that "victory . . . seems most often to have been effectively accomplished by an all-out police-military effort, and not by pushing freedom like a wet noodle from the top down into the countryside," Bashore argued that "the people of a nation under attack must accept discipline and put off or give up many of the rights and privileges that we may hold dear in our democracy. This fact of life, as unpalatable as it may seem, must be fully understood." Rather than pinning one's hopes on building democracies and righting social wrongs, governments would do better, Bashore and Wolf argued, to focus their energies on less glamorous military, organizational, and administrative endeavors. Building roads and distributing land might win friends and influence people, but ultimately police, intelligence, propaganda, and population- and resources-control measures would strangle a guerrilla movement by denying the guerrillas the "inputs" they needed to survive—food, shelter, information, and recruits.[40]

Though they looked at civic action and democracy-building with a jaundiced eye, the pragmatists did not challenge the central tenets of established American doctrine. They acknowledged that genuine reform was both useful and ultimately desirable. They also rejected the more extreme measures—like torture and terror—employed by some French practitioners of *guerre revolutionnaire*. In fact, the actions they recommended—imposing curfews and controlling the distribution of food—were already a part of U.S. doctrine. And, as in existing doctrine, Bashore and Wolf insisted that such measures be legally construed and fairly, if firmly, implemented. They differed from their more idealistic counterparts, therefore, less in the means to be used than in the relative significance to be accorded to hard-versus-soft measures. Still, this was a split that was not readily reconciled.[41]

Nor did the Army resolve it. Previous doctrine had acknowledged the importance of both persuasion and coercion without according unambiguous precedence to either, and champions for every conceivable admixture of the two could be found in the officer corps. This situation would continue, for rather than choose between them, the Army chose to continue to straddle the doctrinal fence. Thus, while the service would place increasing emphasis on practical security and counterinfrastructure measures, it would also cling to the notion that counterinsurgents had to win the loyalty of the people, eschewing purely military and security solutions. Indeed, what is perhaps most interesting about the Army's reaction to the trials and tribulations of the 1960s was that the Army did not seek to abandon the central tenets of the hearts-and-minds approach to counterinsurgency but rather sought ways to execute that philosophy more effectively.

General Johnson's initial concern in this regard focused on the interrelated areas of psychological operations and civil affairs, two disciplines that he believed were central to stability operations. While the new manuals issued in 1966 and 1967 had raised the profile of psychological and civil affairs, many believed the service had yet to achieve the type of cultural and institutional change needed to transform it into a truly effective low intensity force.

One obstacle to improving the Army's political and social capabilities lay in the fact that such activities transcended bureaucratic boundaries, with primary responsibility frequently falling to external agencies that were either coequal with or superior to the Army. A case in point was psychological operations. The U.S. Information Agency bore primary responsibility here, with the Army designated as a supporting agency. After the Dominican intervention had revealed weaknesses in the development, coordination, and execution of U.S. psychological programs, the government had created an Interagency Working Group for Psychological Operations in Critical Areas. The Army was not represented on this body, though it supported the group's efforts to bring structure and uniformity to interagency psychological operations. Unfortunately, bureaucratic wrangling stymied the group's efforts, and by 1968 the Army ruefully concluded that the group had "made no significant progress" in clarifying national policy, doctrine, or organization with regard to social and psychological programs. Frustrated by the inability of higher authorities to clarify national policy and sobered by the fact that in Vietnam the Army was already performing tasks that nominally belonged to civilian agencies, the service began to look for alternatives on its own.[42]

In 1966 a board chartered to review officer education programs had recommended that the Army develop a cadre of stability operations specialists. At the time General Johnson had declined to take such a step, but he revisited the issue after a panel of academics and the deputy chief of staff for personnel endorsed the idea. Between the fall of 1967 and the spring of 1968 the Army Staff would generate a pair of studies advocating a more active role in nation building.

The first study, written by Lt. Col. John H. Johns, a psychological warfare officer in the Office of the Deputy Chief of Staff for Military Operations, was titled "Psychological Operations–Role in Establishing a Sense of Nationhood," or "Psyop-Reason" for short. Johns argued that the Army had no choice but to create its own corps of social engineers and nation-building experts, both because sociopolitical affairs were critical to the success of military operations in low intensity conflicts and because civilian agencies had frequently proved unequal to the task of managing such matters.[43] Johns embraced recent developments in nation-building theory that downplayed material factors in favor of a more holistic approach to social engineering that emphasized people and values over things. The key to nation building, he argued, was to create a sense of community—or nationhood—beginning with individuals and small, intimate social groups at the grass-roots level and gradually expanding to ever larger bodies and institutions. Recent experiences in Asia and Latin America lent credence to such an approach, as billions of dollars worth of economic and material aid had failed to produce viable modern nations. Nowhere was this truer than in Vietnam, where U.S. officials increasingly blamed the war's flagging prospects on the

South Vietnamese government's failure to motivate and mobilize its own populace. Army manuals produced in 1966 and 1967 had already begun to reflect this philosophy, and Johns urged that it be propagated on a wider scale.[44]

The "Psyop-Reason" report received a skeptical reception from Under Secretary of the Army David E. McGiffert. McGiffert believed that the study, like most nation-building literature, was too abstract and was based more on theory than historical analysis. Like General Bruce Palmer, Jr., he doubted whether a universal doctrine for nation building could ever be developed, as each insurgency was the unique product of innumerable historical, social, political, economic, environmental, and military factors. His doubts were bolstered by the report itself, which conceded that "the social sciences as yet have not established a full range of principles upon which information and psychological practitioners can base their programs." Finally, McGiffert objected to the study's assertion that the Army should take the lead on this matter. While stability operations might be a core Army mission, nation building was not. Providing security was one thing; dabbling in the internal political and social affairs of another state was quite another. McGiffert therefore counseled that the Army should not try and carve out a new responsibility for itself, a responsibility that most properly belonged to the Agency for International Development, U.S. Information Agency, the State Department, and other civilian entities involved in overseas assistance programs.[45]

McGiffert's questions did not deter the Army Staff from producing a second paper in favor of greater Army activism in nation building. Prepared under the auspices of the assistant chief of staff for force development (ACSFOR), the study—"Counterguerrilla Operations"— essentially reaffirmed the conclusions of the "Psyop-Reason" report. The study's authors, Lt. Cols. William J. Buchanan and Robert A. Hyatt, criticized the Army's approach to the political side of counterguerrilla warfare. In their opinion, recent manuals, like FM 100–20 (1967) and FM 41–10 (1967), were insufficiently attuned to what they deemed was the focal point of any revolution—the struggle for legitimacy. In a partial rejection of Wolf, they asserted that victory in an insurgency would inevitably accrue to whichever party succeeded in persuading the citizenry that it had a legitimate right to rule. On the other hand, the ACSFOR authors joined with Wolf and Bashore in criticizing earlier American nation-building efforts. Noting that the political struggle "goes beyond good administration and building a viable economy," Buchanan and Hyatt argued that Rostow had erred in viewing the problems of modernization largely from an economic standpoint. "This materialistic view," they declared, "stems from the unfounded belief that the lack of adequate goods and services 'cause' insurgency. With this view, it must follow that provision of the necessary goods and services will solve the problem. This shallow view is unsupportable." They likewise took a dim view of most Army civic action activities, which they believed were "the result of a delusion concerning motivation." Since "the effectiveness of providing minor benefits as a primary source of motivation is not borne out in either scientific behavior theory or in practice," the authors dismissed civic action as a relatively minor propaganda weapon in the broader socio-political struggle.[46]

Rather than tinker around the margins, Buchanan and Hyatt challenged beleaguered governments to fundamentally recast their societies. In the words of the study,

The conduct of a political struggle within a society is revolutionary; that is, the culture and values of the society and its members must be rapidly and permanently changed to establish social control. Time and the insurgent will not permit an evolution of culture and values. . . . What [the government] must understand is that the traditional values will be changed by the insurgent anyhow, and these changes will be detrimental to the government. . . . It is certain that change will take place; it is incumbent on the government to take the necessary steps to insure that the change is orderly, even if revolutionary, and productive of stability. The stability required is related to the regulated motion of a gyroscope, not to the *status quo*.[47]

Once the necessity of fundamental social change was accepted, a government would need a body of highly trained specialists to guide it through the perilous waters of social transformation. To help meet this requirement, Buchanan and Hyatt supported the formation of a uniformed corps of social engineers. They rejected any suggestion of impropriety at having U.S. soldiers involved in overseas nation building, for while nation building might "be incompatible with the concept of not interfering in the internal affairs of nations, it is no more incompatible than the accepted role of teaching an army how to efficiently shoot these same citizens once they are subverted."[48]

If Buchanan and Hyatt disagreed with Wolf over the proper focal point of a counterinsurgency program, they accepted many of the pragmatists' methods. Like Bashore, they insisted that the Army needed to develop a detailed doctrine for waging political warfare. They likewise elevated population security over purely military offensive operations. For the most part, however, they found few faults with the military aspects of contemporary doctrine. Indeed, they believed that the organizational and tactical concepts employed by U.S. combat units in Vietnam were fundamentally sound. The report specifically rejected the idea that the Army could or should attempt to "out-guerrilla the guerrilla," preferring the more traditional approach of blending industrial might with a greater mastery of individual soldier skills to present the guerrilla with a heavily armed, yet savvy, foe.[49]

Since the key to winning an insurgency was to create a more cohesive social system supportive of both modernization and the rule of law, Buchanan and Hyatt frowned on any act that might unduly disrupt social order. They therefore joined existing doctrine in calling for good conduct and condemning actions involving excessive destruction of civilian life and property. Yet like the "PROVN" study of 1966, "Counterguerrilla Operations" insisted on adhering to firepower-intensive tactics, noting that "since the counterinsurgent must keep his casualties to a minimum if he is to retain the capability of fighting a protracted war, the destruction of large enemy units depends on heavy volumes of supporting fires, not on infantry assaults." The report did not explain how one could minimize civilian casualties while simultaneously waging a high-firepower war.[50]

Assistant Chief of Staff for Force Development Lt. Gen. Arthur S. Collins, Jr., reacted favorably to "Counterguerrilla Operations." His only qualm involved the apparent contradiction between firepower-heavy tactics and the need to minimize civil disruption. To resolve this conflict, he recommended that doctrinal materials make clear that the high-firepower tactics endorsed in the study were suitable only for a phase III environment, and then under rules of engagement similar to those employed in Vietnam. He further recommended that the United States refrain from giving third world governments sophisticated equipment and heavy weapons, stating that "I have come to the conclusion that the very nature of our support tends to separate the government . . . from the people." Disillusionment with America's experience in Vietnam also led him to conclude that in future insurgencies the United States should limit itself to providing advice and technical support rather than combat forces. To this end he recommended that the Army delete the combat forces included in the as-yet unimplemented Regional Assistance Command.[51]

Chief of Staff General Johnson's reaction to "Counterguerrilla Operations" was even more positive. "Excellent . . . the most hopeful outlook I've seen" were Johnson's words after he perused the report. Johnson had never accepted General Palmer's 1965 conclusion that it was impossible to codify a universal doctrine for counterinsurgency. By asserting that all revolutions devolved to a political struggle for legitimacy in which the competing factions wielded psychological and organizational tools to recast social groups and institutions, the ACSFOR paper seemed to be offering a scientifically derived basis for the creation of doctrine. Of course the notion that insurgencies were primarily driven by political factors had long held currency in U.S. doctrinal and policy circles. What "Counterguerrilla Operations" brought to the table was a fresh approach to tackling those political issues through the prism of contemporary sociological analysis. General Johnson not only approved the work, but he ordered it distributed throughout the Army's doctrinal and educational system to stimulate thought on how the service could best participate in the "political struggle." Indeed, so important did the Army regard the monograph that *Military Review* devoted the first forty pages of its August 1968 issue to presenting what would ultimately be a two-part, sixty-page distillation of the report. Meanwhile, Johnson used Buchanan and Hyatt's analysis as the basis to launch yet another round of studies to improve Army doctrine, an effort he designated "Refining the Army's Role in Stability Operations," or "REARM-STABILITY."[52]

The only part of the ACSFOR report that General Johnson declined to endorse concerned the recommendation to eliminate combat troops from the Regional Assistance Command. Johnson believed that, no matter how distasteful direct military interventions might be, "we cannot avoid violence, much as we dislike it. We must learn how to control it, without loss of effect on the enemy." Still, a CDC study done as part of the "REARM-STABILITY" effort endorsed deleting the airborne infantry brigade from the Regional Assistance Command while retaining and improving the current Special Action Force organization. All of this proved moot, however, as declining resources and a growing national aversion for overseas interventionism doomed the RAC concept, and it was never implemented.[53]

Fortified by the conclusions of the Army Staff studies of 1967–1968, General Johnson finally decided to establish a cadre of uniformed social engineers. As one of his last actions as chief of staff, Johnson merged the civil affairs and psychological operations career programs into a new career program in 1968. He designated the new career field the Overseas Security Operations (OSO) program, but the name did not stick, and in 1969 it became the Military Assistance Officer Program (MAOP). MAOP officers were to be specialists in politico-military affairs in general and nation building in particular. Army leaders hoped that the new career field would attract the best and brightest officers to politico-military work. To develop the new class of soldier-statesmen, Johnson directed that the Civil Affairs School be moved from Fort Gordon, Georgia, and merged with the Special Warfare Center to form a new Center for Overseas Security

Operations (later renamed the Institute for Military Assistance) at Fort Bragg, North Carolina. From there, MAOP officers would be deployed to military assistance advisory groups, Special Action Forces, headquarters staffs, and units around the world to dispense their knowledge to U.S. and foreign soldiers alike. Johnson emphasized the importance of the new field by authorizing G–5 and S–5 civil-military staff sections for brigades, regiments, groups, and select battalions worldwide, an authorization that heretofore had been limited to Vietnam. He also recommended that every military assistance advisory group in a developing country have at least one officer trained in nation building on its staff. Ultimately, the service hoped to recruit 6,000 officers into the MAOP career field.[54]

General Johnson's retirement in July 1968 removed a determined advocate for expanding the Army's sociopolitical functions. His successor as Army chief of staff, General William C. Westmoreland, was less passionate on this subject. Nevertheless, he too believed that the Army needed to improve its civil affairs, psyops, and nation-building capabilities, and he continued both the MAOP and "REARM-STABILITY" programs.[55]

Between 1968 and 1970 the Army produced a number of doctrinal studies in support of "REARM-STABILITY." One of the first was "Nation Building Contributions of the Army (NABUCA)," written by ODCSOPS' Colonel Johns in 1968. Following recent trends, Johns argued that the single-most important task of nation building was to develop ways and means whereby people could come together to work for common goals. To accomplish this task, American social engineers would have to replace traditional habits and loyalties with "patterns of cooperation" conducive to achieving national unity, social harmony, economic growth, and political liberalization—a process which Johns referred to as institution building.[56]

The "NABUCA" report joined with the "Counterguerrilla Operations" study in criticizing the materialistic orientation of past nation-building and civic action efforts because as Johns conceded, "it does not follow that a farmer assisted with well-building and farm-to-market means will necessarily support the provider of these improvements." With an eye on Vietnam, Johns lamented that "we have failed to generate the enthusiasm and dedication to a cause that is necessary for effective group behavior. Large elements of the population have remained alienated from the mainstream of society."[57]

Colonel Johns thought the Army could do better. He suggested that the Army expand civic action programs and reorientate them toward institution building. Similarly, American training programs should, "with the utmost discretion," imbue foreign military personnel with the ideology of using military resources for constructive societal tasks. He also believed that the military needed to put forth a positive image, though he asserted this truism in unusually strong terms, stating that "purity of motive and honest intentions; good passive troop behavior and good relations with the local power elite are not sufficient. To avoid the image of being an insensitive force, the military must take strong, positive measures to understand the world of the alienated, and demonstrate empathy and compassion for their legitimate plight."[58]

Although Johns strongly supported using advisers and MAOP personnel as social engineers, he shied away from suggesting that U.S. operational forces be committed to nation-building tasks. He also recognized that significant political, ideological, and bureaucratic obstacles existed to the military's playing a more active nation-building role. Thus, while he dismissed most objections to military participation in nation building, Colonel Johns conceded that "there is a limit to the improvements that can be accomplished by unilateral Army action. The suspicion of Army involvement in 'political matters' will continue to inhibit maximum Army contribution to nation building programs until the semantic confusion is cleared. There is legitimate concern with respect to Army politico-military activities, but much of the problem is semantic." He therefore recommended that the Army continue to develop its nation-building capabilities "while avoiding undue criticism for overstepping traditional boundaries." Secretary of the Army Stanley R. Resor and Army Chief of Staff General Westmoreland agreed. They approved the "NABUCA" report for use in developing doctrine and school curriculums but prohibited distribution of the paper outside the Army lest word of the work trigger criticism from civilian agencies that the Army was encroaching on their bureaucratic turf.[59]

The net effect of the 1966–1968 study effort thus had been to create a movement within the Army for strengthening the military's nation-building capabilities. As one report declared, "the day of the Army officer who is professional only in a narrow range of military duties is gone. One of the most important tasks confronting the Army during the period in question will be the development of a new higher level of professional military competence to deal with stability-type operations. The attainment of a high educational level among relatively junior officers in the politico-socio-economic and scientific fields will be a necessity in dealing with other cultures."[60]

Yet the consensus was far from universal, and there remained important obstacles to expanding the Army's nation-building capabilities. Not the least of these was the difficulty of codifying the musings of social and political theorists into meaningful guidance for soldiers because as a council of academics had cautioned in 1967, "the psychological and political dimensions of war cannot by their very nature be rigidly codified. It will, therefore, be impossible to develop doctrine in this area that will be as precise or as rigorous as doctrine usually within the Army."[61]

Doctrinal Developments, 1968–1972

While the theoreticians refined their nation-building concepts, the Army pressed ahead to redress the outstanding gaps identified in the "Counterguerrilla Warfare Doctrine" study. The most notable works to appear in 1968 were three "test" manuals rushed into print to provide interim guidance until more definitive doctrine could be developed—FM 31–36 (Test), *Night Operations*; FM 31–75 (Test), *Riverine Operations*; and FM 31–55 (Test), *Border Security/Anti-Infiltration Operations*. The first two manuals addressed specific challenges in Vietnam, while the third codified recent experience in Korea.[62] Combat Developments Command also continued to disseminate updated stability operations doctrine throughout branch- and functional-level manuals. Examples of this effort included the addition of a new stability operations chapter in FM 31–18, *Long-Range Patrol Company*, that described Vietnam LRRP procedures, and Change 1 to FM 7–11, *Rifle Company, Infantry, Airborne, and Mechanized*, which nearly tripled that manual's coverage of counterguerrilla warfare. By far the most important manual to be revised in 1968, however, was the Army's basic combat manual, FM 100–5, *Operations of Army Forces in the Field*.

The 1968 edition of FM 100–5 incorporated all the new language and terminology that had come into vogue since the manual's last publication in 1962. It identified stability operations as a normal Army function, indicating that early detection and immediate remedial action offered the best chance to eliminate a budding insurgency. Although the manual's chapter on cold war operations stood virtually unchanged, the counterguerrilla chapter was completely rewritten to focus on guerrilla warfare in an insurgency environment as opposed to partisan warfare during limited or general wars. The chapter was also shorter and less detailed than its predecessor due to the publication of many other counterinsurgency-related manuals since 1962.

Perhaps reflecting America's Vietnam experience, FM 100–5 (1968) cautioned that insurgents were "particularly dangerous" when they received outside aid. The manual also added a short section on riverine operations but included scant else from the Vietnam conflict.

Indeed, what is most remarkable about the text is how little it had changed after six years of doctrinal ferment and three years of warfare in Vietnam. With the exception of a phrase here or there, the basic concepts related in this most important manual did not change. Thus FM 100–5 (1968) continued to argue that unresolved grievances caused insurgencies, and that the only way to permanently quell unrest was to redress socioeconomic and political inequities. To achieve this end and "to maintain popular support, accelerated internal development is frequently necessary to satisfy popular needs and demands." On the other hand, FM 100–5 (1968) also adhered to established doctrine in maintaining that "the proper balance of effort between combat and internal development is a command decision based on how best to defeat the insurgency in the specific area of operations," and consequently it refused to prioritize these efforts.[63]

In 1969 Combat Developments Command continued its efforts to ensure that branch and functional manuals kept pace with current concepts and terminology. Usually all this amounted to were minor changes that did little more than reiterate points made in earlier, higher-level manuals. Some manuals, like the 1969 editions of FM 21–50, *Ranger Operations*, and FM 31–5, *Jungle Operations*, emerged substantially unchanged from prewar texts. Others, like FM 41–10, *Civil Affairs* (1969), mirrored current trends by adopting an increasingly sociological flavor and by paying somewhat greater homage to the importance of counterinfrastructure activities. Still others actually curtailed their coverage of stability operations in the name of eliminating redundancy. Thus FM 31–21, *Special Forces Operations—U.S. Army Doctrine* (1969), reduced its coverage of stability operations by 80 percent compared to its 1965 predecessor. The new edition, however, did add a small section on countering urban guerrillas in response to the growth of urban terror movements. According to the manual, the primary mission of Special Forces personnel in urban areas "will be to assist the local government in neutralizing the insurgent political leadership and infrastructure. Good intelligence is the key to identifying and locating hard core insurgent leaders. Apprehending or destroying the hard core leadership is the first step in the fragmentation of the insurgent infrastructure, elimination of centralized direction and control, creating disunity, and the eventual destruction of the insurgent underground apparatus."[64]

While intelligence and counterinfrastructure measures held the key to defeating urban terrorists, experience with rural warfare in Vietnam led the Army to modify its guerrilla-fighting doctrine in a somewhat different way. In 1969 the Army issued a change to FM 31–16,

Counterguerrilla Operations, that incorporated some of the lessons of Vietnam. The new text highlighted the importance of both reconnaissance and firepower in counterguerrilla warfare. It specifically endorsed the DePuy approach of finding the enemy with minimum force and destroying him by fire. This was particularly true when the enemy was fortified, in which case the manual advised commanders to pull back and allow "massed firepower" to overwhelm the enemy. Nearly four years after commanders in Vietnam had begun to employ high-firepower tactics, the Army's primary operational manual for counterguerrilla warfare finally came around to endorsing such techniques.[65]

This modest and incremental approach continued through 1970 and 1971. In 1970 the Army produced two new manuals concerning aspects of defense against guerrillas—FM 31–85, *Rear Area Protection Operations*, which discussed the organization of rear areas during a conventional conflict, and FM 31–81 (Test), *Base Defense*, which related many of the methods used in Vietnam to secure installations against attack. Other Vietnam-induced revisions included Change 1 to FM 21–75, *Combat Training of Individual Soldiers* (1970), which added a chapter on combat intelligence and tracking in a guerrilla environment. The Army also released Change 2 to FM 31–16, which discussed urban counterguerrilla operations. Like earlier manuals, the new urban warfare section counseled discretion in the use of force. Reflecting recent experience during the 1968 Tet offensive, the insert cautioned that guerrillas might choose to fight in a built-up area, "even at the risk of annihilation . . . if they are confident of winning a local or worldwide psychological victory."[66]

Vietnam lessons also provided the rationale for other revisions as well. FM 7–10, *The Rifle Company, Platoons, and Squads* (1970), briefly described Vietnam techniques, while a new edition of FM 6–20–2, *Field Artillery Techniques* (1970), reinforced the trend toward firepower, expanding its coverage of the use of artillery in counterguerrilla warfare nearly sixfold over the 1962 edition. The increase reflected the fundamental shift from maneuver to fire that had occurred in American counterguerrilla tactics during the Vietnam War. The manual reviewed artillery concepts and techniques as they had evolved in Southeast Asia and heartily endorsed using artillery to the maximum extent possible, though it acknowledged the importance of minimizing the adverse consequences of such fires on civilians. Finally, in 1970 the Army produced two manuals devoted exclusively to counterinsurgency. FM 30–31, *Stability Operations—Intelligence*, emphasized the importance of attacking the guerrilla's "parallel" system of social and political control, although it contained few new methods of doing so, while an entirely new manual, FM 19–50, *Military Police in Stability Operations*, addressed the many roles that police organizations played in low intensity conflicts.[67]

Doctrinal Consolidation, 1972–1974

In 1972, after several years of updating derivative branch and functional doctrine, the service returned to the field of fundamental doctrine, producing what would be the third generation of some of its core counterinsurgency manuals. In the interest of streamlining, the Army stripped most of the detail concerning Army counterinsurgency doctrine out of FM 100–20, *Field Service Regulations: Internal Defense and Development*, and placed it into FM 31–23, *Stability Operations: U.S. Army Doctrine*. It likewise folded FM 31–22, *U.S. Army Counterinsurgency Forces*, into FM 31–23, thereby eliminating FM 31–22 entirely and producing two new manuals where there once had been three. FM 100–20 (1972) emerged from this process a hollow shell. Reduced to fifteen pages, the manual provided a cursory overview of the U.S. government's approach to third world development and instability. It reviewed the causes of instability, described the basic philosophy behind America's response, and outlined the roles and missions of the various government agencies involved in overseas internal defense and development work. Little of this was new, as the basic parameters of national policy had remained remarkably constant over the past decade.

Continuity was likewise the theme of the 1972 edition of FM 31–23, *Stability Operations: U.S. Army Doctrine*. The manual perpetuated earlier analyses of both the insurgency challenge and its solution. It emphasized the importance of police countermeasures, especially during the earliest stages of unrest, and included a section on Latin American–style urban insurgency. Its recounting of the Army's three tiers of counterinsurgency forces—the SAF, backup brigades, and the Army as a whole—was virtually unchanged from 1963. FM 31–23 (1972) also adhered to the trend toward conciseness, as it was slimmer than its predecessor despite the fact that it consolidated two manuals and a portion of a third. On the other hand, FM 31–23 (1972) stepped away from the Vietnam experience by purging elements of earlier doctrine that had absorbed some of the flavor of that conflict. Thus the manual dropped much of the 1967 edition's discussion of Communist organization which had been based on the Viet Cong and replaced Vietnam-specific terms like *district* and *province* with more generic words, such as *local* and *state*.

If the 1972 manuals consisted largely of condensed recitations of earlier doctrine, they dutifully incorporated at least one important change in American policy that had transpired since the publication of their predecessor manuals in 1967. In July 1969 the new President of the United States, Richard M. Nixon, had declared that the United States would exercise greater discretion than it had in the past in deciding when, where, and how America would intervene to combat subversion in the third world. Vietnam had cured the United States of its willingness to "pay any price" and "bear any burden . . . to assure the survival of liberty" in remote corners of the globe.[68] The crusade was over, to be replaced by a more cautious strategy of selective engagement. Henceforth, decisions on foreign assistance would be governed by a dispassionate analysis of America's strategic interests rather than Cold War rhetoric. Central to those considerations would be a determination as to the willingness and ability of the afflicted government to fight, for Vietnam had demonstrated the folly of trying to save a nation that lacked the will to save itself. As the president explained in a report to Congress in February 1970,

We cannot expect U.S. military forces to cope with the entire spectrum of threats facing allies or potential allies throughout the world. This is particularly true of subversion and guerrilla warfare, or 'wars of national liberation.' Experience has shown that the best means of dealing with insurgencies is to preempt them through economic development and social reform and control them with police, paramilitary and military action by the threatened government. We may be able to supplement local efforts with economic and military assistance. However, a direct combat role for U.S. general purpose forces arises primarily when insurgency has shaded into external aggression or when there is an overt conventional attack. In such cases we shall weigh our interests and our commitments, and we shall consider the efforts of our allies, in determining our response.[69]

At first glance this seemed nothing new, for national policy and Army doctrine had always maintained that nations bore primary responsibility for their own development and defense. During the heyday of American intervention in Vietnam, however, this principle had tended to be overlooked. Indeed, the 1967 version of FM 100–20 had omitted the 1964 edition's assertion that the threatened country bore primary responsibility for its own defense. Now the pendulum was swinging back to a more cautious approach.[70]

In 1970 Army Chief of Staff General Westmoreland responded to the "Nixon Doctrine" by directing that the Army reexamine its role in stability operations. In response, ODCSOPS produced a study titled "The United States Army's Role in Nation Building." The report endorsed the course the Army had been following over the past few years. It reaffirmed the importance of nation building, both as a tool of U.S. government policy and as an Army mission. The paper supported the Military Assistance Officer Program as a means of developing civil-military and stability operations expertise and advocated the continued use of appropriately orientated MAAGs and training teams to dispense U.S. advice and assistance wherever it was needed.[71]

Yet while the study strongly supported the retention of stability operations capabilities within the Army, it admitted that serious impediments existed to doing so. Perhaps the most fundamental problem was that "our knowledge" of nation building "is still relatively meager." Ten years of effort by thousands of academics and practitioners had yet to decipher the nation-building enigma. While the hard school of experience had given Americans a greater appreciation for nation building's many challenges, the fact remained that the task of building social, political, and economic institutions in alien and unstable environments was more alchemy than science, a magical art that the sorcerers of academia—let alone their uniformed apprentices—only partially understood and imperfectly controlled. Thus, while ODCSOPS believed the Army should continue to study the modernization phenomenon, "it must also recognize its limitations in solving or even understanding the variety of problems facing the LDCs [less developed countries] in their attempts to modernize and must be constantly on the alert to prevent overextending itself in this effort."[72]

If the mysteries of nation building gave Army staffers pause, so too did the more mundane frustrations of governmental organization. A decade of experience with bureaucratic infighting and slipshod coordination notwithstanding, the U.S. government still lacked an effective means of integrating the activities of the many agencies involved in the formulation and execution of internal defense and development policy. Until such a mechanism was created, ODCSOPS believed that much of the Army's activities would go for naught. On the other hand, ODCSOPS also recognized that the service could not blame all of its problems on others, for "there appears to be some inconsistency between stated Army policy and reality. While considerable emphasis has been placed on stability operations, there are indications, particularly in the areas of training and assignments, that these type of operations are not treated on an equal par with the Army's other missions." After years of command emphasis, much of the rank and file still felt uncomfortable with certain aspects of stability operations—most notably its political components. Sociopolitical duty not only violated many soldiers' view of the proper separation of political and military life, but violated their sense of professionalism as well, since no soldier could possibly be an expert in the many diverse roles in which pacification duty cast him. Many soldiers were also convinced, rightly or otherwise, that advisory duty was detrimental to their careers. Sincere and repeated efforts by the Army to dispel this belief, as well as to improve the quality of the advisory effort through career incentives and increased education, never succeeded in overcoming the officer corps' innate aversion for this key component of American policy.[73]

By itself, the lack of enthusiasm exhibited by many soldiers toward stability operations was not an insurmountable obstacle, but it became poisonous when combined with the general malaise that settled over the nation at the close of the Vietnam War. Disillusionment over the Vietnam imbroglio created deep antipathy toward both nation building and overseas interventionism not only within the military, but among politicians, academics, and the general public as well. Antiwar sentiments blended with traditional sensitivity over civil-military relationships to create an added backlash against the Army's participation in nation building. The fact that the 1960s and early 1970s had witnessed a resurgence of military dictatorships in Latin America at a time when the United States was pushing an agenda of military-social activism simply amplified doubts in many people's minds as to the wisdom of military involvement in nation building. Moreover, America was beginning to change its view of the world, replacing the Cold War tendency to regard everything in bipolar terms with a new view that postulated a multipolar world, in which every insurgent was not a Communist and every insurgency ought not trigger an intervention.

The "growing lack of political consensus within the United States" over nation-building and counterrevolutionary activities, when coupled with the Nixon Doctrine and the prospect of rapidly shrinking defense budgets due to postwar downsizing, all led the Army Staff to conclude that the service could neither justify nor afford to maintain a significant stability operations capability, notwithstanding the fact that the Army believed that stability operations would continue to represent its most likely form of activity for the foreseeable future. Consequently, while the Army Staff insisted the Army retain a nation-building capacity through such entities as the MAOP program and the Special Action Forces, it rejected the suggestion that the Army as a whole be structured for stability operations. Instead, ODCSOPS preferred that the Army "concentrate its energies on those activities associated with preparation for land combat."[74]

General Westmoreland approved the ODCSOPS report as Army policy in late 1970 and instructed Combat Developments Command to incorporate its conclusions into doctrine. Together with the Nixon Doctrine, it charted a new direction for the Army. The tide that had borne counterinsurgency upon the Army ten years earlier had begun to ebb. While the service was not willing to disown the internal defense and development mission, henceforth stability operations and nation building would absorb a progressively smaller portion of the service's attention and resources. Gone were the days when enthusiasm for the new frontiers of counterinsurgency and nation building had led the Army to advocate an ever greater role for itself in these most difficult endeavors. Having nearly extricated itself from the Vietnamese quagmire, there was now little enthusiasm for jumping into similar situations anytime soon. Indeed, if the Army had its way, there would never be any quagmires ever again, for while everyone acknowledged that building a nation was a task of years, if not decades, the ODCSOPS report insisted that "in the event that U.S. forces are called upon for nation building activities, they should then be assigned on the basis of a specific mission in a specific time frame in a specific place, and then be withdrawn." This was a heartfelt, if somewhat wistful, declaration.[75]

The 1972 manuals dutifully adopted the new policies. Citing the Nixon Doctrine, FM 100–20 (1972) asserted that "the U.S. military role in stability operations must be primarily advisory. . . . Viable and lasting institutions can be generated only by the host country populace. Neither the U.S. military nor U.S. civilian personnel can create enduring patterns of cooperation among the host country populace." Thus while the basic content of U.S. counterinsurgency doctrine remained relatively unchanged, a new direction had begun to assert itself.[76]

All of the trends of the late 1960s and early 1970s coalesced in the last major counterinsurgency manual of the Vietnam War, FM 100–20, *Internal Defense and Development, U.S. Army Doctrine*, in 1974. Published during the twilight period between the withdrawal of U.S. military forces in 1973 and North Vietnam's conquest of the South in 1975, FM 100–20 (1974) represented the Army's final word of the counterinsurgency era.

The 1974 edition of FM 100–20 superseded not only FM 100–20 (1972), but FM 31–23 (1972) as well. As such, it represented the culmination of the movement to gradually consolidate the four high-level counterinsurgency manuals that had existed in the mid-1960s (FM 100–20, FM 31–15, FM 31–22, and FM 31–23) into a single, authoritative text. After 1974, FM 100–20 became the sole source for overarching U.S. national and U.S. Army doctrine pertaining to internal defense and development. Below FM 100–20 (1974), FM 31–16,

Counterguerrilla Operations (1967 and the changes of 1969 and 1970) provided doctrine for the conduct of combined arms operations at the brigade level and below, while a bevy of branch and functional manuals (listed in an appendix to FM 100–20 [1974]) provided details as to the functioning of each Army branch and service in an internal defense and development environment.

FM 100–20 (1974) set a different tone from earlier manuals in its very first sentence, which stated that "this manual provides U.S. Army concepts and doctrine concerning the conduct of internal defense and development (IDAD) *by host country security forces* to prevent and defeat insurgency, and U.S. Army IDAD advice and assistance to host country security forces." Although the manual's second paragraph conceded that U.S. commanders would follow the same doctrine should U.S. units be deployed to IDAD situations, the manual's initial wording sent a clear signal that advice and assistance, not direct action, would be the Army's primary role in IDAD.[77]

Having confirmed the Army's narrowing role in counterinsurgency, FM 100–20 (1974) stressed the true functions—and limitations—of doctrine. As the manual explained, doctrine

provides fundamental principles that are designed to guide the actions of military forces in the conduct of IDAD operations. In applying the principles, one must be aware that the situation in each developing country faced with an insurgent threat is *unique to that country*. In addition, the situation may vary considerably in different areas of the same country. The IDAD principles, policies, and programs that are applied successfully in one nation (or in one area of a country) may not be applicable in exactly the same manner in another nation (or another area of the same country). Therefore, the principles in this manual only provide a general guide to the conduct of IDAD, and judgment must be used to adapt them to each situation.[78]

This was good advice. While hardly new in concept, it represented a break with those who had asserted that one could fashion a truly definitive and universally applicable doctrine for building nations and suppressing insurgencies.

FM 100–20 (1974) departed from past doctrinal pronouncements in a number of other ways as well. With little fanfare, the manual deleted the term *stability operations* from the Army lexicon, the latest casualty in the seemingly endless war over counterinsurgency-related words. By eliminating the term *stability operations*, the Army finally put an end to General Johnson's ill-conceived foray into lexicography. Henceforth, the Army had only one official term for counterinsurgency—*internal defense and development*—and one upper-level manual to describe it, a situation much improved over the past, when a variety of terms and manuals had vied with each other for doctrinal prominence. Yet the demise of the phrase *stability operations* represented more than just a victory for linguistic and doctrinal clarity, for when the Army jettisoned the term the service also discarded all the connotations Johnson had associated with it. Gone were the assertions that had appeared in the 1967 edition of FM 100–20 that "military activities to promote stability and progress in the modernization process of developing nations have become the U.S. Army's third principal mission. . . . The Army's readiness for such activities commands a full share of its resources and professional military thought and equal priority with readiness for limited and general war missions." The omission clearly signaled counterinsurgency's declining fortunes in the post-Vietnam Army.[79]

FM 100–20 (1974) also reversed the trend toward smaller volumes, and its expanded size allowed it to provide fairly comprehensive coverage of U.S. IDAD policy. The manual adequately explained all of the philosophical, doctrinal, and organizational points that had been covered by its predecessor manuals. It discussed the perils of modernization and the causes of internal conflict, the nature of guerrilla warfare and its Maoist phases, U.S. government organization and policy for foreign assistance, U.S. national strategy for combating overseas insurgencies, and the U.S. Army's own role in IDAD, from providing advisory personnel to the deployment of combat troops. It addressed each of these subjects clearly and concisely. Reflecting the doctrinal studies of the late 1960s, FM 100–20 (1974) embraced a view of the modernization process that blended economic factors with the need to replace outmoded values and build new institutions supportive of political and social comity. According to the manual, "the fundamental thrust of IDAD doctrine is toward preventing insurgencies from escalating to where they present a significant threat and require an inordinate amount of resources to combat," an old lesson driven home by America's unhappy experience in Vietnam. The manual thus pressed for the early identification of problems that could potentially spark an insurgency, and early counteraction, primarily through intelligence, police, and socioeconomic reform actions.[80]

Should an insurgency develop despite the application of these prophylactics, FM 100–20 (1974) adhered to the same basic programs that had characterized the Army's approach to counterinsurgency over the previous quarter of a century. It called for the establishment of a carefully crafted and tightly integrated IDAD plan that would coordinate the activities of U.S. and foreign civil and military agencies to mobilize the populace, develop indigenous sociopolitical systems, and neutralize the insurgent movement. In keeping with past Army philosophy, the manual refused to clearly prioritize these efforts. It maintained that political issues were central and rejected a purely military solution on the one hand, while simultaneously admitting that "the primary objective under this strategy will be the attainment of internal security" first, since mobilizing the population and achieving meaningful development without first protecting people from guerrilla intimidation and violence was impossible. Similarly, while FM 100–20 (1974) never wavered from the cardinal principle that development was the ultimate antidote to internal instability, it conceded that "economic, political, and social changes are inherently dynamic and may promote unrest," a byproduct that was antithetical, at least in the short run, to government objectives. Thus, while the manual did not differ philosophically from previous doctrinal works, it was less strident than some of the 1968 studies in endorsing revolutionary change.[81]

In juxtaposing conflicting objectives, the manual accurately portrayed both existing doctrine and recent U.S. experience. The absence of definitive guidance undoubtedly proved disappointing to those who sought pat solutions and simple "how-to-do-it" instructions. But by painting counterinsurgency issues in shades of gray rather than black and white, the manual was being true to reality, unpleasant as it may have been.

Education

Just as the Army continuously revised and updated its doctrinal publications during the Vietnam years, so too did it seek new ways to bring those publications to life and inculcate their principles into the minds of its officers and men. In 1966 the Army established a special board under Lt. Gen. Ralph E. Haines, Jr., to evaluate the state of the officer education system. The board concluded that counterinsurgency should remain a mandatory element of officer schooling, recommending both an increase in the amount of time devoted to the subject, as well as a partial revision of the curriculum. In the board's opinion, Army schools devoted too much time reviewing the theoretical aspects of counterinsurgency and too little time to applicatory exercises designed to teach and test branch-level techniques. The panel particularly criticized the way intelligence, civil affairs, and propaganda matters were handled in existing instruction. Finally, it stated that the Army needed to improve the quality of instructors assigned to teach counterinsurgency and recommended that the service create a corps of specialists attuned to the cold war's unique political and psychological challenges—the genesis of MAOP.[82]

Although the Haines Board found that the Army needed to do more, it acknowledged that the service had made significant progress since the inception of the national counterinsurgency drive in 1961. In fact, so confident was the board in the Army's progress that it recommended that the Army abolish two courses instituted during the early days of the counterinsurgency movement to bring the officer corps up to speed on the new art—the five-day senior officer orientation course in counterinsurgency and special warfare, and the eight-week counterinsurgency operations course. In the board's opinion these courses—long staples of the Special Warfare School curriculum—had served their purpose. The Special Warfare School objected to the proposal but to no avail, and in 1967 the Army abolished both courses.[83]

The termination of the counterinsurgency course signaled the achievement of at least part of the Army's objectives, yet as the bulk of the report had indicated, the service still had a way to go to achieve optimum understanding of the counterinsurgency phenomenon. For the most part, the Army responded positively to the board's findings. In 1966 Continental Army Command made psychological operations a required subject for all officer candidate, basic, and career courses, while the Command and General Staff College increased its coverage of psychological matters as well. The new course material emphasized the importance of psychological issues in stability operations and enjoined officers to evaluate every action with an eye toward its possible psychological and political effects. The following year, General Johnson issued a special circular that stressed the importance of sociopolitical matters in low intensity conflicts. Under the new guidance, Johnson directed that all military personnel be familiar with civil affairs principles "to insure a proper understanding of the attitudes and cultures of civilian populations, their forms of government, economies and institutions under all conditions of warfare, with emphasis on stability operations." Such training was also to include familiarity with the "rules and conventions governing war, with emphasis on the enforcement of law, preservation of order, and the prevention of wanton destruction of civilian property." Johnson directed that junior officers and noncommissioned officers receive additional training in the organization, function, and relationship of civil affairs elements with other Army activities, while field grade officers were to study comparative systems of government and civil affairs planning. In addition, civil affairs subjects were to be included as much as possible in Army training programs, exercises, and tests. All of these initiatives reinforced concurrent efforts to elevate social, political, and psychological matters in Army doctrine.[84]

*Members of the Reserve Officers' Training Corps undergo
counterinsurgency training in 1971.*

The Army school system followed General Johnson's and the
Haines Board's lead. Most schools increased the amount of time
devoted to counterinsurgency in general, and the Vietnam War in particular. The schools went to great lengths to absorb tactical, technical,
and doctrinal lessons from Vietnam and to relate them to their students.
As both theory and practice evolved during the late 1960s, so too did
classroom instruction. Still, continuity rather than change was the central characteristic of this period, since the basic thrust of U.S. doctrine
changed relatively little during the war.

As during the prewar years, the Army insisted that every soldier
receive some exposure to counterinsurgency. For officers, this exposure began either in ROTC or as cadets at the U.S. Military Academy.
Although the Military Academy had reduced the number of required
classroom hours in counterinsurgency by 1966, the school's counterinsurgency curriculum remained relatively stable thereafter. During
the war all cadets received 30 lessons and 46 hours of field training
in counterinsurgency, plus 73 lessons of related instruction. Much
of this course work appeared in Military Science 401, a required,
senior-level class in which cadets read Mao and examined the lessons of the Indochinese, Malayan, Philippine, and Vietnam wars.
The academy likewise offered another 104 direct and 160 related lessons in counterinsurgency electives, most notably in such courses as
"National Security Problems," "Problems of Developing Nations," and
"Revolutionary Warfare." Annual enrollment in the last named course,

which reviewed the evolution of guerrilla warfare from ancient times to the present, steadily increased from 55 in 1966 to 257 in 1970. The academy supplemented this classroom time by hosting over forty guest speakers on counterinsurgency subjects between 1964 and 1974, including Averell Harriman, Edward Lansdale, Richard Clutterback, and John Paul Vann.[85]

For the most part the West Point curriculum focused on the basic principles of counterinsurgency and nation building rather than the applicatory details, though over time Military Science 401 increasingly described U.S. and Viet Cong tactics. While the academy acknowledged irregular warfare's special challenges, it strongly rejected the notion that guerrilla warfare was exempt from the basic principles that governed all forms of combat. As one academy lecture explained, "there are some officers who are convinced that the counter-guerrilla war is so different from the conventional war that they might as well forget all the principles and fundamentals that they have learned, and burn their books. This couldn't be further from the truth. The fundamentals of combat operations and the related fundamentals of the offense and defense are as valid today as they were twenty-five years ago."[86]

Although West Point instructors did not hesitate to criticize aspects of U.S. operations in Vietnam, the academy maintained that Army doctrine was sound and adequate. At no time did the academy ever teach that large search-and-destroy operations were the only, or even the most important, type of operational method. Rather, the school presented the full range of tactical and operational options, noting the utility of different methods for different conditions. On the other hand, West Point drummed home the moderating principles that were a hallmark of U.S. counterinsurgency philosophy. Noting that "'winning the hearts and minds,' may be a shopworn phrase, but it accurately describes the political and sociological aspects of stability operations," the school impressed upon cadets that counterinsurgency entailed "not only the destruction of the insurgent's infrastructure and military forces but more importantly the elimination of the grievances of the populace. This will ultimately bring about the conditions which will allow the nation and its people to progress; to develop their nation along peaceful lines; and to raise the standard of living without the violence and upheaval attending insurgency." Similarly, while the academy admitted that counterinsurgents needed to regulate the behavior of the population, it embraced the view that such "measures must be limited to those which are absolutely essential and once established must be enforced justly, firmly and with equal vigor on all segments of the population. They must conform to legal codes and should be removed as soon as they have served their intended purpose, for to do otherwise would add to the grievances which could be capitalized upon by the insurgents." Thus political and social considerations lay at the heart of the academy's teachings, existing in uneasy symbiosis with military necessity as the primary drivers of counterguerrilla policy.[87]

Other Army schools mimicked the principles inculcated at West Point, though the amount and content of instruction varied to match each institution's particular mission. All branch-level schools taught a common course on insurgency that related the basic tenets of U.S. counterinsurgency

West Point cadets search a hut as part of counterguerrilla training.

philosophy, but beyond this, coverage continued to vary widely. The Judge Advocate General's School devoted just 1 percent of its classroom time to counterinsurgency, while the School of the Americas—a key element of the nation's Latin America policy—provided extensive coverage of insurgency issues. As one might expect, about 80 percent of the civil affairs officer course at the Civil Affairs School was IDAD related, to include the political and social attributes of developing nations, comparative cultural and religious studies, and the workings of the country team. Meanwhile, the Field Artillery School increased the length of its officer basic course from nine to twelve weeks to expand coverage of artillery techniques as they were being practiced in Vietnam. The school also built two Vietnam-style firebases for instructional purposes and initiated a special field artillery officer orientation course of four to five weeks devoted exclusively to Vietnam tactics and techniques.[88]

As had been the case prior to 1965, the Infantry School led the Army's branch and functional schools in integrating counterinsurgency throughout its curriculum. By 1966 the school was devoting no less than 35 percent of its basic and career courses to counterinsurgency subjects. In that year the school further overhauled its curriculum, increasing coverage of Vietnam-style counterguerrilla, airmobile, and patrol operations. By 1968 nearly half of the infantry officer basic course, which all newly minted infantry officers attended, was devoted to counterinsurgency subjects. Only the

"Guerrillas" enter a mock Viet Cong village used for counterguerrilla training at Fort Bragg, North Carolina.

infantry officer advanced course reduced its counterinsurgency material on the premise that the majority of captains who took the course were Vietnam veterans and thus already familiar with how the war was being fought.[89]

Like other branch schools, Fort Benning naturally focused its instruction on the tactics and techniques of its particular branch of service. Students learned how to conduct checkerboard patrols and how to establish night defensive perimeters. They learned how to search a village and how to conduct airmobile operations in a guerrilla environment. In keeping with the Haines Board's recommendations, theoretical instruction was kept to a minimum. Still, students in the core officer courses spent about a dozen hours reviewing such theoretical subjects as the nature of third world insurgency, the tenets of Maoist revolutionary thought, U.S. national IDAD policy, and the basic principles of Army counterinsurgency doctrine. Students in the advanced course also received approximately three hours of counterinsurgency intelligence training, one hour on the legal aspects of guerrilla warfare, and five hours instruction in foreign counterinsurgency methods, the latter given by the school's British and French liaison officers. Three hours of instruction and twenty hours of practical exercises in civic action and psyops rounded out the nontactical aspects of the course, with additional hours of instruction integrated into applicable portions of the overall curriculum. Throughout, the school emphasized the important role that civic action and psyops played in every action, from squad to brigade. Instructors conceded, however, that the political aspects of counterinsurgency were "probably one of the hardest things to get across to the student. Most of the students who have come here . . . basically are interested in how to go out and kill the guerrilla. This is the main interest of most of them. When we approach them with psychological operations and civic actions per se, we don't get quite the same reactions that we do when we are talking about strictly counterguerrilla operations per se, or combat operations."[90]

As at the Infantry School, counterinsurgency instruction at the Command and General Staff College increased significantly as a result of the Vietnam War, growing from about 92 hours in 1965 to 200 hours in 1968. By the time of the Tet offensive the college's library contained approximately 700 books on counterinsurgency subjects. The quality of instruction improved also, thanks both to Army efforts as well as a steady influx of Vietnam veterans. After 1965 the college routinely had about forty counterinsurgency-qualified instructors, a far cry from 1963 when the school had only six such individuals on its faculty.[91] The school examined past case studies, recent operations, current doctrine, and the latest nation-building theories, with plenty of applicatory exercises in which students put their knowledge to work.[92]

Counterinsurgency studies at the Army's highest educational institution, the Army War College, naturally focused less on technique and more on concept and policy. Between 1965 and 1969 the War College gradually expanded instruction in counterinsurgency and nation building from five to seven weeks, with additional coverage sprinkled through the rest of the curriculum. Like other Army institutions, the college kept abreast of developments, adding Carlos Marighella's *Minimanual of the Urban Guerrilla* to the more traditional readings of Mao and Giap. The school's two deans of counterinsurgency studies— Col. Sam C. Holliday and Col. John J. McCuen—championed a holistic approach to counterinsurgency in which political, administrative, police, intelligence, and population- and resources-security measures predominated over pure combat operations. On the other hand, they recognized that major strikes at guerrilla bases and units were necessary if consolidation operations were to succeed. Consequently, they argued that conducting combat operations was a more suitable mission for U.S. military forces than engaging in police-type activities among the indigenous population, a principle that was already ingrained in U.S. doctrine.[93]

461

Training

While the Army imparted doctrinal precepts through its school system, it drove home those lessons through training. Between 1960 and 1965 the Army had progressively increased the amount of attention devoted to counterinsurgency subjects in its training program, though the degree of emphasis had varied from unit to unit. Although regulations required that units train for assigned contingency missions, most training was to be general in scope and not geared toward any particular country. This meant that units often did not undergo intensive, theater-specific training until after they had been notified of an impending movement overseas. Since units needed to be partially reorganized for counterguerrilla duty and since many units were either understrength or contained soldiers who were ineligible for immediate foreign service due to personnel policies, the first units to be deployed to Vietnam in 1965 and 1966 faced many obstacles. Conditions were frequently chaotic, as commanders scrambled to perform the myriad of training, logistical, and administrative tasks that needed to be accomplished during the few short months between notification of deployment and embarkation. Some units fared better than others, but none emerged from the process unscathed. The experience of the 2d Battalion, 8th Infantry, 4th Infantry Division, exemplifies the predeployment experiences of many units.

In January 1966 the 2d Battalion, 8th Infantry, was at half-strength and had undergone routine small-unit counterguerrilla training. During the spring the unit conducted conventional individual training as it was gradually brought up to full strength. In May the Army notified the battalion that it was heading for Vietnam, triggering two months of intensive Vietnam-oriented training. Included in this regimen was the standard sixteen hours of Vietnam familiarization training prescribed by Continental Army Command for all deploying units and individuals. The course covered such subjects as perimeter defense, ambush drill, sanitation, survival, and Vietnamese culture. The battalion also underwent basic unit training, modified for Vietnam as the commander saw fit, since the Army had not prescribed a specific unit training program, either for Vietnam in particular or counterguerrilla warfare more generally. Finally, the battalion capped off its training by participating in a series of brigade-level exercises that practiced search-and-clear, search-and-destroy, clear-and-hold, and airmobile operations, all based on lessons learned material sent from Vietnam. In July the battalion embarked for Southeast Asia, conducting what training it could aboard ship. When it arrived in August, the battalion was

Troops receiving counterambush instruction prior to deploying to Vietnam

initially "buddied" with veteran troops of the 25th Infantry Division, a common practice that facilitated the transfer of field lore to incoming formations. The unit then served in the field until it withdrew from Vietnam in 1970.[94]

Although the 2d Battalion, 8th Infantry, served for four years in Southeast Asia, its soldiers did not. Rotation policies and casualties brought a steady stream of new men into the unit. In 1965 the Army instituted a special training program for individual infantry replacements destined for Vietnam. New recruits and draftees initially underwent eight weeks of customary basic combat training, during which time they received a one-hour orientation lecture on counterinsurgency and some basic counterguerrilla instruction integrated into conventional training. Upon graduation from basic training, the Army sent its young soldiers to advanced individual training (AIT) where they would learn the particular skills associated with their intended function in the Army. While infantrymen destined for service in the United States or Europe received the conventional eight-week AIT, infantrymen bound for Vietnam received a special Vietnam-oriented AIT program of nine weeks' duration. The course stressed physical conditioning, field craft, weaponry, night operations, and small-unit tactics. In addition to passing through rapid reaction courses and learning search techniques in mock Vietnamese villages, the trainees received the standard two-hour counterinsurgency lecture given to all AIT students, plus the sixteen-hour Vietnam orientation course before the Army shipped them overseas. Upon arrival in Vietnam,

Infantrymen learning how to locate and search Viet Cong tunnels during training at Fort Polk, Louisiana, in 1966

the individual replacement received five to six additional hours of orientation that included the nine rules of conduct among other subjects. The Army then sent the replacements on to their new units where they received further training, frequently of one week's duration. The typical Army draftee thus received about four and a half months of training before seeing combat, a significant sum considering that draftees served for only twenty-four months, no more than twelve of which were to be spent inside Vietnam itself.[95]

Initially, the Army operated only two Vietnam-oriented AIT centers, but as the war progressed and the manpower drain continued, it converted all of its training centers to the Vietnam-based program. Meanwhile, Continental Army Command continued to improve the quality of its training based on reports from the field. Nevertheless, CONARC did not significantly alter the training regimen established during the early 1960s. It continued to require that all units conduct familiarization training in counterinsurgency and practical exercises in counterguerrilla warfare annually, though it adhered to its prewar philosophy of not specifying the exact length and content of training regimens. It did, however, prescribe a list of training subjects for units deploying to Vietnam. Included on this list were the code of conduct and the Geneva Conventions, enemy tactics, intelligence, civil affairs, psychological and pacification operations, airmobility, search-and-destroy operations, clear-and-secure operations, ambush, counterambush, and quick reaction drills, raiding and patrolling, reconnaissance, and fire support coordination. Although Continental Army Command reserved its most intensive counterguerrilla training requirements for units actually assigned counterguerrilla missions, it continued to encourage all commanders to integrate counterguerrilla principles into "all phases of training at every practical opportunity." While the focus of this training was tactical, counterinsurgency principles, including civic action, were covered as well. CONARC particularly enjoined commanders that "individuals must be trained to avoid indiscriminate firing into populated areas and oriented on the problems of discriminating between insurgent/noninsurgent indigenous personnel."[96]

Recognizing a long-standing deficiency, CONARC regulations advised that up to one-half of all field training should be conducted at night. In 1967 the command directed that all combat units develop airmobility and long-range patrol capabilities, with the command operating three reconnaissance and commando schools. In 1968 CONARC further mandated that every infantry battalion and armored cavalry squadron in the United States maintain a cadre of four officers and twelve noncommissioned officers qualified in jungle warfare in order to disseminate knowledge of such operations throughout the Army. Meanwhile, the Army sought to improve the realism of exercise play by issuing an entirely new manual governing the use of "enemy" guerrillas in training. FM 30–104, *Aggressor Insurgent War* (1967), was the first aggressor manual devoted entirely to guerrilla warfare. Unlike earlier manuals whose coverage of irregular warfare had been based largely on Soviet partisan techniques during a conventional conflict, FM 30–104 (1967) depicted the guerrilla enemy entirely within the context of Maoist rural revolutions. The manual stressed the importance of political factors and described guerrilla methods that closely mirrored those used by the Viet Cong.[97]

For the most part, commanders in Vietnam reported satisfaction with the quality of men CONARC sent into the field, at least until morale and cohesion began to erode in the late 1960s. Still, some problems proved particularly resistant to improvement. Among these were deficiencies in land navigation, fire control, camp, sound, and light discipline, nocturnal operations, and small-unit leadership. That these deficiencies persisted was in no small measure due to the tremendous strains that both the draft and rotation policies placed on the Army's overburdened personnel and training systems. By 1968 the Army was rotating about 30,000 men per month into Vietnam. While rotation policies undermined general unit cohesiveness and efficiency, they were particularly pernicious with regard to small-unit leadership.

A "guerrilla" sniper takes aim at a patrol during counterguerrilla training at Fort McClellan, Alabama.

Between July and October 1966, for example, rotation policies stripped the 1st Infantry Division of 60 percent of its company commanders. Other units experienced similar "brain drains," and soon the Army had exhausted its pool of experienced small-unit leaders. Replacement officers and NCOs were frequently hastily trained and devoid of experience, an especially serious handicap in what was essentially a small-unit war. Try as it might, the Army was never able to find a satisfactory solution to this dilemma.[98]

The State of Doctrine at the End of the Vietnam War

During the Vietnam War the Army expended a great deal of effort to redress perceived weaknesses in the content, organization, and presentation of its counterinsurgency doctrine. New manuals were written, old ones refined, and lessons learned or relearned amplified as appropriate. The process was by no means flawless. As in the early 1960s continued friction between Combat Developments Command and Continental Army Command complicated the doctrinal development and dissemination process, as did internal turf battles within CDC itself. While these problems bedeviled the presentation of doctrine, other more substantive issues had also remained unresolved. Differences of opinion continued to be expressed in manuals over civic action, as well as the relative priority of military versus political matters. Moreover, certain stability operation missions, like truce enforcement and peacekeeping, never managed to emerge from the shadow of counterinsurgency and remained relatively undeveloped throughout the period.[99] Nevertheless, these shortfalls should not obscure the fact that changes had occurred. Over time the presentation of counterinsurgency doctrine had become more uniform and complete. Methods were revised based on Vietnam experience and new material incorporated to meet changing conditions. After 1965 the Army made a concerted effort to heighten the visibility accorded to the "softer" side of counterguerrilla warfare—civil affairs, psychological operations, and intelligence. Army doctrinal writings also exhibited a more sophisticated understanding of nation building, one that went beyond material progress and took greater cognizance of the less tangible, social side of modernization. On the whole, therefore, Army doctrine emerged from the war years with a fairly balanced and realistic portrayal of IDAD's many facets and challenges.

Yet, while Army doctrine had evolved between 1965 and 1975, few of the changes had been revolutionary. In fact, what is perhaps the most remarkable thing about the evolution of Army doctrine during the war years was how little it truly did change, notwithstanding the phenomenal outpouring of information and experience from Vietnam. One reason for this was that much of the information coming out of Vietnam was either repetitive in nature or contradictory, as war experiences varied by unit and geographical area. Moreover, most of the lessons learned literature dealt with arcane aspects of technique that did not rise to the level of doctrine. In the Army's opinion, the role of doctrine was to lay down overarching principles. Vietnam-specific information, such as the peculiarities of Viet Cong booby traps, might be discussed in technical publications, but for the most part the Army did not deem such matters worthy of inclusion in doctrinal manuals. Thus, despite calls from soldiers for more how-to-do-it information, Combat Developments Command steadfastly refused to produce a doctrinal field manual specifically devoted to Vietnam, although it did produce a few manuals on aspects of Vietnam service, like riverine operations.[100]

Perhaps the most important reason for continuity in Army doctrine, however, stemmed from the fact that the Army believed that many of the lessons identified in Vietnam reports were not new at all, but rather reaffirmations of principles already embodied in existing manuals and texts. Indeed, throughout the conflict Army officials repeatedly stated that wartime events demonstrated that Army doctrine was fundamentally sound. This attitude reflected both the military's conceptualization of the role of doctrine in general and its acceptance of the core concepts contained in its existing doctrine. Thus, just as unforeseen developments and battlefield failures had not led the Army to change significantly the central tenets of its conventional war doctrine during the Korean and Second World Wars, so too did the Army throughout the Vietnam conflict maintain the essential soundness of its counter-insurgency doctrine. And when setbacks occurred in Vietnam, Army officials tended to ascribe them as they had in wars past to tactical errors; intelligence failings; operational, strategic, and policy misjudgments; misapplications of technique; bureaucratic wrangling; South Vietnamese intransigence; North Vietnamese acumen; and situational factors beyond the Army's control, rather than to conceptual inadequacies. Consequently, despite many adjustments and improvements along the way, Army counterinsurgency doctrine would emerge from the Vietnam War revised and refined, yet essentially unchanged.[101]

Notes

[1] Dennis Vetock, *Lessons Learned: A History of U.S. Army Lesson Learning* (Carlisle Barracks, Pa.: U.S. Army Military History Institute, 1988), pp. 89, 91, 100, 104–15; Alan Armstrong, Utilization of Current Cold War and Limited War Information Within USAIS (Student paper, Infantry School, 1967); Ltr, Lt Gen Albert O. Connor, DCSPER, to Lt Gen Harry W. O. Kinnard, CDC, 24 Oct 67, 732678, RG 338, NARA; Harry Kinnard, "Vietnam Has Lessons for Tomorrow's Army," *Army* 18 (November 1968): 77–80; CONARC Pam 516–3, Counterinsurgency Operations, Counterinsurgency Instructional Training Materials, 10 Mar 66, Historians files, CMH.

[2] CDC Special Warfare Agency, Definitions To Support Counterinsurgency Doctrine, May 65; Routing Slip, Lt Col E. F. Corcoran, Policy Planning Branch, IPD, DCSOPS, to Col Stephanie, CDC, 15 Nov 65, with atchs. Both in 73A2677, RG 338, NARA.

[3] First quote from Gen Johnson, "The Army—Its Philosophy, Its View of Military Strategy, Its Posture," AWC lecture, 11 Jun 65, p. 4, MHI. Second and third quotes from AR 320–5, *Dictionary of United States Army Terms*, 2 Feb 66, p. 215.

[4] Memo, ACSFOR for CDC, 6 Jan 66, sub: Study—Definitions To Support Counterinsurgency Doctrine; Study, Maj David R. Hughes, DCSOPS, 23 Aug 65, sub: New Approach to National "Counterinsurgency" Terminology. Both in 73A2677, RG 338, NARA. Memo, SGS for CSA, 27 Oct 65, sub: Terminology for Counterinsurgency, 68A3306, RG 319, NARA; David Hughes, The Unsettled Language of Counterinsurgency: Symptom of a Strategic Debate (Student paper, AWC, 1967).

[5] Quote from Memo, Col Charles J. Canella for Commandant, CGSC, 7 Oct 65, sub: Draper Report, 11th Annual Human Resources and Development Conference, p. 2, Historians files, CMH. Memo, SGS for CSA, 28 Dec 65, sub: Terminology for Counterinsurgency, CSA, 68A3306, RG 319, NARA.

[6] AR 320–5, *Dictionary of Army Terms*, 31 Oct 67, pp. 224, 396; MFR, Col John Sullivan, Comdr, Internal Defense and Development Field Office, 4 Nov 66, sub: Internal Defense and Development Conference; Memo, CDC for Distribution, 21 Jun 67, sub: Terminology Related to Stability Operations. Both in 73A2677, RG 338, NARA. Billy Wright, Alias Counterinsurgency (Student paper, AWC, 1968), pp. 1–7, 13.

[7] Quote from Ltr, Lt Gen Harry Kinnard, CDC, to Lt Gen Arthur Collins, ACSFOR, 24 Aug 67, 73A2678, RG 338, NARA. Mark Boatner, "Our Widening Military Doctrine Gap," *Army* 20 (August 1970): 20.

[8] As an insurance measure, Combat Developments Command created a temporary entity, the Internal Defense and Development Field Office, to help shepherd counterinsurgency through the transition. Consisting of four people who reported directly to CDC's chief of staff, the office promoted the integration of counterinsurgency into all studies and manuals. CDC closed the office in late 1967. Memos, CDC, 11 Apr 66, sub: Reorganization of USACDC, 71A5349, RG 338, NARA, and CDC for Distribution, 28 Mar 67, sub: Combat Development Responsibilities for Internal Defense and Internal Development, Historians files, CMH.

[9] CDC General Orders 475, 28 Nov 67; Memo, Col Glenn Gardner, CDC Combat Support Group, for CG, CDC, 10 May 67, sub: Study on Most Appropriate Command Organization for the Discharge of Civil Affairs Responsibilities of USACDC, with atchs, Historians files, CMH.

[10] MFR, CDC SWA, 5 Jul 67, sub: SWA Mission and CDC Responsibilities for IDD, Historians files, CMH.

[11] First quote from Study, CDC Special Warfare Agency, Counterguerrilla Warfare Doctrine, Jan 66, p. 6, 73A2677, RG 338, NARA. Second quote from Special Warfare Agency, Doctrinal Literature for Counterinsurgency, 1965, p. 35, 73A2677, CDC, RG 338, NARA.

[12] Quote from Study, CDC Special Warfare Agency, Counterguerrilla Warfare Doctrine, Jan 66, p. A-28, and see also pp. 17, 1-A-29, 2-A-77, 4-A-115, 4-A-122, 4-A-123. FM 31–23, *Stability Operations: U.S. Army Doctrine*, 1967, pp. 49–50.

[13] Study, CDC Special Warfare Agency, Counterguerrilla Warfare Doctrine, Jan 66, pp. 8, 18–22, 1-A-47, 4-A-112, 5-E-165, 5-F-169.

[14] First quote from FM 33–5, *Psychological Operations—Techniques and Procedures*, 1966, p. 22, and see also pp. 23–25, 32. Second quote from ibid., p. 27. Third quote from ibid., p. 29.

[15] Quote from FM 41–5, *Joint Manual for Civil Affairs*, 1966, p. 27, and see also pp. 10, 22, 28, 51.

[16] FM 100–20, *Field Service Regulations: Internal Defense and Development*, 1967, pp. 1-1, 3-3, 5-1 to 5-7, 6-4, 6-7 to 6-13, 7-1.

[17] First quote from FM 31–23, *Stability Operations: U.S. Army Doctrine*, 1967, p. 5. Second quote from ibid., p. 8. Third quote from ibid., p. 10.

[18] First quote from ibid., p. 24, and see also pp. 25, 30–31, 49–50, 56, 91. Second and third quotes from ibid., p. 31.

[19] Quote from ibid., p. 66, and see also pp. 23–24, 64–65, 67, 69, 71.

[20] Ibid., pp. 13–28, 56, 74, 88, 90.

[21] Ibid., pp. 26–31, 34.

[22] Ibid., pp. 23–24, 27, 53–60, 89–90.

[23] Annual Hist Sum, CDC, FY 66, p. 188, copy in CMH.

[24] Quote from FM 31–16, *Counterguerrilla Operations*, 1967, p. 108, and see also pp. 7–8, 18, 36–39, 51, 69–70, 82, 85–86, 89–90.

[25] Quote from ibid., p. 7.

[26] Quote from ibid., p. 50. Memo, Special Warfare Agency for Infantry Agency, 30 Jun 65, sub: Pre-Revision Input to FM 31–16, Counterguerrilla Operations, pp. 2–3, 73A2677, RG 338, NARA.

[27] First quote from FM 31–16, *Counterguerrilla Operations*, 1967, p. 22. Second quote from ibid., p. 35, and see also pp. 90, 96, 104–08, 113–17. Third, fourth, and fifth quotes from ibid., pp. 66, 144, 142, respectively.

[28] The Army replaced the term "free fire zone" with such euphemisms as "specified strike zone" and "restricted area" for similar reasons. Hay, *Tactical and Materiel Innovations*, p. 177; Westmoreland, *A Soldier Reports*, pp. 83–84; Fact Sheets, c. 1971, sub: Background Information on the Term: Search and Destroy, and 11 May 71, sub: Specified Strike Zone. Both in Geo V Vietnam 350 Travel Pack, CMH.

[29] First quote from FM 31–16, *Counterguerrilla Operations*, 1967, p. 50. Second quote from ibid., p. 12, and see also pp. 3, 7, 11, 35–38, 49, 54–58, 63–64, 88.

[30] Quote from FM 21–75, *Combat Training of Individual Soldier and Patrolling*, 1967, p. 78, and see also pp. 77, 134–57, 164–65.

[31] Study, CDC, Intelligence Doctrine and Techniques for Internal Defense and Development (Task 20), 1 Oct 66, Pentagon Library, Va.; CDC, Task 2023 Tentative Conclusions, Part II, n.d., pp. 11–12, 73A2677, RG 338, NARA; Memo, Maj Gen

Joseph A. McChristian, ACSI, for CG, CDC, 6 Nov 68, sub: Intelligence Doctrine and Techniques for Internal Defense and Development (Task 20), with atchs, 73A2677, RG 338, NARA.

[32] Quote from Referral Slip, Lt Col Claud Hamilton, Asst Secy of the General Staff, 28 Sep 66, sub: Civil Affairs Doctrine, Historians files, CMH. Memos, Col Darnell, CDC Special Warfare and Civil Affairs Group, for Maj Gen Harry L. Hillyard, 13 Apr 64, sub: Aftermath of Gen H K Johnson's Viet Nam Visit, CDC, and CSA CSM 67–14 for DCSOPS et al., 11 Jan 67, sub: Improvement of Civil Affairs Capability, both in 73A2677, RG 338, NARA; HQDA Cir 525–1, 20 Apr 67, sub: Military Operations, Improvement of Civil Affairs Capability, Historians files, CMH.

[33] Quote from FM 41–10, *Civil Affairs Operations*, 1967, p. 1, and see also pp. 13, 39.

[34] Quotes from ibid., pp. 43–44.

[35] Quote from ibid., p. 8, and see also pp. 33, 62.

[36] First quote from ibid., p. 46. Second quote from ibid., p. 62. Third and fourth quotes from ibid., p. 45.

[37] Quote from FM 7–20, *The Infantry Battalions*, 1969, p. 7-45. FM 31–75 (Test), *Riverine Operations*, 1968, p. 116.

[38] For examples of critics of American attempts to defeat insurgencies by building democracies and reforming societies, as well as statements by those who continued to believe in the worthiness of "positive programs" but who conceded that such endeavors suffered from many problems, see James Lee, Which Strategy for Advance Insurgency, Pacification or Combat? (Student paper, AWC, 1967), pp. 1–12; George Tanham and Dennis Duncanson, "Some Dilemmas of Counterinsurgency," *Foreign Affairs* 48 (October 1969): 113–22; Irving Heymont, "The U.S. Army and Foreign National Development," *Military Review* 51 (November 1971): 17, 20–23; Barber and Ronning, *Internal Security*, pp. 20, 40–41, 230, 233–34; Garold Tippin, "The Army as Nationbuilder," *Military Review* 50 (October 1970): 11–19; Joseph Cunningham, "The Validity of the Nation Building Concept," *U.S. Army War College Commentary* (December 1967): D-3 to D-7.

[39] Quote from Nathan Leites and Charles Wolf, Rebellion and Authority: An Analytic Essay on Insurgent Conflicts, R–462–ARPA (Santa Monica, Calif.: RAND, 1970), p. 150, and see also pp. 37, 45, 71–75, 149–51, 156. Charles Wolf, Insurgency and Counterinsurgency: New Myths and Old Realities, P–3132–1 (Santa Monica, Calif.: RAND, 1965), pp. 1–14; Boyd Bashore, "The Parallel Hierarchies, Part I," *Infantry Journal* 58 (May–June 1968): 5–8; Boyd Bashore, "The Parallel Hierarchies, Part II," *Infantry Journal* 58 (July–August 1968): 11–15.

[40] First two quotes from Bashore, "Parallel Hierarchies, Part II," p. 11. Third quote from Wolf, Insurgency and Counterinsurgency, p. 10.

[41] Bashore, "Parallel Hierarchies, Part II," p. 11; Leites and Wolf, Rebellion and Authority, p. 33.

[42] Quote from Summary Analyses of Weaknesses in Army Psychological Operations, atch to Study, International and Civil Affairs Directorate, DCSOPS, Progress Psyop—1968, Program to Revitalize, Expand the Scope of, and Strengthen Army Psychological Operations, 1968, p. 4, Historians files, CMH.

[43] Rpt, DCSOPS, 1 Aug 67, sub: Psychological Operations—Role in Establishing a Sense of Nationhood, Psyop-Reason, pp. 29–31, 70A2673, RG 319, NARA (hereafter cited as Psyop-Reason); Rpt of the Ad Hoc Committee on Army Psychological

471

Operations, 21 Apr 67, pp. 5, 8–9, 17–21, 45, atch to Memo, Lt Gen Harry J. Lemley, DCSOPS, for CSA, 11 May 67, sub: Report of the Ad Hoc Committee on Army Psychological Operations, 70A2675, RG 319, NARA.

[44] Psyop-Reason, pp. iii, 15, 21–31, 37, 58; Memo, DCSOPS for CSA, 19 Oct 67, sub: Psyop and Nationhood, with atchs, 70A2673, RG 319, NARA.

[45] Quote from Psyop-Reason, preface. Memo, David McGiffert, Under Secy of the Army, for Lt Gen Harry J. Lemley, DCSOPS, 8 Mar 68, sub: Psychological Operations Role and Establishing a Sense of Nationhood, Historians files, CMH.

[46] First quote from Study, ACSFOR, Counterguerrilla Operations, 19 Mar 68, p. II-10, 73A2677, RG 338, NARA, and see also pp. I-4, III-13 to III-16. Second, third, and fourth quotes from ibid., p. III-12.

[47] Quote from ibid., p. II-9.

[48] Quote from ibid., p. III-18, and see also pp. II-10, II-12, III-17.

[49] Quote from ibid., p. II-4, and see also pp. II-18, III-8.

[50] Quote from ibid., p. II-6, and see also pp. I-23, II-5, II-7, II-8, III-3, III-4, IV-2, IV-3.

[51] Quote from Memo, Lt Gen Arthur Collins, Jr., ACSFOR, for CSA, 30 Apr 68, sub: Counterguerrilla Operations, p. 2. Rationale, atch to Summary Sheet, ACSFOR to CSA, c. May 68, sub: Refining the Army's Role in Stability Operations; Concept Paper, ACSFOR, c. Apr 68, sub: Counterguerrilla Operations, p. 2. All in 71A3100, RG 319, NARA.

[52] Quotes from Summary Sheet, Maj Gen William C. Gribble, Dep ACSFOR, to CSA, 24 Jan 68, sub: Special Study on Counter-Guerrilla Operations. Ltr, Col Daniel Williams, Actg Dir of Doctrine and Systems, ACSFOR, to Distribution, 1 Aug 68, sub: Study, "Counterguerrilla Operations"; Memo, CSA CSM 68–185 for Heads of Army Staff Agencies, 20 May 68, sub: Refining the Army's Role in Stability Operations. All in 71A3100, RG 319, NARA. William Buchanan and Robert Hyatt, "Capitalizing on Guerrilla Vulnerabilities," *Military Review* 48 (August 1968): 3–40; William Buchanan and Robert Hyatt, "Building a Counterinsurgent Political Infrastructure," *Military Review* 48 (September 1968): 25–41.

[53] Quote from Summary Sheet, ACSFOR to CSA, c. May 68, sub: Refining the Army's Role in Stability Operations, 71A3100, RG 319, NARA.

[54] General Johnson also enlarged an intelligence career track, the foreign area specialist (FAS) program, to produce an expanded cadre of third world country and regional specialists. In 1973 the Army merged the two programs into a single foreign area officer (FAO) career track. ARs 614–134, *Military Assistance Officer Program (MAOP)*, 7 Mar 69, and 614–142, *Foreign Area Officer (FAO) Program*, chg 1, 6 Apr 73.

[55] Memo, Westmoreland for McGiffert, 19 Aug 68, sub: Psyop-Reason Study, Historians files, CMH.

[56] Quoted words from Rpt, DCSOPS, Nation Building Contributions of the Army (NABUCA), 1968, p. i, 388.5, Civil Affairs, CMH.

[57] First quote from ibid., p. IV-16. Second quote from ibid., p. IV-17, and see also pp. ii–iii.

[58] First quote from ibid., p. iv. Second quote from ibid., p. II-18, and see also pp. iii, v.

[59] Quotes from ibid., p. IV-18, and see also pp. iii, IV-17. Memo, Adjutant General for Distribution, 16 Jan 69, sub: U.S. Army's Contribution to Nation Building, 388.5, Civil Affairs, CMH.

[60] Quote from Conflict Environment and Implications for the Army, p. 19, atch to Rpt, DCSOPS, 1 Jun 68, sub: Civil Affairs Improvement Program, 72A3468, RG 319, NARA.

[61] Quote from Rpt of the Ad Hoc Committee on Army Psychological Operations, 21 Apr 67, p. 37, and see also pp. 35–36, 38.

[62] The Army eventually published final versions of FM 31–75, *Riverine Warfare*, and FM 31–55, *Border Security/Anti-Infiltration Operations*, in 1971 and 1972, respectively.

[63] First quote from FM 100–5, *Operations of Army Forces in the Field*, 1968, p. 13-1. Second quote from ibid., p. 13-2. Third quote from ibid., p. 13-4, and see also, pp. 1-2, 1-6, 13-7 to 13-9.

[64] Quote from FM 31–21, *Special Forces Operations—U.S. Army Doctrine*, 1969, p. 10-4.

[65] Quoted words from FM 31–16, *Counterguerrilla Operations*, chg 1, 1969, p. 12, and see also pp. 4, 8–11, 13–14. FM 7–20, *The Infantry Battalion*, 1969, pp. 7–44.

[66] Quote from FM 31–16, *Counterguerrilla Operations*, chg 2, 1970, p. 3.

[67] Quoted word from FM 30–31, *Stability Operations—Intelligence*, 1970, p. 2-1.

[68] Inaugural Address, 20 Jan 61, in *Public Papers of the Presidents of the United States: John F. Kennedy, 1961* (Washington, D.C.: Government Printing Office, 1962), p. 1.

[69] Quote from Blaufarb, *Counterinsurgency Era*, p. 293. National Security Decision Memorandum 20 of 10 July 1969 established the Nixon Doctrine. Nixon revealed the basic thrust of the policy in a news conference on Guam on 25 July 1969. W. Bruce Weinrod, "Counterinsurgency: Its Role in Defense Policy," *Strategic Review* 2 (Fall 1974): 37–38.

[70] Compare FM 100–20, *Field Service Regulations, Internal Defense and Development*, 1964, p. 9, with FM 100–20, *Field Service Regulations: Internal Defense and Development*, 1967, p. 4-1, and FM 100–20, *Field Service Regulations: Internal Defense and Development*, 1972, p. 4-1.

[71] Memo, CDC for Institute for Combined Arms and Support et al., 23 Nov 70, sub: ODCSOPS Study "The United States Army's Role in Support of Nation Building," Historians files, CMH.

[72] Quotes from Rpt, DCSOPS, The United States Army's Role in Support of Nation Building, c. 1970, p. 7, Historians files, CMH.

[73] Quote from ibid., p. iv, and see also, pp. v, vii. Clarke, *Final Years*, pp. 371–72; Ricky Waddell, "The Army and Peacetime Low Intensity Conflict, 1961–1993: The Process of Peripheral and Fundamental Military Change" (Ph.D. diss., Columbia University, 1994), p. 218; Peter Dawkins, "The U.S. Army and the 'Other' War in Vietnam: A Study of the Complexity of Implementing Organizational Change" (Ph.D. diss., Woodrow Wilson School of Public and International Affairs, 1979), pp. 63, 68–71, 77–79, 126, 239–43, 247–48.

[74] First quote from Rpt, DCSOPS, The United States Army's Role in Support of Nation Building, c. 1970, p. iv, and see also pp. 4, 9. Second quote from ibid., p. v.

[75] Quote from ibid., p. v, and see also pp. vi–vii.

[76] Quote from FM 31–23, *Stability Operations: U.S. Army Doctrine*, 1972, p. 4-3, and see also p. 4-1. FM 100–20, *Field Service Regulations: Internal Defense and Development*, 1972, p. 4-1.

[77] Quote from FM 100–20, *Internal Defense and Development, U.S. Army Doctrine*, 1974, p. 1-1, and see also pp. 8-2, 8-11.

[78] Quote from ibid., p. 1-1.

[79] Quote from FM 100–20, *Field Service Regulations: Internal Defense and Development*, 1967, p. 1-1. FM 100–20, *Internal Defense and Development, U.S. Army Doctrine*, 1974, p. 1-1.

[80] Quote from FM 100–20, *Internal Defense and Development, U.S. Army Doctrine*, 1974, p. 4-1, and see also pp. 2-1, 4-2 to 4-4.

[81] Quotes from ibid., p. 4-1.

[82] Rpt of the Department of the Army Board to Review Army Officer Schools, 2 vols., Feb 66, 1:54, 634, 636–40.

[83] Ltr, Col Sidney Gritz, Adj Gen, CONARC, to Commandant, Special Warfare School, 13 Feb 67, JFKSWC/HO; Historical Supplement, U.S. Army John F. Kennedy Center for Special Warfare, 1967, p. 68.

[84] First quote from AR 350–25, *Civil Affairs Training*, 28 Apr 67, p. 1. Second quote from ibid., p. 2, and see also p. 3. Rpt, c. 1966, sub: Status Report on the U.S. Army Psychological Operations Improvement Program as of 23 February 1965 [*sic*], CDC, 73A2677, RG 338, NARA; Common Subject Lesson Plan L294, Institute for Military Assistance (IMA), Psychological Operations, Mar 71, pp. LM-4, LM-22 to LM-27, 86–0551, RG 338, NARA.

[85] USMA, Department of Military Art and Engineering, Organizational History and POI files, 1965 to 1974; USMA, Office of Military Instruction, Department of Tactics, POI files, 1965 to 1974; Memo, Brig Gen Richard P. Scott, Commandant of Cadets, for Superintendent, USMA, 7 Apr 66, sub: Counterinsurgency Committee Report, 1966, 10002–02 Training Operations files, USMA; Memo, Scott for Superintendent, USMA, 4 May 67, sub: Counterinsurgency, 10002–02 Training Operations files, USMA.

[86] Quote from Lesson Guide MS 401–8, USMA, The Brigade in Stability Operations, 1970, p. 4.

[87] First quote from Lesson Guide MS 401–4, USMA, Operational Environment of Stability Operations, 1970, p. 4. Second quote from USMA, Notes for the Course in the History of the Military Art, HI 401/402, 1971–72, p. 7-11, History Department, Organizational History and POI files, 1971–72, USMA. Third quote from Lesson Guide MS 401–5, USMA, Military Programs and Tactical Operations in Stability Operations, 1970, p. 11.

[88] Common Subject Lesson Plan, IMA, The Insurgency Problem, Mar 70, 86–0551, RG 338, NARA; Brian Smith, "United States–Latin American Military Relations Since World War II: Implications for Human Rights," in *Human Rights and Basic Needs in the Americas*, ed. Margaret Crahan (Washington, D.C.: Georgetown University Press, 1982), p. 292*n*29; "U.S. Army School of the Americas," *Military Review* 50 (April 1970): 90; Ott, *Field Artillery*, pp. 135–36; POI 5D–8105, Civil Affairs School, Civil Affairs Officer Course, May 71, 85–0301, RG 338, NARA.

[89] Rpt of the Department of the Army Board to Review Army Officer Schools, 2 vols., Feb 66, 1:636; Richard Weinert, The Role of USCONARC in the Army Buildup, FY 66, 1967, pp. 50–52, copy in CMH; Historical Supplement, 1966, U.S. Army Infantry School, 1967, pp. 7, 11–13; POI, IOBC 2–7–C20, Infantry School, Mar 67; POI 2–7–C20, Infantry School, Infantry Officer Basic Course, Jan 68; Historical Supplement, 1967, U.S. Army Infantry School, 1968, p. 8.

[90] Quote from Infantry School, Infantry Instructors' Workshop, Report of Conference, 22–26 August 1966, p. 48, and see also p. 40. POI 2–7–C22, Infantry School, Infantry Officer Advanced Course, Mar 67, p. 30; POI 2–7–C22, Infantry School, Infantry

Officer Advanced Course, Aug 73, p. 4A19; POI 2–7–C20, Infantry School, Infantry Officer Basic Course, Jan 68.

[91] Stephen Bowman, "The Evolution of United States Army Doctrine for Counterinsurgency Warfare: From World War II to the Commitment of Combat Units in Vietnam" (Ph.D. diss., Duke University, 1985), pp. 60–61; Factors To Be Considered in Counterinsurgency Training of U.S. Personnel, p. 3, atch to Briefing, Special Warfare Center, 19 Oct 65, sub: Counterinsurgency Training Review, Historians files, CMH.

[92] CGSC, *Internal Defense: Threat and Response*, RB 31–100, 3 vols. (Fort Leavenworth, Kans.: CGSC, 1970), 1:3-1; An. B, CGSC Capability To Support ICAS in the Development of Doctrine for Stability Operations, atch to Memo, Institute of Combined Arms and Support (ICAS), 3 Jan 68, sub: Doctrine for Stability Operations, Historians files, CMH; Briefing, CGSC, Oct 65, sub: Committee II (Training), President's Review of Counterinsurgency, pp. C-2, D-1, N–13423.355–B–3, CARL.

[93] AWC Curriculum Pamphlets, 1965–1970; Harry Ball, *Of Responsible Command: A History of the U.S. Army War College* (Carlisle Barracks, Pa.: Alumni Association of the U.S. Army War College, 1983), p. 449; AWC, Military Strategy Textbook, vol. 4, 1972, p. 27; AWC, Selected Readings, Academic Year 1969, Military Strategy Seminar, vol. 3, 1969; Sam Holliday, "Stability Operations," AWC lecture, 5 Feb 69, pp. 8–15, Historians files, CMH; Sam Holliday, "Warfare of the Future," *Military Review* 49 (August 1969): 12–17; McCuen, *Art of Counter-Revolutionary War*, pp. 78, 85–122, 196, 206–09, 235, 327.

[94] Annual Hist Supplements, CY 66, 2d Bn, 8th Inf, p. 2; CY 66, 2d Bde, 4th Inf Div, pp. 2-1, 2-2; and CY 66, 1st Bde, 4th Inf Div, pp. 4–5, copies in CMH; John Kilfoil, Army Training Program To Train the Infantry Battalion for Both Conventional and Unconventional Combat (Student paper, IOAC, Infantry School, 1967); Weinert, The Role of USCONARC, 1967, pp. 76–77.

[95] ASubjScds 21–43, Orientation in Counterinsurgency Operations, 9 Jun 66, and 21–43, Orientation in Stability Operations, 17 Oct 69, Historians files, CMH; Common Subject Lesson Plan L296, IMA, Introduction to Internal Defense and Internal Development, Jun 71, NARA; CONARC History, 1965–66, pp. 181, 183, copy in CMH; USARV Reg 350–1, Replacement Training, 71–3078, RG 319, NARA; Earl Cole, "Replacement Operations in Vietnam," *Military Review* 48 (February 1968): 3–8.

[96] First quote from ASubjScd 7–2, Rifle Squad Tactical Training, Dec 65, p. 1. Second quote from ASubjScd 21–43, Orientation in Stability Operations, 17 Apr 69, p. 3. CONARC Reg 350–1, 6 Sep 67, an. B, USCONARC Training Directive, Mandatory, Mission, and Special Emphasis Training, pp. 10–17; CONARC Reg 350–1, 3 Apr 67, ans. M and N to USCONARC Training Directive, Counterguerrilla Training.

[97] CONARC Reg 350–1, 10 Sep 68, chg 2, an. B, Mandatory, Mission, and Special Emphasis Training; Memo, D, FPA, for Johnson, 21 Mar 68, sub: Conversion of Standard AIT Companies to RVN Oriented Infantry AIT Companies, with atchs, 71A3100, RG 319, NARA.

[98] Direct Quotes from Senior Army Officers Visited in RVN, c. Mar 66, 353, 69A2595, RG 319, NARA; Rpt, Col William Towson, CONARC Team Ch, to DCSIT, CONARC, 22 Mar 66, sub: Report of Staff Visit, Infantry School Library; Memo, Maj Gen DePuy, 1st Inf Div, for CG, USARV, 12 Oct 66, 70A2673, RG 319, NARA; Kurt Anderson-Vie, "Company Command in Vietnam: A Comparative Analysis" (Student thesis, CGSC, 1991), pp. 49–56, 70; Shelby Stanton, *The Rise and Fall of an American*

Army: U.S. Ground Forces in Vietnam, 1965–1973 (Novato, Calif.: Presidio Press, 1985), pp. 25–26, 70, 331.

[99] For the relatively static nature of doctrine for non-insurgency related contingency operations, compare FM 100–5, *Field Service Regulations—Operations*, 1962, pp. 155–62, FM 100–5, *Operations of Army Forces in the Field*, 1968, pp. 12-1 to 12-6; FM 61–100, *The Division*, 1962, pp. 4–5, 235–40; FM 61–100, *The Division*, 1965, pp. 3, 146–48; FM 61–100, *The Division*, 1968, pp. 1-2, 12-15 to 12-18.

[100] Criticism over the lack of how-to-do-it information was not limited to counter-insurgency manuals. Combat Operations Research Group, Studies of Doctrinal Field Manuals: A Further Analysis of User Acceptability, CORG–M–252, Oct 66; Ltr, Kinnard to Connor, 13 Nov 67, 73–2678, RG 338, NARA.

[101] DA Pam 350–15–12, *Training Operations–Lessons Learned*, 1 Jan 69, p. 2; Rpt, CDC, Review and Analysis of the Evaluation of Army Combat Operations in Vietnam, 30 Apr 66, pp. 2-II-44 to 2-II-48, Historians files, CMH.

10

THE COUNTERINSURGENCY LEGACY

The Great Retreat: Counterinsurgency in the 1970s

The fall of Saigon in April 1975 marked more than the end of the Vietnam War. It represented the end of an era. If Kennedy's 1961 pledge to "bear any burden" had announced the birth of the counter-insurgency age, then the popular refrain of the early 1970s—"no more Vietnams"—was its eulogy. Bitterly divided over a failed war, preoc-cupied by a sputtering economy and divisive social and political issues at home, and disillusioned by the inability of philanthropic nation-building programs to transform third world countries into prosperous democratic societies, the American body politic turned its collective back on counterinsurgency. The Nixon Doctrine not only remained in force after Nixon's departure from office in 1974, but one federal agen-cy after another set aside its counterinsurgency implements for more conventional tools. During the 1970s, the Central Intelligence Agency gradually shifted its priorities away from counterinsurgency to more customary intelligence-gathering operations. The State Department readily shed some of the operational roles that counterinsurgency had imposed on it for the more comfortable routines of traditional diplo-macy, while the Agency for International Development reverted to emphasizing long-term development programs over the type of short-term, civic action–style projects that had come into vogue during the counterinsurgency era. In 1975 AID also terminated at the direction of Congress its foreign police assistance program. The cancellation, driven by public perceptions that the program had bolstered repressive, right-wing regimes at the expense of human rights, dealt a severe blow to national counterinsurgency policy, which had assigned a prominent role to the creation of effective indigenous police organizations as the first bulwark against subversion.[1]

The Army joined the civilian agencies in downgrading counterinsurgency. As early as 1972, a Department of Defense study had concluded that while the nation needed to maintain a counterinsurgency capability, that capability should be restricted to providing security assistance. The Vietnam experience had discredited direct American action in the eyes of the public. The study also recommended that the counterinsurgency assistance program be separated from the military services "because, if it is not so separated, the dominant traditional U.S. military perceptions and routines will ultimately suffocate it. Thus, if the role is to survive, the resources, organizations, and decision processes that it encompasses will have to be formally decoupled from those concerned with 'direct military intervention' and from the massive arms transfers that are designed to develop conventional forces in 'forward-defense countries.'" Although the Pentagon did create a Defense Security Assistance Agency in 1972, it declined to implement the study's recommendation to create a unified command for low intensity conflict—a step that would not be taken until the defense reforms of the 1980s.[2]

Meanwhile, in 1973 Secretary of the Army Howard H. Callaway and Army Chief of Staff Abrams formed a study group of their own to assess the service's future. Like the studies that had been done under Westmoreland, the Strategic Assessment Group foresaw a multipolar world with diminishing resources being allocated to the Army to perform its many roles. The group complained particularly about the existence of an intellectual and policy elite that was hostile to the military but was still committed to pursuing idealistic agendas abroad, noting that "ironically, the very persons who decry America's past role as a 'world policeman' are the very same persons who demand that the United States 'do something' about massacres in Burundi, civil war in Chile, and unrest on the Indian subcontinent." Still, the report acknowledged that the American people had lost their taste for military interventions and that "for the foreseeable future this repugnance will tend to limit foreign involvement to those areas where hard tangible United States interests are unequivocally involved." Since America's greatest strategic interests lay in Europe and since the greatest threat to those interests was the massive armed might of the Soviet Union, the group concluded that the Army should devote its dwindling resources to the defense of Western Europe by conventional forces. Counterinsurgency, the obsession of the 1960s, would return to the periphery of military affairs.[3]

The study's impact was soon apparent. Although the Army retained the Special Action Forces, it abandoned the more interventionist

Regional Assistance Command concept and deactivated the 8th Special Action Force, which had played a major role in implementing American counterinsurgency assistance in Latin America. The Army blunted the spearhead of the early counterinsurgency movement—Special Forces—reducing it from 13,000 men in 1971 to 3,000 men by 1974. The military did form two Ranger battalions in the early 1970s, but unlike Special Forces, the Rangers trained as elite crisis reaction troops rather than as guerrillas or nation builders. Funding for counterinsurgency research, already on the wane, dried up, as did appropriations for civic action activities.[4]

The Military Assistance Officer Program likewise fell on hard times. Despite General Johnson's intentions, the Army had never fully implemented his decision to create G–5 and S–5 slots in brigades and battalions throughout the Army. By 1973 the program numbered only 433 soldiers, a far cry from the 6,000 Johnson had hoped to recruit. Moreover, the program had become a lightning rod for civilian critics who charged that the Army was trying to create a corps of gauleiters and proconsuls. While there was no truth to the accusations, the criticism compelled the service to review the content of Military Assistance Officer Program training annually to ensure that the program's faculty at Fort Bragg did not put "undue emphasis on the direct or implied role of the Army in such subject areas as political action; social and economic development (nation building); institution building; and psychological operations and civil affairs." The Army further insisted that program instructors instill in their pupils the notion that "the fundamental role of the Army is to defeat enemy forces in land combat, and to gain control of the land and people based on the control and guidance of United States higher civilian authority." By 1973 the luster had fallen off the Military Assistance Officer Program, and the Army combined the program with the foreign area specialist career track to create a new Foreign Area Officer Program. Although the new career track retained civil-military staff features, it was less ambitious than the original program and would take on an increasingly intelligence flavor.[5]

Shifts in the Military Assistance Officer Program were mirrored throughout the Army's training and educational systems. Although a decade of irregular warfare had bequeathed to the service a sizable pool of combat veterans, many of these men lacked conventional warfare training. As one battalion commander complained in 1971, "training problems were compounded by the fact that most of the men in the battalion had no experience in conventional, mid-intensity type tactics. Tactical operations such as delaying actions, manning a combat outpost line, rifle company in the attack, etc., were completely new to the junior officers and NCOs."[6]

The Army responded by reemphasizing conventional training. In 1971 the service deleted stability operations orientation from basic combat courses. The following year Continental Army Command discontinued all Vietnam-oriented advanced individual training, replacing the jungle and counterguerrilla warfare segments with conventional, mechanized warfare drills. The Army likewise dropped the requirement that all combat officers receive Ranger training, turned the Ranger course at Fort Benning toward more conventional applications, and rescinded guidance detailing counterguerrilla warfare training, thereby leaving the Army without a blueprint for such instruction for the first time in twenty years. As the decade progressed fewer and fewer units performed any meaningful counterinsurgency preparation.[7]

The gradual disappearance of counterinsurgency from Army training schedules was replicated in the classroom. As Deputy Chief of Staff for Military Operations Lt. Gen. Richard G. Stilwell noted as early as October 1969, "the question confronting the Army, as a result of congressional and public reaction to Vietnam, is not that we have a third mission, rather how far do we go in carrying out, pragmatically, the application of political, economic, psychological, and sociological factors." The answer proved elusive. A 1971 Continental Army Command query seeking recommendations for curriculum changes found considerable disagreement over whether or not the service should curtail the amount of civil affairs, psyops, and counterinsurgency instruction. Some diminution of coverage was inevitable given America's withdrawal from Vietnam and the apparent unlikelihood that combat units would be sent into similar situations anytime soon, but what the right mix might be was difficult to pinpoint.[8]

In the end, the Army permitted each school to make its own decisions on this question, with varying results. Some schools quickly curtailed counterinsurgency instruction, while others moved at a more measured pace. Ultimately, all dramatically reduced counterinsurgency studies. The Military Academy terminated its mandatory counterinsurgency course—Military Science 401—in 1974. The Infantry School likewise eliminated counterinsurgency studies in its basic course after the war but continued to offer several dozen hours in the advanced course until 1978, when it discontinued that as well. By 1977 the Command and General Staff College was still offering forty hours of low intensity conflict instruction, though this dropped to a mere eight hours in 1979. Still, this was better than the Army War College, where the withdrawal of counterinsurgency material quickly turned into a rout. As early as 1969, school deputy commandant Brig. Gen. Michael J. Greene had predicted that "as time goes by, we will have increasing difficulty justifying 'stability operations' as a separate course" due to changing public and government attitudes toward the subject. By the following year, pressure was developing from within the student body to drop the internal defense and development course because a growing number of officers expressed the opinion that internal defense and development was unsatisfying and "non-military" and hence belonged more to civilian agencies than the Army. By 1972 the War College had reduced internal defense and development instruction to two weeks, but still the students were unhappy, with one commenting that the IDAD course constituted "the worst two weeks of the best year of my life." The college heeded the students' complaints, and by 1975 the school had reduced its coverage of insurgency and counterinsurgency to two days.[9]

Counterinsurgency was not even safe in its cradle, the John F. Kennedy Institute for Military Assistance at Fort Bragg. Named after the patron saint of counterinsurgency and Special Forces, the institute contained separate schools for civil affairs and security assistance, psychological operations, and Special Forces. By 1973 the Special Forces officer course at Fort Bragg was devoting only 10 of its 704 academic hours to stability operations, as the branch turned its back on counterinsurgency in favor of its original unconventional warfare mission. By 1975 the course had reduced its stability operations coverage to a single hour covering the legal aspects of counterinsurgency. Meanwhile, Fort Bragg's Civil Affairs and Security Assistance School eliminated the civic action course from its curriculum altogether. Only the foreign area officer, civil affairs, and civil-military officer courses continued to discuss counterinsurgency-related subjects in any detail, albeit gingerly to avoid civilian criticism. Thus, while counterinsurgency and counterguerrilla doctrine remained on the books, progressively fewer personnel were given the opportunity to study, learn, and practice the tenets of that doctrine.[10]

The Army's doctrinal community was not far behind the training and education systems in marginalizing counterinsurgency. Although the internal defense and development manuals of the early 1970s had begun to distance the Army from what once had been the service's "third principal mission," the true sea change occurred in 1976 when the Army published a new edition of its capstone combat manual, FM 100–5, *Operations*. Written largely by General William E. DePuy, one of the leading tacticians of the Vietnam War, the manual represented a major reorientation in doctrinal thought. Stating that he wanted to help the Army prepare to fight the next war rather than the last one, DePuy produced a manual that was devoted to the defense of Western Europe against the Warsaw Pact. Gone were all references to counter-insurgency, nation-building, civil affairs, and psychological operations, replaced by a single-minded emphasis on the conduct of conventional combat operations in a major war. In contrast to the 1968 edition of FM 100–5, which had stated that "the fundamental purpose of U.S. military forces is to preserve, restore, or create an environment of order or stability within which the instrumentalities of government can function effectively under a code of laws," the very first sentence of the 1976 manual declared unequivocally that "the Army's primary objective is to *win the land battle*—to fight and win battles, large or small, against whatever foe, wherever we may be sent to war." Although such a mandate included fighting guerrillas, the manual returned to an old formulation in arguing that the military should focus its energies on preparing to fight its most dangerous opponent. This was especially true given the lethality of the modern battlefield (as demonstrated by the 1973 Arab-Israeli War) and the precariousness of NATO defenses on the German frontier, factors that led DePuy to believe that the Army had to be able to "win the first battle of the next war." Thus, while he acknowledged that the Army had a wide variety of missions, strategic and tactical necessity dictated a very different prioritization of those missions than had existed just a few years before.[11]

DePuy envisioned that FM 100–5 (1976) would serve as the cap-stone for a whole generation of new subsidiary manuals, each devoted to a particular type of military activity. Forty derivative manuals were planned, including one designated FM 90–8, *Counterguerrilla Operations*. Training and Doctrine Command initially intended to pub-lish the new counterguerrilla manual in 1976, but this did not occur. Instead, soldiers would continue to use the 1967 edition of FM 31–16, *Counterguerrilla Operations* (with the 1969 and 1970 changes), until 1981, when the Army rescinded the Vietnam-era manual without pro-viding a replacement. Not until 1986, after going five years without any type of counterguerrilla combat doctrine, would the service belatedly publish FM 90–8, *Counterguerrilla Operations*.[12]

Over time, many of the Army's branch and functional manu-als followed the lead set by FM 100–5 (1976) and either reduced or eliminated counterguerrilla and IDAD-related material from their pages. This did not mean, however, that the Army was with-out counterinsurgency doctrine during the late 1970s, as both the Army's capstone IDAD manual, FM 100–20, *Internal Defense and Development, U.S. Army Doctrine* (1974), and a number of derivative manuals, including FM 31–16, *Counterguerrilla Operations* (1967); FM 19–50, *Military Police in Stability Operations* (1970); FM 30–31, *Stability Operations—Intelligence* (1970); and FM 31–73, *Advisor Handbook for Stability Operations* (1967), remained in effect into the 1980s, when the Army eventually issued new doctrine in the form of FM 100–20, *Low Intensity Conflict* (1981). Still, the lower profile accorded counterinsurgency throughout the Army's doctrinal, training, and educational establishments relegated the surviving doctrine to relative obscurity.

The Army's disinclination to issue new IDAD manuals after 1975 meant that counterinsurgency doctrine would remain virtually unchanged in the postwar period. Several issues contributed to the decision not to rewrite doctrine after the Vietnam War. A desire to forget the entire unhappy experience was one factor. So too was the policy shift away from foreign interventions, which lessened the urgency for making revisions. The fact that the Army had already incorporated some of the war's lessons into doctrine prior to 1975 also reduced the need for change, while the perceived requirement to address pressing concerns in mid-intensity conflict redirected intellectual energy away from low intensity conflict. Last, change was impeded by the service's belief that the existing doctrine was fundamentally sound and therefore not in need of a major overhaul.

There were of course some attempts to derive lessons after 1975. At the Army War College, students and faculty alike examined the war with a critical eye. When a full-blown "lessons learned" study proved too much for the school to handle, the Army commissioned the BDM Corporation to provide such an analysis. The resulting eight-volume report criticized the way the Army and the nation had conducted the war, but it was so voluminous and arrived so late (1979) that it was relegated to virtual obscurity. A more influential, if controversial, study appeared in 1981, when Col. Harry G. Summers, Jr., published an interpretation of the war titled *On Strategy: The Vietnam War in Context*. Although the Army's Strategic Studies Institute published the work, the book bore a disclaimer that it did not represent the views of the Department of the Army, and like the BDM study, it had no impact on published doctrine.[13]

The absence of any official post-Vietnam assessment did not mean, however, that soldiers were not influenced by the war or its outcome. While each individual held his or her own views regarding the war, several themes seemed to have resonated with large segments of the officer corps. First among these was an aversion for limited war theory, with its gamesmanship, gradual escalations, and piecemeal commitments of U.S. forces. More than anything else, for the Army the phrase "no more Vietnams" meant that the United States should never again seek to commit U.S. troops to combat without the full backing and support of the American people.

The Vietnam experience left soldiers leery of politicians, resentful of civilian micromanagement and media criticism, and skeptical about employing military power to solve certain international problems. Interventions into the internal affairs of foreign nations had proved to be particularly thorny, full of hardship and frustration, with little personal or institutional reward. Unless vital national interests were at stake, few soldiers were anxious to enter into such briar patches again.

If one had to intervene, U.S. soldiers preferred to do so earlier rather than later, before a situation had deteriorated out of hand. Once committed, they also wanted to deploy massive amounts of force to overwhelm the enemy as quickly and decisively as possible so as to pave the way for a rapid restoration of order and an early withdrawal of U.S. troops. Although they acknowledged the importance of political considerations, most soldiers wished to confine the Army's activities to military and security measures, seasoned with some peripheral civic action and community relations programs, but leaving nation building to civilians. Finally, they wanted to operate under clear lines of command, with a single authority capable of unifying the civil-military effort and establishing precise mission statements, concrete, achievable objectives, and a fixed exit strategy. Many of these conditions had appeared on previous wish lists, and not all of them were compatible with each other. Collectively, they represented a conservative approach to the exercise of military power in foreign policy. That these sentiments were not incorporated formally into a manual did not make them any less real, and they would have just as much—if not more—impact on the exercise of American foreign and military policy over the coming decades as official doctrine.[14]

The Evolution of Counterinsurgency Doctrine in Retrospect

The role that counterinsurgency operations played in American strategic thought changed dramatically during the thirty-plus years that spanned the middle of the twentieth century. From relative obscurity in the 1940s, counterinsurgency quietly grew in stature until it erupted with much fanfare in the early 1960s as one of the central tenets of U.S. national security policy. The rapidity with which counterinsurgency made its ascent onto the policy stage in the early 1960s was matched only by the speed of its fall, as a disillusioned nation hastened to return it to the backwaters of strategic thought in the 1970s.

While proponents of low intensity and nation-building operations decried counterinsurgency's demise, shifts in emphasis were neither unreasonable nor unique. During the 1950s, President Eisenhower sought to avoid becoming directly involved in the internal conflicts of foreign nations. A cautious foreign policy, tightening defense budgets, and a philosophy of relying on the threat of massive nuclear retaliation to deter Communist aggression all inhibited the Army from devoting significant attention to counterinsurgency. Not until the later 1950s did Eisenhower begin to react to the threat posed by insurgencies and limited wars. The Army responded as well, with modest steps to improve its ability to operate in "situations short of war." When in 1961 President Kennedy inaugurated a new era of flexible response and foreign policy activism in the third world, the Army again responded, elevating counterinsurgency and nation-building doctrine to unprecedented heights. And when, under the direction of Presidents Nixon and Gerald R. Ford, the nation returned to a more limited, Euro-focused foreign policy, so too did the Army. These fluctuations were matched by changes in organization and equipment, as the Army moved from conventional, World War II–style forces to nuclear-oriented Pentomic divisions and then finally to flexible ROAD divisions. The frequency of these changes was disruptive to the smooth development of doctrine and organization, but the adjustments attested to the Army's willingness to conform to national policy.[15]

Although the Army continuously modified its doctrine and organization to suit civilian policy directives, it steadfastly insisted on keeping one eye on what it regarded as its most important mission, the conduct of major conventional operations. Undoubtedly, the Army would have been better served had it consistently devoted more attention to counterinsurgency and constabulary issues throughout the period, for the Army's mission was and has always been multifaceted. Yet the nation's military leaders also had to make hard judgments as to the allocation of resources, giving priority to those missions that seemed most pressing at the time. If the Army showed some reluctance to recast itself into a low intensity–oriented force, it had good reasons for its reservations. Not only had the nation not relieved the military of the burden of defending Western Europe and Korea, but many soldiers and marines, including Generals Decker, Lemnitzer, Taylor, and Krulak, believed that the guerrilla threat was overblown. Despite the great fanfare given to Communist revolutionary warfare, only a handful of countries would fall to Communist revolutions between 1945 and 1975. With the exception of China, none of these losses posed a significant, long-term threat to American political and economic interests. Rather than heralding the dawn of a new era of warfare, wars of national liberation ultimately proved to be a flash in the pan.[16]

Just as counterinsurgency's fortunes ebbed and flowed in conjunction with the changing tides of national policy, so too did the content of doctrine evolve over the years. Initially, Army counterguerrilla doctrine focused on the threat partisans posed to rear echelon troops during a major war. Counterguerrilla warfare in this context was an adjunct to conventional operations, but one which the Army believed could not be ignored given historical precedent and contemporary Sino-Soviet doctrine. This point of view continued until the late 1950s, when Western soldiers and statesmen increasingly recognized that the Communists might exploit the growing pains of the emerging nations of the third world to the West's disadvantage.

The Army was in the process of moving to meet this threat when President Kennedy launched a national crusade against wars of national liberation. At this point, third world insurgents replaced European partisans as the primary target of counterguerrilla doctrine. Similarly, the traditional military tactics of counterguerrilla warfare—which were being modified by the incorporation of recent experience and technological innovation—were subsumed under a new rubric of counterinsurgency, in which socioeconomic and political considerations were accorded great weight. As the decade progressed, the amount of attention doctrine paid to the noncombat aspects of irregular warfare—civil affairs, intelligence, and propaganda—steadily increased. Not only did civic action and nation building assume an ever greater role in military thought, but the nature of those activities evolved as well, reflecting both the results of experience and the changing hypotheses of the political and social theorists who provided the intellectual basis for much of American policy in the 1960s.

In the emerging national security state, where the boundaries between political and military matters were increasingly blurred, civilian theorists, scientists, and policy makers like Walt Rostow, Robert McNamara, and Robert Osgood had an increasing effect on nearly every aspect of military affairs, from procurement to strategy. The limited war theory that guided much of America's strategic thinking during the Vietnam War was the product of civilian intellectuals, and that counterinsurgency, a subject that involved an intimate intertwining of political and military action, should also reflect a heavy civilian influence was entirely understandable. Much of this influence was positive but not all of it. Although military doctrine traditionally represents the distillation of experience, much of what gave counterinsurgency its distinct flavor in the 1960s came from social science theories that, as George Ball, a State Department official in the Kennedy and Johnson administrations, admitted, were "reeking of the lamp." Based more on hypothesis and conjecture than on in-depth historical analysis, these theories burdened the nation and the Army with relatively untested, ahistorical premises. Among the assumptions that would ultimately prove flawed were that third world populations were thirsting for Western-style modernization, that economic development would inevitably squelch social discontent and produce more equitable societies, that more government intervention in local affairs was inherently preferable to less, that foreigners could adequately diagnose and readily correct another culture's illnesses, that democracy was an exportable commodity, and that military and security matters were of lesser importance to defeating an insurgency than sociopolitical concerns. In the end, many of the assumptions and attributes of what was commonly referred to as the hearts-and-minds approach to insurgency often turned out to be overly optimistic or impractical.[17]

President Kennedy played a particularly prominent role in counterinsurgency's turbulent history. He was largely responsible for pushing the Army to move counterinsurgency from the periphery to the center of military thought in an incredibly short period. He not only compelled the service to address the insurgency issue, but imbued both national policy and military doctrine with a self-assured, crusading spirit. The Army embraced this vision, informing its soldiers that "you are a crusader on the front of a new type of battlefield . . . a battle for the minds of men."[18]

While the champions of enlightened nation building were sincere in their beliefs, tactical considerations also colored their actions. For if idealism is deeply embedded in the American psyche, so too is isolationism, and Kennedy was well aware that the best way to energize the American public was to wrap his foreign policy prescriptions in the mantle of a moral crusade. Truman had done the same thing in the late 1940s, when he justified his aid program to Greece in terms of promoting reform and democracy abroad. Indeed, proponents of change frequently resort to hyperbole to justify their positions. This had been the case during the 1920s and 1930s, when the champions of strategic air power had attempted to win a place in the nation's defense establishment by exaggerating the ability of aircraft to win wars, and the situation was no less true in the 1960s, as the proponents of counterinsurgency pushed their particular agenda. And, as in the case of air power, the broad declarations made by counterinsurgency theorists were aimed not just at the public and Congress, but at the bureaucracy, which the hearts-and-minds advocates believed needed to be prodded into institutionalizing the new creed.

While such behavior was understandable on both human and political grounds, there were some drawbacks to Kennedy's method. Presidential interest precipitated a flood of policy and doctrinal writings as everyone rushed to jump on the counterinsurgency bandwagon. Unfortunately, not all of these writings were well thought out. Not only did this situation breed confusion, but it created a faddish, circus-like atmosphere. Soldiers were just as responsible as civilians for the ensuing state of affairs, as they generated new terms and acronyms with abandon. The consequence was that the emerging doctrine was both overblown and oversold. Proponents of the new doctrine presented a particularly rosy view of countering insurgency and building nations in which enlightened policies and good intentions would inevitably be more powerful than bullets. When these expectations proved difficult to fulfill, cynicism and disillusionment were the result. This disillusionment not only produced a backlash that helped undermine the war effort in Vietnam, but hastened the speed with which government institutions turned their backs on counterinsurgency in the early 1970s.[19]

Ironically, Kennedy's drive to reorient government policy also suffered from the equivocal way in which he pursued his goals. On the one hand, his forcefulness alienated many civilian and military functionaries, who disliked "outsiders" meddling in what they regarded as technical, professional matters. On the other hand, Kennedy failed to bring cohesion to the national crusade. The inability of the Kennedy and Johnson administrations to integrate the competing bureaucracies and disparate programs that contributed to America's counterinsurgency and nation-building effort impeded the execution of American policy in the 1960s. The belated creation of Civil Operations and Revolutionary Development Support in Vietnam represented the nearest approximation of the type of unity of effort that had long been a cardinal principle of Army doctrine, but even that entity was deeply resented by the civilian bureaucracies. Regarded as a temporary expedient for a desperate and unique situation, national policy makers did not formally embrace CORDS as a model for future civil-military endeavors.

Another debatable decision was Kennedy's inclination to treat counterinsurgency as something "special." By attaching a certain mystique to insurgency and counterinsurgency, Kennedy sought to break the "business as usual" cycle and to generate extraordinary attention and effort. A corollary to this formulation was the president's fascination with elite forces. Kennedy's mind-set, however, had the unfortunate effect of encouraging the Army to focus much of its initial effort on Special Forces. This approach was misguided because Special Forces had largely ignored counterinsurgency prior to 1961 and thus had no special knowledge of it. Moreover, the specialist mind-set tended to reinforce the attitude of many soldiers that counterinsurgency was not a mainline mission, but a unique function that could safely be shunted off to a small cadre of experts to handle. This not only undermined Kennedy's larger goal of reorienting the Army as a whole, but relegated proponency for counterinsurgency to a small and bureaucratically weak element within the Army.

President Kennedy and Army leaders created this predicament, but the decision of where to place responsibility for an activity that was at once unique yet also impacted all branches and every level of the Army was difficult. During the mid-1960s, Army Chief of Staff General Johnson tried to undo the harm that had been done by initially categorizing counterinsurgency as being "special." His efforts to make counterinsurgency everyone's business succeeded to an extent, but the organizational question would continue to bedevil the formulation and dissemination of counterinsurgency doctrine throughout the period.

A final weakness of Kennedy's method was that, by politicizing doctrine, he converted it into dogma. The president and his supporters tended to brand those who questioned the hearts-and-minds approach as unenlightened reactionaries whose opinions had no merit. This stifled debate and facilitated the adoption of policies based on what theorists wanted to see happen, rather than on a realistic appraisal of what was possible to achieve.[20]

An example of how dogmatic assertions created inflexibility can be seen in the realm of civil-military relations. One of the cardinal tenets of counterinsurgency theory as it emerged in the 1960s was that insurgency was an inherently political, as opposed to military, activity. One corollary of this principle was that civilians and politics should predominate over soldiers and military considerations in every instance. While the importance of political factors in an internal conflict was indisputable, adhering to a rigid prioritization of roles was neither always possible nor desirable. Civilian officials were frequently incapable of acting in a coherent, unified fashion, while civilian agencies often lacked the resources to carry out their programs. A civil-first approach also did not necessarily mesh with the governments the United States was attempting to assist, particularly if they were dominated by soldiers or had weak civil administrations. Moreover, although political primacy made sense during the early phases of an insurgency, once a rebellion began in earnest, accomplishing socioeconomic and political goals without first achieving security through military operations often proved impractical. Whether in Greece, Vietnam, or even the Philippines, experience demonstrated that military and security considerations were often as important as political matters in successful counterinsurgency operations. By asserting political primacy as an iron-clad rule, however, hearts-and-minds advocates created a doctrinaire mind-set for what should have been a dynamic and flexible relationship.

While Army doctrine during the 1960s took on a distinctive flavor that reflected the intellectual tenor of the day, what is perhaps most remarkable is how little Army doctrine actually changed during the thirty-five tumultuous years covered by this book. This continuity was particularly strong with regard to the military aspects of counterguerrilla warfare. From the beginning, Army doctrine set three fundamental tasks for the counterinsurgent: separating the people physically and spiritually from the guerrillas, separating the guerrillas from external sources of support, and destroying the insurgents. The first objective was to be achieved by an adroit combination of military, police, intelligence, propaganda, population- and resources-control, and sociopolitical measures, while the last two tasks were primarily military in nature.

Operationally, American doctrine throughout the period called for commanders to establish geographical commands, usually based on political boundaries so as to facilitate politico-military coordination. Once deployed, security forces were to remain in a region as long as necessary to pacify the area, a method based on the belief that prolonged service in one area enhanced operations by making commanders more familiar with the local topography, both physical and political. After establishing close relations with the local political and police apparatus, commanders were to wage an aggressive campaign of patrol, raid, and attack with an eye toward driving the guerrillas away from the civilian population, destroying their bases, and wearing them down. As the insurgent threat diminished, military units would break down into progressively smaller units to maintain the pressure. Meanwhile, government authorities were to raise paramilitary forces and purge communities of subversive elements until a level of security and control had been achieved sufficient to permit the regular units to be removed to another locale, where they would repeat the process. Flexibility, adaptability, mobility, intelligence, surprise, security, perseverance, and continuous, offensive operations were the creed that guided all Army doctrinal writings. Although manuals maintained that some form of encirclement represented the best chance of bringing guerrillas to decisive battle, they never elevated a single operational technique, recognizing that both large-unit and small-unit actions had their place under the appropriate circumstances. Aggressive, small-unit infantry action, however, formed the basis of all tactical doctrine, a philosophy that remained unchanged until the mid-1960s, when the danger attendant to rooting out a lethal, well-organized, and deeply entrenched foe led Army leaders to partially reverse the roles of fire and maneuver in Vietnam.

All of this did not mean that Army doctrine did not change. Throughout the period, the advent of new technologies, most notably in the area of aviation, together with lessons derived from experience and foreign example, led the service to adjust its doctrine, especially at the tactical and technical levels. But few of these developments radically altered the basic precepts and overarching concepts of American counterguerrilla doctrine.

Part of the reason why Army counterguerrilla doctrine remained fundamentally unchanged during this period was that much of it was written in general terms. Manuals established guiding principles and concepts, but seldom imposed ironclad rules. This was a practical approach that, if some found unsatisfying, did at least endow soldiers with a flexible instrument.

An equally important factor in the durability of Army counterguerrilla doctrine, however, was the fact that the essential nature of irregular warfare was itself relatively unchanging. Guerrilla movements differed profoundly from each other with respect to size, organization, tactics, and armament, as did the political, social, and topographical milieus in which they occurred. Each case required a unique and tailored response. Nevertheless, most insurgencies shared certain fundamental characteristics. By taking such characteristics into account and by writing doctrine at a broad, conceptual level, the Army succeeded in producing a doctrine that remained useful under a wide variety of circumstances despite the passage of time. That this was true belied the assertions made by some counterinsurgency proponents that modern insurgency was so different from past insurgencies as to make the study of those earlier events irrelevant. In fact, many of the concepts that the Army passed off as "new" doctrine to meet the threat posed by Communist revolutionary warfare in the 1960s were just recycled versions of doctrine that had been written a decade earlier based on Volckmann's analysis of partisan and counter-partisan activities in World War II. The reappearance in subsequent texts of ideas that had first appeared in FM 31–20, *Operations Against Guerrilla Forces* (1951), attested to the value of that original, pre-Maoist doctrine.

American experiences and lessons derived from Chinese, French, and British activities refined, but never replaced, the Army's initial concepts. Thus the counterinsurgency doctrine that emerged in the 1960s was neither an entirely new product nor simply a case of old wine in a new bottle. Rather, it represented a blend of old and new wine—reformulated and repackaged—but retaining much of the fundamental characteristics of the original ingredients.

Just as there was much continuity with regard to the military aspects of counterguerrilla operations, a similar situation existed in relation to pacification and the many civil aspects of irregular warfare. Despite some assertions to the contrary, Army doctrine had always recognized that political factors loomed large in counterguerrilla warfare. Since military action was the service's primary responsibility, it was upon this that the manuals focused. But the manuals never lost sight of the fact that irregular conflicts often originated from and were sustained by the local population, and that consequently the best way to eliminate a rebellion was to redress the political, social, and economic conditions that spawned and perpetuated it. Principles established by Volckmann's 1951 manual included the notions that preventing an insurgency was easier than countering it, that governments should enact policies designed to redress the causes of unrest, and that soldiers should conduct themselves with propriety and decorum when interacting with civilians. From the beginning, Army doctrine called for the formulation of closely integrated plans that took into account the unique political, military, social, economic, and geographical circumstances of the theater of operations. These principles were not the product of some Maoist analysis, rather they were based on long-standing traditions of international law and military government. They were also deeply rooted in a myriad of pacification and civil affairs activities dating back to the founding of the Republic, experiences that the Army first formalized in a doctrinal way in General Orders 100 of 1863. For over a century U.S. forces had been governed by an official creed that held that the purpose of war was peace and that soldiers had a duty to ameliorate the hardships that war inevitably imposed on civilians. General Johnson deliberately tapped into that tradition when he cited General Orders 100 as the basis for his concept of stability operations.[21]

While Army doctrine embraced a general policy of moderation, it also recognized—as had General Orders 100 and most subsequent Army writings—that good deeds alone would not suppress a determined insurrection. No matter how appealing, redressing civilian grievances in a meaningful way was not always possible. Reforms did not necessarily appeal to many hard core revolutionaries, whose true goals were often neither altruistic nor open to compromise. Since irregulars could not survive without some form of civilian cooperation and since positive acts were not always sufficient to prevent a hostile or neutral population from aiding the guerrillas, Army doctrine had long maintained that coercion was an indispensable element in combating an insurrection. Although the service shied away from such unsavory tactics as torture and terror, it embraced all those means sanctioned by international and military law to control people's behavior and restrict their ability to aid and abet the guerrillas. These included curfews; censorship; detention and prosecution (subject to legal proceedings); restrictions over the movement and possession of food, medicine, weapons, and other supplies useful to the guerrillas; the destruction of cover and crops used by irregulars; and, in extreme cases, retaliation. Army regulations also embraced long-standing principles of international law that denied many guerrillas and their supporters the status of legitimate belligerents, though in practice the military frequently afforded mufti-clad combatants some status in an effort to avoid having a conflict descend into a profitless cycle of retaliation and murder. Finally, the Army embraced resettlement in those cases where there was no other way either to protect the local population or sever its cooperation with the guerrillas, though this practice was never accorded a central place in American doctrine.

The Army characterized this carrot-and-stick policy as being firm but fair, a nineteenth-century formulation that the Army would continue to apply to all of its military government, civil affairs, counterguerrilla, and pacification programs during the twentieth century. It was a difficult policy to carry out, since there were few prescribed boundaries as to the degree to which commanders were to rely on persuasion versus coercion. If this was a fault of doctrine, it was a deliberate one, as Army doctrine writers believed that to delineate a fixed relationship that would be equally valid in every circumstance would be counterproductive, if not impossible. As a result, attraction and coercion would sit uneasily side by side in the pages of American manuals.

One of the biggest impacts that the hearts-and-minds philosophy had on doctrine in the 1960s was to shift the delicate balance between persuasion and punishment in favor of the former. The change reflected both the philosophical predisposition of many theorists as well as an increasing intolerance in both international law and world public opinion for actions against civilians. Army doctrine reflected these concerns, adopting additional admonitions as to the importance of good troop conduct and using discretion when employing firepower or imposing restrictive measures. But the tension between force and

493

persuasion remained unabated, as experience continued to demonstrate that repressive steps were often necessary to overcome deeply entrenched guerrilla movements. Consequently, while Army manuals became more effusive about the benefits of the "positive program," they refused to abandon the many practical, if unpleasant, restrictive measures that had proved useful in the past. This approach created some confusion and much criticism. Hearts-and-minds sloganeering further exacerbated the situation by unduly raising expectations about the power of purely positive acts to resolve internecine conflicts with a minimum of unpleasantness. Practical experience, however, repeatedly demonstrated that such expectations were unjustified.

While there were many soldiers who either felt uncomfortable with nation-building activities or who rejected assertions made by Kennedy and others that the Army had to be completely overhauled to perform overseas counterinsurgency functions effectively, there was surprisingly little resistance within the Army to the central tenets of the modernization theory. For the most part soldiers readily accepted Rostow's concepts as well as the other nation-building theories developed by academics. In part, this was because many of these theories were deeply rooted in the American psyche. Despite assertions that the United States was not going to try to recast societies in its own image, the fact of the matter was that most Americans defined modernization in terms of producing more industrial, capitalistic, educated, "liberal," secular, urban, democratic, and socially equitable societies. In short, modernization and nation building looked suspiciously like Westernization, a process that, if taken to conclusion, would produce societies similar to our own.

The counterinsurgency-modernization impulse of the 1960s thus reflected a complex blend of forces that had long characterized American political life—idealism, progressivism, and ethnocentrism. It also resonated with contemporary American thinking about the role of government in a modern society. Initiatives like the Alliance for Progress, civic action, and other nation-building initiatives were the foreign policy equivalents of President Johnson's "Great Society" programs of the 1960s, which employed big government activism to attack at home many of the very same problems—such as racism, unemployment, poverty, ignorance, and malnutrition—that third world nations were experiencing, albeit on a different order of magnitude. Ultimately, U.S. soldiers accepted the "ideology of modernization" because it represented both their cultural heritage and the current mores of their society, a society of which they were very much a part.[22]

This phenomenon was not unique to the 1960s. For nearly a century U.S. soldiers had been approaching overseas pacification and constabulary operations in much the same way. Whether in Cuba and the Philippines in 1900, Greece in 1947, or Vietnam in 1967, U.S. soldiers had gravitated toward a general program of improved public education, economic development, political democracy, and moderate social reform to uplift foreign peoples and quell unrest. Though the specifics of each program varied according to the spirit of the times and the situation and people involved, the extent to which these themes reappeared time after time merely reaffirms the notion that deep-seated cultural and intellectual forces were at play, guiding successive generations of U.S. soldiers as they went about implementing their nation-building, pacification, and constabulary duties.

If this factor helps explain the readiness with which U.S. soldiers accepted many of the precepts of 1960s nation-building and counterinsurgency theory, it also demonstrates the durability of those concepts in postwar doctrine. Despite the general aversion that soldiers and civilians alike exhibited toward undertaking constabulary and pacification missions after Vietnam, doctrine for meeting those contingencies would remain virtually unchanged.[23]

The counterinsurgency era thus bequeathed the post-Vietnam Army an ambiguous legacy. On the one hand, some of the more extreme promises and assumptions that had been made with regard to the political and social aspects of counterinsurgency and nation building had turned out to be either wrong, misguided, or unobtainable. In most cases the United States and its allies had succeeded in defeating Communist insurgents without achieving the profound socioeconomic reforms that some theorists had believed were essential for victory. Nor had American notions of modernization been a panacea for foreign instability. On the other hand, many of the old principles upon which American counterguerrilla doctrine had been based had generally proved to be valid. To the extent that Army manuals of the early 1970s preserved these principles, they would provide useful insights for future doctrine writers and practitioners should the United States once again, as it had done so many times over the past two hundred years, call upon its uniformed men and women to perform counterguerrilla, constabulary, and pacification missions abroad.

Notes

[1] Blaufarb, *Counterinsurgency Era*, pp. 288–89, 292; Shafer, *Deadly Paradigms*, p. 89; Peter Kafkalas, "Low Intensity Conflict and Today's U.S. Army: An Assessment" (Master's thesis, Harvard University, 1984), pp. 14, 51; Thomas Adams, "Military Doctrine and the Organization Culture of the U.S. Army" (Ph.D. diss., Syracuse University, 1990), pp. 445–46.

[2] Quote from H. Heymann and W. W. Whitson, Can and Should the United States Preserve a Military Capability for Revolutionary Conflict? R–940–ARPA (Santa Monica, Calif.: RAND, 1972), p. 65, and see also pp. 1–2, 22, 45, 54–57, 70–71, 80, 92–95.

[3] Quotes from Ricky Waddell, "The Army and Peacetime Low Intensity Conflict, 1961–1993: The Process of Peripheral and Fundamental Military Change" (Ph.D. diss., Columbia University, 1994), p. 193, and see also pp. 194, 212–13. Kafkalas, "Low Intensity Conflict," p. 14; Donald Vought, "Preparing for the Wrong War?" *Military Review* 57 (May 1977): 21–23.

[4] Martin Massoglia et al., Military Civic Action, Evaluation of Military Techniques (Research Triangle Institute, 1971), 2:III-21, III-22; Ltr, Kinnard, CDC, to Fred Wolcott, Vice President, Research Analysis Corporation, 2 Jun 69, 73A2678, RG 338, NARA; Hogan, *Raiders or Elite Infantry*, p. 196; John Waghelstein, "Post-Vietnam Counterinsurgency Doctrine," *Military Review* 65 (June 1985): 46; Adams, "Military Doctrine," p. 447; Waddell, "The Army and Low Intensity Conflict," p. 199.

[5] Quotes from Memo, Brig Gen William R. Bond, Actg Dir, International and Civil Affairs, ODCSOPS, for Vice Chief of Staff, 25 Aug 69, sub: Visit to the JFK Center for Military Assistance, Historians files, CMH. Draft Study, CDC Special Operations Agency, 19 Apr 73, The Civil-Military Operations Study, pp. 2-15, 2-16, Historians files, CMH; *Department of the Army Historical Summary, Fiscal Year 1972* (Washington, D.C.: U.S. Army Center of Military History, 1974), p. 23; *Department of the Army Historical Summary, Fiscal Year 1973* (Washington, D.C.: U.S. Army Center of Military History, 1977), p. 73; Counterinsurgency or Stability Operations Training, pp. 11–12, atch to Summary Sheet, Lt Gen Richard Stilwell, DCSOPS, to CSA, 10 Oct 69, sub: Counterinsurgency or Stability Operations Training, 73–0124, RG 319, NARA; Memo, Maj Gen William Knowlton, SGS, for DCSOPS et al., 17 Nov 69, sub: Internal Defense and Development (IDD)/Counterinsurgency and Stability Operations Training, 73–0127, RG 319, NARA.

[6] Quote from USCONARC History, Fiscal Year 1972, p. 482, and see also p. 514, copy in CMH. Gillespie, *Sergeants Major of the Army*, p. 120.

[7] The Army rescinded ASubjScd 7–12, Anti-Infiltration and Counterguerrilla Training, 9 Apr 68 in June 1976. The evolution of Army aggressor manuals illustrates the trends in training. In 1973 the Army discontinued its first all-guerrilla aggressor manual, FM 30–104, *Handbook on Aggressor Insurgent War*, 1967, merging it back into a new edition of FM 30–102, *Handbook on Aggressor*. Though largely oriented toward conventional operations, the new manual still discussed insurgent warfare. By 1977, however, the irregular warfare segment was reduced to just a few pages on Soviet-style partisans as the Army replaced the 1973 training manual with a new version, FM 30–102, *Aggressor Forces Europe*, that focused exclusively on the European

theater. USCONARC History, Fiscal Year 1972, pp. 523–24; Kafkalas, "Low Intensity Conflict," p. 98.

[8] Quote from Counterinsurgency or Stability Operations Training, p. 5, atch to Summary Sheet, Stilwell to CSA, 10 Oct 69, sub: Counterinsurgency or Stability Operations Training.

[9] First quote from Memo, Brig Gen Michael Greene, Dep Commandant, AWC, for Commandant, AWC, 19 May 69, sub: Final Report, Course 5, Stability Operations, AY 69, in Stability Operations, Course 5, Course of Instruction, Final Report, AWC, 1968/69. Second quote from Stability Operations, Course 4, Course of Instruction, Final Report, AWC, 1969/70, p. 3. Third quote from AWC, Final Report Military Strategy Seminar, Academic Year 1972, MHI. AWC Curriculum Pamphlets, 1969–1975. All in MHI. Ball, *Of Responsible Command*, p. 449; POI files, 1974, USMA, Office of Military Instruction, Department of Tactics, USMA Archives; Vought, "Preparing for the Wrong War?" p. 30; Historical Supplement, 1974, U.S. Army Infantry School, 1975, pp. 16, 22, copy in CMH; POI 2–7–C22, Infantry School, Infantry Officer Advanced Course, Sep 75; Memo, IMA, 4 Mar 74, sub: Internal Defense and Development (IDAD) Training at the United States Army Infantry School (USAIS), Fort Benning, Ga., pp. 1–2, 18–22, Historians files, CMH; Michael Pearlman, "The Fall and Rise of Low-Intensity Conflict Doctrine and Instruction," *Military Review* 68 (September 1988): 78.

[10] POI 2E–F8, IMA, Special Forces Officer Course, Aug 73; POI 2E–F8, IMA, Special Forces Officer Course, Apr 75; POI 7b–F3, IMA, Foreign Area Officer Course, Jun 77; IMA Pam 350–6, Precis of Courses, Jun 75. All in 85–0301, RG 338, NARA.

[11] First quote from FM 100–5, *Operations of the Army in the Field*, 1968, p. 1-6. Second and third quotes from FM 100–5, *Operations*, 1976, p. 1-1, and see also p. 1-2. Paul Herbert, *Deciding What Has To Be Done: General William E. DePuy and the 1976 Edition of FM 100–5, Operations* (Fort Leavenworth, Kans.: Combat Studies Institute, 1988), pp. 6–7, 99–100.

[12] Sheehan, "Preparing for an Imaginary War, Examining Peacetime Functions and Changes of Army Doctrine" (Ph.D. diss., Harvard University, 1988), pp. 175–76, 181, 199.

[13] Harry Summers, "The United States Army's Institutional Response to Vietnam," in *Proceedings of the 1982 International Military History Symposium: "The Impact of Unsuccessful Military Campaigns on Military Institutions, 1860–1980,"* ed. Charles Shrader (Washington, D.C.: U.S. Army Center of Military History, 1984), pp. 300–301; M. J. Brady, "The Army and the Strategic Military Legacy of Vietnam" (Master's thesis, CGSC, 1990), pp. 60–61, 215–16, 222; Harry Summers, *On Strategy: The Vietnam War in Context* (Carlisle Barracks, Pa.: Strategic Studies Institute, 1981).

[14] Petraeus, "The American Military and the Lessons of Vietnam," pp. i–iii, 34, 104, 128–31, 135, 258–59, 300–302.

[15] Kafkalas, "Low Intensity Conflict," p. 14; Doughty, *Army Tactical Doctrine*, p. 47.

[16] Packenham, *Liberal America*, pp. 16, 184; Shy and Collier, "Revolutionary War," in *Makers of Modern Strategy*, ed. Peter Paret (Princeton, N.J.: Princeton University Press, 1986), p. 860; Laqueur, *Guerrilla*, pp. 2, 6, 8; Betts, *Soldiers, Statesmen*, p. 130; Stephen Bowman, "The Evolution of United States Army Doctrine for Counterinsurgency Warfare: From World War II to the Commitment of Combat Units in Vietnam" (Ph.D. diss., Duke University, 1985), pp. 5–6, 85, 121, 134, 177–78, 193; Waddell, "The Army and Low Intensity Conflict," p. 141.

[17] Quote from Betts, *Soldiers, Statesmen*, p. 129. Shy and Collier, "Revolutionary War," pp. 818–19; Packenham, *Liberal America*, pp. 67–68, 242–86; Shafer, *Deadly Paradigms*, pp. 66–69, 126; Massoglia et al., Military Civic Action, pp. v–vii, VIII-1 thru VIII-8; Latham, *Modernization as Ideology*, pp. 5–7, 66, 211.

[18] Quote from Counterinsurgency I, Infantry Career Course 313, Infantry School, Oct 64, p. 1, Infantry School Library.

[19] Paddy Griffith, *Forward into Battle: Fighting Tactics from Waterloo to Vietnam* (Chichester, England: Anthony Bird, 1981), pp. 7–8; Wiarda, *Ethnocentrism in Foreign Policy*, p. 6; Packenham, *Liberal America*, pp. xix–xx.

[20] James Johnson, "People's War and Conventional Armies," *Military Review* 54 (January 1974): 27; DePauw and Luz, *Winning the Peace*, pp. 135–36; Shafer, *Deadly Paradigms*, p. 227; Latham, *Modernization as Ideology*, pp. 71, 197.

[21] Speech, "U.S. Army and Future Strategy," Johnson at AWC, 25 May 65, pp. 1–2, MHI.

[22] Shafer, *Deadly Paradigms*, pp. 3–4, 280; Richard Sutter, "The Strategic Implications of Military Civic Action," in DePauw and Luz, *Winning the Peace*, pp. 133–38; Wiarda, *Ethnocentrism in Foreign Policy*, pp. 9–10, 23. Quote from Latham, *Modernization as Ideology*, p. 71, and see also pp. 93, 214.

[23] Packenham, *Liberal America*, pp. 6, 18–21, 253; Shafer, *Deadly Paradigms*, pp. 49–50, 79; Wiarda, *Ethnocentrism in Foreign Policy*, p. 5.

SELECT BIBLIOGRAPHY

The extensive number of materials used makes a complete bibliography impossible. The following is a listing of the most important sources consulted.

Archival Sources

Carlisle Barracks, Pa. U.S. Army Military History Institute (MHI).
  Army War College (AWC) student papers and curricular materials.
  MACV collection.
  Military document collection.
  Personal papers and manuscript collections of Adams, Paul D.; Almond, Edward M.; Brown, Rothwell H.; DePuy, William E.; Johnson, Harold K.; Lee, Richard M.; Lindquist, Roy E.; Livesay, William G.; Palmer, Bruce, Jr.; Peers, William R.; Powell, Herbert B.; Ridgway, Matthew B.; Rosson, William B.; Van Fleet, James A.; Ward, Orlando; Williams, Samuel T.; Yarborough, William P.
Fort Benning, Ga. Infantry School. Student papers and curricular materials.
Fort Bragg, N.C. Special Warfare School. Curricular materials and history office files.
Fort Leavenworth, Kans. Command and General Staff College (CGSC). Student papers and curricular materials.
Washington, D.C. National Archives and Records Administration (NARA).
  Record Group (RG) 59, Records of the Department of State.
  RG 218, Records of the United States Joint Chiefs of Staff.
  RG 273, Records of the National Security Council.
  RG 319, Records of the Army Staff.
  RG 332, Records of the United States Theaters of War, World War II.
  RG 334, Records of Interservice Agencies.
  RG 335, Records of the Office of the Secretary of the Army.
  RG 337, Records of Headquarters Army Ground Forces.
  RG 338, Records of United States Army Commands.
  RG 472, Records of the United States Army, Vietnam.

Washington, D.C. National Security Archives. Low Intensity Conflict Document Archives.

Washington, D.C. U.S. Army Center of Military History (CMH). Historical Reference Collection.

William C. Westmoreland papers.

West Point, N.Y. U.S. Military Academy (USMA). Curricular materials.

Published Primary Sources

The Declassified Documents Reference System. Woodbridge, Conn.: Research Publications, 1986–1996.

The Declassified Documents Retrospective Collection. Washington, D.C.: Carrollton Press, 1976.

Department of State. *Foreign Relations of the United States [FRUS].* Washington, D.C.: Government Printing Office, 1970–1996.

————. *United States Relations with China.* Washington, D.C.: Government Printing Office, 1949.

Marshall's Mission to China, December 1945–January 1947: The Report and Appended Documents. 2 vols. Arlington, Va.: University Publishers of America, 1976.

The Pentagon Papers: The Defense Department History of United States Decisionmaking on Vietnam. Senator Gravel Edition, 4 vols. Boston: Beacon Press, 1971–1972.

United States–Vietnam Relations, 1945–1967: Study Prepared by Department of Defense. 12 vols. Washington, D.C.: Government Printing Office, 1971.

U.S. Army Field Manuals (FM), by Number

1–100, *Army Aviation*, 1963

6–20, *Field Artillery Tactics and Operations*, 1973

6–20–1, *Field Artillery Tactics*, 1961

6–20–1, *Field Artillery Tactics*, 1965

6–20–2, *Field Artillery Techniques*, 1962

6–20–2, *Field Artillery Techniques*, 1970

7–10, *Rifle Company, Infantry and Airborne Division Battle Groups*, 1959

7–10, *Rifle Company, Infantry and Airborne Battle Groups*, 1962

7–10, *The Rifle Company, Platoons, and Squads*, 1970

7–11, *Rifle Company, Infantry, Airborne Infantry, and Mechanized Infantry*, 1962

7–11, *Rifle Company, Infantry, Airborne, and Mechanized,* 1965

7–15, *Infantry, Airborne Infantry, and Mechanized Infantry Rifle Platoons and Squads,* 1962

7–15, *Rifle Platoon and Squads: Infantry, Airborne, and Mechanized,* 1965

7–17, *The Armored Infantry Company and Battalion,* 1951

7–20, *Infantry, Airborne Infantry, and Mechanized Infantry Battalions,* 1962

7–20, *Infantry, Airborne Infantry, and Mechanized Infantry Battalions,* 1965

7–20, *The Infantry Battalions,* 1969

7–30, *Infantry, Airborne, and Mechanized Division Brigades,* 1962

7–30, *Infantry, Airborne, and Mechanized Division Brigades,* 1965

7–30, *The Infantry Brigades,* 1969

7–40, *Infantry and Airborne Division Battle Groups,* 1959

7–100, *Infantry Division,* 1958

7–100, *Infantry Division,* 1960

17–1, *Armor Operations—Small Units,* 1957

17–1, *Armor Operations,* 1963

17–1, *Armor Operations,* 1966

17–15, *Tank Units, Platoon, Company, and Battalion,* 1966

17–30, *The Armored Division Brigade,* 1961

17–30, *The Armored Brigade,* 1969

17–95, *The Armored Cavalry Regiment,* 1966

17–100, *The Armored Division and Combat Command,* 1958

19–50, *Military Police in Stability Operations,* 1970

21–50, *Ranger Training,* 1957

21–50, *Ranger Training and Ranger Operations,* 1962

21–75, *Combat Training of the Individual Soldier and Patrolling,* 1957

21–75, *Combat Training of the Individual Soldier and Patrolling,* 1962

21–75, *Combat Training of the Individual Soldier and Patrolling,* 1967

27–5, *United States Army and Navy Manual of Military Government and Civil Affairs,* 1943

27–5, *United States Army and Navy Manual of Civil Affairs Military Government,* 1947

27–10, *The Law of Land Warfare,* 1956

30–5, *Combat Intelligence,* 1960

30–5, *Combat Intelligence,* 1963

30–5, *Combat Intelligence,* 1967

31–22, *U.S. Army Counterinsurgency Forces*, 1963
31–23, *Stability Operations: U.S. Army Doctrine*, 1967
31–23, *Stability Operations: U.S. Army Doctrine*, 1972
31–30, *Jungle Operations*, 1960
31–30, *Jungle Training and Operations*, 1965
31–35, *Jungle Operations*, 1969
31–50, *Combat in Fortified and Built-Up Areas*, 1964
31–55 (Test), *Border Security/Anti-Infiltration Operations*, 1968
31–55, *Border Security/Anti-Infiltration Operations*, 1972
31–73, *Advisor Handbook for Counterinsurgency*, 1965
31–73, *Advisor Handbook for Stability Operations*, 1967
31–75 (Test), *Riverine Operations*, 1968
31–75, *Riverine Warfare*, 1971
31–81 (Test), *Base Defense*, 1970
31–85, *Rear Area Protection Operations*, 1970
33–1, *Psychological Operations—U.S. Army Doctrine*, 1971
33–1, *Psychological Operations*, 1979
33–5, *Psychological Warfare in Combat Operations*, 1949
33–5, *Psychological Warfare Operations*, 1955
33–5, *Psychological Operations*, 1962
33–5, *Psychological Operations—Techniques and Procedures*, 1966
33–5, *Psychological Operations—Techniques and Procedures*, 1974
41–5, *Joint Manual of Civil Affairs/Military Government*, 1958
41–5, *Joint Manual for Civil Affairs*, 1966
41–10, *Civil Affairs Military Government Operations*, 1957
41–10, *Civil Affairs Operations*, 1962
41–10, *Civil Affairs Operations*, 1967
41–10, *Civil Affairs Operations*, 1969
57–35, *Airmobile Operations*, 1963
61–100, *The Division*, 1962
61–100, *The Division*, 1965
61–100, *The Division*, 1968
90–8, *Counterguerrilla Operations*, 1986
100–5, *Field Service Regulations, Operations*, 1941
100–5, *Field Service Regulations, Operations*, 1944
100–5, *Field Service Regulations, Operations*, 1949
100–5, *Field Service Regulations, Operations*, 1954
100–5, *Field Service Regulations—Operations*, 1962
100–5, *Operations of Army Forces in the Field*, 1968
100–5, *Operations*, 1976
100–15, *Larger Units, Theater Army-Corps*, 1968
100–20, *Field Service Regulations, Counterinsurgency*, 1964

100–20, *Field Service Regulations: Internal Defense and Development*, 1967

100–20, *Field Service Regulations: Internal Defense and Development*, 1972

100–20, *Internal Defense and Development, U.S. Army Doctrine*, 1974

100–20, *Low Intensity Conflict*, 1981

Dissertations

Adams, Thomas. "Military Doctrine and the Organization Culture of the U.S. Army." Syracuse University, 1990.

Avant, Deborah. "The Institutional Sources of Military Doctrine: The United States in Vietnam and Britain in the Boer War and Malaya." University of California, San Diego, 1991.

Best, Randolph. "A Doctrine of Counterinsurgency." University of South Carolina, 1973.

Bohman, Eric. "Rehearsals for Victory: The War Department and the Planning and Direction of Civil Affairs, 1940–43." Yale University, 1984.

Bowman, Stephen. "The Evolution of United States Army Doctrine for Counterinsurgency Warfare: From World War II to the Commitment of Combat Units in Vietnam." Duke University, 1985.

Carter, Donald. "From G.I. to Atomic Soldier: The Development of U.S. Army Tactical Doctrine, 1945–1956." Ohio State University, 1987.

Dawkins, Peter. "The U.S. Army and the 'Other' War in Vietnam: A Study of the Complexity of Implementing Organizational Change." Woodrow Wilson School of Public and International Affairs, 1979.

Dow, Maynard. "Counterinsurgency and Nation-Building: A Comparative Study of Post–World War II Antiguerrilla Resettlement Programs in Malaya, the Philippines, and South Vietnam." Syracuse University, 1965.

Gray, David. "Black and Gold Warriors: United States Army Rangers During the Korean War." Ohio State University, 1992.

Greenberg, David. "The United States Response to Philippine Insurgency." Fletcher School of Law and Diplomacy, Tufts University, 1994.

Kraemer, Joseph. "The Theory and Practice of Little War." University of Michigan, 1969.

McIntire, Anthony. "The American Soldier in Vietnam." University of Kentucky, 1996.

Marquis, Jefferson. "The 'Other War': An Intellectual History of American Nationbuilding in South Vietnam, 1954–1975." Ohio State University, 1997.

Merrill, John. "Internal Warfare in Korea, 1948–50: The Local Setting of the Korean War." University of Delaware, 1982.

Montgomery, Robin. "Military Civic Action and Counterinsurgency: The Birth of a Policy." University of Oklahoma, 1971.

Pancake, Frank. "Military Assistance as an Element of United States Foreign Policy in Latin America, 1950–68." University of Virginia, 1969.

Petraeus, David. "The American Military and the Lessons of Vietnam: A Study of Military Influence and the Use of Force in the Post-Vietnam Era." Woodrow Wilson School of Public and International Affairs, 1987.

Sereseres, Caesar. "Military Development and the United States Military Assistance Program for Latin America: The Case of Guatemala, 1961–69." University of California, Riverside, 1971.

Sheehan, Kevin. "Preparing for an Imaginary War? Examining Peacetime Functions and Changes of Army Doctrine." Harvard University, 1988.

Waddell, Ricky. "The Army and Peacetime Low Intensity Conflict, 1961–1993: The Process of Peripheral and Fundamental Military Change." Columbia University, 1994.

Books

Alagappa, Muthiah. *The National Security of Developing States, Lessons from Thailand*. Dover, Mass.: Auburn House, 1987.

Andrade, Dale. *Ashes to Ashes: The Phoenix Program and the Vietnam War*. Lexington, Mass.: Lexington Books, 1990.

Appleman, Roy. *South to the Naktong, North to the Yalu*. United States Army in the Korean War. Washington, D.C.: U.S. Army Center of Military History, 1961.

Arnold, James. *The First Domino: Eisenhower, the Military, and America's Intervention in Vietnam*. New York: William Morrow, 1991.

Asprey, Robert. *War in the Shadows: The Guerrilla in History*. 2 vols. Garden City, N.Y.: Doubleday, 1975.

Baclagon, Uldarico. *Lessons from the Huk Campaign in the Philippines*. Manila: M. Colcol, 1960.

Ball, Harry. *Of Responsible Command: A History of the U.S. Army War College*. Carlisle Barracks, Pa.: Alumni Association of the U.S. Army War College, 1983.

Bank, Aaron. *From OSS to Green Berets: The Birth of Special Forces.* Novato, Calif.: Presidio Press, 1986.

Barber, Willard, and Ronning, C. Neale. *Internal Security and Military Power, Counterinsurgency and Civic Action in Latin America.* Columbus: Ohio State University Press, 1966.

Beckett, Ian, ed. *The Roots of Counter-Insurgency: Armies and Guerrilla Warfare, 1900–1945.* New York: Blandford Press, 1988.

Bell, J. Bowyer. *The Myth of the Guerrilla: Revolutionary Theory and Malpractice.* New York: Alfred Knopf, 1971.

Bergerud, Eric. *The Dynamics of Defeat: The Vietnam War in Hau Nghia Province.* Boulder, Colo.: Westview Press, 1991.

————. *Red Thunder, Tropic Lightning.* Boulder, Colo.: Westview Press, 1993.

Betts, Richard. *Soldiers, Statesmen, and Cold War Crises.* Cambridge, Mass.: Harvard University Press, 1977.

Biddiscombe, Perry. *The Last Nazis: SS Werewolf Guerrilla Resistance in Europe, 1944–1947.* Charleston, S.C.: Tempus, 2000.

Birtle, Andrew. *U.S. Army Counterinsurgency and Contingency Operations Doctrine, 1860–1941.* Washington, D.C.: U.S. Army Center of Military History, 1998.

Black, Robert. *Rangers in Korea.* New York: Ivy Books, 1989.

Blasier, Cole. *The Hovering Giant: U.S. Responses to Revolutionary Change in Latin America, 1910–1985.* Pittsburgh, Pa.: University of Pittsburgh Press, 1985.

Blaufarb, Douglas. *The Counterinsurgency Era: U.S. Doctrine and Performance, 1950 to the Present.* New York: Free Press, 1977.

————, and Tanham, George. *Who Will Win?* New York: Crane, Russak and Co., 1989.

Blechman, Barry, and Kaplan, Stephen. *Force Without War: U.S. Armed Forces as a Political Instrument.* Washington, D.C.: Brookings Institution, 1978.

Bolger, Daniel. *Scenes from an Unfinished War: Low-Intensity Conflict in Korea, 1966–1969.* Fort Leavenworth, Kans.: Combat Studies Institute, 1991.

Braestrup, Peter, ed. *Vietnam as History.* Washington, D.C.: University Press of America, 1984.

Brown, Arthur. "The Strategy of Limited War." In *Military Strategy: Theory and Application, A Reference Text for the Department of Military Strategy, Planning, and Operations, 1983–1984*, edited by Arthur F. Lykke, Jr. Carlisle Barracks, Pa.: U.S. Army War College, 1983.

Brownlee, Romie, and Mullen, William. *Changing an Army: An Oral History of General William E. DePuy, USA Retired.* Washington, D.C.: U.S. Army Military History Institute and U.S. Army Center of Military History, 1988.

Buckingham, William. *Operation Ranch Hand: The Air Force and Herbicides in Southeast Asia, 1961–1971.* Washington, D.C.: Office of Air Force History, 1982.

Cable, Larry. *Conflict of Myths: The Development of American Counterinsurgency Doctrine and the Vietnam War.* New York: New York University Press, 1986.

Caldwell, J. Alexander. *American Economic Aid to Thailand.* Lexington, Mass.: D. C. Heath, 1974.

Campbell, Arthur. *Guerrillas.* New York: John Day, 1968.

Carland, John. *Combat Operations: Stemming the Tide, May 1965 to October 1966.* United States Army in Vietnam. Washington, D.C.: U.S. Army Center of Military History, 2000.

Castle, Timothy. *At War in the Shadow of Vietnam: U.S. Military Aid to the Royal Lao Government, 1955–1975.* New York: Columbia University Press, 1993.

Cecil, Paul. *Herbicidal Warfare: The Ranch Hand Project in Vietnam.* New York: Frederick A. Praeger, 1986.

Chandler, Robert. *War of Ideas: The United States Propaganda Campaign in Vietnam.* Boulder, Colo.: Westview Press, 1981.

Cheng, Christopher. *Airmobility: The Development of a Doctrine.* Westport, Conn.: Frederick A. Praeger, 1994.

Clarke, Jeffrey. *Advice and Support: The Final Years, 1965–1973.* United States Army in Vietnam. Washington, D.C.: U.S. Army Center of Military History, 1988.

Clodfelter, Michael. *Vietnam in Military Statistics: A History of the Indochina Wars, 1772–1991.* Jefferson, N.C.: McFarland, 1995.

Clutterbuck, Richard. *The Long, Long War; Counterinsurgency in Malaya and Vietnam.* New York: Frederick A. Praeger, 1966.

Coles, Harry, and Weinberg, Albert. *Civil Affairs: Soldiers Become Governors.* U.S. Army in World War II. Washington, D.C.: U.S. Army Center of Military History, 1964.

Collins, James. *The Development and Training of the South Vietnamese Army, 1950–1972.* Vietnam Studies. Washington, D.C.: Department of the Army, 1975.

Conboy, Kenneth, and Morrison, James. *Shadow War: The CIA's Secret War in Laos.* Boulder, Colo.: Paladin Press, 1995.

Condit, D. M., et al. *A Counterinsurgency Bibliography.* Washington, D.C.: American University, Special Operations Research Office, 1963.

Corr, Edwin, and Sloan, Stephen. *Low-Intensity Conflict: Old Threats in a New World.* Boulder, Colo.: Westview Press, 1992.

Crahan, Margaret, ed. *Human Rights and Basic Needs in the Americas.* Washington, D.C.: Georgetown University Press, 1982.

Cray, Edward. *General of the Army: George C. Marshall, Soldier and Statesman.* New York: W. W. Norton, 1990.

Cumings, Bruce. *The Origins of the Korean War.* 2 vols. Princeton, N.J.: Princeton University Press, 1981–1990.

Dastrup, Boyd. *King of Battle: A Branch History of the U.S. Army's Field Artillery.* Fort Monroe, Va.: HQ, Training and Doctrine Command, 1993.

DePauw, John, and Luz, George, eds. *Winning the Peace: The Strategic Implications of Military Civic Action.* Carlisle Barracks, Pa.: Strategic Studies Institute, 1990.

Doubler, Michael. *Closing with the Enemy: How GIs Fought the War in Europe, 1944–1945.* Lawrence: University Press of Kansas, 1994.

Doughty, Robert. *The Evolution of U.S. Army Tactical Doctrine, 1946–76.* Fort Leavenworth, Kans.: Combat Studies Institute, 1979.

Duiker, William. *The Communist Road to Power in Vietnam.* Boulder, Colo.: Westview Press, 1981.

Dunn, Peter. "The American Army: The Vietnam War, 1965–1973." In *Armed Forces and Modern Counter-Insurgency,* edited by Ian Beckett and John Pimlott. New York: St. Martin's Press, 1985.

Ellis, Joseph, and Moore, Robert. *School for Soldiers: West Point and the Profession of Arms.* New York: Oxford University Press, 1974.

Esterline, John, and Esterline, Mae. *"How the Dominoes Fell": Southeast Asia in Perspective.* New York: University Press of America, 1990.

Ewell, Julian, and Hunt, Ira. *Sharpening the Combat Edge: The Use of Analysis To Reinforce Military Judgment.* Vietnam Studies. Washington, D.C.: Department of the Army, 1974.

Fauriol, Georges, ed. *Latin American Insurgencies.* Washington, D.C.: National Defense University Press, 1985.

Friedrich, Carl, et al. *American Experiences in Military Government in World War II.* New York: Rinehart and Co., 1948.

Galula, David. *Counter-Insurgency Warfare.* New York: Frederick A. Praeger, 1964.

Garland, Albert, ed. *Combat Notes from Vietnam.* Fort Benning, Ga.: Infantry Magazine, 1968.

_____. *A Distant Challenge.* Fort Benning, Ga.: Infantry Magazine, 1971.

_____. *Infantry in Vietnam.* Nashville, Tenn.: Battery Press, 1982.

Gimbel, John. *The American Occupation of Germany*. Stanford, Calif.: Stanford University Press, 1968.

Glenn, Russell. *Reading Athena's Dance Card: Men Against Fire in Vietnam*. Annapolis, Md.: Naval Institute Press, 2000.

Glick, Edward. *Peaceful Conflict: The Non-Military Use of the Military*. Harrisburg, Pa.: Stackpole Books, 1967.

Gray, David. *The U.S. Intervention in Lebanon, 1958: A Commander's Reminiscence*. Fort Leavenworth, Kans.: Combat Studies Institute, 1984.

Greek Army General Staff. Welfare Directorate. *The Nation's Battle*. Athens: Hellenic Publishing, 1952.

Greenberg, Lawrence. *The Hukbalahap Insurrection: A Case Study of a Successful Anti-Insurgency Operation in the Philippines, 1944–1946*. Washington, D.C.: U.S. Army Center of Military History, 1987.

_____. *U.S. Army Unilateral and Coalition Operations in the 1965 Dominican Republic Intervention*. Washington, D.C.: U.S. Army Center of Military History, 1987.

Greene, Thomas, ed. *The Guerrilla, and How To Fight Him*. Washington, D.C.: Frederick A. Praeger, 1967.

Grinter, Lawrence. "Nation Building, Counterinsurgency, and Military Intervention." In *The Limits of Military Intervention*, edited by Ellen Stern. Beverly Hills: Sage Publishing, 1977.

Gross, Liza. *Handbook of Leftist Guerrilla Groups in Latin America and the Caribbean*. Boulder, Colo.: Westview Press, 1995.

Halliday, Jon, and Cumings, Bruce. *Korea, The Unknown War*. New York: Pantheon, 1988.

Hammer, Ellen. *The Struggle for Indochina, 1940–1955*. Stanford: Stanford University Press. 1966.

Hammond, William. *Public Affairs: The Military and the Media*. United States Army in Vietnam. 2 vols. Washington, D.C.: U.S. Army Center of Military History, 1988–1996.

Harrison, Lawrence. *Underdevelopment Is a State of Mind*. Lanham, Md.: University Press of America, 1985.

Hay, John. *Tactical and Materiel Innovations*. Vietnam Studies. Washington, D.C.: Department of the Army, 1974.

Haycock, Ronald, ed. *Regular Armies and Insurgency*. Totowa, N.J.: Rowman and Littlefield, 1979.

Head, William, and Grinter, Lawrence, eds. *Looking Back on the Vietnam War*. Westport, Conn.: Frederick A. Praeger, 1993.

Heginbotham, Eric. *The British and American Armies in World War II: Explaining Variations in Organizational Learning Patterns*.

Cambridge: Center for International Studies, Massachusetts Institute of Technology, 1996.

Heilbrunn, Otto. *Partisan Warfare*. New York: Frederick A. Praeger, 1967.

_____. *Warfare in the Enemy's Rear*. New York: Frederick A. Praeger, 1963.

Hennessy, Michael. *Strategy in Vietnam: The Marines and Revolutionary Warfare in I Corps, 1965–1972*. Westport, Conn.: Frederick A. Praeger, 1997.

Herbert, Paul. *Deciding What Has To Be Done: General William E. DePuy and the 1976 Edition of FM 100–5, Operations*. Fort Leavenworth, Kans.: Combat Studies Institute, 1988.

Hermes, Walter. *Truce Tent and Fighting Front*. United States Army in the Korean War. Washington, D.C.: U.S. Army Center of Military History, 1966.

Herring, George. *America's Longest War: The United States and Vietnam, 1950–1975*. New York: John Wiley and Sons, 1979.

Higham, Robin, ed. *Intervention or Abstention: The Dilemma of American Foreign Policy*. Lexington: University of Kentucky, 1975.

Hogan, David. *Raiders or Elite Infantry? The Changing Role of the U.S. Army Rangers from Dieppe to Grenada*. Westport, Conn.: Greenwood Press, 1992.

Howard, Michael, ed. *The Laws of War: Constraints on Warfare in the Western World*. New Haven, Conn.: Yale University Press, 1994.

Hunt, Richard. *Pacification: The American Struggle for Vietnam's Hearts and Minds*. Boulder, Colo.: Westview Press, 1995.

_____, and Shultz, Richard, eds. *Lessons from an Unconventional War: Reassessing U.S. Strategies for Future Conflicts*. New York: Pergamon Press, 1982.

Johnson, John. *The Military and Society in Latin America*. Stanford, Calif.: Stanford University Press, 1964.

Johnson, Kenneth. *Guatemala: From Terrorism to Terror*. London: Institute for the Study of Conflict, 1992.

Karnow, Stanley. *Vietnam, a History*. New York: Viking Press, 1983.

Kelly, Francis. *U.S. Army Special Forces, 1961–1971*. Vietnam Studies. Washington, D.C.: Department of the Army, 1973.

Kerdphol, Saiyud. *The Struggle for Thailand: Counterinsurgency, 1965–1985*. Bangkok: S. Research Center, 1986.

Kerkvliet, Benedict. *The Huk Rebellion: A Study of Peasant Revolt in the Philippines*. Berkeley: University of California Press, 1977.

Kessler, Richard. *Rebellion and Repression in the Philippines*. New Haven, Conn.: Yale University Press, 1989.

Khuyen, Dong Van. *The RVNAF*. Indochina Monographs. Washington, D.C.: U.S. Army Center of Military History, 1980.

Kinnard, Douglas. *The War Managers*. Hanover, N.H.: University Press of New England, 1977.

Kirk, Donald. *Wider War; The Struggle for Cambodia, Thailand, and Laos*. New York: Frederick A. Praeger, 1971.

Kirkbride, Wayne. *Special Forces in Latin America: from Bull Simons to Just Cause*. Published by Author, 1991.

Kohl, James, and Litt, John. *Urban Guerrilla Warfare in Latin America*. Cambridge: Massachusetts Institute of Technology Press, 1974.

Komer, Robert. *Bureaucracy at War: U.S. Performance in the Vietnam Conflict*. Boulder, Colo.: Westview Press, 1986.

Krepinevich, Andrew. *The Army and Vietnam*. Baltimore, Md.: Johns Hopkins University Press, 1986.

Kyre, Martin, and Kyre, Joan. *Military Occupation and National Security*. Washington, D.C.: Public Affairs Press, 1968.

Lachica, Eduardo. *The Huks: Philippine Agrarian Society in Revolt*. Washington, D.C.: Frederick A. Praeger, 1971.

Lansdale, Edward. *In the Midst of Wars*. New York: Harper & Row, 1972.

Laqueur, Walter. *Guerrilla: A Historical and Critical Study*. Boston: Little, Brown and Co., 1976.

Latham, Michael. *Modernization as Ideology: American Social Science and "Nation Building" in the Kennedy Era*. Chapel Hill: University of North Carolina Press, 2000.

Lee, Lincoln. *The Japanese Army in North China, 1937–1941*. New York: Oxford University Press, 1975.

Levinson, Jerome, and de Onis, Juan. *The Alliance That Lost Its Way*. Chicago, Ill.: Quadrangle Books, 1970.

Lewy, Gunther. *America in Vietnam*. New York: Oxford University Press, 1978.

Linebarger, Paul. *Psychological Warfare*. Washington, D.C.: Combat Forces Press, 1954.

Lobe, Thomas. *U.S. National Security Policy and Aid to the Thailand Police*. Denver, Colo.: University of Denver, 1977.

Lomperis, Timothy. *From People's War to People's Rule*. Chapel Hill: University of North Carolina Press, 1996.

Lowenthal, Abraham. *The Dominican Intervention*. Cambridge, Mass.: Harvard University Press, 1972.

————, ed. *Exporting Democracy: The United States and Latin America*. Baltimore, Md.: Johns Hopkins University Press, 1991.

_____, and Fitch, J. Samuel, eds. *Armies and Politics in Latin America*. New York: Holmes and Meier, 1986.

Lung, Hoang Ngoc. *Strategy and Tactics*. Indochina Monographs. Washington, D.C.: U.S. Army Center of Military History, 1980.

McClintock, Michael. *Instruments of Statecraft: U.S. Guerrilla Warfare, Counter-insurgency, and Counter-terrorism, 1940–1990*. New York: Pantheon Books, 1992.

McCuen, John. *The Art of Counter-Revolutionary War*. Harrisburg, Pa.: Stackpole Books, 1966.

MacGarrigle, George. *Combat Operations: Taking the Offensive, October 1966 to October 1967*. United States Army in Vietnam. Washington, D.C.: U.S. Army Center of Military History, 1998.

McNeill, William. *Greece: American Aid in Action, 1947–1956*. New York: Twentieth Century Fund, 1957.

Maechling, Charles. "Counterinsurgency: The First Ordeal by Fire." In *Low-Intensity Warfare*, edited by Michael Klare and Peter Kornbluh. New York: Pantheon, 1988.

Mansoor, Peter. *The GI Offensive in Europe: The Triumph of American Infantry Divisions, 1941–1945*. Lawrence: University Press of Kansas, 1999.

Mao Tse-tung. *Selected Military Writings of Mao Tsetung*. Peking: Foreign Language Press, 1967.

Marks, Thomas. *Thailand—the Threatened Kingdom*. London: Institute for Conflict Study, 1980.

Masland, John, and Radway, Laurence. *Soldiers and Scholars: Military Education and National Policy*. Princeton, N.J.: Princeton University Press, 1957.

Massachusetts Institute of Technology. Center for International Studies. *U.S. Foreign Policy: Economic, Social, Political Change in the Underdeveloped Countries and Its Implications for U.S. Policy*. Washington, D.C.: Government Printing Office, 1960.

Maullin, Richard. *Soldiers, Guerrillas, and Politics in Colombia*. Lexington, Mass.: D. C. Heath, 1973.

Meade, Edward. *American Military Government in Korea*. New York: Columbia University, 1951.

Melman, Seymour, ed. *In the Name of America*. Annandale, Va.: Turnpike Press, 1968.

Miklos, Jack. *The Iranian Revolution and Modernization: Way Station to Anarchy*. Washington, D.C.: National Defense University Press, 1983.

Mockaitis, Thomas. *British Counterinsurgency, 1919–60*. New York: St. Martin's Press, 1990.

Mossman, Billy. *Ebb and Flow, November 1950–July 1951*. United States Army in the Korean War. Washington, D.C.: U.S. Army Center of Military History, 1990.

Muscat, Robert. *Thailand and the United States: Development, Security, and Foreign Aid*. New York: Columbia University Press, 1990.

Needler, Martin. *The United States and the Latin American Revolutions*. Los Angeles: University of California Press, 1977.

Neel, Spurgeon. *Medical Support of the U.S. Army in Vietnam, 1965–1970*. Washington, D.C.: Department of the Army, 1973.

Ney, Virgil. *Notes on Guerrilla War: Principles and Practices*. Washington, D.C.: Command Publications, 1961.

Nighswonger, William. *Rural Pacification in Vietnam*. New York: Frederick A. Praeger, 1966.

O'Ballance, Edgar. *The Greek Civil War, 1944–1949*. Washington, D.C.: Frederick A. Praeger, 1966.

_____. *The Indo-China War, 1945–1954*. London: Faber and Faber, 1964.

Osanka, Franklin, ed. *Modern Guerrilla Warfare; Fighting Communist Guerrilla Movements, 1941–1961*. Glencoe, Ill.: Free Press, 1962.

Osgood, Robert. *Limited War: The Challenge to American Strategy*. Chicago, Ill.: University of Chicago Press, 1957.

Ott, David. *Field Artillery, 1954–1973*. Vietnam Studies. Washington, D.C.: Department of the Army, 1975.

Packenham, Robert. *Liberal America and the Third World*. Princeton, N.J.: Princeton University Press, 1973.

Paddock, Alfred. *U.S. Army Special Warfare: Its Origins—Psychological and Unconventional Warfare, 1941–1952*. Washington, D.C.: Government Printing Office, 1982.

Paik, Sun Yup. *From Pusan to Panmunjom*. Washington, D.C.: Brassey's, 1992.

Palmer, Bruce, Jr. *Intervention in the Caribbean: The Dominican Crisis of 1965*. Lexington: University of Kentucky Press, 1989.

Palmer, Dave. *Summons of the Trumpet*. San Rafael, Calif.: Presidio Press, 1978.

Paret, Peter. *French Revolutionary Warfare from Indochina to Algeria*. Washington, D.C.: Frederick A. Praeger, 1964.

_____, and Shy, John. *Guerrillas in the 1960s*. New York: Frederick A. Praeger, 1962.

Peterson, Michael. *The Combined Action Platoons*. New York: Frederick A. Praeger, 1989.

Prete, Roy, and Ion, A. Hamish. *Armies of Occupation*. Waterloo, Canada: Wilfred Laurier University Press, 1984.

Prugh, George. *Law at War: Vietnam, 1964–1973*. Vietnam Studies. Washington, D.C.: Department of the Army, 1975.

Pustay, John. *Counterinsurgency Warfare*. New York: Free Press, 1965.

Rabe, Stephen. *Eisenhower and Latin America*. Chapel Hill: University of North Carolina Press, 1988.

————. *The Most Dangerous Area in the World: John F. Kennedy Confronts Communist Revolution in Latin America*. Chapel Hill: University of North Carolina Press, 1999.

Rigg, Robert. *Red China's Fighting Hordes*. Harrisburg, Pa.: Military Service Publishing Company, 1952.

Rogers, Bernard. *Cedar Falls–Junction City: A Turning Point*. Vietnam Studies. Washington, D.C.: Department of the Army, 1974.

Rostow, Walt. *Eisenhower, Kennedy, and Foreign Aid: Ideas and Actions*. Austin: University of Texas Press, 1985.

————. *The Stages of Economic Growth: A Non-Communist Manifesto*. New York: Cambridge University Press, 1960.

Sananikone, Oudone. *The Royal Lao Army and U.S. Army Advice and Support*. Indochina Monographs. Washington, D.C.: U.S. Army Center of Military History, 1981.

Sawyer, Robert. *Military Advisors in Korea: KMAG in Peace and War*. Army Historical Series. Washington, D.C.: U.S. Army Center of Military History, 1962.

Scaff, Alvin. *The Philippine Answer to Communism*. Stanford, Calif.: Stanford University Press, 1955.

Scales, Robert. *Firepower in Limited War*. Washington, D.C.: National Defense University, 1990.

Scheman, L. Ronald, ed. *The Alliance for Progress: A Retrospective*. New York: Frederick A. Praeger, 1988.

Shafer, D. Michael. *Deadly Paradigms: The Failure of U.S. Counterinsurgency Policy*. Princeton, N.J.: Princeton University Press, 1988.

Shrader, Charles. *The Withered Vine: Logistics and the Communist Insurgency in Greece, 1945–1949*. Westport, Conn.: Frederick A. Praeger, 1999.

Shulimson, Jack. *U.S. Marines in Vietnam: An Expanding War, 1966*. Washington, D.C.: Histories and Museums Division, U.S. Marine Corps, 1982.

Shy, John, and Collier, Thomas. "Revolutionary War." In *Makers of Modern Strategy*, edited by Peter Paret. Princeton, N.J.: Princeton University Press, 1986.

Simpson, Charles. *Inside the Green Berets: The First Thirty Years*. Novato, Calif.: Presidio Press, 1983.

Slater, Jerome. *Intervention and Negotiation: The United States and the Dominican Republic.* New York: Harper & Row, 1970.

Smith, Brian. "United States–Latin American Military Relations Since World War II: Implications for Human Rights." In *Human Rights and Basic Needs in the Americas,* edited by Margaret Crahan. Washington, D.C.: Georgetown University Press, 1982.

Sorley, Lewis. *Honorable Warrior: General Harold K. Johnson and the Ethics of Command.* Lawrence: University of Kansas, 1998.

Spector, Ronald. *Advice and Support: The Early Years, 1941–1960.* United States Army in Vietnam. Washington, D.C.: U.S. Army Center of Military History, 1983.

Spiller, Roger. *'Not War But Like War': The American Intervention in Lebanon.* Fort Leavenworth, Kans.: Combat Studies Institute, 1981.

Stanton, Shelby. *The Rise and Fall of an American Army, U.S. Ground Forces in Vietnam, 1965–1973.* Novato, Calif.: Presidio Press, 1985.

Summers, Harry. *On Strategy: The Vietnam War in Context.* Carlisle Barracks, Pa.: Strategic Studies Institute, 1981.

———. "The United States Army's Institutional Response to Vietnam." In *Proceedings of the 1982 International Military History Symposium: The Impact of Unsuccessful Military Campaigns on Military Institutions, 1860–1980,* edited by Charles Shrader. Washington, D.C.: U.S. Army Center of Military History, 1984.

Suter, Keith. *An International Law of Guerrilla Warfare: The Global Politics of Law Making.* New York: St. Martin's Press, 1984.

Taber, Robert. *The War of the Flea: A Study of Guerrilla Warfare Theory and Practise.* New York: Lyle Stuart, 1965.

Tanham, George. *Trial in Thailand.* New York: Crane, Russak and Co., 1974.

———. *War Without Guns: American Civilians in Rural Vietnam.* New York: Frederick A. Praeger, 1966.

Telfer, Gary; Rogers, Lane; and Fleming, V. Keith. *U.S. Marines in Vietnam: Fighting the North Vietnamese, 1967.* Washington, D.C.: History and Museums Division, U.S. Marine Corps, 1984.

Tent, James. *Mission on the Rhine: Reeducation and Denazification in American-Occupied Germany.* Chicago, Ill.: University of Chicago Press, 1982.

Thompson, Robert. *Defeating Communist Insurgency: The Lessons of Malaya and Vietnam.* New York: Frederick A. Praeger, 1966.

Thompson, W. Scott, and Frizzell, Donaldson, eds. *The Lessons of Vietnam.* New York: Crane, Russak and Co., 1977.

Trooboff, Peter, ed. *Law and Responsibility in Warfare: The Vietnam Experience.* Chapel Hill: University of North Carolina Press, 1975.

Valeriano, Napoleon, and Bohannan, Charles. *Counter-Guerrilla Operations: The Philippine Experience.* Washington, D.C.: Frederick A. Praeger, 1962.

Vega, Luis. *Guerrillas in Latin America.* Translated by Daniel Weissbort. New York: Frederick A. Praeger, 1969.

Vetock, Dennis. *Lessons Learned: A History of U.S. Army Lesson Learning.* Carlisle Barracks, Pa.: U.S. Army Military History Institute, 1988.

Volckmann, Russell. *We Remained.* New York: W. W. Norton, 1954.

Wade, Gary. *Rapid Deployment Logistics: Lebanon, 1958.* Fort Leavenworth, Kans.: Combat Studies Institute, 1984.

Walterhouse, Harry. *A Time To Build: Military Civic Action—Medium for Economic Development and Social Reform.* Columbia: University of South Carolina Press, 1964.

Warner, Roger. *Back Fire: The CIA's Secret War in Laos and Its Link to the War in Vietnam.* New York: Simon & Schuster, 1995.

Wedemeyer, Albert. *Wedemeyer Reports!* New York: Henry Holt, 1958.

Wells, Donald. *The Laws of Land Warfare: A Guide to Army Manuals.* Westport, Conn.: Greenwood Press, 1992.

Westmoreland, William. *A Soldier Reports.* Garden City, N.Y.: Doubleday, 1976.

Whiting, Charles. *Werewolf: The Story of the Nazi Resistance Movement, 1944–1945.* Barnsley, England: Pen & Sword Books, 1996.

Wiarda, Howard. *Ethnocentrism in Foreign Policy: Can We Understand the Third World?* Washington, D.C.: American Enterprise Institute for Public Policy Research, 1985.

Wickham-Crowley, Timothy. *Guerrillas and Revolution in Latin America.* Princeton, N.J.: Princeton University Press, 1992.

Wiesner, Louis. *Victims and Survivors: Displaced Persons and Other War Victims in Viet-Nam, 1954–1975.* New York: Greenwood Press, 1988.

Wilson, John. *Maneuver and Firepower: The Evolution of Divisions and Separate Brigades.* Army Lineage Series. Washington, D.C.: U.S. Army Center of Military History, 1998.

Wittner, Lawrence. *American Intervention in Greece, 1943–1949.* New York: Columbia University Press, 1982.

Wolfe, Robert, ed. *Americans as Proconsuls: United States Military Government in Germany and Japan, 1944–1952.* Carbondale: Southern Illinois University Press, 1984.

Wolpin, Miles. *Military Aid and Counterrevolution in the Third World.* Lexington, Mass.: Lexington Books, 1972.

Wyatt, David. *Thailand: A Short History.* New Haven, Conn.: Yale University Press, 1984.

Yates, Lawrence. "A Feather in Their Cap? The Marines Combined Action Program in Vietnam." In *New Interpretations in Naval History,* edited by William Roberts and Jack Sweetman. Annapolis, Md.: Naval Institute Press, 1991.

————. *Power Pack: U.S. Intervention in the Dominican Republic.* Fort Leavenworth, Kans.: Combat Studies Institute, 1988.

Ziemke, Earl. *The U.S. Army in the Occupation of Germany, 1944–1946.* Army Historical Series. Washington, D.C.: U.S. Army Center of Military History, 1975.

Studies and Monographs

Aerospace Studies Institute. U.S. Air Force Air University. Guerrilla Warfare and Airpower in Korea, 1950–1953. 1964.

Baldwin, Ben, et al. Case Study of United States Counterinsurgency Operations in Laos, 1955–1962. RAC–T–435. Research and Analysis Corporation, 1964.

Barton, Fred. Operational Aspects of Paramilitary Warfare in South Korea. ORO–T–25 (FEC). Chevy Chase, Md.: Operations Research Office, Johns Hopkins University, 1952.

————. Salient Operational Aspects of Paramilitary Warfare in Three Asian Areas. ORO–T–228. Chevy Chase, Md.: Operations Research Office, Johns Hopkins University, 1953.

Blaufarb, Douglas. Organizing and Managing Unconventional Warfare in Laos, 1962–1970. RAND–R–919–ARPA. Santa Monica, Calif.: RAND, 1972.

Blumstein, Alfred, and Orlansky, Jesse. Behavioral, Political, and Operational Research Programs on Counterinsurgency Supported by the Department of Defense. Study S–190. Institute for Defense Analyses, 1965.

Boatner, James. American Tactical Units in Revolutionary Development Operations. Report 3570. Air War College, Air University, 1968.

Clark, Dorothy, et al. A History of Insurgency and Counterinsurgency in Thailand. 2 vols. Research and Analysis Corporation, 1970.

Cleaver, Frederick, et al. UN Partisan Warfare in Korea, 1951–1954. ORO–T–64 (AFFE). Chevy Chase, Md.: Operations Research Office, Johns Hopkins University, 1956.

Condit, D. M. Challenge and Response in Internal Conflict. 3 vols. Center for Research in Social Systems, 1968.

Cooper, Chester. The American Experience with Pacification in Vietnam. R–185. 3 vols. Institute for Defense Analyses, 1972.

Daugherty, William, and Andrews, Marshall. A Review of U.S. Historical Experience with Civil Affairs, 1776–1954. Operations Research Office Technical Paper, ORO–TP–29. Chevy Chase, Md.: Operations Research Office, Johns Hopkins University, 1961.

Davison, W. Phillips. Political Side-Effects of the Military Assistance Training Program. RM–2604. Santa Monica, Calif.: RAND, 1960.

_____, and Hungerford, Jean. North Korean Guerrilla Units. RM–550. Santa Monica, Calif.: RAND, 1951.

Department of the Army. Rear Area Security in Russia. DA PAM 20–240. July 1951.

Edwards, T. I. An Index of RAND Corporation Publications on Tactical Warfare and Counterinsurgency. RM 4145–2–PR. Santa Monica, Calif.: RAND, 1986.

Einaudi, Luigi, and Stepan, Alfred. Latin American Institutional Development: Changing Military Perspectives in Peru and Brazil. R–586–DOS. Santa Monica, Calif.: RAND, 1971.

Galula, David. Pacification in Algeria, 1956–1958. RM–3878–ARPA. Santa Monica, Calif.: RAND, 1963.

Gardner, Hugh. Civil War in Greece, 1945–1949. Washington, D.C.: U.S. Army Center of Military History, n.d.

_____. Guerrilla and Counterguerrilla Warfare in Greece, 1941–1945. Washington, D.C.: Office of the Chief of Military History, 1962.

Hanrahan, Gene. Asian Guerrilla Movements. ORO–T–244. Chevy Chase, Md.: Operations Research Office, Johns Hopkins University, 1953.

_____. Chinese Communist Guerrilla Tactics. Columbia University, 1952.

_____. Japanese Operations Against Guerrilla Forces. ORO–T–268. Chevy Chase, Md.: Operations Research Office, Johns Hopkins University, 1954.

Hausrath, Alfred. Civil Affairs in the Cold War. ORO–SP–151. Bethesda, Md.: Operations Research Office, Johns Hopkins University, 1961.

Havron, M. Dean, et al. A Counterinsurgency Guide for Area Commanders: A Criteria Study. Human Sciences Research, 1965.

Hermes, Walter. Survey of the Development of the Role of the U.S. Army Military Advisor. Washington, D.C.: Office of the Chief of Military History, 1965.

Heymann, H., and Whitson, W. W. Can and Should the United States Preserve a Military Capability for Revolutionary Conflict? R–940–ARPA. Santa Monica, Calif.: RAND, 1972.

Hickey, G. C. The American Military Advisor and His Foreign Counterpart: The Case of Vietnam. RM–4482–ARPA. Santa Monica, Calif.: RAND, 1965.

Historical Evaluation and Research Organization (HERO). Isolating the Guerrilla. 3 vols. Washington, D.C.: HERO, 1966.

Hoag, C. Leonard. American Military Government in Korea, War Policy and the First Year of Occupation, 1941–1946. OCMH–76, Washington, D.C.: Office of the Chief of Military History, 1970.

Holbrook, R., et al. Counterinsurgency Studies in Latin America—Venezuela and Colombia. Defense Research Corporation, 1965.

Holliday, L. P., et al. Final Report: Seminar on Area Security and Development (Pacification). RM–5923–ARPA. Santa Monica, Calif.: RAND, June 1969.

Houk, John. Motivating Populations To Support Counterinsurgency. 2 vols. Special Operations Research Office, 1965.

Howell, Edgar. The Soviet Partisan Movement, 1941–1944. DA PAM 20–244, 1956.

Hribar, Arthur. Partisan Warfare. n.d., U.S. Army Center of Military History.

Human Resources Research Institute. The Soviet Partisan Movement in World War II: Summary and Conclusions. Research Memo 26. 2 vols. January 1954.

Kennedy, Robert. German Antiguerrilla Operations in the Balkans. DA PAM 20–243, 1954.

Komer, Robert. The Malayan Emergency in Retrospect: Organization of a Successful Counterinsurgency Effort. R–957–ARPA. Santa Monica, Calif.: RAND, 1972.

Kraemer, Alfred. Promoting Civic Action in Less Developed Nations: A Conceptualization of the U.S. Military Mission Role. Human Resources Research Organization, 1968.

Krepinevich, Andrew. The U.S. Army and Vietnam: Counterinsurgency Doctrine and the Army Concept of War. Fort Bragg, N.C.: U.S. Army John F. Kennedy Special Warfare Center, 1984.

Leighton, Richard, et al. The Huk Rebellion: A Case Study in the Social Dynamics of Insurrection. R–231. Washington, D.C.: Industrial College of the Armed Forces, 1964.

Leites, Nathan, and Wolf, Charles. Rebellion and Authority: An Analytic Essay on Insurgent Conflicts. R–462–ARPA, Santa Monica, Calif.: RAND, 1970.

Lindsay, Michael. China, 1937–1945. Working paper. Special Operations Research Office, 1965.

Lord, John, et al. A Study of Rear Area Security Measures. Special Operations Research Office, American University, 1965.

McMullan, Philip, et al. Military Civic Action. 2 vols. Research Triangle Institute, 1972.

Massoglia, Martin, et al. Military Civic Action, Evaluation of Military Techniques. Research Triangle Institute, 1971.

Operations Research Office. Force-Tie-Down Capabilities of Guerrillas in Malaya. ORO T–72. Chevy Chase, Md.: Operations Research Office, Johns Hopkins University, 1957.

_____. Guerrilla Warfare in the Federation of Malaya. ORO T–44. Chevy Chase, Md.: Operations Research Office, Johns Hopkins University, 1952.

_____. Psychological Warfare and Other Factors Affecting the Surrender and Disaffection Among Communist Terrorists in Malaya. ORO T–296. Chevy Chase, Md.: Operations Research Office, Johns Hopkins University, 1955.

Osanka, Franklin. Counterinsurgency Training: A Select Bibliography. Human Resources Research Organization, 1962.

Pye, Lucian. Lessons from the Malayan Struggle Against Communism. Center for International Studies, Massachusetts Institute of Technology, 1957.

Rambo, A. Terry. The Causes of Refugee Movement in Vietnam: Report of Survey of Refugees in I and IV Corps. Human Sciences Research, 1968.

_____. The Causes of Vietnamese Refugee Movement: An Analysis of Factors Contributing to Refugee Migration in Thuong Duc District, Quang Nam Province. Human Sciences Research, 1967.

RAND. Counterinsurgency: A Symposium, 16–20 April 1962. Santa Monica, Calif.: RAND, 1963.

Ronfeldt, David, and Einaudi, Luigi. Internal Security and Military Assistance to Latin America in the 1970s: A First Statement. R–924–ISA. Santa Monica, Calif.: RAND, 1971.

Siliver, Solomon. Counter-Insurgency and Nation Building: A Study with Emphasis on South East Asia. Washington, D.C.: U.S. Agency for International Development, 1967.

Smith, Robert Ross. The Hukbalahap Insurgency: Economic, Political, and Military Factors. Office of the Chief of Military History, 1963.

Special Operations Research Office. Insurgents and Counterinsurgent Strengths and Tactics in Tunisia, 1952–1956. Washington, D.C.: American University, 1956.

_____. Symposium Proceedings. The U.S. Army's Limited-War Mission and Social Science Research. 26, 27, 28 March 1962. Washington, D.C.: American University, 1962.

Stolzenbach, Darwin, and Kissinger, Henry. Civil Affairs in Korea, 1950–1951. ORO–T–184. Baltimore, Md.: Operations Research Office, Johns Hopkins University, 1952.

Tanham, George. Doctrine and Tactics of Revolutionary Warfare: The Viet Minh in Indochina. RM 2395. Santa Monica, Calif.: RAND, 1959.

Taw, Jennifer. Thailand and the Philippines, Case Studies in U.S. IMET Training and Its Role in Internal Defense and Development. Santa Monica, Calif.: RAND, 1994.

Thayer, Thomas, ed. A Systems Analysis View of the Vietnam War, 1965–1972. Office of the Deputy Assistant Secretary of Defense (Systems Analysis), 1974. U.S. Army Center of Military History.

U.S. Army Forces Far East. Japanese Studies on Manchuria. Book IV. Historical Observations of Various Operations in Manchuria. 1955.

U.S. Army Psychological Warfare School. Guerrilla Warfare. 1953.

Vigneras, Marcel. Impact of Guerrilla Action on Logistics in Limited War. ORO–SP–172. Chevy Chase, Md.: Operations Research Office, Johns Hopkins University, 1961.

Von Luttichau, Charles. Guerrilla and Counterguerrilla Warfare in Russia During World War II. Washington, D.C.: Office of the Chief of Military History, 1963.

Waldman, Eric. German Occupation Administration and Experience in the USSR. ORO–T–301. Chevy Chase, Md.: Operations Research Office, Johns Hopkins University, 1955.

_____. German Use of Indigenous Auxiliary Police in the Occupied USSR. ORO–T–320. Chevy Chase, Md.: Operations Research Office, Johns Hopkins University, 1955.

Williams, T. A., and Homesley, Horace. Small Unit Combat Experience, Vietnam, 1966–1967. Booz Allen Applied Research, 1967.

Wolf, Charles. Insurgency and Counterinsurgency: New Myths and Old Realities. P–3132–1. Santa Monica, Calif.: RAND, 1965.

Wood, Carlton, et al. Civil Affairs Relations in Korea. ORO–T–2464. Baltimore, Md.: Operations Research Office, Johns Hopkins University, 1954.

Foreign Military Studies Monographs

Studies done by former German officers for the U.S. Army. Located at NARA.

Gaisser, Karl. Partisan Warfare in Croatia. P–055b. 1950.
Greiffenberg, Hans von. Small Unit Tactics—Partisan Warfare. P–060E. 1952.
Halder, Franz, et al. Analysis of U.S. Field Service Regulations. P–133. 1953.
Haselmayr, Friedrich. Small Scale Warfare in Western Ukraine. D–261.
Kesselring, Albert. The War Behind the Front: Guerrilla Warfare. C–032. 1950.
Lanz, Hubert. Partisan Warfare in the Balkans. P–055a.
Ratcliffe, Alexander. Lessons Learned from the Partisan War in Russia. P–055c.
_____. Partisan Warfare: A Treatise Based on Combat Experience in the Balkans. P–142. 1953.

Articles

Ahearn, Arthur. "Medicine in Internal Defense." *Military Review* 47 (September 1967): 67–72.
Alpern, Stephen. "Insurgency in Thailand: An Analysis of the Government Response." *Military Review* 55 (July 1955): 10–17.
"Antiguerrilla Operations." *Officer's Call* 3 (March 1951): 1–15.
"Armies Can Be Builders." *Army Information Digest* 20 (February 1965): 16–19.
Arnold, Gary. "IMET in Latin America." *Military Review* 67 (February 1987): 30–41.
Atkinson, James. "The Impact of Soviet Theory on Warfare as a Continuation of Politics." *Military Affairs* 24 (Spring 1960): 1–6.
Auletta, Anthony. "Ten-Nation Progress Report." *Army* 13 (July 1963): 53–59.
Baker, John, and Dickson, Lee. "Army Forces in Riverine Operations." *Military Review* 47 (August 1967): 64–74.
Balcos, Anastase. "Guerrilla Warfare." *Military Review* 38 (March 1958): 49–54.
Barrett, Raymond. "The Development Process and Stability Operations." *Military Review* 52 (November 1972): 58–68.
_____. "Graduated Response and the Lessons of Vietnam." *Military Review* 52 (May 1972): 80–91.
_____. "Updating Civil Affairs Doctrine and Organization." *Military Review* 54 (July 1974): 50–61.
Bartlett, Merrill. "The Communist Insurgency in Thailand." *Marine Corps Gazette* 57 (March 1973): 42–49.

Bashore, Boyd. "Dual Strategy for Limited War." *Military Review* 40 (May 1960): 46–62.

————. "The Name of the Game Is Search and Destroy." *Army* 17 (February 1967): 56–59.

————. "Organization for Frontless War." *Military Review* 44 (May 1964): 3–16.

————. "The Parallel Hierarchies, Parts I and II." *Infantry* 58 (May–June 1968): 5–8, and 58 (July–August 1968): 11–15.

"Battle Lore." *Army Information Digest* 22 (July 1967): 40–43.

"Battle Lore." *Army Information Digest* 22 (September 1967): 17–20.

Beaumont, Roger. "The Military Utility of Limited War." *Military Review* 47 (May 1967): 53–57.

Beebe, John. "Beating the Guerrilla." *Military Review* 35 (December 1955): 3–18.

Bentz, Harold. "Psychological Warfare and Civic Action." *Army* 13 (July 1963): 62–65.

Berry, Sidney. "Observations of a Brigade Commander, Parts I, II, and III." *Military Review* 48 (January 1968): 3–21; 48 (February 1968): 54–66; and 48 (March 1968): 31–48.

Biggio, Charles. "Let's Learn from the French." *Military Review* 46 (October 1966): 27–34.

Bjelajac, Slavko. "Malaya: Case History in Area Operations." *Army* 12 (May 1962): 30–40.

————. "Psywar: The Lessons from Algeria." *Military Review* 42 (December 1962): 2–7.

Blackledge, David. "ROTC Counterguerrillas." *Infantry* 53 (January–February 1963): 49–50.

Block, Thomas. "Quick Fire." *Infantry* 54 (January–February 1964): 18–19.

Boatner, Mark. "The Unheeded History of Counterinsurgency." *Army* 16 (September 1966): 31–36.

Bodron, Margaret. "U.S. Intervention in Lebanon—1958." *Military Review* 56 (February 1976): 66–76.

Bohannan, Charles. "Antiguerrilla Operations." *Annals* 341 (May 1962): 19–29.

Bonesteel, Charles. "U.S.–South Korean Partnership Holds a Truculent North at Bay." *Army* 19 (October 1969): 59–63.

Booth, Waller. "Operation Swamprat." *U.S. Army Combat Forces Journal* 1 (October 1950): 23–26.

————. "The Pattern That Got Lost." *Army* 31 (April 1981): 62–67.

Bourdow, Joseph. "Big War Guerrillas and Counter-Guerrillas." *Army* 13 (August 1962): 66–69.

Bricker, Bill. "The S–2 in Counter Guerrilla Operations." *Infantry* 56 (July–August 1966): 12–15.

Brown, Frank. "Pass on that Combat Lore." *Army* 16 (September 1966): 56–68.

Brown, Michael. "Vietnam, Learning from the Debate." *Military Review* 67 (February 1987): 48–55.

Buchanan, William, and Hyatt, Robert. "Building a Counterinsurgent Political Infrastructure." *Military Review* 48 (September 1968): 25–41.

_____. "Capitalizing on Guerrilla Vulnerabilities." *Military Review* 48 (August 1968): 3–40.

Burke, Robert. "Military Civic Action." *Military Review* 44 (October 1964): 62–71.

Cannon, Michael. "The Development of the American Theory of Limited War, 1945–1963." *Armed Forces and Society* 9 (Fall 1992): 71–104.

Carmichael, Robert, and Eckert, Richard. "Operation New Life." *Infantry* 57 (January–February 1967): 43–47.

"Characteristics of Guerrilla Operations." *Infantry* 52 (May–June 1962): 9, 64–66.

Clingham, James. "'All American' Team Work." *Army Information Digest* 22 (January 1967): 19–23.

Clutterbuck, Richard. "Communist Defeat in Malaya: A Case Study." *Military Review* 43 (September 1963): 63–78.

Codo, Enrique. "The Urban Guerrilla." *Military Review* 51 (August 1971): 3–10.

Cole, Earl. "Replacement Operations in Vietnam." *Military Review* 48 (February 1968): 3–8.

Coles, Harry. "Strategic Studies Since 1945, the Era of Overthink." *Military Review* 53 (April 1973): 3–16.

Collier, Thomas. "Partisans, the Forgotten Force." *Infantry School Quarterly* (August–September 1960): 4–8.

"Considerations in Fighting Irregular Forces." *Infantry* 52 (July–August 1962): 8–9, 39–41.

Cornett, Jack. "Jungle Bashing." *Infantry* 52 (May–June 1962): 18–20.

"Counterguerrilla Units Flourish in ROTC." *Army Reservist* 9 (April 1963): 15.

Curtin, Edwin. "American Advisory Group Aids Greece in War of Guerrillas." *Armored Cavalry Journal* 58 (January–February 1949): 8–11, 34–35.

Daley, John. "U.S. Army Combat Developments Command." *Army Information Digest* 17 (September 1962): 13–18.

Davenport, Robert. "Barrier Along the Korean DMZ." *Infantry* 57 (May–June 1967): 40–42.

"Defense in the Jungle." *Infantry* 52 (March–April 1962): 53–54.

Dexter, George. "Search and Destroy in Vietnam." *Infantry* 56 (July–August 1966): 36–42.

Dials, George. "Find, Fix and Finish." *Infantry* 60 (September–October 1970): 23–25.

Dickerson, William. "Advisor on Combat Operations." *Army* 13 (November 1962): 65–66.

Dillon, Dana. "Comparative Counter-Insurgency Strategies in the Philippines." *Small Wars and Insurgencies* 6 (Winter 1995): 281–303.

Dominguez, Jorge. "Responses to Occupations by the United States: Calibans' Dilemma." *Pacific Historical Review* 48 (1979): 591–605.

Downen, Robert. "Jungle Attacks." *Infantry* 52 (March–April 1962): 40–41.

Downey, Edward. "Theory of Guerrilla Warfare." *Military Review* 39 (May 1959): 45–55.

Easterbrook, Ernest. "Guerrilla Training Is Standard Fare for 25th Division." *Army, Navy, Air Force Journal and Register* 99 (4 August 1962): 15–16.

_____. "Realism in Counterinsurgency Training." *Army Information Digest* 17 (October 1962): 12–21.

Ekman, Michael. "Lessons Learned as a Company Commander." *Infantry* 57 (July–August 1967): 20–22.

Fairbairn, Geoffrey. "Approaches to Counter-Insurgency Thinking Since 1947." *South-East Asian Spectrum* 2 (January 1974): 21–32.

Fall, Bernard. "Indochina: The Last Year of the War, Communist Organization and Tactics." *Military Review* 36 (October 1956): 1–11.

_____. "Indochina: The Last Year of the War, The Navarre Plan." *Military Review* 36 (December 1956): 48–56.

Fisher, Albert. "To Beat the Guerrillas at Their Own Game." *Military Review* 43 (December 1963): 81–86.

Fletcher, James. "Psychology in Civic Action." *Infantry* 53 (November–December 1963): 18–21.

Foland, Frances. "Agrarian Reform in Latin America." *Foreign Affairs* 48 (October 1969): 97–112.

Galvin, John. "Three Innovations: Prime Tactical Lessons of the Vietnam War." *Army* 22 (March 1972): 16–20.

Gann, Lewis. "Guerrillas and Insurgency: An Interpretive Survey." *Military Review* 46 (March 1966): 44–59.

Gates, John. "Peoples' War in Vietnam." *Journal of Military History* 54 (July 1990): 325–44.

Gazlay, John. "Rx the Insurgent: Locate, Isolate, Eradicate." 2 pts. *Armor* 80 (November–December 1971): 39–45; 81 (January–February 1972): 46–52.

"German Antipartisan Operation in Russia: Attack on a Partisan Headquarters." *Infantry* 53 (May–June 1963): 29–32.

"German Antipartisan Operation in Russia: The Forrest Camp." *Infantry* 53 (March–April 1963): 19–21.

"German Tactics of Combating Guerrillas." *Military Review* 24 (June 1944): 104–06.

Gillert, Gustav. "Counterinsurgency." *Military Review* 45 (April 1965): 25–33.

Girouard, Richard. "District Intelligence in Vietnam." *Armor* 75 (November–December 1966): 10–14.

Glick, Edward. "Military Civic Action: Thorny Art of the Peace Keepers." *Army* 17 (September 1967): 67–70.

Graham, Barry. "Mechanized Forces in Vietnam." *Infantry* 59 (July–August 1969): 45–48.

Graves, Patrick. "Observations of a Platoon Leader." 3 pts. *Infantry* 57 (May–June 1967): 34–38; 57 (July–August 1967): 25–29; and 57 (September–October 1967): 42–47.

Gray, David. "When We Fight a Small War." *Army* 10 (July 1960): 26–34.

"The Greek Guerrillas—How They Operate." *Intelligence Review* 156 (March 1949): 27–36.

Greenberg, Lawrence. "The U.S. Dominican Intervention: Success Story." *Parameters* 17 (December 1987): 18–29.

Greenspan, Morris. "International Law and Its Protection for Participants in Unconventional Warfare." *Annals* 341 (May 1962): 30–41.

Griffin, William. "Army Aviation in Support of Counterguerrilla Operations." *U.S. Army Aviation Digest* 8 (September 1962): 9–14.

Griffith, Samuel B. "Guerrilla." 2 pts. *Antiaircraft Journal* 93 (September–October 1950): 15–18, and 93 (November–December 1950): 50–53.

Grimland, Neal. "The Formidable Guerrilla." *Army* 12 (February 1962): 63–66.

Grinter, Lawrence. "How They Lost: Doctrines, Strategies and Outcomes of the Vietnam War." *Asian Survey* 15 (December 1975): 1114–32.

Grossman, Frank. "Artillery in Vietnam." *Ordnance* 52 (November–December 1967): 268–71.

Guelzo, Carl. "The Higher Level Staff Advisor." *Military Review* 47 (February 1967): 92–98.

"Guerrilla Warfare—As the High Command Sees It." *Army* 12 (March 1962): 42–44.

Guthrie, William. "Korea: The Other DMZ." *Infantry* 60 (March–April 1970): 17–22.

Hackworth, David. "Baptism to Command." *Infantry* 57 (November–December 1967): 38–43.

_____. "Guerrilla Battalion, U.S. Style." *Infantry* 61 (January–February 1971): 22–28.

_____. "Hedgerows of Vietnam." *Infantry* 57 (May–June 1967): 3–7.

_____. "No Magic Formula." *Infantry* 57 (January–February 1967): 33–47.

_____. "Target Acquisition Vietnam Style." *Military Review* 48 (April 1968): 73–79.

_____. "Your Mission—Out-Guerrilla the Guerrilla." *Army Information Digest* 23 (July 1968): 61–62.

Hallenbeck, Ralph. "Combat Wedge." *Infantry* 59 (January–February 1969): 43–44.

Hallock, Donald. "No Battle Is Lost." *Army Information Digest* 22 (January 1967): 6–9.

Harmon, Christopher. "Illustrations of 'Learning' in Counterinsurgency." *Comparative Strategy* 11 (January–March 1992): 29–48.

Harrigan, Anthony. "Ground Warfare in Vietnam." *Military Review* 47 (April 1967): 60–67.

Hauser, William. "Fire and Maneuver." *Infantry* 60 (September–October 1970): 12–15.

Heilbrunn, Otto. "A Doctrine for Counterinsurgents." *Marine Corps Gazette* 48 (February 1964): 31–38.

Heiman, Leo. "Guerrilla Warfare: An Analysis." *Military Review* 43 (July 1963): 26–36.

Henry, Tom. "Techniques from Trung Lap." *Army* 14 (April 1964): 35–43.

Heymont, Irving. "Armed Forces and National Development." *Military Review* 49 (December 1969): 50–55.

_____. "The U.S. Army and Foreign National Development." *Military Review* 51 (November 1971): 17–23.

Hilbert, Marquis, and Murray, Everett. "Use of Army Aviation in Counterinsurgency Operations." *U.S. Army Aviation Digest* 8 (October 1962): 3–9.

Hille, Henry. "Eighth Army's Role in the Military Government of Japan." *Military Review* 27 (February 1948): 9–18.

Hoefling, John. "For the Junior Leader: How To Command in Vietnam." *Infantry* 60 (January–February 1970): 41–47.

Holliday, Sam. "An Offensive Response." *Military Review* 43 (April 1963): 16–23.

————. "Warfare of the Future." *Military Review* 49 (August 1969): 12–17.

Hughes, David. "The Myth of Military Coups and Military Assistance." *Military Review* 47 (December 1967): 3–9.

Huppert, G. Harry. "Bullets Alone Won't Win." *Infantry* 54 (July–August 1964): 38–42.

Hurdle, Karl. "Utah Counterguerrillas." *Infantry* 53 (November–December 1963): 62–63.

Iles, Steve. "Cave Hunting Techniques." *Infantry* 56 (July–August 1966): 25–27.

"This Is the Way It Is: Patrolling in Vietnam." *Army Information Digest* 22 (October 1967): 19–21.

Jacobs, Walter. "Mao Tse-Tung as a Guerrilla—A Second Look." *Military Review* 37 (February 1958): 26–30.

————. "This Matter of Counterinsurgency." *Military Review* 44 (October 1964): 79–85.

Jamison, Robert. "Assault Fire." *Infantry* 59 (January–February 1969): 45.

Jarrin, Edgardo. "Insurgency in Latin America—Its Impact on Political and Military Strategy." *Military Review* 49 (March 1969): 10–20.

Jenkins, Brian, and Sereseres, Caesar. "United States Military Assistance and the Guatemalan Armed Forces." *Armed Forces and Society* 3 (Summer 1977): 575–94.

Johnson, Harold. "The Army's Role in Nation Building and Preserving Stability." *Army Information Digest* 20 (November 1965): 6–13.

————. "The Chief of Staff on Military Strategy in Vietnam." *Army Information Digest* 23 (April 1968): 6–9.

————. "Landpower Missions Unlimited." *Army* 14 (November 1964): 41–42.

————. "Subversion and Insurgency: Search for a Doctrine." *Army* 15 (November 1965): 40–42.

Johnson, James. "People's War and Conventional Armies." *Military Review* 54 (January 1974): 24–33.

Jones, Grady. "Dos and Don'ts in Vietnam." *Infantry* 56 (March–April 1966): 25–28.

Jones, Richard. "The Nationbuilder: Soldier of the 1960s." *Military Review* 45 (January 1965): 63–67.

Kauffman, Andrew. "On 'Wars of National Liberation.'" *Military Review* 48 (October 1968): 32–44.

Kee, Robert. "Algiers—1957: An Approach to Urban Counter-insurgency." *Military Review* 54 (April 1974): 73–84.

Kelly, George. "Footnotes on Revolutionary War." *Military Review* 42 (September 1962): 31–39.

Kelly, Joseph. "What Rules for Twilight Wars?" *Military Review* 44 (April 1964): 48–56.

Kinnard, Harry. "Vietnam Has Lessons for Tomorrow's Army." *Army* 18 (November 1968): 77–80.

Klein, William. "Stability Operations in Santo Domingo." *Infantry* 56 (May–June 1966): 35–39.

Koburger, Charles. "Morning Coats and Brass Hats." *Military Review* 45 (April 1965): 65–74.

Kousoulas, Dimitrios. "The Crucial Point of a Counterguerrilla Campaign." *Infantry* 53 (January–February 1963): 18–21.

_____. "The Guerrilla War the Communists Lost." *U.S. Naval Institute Proceedings* 89 (May 1963): 66–73.

Krasin, Chaiyo. "Military Civic Action in Thailand." *Military Review* 48 (January 1968): 73–77.

Kutger, Joseph. "Irregular Warfare in Transition." *Military Affairs* 24 (Fall 1960): 113–23.

Ladd, Jonathan. "Some Reflections of Counterinsurgency." *Military Review* 44 (October 1964): 72–78.

Lansdale, Edward. "Civic Action Helps Counter the Guerrilla Threat." *Army Information Digest* 17 (June 1962): 50–54.

Lenderman, Bob. "Airmobile Tactics and Techniques." *U.S. Army Aviation Digest* 11 (January 1965): 2–6.

Lesh, Burton. "Anti-Guerrilla SOP." *Infantry* 52 (July–August 1962): 30–31.

_____. "Lessons Learned: Thailand." *Infantry* 54 (March–April 1964): 56–59.

Lieber, Albert. "Hide and Seek with Guerrillas." *Infantry* 52 (March–April 1962): 17–18.

Lincoln, George, and Jordan, Jr., Amos. "Limited War and the Scholars." *Military Review* 37 (January 1958): 50–60.

Linebarger, Paul. "They Call 'Em Bandits in Malaya." *U.S. Army Combat Forces Journal* 1 (January 1951): 27–29.

Livingston, George. "Attack of a Fortified Position." *Infantry* 59 (September–October 1969): 13–15.

Livingston, Hoyt, and Watson, Francis. "Civic Action: Purpose and Pitfalls." *Military Review* 47 (December 1967): 21–25.

Long, William. "Counterinsurgency: Some Antecedents for Success." *Military Review* 43 (October 1963): 90–97.

Lubenow, Larry. "Objective Rice." *Infantry* 56 (November–December 1966): 41–42.

Lyon, Hal. "If the Cause Is Right." *Infantry* 54 (March–April 1964): 52–53.

Lyon, Harold. "Cancer Action." *Army* 12 (August 1962): 50–53.

McCuen, John. "Can We Win Revolutionary Wars?" *Army* 19 (December 1969): 16–22.

Mace, James. "Take That Bunker Complex!" *Infantry* 60 (September–October 1970): 6–8.

McEnery, John. "We Can Do Better." *Infantry* 60 (November–December 1970): 42–45.

Machado, J. Bina. "The Making of Brazilian Staff Officers." *Military Review* 50 (April 1970): 75–81.

Mack, Richard. "Hold and Pacify." *Military Review* 47 (November 1967): 91–95.

McNamara, Michael. "Tips for the Delta Advisor." *Infantry* 56 (September–October 1966): 40–43.

Maechling, Charles. "Insurgency and Counterinsurgency: The Role of Strategic Theory." *Parameters* 14 (Autumn 1984): 32–41.

Mangako, Iluminado. "The Constabulary and Rural Development." *Philippine Armed Forces Journal* (March 1956): 43–45.

Manwaring, Max. "Toward an Understanding of Insurgent Warfare." *Military Review* 68 (January 1988): 27–35.

Marr, Lloyd. "Rear Area Security." *Military Review* 31 (May 1951): 57–62.

Matheny, Michael. "Armor in Low-Intensity Conflict: The U.S. Experience in Vietnam." *Armor* 97 (July–August 1988): 9–15.

Merrill, John. "The Cheju-do Rebellion." *Journal of Korean Studies* 2 (1980): 139–98.

Meyer, Richard. "The Ground-Sea Team in River Warfare." *Military Review* 46 (September 1966): 54–61.

"Military Operations Against Irregular Forces." *Infantry* 52 (July–August 1962): 12–13, 44–46.

Millett, Allan. "Captain James H. Hausman and the Formation of the Korean Army, 1945–1950." *Armed Forces and Society* 23 (Summer 1997): 503–39.

Montross, Lynn. "The Pohang Guerrilla Hunt." *Marine Corps Gazette* 36 (January 1952): 19–27.

Moore, Michael. "Improvement of Army Employment in Vietnam." *Armor* 75 (September–October 1966): 4–9.

Moore, Raymond. "Toward a Definition of Military Nationbuilding." *Military Review* 53 (July 1973): 34–48.

Mrazek, James. "Civil Assistance in Action." *Military Review* 35 (October 1955): 30–36.

Murphy, Arthur. "Principles of Anti-Guerrilla Warfare." *Infantry School Quarterly* 39 (July 1951): 52–69.

Nathan, Reuben. "Psychological Warfare: Key to Success in Vietnam." *Military Review* 48 (April 1968): 19–28.

"Nature of the Beast." *Infantry* 52 (May–June 1962): 7–8, 60–61.

Neglia, Anthony. "NVA and VC: Different Enemies, Different Tactics." *Infantry* 60 (September–October 1970): 50–55.

Nichols, Ben. "The Sky's No Limit." *Infantry* 53 (November–December 1963): 3–7, 64–66.

Norman, Lloyd, and Spore, John. "Big Push in Guerrilla Warfare." *Army* 12 (March 1962): 28–37.

Nulsen, Charles. "Retooling for Guerrilla War." *Army* 13 (August 1962): 70.

Nurick, Lester, and Barrett, Roger. "Legality of Guerrilla Forces Under the Laws of War." *American Journal of International Law* 40 (July 1946): 563–83.

O'Brien, James. "Pacification: Binh Dinh's Season of Change." *Infantry* 60 (November–December 1970): 22–24.

Olson, William. "The Concept of Small Wars." *Small Wars and Insurgencies* 1 (April 1990): 39–46.

"Pacification . . . A Many Faceted Thing." *Army Information Digest* 19 (October 1964): 22–23.

Palm, Edward. "Tiger Papa Three: A Memoir of the Combined Action Program." 2 pts. *Marine Corps Gazette* 72 (January 1988): 34–43, and 72 (February 1988): 66–76.

Palmer, Jr., Bruce. "The Army in the Dominican Republic." *Army* 15 (November 1965): 43–44, 136.

_____. "Lessons from the Dominican Stability Operation." *Army* 16 (November 1966): 40–41.

_____, and Flint, Roy. "Counter-Insurgency Training." *Army* 12 (June 1962): 32–39.

Paone, Joseph. "Assault of Enemy Positions." *Infantry* 60 (September–October 1970): 9–11.

Papagos, Alexander. "Guerrilla Warfare." *Foreign Affairs* 30 (January 1952): 215–30.

Papathanasiades, Theodossios. "The Bandits' Last Stand in Greece." *Military Review* 30 (February 1951): 22–31.

Paschall, Rod. "Low-Intensity Conflict Doctrine: Who Needs It?" *Parameters* 15 (Autumn 1985): 33–45.

"On Patrol." *Army Information Digest* 22 (August 1967): 28–31.

Pearlman, Michael. "The Fall and Rise of Low-Intensity Conflict Doctrine and Instruction." *Military Review* 68 (September 1988): 78–79.

Peers, William. "Meeting the Challenge of Subversion." *Army* 15 (November 1964): 95–100.

_____. "Subversion's Continuing Challenge." *Army* 15 (November 1965): 68–71, 136.

Peters, Robert. "So This Is Civic Action." *Army Information Digest* 22 (April 1967): 12–16.

Phillips, Y. Y. "The ROAD Battalion in Vietnam." *Army* 16 (September 1966): 53–56.

Phipps, G. C. "Guerrillas in Malaya." *Infantry* 51 (May–June 1961): 36–40.

Powers, Robert. "Guerrillas and the Laws of War." *U.S. Naval Institute Proceedings* 89 (March 1963): 82–87.

Prillaman, Richard. "Vietnam Update." *Infantry* 59 (May–June 1969): 18–19.

Prosser, Lamar. "The Bloody Lessons of Indochina." *U.S. Army Combat Forces Journal* 5 (June 1955): 23–30.

Pruden, Wesley. "Asia's Other War." *Army* 17 (November 1967): 26–31.

Rast, James. "Highland Fox: The 2d Division's Off-Post Counter-insurgency Exercise." *Infantry* 55 (May–June 1965): 45–49.

Rattan, Donald. "Antiguerrilla Operations: A Case Study from History." *Military Review* 40 (May 1960): 23–27.

Ray, James. "The District Advisor." *Military Review* 45 (May 1965): 3–8.

"Readiness for the Little War, Optimum Integrated Strategy." *Military Review* 37 (April 1957): 14–26.

Rempe, Dennis. "Guerrillas, Bandits, and Independent Republics: U.S. Counter-Insurgency Efforts in Colombia, 1959–1965." *Small Wars and Insurgencies* 6 (Winter 1995): 304–27.

Rigg, Robert. "Get Guerrilla-Wise." *U.S. Army Combat Forces Journal* 1 (September 1950): 7–11.

_____. "Twilight War." *Military Review* 40 (November 1960): 28–32.

Rosen, Stephen. "Vietnam and the American Theory of Limited War." *International Security* 7 (Fall 1982): 83–113.

Rosson, William. "Accent on Cold War Capabilities." *Army Information Digest* 17 (May 1962): 2–7.

Saalberg, John. "Army Nationbuilders." *Military Review* 47 (August 1967): 47–53.

Sananikone, Oudone. "Laos: Case Study in Civic Action, The Royal Lao Program." *Military Review* 43 (December 1963): 44–54.

Scales, Robert. "Firepower and Maneuver in the Second Indochina War." *Field Artillery Journal* 54 (September–October 1986): 47–53.

Selton, Robert. "Communist Errors in the Anti-Bandit War." *Military Review* 45 (September 1965): 66–77.

Shelton, Ralph. "Advice for Advisors." *Infantry* 54 (July–August 1964): 12–13.

Shuffer, George. "Finish Them with Firepower." *Military Review* 47 (December 1967): 11–15.

Slover, Robert. "Action Through Civic Action." *Army Information Digest* 17 (October 1962): 7–11.

————. "This Is Military Civic Action." *Army* 13 (July 1963): 48–52.

————. "The Potential of Civic Action." *Army* 12 (November 1962): 66–67.

Smith, Lynn. "Lebanon—Professionalism at Its Best." *Military Review* 39 (June 1959): 36–46.

Smith, Robert Ross. "The Hukbalahap Insurgency." *Military Review* 45 (June 1965): 35–42.

Smithers, Samuel. "Combat Units in Revolutionary Development." *Military Review* 47 (October 1967): 37–41.

Sorley, Lewis. "The Quiet War: Revolutionary Development." *Military Review* 47 (November 1967): 13–19.

Soutor, Kevin. "To Stem the Red Tide: The German Report Series and Its Effects on American Defense Doctrine, 1948–1954." *Journal of Military History* 57 (October 1993): 653–88.

Souyris, Andre. "An Effective Counterguerrilla Procedure." *Military Review* 36 (March 1957): 86–90.

"Soviet Partisan Warfare." *Army Information Digest* 6 (February 1951): 61–64.

Spence, Larry. "Stay-Behind Ambush." *Infantry* 59 (July–August 1969): 49–51.

Stang, Arthur. "Stand and Fight." *Infantry* 56 (March–April 1966): 32–39.

Stanton, Shelby. "Lessons Learned or Lost: Air Cavalry and Airmobility." *Military Review* 69 (January 1989): 74–86.

Starry, Donn. "La Guerre Revolutionnaire." *Military Review* 47 (February 1967): 60–70.

Stewart, Edward. "American Advisors Overseas." *Military Review* 45 (February 1965): 3–9.

Stilwell, Richard. "Evolution in Tactics—The Vietnam Experience." *Army* 20 (February 1970): 14–23.

Stockell, Charles. "Laos: Case Study in Civic Action, The Military Program." *Military Review* 43 (December 1963): 55–63.

Tanham, George, and Duncanson, Dennis. "Some Dilemmas of Counterinsurgency." *Foreign Affairs* 48 (October 1969): 113–22.

Tilman, Robert. "The Nonlessons of the Malayan Emergency." *Military Review* 46 (December 1966): 62–71.

Tippin, Garold. "The Army as Nationbuilder." *Military Review* 50 (October 1970): 11–19.

Trigg, Harry. "A New ATT." *Army* 13 (February 1963): 35–39.

Turner, Frederick. "Experiment in Inter-American Peace-Keeping." *Army* 17 (June 1967): 34–39.

Van der Kroef, Justus. "Guerrilla Communism and Counterinsurgency in Thailand." *Orbis* 18 (Spring 1974): 106–39.

_____. "Organizing Counter-Insurgency: The Thai Experience." *South-East Asian Spectrum* 2 (January 1974): 45–53.

Venero, Enrique. "Success in Peru: A Case Study in Counterinsurgency." *Military Review* 46 (February 1966): 15–21.

Vought, Donald. "Preparing for the Wrong War?" *Military Review* 57 (May 1977): 16–34.

Waghelstein, John. "Post-Vietnam Counterinsurgency Doctrine." *Military Review* 65 (June 1985): 42–49.

Wallace, J. A. "Counterinsurgency ATT." *Army* 16 (August 1966): 76–77.

Walterhouse, Harry. "Civic Action: A Counter and Cure for Insurgency." *Military Review* 42 (August 1962): 47–54.

_____. "Good Neighbors in Uniform." *Military Review* 45 (February 1965): 10–18.

"The War Against Guerrilla Fighters." *Military Review* 23 (September 1943): 79–80.

Warmbrod, Karlton. "Defense of Rear Areas." *Infantry School Quarterly* 40 (April 1952): 5–15.

Weinrod, W. Bruce. "Counterinsurgency: Its Role in Defense Policy." *Strategic Review* 2 (Fall 1974): 36–40.

Westmoreland, William. "The Fight for Freedom in Viet Nam." *Army Information Digest* 20 (February 1965): 7–15.

Weyand, Frederick. "Winning the People in Hau Nghia Province." *Army* 17 (February 1967): 52–55.

Widder, David. "Ambush." *Army* 12 (November 1961): 38–42.

Williams, Justin. "From Charlottesville to Tokyo: Military Government Training and Democratic Reforms in Occupied Japan." *Pacific Historical Review* 51 (1982): 407–22.

Williamson, Ellis. "Defense of a Firebase." *Infantry* 59 (November–December 1969): 6–12.

Willoughby, William. "Revolutionary Development." *Infantry* 58 (November–December 1968): 4–10.

Wroth, James. "Korea: Our Next Vietnam?" *Military Review* 48 (November 1968): 34–40.

Ximenes. "Revolutionary War." *Military Review* 37 (August 1957): 103–08.

Yarborough, William. "'Young Moderns' Are Impetus Behind Army's Special Forces." *Army* 12 (March 1962): 38–39.

Zacharakis, E. "Lessons Learned in the Anti-Guerrilla War in Greece, 1946–1949." *General Military Review* (July 1960): 179–202.

Zimmerman, Robert. "Insurgency in Thailand." *Problems of Communism* 25 (May–June 1976): 18–39.

GLOSSARY

AARs	After action reports
ACSFOR	Assistant chief of staff for force development
ACSI	Assistant chief of staff for intelligence
ACTIV	Army Concept Team in Vietnam
AFAK	Armed Forces Assistance to Korea
AFB	Air force base
AFP	Armed Forces of the Philippines
AID	Agency for International Development
AIT	Advanced individual training
AMAG	American Mission to Aid Greece
AR	Army regulation
ARCOV	U.S. Army Combat Operations in Vietnam
ARVN	Army of the Republic of Vietnam
ATPs	Army training programs
ATTs	Army training tests
AWC	Army War College
CAP	U.S. Marine Corps Combined Action Platoon
CCP	Chinese Communist Party
CDC	Combat Developments Command
CGSC	U.S. Army Command and General Staff College
CIA	Central Intelligence Agency
CIDG	Civilian Irregular Defense Group
CINCPAC	Commander in chief, Pacific
CIOG	Counterinsurgency Operations Group
CJCS	Chairman, Joint Chiefs of Staff
CMH	U.S. Army Center of Military History
CONARC	Continental Army Command
CORDS	Civil Operations and Revolutionary Development Support
CPT	Communist Party Thailand

CSA	Chief of staff, Army
CY	Calendar year
DA	Department of the Army
DCG, USARV	Deputy commanding general, U.S. Army Vietnam
DF	Disposition form
DMZ	Demilitarized Zone
E	Entry
EDCOR	Economic Development Corps
EIP	Environmental Improvement Program
ELAS	National Popular Liberation Army
EUSAK	Eighth U.S. Army in Korea
I FFV	I Field Force
II FFV	II Field Force
FAO	Foreign area officer
FAS	Foreign area specialist
FM	Field manual
FRUS	*Foreign Relations of the United States*
FYs	Fiscal years
GGS	Greek General Staff
GNA	Greek National Army
GO	General Orders
H&I	Harassment and interdiction
HERO	Historical Evaluation and Research Organization
IAPF	Inter-American Peacekeeping Force
ICAS	Institute of Combined Arms and Support
ID	Intelligence document
IDAD	Internal defense and development
IDAID	Internal defense and internal development
ID/D	Internal defense and internal development
IDD	Internal defense and internal development
ID/DOG	Internal Defense/Development Operations Group
IDEV	Internal development
IDID	Internal defense and internal development

IMA	Institute for Military Assistance
IOAC	Infantry officer advanced course
JCS	Joint Chiefs of Staff
JUSMAG	Joint U.S. Military Advisory Group
JUSMAPG	Joint U.S. Military Advisory and Planning Group, Greece
KMAG	Korean Military Assistance Group
KMT	Nationalist Kuomintang Party
LIC	Low intensity conflict
LL	Lessons learned
LRRPs	Long-range reconnaissance patrols
MAAG	Military assistance advisory group
MACTHAI	Military Assistance Command, Thailand
MACV	Military Assistance Command, Vietnam
MAOP	Military Assistance Officer Program
MATA	Military assistance training adviser
MDA	Mutual Defense Assistance
MDAP	Mutual Defense Assistance Program
MEDCAP	Medical civic action program
MEDCAP II	MEDCAP program expansion
MFR	Memorandum for the record
MHI	U.S. Army Military History Institute
MMAS	Master of Military Arts and Sciences
NARA	National Archives and Records Administration
NDC	National Defense Corps
NIDCC	National Internal Defense Coordination Center
NISC	National Internal Security Committee
NSC	National Security Council
OACS	Office of the Assistant Chief of Staff
OACSFOR	Office of the Assistant Chief of Staff for Force Development
OAS	Organization of American States
OCMH	Office of the Chief of Military History

ODCSOPS	Office of the Deputy Chief of Staff for Military Operations
OIDP	Overseas Internal Defense Policy
ORLL	Operational report-lessons learned
OSO	Overseas Security Operations
OSS	Office of Strategic Services
P&O	Plans and operations
PAVN	*People's Army of Vietnam*
PRD	Partido Revolucionario Dominicano
RACs	Regional Assistance Commands
RG	Record group
ROAD	Reorganization Objective Army Division
ROK	Republic of Korea
ROTC	Reserve Officers' Training Corps
ROTCM	Reserve Officers' Training Corps Manual
SACSA	Special assistant to the chief of staff for special warfare activities
SAFs	Special Action Forces
SCAP	Supreme commander for the allied powers
SEATO	Southeast Asia Treaty Organization
SKLP	South Korean Labor Party
SOP	Standing operating procedure
SORO	Special Operations Research Office
ST	Special text
STARS–70	"Strategic Army Study, 1970"
STRAC	Strategic Army Corps
STRICOM	Strike Command
UAR	United Arab Republic
UN	United Nations
USACDC	U.S. Army Combat Developments Command
USASOC/HO	History Office, U.S. Army Special Operations Command
USFORDR	United States Forces, Dominican Republic
USIA	U.S. Information Agency
USIS	United States Information Service
USMA	U.S. Military Academy
USSR	Union of Soviet Socialist Republics

| WD | War Department |
| WSEG | Weapon System Evaluation Group |

INDEX

543

Alliance for Progress, 294
creation of, 292
results of, 304, 435–36
Almond, Maj. Gen. Edward M., 113, 114
Alvim, Lt. Gen. Hugo Panasco, 209, 213
American Mission to Aid Greece (AMAG), 46
Amnesty programs
doctrinal discussion of, 168
in Thailand, 344
in Vietnam, 325, 398
"Anti-Guerrilla Guerrilla, The" (McGarr), 313
Apache Forces (Vietnam), 377
Arab-Israeli War, 1973, 482
Arana Osorio, Col. Carlos, 301
Area clearance, 97, 136, 167–68, 235. *See also* Oil-spot method (*tache d'huile*); Resettlement.
Armed Forces Assistance to Korea (AFAK), 111–12, 160, 334
Armed Forces of the Philippines (AFP), 61, 63, 64, 65, 81n61
Armor
in Greece, 51
in Korea, 101
role of, in counterinsurgency, 139, 151, 245–46
in Vietnam, 384
Army, Eighth U.S. *See* Eighth U.S. Army in Korea (EUSAK).
Army Field Forces, 131, 149, 150, 231
Army Ground Forces, 231
Army Intelligence Agency, 432–33
Army of the Republic of Vietnam
development of, 308, 309, 311, 312
weaknesses of, 322–23
Army Strategic Studies Institute, 483
Army War College, Carlisle Barracks
lessons-learned study on Vietnam, 483
reduces counterinsurgency instruction, 480–81

Army War College, Carlisle Barracks—Continued
studies counterinsurgency, 152, 212, 266, 461
Artillery, 151, 244–45, 253, 412n47. *See also* Harassment and interdiction.
in training, 274
use of, in Greece, 48, 51
use in Korea, 101, 106
in Vietnam, 380, 381, 382
Assistant Chief of Staff for Force Development (ACSFOR), 439, 442. *See also* Office of the Assistant Chief of Staff for Force Development (OACSFOR).
Atrocities, 236, 253. *See also* Terror; Torture; Troop conduct.
at My Lai (Son My), 404
Aussaresses, Lt. Col. Paul, 230

Balaguer, Joaquin, 203, 210
Ball, George, 487
Barr, Maj. Gen. David G.
and Chinese Civil War, 37, 38, 39, 40, 41
in Korea, 114
Barrio United Defense Corps, 55–56, 58. *See also* Philippines.
Bashore, Lt. Col. Boyd T., 436
BDM Corporation, 483
Beebe, Lt. Col. John, 101, 153
Beirut, marines land at, 184. *See also* Lebanon.
Bell, General J. Franklin, 231
Bohannan, Lt. Col. Charles T. R., 281n16
Bolivia, 300
Bonesteel, General Charles H., III, 330, 334
Boorstin, Daniel, 345–46
Bosch, Juan, 203, 210
Bradley, General Omar, 74n7
Brazil, 298
Brown, Col. Rothwell H., 89

Geneva Convention of 1949—
Continued
on international law, 19
and reprisals, 173n15
soldiers trained in, 403
treatment of captured guerrillas,
112, 147
U.S. ratifies, 20
German counterguerrilla doctrine
encirclement techniques of, 244,
246, 377
Fighting the Guerrilla Bands, 133,
197, 281n15
influences Greek doctrine, 44
influences U.S. doctrine, 133, 138,
229
lessons drawn from World War II
experiences, 132–33, 140, 142,
146
used in Vietnam, 377–78
Germany, occupation of, 15, 16, 17, 18
Giap, General Vo Nguyen, 68, 70,
261, 461
Graduated response, 158
Grady, Henry F., 46, 49
Gray, Brig. Gen. David W., 188, 189,
190, 194
Great Britain, 492. *See also Conduct
of Anti-terrorist Operations in
Malaya.*
counterinsurgency doctrine of, 44,
52, 149
and Greek insurgency, 42, 44, 45,
49, 54
liaison officers in U.S., 460
in Malaya, 162, 168, 229
relationship between British and
American doctrine, 52, 242,
244, 248, 314
Greece, 5, 122, 170, 265, 327, 344,
348
and American assistance, 22, 31
British assistance, 42, 44, 45
economic relief, 48
and Home Guard, 50, 54
insurgency, 42–55

Greece—Continued
internal reform, 119
issue of resettlement, 175n42
National Defense Corps (NDC),
49, 50, 52
use of police forces, 44
and Truman Doctrine, 45, 486
Greek National Army (GNA).
See also Joint U.S. Military
Advisory and Planning Group.
draws on British and German
experience, 44
improvements in, 48, 53
operations of, 45, 48, 53, 54
training of, 48
Greene, Brig. Gen. Michael J., 481
Griswold, Dwight P., 46, 51
Guatemala, 298, 300, 350
accepts U.S. civic action
assistance, 161
and human rights, 302
Guerre revolutionnaire, 163,
180n72, 230, 437. *See also*
Counterinsurgency; Doctrine;
France.
Guerrilla warfare, 4. *See also*
Counterguerrilla warfare;
Field Manual 31–15 (1961);
Field Manual 31–16 (1963);
Field Manual 31–16 (1967);
Field Manual 31–20 (1951);
Field Manuals (FMs); Geneva
Convention of 1949.
and civilian support, 146
destruction of, 363
forms of, 134
German "Werewolf" movement,
9, 133
in Korea, 100
legal status of, 11, 19, 20, 112
Mao develops strategies for rural,
24
nature of, 118
treatment of, 19, 112
Guerrilla Warfare, On (Guevara),
229, 294

Republic of Korea (ROK), 5, 24, 61,
86, 122. *See also* Cheju-do,
Korea.
Army regulations, 90
Chiri mountain region, 86
Combat Police Commands, 102
Communists, 99, 100, 103
counterguerrilla operations,
98–102
counterinsurgency efforts of, 88,
99, 332, 333
Demilitarized Zone, 329, 330, 332
Homeland Defense Reserve, 334
Inch'on landing, 99, 103
internal reform, 119, 329
Japanese colony, 85
Northern infiltration and
incursions into, 329–30, 332
Odae mountain region, 86
Pusan Perimeter, 99, 102
Security Commands, 102
Taebaek mountain region, 86
Republic of Korea Army, 327
III Corps secures South Korea,
105
and counterguerrilla operations,
101–02
regulations, 90
subordinated to American
command, 100
Reserve Officers' Training Corps
(ROTC), 152
Resettlement, 168, 169, 175n42. *See
also* Strategic Hamlet Program.
doctrine, 493
and FM 31–20, 136
in FM 31–22, 249
in FM 31–73, 252
in FM 41–10, 149
in Greece, 149
impact of, 97–98
in Korea, 97, 102, 116, 149
in Philippines, 65, 175n42
in Thailand, 337
in Vietnam, 318, 394
Resor, Stanley R., 444

Revolution of rising expectations,
164, 165, 225, 249, 268, 345,
346, 494. *See also* Rostow,
Walt W.
Revolutionary Development program
(Vietnam), 324
Rhee, Singman, 86, 90, 91, 98, 100,
124n13
Richardson, Maj. Gen. James L.,
200, 201
Ridgway, Lt. Gen. Matthew B., 113,
307, 350
Riggs, Maj. Robert B., 104
Riverine operations, 385, 445
Roberts, Brig. Gen. William L., 90,
124n13
Rogers, Robert, 231
Roosevelt, Franklin D., 18
Roper, Maj. Gen. Harry M., 175n42
Rosson, Brig. Gen. William B., 227
Rostow, Walt W., 258, 292, 435,
439–40, 486
and Kennedy administration, 224
theory of "revolution of rising
expectations," 164, 165, 225,
249, 345, 346, 494
and Vietnam, 315
Rotation policy, 347, 465–66
Roxas, Manuel, 56, 58
Royall, Kenneth C., 49, 74n7
Rules of engagement
in Dominican Republic, 206–07
in Lebanon, 186–87
in Vietnam, 401–02
Russian Civil War, 41

Sandinista Revolution, 298
Santo Domingo, Dominican
Republic, 203, 206, 209, 210.
See also Dominican Republic.
School of the Americas, 304, 459
School for Military Government, 12,
13, 15
Search and clear, 462
Search and destroy
in Korea, 95

Williams, Lt. Gen. Samuel T.—
Continued
importance of military power, 320
on Maoist approach to guerrilla
warfare, 310
Notes on Anti-Guerrilla
Operations, 310, 311
on South Vietnamese troops
performing civic action, 312,
317
Williamson, Brig. Gen. Ellis W., 374
Wilson, Woodrow, 41, 205
"Win in Vietnam" program, 265
Winter Punitive Operation (1949–50)
in Korea, 96

Wolf, Charles, 436, 439

Yarborough, Brig. Gen. William P.,
227, 230, 299
Yemen, 184
Yiafka, 42, 43, 48, 50, 51. *See also*
Democratic People's Army
(Greece).
York, Maj. Gen. Robert H., 208, 213
Yow, Maj. Harold D., 262
Yugoslavia and Greek insurrection,
42, 43, 53, 54

Zachariades, Nikos, 52, 53, 54
Zona operations, 56